SPORTS IN SOCIETY

Issues & Controversies

FIRST CANADIAN EDITION

Jay Coakley, Ph.D.
University of Colorado
Colorado Springs

Peter Donnelly, Ph.D.
University of Toronto

McGraw-Hill
Ryerson

Toronto   Montréal   Boston   Burr Ridge, IL   Dubuque, IA   Madison, WI   New York
San Francisco   St. Louis   Bangkok   Bogotá   Caracas   Kuala Lumpur   Lisbon   London
Madrid   Mexico City   Milan   New Delhi   Santiago   Seoul   Singapore   Sydney   Taipei

McGraw-Hill
Ryerson

Sports in Society: Issues and Controversies
First Canadian Edition

Statistics Canada information is used with the permission of the Minister of Industry, as Minister responsible for Statistics Canada. Information on the availability of the wide range of data from Statistics Canada can be obtained from Statistics Canada's Regional Offices, its World Wide Web site at http://www.statcan.ca, and its toll-free access number 1-800-263-1136.

This book is printed on acid free paper.

ISBN 0-07-091476-1

1 2 3 4 5 6 7 8 9 10 TCP 0 9 8 7 6 5 4

Printed and bound in Canada

Care has been taken to trace ownership of copyright material contained in this text; however, the publisher will welcome any information that enables them to rectify any reference or credit for subsequent editions.

Vice President, Editorial and Media Technology: Patrick Ferrier
Sponsoring Editor: James Buchanan
Developmental Editor: Jennifer DiDomenico
Marketing Manager: Sharon Loeb
Production Coordinator: Mary Pepe
Supervising Editor: Joanne Murray
Copy Editor: Michael Kelly
Permissions Research: Alison Derry/Permissions Plus
Formatter: Anne MacInnis
Cover Design: Dianna Little
Cover Image Credit: © NCC/CCN
Printer: Transcontinental Printing Group

National Library of Canada Cataloguing in Publication

Coakley, Jay J
    Sports in society : issues and controversies/Jay Coakley, Peter Donnelly—1st Canadian ed.
    Previous eds. published under title: Sport in society. Includes bibliographical references and indexes.
    ISBN 0-07-091476-1
    1. Sports—Sociological aspects. I. Donnelly, Peter, 1941- II. Title.
    GV706.5.C63 2003   306.4'83   C2003-904896-9

About the Authors

Jay Coakley

Jay Coakley is currently a professor of sociology at the University of Colorado in Colorado Springs. He was born in Chicago and used an athletic scholarship to fund his undergraduate degree in sociology and psychology. In 1966 he went to the University of Notre Dame where he completed his M.A. and Ph.D. degrees. In 1970, he moved to Arizona to teach at the University of Northern Arizona before moving on to Colorado Springs in 1972. He was the founding editor of the *Sociology of Sport Journal* (1984–89), and he served as Chair of the Sport Sociology Academy of the National Association of Sport and Physical Education (1983) and the North American Society for the Sociology of Sport (1991). His research interests include youth sports, socialization, deviance, gender, and race and ethnicity. He has published many articles and book chapters and consults widely with journalists writing about social issues in sports. His text, *Sport in Society: Issues and Controversies* was first published in the United States in 1978, and it has been revised seven times since then. Other books include the *Handbook of Sport Studies*, edited with Eric Dunning (2000), and *Inside Sports*, edited with Peter Donnelly (1999). He stays active by keeping an eye on three granddaughters and traveling to new places whenever possible.

Peter Donnelly

Peter Donnelly is currently Director of the Centre for Sport Policy Studies, and a professor in the Faculty of Physical Education and Health, at the University of Toronto. He was born in Chester, England, studied physical education as an undergraduate, and taught school for several years. In 1969, he moved to the United States where he completed undergraduate studies in New York City, and then received Master's and Ph.D. degrees in Sport Studies from the University of Massachusetts. In 1976, he moved to Canada, where he taught at the University of Western Ontario from 1976–79 and at McMaster University from 1980–98. He was the second editor of the *Sociology of Sport Journal*, and served as President of the North American Society for the Sociology of Sport in 2000. His research interests include sport politics and policy issues (including the area of children's rights in sports), sport subcultures, and mountaineering (history). He has published numerous scholarly articles on those and other topics. Recent books include: *Taking Sport Seriously: Social Issues in Canadian Sport* (1997; 2nd edition, 2000), and *Inside Sports* (with Jay Coakley, 1999). His current sporting interests include rock climbing/mountaineering (continually proving the inverse relationship between age and risk-taking), hiking, and skiing; he is a novice golfer, and is now enjoying life as an "empty nester."

Contents

Preface   xi

1 The Sociology of Sport: What is it and why study it?   1

What Is Sociology?   2
  Culture   3
  Society   3

What Are Sports?   4
  An Alternative Approach to Defining Sports   8
  REFLECT ON SPORTS: Sports as Contested
    Activities   10

What Is the Sociology of Sport?   11
  Differences between the Sociology of Sport and
    the Psychology of Sport   12
  Using the Sociology of Sport   13
  Controversies Created by the Sociology
    of Sport   14

Why Study Sports as Social Phenomena?   16
  Sports Are Part of People's Lives   16
  Sports Are Tied to Social Structure and Cultural
    Ideology   17
  Sports Are Connected to Major Spheres of Social
    Life   20
  REFLECT ON SPORTS: The Body and the
    Sociology of Sport   21

**What Is the Current Status of the Sociology
  of Sport?   24**
  Professional Associations and Journals   24
  Disagreements in the Sociology of Sport   25

Summary: Why Study Sports?   27

2 Using Social Theories: What can they tell us about sports in society?   30

**What Are Theories and Why Do We Need
  Them?   31**

**Functionalist Theory: What Do Sports
  Contribute to Society?   32**
  Functionalist Theory and Research
    on Sports   36
  Using Functionalist Theory in
    Everyday Life   36
  Weaknesses of Functionalist Theory   37

**Conflict Theory: Are Sports All about Money
  and Economic Power?   37**
  Conflict Theory and Research on Sports   38
  Using Conflict Theory in Everyday Life   38
  Weaknesses of Conflict Theory   39
  Beyond the Needs of Society   40

**Interactionist Theory: How Do People
  Experience Sports?   40**
  Interactionist Theory and Research
    on Sports   40
  Using Interactionist Theory in
    Everyday Life   41
  Weaknesses of Interactionist Theory   42

**Critical Theories: How Are Sports Involved in
  Creating and Changing Social Relations
  and Culture?   42**
  Critical Theories and Research on Sports   44
  REFLECT ON SPORTS: Sports Are More
    Than Reflections of Society   45

Using Critical Theories in Everyday Life   46
REFLECT ON SPORTS: Critical Feminist
    Theories: Assessing Gender Relations and
    Sports   47
Weaknesses of Critical Theories   48

**Figurational Theory: Understanding Sports in
    Terms of Historical and Global Processes   49**
Figurational Theory and Research on Sports   50

**Summary: Is There a Best Theoretical Approach
    to Use When Studying Sports?   51**

3   A Look at the Past: Does it help us understand sports today?   54

**Understanding History while Studying Sports in
    Society   55**

Sports Vary by Time and Place   56

**Contests and Games in Ancient Greece: Beyond
    the Myths (1000 B.C.E. to 100 B.C.E.)   57**

**Roman Contests and Games: Spectacles and
    Gladiators (100 B.C.E. to C.E. 500)   59**

**Tournaments and Games in Medieval Europe:
    Separation of the Masters and the Masses
    (500 to 1300)   60**

**The Renaissance, Reformation, and
    Enlightenment: Games as Diversions
    (1300 to 1800)   62**
The Renaissance   62
The Reformation   62
The Enlightenment   64

**The Industrial Revolution: The Emergence of
    Organized Competitive Sports
    (1780 to the present)   64**
REFLECT ON SPORTS: Lessons from History:
    Distorted Views of Sports among Native North
    Americans   65
The Early Years: Limited Time and Space   65
The Later Years: Changing Interests, Values,
    and Opportunities   67
REFLECT ON SPORTS: The Characteristics
    of High-Profile Organized Competitive
    Sports   69

**Summary: Can We Use History to Understand
    Sports Today?   79**

4   Sports and Socialization: Who plays and what happens to them?   83

What Is Socialization?   84
A Functionalist Approach to Socialization   84
A Conflict Theory Approach to Socialization   85
New Approaches to Socialization   86

**Becoming Involved and Staying Involved
    in Sports   86**
The Process of Becoming a High-Performance
    Athlete   87
The Process of Being Accepted as an Athlete   88
To Participate or Not to Participate   89

Changing or Ending Sport Participation   90
Jay Coakley's Study of Burnout among
    Young Athletes   91
Getting Out of Sports and Getting On
    with Life   91
Changing Personal Investments in
    Sport Careers   92

Being Involved in Sports: What Happens?   93
Do Sports Build Character?   93
REFLECT ON SPORTS: Power and
    Performance versus Pleasure and
    Participation: Different Sports, Different
    Experiences, Different Consequences   96
How Do Sports Affect Our Lives?   98
Real-Life Experiences: Sport Stories from
    Athletes   98
Social Worlds: Living in Sports   101
Ideology: Sports as Sites for Struggling over How
    We Think and What We Do   104

**What Socialization Research Does Not Tell
    Us   109**

Summary: Who Plays and What Happens?   110

5   Sports and Children: Are organized programmes worth the effort?   113

**Origin and Development of Organized Youth
    Sports   114**
Organized Sports and Changes Related to
    Society, Family, and Childhood   116

Problems in Adult-Organized Youth Sports and "Made in Canada" Solutions   118
  Assumption 1: Children Play Sports to Entertain Adults   118
  Assumption 2: Games and Sports for Kids Must Be Organized and Controlled by Adults If They Are to Be of Real Value   120
  Assumption 3: Kids Are Miniature Adults   123
  Assumption 4: The Real Value in Sport Lies In Learning to Be a Winner…   124

Children in High-Performance Sports   125
  REFLECT ON SPORTS: Solving the Problems in Children's High-Performance Sports   127

Sociological Questions about Youth Sports   129
  When Are Children Ready to Play Organized Competitive Sports?   129
  What Are the Dynamics of Family Relationships in Connection with Organized Youth Sports?   130
  How Do Social Factors Influence Youth Sport Experiences?   131

Major Trends and Recommendations   133
  Major Trends in Youth Sports Today   133
  REFLECT ON SPORTS: Different Experiences: Informal, Player-Controlled Sports versus Organized, Adult-Controlled Sports   137
  Recommendations for Changing Children's Sports   139

Summary: Are Organized Youth Sport Programmes Worth the Effort?   143

6 "Deviance" in Sports: Is it out of control?   147

Problems Faced When Studying "Deviance" in Sports   149

Defining and Studying "Deviance" in Sports: Three Theoretical Approaches   153
  Using Functionalist Theory: "Deviance" Disrupts Shared Values   153
  Using Conflict Theory: "Deviance" Interferes with the Interests of Those with Economic Power   154
  Using Interactionist and Critical Theories:

  "Deviance" Is Based in Social Processes and Power Relations   155
  REFLECT ON SPORTS: Just (Over)do It: The Sport Ethic in Nike Ads   161
  REFLECT ON SPORTS: Hazing and University Policy   164

Research on "Deviance" among Athletes   166
  "Deviance" on the Field and in Sport Settings   167
  "Deviance" off the Field and Away from Sports   168
  Why Focus Only on "Deviance" among Athletes?   170
  REFLECT ON SPORTS: Is Sport Participation a Cure for "Deviant" Behaviour?   171

Performance-Enhancing Substances: A Case of "Deviant" Overconformity in Sports   173
  Defining and Banning Performance-Enhancing Substances   174
  REFLECT ON SPORTS: Ben Johnson, the Dubin Commission, and Drug Testing in Canada   175
  Why Is the Challenge of Substance Control So Great in Sports Today?   178
  Drug Testing as a Deterrent   179
  Controlling Substance Use in Sports: Where to Start?   180

Summary: Is "Deviance" in Sports out of Control?   183

7 Violence in Sports: How does it affect our lives?   186

What Is Violence?   187

Violence in Sports through History   188

Violence on the Field   189
  Types of Violence   189
  Violence as "Deviant" Overconformity to the Norms of the Sport Ethic   190
  REFLECT ON SPORTS: Brashear and McSorley: A Case of Criminal Violence?   191
  Commercialization and Violence in Sports   192
  Violence and Masculinity   194
  Violence, Gender, Social Class, and Race   195

The Institutionalization of Violence in
   Sports   196
Pain and Injury as the Price of Violence   198
Controlling on-the-Field Violence   199

Violence off the Field   200
Do Violent Strategies Learned in Sports Carry
   Over to the Rest of Life?   200
REFLECT ON SPORTS: Sexual Harassment
   and Abuse   202
REFLECT ON SPORTS: Fair Play
   Leagues   205
Impact of Violence in Sports on Gender
   Ideology: Reproducing the Connection
   between Masculinity and Physical
   Domination   206

Violence among Spectators   206
Violence among Television Viewers   207
Violence at Sport Events   207

**Summary: Does Violence in Sports Affect Our
   Lives?   214**

8 **Gender and Sports:
   Does equity require ideological
   changes?   217**

Participation and Equity Issues   218
Reasons for Increased Participation   218
Reasons to Be Cautious When Predicting Future
   Participation Increases   222
Gender and Fairness Issues in Sports   225
REFLECT ON SPORTS: Girls Playing on
   Boys' Teams: The Justine Blainey
   Case   231
Strategies to Achieve Equity and Fairness   234

Ideological and Cultural Issues   237
Gender Logic in Society   238
Gender Logic in Sports   240
REFLECT ON SPORTS: Women
   Bodybuilders: Expanding Definitions
   of Femininity?   243
Strategies for Changing Ideology and
   Culture   248

**Summary: Does Equity Require Ideological
   Changes?   251**

9 **Race and Ethnicity: Are they
   important in sports?   255**

**Definitions of *Race*, *Ethnicity*, and *Minority
   Group*   256**
Origins and Implications of the Concept
   of Race   258

Race Logic   260
Origins of Race Logic   260
Race Logic in Sports   261
Race Logic, Gender, and Social Class   263

Racial and Ethnic Relations in Canada   263
A Snapshot of the Canadian Population,
   2001   267
Canadian and U.S. Differences in Racial and
   Ethnic Logic   269

**The Dynamics of Ethnic and Racial Relations in
   Canadian Sports   270**
Francophone and Anglophone Relations   271
Native and Non-Native Relations   276
REFLECT ON SPORTS: Sports and
   Bilingualism   278
Colonizing Nations and Immigrant
   Relations   281

**The Challenges of Racial and Ethnic Relations
   in Canadian Sports   286**
Eliminating Racial and Ethnic Exclusion in Sport
   Participation   287
Dealing With and Managing Racial and Ethnic
   Diversity in Sports   288
Integrating Positions of Power in Sport
   Organizations   289
Prospects for Change   290

**Summary: Are Race and Ethnicity Important in
   Sports?   291**

10 **Social Class: Do money
   and power matter in
   sports?   294**

Social Class and Class Relations   295
Sports and Economic Inequality   296
The Dynamics of Class Relations   297

Class Relations and Those Who Have the Power
in Sports   298
Sports as a Vehicle for Transferring Public
Money to Wealthy Individuals and
Private Corporations   301
**Social Class and Sport Participation
Patterns   303**
Homemaking, Child Rearing, and Earning a
Living: What Happens When Class and
Gender Relations Come Together in Women's
Lives   307
Getting Respect and Becoming a Man: What
Happens When Class and Gender Relations
Come Together in Men's Lives   308
Class Relations in Action: The Decline of School
Sports and Physical Education, and the
Increase of User Fees   309
Class Relations in Action: The Cost of Attending
Sport Events   310
**Economic and Career Opportunities
in Sports   312**
Career Opportunities Are Limited   312
REFLECT ON SPORTS: The Odds of
Becoming a Professional Athlete   313
Opportunities for Women Are Growing
but Limited   314
Opportunities for Racial and Ethnic Minorities
Are Growing but Limited   316
**Sport Participation and Occupational Careers
among Former Athletes   317**
Highly Paid Professional Athletes and Career
Success after Playing Sports   318
Athletic Grants and Occupational Success   320
**Summary: Do Money and Power Matter in
Sports?   322**

11   Sports and the Economy: What are the characteristics of commercial sports?   325

**The Emergence and Growth of Commercial
Sports   327**
General Conditions   327
Class Relations and Commercial Sports   327
The Creation of Spectator Interest in
Sports   328

Economic Motives and the Globalization of
Commercial Sports   330
**Commercialization and Changes in
Sports   336**
Structure and Goals of Sports   336
Orientations of the Athletes, Coaches, and
Sponsors   338
Organizations That Control Sports   341
**Owners, Sponsors, and Promoters in
Commercial Sports   341**
Professional Sports in North America   341
REFLECT ON SPORTS: Stadium
Construction: A Tale of Two Cities   348
Amateur Sports in North America   352
**The Legal Status and Incomes of Athletes in
Commercial Sports   353**
Professional Athletes   354
Amateur Athletes in Commercial Sports   360
**Summary: What Are the Characteristics of
Commercial Sports?   362**

12   Sports and the Media: Could they survive without each other?   365

Characteristics of the Media   366
Characteristics of the Internet   371
Characteristics of Video Games and Virtual
Sports   373
**Sports and the Media: A Two-Way
Relationship   373**
Do Sports Depend on the Media?   373
Do the Media Depend on Sports?   377
Sports and the Media: A Relationship Fuelled by
Economics and Ideology   384
Images and Messages in Media Sports   385
How the Media Construct Sports   385
Themes Underlying Media Images and
Messages   387
REFLECT ON SPORTS: Sydney 2000:
The Disappointment Games?   388
Media Impact on Sport-Related
Behaviours   395
Audience Experiences with Media Sports   397

The Profession of Sports Journalism 397
  Journalists on the Job: Relationships with
    Athletes 397
  Sportswriters and Sports Announcers:
    A Comparison 399
**Summary: Could Sports and the Media Survive
  without Each Other? 400**

13 Sports and Politics: How do governments and globalization influence sports? 403

The Sports-Government Connection 404
  Safeguarding the Public Order 405
  Maintaining Health, Fitness, and Physical
    Abilities 409
  Promoting the Prestige and Power of a Group,
    Community, or Nation 410
  Promoting a Sense of Identity, Belonging, and
    Unity 411
  Emphasizing Values Consistent with the
    Dominant Ideology 413
  Increasing Support for Political Leaders and
    Government 414
  Promoting Economic Development 415
  Conclusion and Qualification: Critical Issues and
    Government Involvement in Sports 415
Sports and Global Political Processes 416
  International Sports: Ideals versus
    Realities 416
  REFLECT ON SPORTS: Sport Boycotts and
    the End of Apartheid 418
  Nation-States, Sports, and Cultural
    Ideology 419
  REFLECT ON SPORTS: The Olympic Games:
    Are They Special? 420
  New Political Realities in an Era of Transnational
    Corporations 421
  Other Global Political Issues 425
  Making Sense of New Political Realities 428
Politics in Sports 428
  What Qualifies as a Sport? 429
  What Are the Rules of a Sport? 432
  Who Makes and Enforces the Rules in
    Sports? 432

  Who Organizes and Controls Games, Meets,
    Matches, and Tournaments? 433
  Where Do Sport Events Take Place? 433
  Who Is Eligible to Participate in a Sport? 435
  How Are Rewards Distributed to Athletes and
    Other Organization Members? 435
**Summary: How Do Governments and
  Globalization Influence Sports? 436**

14 Sports in High School and University: Do interscholastic sport programmes contribute to education? 440

**Comparison between Canadian and U.S.
  Interscholastic Sports 442**
**Arguments for and against Interscholastic
  Sports 445**
**Interschool Sports and the Experiences of High
  School Students 445**
  High School Student-Athletes 445
  Student Culture in High Schools 450
  Additional Effects of High School Sports 452
**Interuniversity Sports and the Experiences of
  Students 453**
  The Diversity of Student-Athlete
    Experiences 453
  Grades and Graduation Rates: How Do Student-
    Athletes Compare with Other Students 454
**Do Schools and Universities Benefit from
  Interscholastic Sport Programmes? 455**
  School Spirit 455
  School Budgets 456
**High School Sports: Problems and
  Recommendations 457**
  Restricted Budgets 457
  Overemphasis on "Sport Development"
    Models 458
  Limited Participation Access 460
**Interuniversity Sports: Problems and
  Recommendations 463**
  Athletic Scholarships 463
  Relationships with High-Performance
    Sports 464

Gender Equity   464
Restricted Budgets   466
**Summary: Are Interscholastic Sports
Educational?   467**

15 Sports in the Future: What can we expect?   470

Major Sport Forms in the Future   471
Power and Performance Sports   472
Pleasure and Participation Sports   472
Future Trends in Sports   473
The Ongoing Dominance of Power and
Performance Sports   473
The Growth of Pleasure and Participation
Sports   475
Specific Forecasts   479
Professional Sports   479
High School and University Sports   480
Youth Sports   481
Spectators and Spectator Sports   481
Participant Sports   482

Technology and Media   483
Organization and Rationalization   484
Commercialism and Consumerism   484
Gender Equity and Ethnic Diversity   485
The Challenge of Making the Future   486
Theories Used to Form Visions and Develop
Strategies   486
Change Means Different Things to Different
People   489
Four Vantage Points for Making Changes   489
REFLECT ON SPORTS: Athletes as Change
Agents: Does It Ever Happen?   491
**Summary: What Can We Expect in the
Future?   492**

Credits   495

References   497

Name Index   530

Subject Index   536

Preface

PREFACE TO THE FIRST CANADIAN EDITION

As many observers have noted, Canada is such an unlikely country. Unlike most other countries, the population does not share an ethnicity or even have a common language. It is complicated in terms of climate, size, geography, and population, as well as in the distribution of that population. It has two or three founding nations (depending on who is counting); two official languages; a complex sharing of governmental power between the federal government and ten provinces and three territories; and more spiritual, ethnic, and racial diversity and a higher rate of immigration than any country in the world.

In many ways, sports in Canada are different from sports in the United States:

- The history of sports since European contact is quite different.
- The ways in which Canada has dealt with issues of violence in sports, drug abuse in sports, problems relating to children in sports, and legal issues regarding gender relations in sports are quite different from the United States.
- The racial, ethnic, and social class structure of Canada, the way in which Canada deals with diversity, and the implications of those differences for sports are quite different from the United States.

- The Canadian economy and media have distinct differences from the United States, and the political system in Canada (together with the involvement of politics in sports) is distinctly different.
- The ways in which sports are organized in high schools and universities in Canada are different from the United States.
- The relative lack of emphasis on religion in Canadian society represents a distinct difference from the United States.

And yet, there are also many similarities between Canada and the United States. For this reason it has been possible to use U.S. sociology of sport text books in Canada when no viable alternatives were available. Instructors often supplemented those texts—the most popular of which was Jay Coakley's *Sports in Society*—with Canadian readings and lecture materials.

PURPOSE OF THE TEXT

The first Canadian edition of *Sports in Society: Issues and Controversies* grew out of discussions between both authors, and discussions with numerous Canadian colleagues who have used the U.S. editions of *Sports in Society*. We all agreed that, while the U.S. edition had many features that were attractive to Canadian students, there were just too many differences between Canada and the United States, in terms of both sports and society, which could not be captured by the U.S. edition. This Canadian adaptation is designed to meet this need. While the overall scope and goals of the text remain the same, Canadian examples and photos have been included, Canadian research has been cited, and major changes have been made when the "issues and controversies" in Canada are different from those in the United States.

In addition to providing Canadian students with Canadian materials, there are three further aims of this first Canadian edition. First, it is designed to show students how sociology can be used to study sports in society. Second, it is written to encourage students to ask questions and think critically about sports as parts of social life. Third, it is organized to facilitate the use of published literature combined with the Internet and the World Wide Web to learn about sports in society.

We organize the chapters around issues and questions designed to arouse curiosity, and then discuss them in terms of recent research and theory in the sociology of sport. Although the concepts and source materials are not taken exclusively from sociology, discussions throughout the book are grounded in a sociological approach. Therefore, the emphasis is clearly on sports and sport-related actions as they occur in social and cultural contexts. Current issues and controversies are also highlighted in Reflect on Sports boxes throughout the text, which are designed to provoke student interest and stimulate critical thinking. Each chapter concludes with a list of fully updated Suggested Readings and Website Resources to acquaint students with Canadian and international research literature.

Throughout the book, we tend to use the term sports rather than sport. We do this to emphasize that the forms and meanings of sports vary from place to place and time to time. We want to avoid the inference that sport has an essential and timeless quality apart from the

contexts in which people invent, develop, define, plan, package, promote, and play sports.

FOR WHOM IS THIS BOOK WRITTEN?

Sports in Society is written for those taking their first look at sports as parts of culture and society. The content of each chapter is presented so that it can be understood by first year university students who have not taken other courses in sociology or sport sciences. Discussions of issues do not presume in-depth experiences in sports or detailed knowledge of sports (or sociological) jargon and statistics. Our goal is to encourage students to think more critically about sports and how sports are related to their social lives. We use concepts, theories, and research as tools that enable us to dig into sports and see them as more than activities that simply reflect the world in which we live.

Since the book is organized in terms of an issues approach, the content of many chapters is useful for those concerned with sport-related policies and programme administration. Our emphasis throughout the book is on making sports more democratic and making sport participation more accessible to all people.

Given that there are so few books written about sports in Canadian society, we also believe that this Canadian edition will be useful for non-Canadians interested in sports in Canadian society, and for students and scholars who may be interested in taking a comparative approach to studying issues and controversies in sports in Canada and other societies.

WHAT IS NEW IN THE FIRST CANADIAN EDITION?

This edition is a total adaptation of the U.S. seventh edition; each chapter has been revised line-by-line. Our goal has been to preserve all of the best features of the seventh edition and to include Canadian materials and draw international comparisons when appropriate.

For the most part, the essential organization of the text has been preserved; however, religion, one of the institutions included in the U.S. edition, has been excluded from the Canadian edition. There are several reasons for this. First, recent survey data in Canada indicate that organized religion has far less significance in the country than it has in the United States. This does not mean that Canadians are not spiritual, or that there is no relationship between sport and religion in Canada. However, the relationships are not nearly as evident as in the United States and, as a consequence, there is very little Canadian research on the topic (some of that research is incorporated into Chapter 4).

Second, removing a chapter has facilitated the inclusion of additional Canadian information without the loss of important U.S. material.

Third, a fifteen-chapter text better fits the length of a Canadian university term. For those who are interested in the relationships between religion and sports, we have included the chapter from the U.S. edition on the Online Learning Centre (www.mcgrawhill.ca/college/coakley). The organization of the first Canadian edition is as follows:

- Chapters 1–3 deal with introductory materials: definitions, theories, and the historical development of sports.
- Chapters 4–7 deal with socialization and the character of sports: children's involvement, "deviance," and violence.
- Chapters 8–10 deal with equity issues: gender, race/ethnicity, and social class, and how these affect participation in sports.
- Chapters 11–14 deal with social institutions and their relationships with sports: the economy, media, politics, and education.

- Chapter 15 provides concluding materials and proposals about how sports might look, and how we might make them look, in the future.

The first Canadian edition incorporates over 175 new references, approximately 55 new photographs, and 11 new Reflect on Sports boxes to illustrate Canadian approaches to sports and to the sociology of sport. Below is a chapter-by-chapter summary of just some of the content changes in this adaptation.

Chapter 1: The Sociology of Sport: What is it and why study it?

- Reorganized the location of the definition of "sports" for clarity
- Simplified discussion of basic and applied research

Chapter 2: Using Social Theories: What can they tell us about sports in society?

- Reduced coverage of figurational theory to reflect its limited use in Canadian sociology of sport
- Added material to reflect Canadian contributions to sociological theory, and to theoretical developments in the sociology of sport

Chapter 3: A Look at the Past: Does it help us understand sports today?

- Made minor changes to first half of the chapter (sports in Europe before "contact")
- Made substantial changes with regard to "post-contact" development of sports to reflect the specific developments in Canada

Chapter 4: Sports and Socialization: Who plays and what happens to them?

- Replaced many of the extended examples of socialization research with Canadian examples

Chapter 5: Sports and Children: Are organized programmes worth the effort?

- Rewritten to reflect the particular nature of children's organized sports in Canada and a number of "made in Canada" solutions
- Added a Reflect on Sports box on "Solving the Problems in Children's High Performance Sports"
- Incorporated material on "Informal Player-Controlled Sports versus Organized Adult-Controlled Sports" into a Reflect on Sports box

Chapter 6: "Deviance" in Sports: Is it out of control?

- Revised to reflect the theoretical problems with using the term "deviance" in a book advocating a critical approach to sociology
- Included Canadian examples throughout
- Added two new Reflect on Sports boxes: "Hazing and University Policy" and "Ben Johnson, the Dubin Commission, and Drug Testing in Canada"

Chapter 7: Violence in Sports: How does it affect our lives?

- This chapter has been revised to incorporate Canadian examples and approaches to controlling violence in sports
- Added three new Reflect on Sports boxes: "Brashear & McSorley: A Case of Criminal Violence?", "Sexual Harassment and Abuse," and "Fair Play Leagues"

Chapter 8: Gender and Sports: Does equity require ideological changes?

- This chapter has been extensively revised as it was frequently cited as an example of the need for a Canadian adaptation—instructors told us, "our students think Title IX applies in Canada!"
- Included Canadian human rights and gender equity legislation and policies
- Incorporated Canadian examples and approaches to gender and sports issues and controversies

- Added a new Reflect on Sports box: "Girls Playing on Boys' Teams: The Justine Blainey Case"

Chapter 9: Race and Ethnicity: Are they important in sports?

- This chapter has been substantially re-written to reflect the particular racial and ethnic structure of Canada
- Provided Canadian census data, and focused on three major sets of racial/ethnic relations in Canada: anglophone/francophone relations, Aboriginal/non-Aboriginal relations, and immigrant/non-immigrant relations
- Added a new Reflect on Sports box on "Sport and Bilingualism"

Chapter 10: Social Class: Do money and power matter in sports?

- Canadian sociological researchers have dealt more often with issues and controversies related to social class than their U.S. counterparts, and this is reflected in the material and examples presented in this chapter
- Added a new Reflect on Sports box on "The Odds of Becoming a Professional Athlete" to incorporate Canadian data on becoming an NHL player or a PGA golfer
- New table assessing the status of prominent figures in Canadian sports

Chapter 11: Sports and the Economy: What are the characteristics of commercial sports?

- Modified to reflect the "branch plant" nature of the Canadian economy in the globalized economy of sports
- Included new Canadian examples, information, and data, such as tobacco sponsorship legislation in Canada
- Added a new Reflect on Sports box on "Stadium Construction: A Tale of Two Cities"

Chapter 12: Sports and the Media: Could they survive without each other?

- Outlined the structure of media in Canada, particularly the widespread exposure of Canadians to U.S. media and the place of public broadcasting in Canada
- Included Canadian data and examples on issues ranging from Olympic rights fees to gender representation
- Added a new Reflect on Sports box on "Sydney 2000: The Disappointment Games?" to reflect themes developed in Canadian media

Chapter 13: Sports and Politics: How do governments and globalization influence sports?

- Revised to reflect the political structure of sports in Canada, and federal and provincial government involvement in sports
- Added a new Reflect on Sports box: "Sport Boycotts and the End of Apartheid" to indicate Canadian involvement in this major social change

Chapter 14: Sports in High School and University: Do interscholastic sport programmes contribute to education?

- Substantially re-written to reflect the relationships between sports and education in Canada
- Focused mostly on sports in high schools and universities, and developed the comparison between sports and education in the U.S. and in Canada
- Provided an up-to-date account of crises in high school sports, and the controversy over the introduction of athletic scholarships in Canada

Chapter 15: Sports in the Future: What can we expect?

- Incorporated of David Foot's demographic research regarding the future of sports and

physical activity in Canada's "greying" and "greening" population
- Included Canadian examples

INSTRUCTOR RESOURCES

i-Learning Sales Specialist

Your *Integrated Learning Sales Specialist* is a McGraw-Hill Ryerson representative who has the experience, product knowledge, training, and support to help you assess and integrate any of the below-noted products, technology, and services into your course for optimum teaching and learning performance. Whether it's how to use our test bank software, helping your students improve their grades, or how to put your entire course on-line, your *i*-Learning Sales Specialist is there to help. Contact your local *i*-Learning Sales Specialist today to learn how to maximize all McGraw-Hill Ryerson resources!

iLearning Services Program

McGraw-Hill Ryerson offers a unique iServices package designed for Canadian faculty. Our mission is to equip providers of higher education with superior tools and resources required for excellence in teaching. For additional information visit www.mcgrawhill.ca/highereducation/eservices/.

Instructor's Manual and Test Bank

This supplement has been fully adapted to accord with the first Canadian edition text. It includes chapter outlines, multiple choice and true-false test questions, and discussion/essay questions for each chapter.

Computerized Test Bank

The questions in the Test Bank are also available on Brownstone, a powerful, accessible test-generating program on a hybrid CD-ROM. With Brownstone, instructors can easily select questions and print tests and answer keys. Instructors can also customize questions, headings, and instructions; add or import their own questions; and print tests in a choice of printer-supported fonts.

Online Learning Centre

The Online Learning Centre for *Sports in Society*, First Canadian Edition (www.mcgrawhill.ca/college/coakley), features a variety of instructor resources, including excerpts from past editions that add depth and background to current chapter topics, downloadable supplements, and Web links, in a passcode-protected environment.

PageOut

PageOut™

Build your own course website in less than an hour. You don't have to be a computer whiz to create a website, especially with an exclusive McGraw-Hill product called PageOut. It requires no prior knowledge of HTML, no long hours of coding, and no design skills on your part. With PageOut, even the most inexperienced computer user can quickly and easily create a professional-looking course website. Simply fill in templates with your information and with content provided by McGraw-Hill, choose a design, and you've got a website specifically designed for your course. Visit us at www.pageout.net to find out more.

STUDENT RESOURCES

Online Learning Centre

The Online Learning Centre for *Sports in Society*, First Canadian Edition (www.mcgrawhill.ca/college/coakley), features learning and study tools such as chapter quizzes, additional readings, and Web links.

PowerWeb: Health & Human Performance

This unique online tool provides students with premium content such as current articles, curriculum-based materials, weekly updates with assessment, informative and timely world news, web links, research tools, study tools, and interactive exercises.

ACKNOWLEDGEMENTS

A great many people are involved in adaptations such as this, but particular thanks must go to Jay Coakley for his generosity of spirit and academic integrity in permitting this Canadian adaptation of a text that he has nurtured so carefully through eight editions.

Our students have helped to write this text in many ways that they could not imagine, but especially in providing constructive critiques of our ideas, and in opening our eyes to new ways of looking at sports as social phenomena.

Special thanks go to friends and colleagues who helped in so many ways with this adaptation: Louise Donnelly for her love and support, and for her tolerance of my use of the dining room table; Yuka Nakamura for her invaluable help on chapter 9; Margaret MacNeill for her help on chapter 12 and her help with photographs; Parissa Safai for her help on chapter 14; and Graham Knight for his help on the Disappointment Games box in chapter 12. Other colleagues and graduate students at the University of Toronto—Bruce Kidd, Brian Pronger (get well soon), Russell Field, Caroline Fusco, Ted Norman, and LeAnne Petherick, have helped in all kinds of ways, as have colleagues and friends in the sociology of sport community across Canada, especially Mike Atkinson, James Gillett, Jean Harvey, Nancy Theberge, Phil White, Brian Wilson, and Kevin Young. Many individuals and agencies also helped with fact-checking, especially Stephen Wenn at Wilfred Laurier University, the CFL, and the Canadian Olympic Committee.

Our appreciation goes to the publisher's reviewers, whose suggestions were crucial in the planning and writing of this adaptation. They include:

Robert Argue, M.A., Ryerson University
Michael Atkinson, Ph.D., McMaster University
Rick Bevis, M.A., Malaspina University College
Dayna Daniels, Ph.D., University of Lethbridge
Susan L. Forbes, Ph.D., Brock University
Jean Harvey, Ph.D., University of Ottawa
Carl James, Ph.D., York University
Ann Oishi, M.H.K., College of New Caledonia
Robert Pitter, Ph.D., Acadia University
Christopher Stevenson, Ph.D., University of New Brunswick
Louis Svenningsen, M.Sc., University of Manitoba
Nancy Theberge, Ph.D., University of Waterloo
Kevin Young, Ph.D., University of Calgary

Thanks also to the staff at McGraw-Hill Ryerson—Jennifer DiDomenico, Senior Developmental Editor, and Joanne Murray, Supervising Editor—and their freelancers, Permissions Researcher Alison Derry and Copy Editor Mike Kelly.

Peter Donnelly
Burlington, ON

Online
LearningCentre

www.mcgrawhill.ca/college/coakley

FOR THE STUDENT

- Want to get higher grades?

- Want instant feedback on your comprehension *and* retention of the course material?

- Want to know how ready you *really* are to take your next exam?

- Want the extra help at *your* convenience?

Of course you do!

Then check out your
Online Learning Centre!

- Online Quizzes
- Additional Readings
- Web Research

FOR THE INSTRUCTOR

- Want an easy way to test your students prior to an exam that *doesn't* create more work for you?

- Want to access your supplements *without* having to bring them all to class?

- Want to integrate current happenings into your lectures *without* all the searching and extra work?

- Want an *easy* way to get your course on-line?

- Want to *free up more time* in your day to get more done?

Of course you do!

Then check out your
Online Learning Centre!

- Downloadable Supplements
- PageOut
- Online Resources

McGraw-Hill Ryerson

Higher Learning. Forward Thinking.™

Sculpture outside Hockey Hall of Fame
(CP/Steve White)

The Sociology of Sport

What is it and why study it?

Sport is all hoke and hype, but I find it outrageous and wonderful.

> —**Dick Beddoes, Canadian sportswriter (1975)**

Sport is no longer just sport for individual expression. Rather, it has become spectacle, with a jaundiced eye on the profit margin.

> —**Robert Rinchart, author, *Players All* (1998)**

The rituals of sport engage more people in a shared experience than any other institution or cultural activity today.

> —**Varda Burstyn, author, *The Rites of Men* (1999)**

 Online Learning Centre Resources

Visit *Sports in Society's* Online Learning Centre at **www.mcgrawhill.ca/college/coakley** for additional information and study material for this chapter.

WHAT IS SOCIOLOGY?

Most of you reading this book have experienced sports personally, as athletes or spectators or both. You probably are familiar with the physical and emotional experiences of sport participation, and you may have extensive knowledge of the rules and regulations of certain sports. You probably know about the lives, on and off the field, of high-profile athletes in your community or country. It is likely that you have followed certain sports by watching them in person and on television, reading about them in the print media or on web pages, or listening to discussions of them on the radio.

This book is written to take you beyond the scores, statistics, and personalities in sports. The goal is to focus on the "deeper game" associated with sports, the game through which sports become an integral part of the social and cultural worlds in which we live.

Fortunately, we can draw on our personal emotions and experiences as we consider this deeper game. Let us use our experiences with community sports in Canada as an example. When young males play junior hockey, we know that team membership may affect their status in school and the way teachers and fellow students treat them. We know it may have implications for their prestige in the community, for their self-images, and for their self-esteem. We know that it may affect even their future relationships, their opportunities in education and the workforce, and their overall enjoyment of life.

Building on this knowledge enables us to move further into this deeper game associated with sports. For example, we might ask why Canadians place such importance on professional sports and high-performance athletes. What does that say about our institutions, our communities, and our values? We might study how sport programmes are organized and how they are related to the way many people think about masculinity and femininity, about achievement and competition, about pleasure and pain, about winning and fair play, and about many other things important to those who endorse and promote the programmes. We might ask how sports influence the status structure that exists in our institutions, our communities, and our society, and how athletes fit into that structure. We also might ask if the organization of sports is influenced by new forms of corporate sponsorships and examine athletes' ideas about the corporations whose names and logos are on their uniforms and on the surfaces of their sport facilities.

In other words, sports are more than just games and meets; they are also **social phenomena**[1] that have meanings that go far beyond scores and performance statistics. In fact, sports are related to the social and cultural contexts in which we live; they provide the stories and images that many of us use to explain and evaluate these contexts, the events in our lives, and our connections to the world around us.

People who study sports in society are concerned with the deeper meanings and stories associated with sports in particular cultures. They use their research to develop an understanding of (1) the societies in which sports exist, (2) the social worlds that are created around sports, and (3) the experiences of individuals and groups associated with sports.

Sociology[2] is important when it comes to studying sports as social phenomena. It provides concepts, theoretical approaches, and research methods to describe and understand behaviour and social interaction as they occur in particular social and cultural contexts. Sociology gives us the tools we need to examine social life *in context*, in its "social location." These tools enable us to "see" behaviour as it is connected with

---

[1]Social phenomena are occasions or events involving social relationships and collective action and having relevance in the social lives of particular collections of people.

[2]Important concepts used in each chapter are identified in **boldface.** Unless they are accompanied by a footnote that contains a definition, the definition is given in the text itself. This puts the definition in context rather than separating it in a glossary.

history, politics, economics, and cultural life. In this book, we use sociology to see sports as a part of social and cultural life and to describe and understand social issues related to sports. As we do this, it is important that we know what the terms *culture* and *society* mean.

Culture

Culture consists of the ways of life people create in a particular society. These ways of life are complex. They come into existence and are changed as people in a society come to terms with and sometimes struggle over how to do things, how to relate with one another, and how to make sense out of the things and events that make up their experiences. Culture is not something that is imposed by some people on others; rather, it is a creation of people interacting with one another. It consists of all the socially invented ways of thinking, feeling, and acting that emerge in particular groups as people try to survive, meet their needs, and achieve a sense of significance in the process. Of course, some people have more power and resources than others to use in the "culture creation" process.

Sports are parts of cultures. Therefore, many sociologists refer to sports as **cultural practices.** Like other cultural practices, sports are human creations that come into being as people struggle over what is important and how things should be done in their groups and societies. This is why sports have different forms and meanings from one place to another and why they change over time: people never come to once-and-for-all-time definitions of the ways things should be in their lives. For example, traditional martial arts and sumo wrestling in Asia have different meanings, organizations, and purposes than individual sports such as boxing and wrestling in Canada. Basketball's meaning, organization, and purpose have changed considerably since 1891, when it was developed at a YMCA in Massachusetts as an indoor exercise activity to occupy the time of young men during

winter evenings. Canadian James Naismith, who invented basketball as part of an assignment in a physical education course, would not recognize his game if he were to see Vince Carter slam dunk during the Olympics while a billion people watch on television and thousands of others pay hundreds of dollars to see the game in person. It is important to know about these cultural and historical differences when we study sports as social phenomena.

Society

In this book, the term **society** refers to a collection of people living in a defined geographical territory and united through a political system and a shared sense of self-identification that distinguishes them from other collections of people. For example, as separate societies, Canada and Japan have different cultures, or ways of life. Canada and the United States are also different societies with different cultures, although there are some important similarities between them. We can understand the forms and meanings of sports in Japan only in connection with Japanese history, society, and culture. The same is true for other sports in other societies, even in societies that have cultural similarities.

As you read this book, keep in mind that sports have different forms and meanings from place to place and time to time. This is the case because sports are **social constructions.** In other words, sports are activities to which human beings give form and meaning as they live their lives with one another. Because sports are social constructions, they can be changed and given different forms and meanings (socially re-constructed). Also, because sports are social constructions, sociologists study them in connection with social relationships and social, political, and economic processes. Thus, sociologists ask questions about why particular groups and societies have identified some physical activities as sports and not others. They ask why sports are organized in particular

The notion that sports are social constructions implies that human beings create them and human beings can change them. This leads some people to identify things about sports that should be changed; others resist this notion because they benefit from sports as they are currently organized.

ways, why different groups and societies associate different meanings with sports and sport participation, and who benefits from the organization and definition of sports in society.

In summary, sports are cultural practices that differ from place to place and time to time. How they are defined, organized, and integrated into social life varies from group to group. The types of sports played in a particular group or society, the organization of sports, the resources dedicated to sports and sport programmes, who plays sports, the conditions under which sport participation occurs, who sponsors and controls sports, the definition of an "athlete," and the meanings associated with sport participation are all determined through social interaction within a cultural context. This means that to understand sports we must view them as social phenomena. Sociology provides us with the analytical tools that will help us do this as we discuss major issues related to sport in society in this book.

The remainder of this chapter focuses on four additional questions:

1. What are sports, and how are they related to similar activities, such as play and dramatic spectacle?
2. What is the sociology of sport?
3. Why study sports as social phenomena?
4. What is the current status of the sociology of sport?

The answers to these questions are guides for understanding the material in chapters 2 through 15.

WHAT ARE SPORTS?

This question may seem elementary. We certainly have a good enough grasp of the meaning of sports to talk about them with others. However, when we study sports systematically, it helps to have a precise definition of what we are talking about. For example, can we say that two groups of children playing road hockey in an Alberta town and a pickup game of soccer on a Mexican beach are engaged in sports? Their activities are quite different from what occurs during games in the Little League World Series, or in the Air Canada Centre, or in soccer's World Cup tournament. These differences become significant when parents ask if playing sports is good for their children, or when community leaders ask if they should fund sports with public money, or when school officials ask if sports contribute to the educational missions of their schools.

Students ask us if jogging and skipping are sports. How about weight lifting? hunting? scuba diving? darts? automobile racing? ballroom dancing? chess? professional wrestling? skateboarding? the X Games? paintball? a piano competition? Should any or all of these activities be called sports? In the face of such a question, many scholars feel that we should think about the social organization, social dynamics, and social implications of certain activities to determine which ones are similar enough to be grouped together when we do sociological research. For this reason, many people in the sociology of sport have decided that a precise definition of **sports** is needed. Then we can study sports as distinct from other activities, which may have different social dynamics and social implications, and we can share our research with others who have similar interests.

Although definitions of *sports* vary, those who offer definitions tend to emphasize that *sports are institutionalized competitive activities that involve rigorous physical exertion or the use of relatively complex physical skills by participants motivated by personal enjoyment and external rewards.* Parts of this definition are clear, but other parts need explanations.

First, sports are *physical activities.* Therefore, according to the definition, chess probably is not a sport, since playing chess is more cognitive than physical. Are darts and pool physical enough to qualify as sports under this definition? Making this determination is arbitrary, since there are no objective rules for how "physical" an activity must be to qualify as a sport. Pairs ice dancing is considered a sport in the Winter Olympics, so why not add ballroom dancing to the Summer Games? This question was asked by members of the International Olympic Committee (IOC) in connection with the 2000 Games in Sydney.

Second, sports are *competitive activities*, according to this definition. Sociologists realize that competitive activities have different social dynamics from cooperative or individualistic activities. They know that when two girls kick a soccer ball to each other on the grass outside their home, it is sociologically different from what happens when the Canadian women's soccer team plays the U.S. national team in the under-19 World Cup, so it makes sense to separate them for research purposes.

Third, sports are *institutionalized activities.* **Institutionalization** is a sociological term referring to the process through which behaviours and organization become patterned or standardized over time and from one situation to another. Institutionalized activities have formal rules and organizational structures, which people use to frame and guide their actions from one situation to another. When we say that sports are institutionalized activities, we distinguish what happens when two skiers decide to race each other down their favourite ski slope while vacationing in Whistler from what happens when skiers race each other in a World Cup giant slalom event, which has been highly organized according to strict rules laid down by the Fédération Internationale de Ski (FIS). When it comes to defining *sports*, many sociologists would say that the process of institutionalization includes the following:

1. *The rules of the activity become standardized.* This means that sports have rules that are not simply produced by a single group getting

together on an informal basis. Rules in a sport are based on more than spontaneous expressions of individual interests and concerns. In sports, the rules of the game define a formal and official set of behavioural and procedural guidelines and restrictions. They permit competition to occur between teams and individuals who may not share the same language or other cultural traditions.

2. *Official regulatory agencies take over rule enforcement.* When the physical performances of teams or individuals are compared from one competitive event to another, it is necessary for a regulatory agency to sanction games and meets and to ensure that standardized conditions exist and rules are enforced. Regulatory agencies could include everything from a local rules committee for a children's softball league to the central office of Canadian Interuniversity Sport (CIS).

3. *The organizational and technical aspects of the activity become important.* When competition is combined with external rule enforcement, an activity becomes increasingly *rationalized*. This means that players and coaches come to develop strategies and training schedules to improve their chances for success within the rules. Additionally, equipment and technologies are developed and manufactured to enhance performance and to maximize the range of experiences available through participation.

4. *The learning of game skills becomes formalized.* This occurs for two major reasons. First, as the organization and the rules of the activity become more complex, they must be presented and explained to people in systematic ways. Second, as the stakes associated with competitive success grow,

> What disqualifies war from being a true game is probably what also disqualifies the stock market and business—the rules are not fully known nor accepted by all the players.
> —Marshall McLuhan, author, *Understanding Media* (1964)

participants at various skill levels begin to seek guidance from experts. Instructors or coaches are often supplemented by others, such as trainers, dietitians, sport scientists, managers, and team physicians.

Fourth, according to this definition, sports are *activities played by people for personal enjoyment and external rewards.* This means that participation in sports involves a combination of two sets of motivations. One is based in the internal satisfactions associated with expression, spontaneity, and the pure joy of participation; the other motivation is based in external satisfactions associated with displaying physical skills in public and receiving approval, status, or material rewards (trophies, medals, prizes, salaries) in the process. When we define sports in this way, we can distinguish them from both play and dramatic spectacle (see the photos on the next page). **Play** involves expressive activity done for its own sake; it may be spontaneous or guided by informal norms. An example of play is three four-year-olds who, during a recess period at school, spontaneously run around a playground, yelling joyfully while throwing playground balls in whatever directions they feel like throwing them. Of course, it makes sociological sense to distinguish this type of behaviour, motivated *primarily* by personal enjoyment and expression, from what happens in sports. **Dramatic spectacle** involves performances to entertain an audience. An example of dramatic spectacle is four professional wrestlers paid to entertain spectators by staging a skillful and cleverly choreographed tag-team match in which outcomes are designed for audience entertainment. It also makes sociological sense to distinguish this type of physical activity, motivated *primarily* by a desire to

Many sociologists define *sports* in precise terms, so they can distinguish sports from other activities, such as informal play and dramatic spectacle. Interschool wrestling is sociologically different both from wrestling that might occur in a backyard or in the televised spectacle "Raw Is War." We used "action figures" to represent dramatic spectacle, partly because pro wrestling organizations exercise restrictive control over the images of their events and "personalities." (Jay Coakley)

perform for the entertainment of others, from what happens in sports.

Does this mean that sports do not involve elements of play and spectacle? No, it means that

sports involve combinations of both. It is the combination of intrinsic enjoyment and the desire to display physical skills, and the effort to preserve some sort of balance between these two factors, that distinguishes sports from either play or dramatic spectacle. People who define *sports* in this way might complain when physical activities are not "organized enough" to enable them to know what's going on. They also might complain that, when activities are choreographed so carefully for entertainment purposes, they seem to be "staged."

In summary, many sociologists feel it is important to define *sports* in order to distinguish them from other activities that are sociologically dissimilar. This is a practical approach, but it has potentially serious problems associated with it. For example, when we focus our attention on institutionalized, competitive activities, we may overlook physical activities in the lives of many people who have neither the resources to formally organize those activities nor the desire to make their activities competitive. In other words, we may spend all our time considering the physical activities of relatively select groups in society, because those groups have the power to formally organize physical activities and the desire to make those activities competitive. If this happens, we can create the impression that the activities of these select groups are more important parts of culture than the activities of other groups. This, in turn, can contribute to the marginalization of groups who have neither the resources nor the time to play organized sports or who are not attracted to competitive activities.

Ironically, this outcome would reinforce the very ideas and organization that may have disadvantaged these groups in the first place, and we would be doing this in the name of science. But, if we are aware of this potential problem, we can continue to ask critical questions about how sports have become what they are in particular societies and what social purposes they serve. We also can ask questions about how sports are connected to power, privilege, and social relations and about the changes needed to involve more people in the determination of what sports could and should be in society. However, when we ask such questions, we may begin to wonder if there is another way to deal with the definition of *sports*,

a way that does not give priority to organized sports. This has led some scholars to seek an alternative approach to defining *sports*.

An Alternative Approach to Defining Sports

Instead of using a single definition of *sports*, some scholars ask two definition-type questions about sports in a particular society:

1. What activities are counted as sports in a society?
2. Whose sports count the most when it comes to obtaining support and resources?

Asking these questions does not limit the analysis of sports in ways that might happen when a precise definition is used. In fact, asking these questions leads researchers to dig into the social and cultural contexts in which ideas are formed about physical activities. The researchers must explain how and why some physical activities come to be defined as sports and then become culturally important activities in the social life of a particular group or society.

Those who use this alternative approach do not describe sports with a single definition. When they are asked, "What is sport?" they say, "Well, that depends on whom you ask, when you ask, and where you ask." They explain that not everyone has the same way of looking at and defining *sports* and that ideas about sports vary over time and from one place to another. For example, they might note that many people who grew up at the end of the nineteenth century in England, a time when amateur and fair play codes were extremely important, would be horrified, confused, or astonished by what people in Canada today consider to be sports. Similarly, the people who watch CFL football games today would look at many activities that were considered sports in nineteenth-century England and say they were not "real" sports because participants did not train, compete according to schedules, or play in leagues. Maybe people in the year 2100 will define activities played in virtual reality as sports and see what we defined as sports today as backwards, overorganized, and funless activities geared to the physical abilities of the few rather than the interests and fantasies of everyone.

Those who use this alternative approach to defining *sports* also note numerous cultural differences in how people identify sports and include them in their lives. In cultures that emphasize cooperative relationships, the idea that people should compete with each other for rewards might be defined as disruptive, if not immoral. For people in cultures that emphasize competition, physical activities and games that have no winners may seem pointless. These cultural differences are important to understand. Instead of letting a definition of *sports* shape what should be studied, those who use this alternative approach would do research based on what the people in particular cultural settings think is important in their own lives (see Martin and Miller, 1999; Rail, 1998; Rinehart, 1998).

The assumption underlying this approach is that sports themselves are "contested activities." In other words, there is no universal agreement about the meaning, purpose, and organization of sports; there is no universal agreement about who will participate in sports, about the circumstances under which participation will occur, or about who will sponsor sports or the reasons underlying sponsorship. All of these vary over time from group to group and society to society. The most important sociological issue to recognize when we use this approach is that people in particular places at particular times struggle over *whose* ideas about sports will count as *the* ideas in a group or society. A guide for thinking about these issues is in the Reflect on Sports box titled "Sports as Contested Activities" on pages 10–11.

Struggles over whose ideas count when it comes to the meaning, organization, and purpose of sports are much more common than you might think. Consider the different ways

sports might be defined and the different meanings associated with those definitions in connection with the following decisions:

- Whether children younger than six years old should be allowed to play sports, and how sports ought to be organized and what they ought to mean for young children
- Whether money from a local youth sport budget ought to be given to a programme in which young girls are taught skipping or to a programme in which boys and a few girls compete in a roller hockey league at a local arena
- Whether the provincial high school athletic associations ought to include cheerleading as an official high school sport
- Whether skateboarding and hacky sack ought to be supported through a university intramural sport programme
- Whether tenpin bowling, darts, or men's synchronized swimming ought to be recognized as Olympic sports
- Whether a permit to use a sport field in a public park ought to be given to a group that wants to throw Frisbees freely for a couple of hours or to a softball team that plays in an organized community league
- Whether synchronized swimming events ought to be covered in the sports section of a city newspaper, or in the lifestyle section
- Whether an editor ought to assign a sport reporter to a cheerleading clinic attracting hundreds of local girls or to a press conference with boxer Lennox Lewis
- Whether a corporate sport sponsorship should be awarded to a beach volleyball league or to a fitness walking programme for older people
- Whether the WWE wrestler Chris Jericho could be nominated for a "sports person of the year" award

These issues raise important questions about what activities are counted as sports in certain societies at certain points in time. They also raise questions about the usefulness of a single definition of

| REFLECT ON SPORTS | **Sports as Contested Activities** |

When sociologists say that sports are contested activities, they mean that, through history, people have disagreed about what sports could and should be. These disagreements have led to struggles over three major questions about sports and a number of related questions. As you read the following questions, remember that there are many possible answers to each. Sociologists are concerned with how people in different groups and societies arrive at particular answers at various points in time.

1. WHAT IS THE MEANING, PURPOSE, AND ORGANIZATION OF SPORTS?

The struggles related to this question have raised other questions, such as the following:

- What activities will be defined as "official" sports?
- What will be the relative importance of different types of physical skills in those activities? Will strength, size, and speed, for example, be more important than flexibility, balance, and endurance?
- How will sport experiences be evaluated? Will emotional enjoyment be more important than competitive success? Will fun and physical pleasure be more important than performance outcomes? How will participants define *fun?*
- What types of performance outcomes will be important, and how will success be defined, measured, and rewarded? Will external rewards go to the person who completes an event, the one who achieves a personal best, the one who outscores or dominates others in terms of scores or another measure, or the one who lives through the experience without being seriously injured or killed?
- How will excellence be defined—in terms of one's abilities to be tough, aggressive, and dominate others; in terms of all-around abilities to do different things well; in terms of being able to perform a narrowly defined set of skills extremely well; or in terms of being able to maximize enjoyment for self and others?

2. WHO WILL PARTICIPATE IN SPORTS, AND UNDER WHAT CONDITIONS WILL THIS PARTICIPATION OCCUR?

The struggles related to this question have raised other questions, such as the following:

- Will females and males be involved in the same sports? Will they play at the same time or be segregated by sex? Will some sports be defined as girls' and women's sports, while others are defined as boys' and men's sports? On what basis will people make such distinctions? Will rewards for achievement be the same for females and males?
- Will sport participation be open to people regardless of their social class and wealth? Will the rulers and the ruled, the wealthy and the poor, the powerful and the powerless play and watch sports together? Will they be segregated, and for what reasons? Will participation opportunities be equal? Will sponsors support participation for some or all?
- Will sport participation be related to skin colour or ethnicity? Will people from different racial and ethnic backgrounds be allowed or encouraged to play together? Will they be segregated? Will the meanings given to skin colour or ethnicity influence participation patterns or access to participation?
- Will age be a factor in whether people are encouraged or discouraged from participating in sports? Will expectations vary for people of different ages? Will older and younger people play sports together or separately? Will people of different ages have the same access to participation opportunities?
- Will people with able bodies and people with various types of disabilities have the same opportunities? Will they play together or be segregated? For what reasons will integration or segregation occur, and who will benefit from what is decided? How will people define the accomplishments of athletes with disabilities?

Continued

- Will gay men and lesbians be included in sports in the same ways that heterosexual people are? Will homosexual persons be encouraged to participate in all sports?
- Will athletes be in control of the conditions under which they play sports? Will they have the rights and the power to change those conditions to meet their own needs and interests? Will they be paid? Will they be rewarded in noncash terms? How much will players be rewarded, and how will this be determined?

3. HOW WILL SPORTS BE SPONSORED, AND WHAT WILL BE THE REASONS FOR SPONSORSHIP?

The struggles related to this question have raised other questions, such as the following:

- Will sports be sponsored by public agencies and organizations for the sake of the "public good"? Who will determine the public good, and how is *public good* defined?
- Will sports be sponsored by nonprofit groups and organizations? Will the reasons for their sponsorship be related to organizational philosophies? Will the reasons be related to the interests of all group members, or to the interests of some over others?

- Will sports be sponsored by private commercial organizations? To what extent will private sponsorships be designed for the benefit of athletes and communities or for the purpose of maximizing profits and increasing the power of private individuals and corporations in society?
- To what extent will sponsors control the sports and the athletes they support? What will be the legal rights of the sponsors relative to those of the athletes and others involved in sports?

As you can see, sports are indeed contested activities! They may take many forms and have varying consequences in society, depending on how these questions are answered. Furthermore, answers to these questions are never permanent. New answers replace old ones as interests change; as power shifts; as the meanings associated with age, skin colour, ethnicity, gender, and disability change; and as economic, political, and legal forces take new and different forms.

This means that any definition of *sports* reflects the structure and organization of relationships and social life in a particular society at a particular point in time. Of course, definitions can be helpful, but they should always be used with caution. *What do you think?*

....

sports. For example, if sports are institutionalized, competitive physical activities played to achieve internal and external rewards, then why are competitive dancing, aerobics, skipping, and cheerleading not counted as sports? They fit the definition. The fact that they are not considered sports when it comes to important issues such as sponsorships, funding, and formal recognition raises two questions: what is counted as a sport in a society, and how do people determine what is counted as a sport? Answering these questions requires a careful analysis of the cultural context in which

decisions are made in everyday life. The issues raised by asking what activities are counted as sports are challenging. They force us to look at the cultures in which people live their lives and make decisions about what is important.

WHAT IS THE SOCIOLOGY OF SPORT?

This question is best answered at the end of the book instead of the beginning. However, you should have a clear preview of what you will be reading for the next fourteen chapters.

What activities are counted as sports in society? Discussions of this question emphasize that sports cannot be understood apart from cultural values and power relations in a society. As ideas about gender have changed over the past three decades, physical activities such as synchronized swimming have come to be considered sports, despite resistance from some who believe that "real" sports must reflect "manly" attributes. Women athletes and spectators have more power in society today than they have had in the past. (CP/Brendon Dlouhy/*Edmonton Sun*)

1. Why have certain activities (rather than others) been selected and designated as sports in particular groups?
2. Why have sports in particular groups and societies been created and organized in certain ways?
3. How are sports and sport participation included in our personal and social lives, and how do they affect who we are, how we are connected with other people, and how we define those connections?
4. How do sports and sport participation affect our ideas about our own bodies, what is "natural" and "unnatural," masculinity and femininity, social class, race and ethnicity, work, fun, ability and disability, achievement and competition, pleasure and pain, youth and old age, and aggression and violence?
5. How are the meaning, organization, and purpose of sports connected with social relations, material conditions, and the dynamics of power in groups and societies?
6. How are sports related to important spheres of social life, such as family, education, politics, the economy, and the media?
7. How can people use their knowledge about sports and what sports could and should be as a basis for changing them to make social life more fair and democratic?
8. How can people use their knowledge about sports as social phenomena to understand the organization and dynamics of society and social life and then participate as effective agents of progressive change in today's world?

Most people in the sociology of sport agree that the field is the subdiscipline of sociology that studies sports as parts of social and cultural life. The focus of much research and writing in this field is on what many of us refer to as "organized, competitive sports," although many in the field are studying other physical activities as well (Beal, 1999; Markula, 1995; Rinehart and Sydnor, 2003). The people who carry out this research and writing use sociological concepts, theories, and research to answer questions such as the following:

Differences between the Sociology of Sport and the Psychology of Sport

One way to understand the sociology of sport is to contrast it with another discipline that studies sports and behaviour. Consider psychology as a comparison discipline.

Psychologists study behaviour in terms of attributes and processes that exist *inside* individuals. Psychologists focus on motivation, perception, cognition, self-esteem, self-confidence, attitudes, and personality. Psychologists also deal with interpersonal dynamics, including communication, leadership, and social influence, but they usually discuss these things in terms of how they affect attributes and processes that exist inside individuals. Therefore, they might ask a research question such as this: "How is the motivation of athletes related to their personality characteristics and perceptions of their own competence as athletes in their sports?"

Sociologists study behaviour in terms of the social conditions and cultural contexts in which people live their lives. Sociologists focus on the reality *outside and around* individuals. Therefore, sociologists deal with how people form relationships with one another and create social arrangements that enable them to survive and exert some control over their lives. Sociologists also ask questions about how behaviour, relationships, and social life are related to characteristics that are defined as socially relevant by people in particular groups. This is why they often deal with the social meanings and dynamics associated with age, social class, gender, race, ethnicity, disability, sexuality, and nationality. A sociologist might ask a question such as this: "How do prevailing cultural definitions of masculinity and femininity affect the way sport programmes are organized and who participates in sports?"

When it comes to the application of their knowledge, psychologists focus on the personal experiences and the personal troubles of particular individuals. Sociologists may emphasize the ways in which personal troubles are related to public issues (Mills, 1959). They focus on group experiences and the social issues that have an impact on entire categories or groups of people. For example, when studying burnout among young athletes, psychologists would look at factors that exist *inside* the athletes themselves. Because stress has been identified as a key "inside factor" in human beings, psychologists would focus on the existence of stress in the lives

of individual athletes and how stress might affect motivation, performance, and burnout (Smith, 1986). They might use strategies to help individual athletes manage stress through goal setting, personal skill development, and the use of relaxation and concentration techniques.

Sociologists, on the other hand, study burnout in connection with how sport programmes are organized, the treatment of athletes in sport programmes, and athletes' relationships with parents, peers, and coaches. Since burnout often occurs when athletes feel they have lost control over their lives and feel they have no power to make decisions about important things in their lives, sociological intervention would emphasize the need for changes in the organization of sport programmes and athletes' relationships (Coakley, 1992). Such changes might emphasize giving athletes more power within sport organizations and more control over important parts of their lives.

Of course, both approaches have potential value (Gould, 1996). However, some people may see the sociological approach as too complex and too disruptive. They may conclude that it is easier to change individual athletes and the ways in which athletes deal with external conditions than to change the external conditions in which athletes live their lives. This is one of the reasons that those who have power and control in sport organizations often resist sociological approaches. They are uncomfortable with recommendations calling for changes in how they exercise power and control within their organizations. Parents and coaches also might resist approaches that call for changes in their relationships with athletes, especially since they have developed those relationships in ways they feel are best, from their point of view, for everyone involved.

Using the Sociology of Sport

The insights developed through sociological analyses are not always used to make changes in favour of the people who lack power in society.

Like any science, sociology can be used in various ways. For example, research findings can be used to assist powerful people as they try to control and enhance the efficiency of particular social arrangements and organizational structures. Research findings also can be used to assist people who lack power as they attempt to change social conditions and achieve greater opportunities to make choices about how they live their lives (Ingham and Donnelly, 1990).

In other words, sociologists must consider the possible consequences of their work, as well as how they do sociology. Sociologists cannot escape the fact that social life is complex and that the interests of different groups of people in society are not always the same. Sociologists, like the rest of us, must recognize that social life is at least partly shaped by who has power and who does not. Therefore, using sociology is not a simple process that always leads to good and wonderful conclusions for all humankind. This is the reason we must think critically about what we want sociology to do for us when we study sports.

As a result of our thinking about sports in society, we have written this book to help you use sociology to do the following:

1. Think critically about sports, so you can identify and understand social problems and social issues associated with sports in society.
2. Look beyond issues of physical performance and scores to see sports as social phenomena having relevance for the ways people feel, think, and live their lives.
3. Learn things about sports that you can use to make informed choices about your own sport participation and the place of sports in the communities and societies in which you live.
4. Think about how sports in your schools and communities might be transformed so they do not contribute to ideas or conditions that systematically disadvantage some categories of people while privileging others.

Controversies Created by the Sociology of Sport

We view sociology as a critical science. This means that we do not accept the way things are in society as natural or normal or as common sense. Often, the way things are has been socially constructed in a manner that is an advantage to some and a disadvantage to others.

As we have noted, the conclusions sociologists reach sometimes create controversy. This occurs because those conclusions often call for changes in the organization of sports and the structure of social relations in society as a whole. These recommendations often threaten certain people, including those in positions of power and control in sport organizations, those who benefit from the current organization of sports, and those who think the current organization of sports is "right and natural," regardless of its consequences. These are the people with the most to lose if changes are made in social relations and social organization. After all, people with power and control in society know that changes in important parts of society could jeopardize their positions and the privilege that comes with them. This leads many of these people to favour approaches to sports that explain problems in terms of the characteristics of individuals rather than in terms of social conditions and social organization. If theories put the blame for problems on individuals, the solutions will emphasize better ways of controlling people and teaching them how to adjust to society as it is, rather than emphasizing changes in how society is organized (Donnelly, 1999; Scraton, 1999).

The potential for controversy that results from a sociological analysis of sports can be illustrated by looking at some of the research findings on sport participation among women in many countries around the world. Research shows that women, especially women in low-income households, have lower rates of sport participation than other categories of people. Research also shows that there are many reasons for this. The most obvious is that women are less likely than men to have the resources they need to play sports, and they are less likely to have the time and freedom to play sports on a regular basis. Women do not often control the facilities where sports are played, or the programmes in those facilities. The demands of jobs combined with the demands of homemaking and childrearing often cause women to have less free time than men. Women also have less access to transportation and less overall freedom to move around at will and without fear, and they may be expected to take full-time responsibility for the social and emotional needs of family members—a job that can never be completed or done perfectly! Furthermore, the sport programmes that do exist in societies around the world are grounded primarily in the values, interests, and experiences of men. They are controlled by men and geared to the way men have learned to think about their bodies, their relationships to other people, and the way the world operates. To the extent that this is the case,

many men may choose not to support women's participation, by taking care of children, for example. Furthermore, many women may not see sports as appropriate activities for them to take seriously, and the men in their lives may encourage them to continue thinking this way.

It is easy to see the potential for controversy associated with these conclusions. For example, sociologists might use these conclusions to suggest that opportunities to play sports should be increased for women, that resources for women's programmes should be increased, that women and men should share control over sports, and that new variations of sports based on the values and experiences of women should be developed. Other suggestions might call for changes in gender relations, family structures, the organization of work, and the distribution of resources in society. They also might call for changes in who takes care of children, for revised and expanded definitions of femininity and masculinity, and for new forms of social

Local youth sport events are rich contexts for studying the meanings of sports in a culture and the place of sports in community and family life. Issues related to gender, social class, and race and ethnicity often are apparent at these events. (Peter Donnelly)

organization that are more sensitive to how women live their lives in particular cultures.

When sociologists make recommendations about how to increase sport participation among women or how to achieve gender equity in sport programmes, they may not receive positive responses from certain people. In fact, their recommendations may threaten those who benefit from the existing organization of sports and social life. Recommendations also may threaten those who believe that sports and social life were "naturally intended" to be as they are now, regardless of who benefits and who does not. For this reason, some people see the sociology of sport as either too critical and negative, or too idealistic.

Our response to this is that when we study sports as social phenomena, we are obligated to take a skeptical and critical look at the social conditions that affect our lives on and off the playing field. This helps us understand more about our world, even if it makes some people think we are too negative. As we study sports with a critical eye, we must be idealistic as we think about and form images of what sports and society could and should be in the future. Without these images, what would motivate and guide us as we become active citizens in our communities, societies, and world? Of course, it is important to be practical and ready to compromise as we deal with complex issues, but being skeptical and idealistic is important if we want to make a real difference in the world.

WHY STUDY SPORTS AS SOCIAL PHENOMENA?

Sports Are Part of People's Lives

Studying sports is a logical thing for sociologists to do. Sports clearly are an important part of cultures and societies around the world. As we look around us, we see that the Olympic Games, soccer's World Cup, the Tour de France, the tennis championships at Wimbledon, the Stanley Cup, and American football's Super Bowl are now worldwide events capturing the interest of billions of people. Some of these events are televised in over two hundred countries. Children around the world grow up with vivid images of televised sports and sport figures, they play video games based on these sports, and they are encouraged to participate in sports by parents, teachers, and the elite athletes who often are presented as role models in their lives.

People of all ages connect with sports through the media. Newspapers in most cities devote entire sections of daily editions to the coverage of sports. This is especially true in North America, where space given to sports coverage frequently surpasses space given to the economy, politics, or any other single topic of interest. Radio talk shows about sports capture the attention of numerous listeners every day in some countries. Satellites and Internet technology now enable millions of people around the world to share their interest in sports and to have "interactive" experiences while they watch sports. People around the world recognize high-profile sport teams and athletes, and this recognition fuels everything from product consumption to tourism. Team logos are imprinted on hats, shirts, posters, jackets, and other memorabilia and sold around the world. Sales vary with the ebb and flow of popularity among teams and athletes. People schedule not only their vacations but also their weekends and other free time around playing and watching sports. Even when individuals do not have an interest in sports, the people around them may insist on bringing them to games and talking with them about sports to such a degree that they are forced to make sports a part of their lives.

Sport images are so pervasive today that many young people are more familiar with the hairstyles and tattoos of their favourite sport celebrities than they are with the local politicians who make policies that have a significant impact on their lives. At the same time, there are legal fights over who owns the right to profit from selling sport images, especially images that represent the identity or persona of a particular athlete. The media coverage and marketing of celebrity-athletes is another way that sports enter our lives. Clearly, the attention given to certain athletes has turned them into celebrities at least, if not cultural icons and heroes.

People around the world increasingly talk about sports—at work, at home, in bars, on dates, at dinner tables, in school, with friends and family members, and even with strangers at bus stops, in airports, and on the street. Comments about sports provide nonthreatening "conversation openers" with strangers. Relationships often revolve around sports, especially among men, and among an increasing number of women as well. People often identify with teams and athletes so closely that what happens in sports may influence their moods and overall senses of identity and well-being. In fact, people's identities as athletes and fans may be more important to them than their identities related to education, career, religion, or family.

Overall, sports and sport images have become a pervasive part of our everyday lives, especially for those of us living in countries where resources are relatively plentiful and the media are widespread. For this reason, sports are logical topics for the attention of sociologists and anyone else concerned with social life today.

Sports Are Tied to Social Structure and Cultural Ideology

Studying sports as social phenomena is also appropriate because sports are closely tied to **cultural ideology**. Cultural ideology consists of the general perspectives and ideas that people use to make sense of the social world, discover their place in that world, and determine what is important or unimportant and what is right and natural in the world (Hall, 1985). We could say that cultural ideology is a window into the

> Hockey is our national glue. It defines Canada and Canadians. We have so few people in such a large land…But hockey holds us together.
> —Roy Green, host of a Toronto talk radio programe (1996)

underlying "everyday logic" of how people live their lives in a society.

Cultural ideology does not come in a neat package, especially in highly diverse and rapidly changing societies. Different groups in any society develop their own perspectives and ideas for making sense of the social world, and they may not always agree with one another. In fact, different groups often struggle over whose way of making sense of the world is the best way, or the right way, or the moral way. This is where sports become sociologically relevant. Sports consist of activities and situations that either embrace or challenge particular ideologies. As sports are created by people, they may develop around particular ideas about the body and human nature, about how people should relate to each other, about expression and competence, about human abilities and potential, about manhood and womanhood, and about what is important and unimportant in life. These ideas usually support and reproduce what might be called the **dominant ideology**, an ideology that attempts to sustain the power differences in a society. Dominant ideology is built on the perspectives and ideas favoured and promoted by dominant and powerful groups in a society, and it serves the interests of those groups (Theberge, 2000a).

We can use gender ideology in Canada to show how sports are connected with general cultural ideology. In Canadian culture, there are many different perspectives and ideas about gender, about masculinity and femininity, and about relationships between men and women. As sports were developed and became increasingly organized, they were associated with a **gender logic** that was consistent with dominant forms of gender ideology in the culture as a whole. This gender logic usually worked to the advantage of men, while it disadvantaged women. Therefore, when people participated in sports, they often learned a form of "common sense" that led to the conclusion that women were "naturally" inferior to men in any activity requiring strength, physical skills, and emotional control.

This conclusion about male superiority and female inferiority even informed the vocabulary used in connection with many sports. When someone threw a ball correctly, many people would say that he or she threw "like a boy" or "like a man." When someone threw a ball incorrectly, many would say that he or she threw "like a girl." The same was true when running or other physical skills were assessed. If the skill was done correctly, it was done the way a boy or man would do it. If it was done incorrectly, it was done the way a girl or woman would do it. In fact, people generally understood that doing sports, especially sports that were physically demanding, would make a

Billboard showing Nike ad on building at Olympic games in Sydney. (M. MacNeill)

boy into a man. When women excelled at these sports, ideology led many people to say that playing sports was "unnatural" for "real" women. Their gender logic even led them to see strong, competent women athletes as "dykes," or lesbians. They thought that heterosexual femininity and excellence in sports, especially physically demanding and heavy contact sports, could not go together.

This gender logic became such a central part of many sports that some coaches of men's teams even used it to motivate players. These coaches criticized male players who made mistakes or did not play aggressively enough by "accusing" them of "playing like a bunch of girls." Thus, according to the gender logic they used, being a female meant being a failure. This "logic" clearly served for many years to privilege boys and men in sports and disadvantage girls and women, who were never considered to be equal to males when it came to allocating resources and providing opportunities and encouragement to play sports. Although this gender logic has been challenged and discredited in recent years, its legacy continues to privilege some boys and men and disadvantage some girls and women.

The traditional gender logic used in sports has helped to promote or reproduce dominant gender ideology in the society as a whole, which has, in turn, privileged men and disadvantaged women in economic, political, legal, and educational spheres of life. Similarly, the gender logic in many sports over the years has reproduced ideas about masculinity, promoting the notion that manhood is based on being hard, big, tough, strong, aggressive, and willing to endure pain without showing weakness (Burstyn, 1999).

However, cultural ideology is never established permanently. People constantly question it and struggle over it. They challenge the cultural logic used by others, and they even may mount challenges that produce changes in deeply felt and widely accepted perspectives and ideas. In the case of gender ideology, sports have been a "social place"[3] for mounting such challenges to dominant ideas about what is natural and feminine. The history of these struggles over the meaning and implications of gender in sports is complex, but recent challenges by both women and men who do not accept the logic used widely in the past have led to important revisions in dominant cultural ideology. Women athletes have illustrated clearly that females can be physically powerful and capable of noteworthy physical achievements surpassing those of the vast majority of men in the world. Furthermore, the accomplishments of women athletes have raised serious questions about what is "natural" when it comes to gender. We discuss issues related to gender logic in sports in nearly every chapter, but especially chapter 8. The Reflect on Sports box on pp. 21–22, "The Body and the Sociology of Sport," presents issues related to what we consider to be natural when it comes to the body.

Other Ideological Struggles Studying sports as social phenomena is important because sports are sites for many important ideological struggles. For example, ideas about socioeconomic differences and social class are built into dominant forms of sports in many cultures. In other words, many sports are associated with a **class logic.** This class logic serves as a basis for explaining economic success and failure, generally leading to favourable conclusions about the characters and qualifications of those who are wealthy and powerful, as well as to negative conclusions about the characters and qualifications of poor people and those who lack power in society. We discuss this in chapter 10 and in other chapters.

Many sports also are associated with a **race and/or ethnic logic** related to dominant ideas about racial and ethnic categories and sport-related physical skills. When using race logic, people often have associated light or "white" skin with certain athletic abilities and dark or

"black" skin with other athletic abilities. Like other forms of cultural ideology, this race logic varies from one culture to another. However, it can be a very powerful force in social relations. We discuss race and ethnic logic in chapter 9.

People also associate what we might call **character logic** with sports in certain cultures. For example, many sport programmes in Western Europe and North America have been organized around particular beliefs about what character is and how it is developed and expressed. Consequently, many people assume that playing sports teaches people valuable lessons and develops positive character traits. We discuss this issue in connection with questions related to "socialization and sports" in chapters 4 through 7.

As we think about sports and cultural ideology, we must remember that ideology is complex and sometimes inconsistent. Therefore, sports connect with ideology in various and sometimes contradictory ways. We saw this in the example showing that sports are sites for simultaneously reproducing *and* challenging dominant gender ideology in society. Furthermore, sports come in many forms, and those forms can have many social meanings associated with them. For example, baseball is played by similar rules in Japan and Canada and the United States, but the meanings associated with baseball, with games, and with athletes' performances are different in Japanese and North American cultures. Team loyalty is highly prized in Japan and emotional displays by players or coaches are frowned upon, while in Canada and the U.S. individualism is emphasized and emotional displays are accepted and defined as entertaining. Japanese baseball games may end in ties, while many sports in Canada and the U.S. often make every attempt to have clear winners and losers, even if it means playing extra innings, overtime, and "sudden death" periods. This is the case because sports are cultural practices as well as games. Therefore, it is difficult to generalize

---

[3]Sociologists often refer to the "social places" or "social locations" where significant social occasions or developments occur as *sites*.

about the consequences of sports in society. Sports have the social potential to do many things. This is another reason for studying them as social phenomena.

Sports Are Connected to Major Spheres of Social Life

Another reason to study sports as social phenomena is that they are clearly connected to major spheres of social life, including the family, the economy, the media, politics, education, and religion. We discuss these connections in various chapters in this book, but it is useful to highlight them at this point.

Sports and Family Sports are closely related to the family. In Canada, for example, hundreds of thousands of children are involved in a variety of organized sport activities. It is primarily their parents who organize leagues, coach teams, attend games, and serve as "taxi drivers" for child athletes. Family schedules are altered to accommodate practices and games. These schedules also may be affected by the patterns of sport involvement among adult family members. The viewing of televised sport events sometimes disrupts family life and at other times provides a collective focus for family attention. In some cases, relationships between family members are nurtured and played out during sport activities or in conversations about these activities.

Sports and the Economy The economies of most countries, especially wealthy postindustrial countries, have been affected by the billions of dollars spent every year for game tickets, sports equipment, participation fees, athletic club membership dues, and bets placed on favourite teams and athletes. The economies of many local communities have been affected by the presence of sport teams. Some countries use public monies (taxes) to subsidize teams and events. In fact, sports and commerce have fused together, have expanded into public spaces, and have

defined those spaces on their terms (Burstyn, 1999). For example, corporate logos are tied to sport teams and athletes and are displayed prominently in schools, arenas, and parks, among other public and quasi-public areas.

Some athletes make impressive sums of money from various combinations of salaries, appearance fees, and endorsements. Corporations have paid as much as US$100 million to be international Olympic sponsors and have their corporate names associated with the Olympic name and symbol for four years. Many sport stadiums, arenas, and teams are now named after corporations instead of people or images with local cultural or historical relevance. Sponsorships and commercial associations with sports have been so effective that many people around the world now believe that, without Adidas, Coca-Cola, McDonald's, Panasonic, Nike, and other transnational corporations, sports would not exist.

Finally, the fact that average per capita income around the world at the close of the twentieth century was under US$6,000 per year, while a few athletes in North America and Europe were making from US$5 million to US$30 million per year in salary and more than US$10 million per year in endorsements, indicates that sports are cultural practices deeply connected with the material and economic conditions in society.

Sports and the Media Television networks and cable stations may now pay millions of dollars for the rights to televise major games and events. As U.S. television networks drive these rights fees ever higher, even public broadcasters such as the Canadian Broadcasting Corporation and its counterparts in countries such as the U.K. and Australia are obliged to pay increased fees to broadcast events such as the Olympics and the World Cup of soccer. People in sport organizations that depend on spectators are keenly aware that without the media their lives would be different. Also, the images and messages presented

REFLECT ON SPORTS   The Body and the Sociology of Sport

Until recently, most people viewed the body as a fixed, unchanging fact of nature. They saw the body in biological terms rather than social and cultural terms. But more people in various academic fields now recognize that we cannot fully understand the body unless we consider it in social and cultural terms (Blake, 1996; Brownell, 1995; Cole, 2000a; Loy et al., 1993; Shilling, 1994; Turner, 1997). For example, medical historians recently have shown that the body and body parts have been identified and defined in different ways through history and from one culture to another. They also have shown that this is important because it affects medical practice, government policies, social theories, and the everyday experiences of human beings (Fausto-Sterling, 2000; Laqueur, 1990; Lupton, 2000).

Changes in the ways bodies have been socially defined (or "constructed") over the years have had implications for how people think about sex, sex differences, sexuality, ideals of beauty, self-image, body image, fashion, hygiene, health, nutrition, eating, fitness, racial classification systems, disease, drugs and drug testing, violence and power, and many other things that affect our lives. In fact, body-related ideas influence how people view desire, pleasure, pain, and the quality of life. For example, nineteenth-century Europeans and North Americans used insensitivity to pain as a physiological indicator of general character defects in a person and saw muscular bodies as indicators of criminal tendencies and lower-class status (Hoberman, 1992). Today, however, partly in connection with how sports have been defined, people in Europe and North America see the ability to ignore pain as an indicator of strong character, instead of a sign of deviance and defective character. They now regard a muscular body as an indicator of self-control and discipline rather than criminality.

When it comes to sports, the physical body is social in a number of ways. Sociologist John Wilson explains this in the following way:

[In sport] social identities are superimposed upon physical being. Sport, in giving value to certain physical attributes and accomplishments and denigrating others, affirms certain understandings of how mind and body are related, how the social and natural worlds are connected. The identity of the athlete is not, therefore, a natural outgrowth of physicality but a social construction. . . . Sport absorbs ideas about the respective physical potential of men versus women, whites versus blacks, and middle-class versus working-class people. In doing so, sport serves to reaffirm these distinctions. (1994: 37–38)

In fact, sport science has invented new ways to see bodies as complex performance machines with component parts that can be isolated and transformed to enhance specialized competitive performances. This, in turn, has led to an emphasis on monitoring and controlling bodies. Body monitoring and controlling take forms such as weigh-ins, tests for aerobic capacity, muscle biopsies and tissue analysis, the identification of responses to various stressors, hormone testing, the administration of drugs and other chemical substances, drug testing, blood boosting, blood testing, diet regulation and restriction, vitamin regulation, and the measurement of body fat percentage, muscle size, anaerobic capacity, and on and on. In the future, we are likely to see brain manipulations, hormonal regulation, DNA testing, body part replacements, and genetic engineering (Hoberman, 1992). Therefore, the body is cultural in the sense that it is now interpreted and understood in terms of performance outcomes rather than in terms of how people experience and enjoy their bodies. In many sports today, pain rather than pleasure has become the indicator of the "good body," and limiting the percentage of body fat has become such a compulsion that bodies are starved to be "in good shape."

This new way of thinking about the body in cultural terms has challenged traditional Western ideas about the separation of mind and body. It also has raised new questions and issues in the sociology of sport. Some people in the sociology of sport are now working with colleagues in other disciplines who

. . . .

Continued

REFLECT ON SPORTS   The Body and the Sociology of Sport continued

share interests in the body. In fact, their research is based on the notion that culture is *embodied* and that we can learn about culture by studying bodies. They are asking critical questions such as the following:

1. How do people form ideas about what is natural or unnatural, ideal or imperfect, and aesthetically pleasing or ugly and deviant when it comes to bodies in sports and in the culture as a whole?
2. What are the moral, cultural, and sociological implications of how bodies are protected, probed, monitored, tested, trained, disciplined, evaluated, manipulated, and rehabilitated in sports?

3. How are bodies in sports marked by gender, race, (dis)ability, and age, and what are the social consequences of such marking?
4. How are bodies in sports represented in the media and popular culture in general?

These are crucial questions, although they make many people associated with sports uncomfortable because the answers often challenge taken-for-granted ideas about nature, beauty, health, and the organization and purpose of high-performance, competitive sports. We think it is important to ask these questions. *What do you think*?

. . . .

in the media coverage of sports emphasize particular ideological themes, and they influence the ways people see and think about sports and social life. For example, television's use of zoom lenses, special camera angles, filters, isolated coverage of action sequences, slow-motion replays, diagrammatic representations of action, commentary intended to enhance drama and excitement, and "delayed live" coverage all influence how people "see" sports. For those who do not play sports or attend games in person, the mediated versions of sports are the only versions they know.

Over a few decades, the media have converted sports into a major form of entertainment in many societies. Satellite technology makes it possible for the images and messages associated with a single competitive event to be witnessed simultaneously by billions of people. Athletes become global entertainer-celebrities in the process, and powerful corporations sponsor these media events to imprint their logos in people's minds and promote a lifestyle based on product consumption. This certainly raises issues related to values, power, and culture.

Sports and Politics People in many societies link sports to feelings of national pride and a sense of national identity. Despite frequent complaints about mixing sports and politics, most people around the globe have no second thoughts about displaying national flags and playing national anthems at sporting events. Political leaders at various levels of government promote themselves by associating with sports as both participants and spectators. Former athletes have even been elected or appointed to powerful political positions because of their name recognition and reputation from sports.

In Canada, the state is central to the amateur sport system, and has even intervened at the professional sport level. Since the 1960s, the federal government and, to a lesser extent, provincial governments have developed laws and policies that have a major impact on the conduct of sports. International sports have become hotbeds of political controversy in recent years, and many countries around the world have used sports actively to enhance their reputations in global political relationships.

Furthermore, sports involve political processes associated with issues such as who controls sports and sport events, the terms of eligibility and team selection, rules and rule changes, rule enforcement, and the allocation of rewards and punishments. Sports and sport organizations are political because they involve the exercise of power over people's lives.

Sports and Education Sports have become integral parts of school life for many students around the world. In many countries, sports are taught and played in physical education classes. Schools in a few countries have interschool sport teams, and some of these teams attract more attention among students than academic programmes, especially in the United States. At the same time, many of these schools have eliminated or are in the process of eliminating physical education for their student bodies as a whole. As many Canadian scholarship athletes know, some U.S. universities may use their interuniversity teams to promote the quality of their academic programmes while the athletes come to recognize the difficulties of being a serious student in these "big time" programmes. Athletic scholarships have recently become a significant and divisive issue in Canadian Interuniversity Sport (CIS). The interschool sports sponsored by schools in most countries take the form of low-profile, club-based teams that emphasize participation and student control.

Sports and Religion Although formal organized religion has far less significance in Canada than in the United States, with significantly fewer Canadians attending religious services regularly, and a great deal less likelihood that politicians will be identified by their

"This won't take long, will it?"

(Peter Donnelly)

Families and family schedules often are influenced by sport involvement. Sometimes this involvement disrupts family life and interferes with family relationships (left); sometimes it brings family members together in enjoyable ways (right).

religion or use it in their work, there are still some associations between sports and religion. For example, local churches and church groups may sponsor athletic teams and leagues, and the YMCA and other community centres with religious affiliations are widely associated with physical fitness activities. Also, following the U.S. lead, some athletes in Canada have become increasingly likely to display religious beliefs in connection with their sport participation, and may define their sport participation in religious terms (see *Sports in Society* Online Learning Centre [www.mcgrawhill.ca/college/coakley] for a bonus chapter on "Sports and Religion").

In summary, there is no shortage of reasons for studying sports as social phenomena: they are part of our everyday lives, they influence cultural ideology, and they are connected with major spheres of social life.

WHAT IS THE CURRENT STATUS OF THE SOCIOLOGY OF SPORT?

Research and interest in the sociology of sport have grown as organized sports have become increasingly visible and popular in many societies around the world. For example, if you go to www.amazon.ca on the Internet, you will see several hundred books listed in the "Sociology of Sport" and "Sport in Society" categories. However, the growth of the field has been constrained by long-standing intellectual traditions in much of Europe and North America. Because social scientists have traditionally made clear distinctions between leisure and work, and between physical and intellectual activities, they have tended to define play and sports as nonserious, nonproductive activities that did not deserve scholarly attention. However, as social scientists have turned more attention to research on everyday experiences, gender, and the media in society, they have been more likely to study sports in the process.

These intellectual traditions in Europe and North America have exerted more influence in sociology than they have in physical education and kinesiology. Therefore, the roots of the sociology of sport are grounded more firmly in the field of physical education than in sociology itself. In fact, those doing research and teaching courses on sports in society are more likely to have their degrees in physical education, kinesiology, or sport science than in sociology. There are only a handful of departments around the world that declare a formal Ph.D. emphasis in the sociology of sport, and several of these are in Canada (e.g., University of Alberta, University of Toronto, and l'Université de Montréal). Opportunities to study sports in graduate programmes are more prevalent in physical education, kinesiology, and sport science programmes. However, many of these programmes still give higher priority to research on motor learning, exercise physiology, and physical performance than they give to research on social, historical, and philosophical issues and questions.

Professional Associations and Journals

Much of the growth in the sociology of sport has occurred since 1980, and it has been fuelled partly by the formation of professional associations and academic journals devoted to the field. These associations and journals have enabled scholars from different disciplines to meet with each other and to present and publish their ideas and research on sports in society. The journals related to the field are listed in table 1.1. The major organizations are the following:

1. *The International Sociology of Sport Association (ISSA)*. This is the first organization in the field, formed in 1964 and originally known as the International Committee for the Sociology of Sport. It is affiliated with the International Council of Sport Science and Physical Education (ICSSPE) and the International Sociological Association (ISA),

and through both of these organizations with the United Nations Educational, Scientific and Cultural Organization (UNESCO). ISSA meets annually, attracting scholars from all over the world. Since 1965, it has sponsored publication of the *International Review for the Sociology of Sport.*

2. *The North American Society for the Sociology of Sport (NASSS).* This is the principal organization for scholars in the sociology of sport in Canada and the United States. It was formed in 1978, and has held conferences every year since 1980. NASSS has sponsored publication of the *Sociology of Sport Journal* since 1984.

3. *Other organizations.* Many countries and regions have their own sociology of sport organizations. Sometimes, these are informal groups of scholars who meet occasionally, but more often they form official national associations in countries such as Japan, Korea, and Spain. The recently formed Société de Sociologie du Sport de la Langue Française includes members from France, Canada, Belgium, Switzerland, and North Africa. Sociology of sport scholars also meet and present their research at a variety of physical education, sport sciences, and sociology conferences around the world.

Future growth in the sociology of sport depends largely on whether those in the field can conduct and publish research that proves useful for understanding social life in ways that help make the world a better place. However, the scholars in the sociology of sport do not always agree on what is "better" or what types of research will accomplish this goal (Ingham and Donnelly, 1997).

Disagreements in the Sociology of Sport

As in most other sciences, sociology (including the sociology of sport) has both "basic" and "applied" research traditions. In the basic tradition, sociologists are involved in collecting data and developing theoretical interpretations of those data. They want to understand sports, and their place in human behaviour, social relations, culture, and ideology. They differ in terms of their theoretical approaches, and disagreements sometimes occur about how data should be interpreted (see chapter 2). However, those who limit themselves to the basic tradition believe that such practical/applied issues as policy development and interventions that affect the practice of sports should be left to others. Some basic researchers even see the applied approach as controversial in the sociology of sport. They believe that all social interventions have unintended consequences, and that we should always hold back from involvement until we have a great deal more knowledge.

Those who believe that sociologists should "apply" their research to practical issues and problems tend to fall into two types who also disagree. Some researchers declare themselves to be **sport sociology experts**, and sell their expertise as consultants with, for example, sport organizations or sporting goods manufacturers. Others recognize the need for critical scientific and policy expertise at all levels of sports, and not just for those who can afford to pay. They are concerned about those who seem to be aligning the sociology of sport with people who have the money and power to hire experts. Since people with money and power rarely want to ask tough, critical questions about sports and the way they are organized, some sociologists of sport see this as a violation of the critical principles of sociology (Ingham and Donnelly, 1990).

This basic and applied distinction has not been very evident in the sociology of sport in Canada in recent years. Many researchers are involved with social, theoretical, and cultural issues, *and* they also devote research, time, and expertise to resolving issues at all levels of sports. These include concerns about equity in sports participation, problems relating to children's involvement

Table 1.1   Publication Sources for Sociology of Sport Research

JOURNALS DEVOTED PRIMARILY TO SOCIOLOGY OF SPORT ARTICLES

International Review for the Sociology of Sport (quarterly)
Journal of Sport and Social Issues (quarterly)
Sociology of Sport Journal (quarterly)

SOCIOLOGY JOURNALS THAT SOMETIMES INCLUDE ARTICLES ON OR RELATED TO SPORTS

Body & Society
British Journal of Sociology
Canadian Journal of Sociology
Canadian Review of Sociology and Anthropology
Sociology of Education
Theory, Culture and Society

INTERDISCIPLINARY, SPORT SCIENCE, AND PHYSICAL EDUCATION JOURNALS THAT SOMETIMES INCLUDE ARTICLES ON OR RELATED TO SOCIOLOGY OF SPORT TOPICS

Avante
CAHPER Journal
Culture, Sport, Society
European Journal of Physical Education
Journal of Physical Education, Recreation & Dance
Journal of Sport Behavior
Quest
Research Quarterly for Exercise and Sport

Sport, Education and Society
Sport Science Review
Women in Sport & Physical Activity Journal

JOURNALS IN RELATED FIELDS THAT SOMETIMES INCLUDE ARTICLES ON OR RELATED TO SOCIOLOGY OF SPORT TOPICS

Adolescence
Aethlon: The Journal of Sport Literature
The British Journal of Sport History
The European Sports History Review
International Journal of the History of Sport
International Journal of Sport Psychology
Journal of Human Movement Studies
Journal of Leisure Research
Journal of the Philosophy of Sport
Journal of Popular Culture
Journal of Sport and Exercise Psychology
Journal of Sport History
Leisure Sciences
Leisure Studies
Olympika: The International Journal of Olympic Studies
Soccer and Society
Loisir et Societé/Society and Leisure
The Sport Psychologist
Sport History Review
Sporting Traditions
The Sports Historian
Youth & Society

---

in sports, and violence and injury in sports. They are also often involved in the development of sport policy at all levels of sports.

Knowledge is a source of power in our complex world, and power has an impact on how knowledge is produced. In other words, doing research to build knowledge in the sociology of sport has political implications because it has an impact on how people see sports, and how they think about their lives and the world around them. Unless people in the sociology of sport think about these things when they do their work, they will limit their understanding of the diverse meanings that people give to sports in their lives and of the impact that sports and sport participation have on individuals, communities, and societies.

SUMMARY

WHY STUDY SPORTS?

Sociology is the study of the social arrangements that people create as they live together and make sense of their lives. Sociologists are concerned with social issues, social relationships, social organization, and social change. Their overall goal is to enable people to understand, control, and change their lives so human needs among all categories of people are met at both individual and group levels.

Before considering an analysis of *sports*, it is necessary to be clear about what is meant by that term. Some scholars in the field define *sports* as activities involving (1) the use of physical skill, prowess, or exertion; (2) institutionalized competition; and (3) the combination of intrinsic and extrinsic reasons for participation. Such a definition is problematic unless it is seen as a limited tool for distinguishing among different forms of socially important activities in people's lives. A sociologist who takes a single definition of sports too seriously may focus attention primarily on the lives of people who have the resources and the desire to develop formally organized and competitive physical activities. For this reason, some scholars recommend that, instead of using a single definition of *sports*, we should ask what activities are counted as sports in different cultures at different points in time. This question focuses attention on the relationship between sports and power and privilege in society and leads more directly to the consideration of transforming social life so that more people have access to the resources they need to control their lives and make them meaningful.

Sociologists study sports as parts of culture. They look at sports in terms of their importance in people's lives, how they are organized, and their connections to cultural ideology and major spheres of social life. Research in the sociology of sport helps us understand sports

as social phenomena but, beyond that, often leads to the discovery of problems based in the structure and organization of either sports or society. When this happens, the recommendations sociologists make may threaten those who want sports and sport programmes to remain as they are now. Therefore, sociology sometimes creates controversies.

The sociology of sport uses the concepts, theories, and research methods of sociology, but it draws much of its organizational support from scholars associated with physical education, kinesiology, and sport science departments in universities. Continued growth depends primarily on whether those in the field are able to make meaningful contributions to the way people live their lives. Complicating the issue of future growth is the fact that not everyone in the field agrees on how to "do" sociology of sport. Some carry out "basic" research focusing on social, theoretical, and cultural issues. Others carry out "applied" research, using either an entrepreneurial *scientific expert* approach, or working as members of the community who are able to contribute critical social scientific and policy expertise more equitably. Many sociologists of sport in Canada combine this latter approach with a "basic" interest in social, theoretical, and cultural issues. Differences among these three approaches raise important questions about the production and use of scientific knowledge (see chapter 2). These questions produce ongoing debates in the field.

 ### SUGGESTED READINGS

Brownell, S. 1995. *Training the body for China: Sports in the moral order of the People's Republic.* Chicago: University of Chicago Press (participant observation study of the body and sports in Chinese culture; shows clearly through firsthand examples that sports must be studied in historical and cultural context to be understood as social phenomena).

Burstyn, V. 1999. *The rites of men: Manhood, politics, and the culture of sport.* Toronto: University of Toronto Press (thorough analysis of the institutionalized world of sports and how it is connected with and informed by a combination of masculinism and capitalism; there is a consistent focus on how hypermasculinity in North American culture in particular is perpetuated through a web of interlocking organizations, which includes sports, the media, industry, and government).

Coakley, J., and E. Dunning, eds. 2000. *Handbook of sports studies.* London: Sage (forty-two chapters on the ways sports are studied as social phenomena and on the sociology of sport in various countries and regions around the world).

Dunning, E. 1999. *Sport matters: Sociological studies of sport, violence, and civilization.* London: Routledge (an introduction to selected research on sport and society; analyses, guided by figurational theory, of the emergence of modern sports with special emphasis on soccer, emotions in sports, soccer hooliganism and crowd violence, racial stratification, and gender relations).

Gruneau, R., and D. Whitson. 1993. *Hockey Night in Canada: Sport, identities, and cultural politics.* Toronto: Garamond Press (a thorough analysis of hockey in Canada, from its origins and the clash between amateurism [character building and moral entrepreneurs] and professionalism [commercial and entertainment] to the rise of the NHL, and current issues in the Canadian game—media, violence, women's participation, nationalism; all presented within a broader context of Canada and Canadian identity).

Horne, J., A. Tomlinson, and G. Whannel. 1999. *Understanding sport: An introduction to the sociological and cultural analysis of sport.* London: E & FN Spon (focuses on sports in Britain; provides historical material along with overviews of research on sports and stratification, socialization, the media, the state, work, and commercialization).

Wilson, J. 1994. *Playing by the rules: Sport, society, and the state.* Detroit, MI: Wayne State University Press (chapters 1 and 2 offer definitions and descriptions of major sociological concepts used in traditional studies of sports in society).

WEBSITE RESOURCES

Note: Websites often change. The following URLs were current when this book was printed. Please check our Online Learning Centre website (www.mcgrawhill.ca/college/coakley) for updates as well as for additional resources and study tools.

www.ucalgary.ca/library/ssportsite/ (a guide to online "Scholarly Sport Sites"; this is the most useful starting point we have found as we look for online information)

www.uwm.edu/~aycock/nasss/nasss.html (official site for the North American Society for the Sociology of Sport; contains a list of experts in the field, along with graduate programs specializing in the sociology of sport)

http://u2.u-strasbg.fr/issa/ (the official site of ISSA, the International Sociology of Sport Association; this organization is a subcommittee of ICSSPE, the International Council of Sport Science and Physical Education, and is affiliated with UNESCO, the United Nations Educational, Scientific and Cultural Organization)

www.sportinsociety.org (Center for the Study of Sport in Society; complete information on all the center's programs: Athletes in Service to America, Mentors in Violence Prevention Program, Project TEAMWORK, Urban Youth Sports, SportsCAP, and Additional Outreach Programs; the CSSS is the most active organization in the world when it comes to promoting socially responsible changes in and through sports)

www.sportdiscus.com (a comprehensive international database of sport and fitness information, containing over a half million references, which can be searched by using subject-related keywords; this site provides direct links to additional websites that contain articles.)

http://physed.otago.ac.nz/sosol/home.htm (*Sociology of Sport Online* is an international electronic journal based in England; it publishes articles by authors from around the world)

http://europa.eu.int/comm/sport/index_en.html (the site of Sport and European Union covers issues related to the development of sport through the new European Union)

www.sportquest.com/naslin/ (links to many
   electronic journals dealing with sports; the
   journals represent many disciplines; sociology
   references can be found, although they are scarce)
www.abc.net.au/sport/abc (Radio National of the
   Australian Broadcasting Corporation presents a
   weekly show, *The Sports Factor* with Amanda
   Smith, which regularly covers topics of interest
   to people in the sociology of sport; program
   transcripts are available, or the audio can be
   heard if the appropriate software is downloaded
   through the site.)
www.aafla.org (Amateur Athletic Foundation, Los
   Angeles; much of the information at this site is of
   interest to sport scholars, including people in the
   sociology of sport)

Chantal Petitclerc, Olympic wheelchair track and field
(CP/ Ryan Remiorz)

Using Social Theories

What can they tell us about sports in society?

Today, sports has come to pit race against race,
men against women, city against city, class against
class, and coach against player.

—Frank Deford, sportswriter (1998)

Hockey is the Canadian metaphor, the rink is this
country's vast stretches of water and wilderness, its
extremes of climate, the player a symbol of our
struggle to civilize such a land. Some people call it
our national religion. Well, what better?

—Bruce Kidd and John Macfarlane, authors,
The Death of Hockey (1972)

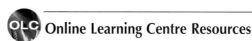 **Online Learning Centre Resources**

Visit *Sports in Society's* Online Learning Centre at
www.mcgrawhill.ca/college/coakley for additional
information and study material for this chapter.

Those of us who study sports in society want to understand the social and cultural contexts in which sports exist and how those contexts are influenced by sports. We also want to understand the social worlds that people create in connection with sports and the experiences of individuals and groups associated with those social worlds. We are motivated by various combinations of curiosity, interests in sports, and concerns about social life and social issues. Most of us also want to use what we know about sports in society to promote social justice, expose and challenge the exploitive use of power, and empower people so they might resist and transform oppressive social conditions.

As we engage in this project of studying and changing sports, we use social and cultural theories to assist us. These theories help us identify issues and problems to study. They provide frameworks for asking research questions, interpreting information, and uncovering the deeper meanings and stories associated with sports in particular cultures. They also enable us to be more informed citizens as we apply what we learn in our research to the world in which we live. Because those of us who study sports in society come from many different academic backgrounds and because social life is so diverse and complex, we use a wide variety of theories to guide our work.

The two goals of this chapter are to

1. Identify and describe the theories that have been used most widely to study sports in society
2. Explain how various theories assist us in our efforts to understand sports as social phenomena as well as the society and culture in which we live

WHAT ARE THEORIES AND WHY DO WE NEED THEM?

Whenever we ask why our social world is the way it is and then imagine how it might be changed,

we are "theorizing" (Hooks, 1992). Theorizing involves a combination of description, reflection, and analysis. When we theorize, it is not necessary to use complex terminology. In fact, the best theories are those we understand so clearly that they help us make sense out of the social world and become involved in the world as informed citizens. When we study sports in society, the best theories are the ones that help us ask questions and seek information that enable us to see sports in new ways, understand the relationship between sports and social life, and make informed decisions about sports and sport participation in our lives, families, communities, and societies.

Many people think that theories do not have practical applications. This is not true. Most of our actions are based on our predictions of their possible consequences, and predictions are based on our personal theories about social life. Our personal theories may be incomplete, poorly developed, based on limited information, and biased to fit our own needs, but we still use them to guide our behaviour. The more accurate our theories, the more accurate our predictions and the more effective we become in relating with others and controlling what happens in our lives. When we make decisions about sports, formulate policies, or decide whether to fund or cut money from sport programmes, we usually base our decisions on our personal theories about sports and their connections to social life.

None of the theories discussed in this chapter is perfect, but each can be useful as we move beyond our limited personal perspectives and develop a more broadly informed set of ideas about sports in society. Theories about society and social life are based on a combination of systematic research and deductive logic. Ideally, they are presented in published books and articles, so that other people may evaluate, test, use, and revise them. Most theories are the products of more than one person. They may be refined and improved over time as people test them in research, or they may be abandoned as people discover that they are not very useful in their efforts to understand social life.

Theories of all types are very important in our lives. They help us ask questions, seek answers, make decisions, take action, and evaluate what we do. Without theories we lack the frameworks we need to make sense out of life and learn from our experiences.

Many theories and theoretical approaches have been used to study sports in society. This theoretical diversity reflects the diversity and complexity of social life itself. All societies have their own histories, dynamics, and cultures, and they can be viewed from many perspectives. Although this can be confusing, it also reminds us that no single theoretical approach can tell us all we may want to know about sports or about social life.

Six major theories have been used to study sports in society:

- Functionalist theory
- Conflict theory
- Interactionist theory
- Critical theories
- Feminist theories
- Figurational theory

While there are important differences among the theories outlined here, there are many points at which two or more of them converge and overlap. This is because people read and respond to the ideas of others as they develop their own ideas about society and social life. Therefore, even though we summarize these six theories in separate sections, we should remember that all social theories are fluid, changing sets of ideas about how the social world works; they are *not* completely separate frameworks that have nothing in common with each other (Calhoun, 1998)

All of these six theories have their origins in European and U.S. sociology. However, Canadian social scientists such as Fernand Dumont, Margrit Eichler, Erving Goffman, Harold Innis, Marshall McLuhan, C.B. McPherson, John Porter, and Dorothy Smith have made important contributions in the development of social theory both on a global basis and in the Canadian context. Moreover, a particular tradition that is often thought to characterize Canadian sociology is **political economy**, a term that, in its modern sense, captures elements of conflict and critical theories, and which has more recently been combined with interactionist and feminist theories.

Canadian sociologists of sport such as Rick Gruneau at Simon Fraser University and Nancy Theberge at the University of Waterloo have been at the forefront in the development of social theory to increase our understanding of sports in society. The political economy tradition is also well represented in Canadian sociology of sport by scholars such as Gruneau, Jean Harvey at the University of Ottawa, and Bruce Kidd at the University of Toronto. It is acknowledged internationally that Canadian contributions to the sociology of sport are far more significant than might be expected from a country of only 30 million people.

The following sections describe each theory, provide examples of how each has been used to inspire and guide discussions and research on sports as social phenomena, explain how each theory might be used to take action or make policies about sports in our everyday lives, and point out the weaknesses of each theory. To assist you in learning about these theories and understanding how they have been used to guide discussions and research, table 2.1 provides a general comparison that summarizes the theories (see pages 34–35).

FUNCTIONALIST THEORY: WHAT DO SPORTS CONTRIBUTE TO SOCIETY?

Functionalist theory is based on the assumption that it is possible to study society, discover scientific "truths" about how societies operate, and then develop a system of "social laws" that we might use to understand, control, and even

One assumption underlying functionalist theory is that social order depends on consensus and common values. Functionalists assume that established social institutions, such as sports, contribute to consensus and common values. (CP/Adrian Wyld)

change society for the better. Those using functionalist theory view society as an organized system of interrelated parts held together by shared values and social processes that minimize differences and promote consensus among people. According to functionalist theory, the driving force underlying all social life is the tendency for any social system to maintain itself in a state of balance, so that it continues to operate efficiently. This balance is achieved "naturally" as groups of people develop consensus, common values, and coordinated organization in the major spheres of social life, such as the family, education, the economy, the media, politics, religion, leisure, and sport.

When sociologists use functionalist theory to explain how a society, community, school, family, sport team, or other social system works, they focus attention on how each part in the system contributes to the system's overall operation. For example, if Canadian society is the system being studied, a person using functionalist theory is concerned with how the Canadian family, economy, government, education, media, religion, and sport are related to each other and how they work together in contributing to the smooth operation of the society as a whole. Analysis focuses on how each of these spheres of social life helps keep the larger social system operating efficiently.

According to functionalist theory, social systems operate smoothly when they have efficient mechanisms for doing four things: (1) socializing people to learn and accept important cultural values, (2) promoting social connections between people, (3) motivating people to achieve cultural goals through accepted methods, and (4) protecting the system from disruptive outside influences. Functionalists assume that if these four "system needs" are satisfied, social order will be maintained and everyone will benefit. The first column in table 2.1 on page 34 summarizes functionalist theory.

Table 2.1 Using social theories to study sports in society: a summary and comparison

Functionalist Theory	Conflict Theory	Interactionist Theory
ASSUMPTIONS ABOUT THE BASIS FOR SOCIAL ORDER IN SOCIETY		
Social order is based on consensus and shared values, which hold all the interrelated parts of society together. All social systems tend toward a state of balance.	Social order is based on economic interests and the use of economic power to exploit labour. Social class shapes social structures and relationships.	Social order is created from the bottom up through intentional social interaction.
MAJOR CONCERNS IN THE STUDY OF SOCIETY		
How do the individual parts of social systems contribute to the satisfaction of major system needs and the overall operation of the system?	How is economic power distributed and used in society? What are the dynamics of social class relations? Who is privileged and exploited in class relations?	How are meanings, identities, and culture created through social interaction? How do people define the reality of their own lives and the world around them?
MAJOR CONCERNS IN THE STUDY OF SPORT		
How do sports fit into social life and contribute to social stability and efficiency? How does sport participation influence personal development? How do sports contribute to social integration and the maintenance of social order?	How do sports reflect class relations? How are sports used to maintain the interests of those with power and wealth in society? How has the profit motive distorted sports?	How do people become involved in sports, become defined as athletes, derive meaning from participation, and make transitions out of sports into the rest of their lives?
MAJOR CONCLUSIONS ABOUT THE SPORT-SOCIETY RELATIONSHIP		
Sport is a valuable social institution that benefits society as well as individuals in society. Sports are sources of inspiration on both personal and social levels.	Sports are forms of physical activity that are distorted by the needs of capital. Sports are opiates that distract attention away from the problems that affect those without economic power.	Sports are forms of culture created through social interaction. Sport participation is grounded in the decisions made by people in connection with their identities and their relationships.
SOCIAL ACTION AND POLICY IMPLICATIONS		
Develop and expand sport programmes that will promote traditional values, build positive character, and contribute to order and stability in society.	Raise class consciousness and make people aware of their own alienation and powerlessness. Eliminate the profit motive in sports and allow sport participation to be a source of expression, creative experience, and physical well-being.	Allow individuals to shape sports to fit their definitions of reality. Make sport organizations more democratic and less hierarchically organized. Focus on the culture and organization of sports, rather than individual athletes when trying to control "deviance" in sports.
MAJOR WEAKNESSES		
It overstates the positive consequences of sports. It ignores that sports serve the needs of some people more than those of others. It does not acknowledge that sports are social constructions.	It overstates the influence of economic forces in society. It assumes that people who have economic power shape sports to meet their interests. It ignores that sports can be sites for creative and liberating experiences.	It fails to explain how meaning, identity, and interaction are related to social structures and material conditions in society. It ignores issues of power and power relations in society.

Critical Theories	Critical Feminist Theories	Figurational Theory
Social order is negotiated through struggles over ideology, representation, and power. Social life is full of diversity, complexities, and contradictions.	Social order is based primarily on the values, experiences, and interests of men with power. Social life and social order are gendered.	Social order is based on interdependencies among individuals and groups. Connections between people take the form of social figurations.
How is cultural ideology produced, reproduced, and transformed? What are the conflicts and problems that affect the lives of those who lack power in society?	How is gender ideology produced, reproduced, and transformed? How do dominant forms of gender relations privilege men over women and some men over other men?	How do social figurations emerge and change? How do power balances within figurations influence relationships between individuals and groups?
How are power relations reproduced and/or resisted in and through sports? Whose voices are/are not represented in the narratives and images that constitute sports?	How are sports gendered activities, and how do they reproduce dominant ideas about gender in society? What are the strategies for resisting and transforming sport forms that privilege men?	How did modern sports emerge and become so important in society? What are the social processes associated with the commercialization of sports, expressions of violence in sports, and forms of global sports?
Sports are social constructions. Sports are sites where culture is produced, reproduced, and transformed. Sports are cultural practices that repress and/or empower people.	Sports are grounded in the values and experiences of powerful men in society. Sports reproduce male power and distorted ideas about masculinity. Sports produce gendered ideas about physicality, sexuality, and the body.	Sports are exciting activities that relieve boredom and control displays of violence. Sports celebrate masculinity and male power. Global sports are complex activities with local and national significance.
Use sports as sites for challenging and transforming forms of exploitation and oppression. Increase the range and diversity of sport participation opportunities. Challenge the voices and perspectives of those with power.	Use sports as sites for challenging and transforming oppressive forms of gender relations. Expose and resist all expressions of homophobia and misogyny in sports. Transform sports to emphasize partnership over competition and domination.	Develop a fund of valid knowledge, which can be used to enable people to control expressions of violence, exploitation, and the abuse of power. Increase access to sport participation among those who have lacked power through history.
There are no clear guidelines for identifying and assessing forms of resistance and the value of ideas and actions across situations. There are no unified strategies for dealing with problems, conflicts, and injustice.	There are no clear guidelines for identifying and assessing forms of resistance and the value of ideas and actions across situations. Little attention is given to connections between gender and some other categories of experience.	It gives too little attention to problems and struggles that affect day-to-day lives. It understates the immediate personal consequences of oppressive power relations. It gives little attention to the experiences of women and to gender inequities.

Functionalist Theory and Research on Sports

Functionalist theory usually inspires discussions and research about how sports fit into social life and contribute to stability and social progress in organizations, communities, and societies. In fact, people have often used functionalist theory to guide their thinking as they study many of the issues discussed in the following chapters of this book. Examples include the following:

1. Do sports and sport participation influence social and personal development? This issue is discussed in chapters 4 through 7.
2. Do sports and sport participation foster the development of social integration in groups, communities, and societies? This issue is discussed in chapters 9, 10, 13, and 14.
3. Does playing sports have a positive impact on success in school and work, and does it teach people to follow the rules as they strive for success? This issue is discussed in chapters 4, 6, 7, 10, and 14.
4. Do sports contribute to health and wellness and the strength of society as a whole? This issue is discussed in chapters 7 and 13.

Functionalist theory focuses attention on how sports help to keep societies, communities, organizations, and groups operating smoothly, as well as how they influence individuals to contribute to the social systems in which they participate. This is why a functionalist way of understanding is often popular among people who have a vested interest in preserving the status quo in society. These people want sociologists to tell them how sports contribute to the smooth operation of the societies, communities, organizations, and groups in which they live. Many people like functionalist theory because it fits with how they have learned to view the social world and because it leads to the conclusion that sports are popular because they serve as a source of inspiration for individuals and societies.

Using Functionalist Theory in Everyday Life

Around the world, many people use popularized forms of functionalist theory to make decisions about sports and sport programmes at national and local levels. They view sports as having particular "functions." Thus, people promote the development and growth of organized youth sports (to build values), fund sports in schools and communities (to promote organizational loyalty and attachments to schools and communities), develop sport opportunities for girls and women (to increase achievement motivation among girls and women), include sports in military training (to increase military preparedness and the fitness of soldiers), and fund and televise the Olympic Games (to build international goodwill and unity).

Functionalist theory leads people to promote changes in sports that emphasize what they see as traditional values in society. If individualism, competition, and success are important values in society, a person using functionalist theory would call for changes leading to increases in individual achievement, winning records, and overall participation in competitive sports. Since functionalist theory generally leads to the conclusion that sports build the kind of character valued in the society as a whole, it also leads to policy recommendations for more organized competitive programmes, more structured sport experiences, more supervision of athletes, more coaching education programmes, the development of more training centres for top-level athletes, and increased surveillance and drug testing to control disruptive deviance among athletes. In the case of youth sports, for example, functionalist theory would emphasize actions to increase developmental sport programmes, coaching certification requirements, and a sport system that promotes success at elite levels of competition. Functionalist theory leads people to look for and do research on how sports contribute to the development of individuals and society as a whole.

Since many people use a "systems model" to understand how the social world works, their view of sports fits with functionalist theory. In other words, they assume that society is held together by shared values, and they see sports as contributing to the order and stability of society. This is the viewpoint that many students have when they take courses in the sociology of sport, and it leads many of them to feel comfortable with questions, ideas, and research based on functionalist theory and to be uncomfortable with questions, ideas, and research based on other theoretical approaches. Those with power and influence in a society also favour functionalist theory because it provides guidance for maintaining society the way it is, and people with power and influence like to keep things the way they are so that the basis for their power and influence is preserved.

Because elements of the functionalist approach are so widely used in popular explanations, everyday discussions, and media coverage of sports in society, it is important for us to know the major weaknesses of functionalist theory.

Weaknesses of Functionalist Theory

Functionalist theory has three major weaknesses when it is used to study sports in society. First, it leads to overstatements about the positive effects and understatements about the negative effects of sports in society. For example, functionalist theory would not help us understand that the emphasis on physical power and the domination of opponents that is so common in many sports has worked to the disadvantage of women in society. Nor would it help us understand how sport teams in some schools and communities may actually undermine social integration and lead some individuals to feel marginalized because of status systems that may favour athletes.

Second, functionalist theory is based on the assumption that the needs of all groups within a society are the same as the needs of the society as a whole. This causes us to underestimate the existence of differences and conflicts of interest within a society and to ignore cases where sports benefit some groups more than others. This limits our understanding of difference, conflict, and the dynamics of change in societies.

Third, functionalist theory does not account for the fact that sports are "social constructions" created and defined by human beings as they make decisions about what is important in their lives and how they are connected with others. Therefore, the functionalist approach often overlooks how sports are usually organized to promote the interests of those with power and wealth, and how sports contribute to disruptive forms of social inequality in societies.

One of the theories concerned with issues of social problems, changes, and inequalities in society is conflict theory.

CONFLICT THEORY: ARE SPORTS ALL ABOUT MONEY AND ECONOMIC POWER?

Conflict theory is based on the ideas of Karl Marx. People using conflict theory view society as a system of social structures and relationships that are shaped ultimately by economic forces. They assume that money, wealth, and economic power shape how society is organized and how it operates. They assume that social life revolves around economic interests and that people use their economic power to coerce and manipulate others to accept their view of the world as the correct view. This means that anyone using conflict theory is concerned with "class relations," that is, social processes revolving around who has economic power, how economic power is used, and who is advantaged or disadvantaged by economic organization and economic forces in society. Studies of class relations focus on the consequences of social inequality and the processes of change in society.

The main goal of conflict theory is similar to the main goal of functionalist theory: to develop a general theory about how society operates as a system. Thus, conflict theory is designed to show that economic power in capitalist societies is entrenched so deeply that progressive changes are possible only if people without economic power become aware of the need for change and then take action to make radical changes in the organization of the economy and society.

Conflict theorists assume that major forms of sport in a society ultimately promote the interests of people with money and economic power. Sports, they argue, focus the emotions and attention of the have-nots in society on escapist spectator events that distract them from the need to change the economy. In fact, sports, especially spectator sports, are organized and sponsored by those with money and economic power in an effort to affirm the capitalist values of competition, production, and consumption. Thus, conflict theorists see sports as an opiate in society, as activities and spectacles that deaden awareness of economic exploitation among those without power while perpetuating the privilege and position of those who control wealth and the economy.

Conflict Theory and Research on Sports

Conflict theory usually inspires discussions and research about how sports perpetuate the power and privilege of elite groups in society, as well as how sports serve as tools of economic exploitation and oppression. Those using conflict theory have studied and discussed the following issues:

1. How and when do athletes become alienated from their own bodies? This issue is discussed in chapters 4 through 7.
2. How do sports contribute to the existence of socioeconomic inequality in society? This issue is discussed in many chapters— especially chapters 8 through 11.
3. How do the processes of commercialization change sports and influence social relationships in society? This issue is discussed in chapters 10 through 13.

4. How do people with economic power use sports to further their own interests? This issue is discussed in chapters 10 through 13.

Conflict theory focuses attention on how powerful people use sports to promote attitudes and relationships that enable them to maintain power and privilege. Like functionalist theory, it is based on the assumption that social life is driven and shaped by specific societal needs, although conflict theory emphasizes the "needs of capital" rather than the general "needs of social systems." Conflict theory also focuses attention on how sports reflect and perpetuate the unequal distribution of power and economic resources in societies. This leads to an emphasis on the negative consequences of sports and the conclusion that radical changes are needed in sports and society as a whole. According to conflict theorists, the goal of these changes is to bring about the development of a humane and creative society, so that sports can become sources of expression, creative energy, and physical well-being.

Most people in countries with capitalist economies are not comfortable with the assumptions and conclusions of conflict theory. They say that the negative tone of conflict theory does not fit with their ideas about sports or society, and they are uneasy with conclusions that threaten the current structure and organization of sports and society. However, conflict theory has been very useful in calling attention to important economic issues in sports and to forms of inequality that create conflict and tensions in society as a whole.

Using Conflict Theory in Everyday Life

Conflict theory leads people to focus attention on economic factors, class inequality, and the need for changes in how society and sports are organized. These changes emphasize making athletes and spectators aware of how they are manipulated and oppressed for the profit and personal gain of the economic elite in society.

Conflict theory leads to the conclusion that problems in sports exist because power does not rest in the hands of people who play sports or might play if sports were organized to reflect the public good rather than the economic good. Therefore, it would lead people to support policies and programmes that regulate or eliminate economic profit motives in sports, and it would promote the idea that athletes should have more control over sports and the conditions of their sport participation.

Conflict theory would lead people to call for more emphasis on play in sports and less emphasis on business, so that sport participation could become more liberating and empowering for a greater number of people. It would lead people to favour players' unions, as well as organizations that represent the interests of fans and people in communities where large amounts of public money are used to subsidize wealthy team owners. Actions and policies inspired by conflict theory would emphasize the material conditions of those who lack money and power and the need for radical changes in the overall organization of sports. These actions and policies would discourage the development and growth of spectator sports and would promote the idea that physical games should be for the players themselves. Finally, these actions and policies would promote new sports organized at the grassroots level for fun, and they would promote doing away with sports organized by people with money for economic profit.

> **In America, it is sport that is the opiate of the masses.**
> —Russell Baker, columnist, *The New York Times* (1967)

Weaknesses of Conflict Theory

Conflict theory has three major weaknesses. First, it assumes that all social life is driven and shaped by economic factors, by the needs of capital in society. It focuses on the relationship between the economic haves and have-nots, and it assumes that the haves always use their power to control and exploit the have-nots. It also assumes that the have-nots live their lives in a state of powerlessness and alienation. These assumptions lead people who use conflict theory to focus exclusively on economic factors when they study sports. However, many sports, especially those emphasizing recreation and mass participation, cannot be explained totally in terms of economic interests or economic power in society.

Second, conflict theory ignores the importance of gender, race, ethnicity, age, sexual orientation, and other factors when it comes to explaining how people identify themselves, relate to others, and organize social life. Conflict theory emphasizes that all history and social organization revolves around economic factors. Therefore, those who use it to study sports often overlook the possibility that inequalities in society are based also in forms of social relations that are not shaped exclusively by struggles revolving around social class and economic differences. This means they ignore or underestimate the importance of struggles related to gender, race, ethnicity, age, religion, sexual orientation, and physical ability (being able-bodied or disabled).

Third, conflict theory ignores cases where sport participation consists of experiences that empower individuals and groups in capitalist societies. Testimonials from athletes indicate that sports do more than alienate people from their bodies, despite the fact that some athletes take harmful drugs and use their bodies as tools of production. In fact, sport participation is sometimes a personally creative and liberating experience. Furthermore, sports may serve as sites for challenging and resisting the interests of economically powerful groups, and in some cases they could even be sites for transforming the way power is distributed in an organization or a community. Conflict theorists generally ignore these possibilities.

Beyond the Needs of Society

Functionalist theory and conflict theory both focus on societal needs and how sports are related to the satisfaction of those needs. In a sense, they give us a picture of sports in society from the top down. They do not tell us much about sports in everyday life or how people create sports and the overall society in which they live their lives. They ignore a view of society from the bottom up, from the perspectives of people who "do" sports and give meaning to sports as parts of their everyday lives. They also ignore the complexities of everyday social life and the fact that sports and society are social constructions that emerge in connection with multiple struggles over what is important in people's lives. The theories that focus attention on various aspects of these issues are interactionist theory and various forms of critical theory, which we discuss in the following sections.

INTERACTIONIST THEORY: HOW DO PEOPLE EXPERIENCE SPORTS?

Interactionist theory, drawn from the work of George Herbert Mead and Herbert Blumer, focuses on issues related to meaning, identity, social relationships, and subcultures in sports. It is based on the idea that human behaviour involves choices and that choices are based on the definitions of reality that people form as they interact with others. According to interactionist theory, we humans do not simply respond in an automatic fashion to the world around us. Instead, we actively make decisions about our behaviour based on the consequences that we think our behaviour will have on our lives, the people around us, and the social world in which we live. Furthermore, as we interact with others, we create the norms, roles, relationships, and structures that make up society itself.

According to interactionist theory, our ability to reflect on and assess our decisions and actions enables us to develop a sense of who we are and how we are connected to the social world. This sense of who we are in the social world is our **identity**. Identities are key factors as people interact with each other and construct their social worlds. In other words, identity is a basis for self-direction and self-control in our lives. Identity is never formed permanently, because it emerges out of our relationships, and our relationships are constantly changing as we meet new people, as people change, and as we face new situations.

Research based on interactionist theory helps us to understand how human beings define and give meaning to themselves, their behaviour, and the world around them. It also helps us to understand how those meanings are connected with identity and social interaction. Therefore, when people use interactionist theory, they study human beings as choice makers and creators of meaning, identity, and relationships; they do research that focuses on "seeing" the world through the eyes of the people they observe, interview, and interact with. They often study particular groups of people or identifiable subcultures, and try to understand them from inside, from the perspectives of the people themselves. In a sense, they view society from the bottom up rather than the top down.

Interactionist Theory and Research on Sports

Interactionist theory usually inspires discussions and research about the experiences of athletes and how the athletes define and make sense out of their participation in sports. A common goal of interactionist research is to reconstruct and describe the reality that exists in the minds of athletes, coaches, spectators, and others involved with sports in society.

Interactionists use research methodologies designed to gather information about how people see their social worlds and their connections to those worlds. Therefore, they do studies that involve participant observation and in-depth

Interactionists study the meanings and identities associated with sports and sport participation. Meanings associated with youth sports vary from one cultural setting to another, as do the lessons players learn in connection with participation. (Jay Coakley)

interviews. These are the best methods for understanding how people define situations and use those definitions to form identities and make choices about their behaviour.

Those who use interactionist theory have focused on the following issues:

1. What are the social processes through which people become involved in sports?
2. How do people come to define themselves and be defined by others as athletes?
3. How do people give meaning to and derive meaning from their experiences in sports?
4. What happens when people retire from sport and make the transition into the rest of their lives?
5. What are the characteristics of sport subcultures, how are they created by the people involved in sports, and how do they influence identity and behaviour on and off the field?

These issues are discussed directly in chapters 4 and 6. They are also discussed in various ways in many other chapters. This is because we feel that interactionist research provides vivid descriptions of sport experiences, which we can use to understand behaviour and social life.[1]

Using Interactionist Theory in Everyday Life

Interactionist theory focuses on the meanings and interaction associated with sports and sport participation. It emphasizes the complexity of human behaviour and the need to understand behaviour in terms of how people associated with sports define situations through their relationships with others. Those using this theory would

---

[1]We have edited a book entitled *Inside Sports* (Coakley and Donnelly, 1999), in which examples of this type of research are described specifically for students interested in studying sports to learn about the social world.

call for changes in sports that reflect the per-spectives and identities of those who play sports. Many argue that the best way of affecting these changes is to restructure sport organizations, so that all those involved, especially athletes, have opportunities to raise issues about the purposes and conditions of sport participation. Therefore, they would call for sport organizations to be changed to make them more democratic, less autocratic, and less hierarchically organized.

For example, in the case of youth sports, those using interactionist theory would call for changes in games that reflect the needs and interests of children, rather than the needs and interests of adults. They would caution parents and coaches about problems that occur when young people develop identities and relationships that overemphasize sports to the exclusion of other identities and relationships. In the case of other sports, they would call for changes that discourage athletes from defining pain and injury as normal parts of the sport expe-rience. They would see the use of performance-enhancing substances as connected with identi-ty and sport culture, and they would argue that controlling the use of these substances demands changes in the norms and culture of sports. Identifying users as "bad apples" and punishing them as individuals will not change the culture in which athletes learn to sacrifice their own bodies for the sake of the team.

Weaknesses of Interactionist Theory

Interactionist theory has inspired many informa-tive studies of meaning, identity, interaction, and subcultures in sports. However, its major weak-ness is that it focuses our attention almost exclu-sively on relationships and personal definitions of reality without explaining how interaction processes and the construction of meaning in sports are related to social structures and mater-ial conditions in society. Interactionist research has generally ignored connections between sport experiences and sport subcultures, on the one

hand, and the systems of power and inequality that exist in societies, communities, organiza-tions, families, and small groups, on the other hand. Therefore, interactionist theory does not tell us much about how sports and sport experi-ences are related to issues of power and power relations in society as a whole. Furthermore, it does not provide us with a critical vision of what society could and should be when it comes to social organization.

A number of theories deal directly with issues of power and critical visions of what society could and should be, and they are discussed under the following general category of *critical theories*.

CRITICAL THEORIES: HOW ARE SPORTS INVOLVED IN CREATING AND CHANGING SOCIAL RELATIONS AND CULTURE?

Most people who study sports in society today use critical theories. Although critical theories take many forms, they focus primarily on explanations of culture, power, and social relations.[2] They consist of various approaches designed to understand where power comes from, how it operates in social life, and how it shifts and changes as people struggle over the many issues that affect their lives and their rela-tionships with each other (Gruneau, 1999; McDonald and Birrell, 1999; Tomlinson, 1998).

Critical theories also offer a range of explana-tions of the following: (1) how culture is produced and reproduced; (2) how power relations operate in the processes of cultural production and repro-duction; and (3) how people struggle over the ideas and meanings they use to make sense out of the world, form identities, interact with others, and transform the conditions of their lives. People using functionalist and conflict theories often say, "Sport is a reflection of society," but those using critical theories explain that sports are much more than that. They say that sports are social places (sites) where society and culture are produced and reproduced, and this makes them much more important than they would be if they were mere reflections of society. This issue is discussed in the Reflect on Sports box, "Sports Are More Than Reflections of Society," on page 45.

Unlike people who use functionalist or conflict theory, those using critical theories do not believe that it is possible to discover a universal explanation of social life, which we can use to understand all societies at all points in the past, present, and future. In fact, they feel that such a goal inevitably leads us to ignore the diversity, complexity, contradictions, and changes that are inherent in all forms of social life. Furthermore, they realize that there are many perspectives and standpoints from which to study and understand social life and that the search for general social laws or social truths about society and social life is fruitless. This makes them very different from those who use functionalist and conflict theories, even though they may borrow and use ideas from these theories as they extend and revise their own ideas.

According to critical theories, the relationship between sports and society is never set once and for all time: sports change as historical conditions and political and economic forces change. Sports change with new developments in government, education, the media, religion, and the family. Sports change with new ideas about masculinity and femininity, race, ethnicity, age, sexual orientation, and physical ability. And sports change with new narratives and discourses that offer visions of culture and social life, which people use to make sense of the world around them.

Critical theories are also about action and political involvement. All forms of critical theory have grown out of desires to identify issues and problems and to make social life more fair, democratic, and open to diversity. Critical theories have been valuable tools in identifying and studying specific social problems and in thinking about and putting into action practical programmes and processes that eliminate oppression and exploitation and promote equity, fairness, and openness. Most people who use critical theories are interested in explaining that all social relationships are grounded in political struggles over how social life should be defined and organized. They realize that dominant forms of sport in most societies have been socially constructed in ways that systematically and arbitrarily privilege some people over others. Their goals are to study and explain all the ways that this occurs, to expose them, and to inspire new ways of talking about, defining, organizing, and playing sports.

---

[2] Because this chapter is written as a basic introduction to using theories, we present "critical theories" as a general category. Our goal is to give a brief general description of the valuable analyses being done by those who would say they are engaged in a critical analysis of sports in society. Therefore, we attempt to pull together major ideas from the following theories and theoretical frameworks: *neo-Marxist theories*, *traditional critical theory* (combining ideas of Marx and Freud), *hegemony theory* (based on the ideas of Italian Marxist, Antonio Gramsci), *cultural studies* (based on applications of hegemony theory to the study of culture, power, and ideology as they are contested and struggled over in everyday life), *feminist theories* (primarily those informed by critical theory, cultural studies, or poststructuralism), *poststructuralism* (based on cultural studies, semiotics, and forms of literary analysis dealing with language and the construction of power, meaning, representation, and consciousness under the unstable, "disunified," and fragmented conditions of postmodern life), and *queer theory* (combining feminist cultural studies and poststructuralism). Of course, none of these frameworks is done justice in our summary. However, our goal is to highlight the exciting issues and questions that various scholars have discussed and analyzed while using one or more of these critical theoretical approaches, as well as to give you a basis for entering these discussions and analyses and learning more about sports and society in the process.

Critical Theories and Research on Sports

Critical theories are diverse and deal with many dimensions of our lives. Therefore, they have inspired and guided a wide range of discussions and research on sports in society.

Those who use critical theories to study sports generally focus on one or more of the following issues:

1. Whose ideas about the meaning and organization of sports are most important when it comes to determining what sports will be funded, who will participate in them, how they will be covered in the media, and how they will be used for social, political, and economic purposes?
2. How are sports and sport experiences (as parts of culture) tied to various forms of power relations in society and to overall processes of social development?
3. When do sports reproduce systems of power and privilege, and whom do sports privilege and whom do they disadvantage in society?
4. How are sports related to popular ideas about economic success or failure, work and fun, physical health and well-being, and ideas about gender, race and ethnicity, sexual orientation, and physical ability and disability, and what is natural and "deviant" in society?
5. What are the ways that people struggle over the organization and meanings of sports in their lives?
6. When do sports become sites for challenging, resisting, and even transforming how social life is organized?
7. What are the discourses and images that people use to construct sports and to connect sports and sport experiences to their lives and to culture in general?
8. Whose voices are represented and whose perspectives are used to frame the dominant discourse about sports in society, and whose voices and perspectives are not represented or are silenced in that discourse?
9. How might systems of power relations, as well as everyday discourses and images, be disrupted and transformed to give voice to those who lack power and representation in a society, a community, an organization, or a group?

One or more of these issues are discussed in all the following chapters of this book. We give priority to these issues because we think that critical theories inspire the most interesting and provocative discussions and analyses of sports in society. Research guided by critical theories emphasizes that sports are more than mere reflections of society. This research is based on the assumptions that sports have never been developed in a neatly ordered, rational manner and that there are no simple or general rules for explaining sports as social phenomena. The intent of research based on critical theories is to expose how the structure, organization, and meaning of sports vary with the complex and constantly changing relationships in and between groups possessing different amounts of power and resources in a particular culture at a particular point in time.

In addition to being concerned with how sports come to be what they are in society, critical theorists study how sports affect the processes through which people develop and maintain **cultural ideology**—that is, the orientations and beliefs they use to explain what happens in their lives. Critical theorists also want to know how and when sports become sites for questioning, opposing, and challenging dominant forms of cultural ideology and for transforming how people see and interpret the social world around them. One of the mottos of critical theorists (see Hargreaves and MacDonald, 2000) is a statement made by C. L. R. James, a native of the West Indies, who learned to play cricket from the British colonists of his homeland. James said, "What do they know of cricket who only cricket know?" (James, 1984, preface). Critical theorists would say, "We know

REFLECT ON SPORTS   Sports Are More Than Reflections of Society

When people study sports in society, they sometimes say, "Sports are reflections of society." This idea is helpful to someone who is just beginning to think about sports as parts of society and culture. However, it is not very helpful to those of us who want to do in-depth studies of sports. The problem with assuming that sports are reflections of society can be demonstrated by shifting our attention away from sports and onto another sphere of social life: the family.

Like sports, families are reflections of society, but our personal experience tells us that everyday family life is more than that. Families are the creations of people interacting with one another in a variety of ways depending on their abilities, resources, levels of power, and definitions of family life. Of course, the opportunities and choices available to the members of any particular family are influenced by factors in the larger society, including laws; economic conditions; government policies; general beliefs about how husbands, wives, parents, and children should relate to one another; and even the words we use when we talk about families. This means that there are similarities among many families in the same society, but it does not mean that all families are destined to be the same or to be mere reflections of society.

Society serves as a context in which individuals produce, define, and reproduce specific family practices. Families are not determined or shaped by society. In reality, they are sets of relationships that are produced by people in society. This is why each family has its own unique way of life. People create families, and they reproduce or challenge ideas about family every day as they go about their lives.

At times, families become sites (social locations) for raising questions about how family life should be organized. Some of these questions force people to rethink larger issues related to cultural values and the organization of society as a whole. In this way, what we do in our families becomes part of a general process of cultural production, the impact of which goes far beyond family life. For example, during the mid-twentieth century, when people in Canada asked questions about individual rights, marriage, and family, there were discussions that ultimately led to changes in divorce laws. These

and other discussions also encouraged people to rethink their ideas about intimate relationships, gender, women's rights, parent-child relationships, children's rights, and even the ways in which community social services should be organized and delivered. In other words, families have always been much more than reflections of society. They are the creations of human beings, as well as sites for producing and transforming the ways of life that constitute culture.

This means that human beings are agents of social change, not just in their immediate family lives, but also in the larger social settings in which they live. Through the things they do in their families, people produce and reproduce the culture of which they are a part.

So it is with sports and all of those associated with sports. Sports are more than reflections of society. They are the creations of people interacting with one another. No voice comes out of the sky and says, "I am society, and this is the way sports should be." Of course, social conditions have an impact on the structure and dynamics of sports, but, within the parameters set by those conditions, people can change sports or keep them the way they are. In fact, it is even possible for people to create and define sports in ways that differ from or even defy dominant ideas and norms and, in the process, to turn sports into sites for the transformation of the very culture of which they are a part.

This is a helpful way of thinking about sports in society. It recognizes that sports can have both positive and negative effects on participants, that people define and create sports in their own lives, and that sports are involved in either reproducing culture or standing in opposition to dominant ideology and forms of social relations in society.

This means that sports are very important in a sociological sense. Instead of just being the mirrors that reflect society, they are the actual "social stuff" out of which society and culture come to be what they are. When we understand this, we become aware of our capacity as agents of cultural production. This awareness helps us realize that we are not destined to do sports in a particular way or define sports as they are defined in the images promoted by Nike or Molson. We create culture and sports. *What do you think?*

nothing about sports if sports is all we know." In other words, if we want to know about sports, we must also know about the cultural context in which they exist.

Using Critical Theories in Everyday Life

Critical theories are based on concerns for fairness and desires to understand, confront, and transform systems of exploitation and oppression in social life. They lead to concerns about how sports either reproduce or transform the societies in which they exist. Those using some forms of critical theory emphasize that changes in sports depend on more than simply shifting the control of sport to the participants themselves. They note that many people are aware of who controls sports in their societies and have learned to accept those systems of control and to define them as correct. Therefore, policies based on critical theories would usually call for an increase in the number and diversity of sport participation alternatives available in society. The goal of such policies would be to provide people with opportunities to participate in many sports and, in the process, would enable them to use their experiences to create the critical abilities that lead to progressive transformations in their relationships, organizations, communities, and societies. As Peter Donnelly has suggested, "the struggle to achieve…fully democratized sport…might result in the capacity to transform communities. People could learn initiative, community endeavour, collective rather than individual values, self-determination, etc., that could permit them to begin to take charge of their own lives and communities" (1993, p. 428).

Critical theorists also raise questions about the stories told about sports in a culture. They challenge those whose voices and perspectives dominate those stories, and they make space for voices that have been silenced and for perspectives that are not represented in those stories. For example, critical feminist theories emphasize the need to critically assess and trans-

First nation canoer at 1984 Olympics with eagle feather (CP/Crombie McNeil)

form the ideology and organization of sports, so that sports give voice to and represent the perspectives and experiences of women in society. Those who use these feminist theories argue that, unless ideological and organizational changes are made, there will never be true gender equity in sport or in society as a whole. "Critical Feminist Theories" are discussed in the Reflect on Sports box on pages 47–48.

Critical theories force us to question what sports are and to think of what they might be from a variety of standpoints and perspectives. This can be either exciting or threatening, depending on your willingness to see sports in new and different ways.

REFLECT ON SPORTS

Critical Feminist Theories
Assessing Gender Relations and Sports

Feminist theories represent a diverse set of interpretive frameworks. However, they are all based on the assumption that, if we want to understand human behaviour and social life, we must understand the meanings that people give to gender and the ways that those meanings come to be incorporated into social experience and the organization of society.

Feminist theories in all disciplines have grown out of a general dissatisfaction with the intellectual traditions that base knowledge on the values and experiences of men and ignore women or do not take seriously the experiences and insights of women. Feminist theories are grounded in the awareness that women have been systematically devalued and oppressed in many societies and that there is a need to develop political strategies to eliminate oppression and to empower women to transform the cultures in which they are devalued.

Critical feminist theories are concerned primarily with issues of power and the dynamics of gender relations in social life. They pay close attention to how gender relations privilege men over women and some men over other men. They study how gender ideology (i.e., dominant ideas about masculinity and femininity) is formed, reproduced, resisted, and transformed in and through the everyday experiences of men and women.

Critical feminist approaches to sports in society are based on the assumption that sports are *gendered activities*. In other words, the meaning, organization, and purpose of sports are grounded in the values and experiences of men and are defined to celebrate the attributes and skills associated with masculinity in society (Birrell, 2000; Burstyn, 1999). Therefore, in the world of sports, a person is defined as "qualified" as an athlete, a coach, or an administrator if he or she is tough, aggressive, and emotionally focused on competitive success. If a person is kind, caring, supportive, and emotionally responsive to others, he or she is qualified only to be a cheerleader, a volunteer worker, or possibly an assistant in marketing and public relations; these qualities, often associated with women and men who did not fit the criteria outlined above, are not valued qualities in most sport organizations.

Research done by those who use critical feminist theories generally focuses on one or more of the following issues (see Birrell, 2000):

1. How are sports involved in the production of ideas about what it means to be a man in society, as well as in the production of a system of gender relations that privileges tough and aggressive men?
2. How are women and men represented in media coverage of sports, and how do those representations reproduce dominant ideas about femininity and masculinity in society?
3. What are the strategies used by women to resist or challenge the dominant gender logic that is promoted and reproduced through most organized competitive sports?

"How can feminists say that sports revolve around the values and interests of men with power?"

Feminists argue that dominant sports traditionally have been organized to reproduce cultural ideas that work to the advantage of men with power and influence in society.

Continued.

REFLECT ON SPORTS

Critical Feminist Theories continued

4. How are sports and sport participation involved in the production of gendered ideas about physicality, sexuality, and the body?

When critical feminists do research, they often have a clear political agenda: they want to use sports as sites for challenging and transforming oppressive forms of gender relations, and they want to expose and resist expressions of sexism and homophobia in sports. For many critical feminists, the goal is to change the meaning, organization, and purpose of sports to emphasize the notion of partnership and competition with others; they are opposed to sports that emphasize the notion of dominating and competing *against* others.

Critical feminist theories are not without weaknesses. In fact, they have most of the same weaknesses of critical theories generally. Additionally, because of their focus on gender as a category of experience, they often have ignored or given too little attention to other categories of experience that are connected with gender in important ways. These include age, race and ethnicity, social class, disability, religion, and nationality. Recent research has focused on the intersections of gender, race, and social class, but much remains to be done to explore the experiences and the problems faced by women of different ages, abilities, religions (for example, Muslim women), and nationalities.

Critical feminist research and theories have had a major impact on all of us who study sports in society. They have increased our understanding of sports as a part of culture, and they have made us aware of many other important questions to ask about gender and sports. For example, why do so many men around the world continue to resist efforts to promote gender equity in sports? Why do some women fear being called lesbians if they are strong and powerful athletes? Why are some men's locker rooms full of homophobia, gay-bashing jokes, and comments that demean women? Why are we not more concerned when more than forty thousand young men are carried off North American football fields every year with serious knee injuries? Why do church-going mothers and fathers who support "get tough" anticrime policies take their children to hockey games and cheer for young men charged and sometimes convicted of physical and sexual assault? Why do so many people assume that men who play sports must be heterosexual? Why has an openly gay male athlete never been featured on the cover of *Sports Illustrated*? Why are so many women's high school and university teams still called "Lady so-and-so's" or the "Something-ettes"? For example, note the "Lady Wesmen" of the University of Manitoba, or the "Vikettes" of the University of Victoria.) These questions, inspired by critical feminist theories, are worth serious attention. They deal with issues that affect our lives every day. In fact, if we do not have thoughtful responses to these questions, we really do not know much about sports in society. *What do you think?*

Weaknesses of Critical Theories

Because there are so many variations of critical theories used by those who study sports in society, it is difficult to neatly summarize their weaknesses.

One of the general weaknesses of critical theories is that they do not provide clear guidelines for determining when sports reproduce dominant forms of social relations in society and when they become sites for resisting and transforming social relations. Although recent research based on critical theories has focused on cases when sports are sites for resistance, it has not identified general guidelines for promoting the forms of resistance that lead to social transformations in sports or social relations. This is partly because most critical theorists give a higher priority to analyzing problems and taking political action to promote change than they do to building a general theory of social life. They say that all knowledge and truth depend on the cultural and social perspective through which they are constructed. Therefore, different problems and conflicts always call for different strategies and different forms of intervention. Of course, this can be a useful approach when dealing with a particular problem, conflict, or injustice, but it does not encourage the building of social theories that might have political and moral value from one situation to another.

A related weakness is that, because critical theories emphasize resistance and transgression, there is a tendency to see value in all resistant discourses and all behaviours that do not conform to dominant norms, especially when they represent the interests of marginalized segments of society. However, it is clear that dominant norms are not always unfair or oppressive and that the voices and perspectives of some marginalized and disadvantaged groups are not based on concerns about fairness, liberation, and tolerance of differences. It is important to respect the voices and creative potential of marginalized and oppressed groups, but it is not politically or morally wise to assume that the contributions of all groups have equal value when it comes to transforming social life. Many critical theorists have not identified criteria to prioritize ideas and forms of intervention that have an impact on people's lives. Therefore, they have a difficult time assessing the value of ideas and actions from one situation to the next.

A third weakness is that critical theories are so diverse that it is often difficult to understand their similarities and differences. Some use vocabularies that are confusing and that interfere with merging different critical ideas into more useful frameworks for social intervention and social change. Fortunately, some critical theorists are aware of this weakness and advocate coordinated critical analyses that reveal the dynamics of power relations in various cultural contexts and that can serve as a basis for effective forms of social intervention (McDonald and Birrell, 1999).

FIGURATIONAL THEORY: UNDERSTANDING SPORTS IN TERMS OF HISTORICAL AND GLOBAL PROCESSES

Figurational theory, which has its roots in European-history-based intellectual traditions, is rarely used directly in North American sociology of sport. It is more common in the U.K. and western Europe, and increasingly in Japan. However, it has influenced a number of Canadian theorists and researchers in the sociology of sport, and for that reason, a brief description is included here, and figurational theory is included in table 2.1.

Figurational theory is a comprehensive theory based on the notion that social life consists of networks of interdependent people. Those who use this theory focus on the historical processes through which these networks, or sets of interconnections between people, emerge and change over time. These sets of interconnections are called "figurations."

Those who use figurational theory view social life in terms of figurations. They study the long-term processes through which the relatively autonomous actions of many individuals and collections of people influence and constrain each other. These processes are complex and dynamic, and they involve a wide range of outcomes, which no single individual or group has chosen, designed, planned, or intended. These outcomes may be enabling or constraining for different individuals and groups, but they are never permanent. They shift and change as power balances within figurations shift and change over time. Power balances shift and change over time in connection with changes in the economic, political, and emotional dimensions of social life (Murphy et al., 2000).[3]

Figurational Theory and Research on Sports

Figurational theory has inspired much research and discussion about sports in society. It offers useful analyses of the following topics:

1. What are the historical, economic, political, and emotional factors that account for the emergence of modern sports during the eighteenth and nineteenth centuries in much of Europe?
2. What are the historical and social processes through which sport participation became increasingly serious in people's lives and through which sports became professionalized and commercialized in various societies during the twentieth century?
3. What are the historical and social dynamics of violence and efforts to control violence in sports, especially in connection with soccer in England and around the world?
4. What are the relationships among sports, national identity, and the dynamics of globalization processes in which the media, economic expansion, and consumerism play important roles?

Unlike other social theories, figurational theory gives close attention to sports in society. Sports are important because they are "collective inventions," which provide people, especially men, in highly regulated modern societies with forms of enjoyable excitement that reduce boredom while limiting the excessive and destructive

It does matter what theoretical framework is used to study an issue or a question. This researcher and intern are in Canada, so they do not have figurational theory "on the shelf."

violence that characterized many folk games in premodern Europe (Dunning, 1999).

Furthermore, the concept of figurations has been especially useful in studies of the complex economic, political, and social processes associated with global sports. Figurational research on the global migration of elite athletes, the global sport industry, the global media-sport complex, the impact of global sport on identity politics, and the ways that sports are incorporated simultaneously into local cultures and global processes have helped us understand sports in a global perspective (Maguire, 1999).

Canadian researchers have paid particular attention to figurational research on the origins and development of sports, on sports violence, and on various aspects of globalization.

---

[3]Figurational theory grew out of the work of Norbert Elias, a German Jew who fled Nazi Germany in 1933 and continued his sociological research in England until he died in 1990. Elias' theory of civilizing processes in western Europe is based on extensive historical research (see Elias, 1978, 1982). When Elias turned his attention to sports and leisure, much of his work was done with Eric Dunning (Elias and Dunning, 1986). Dunning has influenced students around the world through his writing and his lectures at Leicester University in England and many other universities.

SUMMARY

IS THERE A BEST THEORETICAL APPROACH TO USE WHEN STUDYING SPORTS?

Theories are tools that provide us with frameworks for asking questions, identifying problems, gathering information, explaining social life, prioritizing strategies to deal with problems, and anticipating the consequences of our actions and interventions.

In our experience as involved citizens, as sociologists, and as people who have played and watched sports with friends and family, we have found all the frameworks discussed in this chapter useful. Each of them has made us aware of questions and issues that are important in our lives or in the lives of those with whom we work and play. (See table 2.1.)

In much of our own research, we have used *interactionist theory* because we wanted to view sports from the inside, from the perspectives of those who make decisions to play or not to play and who integrate sport participation into their lives in various ways. However, we have also been influenced strongly by *critical theories*, including *critical feminist theories*. This combination has helped us become more aware of the social and cultural contexts in which people make decisions about sport participation, and it has enabled us to see how access to participation opportunities is influenced by economic, political, and cultural factors. Furthermore, *critical* and *feminist theories* have helped us think about very practical issues, such as how to become politically involved on proposals to fund new parks or professional sports stadiums and arenas. They have helped us to think about policies related to organizing sport programmes for at-risk youth and for keeping sports as a part of high school extracurricular activities.

Functionalist theory helps us understand how other people think about sports in society, but it does not help to identify the issues and controversies connected with sports in our communities and in the sport organizations where we work with coaches and administrators. *Conflict theory* alerts us to social class and economic issues, but *critical theories* help us to go beyond those issues to also consider factors related to gender, race and ethnicity, disability, sexuality, and media coverage of sports and sports figures. *Figurational theory* has helped us understand historical and global issues more clearly, and we have used figurational research findings to help our thinking about power and politics in a global perspective.

Critical and *feminist theories* offer useful frameworks for thinking about how to change sports and make sport participation more accessible to a wider range of people in society. We are much more interested in increasing choices and alternatives for people in sports than we are in making sports a more efficient means of maintaining the status quo in society (a goal of *functionalist theory*) or in dismantling the current system of sports altogether (a goal of *conflict theory*). We think that many aspects of the status quo in Canada and in other societies are in need of change and that sports can be useful sites for making people aware of what changes are needed and the forms they might take.

Creating alternative ways of doing sports requires an awareness of the values underlying dominant forms of sports in society today, as well as a vocabulary for thinking about creative possibilities for the future. A combination of *critical* and *feminist theories* is especially helpful in critically assessing those values and providing the vocabulary we need to assess existing sport forms and to develop new forms that offer human beings new possibilities for organizing their thoughts about the world and their connections with each other.

Our theoretical preferences often conflict with the preferences expressed by students and people who work for sport organizations. Students who would like to work in sport organizations know that most of the people in those organizations see sports in functionalist terms, so they prefer *functionalist theory*. However, we try to remind these students that, if they are familiar with issues of power and culture, they will be able to critically assess organizational policies in terms of their impact on various groups of employees in the organization and on various segments of the surrounding community. When we work with coaches and sport administrators, they often tell us that our critical approach has helped them see things in their lives in new and helpful ways.

Finally, we believe that true empowerment involves enabling people to position themselves as subjects so they can effectively "challenge and change unequal power relationships" (Mahiri, 1998). As we try to live by this belief, we find that critical and feminist theories, combined with interactionist theory, are especially helpful.

Despite their limitations and weaknesses, social theories are helpful as we explore issues and controversies in sports and as we assess the research and ideas on sports in society. We do not have to be theorists to use theory to help us organize our thoughts and become more informed citizens in our schools and communities.

 SUGGESTED READINGS

Sports and Social Theory

Maguire, J., and K. Young (eds.) 2002. *Theory, sport & society*. Oxford: JAI/Elsevier Science (provides a comprehensive overview of the six theories discussed in this chapter, and a number of other theories that have been used in the study of sports in society).

Functionalist Theory

Loy, J., and D. Booth, 2000. Functionalism, sport and society. In J. Coakley and E. Dunning, eds., *Handbook of sports studies* (pp. 9–27). London: Sage (overview of functionalism and research informed by functionalism in the sociology of sport).

Conflict Theory

Rigauer, B. 2000. Marxist theories. In J. Coakley and E. Dunning, eds., *Handbook of sports studies* (pp. 28–47). London: Sage (overview of Marxist theory and research in the study of sport; special emphasis on sport as a form of work in capitalist societies).

Interactionist Theory

Coakley, J., and P. Donnelly. 1999. *Inside sports*. London: Routledge (many of the twenty-two articles in this collection use interactionist theory to guide qualitative research on sport participation and sport experiences; highlights processes of becoming involved in sports, developing an athlete identity, participating in sports, and making the transition out of sports).

Donnelly, P. 2000. Interpretive approaches to the sociology of sports. In J. Coakley and E. Dunning, eds., *Handbook of sports studies* (pp. 77–91). London: Sage (overview of interactionist and other interpretive approaches to studying sports).

Critical Theories and Feminist Theories

Birrell, S. 2000. Feminist theories for sport. In J. Coakley and E. Dunning, eds., *Handbook of sports studies* (pp. 61–76). London: Sage (overview of how feminist theories have been used in sport studies; traces the history of this use and discusses critical feminist cultural studies as used by many people in recent years).

Gruneau, R. 1999. *Class, sports, and social development*. Champaign, IL: Human Kinetics (considered to be one of the most important theoretical works in the sociology of sport, a book that signalled the shift to critical approaches that are now so widespread in the field).

Hall, M. A. 1996. *Feminism and sporting bodies: Essays on theory and practice*. Champaign, IL: Human Kinetics (overview of feminist approaches to the study of sport and culture; discusses feminist theories in connection with other forms of cultural theories).

Hargreaves, J., and I. MacDonald. 2000. Cultural studies and the sociology of sport. In J. Coakley and E. Dunning, eds., *Handbook of sports studies*. (pp. 48–60). London: Sage (overview of critical theories and research informed by Gramsci and Cultural Studies in the study of sports).

Pronger, B. 2002. *Body fascism: Salvation in the technology of physical fitness*. Toronto: University of Toronto Press (a critical poststructuralist analysis of the fitness movement, which develops a theory of science and the body, and draws a striking parallel between the effects of technology on the environment and the effects of technology on the body).

Figurational Theory

Dunning, E. 1999. *Sport matters: Sociological studies of sport, violence, and civilization.* London: Routledge (definitive introduction to the study of modern sport from a figurational perspective; figurational theory is clearly distinguished from other theoretical approaches in each of the chapters).

Elias, N., and E. Dunning. 1986. *Quest for excitement.* New York: Basil Blackwell (uses figurational theory to guide discussions of sport as a form of pleasurable excitement that counterbalances the stress-tensions in the rest of people's lives).

Maguire, J. 1999. *Global sport: Identities, societies, civilizations.* Cambridge: Polity Press (presents a model for understanding the emergence of global sports and issues associated with the global diffusion of sports; case studies of the migration of elite athletes, the role of the media in the global expansion of sports, the global sports industry and capitalist expansion, and identity politics and global sports).

Murphy, P., K. Sheard, and I. Waddington. 2000. Figurational sociology and its application to sports. In J. Coakley and E. Dunning, eds., *Handbook of sports studies* (pp. 92–105). London: Sage (overview of figurational sociology in the study of sport and society).

WEBSITE RESOURCES

Note: Websites often change. The following URLs were current when this book was printed. Please check our Online Learning Centre website (www.mcgrawhill.ca/college/coakley) for updates, as well as for additional resources and study tools.

www.mcmaster.ca/socscidocs/w3virtsoclib/theories. htm (research source for information on sociological theory and theorists; it is not sport-related, but it provides numerous links to sites around the world)

www.socqrl.niu.edu/FYI/theory.htm (valuable links to helpful sites on social theory)

www.soc.qc.edu/gramsci/ (offers resources on Antonio Gramsci, whose work influences much of critical theories)

www.feminist.org/research/sports2.html (special coverage of "Empowering Women in Sports"; this site not only is a good example of applied feminist theories but it also highlights the issues that are most important in a feminist analysis of sports)

www.usyd.edu.au/su/social/elias.html (one of a number of sites devoted to Norbert Elias and figurational theory; provides links to many European sources)

A Look at the Past

Does it help us understand sports today?

There is no game as Canadian as lacrosse. Hockey is really an ice version of bandy, played by the English years before it was adapted for Canada. Basketball was invented by a Canadian, but he invented it in the United States. Lacrosse was the natives' game. Its origins are unclear, but it was played long before the Europeans arrived.

—**William Humber, Canadian sports historian (1989)**

They who laid the intellectual foundations of the western world were the most fanatical players and organizers of games that the world has ever known.

—**C.L.R. James, West Indian writer and cricket player (1963)**

Sports have been revered by fascists and communists, by free-marketers and filibusters. They have also been, paradoxically, reviled by all those political factions. Sports may be among the most powerful human expressions in all history.

—**Gerald Early, Professor of Modern Letters, Washington University, St. Louis (1998)**

 Online Learning Centre Resources

Visit *Sports in Society's* Online Learning Centre at **www.mcgrawhill.ca/college/coakley** for additional information and study material for this chapter.

To understand sports as social phenomena in today's world, we should have a sense of what physical games, contests, and sport activities were like in past times. Therefore, this chapter presents brief social overviews of sport activities in different cultural and historical settings. Our intent is *not* to provide an integrated overall history of sports. Such a history would look at the development and organization of physical activities and games across all continents from one cultural group to another over time. This would be an ambitious and worthy project, but it is far beyond the scope of this book.

The material we present focuses on (1) the ancient Greeks, (2) the Roman Empire, (3) the Middle Ages in parts of Europe, (4) the Renaissance through the Enlightenment in parts of Europe, and (5) the Industrial Revolution through recent times, with special emphasis on Canada. It is important that we do not conclude that this material somehow represents either the entire world or the most important part of the world. We have chosen these times and places because they are familiar to many of us, and they are examples of how sports are cultural practices connected clearly with the ideology and social structures of the societies in which they exist.

The goal of this chapter is to show that, for each of these times and places, our understanding of sports depends on what we know about the social lives of the people who created, defined, played, and integrated them into their everyday experiences. As critical theories suggest, it is especially important to know how people used their power and resources as they struggled with one another to shape physical activities that fit their needs and interests.

When we view sports from the past in this way, dates and names are not the most important pieces of information. Instead, we focus primarily on what sport activities tell us about relationships between various groups of people at particular times and places. This is the focus throughout the chapter.

UNDERSTANDING HISTORY WHILE STUDYING SPORTS IN SOCIETY

When we think about history, many of us think about a chronological sequence of events that build on each other and gradually lead to a better, or more "modern," society. Even the terminology used in many discussions of history leads us to think this way. For example, many historical accounts are full of references to societies that are traditional or modern, primitive or civilized, underdeveloped or developed, preindustrial or industrial. This terminology implies that history is moving in a particular direction and that, as it moves, cultural forms, social institutions, and material conditions are improving and becoming more modern and developed. In other words, history is frequently presented as linear and progressive—always following a line that moves forward and upward.

This approach enables some people today to feel superior because they conclude that they are the most modern, civilized, and developed people in history. However, such a conclusion is not historically accurate. In the case of sports, there are literally thousands of "histories" of physical activities among thousands of human populations in different places around the world. These histories involve patterns of changes that many people would not describe as progressive. Furthermore, even the definitions of *progress* that different people use are products of particular cultural experiences.

Historical evidence suggests that physical activities and games have existed in all cultures. The specific forms of these activities and games, along with the meanings that people gave to them, were shaped through struggles over the organization and purpose of the activities, over who should play them and who should not, and over how they should be integrated into people's lives. To say that physical activities and games over the years have evolved to fit a pattern of progress, or modernization, is to distort the life experiences of people all over the world

(Gruneau, 1988). There may be decreasing contrasts among the games that different people play today, but this does not mean that sports are "evolving" to fit a grand scheme for how physical activities should be organized or what they should mean in people's lives (Maguire, 1999). Instead, decreasing contrasts around the globe are due to processes of cultural diffusion combined with recent concentrations of global power and influence among corporations, which have the power to define, organize, sponsor, promote, and present through the media particular sports and sport forms.

One clear illustration of the importance of global power relations in sports is the process through which new events are added to the Olympic Games. New events usually reflect the interests of groups or organizations that are able to exert influence on the members of the International Olympic Committee. This is the reason that events and games originating in Africa, Latin America, and Asia are seldom included in the Olympics. When beach volleyball was included as a new sport in the 1996 Summer Games in Atlanta, it was primarily because it represented the interests of sport groups, corporate sponsors, and media organizations from wealthy countries. To call this progress is to make a political statement, not a historical one—although Coca-Cola, Nike, and Cuervo Tequila (a sponsor of beach volleyball in the United States) would like us to think otherwise.

Therefore, do not conclude that this chapter is a story of progress. Instead, read it as stories about certain people at different times and in different places struggling over and coming to terms with what they wanted their physical activities to be and how they wished to include them in their lives. Certainly, there is some historical continuity in these processes and struggles in particular cultures, but continuity does not always mean that the structure and organization of sports equally represent the interests of all people in a culture. Human history does not follow any grand plan of progress. When progressive

changes do occur, it is because people have made them happen at a particular time, and these people usually realize that, unless they keep an eye on things, the progress will be only temporary.

SPORTS VARY BY TIME AND PLACE

People in all cultures have engaged in physical activities and used human movement as a part of their ritual life. As we look at cultural variations, it is necessary to remember that few cultures have had physical games that were characterized by formal organization, rule-governed competition, and record keeping.

In prehistoric times, there were no sports as we know them today. Physical activities were often tied directly to the challenge of survival and the expression of religious beliefs. People hunted for food and sometimes used their physical abilities to defend themselves or establish social control and power over others. Archaeological evidence suggests that people on each continent of the globe created unique organized forms of physical challenges for the purpose of appeasing their gods. These activities involved acting out events that had important symbolic or real meaning in their everyday lives, and, even though they may have taken the form of games, they were inseparable from sacred rituals and ceremonies. In fact, they often were performed as forms of religious worship, and sometimes their outcomes were determined by religious necessity rather than the physical abilities of the people involved (Guttmann, 1978).

The first forms of organized games around the world probably emerged from this combination of physical challenges and religious rituals. From what we can tell, these games were connected closely with the social structures, social relations, and belief systems of the societies in which they existed, and they usually re-created and reaffirmed dominant cultural practices in those societies. But this was not always the case. Sometimes they served as sources of protest or opposition

SIDELINES

©1982 M.T.F.-T.W.S.-Lakewood, CO

"How can you stop to shoot pool on the way home when it won't be invented for another 10 million years?"

In early human history, there were no sports as we define and play them today. People used their physical abilities for survival. Physical activities occasionally were included in community and religious rituals, but their purpose probably was to appease the gods, rather than to entertain or build character.

against dominant ways of thinking about and doing culture in particular groups or societies.

Historical and cultural variations in the form and dynamics of physical activities remind us that all cultural practices, even sports, can serve a variety of social purposes. This raises the question of how the definition and organization of sports in any society promote the interests of various groups within that society. People create sport activities within the constraints of the social world in which they live. Therefore, not everyone has an equal say in how those activities are defined and organized. People with the strongest vested interests and the most *power* in a group or society generally have the greatest impact on how sports are defined, organized, and played in that group or society. Sport activities do not totally reflect their desires, but sports represent the interests of the powerful more than they represent the interests of other groups in society.

This critical theory approach to studying sports in history calls attention to the existence and consequences of social inequality in

societies. Social inequality has always had a significant impact on how sport activities are organized and played in any situation. The most influential forms of social inequality are those related to wealth, political power, social status, gender, age, and race and ethnicity. We pay special attention to these in the following discussions of times and places. We should also point out that the following descriptions are partial, and extremely Eurocentric, primarily because the dominant forms of contemporary sports trace their origins to Europe. In a colonial and multicultural society such as Canada, it is important to remember that there are rich traditions of physical culture among aboriginal peoples, and from other parts of the world, such as various regions of Africa and Asia.

CONTESTS AND GAMES IN ANCIENT GREECE: BEYOND THE MYTHS (1000 B.C.E. TO 100 B.C.E.)[1]

The games played by the early Greeks (circa 900 B.C.E.) were grounded in mythology and religious beliefs. They usually were held in conjunction with festivals, which combined prayer, sacrifices, and religious services, along with music, dancing, and ritual feasts. Competitors in these early games were from wealthy, respected Greek families. They were the only people who could afford to hire trainers and coaches and who had the time and resources to travel to various games. Events that we know about were based on the interests of young males. They consisted primarily of

---

[1] The terms C.E. (common era) and B.C.E. (before the common era) are used here rather than the more traditional A.D. (*anno Domini*—the year of our Lord) and B.C. (before Christ) because such usage is now becoming the norm in the academy. This is in recognition of the fact that Christian traditions should no longer predominate in a secular, multicultural society. As is traditional, however, when there is no designation (e.g., 1922), it refers to the common era.

warrior sports, such as chariot racing, wrestling and boxing, javelin and discus throwing, foot racing, archery, and long jumping. Violence and serious injuries were commonplace, in comparison with today's sport events (Elias, 1986; Kidd, 1984, 1996b). Greek women, children, and older people occasionally played sports in these festivals, but they never played in the games held at Olympia.

The locations and dates of the Greek festivals also were linked to religious beliefs. For example, Olympia was chosen as one of the festival sites because it was associated with the achievements and activities of celebrated Greek gods and mythological characters. In fact, Olympia was dedicated as a shrine to the god Zeus in about 1000 B.C.E. Although permanent buildings and playing fields were not constructed until 550 B.C.E., the games at Olympia were held every four years. Additional festivals involving athletic contests were also held at other locations throughout Greece, the principal ones being at Delphi, Isthmia, and Nemea, but the Olympic Games became the most prestigious of all athletic events.

Women were prohibited from participating as athletes or spectators in the Olympic Games. However, women held their own games at Olympia. Dedicated to the goddess Hera, the sister-wife of Zeus, these games grew out of Greek fertility rites. According to some estimates, the Heraean Games even predated the exclusively male Olympic Games. Serious women athletes often risked their reputations in the eyes of males when they engaged in sports. Physical prowess was not consistent with dominant definitions of heterosexual femininity among the Greeks, so many people raised questions about the sexuality of strong and physically skilled women,

> **Of the thousands of evils...in Greece there is no greater evil than the race of athletes....Since they have not formed good habits, they face problems with difficulty. They glisten and gleam like statues ...when they are in their prime, but when bitter old age comes...they are like tattered and threadbare old rugs.**
>
> —Euripides, Greek dramatist (fifth century B.C.E.)

including the goddesses in Greek mythology (Kidd, 1984).

The discrimination against women who participated in sports was rooted in a patriarchal family structure in which females had no legal rights and only limited opportunities for experiences outside their households. Although some women from well-to-do Greek families did become regular participants in games at certain sites, their involvement was limited and their achievements were usually ignored.[2]

The games at Olympia took on political significance as they grew in visibility and popularity. Winning became connected with the glory of city-states, and physically skilled slaves and young men from lower-class backgrounds were forced to become athletes, or wealthy patrons and government officials hired them to train for the Olympics and other games. Victories brought prizes of cash, along with subsidies for living expenses, for these slaves and hired athletes. Victories also earned them reputations, which they could convert into monetary rewards when competing in other popular Greek games. Contrary to myths of ama-

---

[2] Interestingly, some of the earliest recorded winners of events at Olympia were women: owners of winning horses were listed as winners, and these were sometimes women. This introduces a note of caution with regard to our subsequent comments about the involvement of girls and women in sports. When the historical record is primarily a record of, and by, the wealthy and powerful, usually males, as is overwhelmingly the case for the Greek, Roman, Medieval, and Renaissance periods, it does not necessarily mean that those who have not left a record were not involved. We report the weight of evidence suggesting that women were usually discouraged, even prohibited, from involvement, but there are regular examples of girls and women finding a way to be involved in sports and physical activities (see, for example, Simri, 1983).

teur ideals among the Greeks, these male athletes saw themselves as professionals. During the second century B.C.E., they even organized athletic guilds so they might bargain for rights, for control over the conditions of their sport participation, and for material security when they had to retire from competition (Baker, 1988).

Greek athletes became so specialized in their physical skills that they made poor soldiers. They engaged in warrior sports, but they lacked the generalized skills of warriors. Furthermore, they concentrated so much on athletic training that they ignored intellectual development. This evoked widespread criticism from Greek philosophers, who saw the games as brutal and dehumanizing and the athletes as useless and ignorant citizens.

Unfortunately, representatives of the modern Olympics have romanticized and perpetuated myths about Greek games in an attempt to connect the modern Olympics to a positive legacy from the past. Although Plato may have philosophized about connections between mind and body, Greek athletes often maimed or killed one another in the pursuit of victories and the rewards that came with them. Fairness was not as important as honour, violence was common, and athletic contests were closely connected with a cultural emphasis on warfare (Dunning, 1999).

Physical contests and games in Greek culture influenced art, philosophy, and the everyday lives of many people, especially those wealthy enough to train, hire professionals, and travel to games. However, Greek contests and games were different from the organized competitive sports of today (Guttmann, 1978; see also the Reflect on Sports box, "The Characteristics of High-Profile Organized Competitive Sports," pages 69–70). First, they were grounded in religion; second, they lacked complex administrative structures; and, third, they did not involve measurements and record keeping from event to event. However, there is one major similarity: they often reproduced dominant patterns of social relations in the society as a whole. The power and

advantages that went with being wealthy, male, and young in Greek society shaped the games and contests in ways that limited the participation of women, older people, and those without economic resources. In fact, even the definitions of excellence used to evaluate performance reflected the abilities of young males. This meant that the abilities of others were substandard by definition—if you could not do it as a young male could do it, then you could not do it right.

ROMAN CONTESTS AND GAMES: SPECTACLES AND GLADIATORS (100 B.C.E. TO C.E. 500)

Roman leaders used physical contests and games to train soldiers and provide mass entertainment spectacles. They borrowed events from Greek contests and games, but they geared athletic training to the preparation of obedient military men. They were critical of the Greek emphasis on individualism and the development of specialized physical skills that were useless in battle. They packaged their physical activities in ways that would appeal to spectators.

Through the first century C.E., Roman contests and games increasingly took the form of circuses and gladiatorial combat. Chariot races were the most popular events during the spectacles. Wealthy Romans recruited slaves as charioteers. Spectators bet heavily on the races and, when they became bored or unruly, the emperors passed around free food to keep them from becoming hostile. In some cases, free raffle tickets for attractive prizes were distributed to spectators to prevent riots, which could start when people became overexcited. This tactic pacified the crowds and allowed the emperors to use the spectator events as occasions to celebrate themselves and their positions of power. Government officials in Roman provinces and colonies also used similar events to maintain control in their communities.

As the power and influence of the Roman Empire grew, these spectacles, consisting of contests and games, became increasingly important as diversions for the masses. By C.E. 300, half of the days on the Roman calendar were public holidays. Because of the system of slavery, many free workers held only part-time jobs, and unemployment was extremely high. Activities other than the standard chariot races, boxing matches, and other such contests were needed to keep events interesting. Bearbaiting, bullbaiting, and animal fights were added to capture spectator interest. Men and women were forced into the arena to engage in mortal combat with lions, tigers, and panthers. Condemned criminals were sometimes dressed in sheepskins and thrown in with partially starved wild animals. Gladiators, armed with a variety of weapons, were pitted against one another in gory fights to the death. These spectacles achieved two purposes for the Romans: they entertained an idle populace and disposed of socially "undesirable" people, such as thieves, murderers, and Christians (Baker, 1988).

Some Romans criticized these spectacles as tasteless activities, devoid of cultural value. However, the criticisms were not based on concerns for human rights as much as they were based on an objection to events where the upper and lower social classes fraternized with one another. In other words, the objections were based on prejudice against the lower classes. Other than some outspoken Christians, few people objected to the spectacles on moral or humanitarian grounds. The objections coming from the Christians had little effect on the fate of the events. In fact, the demise of Roman spectacles went hand in hand with the fall of the Roman Empire. As the Roman economy went deeper and deeper into depression, and as wealthy people moved away from cities, there were not enough resources to support such spectacles (Baker, 1988).

Women were seldom involved in Roman contests and games. They were allowed in the arenas to watch and cheer male athletes, but few had opportunities to develop their own athletic skills. Within the Roman family, women were legally subservient to and rigidly controlled by men. Like women in ancient Greece, they were discouraged, though not always successfully (see Note 2), from pursuing interests beyond the household.

Although local folk games and other physical activities existed in the Roman Empire, we know little about how they were organized and played and what they meant in people's lives. The spectacles did not capture the interest of everyone, but they attracted considerable attention in major population centres. Roman contests and games differed from organized sports today in that they sometimes were connected with religious rituals, and they seldom involved the quantification of athletic achievements or the recording of outstanding accomplishments (see the Reflect on Sports box, "The Characteristics of High-Profile Organized Competitive Sports," pages 69–70).

TOURNAMENTS AND GAMES IN MEDIEVAL EUROPE: SEPARATION OF THE MASTERS AND THE MASSES (500 TO 1300)

Sport activities during Medieval Europe consisted of folk games played by local peasants, tournaments staged for knights and nobles, archery contests, and activities in which animals were brutalized (Dunning, 1999). The folk games, often violent and dangerous, and activities that involved the maiming or killing of animals emerged in connection with local peasant customs. The tournaments and archery contests were tied to military training and the desire for entertainment among the feudal aristocracy and those who served them.

Some of the local games of this period have interesting histories. As Roman soldiers and government officials moved throughout Europe during the fourth and fifth centuries, they built bathing facilities to use during their leisure time. To loosen up before their baths, they engaged in various forms of ball play. Local peasants during the early medieval period adopted the Roman activities and gradually developed their own forms of ball games. They often integrated these games into local religious ceremonies. For example, tossing a ball back and forth sometimes represented the conflict between good and evil, light and darkness, or life and death. As the influence of the Roman Catholic Church spread through Europe during the early years of the medieval period, these symbolic rituals were redefined in terms of Roman Catholic beliefs; thus, in these cases sport and religion were integrally connected.

During most of the medieval period, the Roman Catholic Church accepted peasant ball games, even though they occasionally involved violence. In fact, local priests encouraged games by opening church grounds on holidays and Sunday afternoons to groups of participants, so the games became a basic part of village life. People played them whenever there were festive community gatherings. They were included with the music, dancing, and religious services held in conjunction with seasonal ceremonies and saints' feast days. An interesting note is that these local ball games contained the roots for many contemporary games, such as soccer, field hockey, football, rugby, bowling, curling, baseball, and cricket. However, the games played in rural villages had little structure and few rules. Local traditions guided play, and these traditions varied from one community to the next.

The upper classes in medieval Europe paid little attention to and seldom interfered in the leisure of peasants. They saw peasant games and festivities as safety valves defusing mass social discontent. The sport activities of the upper classes were distinctively different from those of the peasants. Access to equipment and facilities allowed the nobility to develop early versions of billiards, shuffleboard, tennis, handball, and jai alai. Ownership of horses allowed them to develop various forms of horse racing, while their stable hands developed a version of the game of horseshoes. On horseback, they also participated in hunting and hawking. Owning property and possessing money and servants had an impact on their sports.

Through much of the medieval period, the popular sporting events among upper-class males

were tournaments consisting of war games designed to keep knights and nobles ready for battle. Some tournaments differed very little from actual battlefield confrontations. Deaths and serious injuries occurred, victors carried off their opponents' possessions, and losers often were taken as prisoners and used as hostages to demand ransoms from opposing camps. Later versions of tournaments were not quite so serious, but they still involved injuries and occasional deaths. Gradually, colourful ceremonies and pageantry softened the warlike tournaments, and entertainment and chivalry took priority over military preparation and the use of extreme violence.

Throughout the period, women were less apt than men to be involved in physical games and sport activities. Gender restrictions were grounded in a combination of religious dogma (the Roman Catholic Church taught that women had inferior status) and a male-centred family structure. A woman's duty was to be obedient and submissive. This orientation did not change much through the medieval period; however, peasant women were involved in some of the games and physical activities associated with the regular rounds of village events during the year. Among the aristocracy, gender relations were patterned so that men's activities and women's activities were clearly differentiated. Aristocratic women did little outside the walls of their dwellings, and their activities seldom involved rigorous physical exertion for the purpose of self-entertainment. Women in the upper classes sometimes engaged in "ladylike" games and physical activities, but, because they were subject to men's control and often viewed as sex objects and models of beauty, their involvement in active pursuits was limited. Feminine beauty during this time was defined in passive terms: the less active a woman, the more likely she was perceived as beautiful. In meeting expectations for beauty, women usually avoided all but very limited involvement in physical exercise (although, see Note 2).

Even though some sports in Europe and North America today can trace their roots back to the contests and games of the medieval period, the tournaments and games of that time were not much like today's organized sports. They lacked specialization and organization, they never involved the measurement and recording of athletic achievements, and they were not based on a commitment to equal and open competition among athletes from diverse backgrounds (see the Reflect on Sports box, "The Characteristics of High-Profile Organized Competitive Sports," pages 69–70). Guttmann has vividly described this last point:

> In medieval times, jousts and tournaments were limited to the nobility. Knights who sullied their honor by inferior marriages—to peasant girls, for instance—were disbarred. If they were bold enough to enter a tournament despite this loss of status, and were discovered, they were beaten and their weapons were broken. Peasants reckless enough to emulate the sport of their masters were punished by death. (1978, p. 30)

Although some characteristics of medieval sport activities may be seen in the games and contests of the Renaissance, Reformation, and Enlightenment periods, these later periods involved important transformations, which shaped the forms and meanings of physical activities and games.

THE RENAISSANCE, REFORMATION, AND ENLIGHTENMENT: GAMES AS DIVERSIONS (1300 TO 1800)

The Renaissance

Wars throughout Europe during the fourteenth and fifteenth centuries encouraged some monarchs, government officials, and church authorities to increase their military strength. To do this, they often enacted new rules prohibiting popular peasant pastimes. Those in authority saw the time peasants spent playing games as time they could spend learning to defend the lands and lives of their masters. But, despite the pronouncements of bishops and kings, the peasants did not readily give up their games. In fact, the games sometimes became rallying points for opposition to government and church authority.

About the same time that the peasants were being subjected to increased controls in many locations, the "scholar-athlete" became the ideal among many of the aristocrats and the affluent. They saw the "Renaissance man" as someone who was "socially adept, sensitive to aesthetic values, skilled in weaponry, strong of body, and learned in letters" (Baker, 1988, p. 59).

Throughout the Renaissance period, women had relatively few opportunities to be involved in tournaments and sport activities. Although peasant women sometimes played physical games, their lives were restricted by the demands of work in and out of the home. They often did hard physical labour, but they were not encouraged to engage in public activities that called special attention to their physical abilities and accomplishments.

Upper-class women sometimes participated in activities such as bowling, croquet, archery, and tennis, but their involvement was limited because women were seen during this time as "naturally" weak and passive. Some of these "Renaissance women" may have been pampered and put on proverbial pedestals, but men maintained their power by tightly controlling the lives of women, partly by promoting the idea that women were too fragile to leave the home and do things on their own.

The Reformation

During the Protestant Reformation, a growth in negative attitudes regarding games and sport activities adversely affected the participation of both men and women, especially in locations where either Calvinism or Puritanism was popular. For example, between the late 1500s and the 1600s, the English Puritans worked hard to eliminate or control leisure activities, including physical contests and games, in everyday life in

England. The Puritans were devoted to the work ethic and, according to Robert Malcolmson, a social historian at Queen's University, this is how they viewed sports:

> [Sports] were thought to be profane and licentious—they were occasions of worldly indulgence that tempted men from a godly life; being rooted in pagan and popish practices, they were rich in the sort of ceremony and ritual that poorly suited the Protestant conscience; they frequently involved a desecration of the Sabbath and an interference with the worship of the true believers; they disrupted the peaceable order of society, distracting men from their basic social duties—hard work, thrift, personal restraint, devotion to family, [and] a sober carriage. (Malcolmson, 1984, p. 67)

The primary targets of the Puritans were the pastimes and games of the peasants. Peasants did not own property, so their festivities occurred in public settings and attracted large crowds. The Puritans did their best to eliminate them—especially festivities scheduled on Sunday afternoons. It was not that the Puritans objected to the games themselves, but they disapproved of the drinking and partying that accompanied the games and did not like the idea of promoting physical pleasure on the Sabbath. The physical activities and games of the affluent were less subject to Puritan interference. Activities such as horse racing, hunting, tennis, and bowling took place on the private property of the wealthy, making it difficult for the Puritans to enforce their prohibitions. As in other times and places, power relations had much to do with who played what activities under what conditions.

Despite the Puritans and social changes affecting the economic structure and stability of English village life, many peasant people maintained their participation in games and sports. This was especially the case in locales where Martin Luther's ideas had been more influential than John Calvin's ideas. However, some traditional peasant activities were adapted so they could be played in less public settings.

During the early 1600s, King James I formally challenged Puritan influence in England by issuing *The King's Book of Sports*. This book, reissued in 1633 by Charles I, emphasized that Puritan ministers and officials should not discourage lawful recreational pursuits among English people. Charles I and his successors ushered in a new day for English sporting life. They revived traditional festivals and actively promoted and supported public games and sport activities. A few sport activities, including cricket, horse racing, yachting, fencing, golf, and boxing, became highly organized during the late 1600s and the 1700s, although participation patterns reflected and reproduced social class divisions in society.

In colonial Canada, British and French influences were strong in the Maritimes and Upper and Lower Canada. Many of the colonists were not necessarily playful people; hard work was necessary for survival. However, as the lifestyles of the colonists became established, and as free time became available, there was a growing desire to introduce games from the past into life in the new colonies. Voyageurs engaged in the fur trade and troops garrisoned in Canada also found time to play. As the colonies became more established, the class structures of Europe, especially Britain, began to be re-created in the playing styles of landowners and workers (Bouchier, 2003).

During this period, although there was extensive contact between native peoples and colonists, there is little evidence that the games of colonists were affected by the influence of natives, or vice versa. However, the widespread adoption of the canoe as a means of transportation by colonists certainly meant that informal races occurred; and a later fascination with baggataway led to its incorporation as lacrosse.

Native peoples continued to play the games that had been a part of their cultures for centuries. In fact, sports and sport participation have many histories across North America. This reminds us to keep in mind whose voices and perspectives are represented in various historical accounts of games, contests, and

SIDELINES

"Why don't we settle this in a civilized way? We'll charge admission to watch!"

Dominant forms of sport in many societies have been created by and for men. These sports often have celebrated a particular form of masculinity, emphasizing aggression, conquest, and dominance.

sports. The Reflect on Sports box, "Lessons from History," on pages 65–66, emphasizes that we should be skeptical of historical accounts that do not represent the experiences and perspectives of those who lack the power to tell their stories in a public forum.

The Enlightenment

During the Enlightenment period (1700 to 1800), many games and sport activities in parts of Europe and North America began to resemble sport forms that we are familiar with today (Guttmann, 1978). With some exceptions, they were no longer grounded in religious ritual and ceremony; they involved some specialization and some degree of organization; achievements sometimes were measured; and records occasionally were kept. Furthermore, the idea that events should be open to all competitors, regardless of background, became increasingly popular. This commitment to equality and open participation, along with other forces and ideas,

gave rise to world-changing revolutions in France and the United States.

However, sport activities during the Enlightenment period were different from the dominant sport forms of today in at least one important respect: they were defined strictly as diversions—as interesting and often challenging ways to pass free time. People did not see them as having any utility for athletes in particular or society in general. No one seriously thought that sports and sport participation could change how people developed or acted, or how social life was organized. Therefore, there were no reasons for people to organize sport activities for others or to build sport organizations to oversee the activities of large networks of participants. People formed a few sport clubs, and they occasionally scheduled contests with other groups, but they did not feel compelled to form leagues or national and international associations. All this began to change during the Industrial Revolution.

THE INDUSTRIAL REVOLUTION: THE EMERGENCE OF ORGANIZED COMPETITIVE SPORTS (1780 TO THE PRESENT)

It would be an oversimplification to say that the organized competitive sports of today are simply a product of the Industrial Revolution (Dunning, 1999; Gruneau, 1988). They clearly emerged during the process of industrialization, but they were actually social constructions of people themselves—people who were trying to play their games and maintain their sport activities while they coped with the realities of everyday life in their rapidly changing families, communities, and societies. Of course, the realities of everyday life included economic, political, and social forces that either enabled or constrained people, depending on their position in society.

It is difficult to pinpoint the beginning of the Industrial Revolution. It is not marked by a

REFLECT ON SPORTS

Lessons from History
Distorted Views of Sports among Native North Americans

The history of sports is noteworthy for what it does *not* tell us as much as for what it does tell us. This is especially true when it comes to the physical activities, games, and sports of native peoples in North America. Joseph Oxendine (1988), a physical educator and Lumbee Indian, notes that there is a lack of recorded history about Native North Americans. Prior to the arrival of Europeans, the history of native peoples was kept in oral rather than written form. It was not until the late eighteenth century that accurate information about native cultures was recorded. However, by that time they had been influenced greatly by European explorers and settlers.

> **Just as the dominant class writes history, so that same class writes the story of sport.**
>
> —James Riordan, social historian and former soccer player (1996)

When the oral history and mythology of native peoples are combined with information written by archaeologists and anthropologists, it is possible to formulate hypotheses and general ideas about physical activities and games in traditional native cultures. However, many of the so-called scientific reports about native peoples over the past two hundred years provide only distorted descriptions of their games and sports. This is because their lives and cultures were disrupted by conflicts with Europeans, missionaries, the westward push of European settlers, and mistreatment at the hands of those who did not respect or take seriously native peoples or cultures. The accounts that were recorded during these times tell us little about traditional patterns of games and sports and how they were integrated into the diverse cultures that existed on the North American continent before European contact.

For the most part, it was impossible for Europeans to observe authentic expressions of traditional native cultures. When they did make observations, it was often under strained circumstances during which native peoples were unwilling to spontaneously reveal their customs while being watched by outsiders who often viewed them as "oddities." Observations were also reported from a European perspective, making no attempt (in contrast to usual practice in present-day anthropology) to see culture from the perspective of those producing it. By the time native peoples could describe their own activities in English or French, their cultures had changed in appreciable ways. It is known that some games of native peoples were forms of religious rites rather than spontaneous forms of play (as play is defined in chapter 1). Therefore, outsiders were seldom allowed to observe them in their authentic, traditional forms, and recorded information about them is frequently distorted.

Continued

single event, but it was associated with the development of factories and the mass production of consumer goods. It resulted in the development of cities and an increased dependence on technology. It involved changes in the organization and control of work and community life and was generally accompanied by an increase in the number of middle-class people in the societies in which it occurred. The Industrial Revolution first began in England around 1780. Shortly after that time, it became a part of life in other European countries; in Canada and the United States, it started around 1820.

The Early Years: Limited Time and Space

During the early years of the Industrial Revolution, it was difficult for all people except the wealthy to play games and sport activities regularly. Those who worked on farms and in factories had little free time, although workers were sometimes able to negotiate time by not

More recently, it has been difficult to describe the games and sports of native peoples because there is not one agreed upon definiton of who is a native person. Since the mid-twentieth century, native peoples have participated in a wide range of organized amateur and professional sports in Canada and the United States. In some cases, they have been identified and recognized in terms of their heritage, but in many cases they have not. "Who counts as a native person" is a contentious issue across North America. As native peoples in both Canada and the United States have interacted with other people, many have intermarried, with some maintaining traditions as Métis people (another category that is contentious in terms of definition), and many have become acculturated to the point that traditional forms of native cultures are nearly invisible, except on or near reserves. In other cases, native peoples have expressed their traditional ways only in private so as to avoid curiosity or discrimination or both.

Oxendine's book *American Indian Sports Heritage*, along with Peter Nabokov's book *Indian Running* (1981), highlights the fact that social, political, and economic forces influence what we know about the history of sports. Therefore, if we want to understand the importance of a historical event such as the establishment of the Iroquois National Lacrosse Team (in 1983), we must know about the following: the history and cultures of specific Native North American nations and the six nations of the Iroquois Confederacy, political relations between first nations people and the governments of Canada and the United States, and the experiences of first nations people as they have struggled to maintain their culture and survive in a society where powerful others have tried to strip them of their dignity, language, religion, and customs through deliberate attempts to assimilate the people into European culture (e.g., residential schools).

History is clearly much more than a chronological series of events, and we can view it from many perspectives. Therefore, when we study the history of sports, we must be aware of whose voices, perspectives, and theories are being represented and whose are being ignored or silenced. Information about sports and sport experiences among people from ethnic minority groups is scarce in most societies. There may be statistics about the number of participants but little in-depth information about the meanings given to sports by people in many ethnic minority populations and communities. This scarcity has diminished our awareness of sports history around the world. When history does not include the experiences and perspectives of minorities, it is always incomplete, usually erroneous, and sometimes dangerous because it reproduces stereotypes and justifies discrimination. This is why some people call for a revision of history books and curricula in high schools and universities. *What do you think?*

showing up for work on some Monday mornings. This tradition, widely known in the U.K. as St. Monday—i.e., the feast of St. Monday, recalling the traditional Saints' Days (holidays) that had dominated the calendar in days before the Industrial Revolution—survived until factory discipline became fully established. The workdays, even for many child workers, were often long and tiring. People who lived in cities had few open spaces in which they could play sports. Production took priority over play in the plans of industrialists and city leaders. Parks and public play spaces did not exist. Furthermore, working people were discouraged from getting together in large groups outside the workplace. People in authority perceived such gatherings as dangerous because they wasted time that could be used for work and because they provided opportunities for workers to organize themselves and challenge the power of the owners of factories and other means of production (Gruneau, 1999; Metcalfe, 1987; Palmer, 1979).

In most industrializing countries, the clergy also endorsed the containment of popular games and gatherings. Ministers preached about the moral value of work and the immorality of play and idleness. Many even banned sports on Sundays and were supported by the state in the notorious "blue laws." Anyone who was not totally committed to work was accused of being lazy. In the religious belief systems of the time, work was a sign of goodness. Not everyone agreed with this way of looking at things, but working people had few choices. For them, survival depended on working long hours, regardless of what they thought about work, and they had little power to change these definitions of work or what they needed to do to survive. The so-called blue laws, which in some Canadian jurisdictions lasted until well into the twentieth century, prohibited play, sports, and commercial entertainment on Sundays, and obliged taverns to close. Since Sunday was the only free day for workers, the laws were regularly disregarded by the latter part of the nineteenth century, and Metcalfe (1978) describes a widespread "Sunday subculture" of sports and gambling that developed in Montreal.

In most countries, games and sport activities during this period existed *despite* the Industrial Revolution, *not* because of it. People in small towns and farm communities still had opportunities to play games and sport activities during their seasonal festivities, holidays, and public ceremonies. Most city people had few opportunities to organize their own games and sports, although people with great wealth maintained highly publicized "lives of leisure" (Veblen, 1899). Among the working classes, sport involvement seldom went beyond being spectators at new forms of commercialized sport events. Of course, there were variations from one country to the next, but urban workers tended to watch a combination of cricket, horse racing, boxing and wrestling, footraces, rowing and yachting races, cockfighting, bullbaiting, and circus acts, among other events.

Rules against congregating in large crowds often were suspended when people participated in controlled commercialized spectator events. A fear of riots had led to restrictions on many neighbourhood events that might have attracted crowds, but organized commercial events seldom met objections in most industrial societies, even when they attracted large groups; these events were controlled and organized to benefit the interests of the powerful.

Some sport participation did occur among urban workers, but it was relatively rare during the early days of the Industrial Revolution. In Canada, for example, it usually was limited to various tavern games, played mostly by men. The constraints of work and the lack of material resources made it difficult for working-class people to engage in anything but informal games and sport activities. There were some exceptions, but they were rare.

Around the middle of the nineteenth century, things began to change. Reformers in parts of Europe and North America became concerned about the physical health of workers. Some of this concern was based on the awareness that workers were being exploited, and some was based on the recognition that weak and sickly workers could not be productive, so people began calling for new open spaces and externally sponsored "healthy" leisure pursuits. Fitness became highly publicized, and there was an emphasis on calisthenics, gymnastics, and outdoor exercises, and an effort to limit tavern games.

The emergence of formally organized competitive sports would require more than increased freedom and limited support for healthy leisure activities, but this was the time during which their foundations were established. In discussing more recent issues related to sports in society, we focus in the next section on events in Canada.

The Later Years: Changing Interests, Values, and Opportunities

From the late nineteenth century until today, there has been a growing emphasis on rationality and organization in Canadian society.

For example, during the mid-1800s, common interests in sport activities led to the establishment of organized clubs, which sponsored and controlled sport participation. Club membership usually was limited to wealthy men, and sometimes women, in urban areas. Metcalfe (1987) notes, for example, that there were 24 sports clubs in Montreal in 1860, mostly for wealthy anglophones in the sports of cricket, curling, lacrosse, and snowshoeing. However, the clubs did sponsor competitions, which often attracted spectators from all social classes.

The rapidly expanding middle classes during this time, particularly in the major cities such as Montreal and Toronto, were a key element in the development and spread of organized sports. As Hall, et al., point out with regard to the rapid increase in the number of urban sports clubs between the 1860s and the end of the century:

> [A]s the mercantile middle class (businessmen, merchants, storeowners, bookkeepers, clerks, and sales personnel) grew, so did the sports clubs, particularly in team sports like lacrosse, baseball, hockey, and football. The original political and commercial elite who had dominated the earlier clubs retreated to their socially oriented golf, tandem, and hunt clubs, leaving the organization and administration of the more competitively focused clubs to the middle class (1991, p. 57).

The rapidly expanding middle classes sought to bring a new cultural logic to sports—order, seriousness, new meanings, and regulation (see following sections on character and gender). The reformers of the "rational recreation" movement were from the middle classes, and, in addition to parks, playgrounds, public libraries, and museums, they developed organizations such as the YMCA, founded in 1844 in England. The YMCA did much to change the popular notion that physical conditioning through exercise and sports was anti-Christian and to promote recreational physical activity to lower-middle-class and working-class males.

The games and sport activities of workingclass people did not usually occur under the sponsorship of clubs or organizations, and they seldom received any publicity.

As sport activities became more organized, they generally reinforced existing class distinctions in society. Upper-class clubs emphasized achievement and "gentlemanly" involvement—an orientation that ultimately provided the basis for later definitions of amateurism (which originated in England). These definitions of the "amateur" then became tools for excluding working-class people from the sport events organized to express the interests of upper-class participants (Bouchier, 2003; Gruneau, 1999; Metcalfe, 1987). The activities of the working classes, by contrast, were much more likely to involve folk games and commercialized sports—a combination that ultimately led to professionalization. This two-phased development of amateurism and professionalization occurred in slightly different ways in different countries (Dunning, 1999).

The Seeds of New Meanings Underlying the growing organization of sport activities during the second half of the nineteenth century was a new emphasis on the seriousness of sports. Instead of defining sports simply as enjoyable diversions, new middle-class values began to be imposed and people gradually came to see physically strenuous, organized competitive games as tools for achieving economic progress and social development. Many people linked sport participation with economic productivity, national loyalty, and the development of admirable character traits, especially among males. This new way of looking at organized sports was grounded in a wide array of changes in every segment of industrial society: the economy, politics, family life, religion, education, science, philosophy, and technology. See the Reflect on Sports box, "The Characteristics of High-Profile Organized Competitive Sports," on pages 69–70.

REFLECT ON SPORTS

The Characteristics of High-Profile Organized Competitive Sports

The organized competitive sports so popular in many parts of the world today are very different from the folk games played before the Industrial Revolution. Allen Guttmann's study of sport activities through history shows that *dominant sport forms (DSFs)* today comprise seven interrelated characteristics, which have never before appeared together in past physical activities and games.[1] These characteristics are

1. *Secularism.* Today's DSFs are not directly linked to religious beliefs or rituals. They are sources of diversion and entertainment, not worship. They are played for personal gains, not the appeasement of gods. They embody the immediacy of the material world, not the mysticism of the supernatural.
2. *Equality.* Today's DSFs are based on the ideas that participation should not be regulated by birthright or social background and that all contestants in a sport event should face the same competitive conditions, regardless of who they are and where they come from.
3. *Specialization.* Today's DSFs are dominated by the participation of specialists. Athletes often dedicate themselves exclusively to participation in a single event or position within an event. Positions often are defined and distinguished from one another by skills and responsibilities. Equipment, such as shoes and clothing, is specialized to fit the demands of particular activities.
4. *Rationalization.* Today's DSFs consist of complex sets of rules and strategies. Rules specify goals and how athletes should pursue goals. Rules also regulate equipment, playing techniques, and the conditions of participation. Strategies inspire rationally

[1]Eric Dunning and Kenneth Sheard compare medieval folk games with modern sports in Europe in their social historical analysis presented in the book *Barbarians, Gentlemen, and Players* (1979: 33–34). Their analysis, like Guttmann's, highlights the characteristics of modern sports as they emerged in nineteenth-century Europe.

Organized competitive sports are characterized by an emphasis on quantification, among other things. Everything that can be defined in terms of time, distance, or scores is measured and recorded. The clock is key in sports. (Bob Jackson, *Colorado Springs Gazette*)

Continued.

REFLECT ON SPORTS

The Characteristics of High-Profile Organized Competitive Sports continued

controlled training methods, which affect the experience of sport participation and the evaluation of athletes.

5. *Bureaucratization.* Today's DSFs are controlled by complex organizations on the international, national, and local levels. The people in these organizations oversee and sanction athletes, teams, and events. They make up and enforce rules, organize events, and certify records.

6. *Quantification.* Today's DSFs feature an abundance of measurements and statistics. Everything that can be reduced to a time, distance, or score is measured and recorded. Standards of achievement are discussed in measurable terms, and statistics are used as proof of achievements.

7. *Records.* Today's DSFs emphasize setting and breaking records. Performances are compared from one event to another, and records are published for individuals, teams, leagues, events, communities, states, provinces, and continents. Most important, of course, are world records or world standings.

One or more of these traits have characterized physical games during previous historical periods, but not until the nineteenth century did all seven appear together in what might be called modern sports (Dunning, 1999). This does not mean that today's organized competitive sports are somehow superior to the games and activities of the past. It means only that they are different in the way they are organized and integrated into people's lives. Sociologists study these differences in terms of their impact on the organization and dynamics of social life.

Table 3.1 summarizes Guttmann's historical comparison of physical games and sports in terms of these seven characteristics. The table shows that today's DSFs are different from the physical games played by people in times past. However, it does not explain why the differences exist or the social implications of the differences.

Finally, we should remember that these seven characteristics are not found in all sports today. Sports are social constructions. They change as social, economic, and political forces change and as people seek and develop alternatives to dominant sport forms. In fact, fifty years from now, sports may have characteristics that are quite different from these seven. *What do you think?*

Table 3.1 Historical comparison of organized games, contests, and sport activities*

Characteristic	Greek Games and Contests (1000 B.C.E. to 100 B.C.E.)	Roman Sports Events (100 B.C.E. to C.E. 500)	Medieval Games and Tournaments (500 to 1300)	Renaissance and Enlightenment Games and Sport Activities (1300 to 1800)	Modern Sports
Secularism	Yes and no**	Yes and no	Yes and no	Yes and no	Yes
Equality	Yes and no	Yes and no	No	Yes and no	Yes
Specialization	Yes	Yes	No	Yes and no	Yes
Rationalization	Yes	Yes	No	No	Yes
Bureaucratization	Yes and no	Yes	No	No	Yes
Quantification	No	Yes	No	Yes and no	Yes
Records	No	No	No	Yes and no	Yes

*Modified version table 2 in Guttmann (1978).
** This characteristic existed in some sports during this time, but not in others.

The leisure activities of the wealthy at the turn of the twentieth century included sports. Systems of gender exclusion in sports have varied through history, and from one sport to another. Sports played by girls and women during the nineteenth and twentieth centuries often involved balance and coordination, which were defined as "ladylike" qualities, and they often included nets or other barriers, so that there would be no physical contact between female players. (H. Armstrong Roberts)

The Growth of Elite, Competitive Sports in Canada: 1880 to 1920

POWER AND WEALTH IN ACTION The years between 1880 and 1920 were crucial for the development of elite competitive sport forms in Canada (Howell, 2001; Kidd, 1996b; Metcalfe, 1987). During this time, wealthy people developed lives of leisure, in which sport activities played a major part. In fact, the rich used participation in certain sports to prove to the world that they were successful enough to have the luxury of "wasting" time by engaging in frivolous, nonproductive activities (Veblen, 1899). Although the wealthy often used sports to rein-

force status distinctions between themselves and the rest of the population, they also influenced how sports were played and organized by others, especially those in the middle class who aspired to enter the ranks of the rich and powerful.

Upper- and upper-middle-class influence affected various dimensions of sports, including the sport norms for players and spectators, the standards for facilities and equipment, and the way in which people in lower social classes defined sports and integrated them into their leisure patterns. Gruneau and Whitson (1993) identify two different trajectories to their influence. The first they term "moral entrepreneurs," who were promoting the reformist and positive recreational aspects of sports and physical activity—strict amateurism, and the idea that participation would make you into a "better" person (in terms of both health and character). The second were the "economic entrepreneurs," who saw sports both as commercial opportunities and as ways to promote one's community. Sports became part of the entertainment industry with the emergence of professional leagues and barnstorming teams, and the promotion of events such as boxing matches. Having a representative team in one's community was an aspect of civic boosterism that was characteristic of the newly developed towns growing all over Canada. These two views of sports clashed continually over the issue of amateurism and professionalism, eventually coming to a head in what came to be known as "the athletic war" in 1906–08 (Morrow, 1986; Metcalfe, 1987).[3]

The two forms of entrepreneurialism came together in an interesting way as wealthy people used their economic resources to encourage others to define sports as *consumer activities* to be played in *proper* attire, using the *proper* equipment in a *proper* facility, and preceded or followed by *proper* social occasions separated from employment and the workplace. Through this process of "encouragement" and the development of consensus about the forms and meanings of sports (described as *hegemony* by sociologists; see chapter 4, page 106), sports became connected with the economy. The connection was subtle because sports involved widespread consumption and a commitment to rules and productivity, while being popularly defined as "nonwork" activities, separate from the economy.

The emergence of these ideas about how sports "should be" played was important, because it enabled people with power to reproduce their privilege in society without overtly coercing workers to think and behave in certain ways. Instead of maintaining their privilege by force, people with economic power promoted sport forms that were entertaining and fun while reinforcing the values and orientations that promoted capitalist business expansion. As critical theories have emphasized, this is a good example of how sports can be political and economic activities, even though most people see them just as cultural events, fun physical activities, and competitions.

From 1880 to 1920, middle- and working-class people, especially white males, had increased opportunities to play sports. Labour unions, progressive government legislation, and economic expansion combined to improve working and living conditions. The efforts of unions and social reformers gradually led to increases in the free time and the material resources available to many working-class people. This process was complemented by the expansion of the middle class, a collection of people with at least some leisure resources. The spirit of reform around the turn of the century also was associated with the development of parks, recreation programmes, and organized playground activities for urban residents, especially children (Kidd, 1996b).

IDEAS ABOUT SPORT PARTICIPATION AND "CHARACTER DEVELOPMENT." Early in the twentieth century, opportunities for sport involvement increased, but the kinds of opportunities available to most people were shaped by factors beyond the interests of the participants themselves. Important changes in how people thought about human behaviour, individual development, and social life led to an emphasis on organized competitive sports as "character-building" activities.

Until the latter part of the nineteenth century, most people believed human behaviour was unrelated to environmental factors. They believed that fate or supernatural forces dictated individual development and that social life was established by a combination of God's will, necessity, and coincidence. However, these ideas began to change as people became aware of the

---

[3] This war continued to be fought, on and off, and in various ways, through most of the twentieth century. It only came to an end as the Olympics began to embrace Western notions of professionalism at the 1984 Los Angeles Games.

TITLES b...
... .com.. McMASTER UNIVERSITY
McMaster serving the
12:54:21 unity...
TRANS NO: 1.AP 2007
                    84909
CLERK: LC

PURCHASE

Raincheck # R02763
1 SOCIOL 3GG3 MANAGING A   36.95 GX
2900666272743
2 SPORTS IN SOCIETY   75.00 XX
2900070914765

       PRICE SUBTOTAL   111.95
       FEDL GST   2.22

       TOTAL   114.17

       MASTERCARD ------   114.17
          Card# ***********8034
01 Approved - Thank You 027

Date/Time : 09/11/07 12:56:01
Reference # : 66045336 0012993090 S
Authorization # : 125602
         This is your receipt.
     You should retain this for
  comparison with your statements.
      GST REG. NO. R119 035 988

links between the environment and behaviour and that it was possible to intentionally change how social life was organized.

This new "character logic" within the culture was a crucial catalyst in the growth of modern sports. It made sports into something more than just enjoyable pastimes. Gradually, sports were defined as potential educational experiences— experiences with important consequences for individuals and society as a whole. This change, based on the functionalist and evolutionary ways of thinking, which were dominant at the time, provided a new basis for organizing and promoting sport participation. For the first time in history, people saw sports as tools for positively changing behaviour, shaping character, building unity and cohesion in an ethnically diverse population, and creating national identity.

People began to think about the meaning and purpose of sports in new and serious terms. For example, some religious groups, later referred to as "muscular Christians" (see the "Sports and Religion" chapter on the Online Learning Centre), suggested a link between physical strength and the ability to do good works; they promoted sport involvement as an avenue for spiritual growth. Others saw sports as tools for teaching immigrant children lessons that would make them into contributing members of a corporate-bureaucratic-democratic society; they promoted organized playground programmes that used team sports to undermine traditional ethnic values and replace them with an emerging Canadianized way of looking at the world. Those interested in economic expansion tended to see organized sports as tools for generating profits and introducing untrained workers to activities emphasizing teamwork, obedience to rules, planning, organization, and production; they promoted sports for the purpose of creating good workers who could tolerate stressful working conditions.

In large part, organized sports became important because they could be used to train loyal and hardworking people dedicated to achievement and production for the glory of God and country. Sports were socially constructed and defined in ways that people believed would promote this type of character development.

ORGANIZED SPORTS AND IDEAS ABOUT MASCULINITY AND FEMININITY The new belief that sport participation built character was applied primarily to males. Those who organized and sponsored new programmes thought they could use organized sports, especially team sports, to tame what they perceived as the savage, undisciplined character of young, lower-class males. Their intent was to create orderly citizens and cooperative workers. At the same time, they used sports for young males from upper- and middle-class backgrounds to counteract what many believed was the negative influence of female dominated home lives. Their goal was to turn "overfeminized" boys into assertive, competitive, achievement-oriented young men, who would become effective leaders in business, politics, and the military. In these ways, contemporary sports were heavily grounded in the desire of those in the dominant social classes to exercise control over the working classes, while preparing their own sons to inherit their positions of power and influence (Burstyn, 1999; Kidd, 1996b).

Although an increasing number of women participated in sport activities between 1880 and 1920, many sport programmes ignored, or actively opposed, females (see boxed quotation on page 74). Organizers and sponsors did not see sport participation as an important factor in the character development of girls and women. They sometimes included young girls with boys in the organized games in playground programmes, but they discouraged sex-integrated sport activities for children nearing the age of puberty. There were strong fears that, if boys and girls played sports with one another, they might become good friends and that, if they were friends, their relationships would lose the mystery that led people to be interested in getting married and having children. (We may laugh at such ideas today, but, in the last ten years, we have heard people say similar things about possible problems of allowing women to play on men's football, hockey, and wrestling teams.)

While boys were taught to play a number of sports on the playgrounds after the turn of the century, girls often were given shady places, where they could rest and preserve their energy. Helen Lenskyj (1986), of the University of Toronto, and Patricia Vertinsky (1990), of the University of British Columbia, have both documented the ways in which the medical profession was implicated in preventing girls and women from becoming involved in sports and physical activity, warning that involvement would sap the energy needed to conceive and bear healthy children. However, despite a continuous barrage of warnings from physicians:

> There is no reason to think that a healthy woman can be injured [cycling]… provided she does not over-exert herself by riding too long a time, or too fast, or up too steep hills, and provided she does not ride when common sense and physiology alike forbid any needless exertion (Dr. J. West Roosevelt, 1895; cited by Lenskyj, 1986, pp. 24–25).

women became increasingly involved. In the same year as Roosevelt's warning, Dr. Grace Ritchie, writing in the *National Council of Women of Canada Yearbook, 1895*, pointed out that:

> Every year, some new avenue, some new form of physical exercise is being opened to women. What was once frowned down upon as unladylike,

…we, the members of the Queen's College Snowshoe Club after much anxious thought, do hereby seriously but heartily resolve, that owing to the dire and disastrous effects of co-education, at the Royal College, that no 'female woman' whatsoever, be allowed, no matter in what capacity to participate in any manner in our tramps. That we shall not peril the prosperity of this Club by subjecting it to their baleful influences

—(*Queen's University Journal*, 1883; cited by Cochrane, et al., 1977, p. 26).

trivial and shocking, is now done openly and with the approval of the beholders. Perhaps nothing illustrates this so much as the riding of the bicycle (1896, p. 117; cited by Lenskyj, 1986, pp. 24–25).

Ann Hall (1999, 2002), of the University of Alberta, has pointed out how key cycling was in the political and cultural emancipation of women.

Still, organized activities for girls often consisted of domestic science classes designed to make them good homemakers and mothers. When playground organizers did provide opportunities for girls to play games and sports, they designed activities that would cultivate "ladylike" traits, such as poise and body control. This is why so many girls participated in gymnastics, figure skating, and other "grace and beauty" sports (Burstyn, 1999; Hart, 1981). Another goal of the activities was to make young women healthy for bearing children. Competition was eliminated or controlled, and the activities emphasized personal health, the dignity of beauty, and good form. In some cases, the only reason games and sports were included in girls' activities was to provide the knowledge they would need in the future to introduce their sons to active games.

Limited opportunities and a lack of encouragement did not stop women from participating in sports, but they certainly restricted the extent of their involvement (Vertinsky, 1994). Some middle- and upper-class women engaged in popular physical exercises and recreational sport activities such as cycling, but, apart from a limited number of interuniversity games and private tournaments, they had few opportunities to engage in formal competitive events.

(City of Toronto Archives, Fonds 1244, item 477)

The participation of girls and women from lower-income groups was restricted to informal street games, a few supervised exercise classes, and play days in public schools. Ideas about femininity were changing between 1880 and 1920, but traditional gender ideology and numerous misconceptions about the physical and mental effects of strenuous activities on females prevented the "new woman" of the early twentieth century from enjoying the same participation opportunities and encouragement males received (Lenskyj, 1986). In fact, medical beliefs did more to subvert the health of women during these years than to improve it (Vertinsky, 1987).

ORGANIZED SPORTS AND IDEAS ABOUT SKIN COLOUR AND ETHNICITY. The previous sections have focused primarily on anglophone sport development in Canada. By this time, however, clubs and teams were beginning to be formed around various ethnic affiliations as new waves of immigrants reached Canada. Of the "two" colonizing nations of Canada, the Montreal anglophone community figures prominently in Canadian sport history, but, as Harvey (1999) notes, "Although they took longer to get organized, a modernist and liberal faction of the French Canadian community also decided to use sport as a means for the promotion of its nationalist interests with the creation, in 1894, of the Association Athlétique d'Amateurs Le National" (p. 31). However, while sports remained a major interest of francophones in larger communities, where they were well represented in organized sports, several researchers have pointed out that the major influence of the Catholic Church (especially in smaller communities) resulted in a somewhat different pattern of sport development in francophone Quebec (Bellefleur, 1986, 1997; Harvey, 1988). Indeed, for the francophone Catholic hierarchy in Quebec, sports under the control of anglophones posed a danger of assimilation. Unable to prevent the growing interest of francophones in sports, the clergy took the initiative to create a separate sport system with a less competitive set of values. This was to have interesting consequences for the development of sports in Quebec until the "Quiet Revolution."

The first nations/aboriginal Canadians, fared less well. Native sports such as snowshoeing and baggataway were incorporated and transformed into precisely the types of DSFs outlined in the Reflect on Sports box, "The Characteristics of High-Profile Organized Competitive Sports," on pp. 69–70, and aboriginal peoples were prevented from joining the clubs where competitions took place. At one point, all native Canadians were designated as "professionals" in order to prevent them from competing against the amateur clubs. Eddington (2000) points out that it took twenty years, until 1887, before the Iroquois Nationals became the first native team to join the International Lacrosse Federation. Native skill at running was also exploited, and Bruce Kidd (1980, 1983) has documented the vicious racist treatment experienced by one of the best known native Canadian runners, Tom Longboat.

Other visible minorities in Canada received similar treatment at this time, with few opportunities for participation for, for example, Asian immigrants. And, despite a different history of relations with African Canadians, they fared no better than African Americans at this time. Following a period of emancipation after the Civil War, the segregation of African Americans was reinstated at the end of the nineteenth century with the "Jim Crow laws." These laws were imitated in Canada, leading to the appearance of a number of segregated baseball and hockey teams. The treatment of francophones and visible minorities by the anglophone majority was a manifestation of the prevailing race and ethnic logics at the time. Non-Europeans and non-anglophones were considered to be inferior, and it was undignified to be beaten at sports by one's social "inferiors."

ORGANIZED SPORTS AND IDEAS ABOUT AGE AND DISABILITY.   Aging involves biological changes, but the connection between aging and sport participation depends on the social meanings given to those changes. Because developmental theory around the turn of the twentieth century emphasized that development occurs during childhood and adolescence, sport programmes were created and sponsored for young people, not for older people. Theories suggested that older people were already developed: they were "grown up," and their characters could no longer be shaped.

Medical knowledge at the time also discouraged older people from engaging in sports. Many people believed that strenuous activities might put too many demands on the heart and other muscles in aging bodies. This did not stop older people from participating in certain forms of sport activities, but it did prevent the establishment of organized sport programmes for older people. Furthermore, when participation did occur among older people, it was usually in age-segregated settings.

People with most forms of physical or mental disability during this time were either denied the opportunity to participate in or actively discouraged from engaging in most physical activities, especially sports. People were unsure about the effects of strenuous exercise on their behaviour or physical wellness. Definitions of mental and physical disability often gave rise to fears and prejudices. Some people thought it was dangerous to physically excite people with disabilities; therefore, programmes to build their bodies were discouraged. This policy meant that people with disabilities were either isolated or seen as unworthy of any serious attention related to their physical development.

1880 TO 1920—A KEY PERIOD. Although opportunities for participation in organized, competitive sports between 1880 and 1920 were not equally distributed by social class, gender, skin colour, ethnicity, age, or ability, participation among most categories of people increased dramatically. This was the case in most industrializing societies. In most Western cultures, the organizational attributes that we associate with today's high-profile organized sports became clearly established during this time. The games people played featured a combination of secularism, a growing commitment to participation among competitors from all socioeconomic backgrounds, increased specialization, rationalization, bureaucratization, quantification, and the quest for records. As noted in the box "The Characteristics of High-Profile Organized Competitive Sports" (pages 69–70), these are some of the sociologically relevant characteristics that have become the foundation of what many people define as sports today.

Since 1920, the resources devoted to organized, competitive sports have increased in many societies around the world. Technology has been used to change sport experiences for participants and spectators, and tremendous growth has occurred in sport-related industries and the government sponsorship of sports. Many of today's struggles about the organization, meaning, and purpose of sports and how sports should be integrated into people's lives were visible in some form eighty years ago.

Since the 1920s: Struggles Continue By the 1920s, major cultural links had been established between sports and Canadian society. The desire to make or raise money had led to the creation and marketing of spectator sports on the professional level. Entertainment had become at least as important as the development of moral character in the sponsorship of sports. The most heavily promoted sports were hockey, football, and baseball. Each was native to North America; each celebrated a form of masculinity, emphasizing aggression, domination, and emotional control; and each was used to generate profits and national loyalties (Burstyn, 1999). Commercial interests had promoted an emphasis on competition, winning, and record setting.

Basic organizational structures for professional sports had been established. Universities had formed athletic conferences and a national association to govern interuniversity sports. There were numerous other national associations connected with a wide variety of amateur and professional sports, and the Olympics had been revived and held on six occasions: once in Greece, four times in Western Europe, and once in the United States. Newspapers promoted and sensationalized sport events to boost their circulation, and radio broadcasts brought sports into people's homes and maintained spectator interest in both urban and rural areas.

Interuniversity teams were elitist and sexist. Universities and schools generally ignored the participation interests of female students, providing them with sport "play days" at best. Some women struggled to make changes in these traditions, but they had limited success; resisting dominant norms often led to questions about their sexuality.

Coaching emerged as a specialized, technical profession, and coaches were hired to supervise teams and maintain winning records. The control of teams had shifted from the players to coaches, managers, owners, and top administrative staff members.

Rules had become standardized on a national level so that commercially attractive intersectional competitions could be held. Sponsoring organizations kept records and statistics, frequently publishing them in newspapers and discussing them in radio broadcasts. The broadcasters used flair and exaggeration to dramatize events and enhance their own images and reputations.

Bruce Kidd points out that, in 1920, there were a number of serious divisions—"between amateur and professional, east and west, male and female, 'bourgeois' [middle class] and workers organizations" (p. 266). These divisions led to struggles for supremacy, and, for a time during the 1920s and 1930s, workers' sports and "girls' sports run by girls" were in the ascendancy in this era of democratically organized and participant-oriented sports. The major struggle was between this form of sports, and the "well-publicized commercial, continentalist, and exclusively male sector" (p. 266) best represented by the NHL. Of course, the NHL and sports as entertainment triumphed, and participant-oriented sports continue to struggle in Canada.

Fifty years later, the sporting scene in Canada changed dramatically. National hockey teams were doing poorly in international competitions, and Montreal was about to host Canada's

first Olympic Games. The federal government became involved in sports for a variety of reasons—fitness, national unity, international prestige—and began eventually to re-establish some democratic traditions. Frank Hayden at McMaster University was proposing a plan that eventually became the Special Olympics, and Bob Steadward at the University of Alberta was to play a significant part in the development of the Paralympics. Government involvement led to funding for athletes, and the construction of facilities, to overcome some of the class barriers to participation; equity policies for gender, language, and athletes with a disability; widespread drug testing in an attempt to ensure that Canada's athletes would be "clean"; and most

During the twentieth century, sports clearly were linked to political and racial ideologies. During the 1936 Olympic Games in Berlin, Hitler and the Nazi Party used the games to promote their ideas about the superiority of the "Aryan race." This historic photo shows a German official giving the Nazi salute and Jesse Owens, the African American sprinter who won four gold medals during the games, giving the U.S. salute. The success of Owens had challenged Hitler's ideas about Aryan supremacy in sports. (USOC Archives)

recently, the introduction of policies to combat sexual harassment. Not all of these have been completely successful, but Canada's sports system is often considered to have been progressive and innovative, and has been widely imitated (perhaps most successfully by Australia).

Sports in the 1920s contained the cultural seeds of today's sports. Things have changed over the past eighty years: sports are more visible and culturally influential than in the past, but they continue to be socially constructed through the struggles of various groups to integrate physical activities into their lives in ways that meet their interests.

Today, sports remain organized and competitive, strongly linked to commercial interests, and closely tied to an ideology in which toughness, aggression, individualism, and success are highly valued. However, sports also continue to be contested activities, and people continue to struggle over how they can and should be defined and organized. Some people want their activities and teams to be more organized and competitive, while others want to eliminate formal structure and competition. Some people want women's sports to resemble men's sports, while others want to develop new sport forms that emphasize partnership rather than domination. Many people struggle because they still confront issues of exclusion based on social class, race, skin colour, and ethnicity. People with disabilities struggle for resources to enable them to play sports with each other and with able-bodied athletes. Gay and lesbian athletes struggle over issues of homophobia, identity disclosure, and opportunities to play sports without hiding their sexuality. Professional athletes organize themselves into unions and even call strikes to gain more control over the conditions of their own sport involvement, and owners lock players out and collude with one another to maintain their power.

These things all happen in social, political, and economic contexts that influence the range of alternatives and choices that are available to different individuals and groups. The sociology of sport is concerned with these contexts and the struggles that occur as people make and pursue their choices. In fact, these are many of the issues and controversies that we discuss in the following chapters.

SUMMARY

CAN WE USE HISTORY TO UNDERSTAND SPORTS TODAY?

Our selective look at different times and places shows us that physical games, contests, and sport activities are integrally related to social relations and social forces in societies. As social life changes and as power shifts in any society, there are changes in the organization and meanings of games and sport activities, as well as in the people who participate in, watch, and sponsor them.

In ancient Greece, games and contests were grounded in mythology and religious beliefs. They focused on the interests of young males from wealthy segments of society. As the outcomes of organized games took on political and social implications beyond the events, athletes were recruited from the lower classes and paid for their participation. The existence of professional athletes, the use of violence during contests and games, the heavy emphasis on victory, and the low priority given to fairness shows us a side of sports in ancient Greece that contradicts many popular beliefs. It also indicates that fairness and democracy are not achieved in sports without commitment and effort.

Roman contests and games emphasized mass entertainment. They were designed to celebrate and preserve the power of political leaders and to pacify masses of unemployed and underemployed workers in Roman cities and towns. Many athletes in Roman events were slaves recruited for the events, or "troublemakers" coerced into jeopardizing their lives in battle with one another or with wild animals. These spectacles faded with the demise of the Roman

Empire. Critically assessing the spectacle-like contests and games of this period makes us more aware of the interests that powerful people may have in promoting large sport events.

Folk games and tournaments in medieval times clearly reflected and reproduced gender and social class differences in European cultures. The peasants played local versions of folk games in connection with seasonal events in village life. The knights and nobles engaged in tournaments and jousts. Other members of the upper classes, including the clergy, often used their resources to develop games and sport activities to occupy their leisure time. Studying this time period alerts us to the importance of gender and class differences in our efforts to understand sports and sport experiences today.

The patterns from the medieval period continued through the Renaissance in parts of Europe, although the Protestant Reformation generated negative attitudes about any activities that interfered with work and religious worship. Peasants felt the impact of these attitudes most sharply, because they did not have the resources needed to avoid the restrictive controls imposed by government officials who were inspired by Calvinist or Puritan orientations. The games and sports of the wealthy generally continued within the safe confines of their private grounds. The Enlightenment was associated with increased political rights and freedom to engage in diversionary games and physical activities. Studying these historical periods alerts us to the importance of cultural ideology and government policies when it comes to who plays sports under what conditions.

During the early days of the Industrial Revolution, the demands of work and the absence of spaces for play generally limited sport involvement to the wealthy and to people in rural areas. This pattern began to change in Canada from the mid-1800s to the early 1900s, when the combined influence of labour unions, progressive legislation, and economic expansion led to the creation of new ideas about the consequences of sport participation and new opportunities for involvement.

However, opportunities for involvement were shaped primarily by the needs of an economy emphasizing mass production and mass consumption. It was in this context that people developed what we now refer to as organized competitive sports. Studying this period shows us that the origins of today's sports were tied closely to complex social, political, and economic factors.

Sports have never been so pervasive and influential in the lives of people as they are in many societies today, and never before have physical activities and games been so closely linked to profit making, character building, nationalism, and personal health. Organized sports in Canada have become a combination of business, entertainment, education, moral training, masculinity rituals, technology transfer, declarations of identity, and endorsements of allegiance to nations and corporate sponsors. However, sports are also activities through which people seek physical challenges and exciting expressive experiences, seldom available in the rest of their lives (Dunning, 1999; Elias and Dunning, 1986). All these things have combined to make organized competitive sports important social phenomena in the past, the present, and very likely the future.

SUGGESTED READINGS

Baker, W. J. 1988. *Sports in the western world.* Urbana: University of Illinois Press (a survey and analysis of European and North American sports, starting with the ancient Greeks and ending with contemporary commercial sports).

Bouchier, N. 2003. *For the love of the game: Amateur sport in small-town Ontario, 1838–1895.* Montreal & Kingston: McGill-Queen's University Press (documents the nineteenth-century changes in Canadian sport that are outlined in this chapter—the shift from popular recreations to rational recreations, and the growing control of elites through the imposition of strict amateurism—and does so in the context of two small towns in Ontario: Ingersoll and Woodstock).

Cochrane, J., A. Hoffman, and P. Kincade. 1977. *Women in Canadian life: Sports.* Toronto: Fitzhenry & Whiteside (part of the publisher's series on women in Canadian life, and written at the height of the second wave of feminism, this is one of the first books to explore the challenges faced by and achievements of women in sport in Canada; good illustrations and historical information; the second author, Abby Hoffman, was Director General of Sport Canada).

Dunning, E. 1999. *Sport matters: Sociological studies of sport, violence, and civilization.* London: Routledge (development and change in sports are viewed in connection with historical developments and changes; clear examples of how figurational sociology uses historical data as integral to a sociological analysis of civilizing processes and sport).

Gruneau, R. 1988. Modernization or hegemony: Two views of sport and social development. In *Not just a game*, edited by J. Harvey and H. Cantelon. Ottawa: University of Ottawa Press (a concise critique of conceptual approaches to the history of sport; read this article before reading any of the "historical accounts" of sport events in this list).

Guttmann, A. 1978. *From ritual to record: The nature of modern sports.* New York: Columbia University Press (a comparative analysis of the characteristics of sports in different historical periods).

Gruneau, R. and D. Whitson. 1993. *Hockey night in Canada: Sport, identities, and cultural politics.* Toronto: Garamond (although not exclusively a history book, it provides a thorough documentation of the growth of hockey in Canadian culture, locating it in the processes described in this chapter—the growth of ideas about character building, and the growth of commercialism and commercial entertainment).

Hall, A. 2002. *The girl and the game: A history of women's sport in Canada.* Peterborough, ON: Broadview Press (probably the most comprehensive history of women's organized sports in Canada, this book links well with the theme of cultural struggles over the form and meanings of sports outlined in this chapter).

Kidd, B. 1980. *Tom Longboat.* Toronto: Fitzhenry & Whiteside (a short, illustrated and accessible biography of Longboat that should be read in conjunction with Kidd's [1983] article in order to understand the achievements of this Onondagan athlete, and the context in which they were accomplished).

Kidd, B. 1997. *The struggle for Canadian sport.* Toronto: University of Toronto Press (focuses on key struggles over the meaning and organization of Canadian sports, primarily during the first half of the twentieth century; analysis centres on four major sport organizations and how they fared in connection with major social and cultural transformations).

Kruger, A., and J. Riordan, eds. 1996. *The story of worker sport.* Champaign, IL: Human Kinetics (an overview and ten accounts of the history of the worker sport movement, which, between 1912 and the late 1940s, provided for workers around the world an alternative to sport forms emerging in connection with capitalist economic expansion).

Metcalfe, A. 1987. *Canada learns to play: The emergence of organized sport.* Toronto: McClelland & Stewart (explores the growth of organized sports in Canada, focusing on both the part played by anglophone elites [especially in Montreal] and the working-class challenges and adaptations to the newly formed organizations; this book summarizes much of that work).

Mott, M., ed. 1989. *Sports in Canada: Historical readings.* Toronto: Copp Clark Pittman (a useful collection of articles covering topics from colonial times until the late twentieth century).

Norcliffe, G. 2001. *The ride to modernity: The bicycle in Canada, 1869-1900.* Toronto: University of Toronto Press (a fascinating account of the development of the bicycle and cycling in Canada during the period of rapid social change in the second half of the nineteenth century; shows how these developments were interconnected with, and paved the way for, a number of other technological and cultural changes).

Struna, N. 2000. Social history and sport. In *Handbook of sports studies*, edited by J. Coakley and E. Dunning. London: Sage (a critical overview of historical studies of sports; emphasizes the need to view sports as social practices and social formations that are constitutive of societies over time).

WEBSITE RESOURCES

Note: Websites often change. The following URLs were current when this book was printed. Please check our Online Learning Centre website (www.mcgrawhill.ca/college/coakley) for updates, as well as for additional resources and study tools.

http://depthome.brooklyn.cuny.edu/classics/gladiatr/index.htm (site developed by Roger Dunkle, an expert on Roman sports; excellent information and visuals related to the spectacles in which gladiators participated)

www.studies.org (The Institute for Mediterranean Studies; site summarizes and sells audiotapes on the Olympic Games in ancient Greece and on sports in the Roman world)

www2.umist.ac.uk/sport/ishpes2.html (International Society for the History of Physical Education and Sport provides links to many other sites for sports history)

www2.umist.ac.uk/sport/index2.html (British Society of Sports History)

www.nassh.org (North American Society for Sport History)

Young girl in figure skating class
(Anne-Marie Weber/Taxi/Getty Images)

Sports and Socialization

Who plays and what happens to them?

Athletics taught me so much about life that it's
hard to know where to begin.

—**Elaine Tanner, Canadian swimmer (1979)**

I love the self-discovery. Life off ice is so
complicated, its outcomes smudged, its
motivations rationalized and finessed, the picture
you get of yourself so unclear. On the ice, you see
your elemental self, whether you like it or not—
do you try hard? do you quit? are you fair? are
you selfish? do you give? are you willing to take
risks? do you care too much or too little? do you
fit in with a team on the ice, and off?

—**Ken Dryden, hockey player, author, *Home
Game* (1989)**

 Online Learning Centre Resources

Visit *Sports in Society's* Online Learning Centre at
www.mcgrawhill.ca/college/coakley for additional
information and study material for this chapter.

Socialization is a popular topic today in discussions about sports. When we ask any of the following questions, we are concerned about sports and socialization issues:

- Why are some people fanatically interested in playing and/or watching sports, while others do not seem to care about sports?
- How and why do some people see themselves as athletes and dedicate themselves to playing particular sports?
- When and why do people stop playing competitive sports, and what happens to them when they do?
- What impact do sports and sport participation have on people's lives, characters, behaviours, thoughts, relationships, and careers?

Many of us in the sociology of sport have carried out research to find answers to one or more of these questions. The search for answers has taken us in different directions, depending on the theoretical frameworks we have used to guide our thinking about sports and sport participation. The influence of theoretical perspectives is discussed in the first section of this chapter. Then we consider three topics that are central to discussions of sports and socialization:

1. The process of becoming involved and staying involved in sports
2. The process of changing or ending sport participation
3. The impact of being involved in sports

In connection with these topics, we explain how the questions previously listed have been answered in the sociology of sport. As you read the chapter, you will see that most of the answers are incomplete and many others are so complex that discussions about them will carry over into other chapters.

The chapter closes with information about new approaches to socialization. These approaches are based on critical theories that emphasize socialization as a community and cultural process rather than an individual and personal process.

WHAT IS SOCIALIZATION?

Socialization is an active process of learning and social development, which occurs as we interact with one another and become acquainted with the social world in which we live. It involves the formation of ideas about who we are and what is important in our lives. We are *not* simply passive learners in the socialization process. We actively participate in our own socialization as we influence those who influence us. We actively interpret what we see and hear, and we accept, resist, or revise the messages we receive about who we are, about the world, and about what we should do as we make our way in the world. Therefore, socialization is *not* a one-way process of social influence through which we are moulded and shaped. Instead, it is an interactive process through which we actively connect with others, synthesize information, and *make decisions* that shape our own lives and the social world around us.

This definition of *socialization*, which we use to guide our research, is based on a combination of *critical* and *interactionist* theories. Therefore, not all sociologists would agree with it. Those using functionalist or conflict theory approaches, for example, would define *socialization* in slightly different terms. Their definitions have an impact on how they do research and the questions they ask about sports and socialization.

A Functionalist Approach to Socialization

When *functionalist theory* is used to guide research, socialization is viewed as a process through which we develop social characteristics that enable us to fit into society and contribute to its operation. Functionalists assume that socialization conforms to an *internalization model* (see Coakley, 1993a, b). In other words, as we grow up in our families, go to school, interact with peers, and receive messages from the media, we learn the rules we should follow and the roles we should play in society.

When researchers use an internalization model to guide their studies, they focus attention on three things: (1) the characteristics of those being socialized, (2) the people and social institutions that *do* the socializing, and (3) the specific *outcomes,* or results, of socialization. In most studies of sports and socialization, researchers focus on athletes as the people being socialized. The studies are designed to identify *who* socializes athletes. The primary agents of socialization include fathers, mothers, brothers, sisters, teachers, coaches, peers, and occasionally certain role models. The most central and influential "socializers" are described as **significant others.** In some cases, socializing institutions such as the family, education, and the media are also studied in connection with sport participation. The socialization outcomes, or results, that are studied include the personal attitudes, values, and skills that are considered functional for the society as a whole.

"I know this is starting early, but I can't let him get too far behind the other kids if he's ever going to make a team in high school."

Those who use a functionalist approach have often studied who and what *caused* people to participate in sports and how participation prepared young people to be productive members of society. These studies primarily used quantitative research methods. Numerous functionalist studies have been done and thousands of questionnaires have been sent to people, especially children and high school students, in an effort to find out how people become involved in sports and what they learn when they play sports. The analyses in these studies have compared those who play organized sports with those who do not play organized sports. The researchers have tried to identify (1) who or what might influence a person to play sports and (2) what personal characteristics might be attributed to sport participation.

Some of these studies have helped us understand certain aspects of sports and socialization, but many of them have presented inconsistent and contradictory findings. With notable exceptions,[1] data on the causes and benefits of playing sports have tended to be superficial, and they have told us little about sport socialization as an ongoing process in people's lives. The exceptions include a series of studies carried out over a number of years by Jim Curtis and his colleagues at the University of Waterloo. The studies use strong sets of data from national surveys, and involve thorough and thoughtful analyses. Recent examples have explored the effects of participating in interschool sports on sport participation in later life (Curtis, McTeer, and White, 1999), and the effects of participating in interschool sports on adult income (Curtis, McTeer, and White, 2003). See chapter 14 for additional socialization outcomes related to participating in high school sports.

A Conflict Theory Approach to Socialization

Studies based on conflict theory have also used an internalization model of socialization. However, they have emphasized how socialization processes in sports serve the economic needs of capitalist systems by influencing people in society to become compliant workers and eager consumers of goods and services. Conflict theorists assume that people with economic power direct and use economic forces to maintain their privileged positions in society. Therefore, studies based on this theoretical approach have focused on research issues such as these: (1) Does participation in organized competitive sports create apolitical, militaristic, sexist, and racist orientations among players and spectators? (2) Are people from low-income and working-class backgrounds systematically denied opportunities to play sports on their own terms and in their own ways? (3) Are athletes, especially those from poor, minority backgrounds, victims of a profit-driven, win-at-all-cost sport system in which they have no rights? (4) Do people with money and power control the conditions of sport participation and exploit others to make money and maintain their own interests?

Overall, these studies have emphasized how elitist, oppressively organized sport programmes and autocratic, military-style coaches produced athletes who were obedient, politically conservative, and willing to engage in violence to achieve goals approved by those with power in the society. Some of these studies also have described how sport participation has jeopardized the health of athletes and has alienated athletes from their own bodies to the point that they have been willing to play while injured.

New Approaches to Socialization

Many sociologists have become dissatisfied with the assumptions inherent in the internalization model of socialization used in research by functionalists and conflict theorists. They are not comfortable with the idea that we humans are either products of society and its system needs or are victims of economic forces. Therefore, many researchers have turned to *interactionist models* of socialization and use new methods to study socialization processes.

Recent research on sports and socialization tends to be based on various combinations of critical and interactionist theories. Therefore, socialization is defined as it is defined at the beginning of this section, and researchers are likely to use qualitative rather than quantitative research methods. Instead of using questionnaires to obtain statistical data from large numbers of people, researchers using critical and interactionist theories are more likely to use in-depth interviews and field observations. Their goal is to obtain detailed descriptions of sport experiences as they occur in people's lives. They seek information on how people actively make decisions about their sport participation and about how they derive meaning from playing sports. Finally, they seek to connect those meanings with the larger cultural context in which sports and sport participation exist. The rest of this chapter draws on both old and new approaches in an effort to outline what we know about sports and socialization today.

BECOMING INVOLVED AND STAYING INVOLVED IN SPORTS

Research based on functionalist theory tells us that sport participation is related to three factors: (1) a person's abilities and characteristics; (2) the influence of significant others, including parents, siblings, teachers, and peers; and (3) the availability of opportunities to play and experience success in sports. These are the snapshots that we have of *socialization into sports*. However, a fuller description of the ongoing process of becoming and staying involved in sports emerges when we obtain detailed stories from people about their sport participation. These stories are more like videos than snapshots.

Studies using in-depth interviews, fieldwork, participant observations, and strategic conversations indicate that sport participation is connected with many ongoing processes that make up people's lives, and it occurs as people actively make decisions about their lives in connection with those processes. In other words, people continually make decisions about sport participation; they do not make decisions once and for all time. As social conditions change, so do people's decisions. Furthermore, as people stay involved in sports, their reasons for participating on one day may be different from the reasons for participating on the next day, or the next. When there is no reason, they may discontinue or change their sport participation.

We can best understand the process of becoming and staying involved in sports by looking at examples of research. The following studies give us sociological videos of how people have integrated sport participation into their lives on an everyday basis. These videos help us develop a sense of socialization processes in people's lives.

The Process of Becoming a High-Performance Athlete

Chris Stevenson, from the University of New Brunswick, is interested in how people become athletes. Using a symbolic interactionist approach, he interviewed and collected stories from elite athletes about how they were introduced to their sports and became committed to sport participation. As he analyzed the stories, he noticed that they sounded much like descriptions of careers. In other words, they had identifiable beginnings, followed by a process of development, and ultimately an end. Stevenson felt that he could understand these careers in terms of the decisions the people made about sport participation in connection with other things that were important in their lives over time.

In one of his studies, Stevenson (1999) interviewed twenty-nine Canadian and British international athletes. At first he was struck by the diversity of the stories the athletes told him. But then he detected two processes that were common in the stories. First, there was a process of **introduction and involvement,** during which young people received support as they tried

Young boy with parents trying to ski.
(Photomondo/Taxi/Getty Images)

certain sports. His interviewees talked about being introduced to sports bit-by-bit over time through important relationships in their lives. Gradually, they chose to specialize in a particular sport based on an evaluation of their potential for success and on how much they liked the people associated with the sport. Second, there was a process of **developing a commitment** to sport participation. This process occurred as the athletes formed a web of personal relationships connected with their participation and gradually established personal reputations and identities as athletes in their sports. Their relationships and identities figured prominently in how they set priorities and made decisions about sport participation. Their participation over time depended on active and thoughtful efforts to develop identities as athletes. As this happened, and as people who were important in the lives of these young people gave them recognition and respect as athletes, they became more deeply committed to their sports and to living the life of an athlete.

Stevenson found that these processes did not occur automatically. The young people themselves helped them happen. Becoming and staying involved in sports was a complex process. The young people realized that they could not take for granted the social support they received for playing sports and being athletes. They knew that the resources needed for participation could disappear or that changes in other parts of their lives could force them to alter the importance of sport participation. Therefore, they made decisions to stay involved in sports day by day, and, as they stayed involved, they impressed and influenced those who supported and influenced them.

Stevenson's research shows that the socialization process is *interactive* and that each of us actively participates in our own socialization.

The Process of Being Accepted as an Athlete

Peter Donnelly, from the University of Toronto, and Kevin Young, from the University of Calgary, are sociologists who have studied sports as "social worlds," or subcultures where people develop their own ways of doing things and relating to one another. In their research, they paid special attention to how people become a part of those subcultures. They have taken a closer look at some of the things studied by Stevenson (Donnelly and Young, 1999).

On the basis of stories that Donnelly collected from rock climbers in the U.S. and U.K., and that Young collected from rugby players in

Canada, they determined that playing sports occurs in connection with complex processes of identity formation. They explain that entering and becoming an athlete in a particular sport subculture involves the individual in a process of *constructing* an appropriate subcultural identity, and the *confirmation* of that identity by established members of the subculture. This occurs through a four-phase process:

1. Acquiring knowledge about the sport
2. Associating with people involved in the sport
3. Learning how those people think about their sport and what they do and expect from each other
4. Becoming recognized and fully accepted into the sport group as a fellow athlete

This description of sport socialization extends our understanding of what is involved in developing a commitment to a sport. Donnelly and Young discovered that becoming involved in a sport depends on learning to "talk the talk and walk the walk," so that one is identified and accepted as an athlete by others who are athletes. This identification and acceptance do not happen once and for all time; it is a continuous process. When we lose touch and are no longer able to talk the talk and walk the walk, acceptance wanes, our identities become difficult to maintain, and overall support for our participation becomes weak. We are not athletes forever.

To discover part of what Donnelly and Young found in their study, just observe a sport group such as skateboarders ("street skaters," "ramp skaters," or "curbheads"), in-line skaters, snowboarders, or beach volleyball players. Each group has its own vocabulary and its own way of referring to themselves and what they do. The terms they use are not found in dictionaries. They also have unique ways of thinking about and doing their sports, and they have special understandings of what they can expect from others in their group. New participants in these sports may be tested and "pushed" by the "veterans" before being accepted and defined as true skaters, riders, or volleyball athletes. Vocabularies may change over time, but this process of becoming accepted and gaining support for participation exists in basketball, hockey, gymnastics, and golf—in every sport. Many people have discovered that, if they do not establish social connections and acceptance in a sport, their sport participation may not be very regular or long term. Becoming involved in sports clearly is part of a complex, *interactive* socialization process.

To Participate or Not to Participate

Anita White is a sport sociologist and former director of sport development at the British Sports Council. Before she began working at the Sports Council, White and Jay Coakley carried out a study of sport participation patterns among British adolescents in a working-class area east of London (Coakley and White, 1999). The goal was to provide coaches and programme organizers with information about why some young people participated in council-sponsored sport programmes, while most did not.

In-depth interviews with thirty-four young men and twenty-six young women indicated that their participation or lack of participation in sports was the result of decisions based on a combination of factors. In the lives of British teenagers, these factors included the following:

1. Their ideas about how sport participation was related to other interests and goals in their lives
2. Their desires to develop and display competence in ways that would gain them recognition and respect from others
3. Social support for participation and access to the resources needed for participation (time, transportation, equipment, and money)
4. Memories of past experiences with physical activities and sports
5. General cultural images and messages about sports that they had in their minds

They found that the young people made decisions to play sports when it helped them extend control over their lives, become what they wanted to be, and present themselves to others as competent. They also found that the young women were less likely than the young men to imagine that sport participation could do these things for them. Therefore, the young women participated in organized sports less often and less seriously.

The young people in the study did not simply respond to the world around them. Instead, they actively thought about how sports might fit with the rest of their lives and what they wanted out of their lives in the future. Their decisions were based on their conclusions. Their sport participation patterns shifted over time, depending on their access to opportunities, changes in their lives, and changes in the way they saw themselves and their connections to the world. Therefore, socialization into sports was a *continuous, interactive process* grounded in the social and cultural contexts in which the young people lived.

The stories heard in the study showed that people make decisions to participate in sports for different reasons at different points in their lives. This fits with theories telling us that developmental tasks and challenges change as we move through childhood, adolescence, young adulthood, and adulthood. Therefore, the issues considered by seven-year-olds who make decisions about sport participation are different from the issues considered by fourteen-year-olds or forty-year-olds (see Porterfield, 1999; Stevenson, 2002). Furthermore, when seven-year-olds make decisions about sport participation today, they do so in a different cultural context than the context in which seven-year-olds lived in 1970 or will live in 2010.

Sport participation decisions at all points during the life course and through history also are tied to the perceived cultural importance of sports and the links between playing sports, general social acceptance, and the achievement of personal goals. Therefore studies of socialization into sports must take into account the ways in which sport participation is related to individual development, the organization of social life, and cultural ideology (Ingham et al., 1999).

In summary, these studies provide three videos about becoming involved and staying involved in sports. They show that sport participation is grounded in decision-making processes involving self-reflection, social support, social acceptance, and cultural issues. People never make decisions about sport participation once and for all time. They make them day by day as they consider how sports are related to their lives. In fact, they sometimes make them moment by moment when coaches are making them run wind sprints and they are sucking air at the starting line! These decisions are mediated by the social and cultural contexts in which the people live. Therefore, the social meanings attached to gender, class, race, age, and physical (dis)abilities influence decision-making processes; and political, economic, social, and cultural forces influence social meanings.

> **In gym, when we start basketball or volleyball, most of the girls go to the benches and just talk. All the guys are on the court…That's why I think most of the guys from my school figure the girls can't play sports.**
>
> —David, high school student (1996)

CHANGING OR ENDING SPORT PARTICIPATION

Questions about becoming and staying involved in sports often are followed by questions about changing or ending involvement. Much of the research on this latter issue has been guided by "role theories" inspired by functionalist theory, or "alienation theories" inspired by conflict theory (see Coakley, 1993b).

Researchers using *functionalist theory* have been concerned with identifying who was dropping out of sports and what could be done to keep them in sports, so that they would learn the positive lessons that come with sport participation. This was a very popular research topic when millions of baby boomers were flooding playgrounds and elementary schools, and parents wanted to know how to control and build character in their children. Research based on functionalist approaches also has focused on how to make sport programmes more efficient in developing skills and preparing young people to move to higher levels of competition. This remains a popular topic among people in sports, since they have an interest in creating winners on interuniversity, international, and professional teams.

Researchers using *conflict theory* generally have focused on the possibility that rigidly organized, win-oriented programmes turned children off participation. These programmes, along with autocratic, command-style coaches, alienated many young athletes and caused them to drop out. Older athletes dropped out because of injuries or alienation caused by years of exploitation. Research explored how athletes in elite sports were victims of exploitation and how specialized, long-term sport participation itself could be a socially alienating experience, causing athletes to drop out and to have serious personal problems when they did.

After reviewing dozens of these studies grounded in functionalism and conflict theory, we've concluded that they tell us the following important things:

- When people drop out of particular sports, they do not drop out of all sports forever, nor do they cut all ties with sports. In fact, many play different and less competitive sports or move into other sport roles, such as coach, programme organizer or administrator, referee/judge, or sports businessperson.

- Dropping out of sports is usually part of a process involving changes and transitions in the rest of a person's life (changing schools, graduating, getting a job, getting married, having children, etc.).
- Dropping out of sports is not always the result of victimization or exploitation, although injuries and negative experiences can and do influence decisions to change or end participation.
- Problems may occur for those who end long careers in sports, especially those who have no identity apart from sports or who lack the social and material resources they need to make transitions into other careers and social settings.

Recent studies, especially those using qualitative methods and informed by critical interactionist models of socialization, have built on these findings and extended our understanding. Following are three examples of these studies.

Jay Coakley's Study of Burnout among Young Athletes

Jay Coakley's work with coaches combined with his interest in identity issues led him to carry out a study of young people who, after being age-group champions with the potential to succeed in their sports, had made the decision to quit playing their sports (Coakley, 1992). Since the term *burnout* often was used to describe this phenomenon, Jay decided to interview former elite athletes identified by themselves or others as cases of burnout; all were adolescents.

Data from in-depth interviews led him to conclude that burnout was grounded in the organization of the high-performance sports in which these young people had played. It occurred when the young people felt they had lost control over their lives and felt they could not explore and develop identities apart from sports. The athletes associated this combination of having no control and having a unidimensional identity with high

levels of stress and a decline in the amount of fun they had in their sports. As stress increased and fun decreased, they burned out.

This study showed that stress and fun were connected with how sport programmes were organized and how sport experiences were connected with developmental issues during adolescence. When being a young athlete, especially a highly successful one, interfered with accomplishing important developmental tasks during adolescence, burnout was likely. Teaching young athletes how to manage stress is important in preventing burnout, but it is also important to empower athletes and change the social organization of the sport contexts in which they train and compete (Gould et al., 1997).

Getting Out of Sports and Getting On with Life

Derek Swain (1991, 1999) is a psychologist in Vancouver who joined a number of other researchers (e.g., Coakley, 1983; Curtis and Ennis, 1988) in critiquing the view that retirement from sports was always a traumatic experience. Swain conducted multiple in-depth interviews with ten men who were former professional athletes in Canada (hockey players, jockeys, football players, and racquetball players). All of these men were accomplished athletes in their sports, although none held million-dollar contracts. His research emphasizes the idea that retirement from high-performance sports is a process that occurs gradually over a long period of time. Thus, retirement is not an *event* but a *process*—starting soon after they became involved in their professional careers, for many of the athletes interviewed. These men initiated the process when they realized that they could not play forever, and that there was life after sports. They anticipated problems as they ended their careers, but they were often ready for retirement because they had become increasingly tired of training and competition, and concerned about the toll that sport participation was taking on their bodies. They began to seek new careers and plan for the future. They all viewed retirement with mixed feelings, but gradually accepted it as it became a reality, and settled into their new lives after sports. (For another example of the *process* of retirement, see the Koukouris [1991] example on the Online Learning Centre.)

Swain reports that these former athletes did experience a strong sense of loss as their careers ended. On the one hand, they felt alienated and worried about their futures, and it was difficult for them to give up the celebrity status they had as athletes. On the other hand, they appreciated the new opportunities and improved health that came with retirement, and enjoyed the chance to connect in new ways with their families. Overall, the former athletes were ready to move on in their lives, but they also made efforts to stay connected with sports at a recreational level or in supporting roles in sport organizations. This enabled them to retain part of their sport-related identities as they developed additional ones through new relationships and activities.

Swain also found that the athletes' wives, girl-friends, and other family members sometimes had problems adjusting to their loss of celebrity status when the athletes retired. This reminds us that athletes often receive emotional and social support from others during their playing careers and through the retirement process. The experiences of those who provide this support has seldom been acknowledged (see McKenzie, 1999).

Changing Personal Investments in Sport Careers

Garry Wheeler from the University of Alberta is concerned with the careers of athletes with disabilities and what happens when their playing careers end. Building on a study with Canadian paralympic athletes (Wheeler et al., 1996), Wheeler and his fellow researchers gathered data through interviews with forty athletes from Israel, the United Kingdom, Canada, and the United States (Wheeler et al., 1999). Data indicated that

Although people may drop out of sports at one point in the life course, they may return at a later point. (Robert E. Daemmrick/Stone/Getty Images)

patterns among the athletes with disabilities were similar in each of the countries. The athletes tended to become deeply involved in their sport participation, and they often achieved a high level of success in a relatively short time. Through sports, they found meaning, developed a sense of personal competence, and established identities as elite athletes. Their intense investment in sport participation and their sport identity brought both rewards and costs.

Withdrawal from participation and the transition into the rest of life presented challenges for many. About one in ten experienced serious emotional problems during this process. Retirement often came quite suddenly and was accompanied by a process of reinvesting time and energy into other spheres of their lives. There was a focus on reconnecting with family members and friends, going back to college or university, and getting on with occupational careers. However, most stayed connected with sports and sport organizations as coaches, administrators, or recreational athletes. Those few who hoped they might compete again often experienced difficulties during the retirement transition, but most of those interviewed accepted and adjusted to ending their competitive careers.

In summary, research shows that ending or changing sport participation often involves the

Many factors can encourage people to decide to drop out of sports or shift their participation from one sport to another. Identity changes, access to resources, and life course issues are also involved. As circumstances change, so do our ideas about ourselves and about sports and sport participation.
(CP/Preston Brownschlaigle/*Edmonton Sun*)

same interactive and decision-making processes that underlie becoming and staying involved in sports. Just as people are not simply socialized into sports, neither are they simply socialized out of sports. Changes in participation are grounded in decision-making processes tied to the lives, life courses, and social worlds of those involved. It is difficult to explain changes in sport participation without knowing about the identity issues and the developmental and life course issues that are involved (Dacyshyn, 1999; Drahota and Eitzen, 1998). It also is important to know about the resources that athletes possess and can use as they make transitions to other relationships, activities, and careers. Some people have problems when they retire from sports, but, to understand those problems, we need information about how sports fit into their lives. Our conclusion is that, if sport participation expands a

person's identity, experiences, relationships, and resources, the retirement transition will be smooth. Difficulties are most likely to occur when a person has never had the desire or the chance to live outside the culture of elite sports (Murphy et al., 1996).

BEING INVOLVED IN SPORTS: WHAT HAPPENS?

Do Sports Build Character?

Although beliefs about the consequences of sport participation vary from culture to culture, the notion that playing sports builds character has been and continues to be widely accepted in many cultures. This form of **character logic** has been used as a basis for encouraging children to play sports, for funding sports programmes, for building stadiums, for promoting teams and leagues, and for sponsoring events such as the Olympic Games.

For nearly fifty years, people have done research to test the validity of this logic. Much of this research involves comparisons of the traits, attitudes, and behaviours of people who participate in particular organized competitive sports at a particular time with the traits, attitudes, and behaviours of those who do not. Most of these comparisons look at differences between the members of U.S. high school teams and other students, who are not on teams, at a particular time. These snapshot comparisons have provided inconsistent and confusing results. This is because "character" is difficult to measure, and researchers have used multiple definitions of *character* in their studies (Stoll and Beller, 1998). Furthermore, many researchers have based their studies on two faulty assumptions about sports and sport experiences (McCormack and Chalip, 1988). First, researchers have wrongly assumed that *all* organized competitive sports involve similar character-shaping experiences for *all* athletes. Second, they have wrongly assumed that the character-shaping experiences in organized sports are so unique that people who do not play sports are at a disadvantage when it comes to developing certain positive traits, attitudes, and behaviours.

A third characteristic of such studies is the assumptions made by researchers with regard to what are valuable character traits. Characteristics that are likely to lead an individual to be a "team player" and to be obedient were highly valued—especially by coaches who rated individuals in terms of their "coachability." Character traits such as independence, stubbornness, and creativity tend to be less valued if they might lead athletes to question or reject certain practices. As Donnelly (1981) noted in a critique of the character building

> **What do kids know about us? They only know that we play sports. They don't know who we are as people. You don't learn the important things about life by watching a person play football.**
>
> —Emmitt Smith, NFL player (1996)

aspects and assumptions of some outdoor education courses, "[t]hose individuals who refuse to engage in certain activities in the face of enormous social pressures may actually be showing more courage [and character] than those who comply. But they are never made to feel that way" (p. 23).

Over the years, these faulty assumptions have led many researchers to overlook the following characteristics as they have studied sports and socialization by using statistical comparisons of athletes and nonathletes:

1. Sports are organized in vastly different ways across programmes, teams, and situations and thus offer many *different experiences* to participants. Therefore, sport participation involves a wide range of possible socialization experiences. (This point is explained in the Reflect on Sports box, "Power and Performance versus Pleasure and Participation," pages 96–97.)

2. People who choose or are selected to participate in sports may be different in certain ways from those who do not choose or are not selected to participate. Therefore, sports may not *build* character as much as they are organized to *select* people who already have certain character traits to play on teams.

3. Different people define sport experiences in different ways, even when they are in the same programmes or on the same teams. Therefore, the lessons learned in sports and the applications of those lessons to everyday life vary from one person to the next.

4. The meanings that people give to sport experiences often change over time as they grow older and change how they view themselves and the world. Therefore, the lessons that people learn while playing sports may change in the future as they learn

new ways to evaluate their past experiences, including experiences in sports.

5. Socialization occurs through the social interaction that accompanies sport participation. Therefore, the meaning and importance of playing sports is derived through a person's social relationships and the social and cultural context in which participation occurs.

6. The socialization that occurs in sports may also occur in other activities. Therefore, people who do not play sports may participate in other activities that involve valuable socialization experiences.

Due to these oversights, studies that have compared so-called athletes with so-called nonathletes have not provided consistent evidence about the complex socialization processes that occur in connection with sports and sport participation.

Our review of these studies leads us to conclude that sport participation is most likely to have positive effects on people's lives when it is associated with the following:

- Opportunities for testing and developing identities apart from playing sports
- Knowledge of the world and how it works
- Experiences that go beyond the locker room and the playing field
- Formation of new relationships, including relationships outside of sports
- Clear lessons about how sport experiences can be used as a basis for dealing with challenges outside of sports
- Opportunities for other people to see, define, and deal with a person as more than just an athlete
- Opportunities to develop competence and become responsible in activities outside of sports

On the other hand, when playing sports *constricts* a person's opportunities, knowledge, experiences, and relationships, we can expect that negative socialization consequences will accompany participation. Of course, none of this should come as a surprise. Neither good nor bad socialization outcomes occur automatically in connection with sport participation. In fact, the impact of all our experiences in sports is mediated by the social and cultural context in which we live.

The mere fact that people do or do not play sports tells us little about their overall lives and how they go about developing their sense of who they are, how they are connected with others, and what is important in their lives. This is why hundreds of studies have not given us the evidence we need to determine whether sports do or do not build character (Miracle and Rees, 1994; Sage, 1998a; Shields and Bredemeier, 1995; Stoll and Beller, 1998). The snapshots provided by comparisons of so-called athletes and nonathletes have helped us develop hypotheses about what happens in sports, but they have not provided the videos we need to understand all the positive and negative consequences that can occur in such dynamic socialization processes.

The failure to find consistent, measurable effects of sport participation on specific character traits *does not mean* that sports and sport experiences have no impact on people's lives. We know that the discourses, images, and experiences associated with sports in many parts of the world are vivid and powerful. Sports do have an impact on us and on the world around us. However, we cannot separate that impact from the meanings we give to sports and the ways we integrate sport experiences into our lives, relationships, and culture. Therefore, if we want to know what happens in sports, we must study sport experiences in the social and cultural contexts in which they occur. This type of research is exciting, and it provides helpful insights into the many ways that sports are involved in socialization processes. See the Reflect on Sports box, "Power and Performance versus Pleasure and Participation," on pages 96–97, for the differences in sport experiences.

REFLECT ON SPORTS	**Power and Performance versus Pleasure and Participation** *Different Sports, Different Experiences, Different Consequences*

Sport experiences vary with the conditions under which sports are organized and played. To assume that all sports are organized around the same goals and emphasize the same orientations and behaviours is a mistake. In North America, for example, there are highly organized competitive sports, informal sports, adventure sports, recreational sports, extreme sports, alternative sports, cooperative sports, folk sports, contact sports, artistic sports, team sports, individual sports, and so on, and there are various combinations of these types. However, at this time, it seems that the dominant sport form in many societies is organized around what we call a **power and performance model.**

Power and performance sports are highly organized and competitive. Generally, they emphasize the following:

- The use of strength, speed, and power to push human limits and aggressively dominate opponents in the quest for victories and championships
- The idea that excellence is proved through competitive success and achieved through intense

dedication and hard work, combined with making sacrifices, risking one's personal well-being, and playing in pain
- The importance of setting records, defining the body as a machine, and using technology to control and monitor the body
- Selection systems based on physical skills and competitive success
- Hierarchical authority structures, in which athletes are subordinate to coaches and coaches are subordinate to owners and administrators
- Antagonism to the point that opponents are defined as enemies

Of course, becoming involved in and playing sports with these characteristics would be different from becoming involved in and playing sports with other characteristics.

Although power and performance sports have become the standard for determining what sports should be in many countries, they have not been accepted by everyone. In fact, some people have

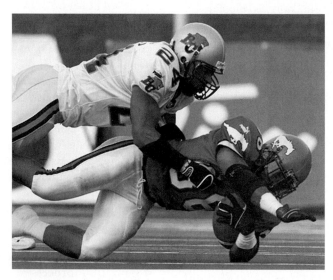

Power and performance sports involve the use of strength, speed, and power to dominate opponents in the quest for competitive victories. (CP/Adrian Wyld)

Pleasure and participation sports may involve competition, but the primary emphasis is on connections between people and on personal expression through participation. (CP/Jeff Stokoe/*Red Deer Advocate*)

maintained or developed other forms of sports grounded in a wide range of values and experiences. Some of these are spin-offs or revisions of dominant forms, while others represent alternative or even oppositional sport forms. These alternative and oppositional forms are diverse, but many fit what we call a **pleasure and participation model**.

Pleasure and participation sports represent a diverse collection of physical activities, but they generally emphasize the following:

- Active participation revolving around a combination of types of connections—connections between people, between mind and body, and between physical activity and the environment
- An ethic of personal expression, enjoyment, growth, good health, and mutual concern and support for teammates and opponents
- Empowerment (not power) created by experiencing the body as a source of pleasure and well-being
- Inclusive participation based on an accommodation of differences in physical skills
- Democratic decision-making structures characterized by cooperation, the sharing of power, and give-and-take relationships between coaches and athletes
- Interpersonal support around the idea of competing *with*, not against, others; opponents are not enemies, but those who test each other

These two sport forms do *not* encompass all the ways that sports might be organized and played. In fact, some people play sports that contain elements of both forms and reflect many ideas about what is important in physical activities. However, power and performance sports remain dominant today in the sense that they receive the most attention and support.[1]

It is reasonable to hypothesize that, when people play or watch these sports, their experiences are different than when they play or watch pleasure and participation sports. Not all sports are the same when it comes to socialization. *What do you think?*

----

[1] On the Online Learning Centre (www.mcgrawhill.ca/college/coakley), you will find a feature suggesting why power and performance sports are dominant today. Also, since one of the distinguishing characteristics between power and performance sports and pleasure and participation sports is the intensity of and meaning attached to competition, you will also find additional information specifically on competition and cooperation.

How Do Sports Affect Our Lives?

Sports and sport participation do have an impact on people's lives. We are learning more about this impact through three types of studies based on a combination of critical, feminist, and interactionist theories:

1. Studies of sport experiences as explained through the voices of sport participants
2. Studies of the social worlds that are created around sports
3. Studies of sports as sites for the formation of ideology and for struggles over ideological issues

Taken together, these studies have led many of us who are concerned with sports in society to rethink socialization issues. Now we view sports as *sites for socialization experiences*, rather than as *causes of specific socialization outcomes*. This is an important distinction. It highlights two things. First, sports are social locations rich in their potential for providing memorable and meaningful personal, social, and cultural experiences. Second, sports *by themselves do not cause particular changes in the character traits, attitudes, and behaviours of athletes or spectators*. In other words, when positive or negative socialization occurs in association with sports, we cannot just say it is caused by sports; instead, we treat sports as sites for experiences and then search for and explain the specific social processes through which socialization occurs.

A summary of some of this research illustrates how it helps us to understand what happens in sports and how sports are connected with larger social issues in society.

Real-Life Experiences: Sport Stories from Athletes

The following examples provide what we would describe as socialization videos. They illustrate what happens in sports from the perspectives of the participants themselves, and they show us how

"I've got a bad feeling about his 'boxing for Jesus' approach."

Meanings given to sports may vary from one person to another. However, many power and performance sports are organized to encourage orientations that emphasize domination over others. Those who do not hold this orientation may not fit very well in these sports.

people make sense out of sport experiences and integrate them into their lives on their own terms.

The Moral Lessons of Sports   Chris Stevenson, from the University of New Brunswick, spent a number of years conducting in-depth interviews with Christian athletes in various settings—current and former professional and college athletes who are members of Athletes in Action in western Canada (Stevenson, 1991, 1997), and members of a church-sponsored hockey league in New Brunswick (Dunn and Stevenson, 1998). These individuals had been socialized as both Christians and athletes, and Stevenson was interested in how they resolved any conflicts that may exist between their participation in **power and performance sports** and their Christian beliefs and values. (Hoffman [1992, 1999] has argued convincingly that such conflicts exist.) Dilemmas such as these, described as *role conflict* in interactionist theory, are important because the ways humans attempt to resolve them provide insights into human behaviour and the processes of socialization.

The resolutions took various forms. Players in the church-sponsored hockey league adopted many aspects of a **pleasure and participation** approach to sports in an attempt to play hockey in a way that reflected their Christian values:

- There was a stated commitment in the league to fair play.
- The players agreed to ban body contact, fights, swearing on the ice, and beer in the locker room.
- There was public prayer before each game.
- There were no official league standings, although scores were kept in games.

The players were not always successful in the attempt—especially when they became caught up in the action—but, in general, they managed to maintain their values in sport.

The Athletes in Action resolved their *role conflict* in three distinct ways:

- One response was to completely *segregate* the two roles: when you are in a sporting context, you are only an athlete, with athletes' values; when you are in other settings, you are a Christian.
- The majority were *selective* in the way they accommodated the two roles, giving preference to the athlete role in athletic settings, but maintaining some of their religious values to the extent that they were able.
- The smallest group remained *committed* to their Christian values even in the sports setting, although in practice they admitted to some aspects of *selectivity*.

Stevenson's studies highlight the strong influence of power and performance sports, and the way that they oblige athletes to find ways to accommodate and resolve their religious beliefs and value systems.[1]

Lessons in the Locker Room Sociologist Nancy Theberge (1995, 2000b) spent two years studying an elite women's ice hockey team in Ontario. As she observed and interviewed team members, she noted that their experiences and orientations enabled them to form a community based on their shared passion for hockey. This community was defined by a professional approach to participation. They focused on hockey and were serious about being successful on the ice. In the process, they developed close connections with one another. The team became a community with its own dynamics and internal organization. Within the context of this "constructed community," the athletes learned things about hockey, about themselves, and about one another. The definitions and meanings that the players gave to their hockey experiences and the ways they linked them to their lives emerged as they interacted with one another on and off the ice.

The locker room was a key place for the interaction through which the team members bonded with each other and worked out their personal definitions and meanings of sport participation. The emotional climate of the locker room, especially *after* a practice or game, encouraged talk that focused on who the athletes were as people and how they saw their connections with the world. This talk gave shape and meaning to what they did on the ice, to their sport experiences. It also served as a means for expressing feelings and thoughts about men, sexuality/homosexuality, male partners and female partners, and families. The women talked and joked about men but did not degrade or reduce them to body parts in their comments. They made references to sex and sexuality in their conversations, but the substance of these references promoted inclusiveness rather than

---

[1] On the Online Learning Centre, you will find Coakley's full chapter on "Sports and Religion." It includes a figure outlining a model of conflict, doubt, and resolution that demonstrates the conflict between Christian beliefs and power and performance sports.

hostility or stereotypes. This was very different from what has reportedly occurred in many men's locker rooms (Curry, 1993).

Theberge's study shows us that playing sports is a social as much as a physical experience. The socialization that occurs in sports occurs *through social relationships.* Theberge focused on relationships between the athletes, but also important were their relationships with coaches, managers, trainers, friends, family members, sport reporters, and even fans. If we want to know what happens in sports, we must understand what happens in all those relationships. It is through them that players give meaning to what happens on the playing field, regardless of whether they win or lose, play well or make mistakes.

Stories about Gay Male Athletes   The meanings given to sport experiences emerge in connection with social relationships. Meanings vary from one person to another because social relationships are influenced by social definitions given to age, gender, social class, ethnicity, skin colour, (dis)abilities, and sexuality. This is one of the points highlighted in Dan Woog's (1998) book about gay male athletes in the United States. Woog, a journalist, felt it was important to give voice to gay men in sports and hear what they had to say about themselves and their sport experiences. Using data collected in interviews, Woog tells twenty-eight stories about athletes, coaches, referees, administrators, and others in sports.

The stories indicate that the social worlds created around sports hinder the coming out process. Successfully combining a gay identity with an athlete identity was a challenging process for nearly all the interviewees. Woog observed that the social contexts and relationships associated with individual sports, such as running and swimming, generally were more gay-friendly than team sports, although a cosmopolitan sport such as soccer provided a more gay-friendly context than "a mechanized, play-by-rote game like football." Being out was liberating for most of the gay men, but it was also dangerous for some of them. These men cared deeply about sports, and they often feared that being out could lead them to be excluded from sport teams and programmes. Positive experiences for the gay athletes were enhanced when there were organizations that acknowledged and supported them on and off the field, when there was overt support from family and friends, and when someone in their sport, such as a teammate or coach, served as their advocate.

Brian Pronger's (1990a, 1990b) interviews with gay male athletes in Canada produced some different results. While the primary concern of U.S. athletes seems to be coming out, the Canadian athletes were also likely to be struck by the irony of "passing" as a heterosexual athlete when naked in a locker room with other males. While the Canadian athletes interviewed by Pronger have the same concerns about coming out, and recognize the potential danger of passing, they are also conscious of the humour of the situation. Being a gay male athlete on a heterosexual team, or in a social world of sports in which "compulsory heterosexuality" appears to be the norm, represents another situation where *role conflict* may occur. As with the Christian athletes noted previously, gay athletes may employ different strategies to resolve the conflict. For those interviewed by Woog, the ideal strategy seems to be coming out, although most gay athletes have not chosen this route. Pronger's subjects seem to have opted to keep the two roles separate, while also finding humour in the assumption of heterosexuality made by heterosexual teammates. (See Fusco [1995] for some stories of lesbian athletes in Canada.)

Of course, there are many similarities between the experiences of gay men and those of straight men in sports. However, the meanings given to those experiences and the ways in which they are integrated into people's lives differ in important ways because of how *heterosexuality* and *homosexuality* are defined by many people. Those definitions influence what happens in sports and how people are affected by their sport experiences (see also Anderson, 2000).

In summary, these studies show that people define and give meaning to their sport experiences in connection with their social relationships. Meanings given to sport experiences are also grounded in the cultural context in which they occur. Prevailing definitions of social characteristics often influence the importance of sports in people's lives. As these definitions change, so do the meanings of sport experiences.

Social Worlds: Living in Sports

Although sociologists study sports mostly as parts of the societies and cultures in which they exist, some research has focused on sports as **social worlds,** a term used in interactionist theory to refer to a way of life and an associated mindset that revolve around a particular set of activities and envelop all the people and relationships connected with the activities.[2] We use this term to explain that we cannot understand who athletes are, what they do, and how sport influences their lives unless we view them in two contexts: (1) the social world of their sport and (2) the overall society and culture in which the sport world exists. Unless we know about these contexts, we have difficulty making sense of sport experiences and their impact on people. This is especially the case when we study people whose lives revolve completely around a particular sport, i.e., when the social world of their sport is their entire world.

Studies of social worlds that are created in connection with specific sports provide useful information about socialization processes and experiences. Following are a few examples.

Learning to Be a Pro Sociologist Michael Robidoux, who teaches at the University of

Ottawa, spent a season travelling with and studying an American Hockey League (AHL) team. The AHL is now the primary farm system for NHL teams, and the majority of the professional players in the AHL aspire to play in the NHL; only a few actually do. Robidoux (2001) documented the daily lives of the players and the team: practices, games, initiation ceremonies for rookies, the training room, and travel. He was struck by three significant, and interconnected, features of working life at this level of professional sports as these players—mainly from the Canadian junior system, but also from U.S. universities and Europe—learned to be pros.

The first is what Robidoux terms "homogenized masculinity." Rookie players must endure an initiation ceremony that, if successful, permits them to be a part of the team as a professional player. But a second, and more implicit, part of the process is that players must adopt a very limited view of what it is to be a man. While the job itself, particularly given the style of play that is expected in the AHL, involves adopting a physically dominant style of masculinity, that demand is repeated also for off-ice behaviour. Adopting that style is rewarded by acceptance from established players and by management; but it means that players must abandon other aspects of their identity and their personal development.

Once the players have accepted this limited view of themselves as human beings, they must face the second significant feature of life as players at this level of professional sport—becoming a "commodity." This is a relatively standard critique of professional sports—many players are highly rewarded, but they are bought and sold, that is, drafted and traded, just like commodities. However, this notion takes on much greater significance in the AHL. Because the AHL is the farm system for the NHL, "[t]he players are literally cultivated on the farm; only those with suitable qualities are 'picked' to be used in the NHL market. The cultivation period, moreover, is limited, and

---

[2]We use the term *social world* in the same way that others use the term *subculture* (see Crosset and Beal, 1997; Donnelly, 1988b).

those who do not develop sufficiently are eventually replaced with new 'stock'" (p. 190).

The third feature is the players' powerlessness in the face of a totally controlling, continually demanding management. The players are living out their dream, and the dream of many Canadian boys—they are professional hockey players, about as close as you can get to the NHL. They are totally committed (on an average salary of about US$55,000 a year), and their commitment is easy to exploit. Robidoux (p. 193) lists the price that players pay for such commitment:

- They deprive themselves of occupational and other experiences outside of hockey, limiting their employment opportunities when their careers end.
- They deprive their families of their presence, and themselves of family support.
- They endure injuries on a regular basis, and often suffer from more long-term debility as a consequence of their injuries.
- Their education is limited, with many not having completed high school.
- They have difficulties in finding meaningful relationships outside hockey.

Robidoux's study takes us into the heart of professional sports, where players are attempting to live out their dreams. But they cannot even point to the million-dollar salaries as justification for the costs incurred.

Realizing Image Isn't Everything Anthropologist Alan Klein studied the social world of competitive bodybuilding for seven years. In his book *Little Big Men* (1993), he explains that much of the lives of the bodybuilders revolved around issues of gender and sexuality. The bodybuilders, both male and female, learned to project public images of power and strength while privately they experienced serious doubts about their identities and self-worth. The social world of bodybuilding seemed to foster a desperate need for attention and approval from others, especially fellow bodybuilders. Ideas about masculinity within the social world of bodybuilding were so narrow and one-dimensional that the male bodybuilders developed homophobic attitudes and went to great lengths to assert their heterosexuality in public. Also, the focus on body size and hardness created such insecurities that the men learned to present and even define themselves in terms of exaggerated caricatures of masculinity—like comic-book depictions of men. Overall, bodybuilding was a site for powerful socialization experiences in their lives. However, due to gender relations in the culture at large, these experiences took on different meanings for the women bodybuilders than they did for the men (see the Reflect on Sports box, "Women Bodybuilders: Expanding Definitions of Femininity," in chapter 8, pages 243-244).

Working in the LPGA Two sociologists carried out studies—almost twenty years apart—of the golfers on the LPGA tour. Nancy Theberge (1977, 1981), now at the University of Waterloo, conducted observations, interviews, and surveys in the mid-1970s, and was struck by the *structured uncertainty* faced by women golfers as a result of their work, especially on a tour which was struggling for recognition, and on which the prizes were significantly less than those available today. Their work routines were characterized by "extreme variability and indeterminacy": financial (since most golfers could not win enough to support their careers, they were obliged to find other sources of income); courses and competition (every week, golfers have to contend with new courses and must learn course management); relationships (with other golfers, caddies, coaches, and spectators); and lifestyle (constant travel, living in hotels, etc.). Theberge cites golfer Amy Alcott: "In professional golf, you have to stay on top every week, adjust to travel, to practice schedules; you learn to deal with people, with weather. It's all a big mystery at first, but if you want to remain on tour, you learn to cope." Theberge

(1981) documents the ways in which professional golfers learn to cope with this *structured uncertainty* as they become socialized into the culture of the LPGA tour. And what the surviving golfers learn more than anything is to resolve the uncertainty by attempting in every way possible to standardize their work situation. They establish routines, attempt to develop a stable source of income, develop course management skills, and standardize as much as possible their relationships with those with whom they must interact.

Todd Crosset (1995), who teaches sport management at the University of Massachusetts, focuses more specifically on gender relations in the LPGA. He spent fourteen months traveling and living in his pick-up truck while studying the social world of women's professional golf. He found that being on the LPGA tour created and, in fact, required a complete mindset revolving around the commitment to using physical competence as a basis for evaluating self and others on the tour. He described this

Sports in many cultures are no longer seen as exclusively masculine activities. However, traditional gender definitions may still keep some girls out of the action. (Jay Coakley)

mindset as "an ethic of prowess." This ethic of prowess existed partly because the women were very concerned about neutralizing the potentially negative effects that dominant ideas about gender could have if these ideas were to enter the social world of women's professional golf. One golfer he interviewed said that much of what she did in her life was a response to the notion that "*athlete* is almost a masculine noun" in this society. The impact of being a pro golfer was summarized by one woman, who said, "We are different than the typical married lady with a house full of kids in what we think and do." Both studies emphasize that we can understand the meaning of this statement only in the context of the social world of the LPGA and that we can understand the social world of the LPGA only in the context of gender relations in North American culture at the turn of the twenty-first century.

Sport Worlds Portrayed in the Media
Laura Robinson (1998), Joan Ryan (1995), and Christine Brennan (1996) are journalists who have studied and written about the social worlds of high-performance sports. Their research methods and writing styles are different from those of academic scholars, but they contribute to what we know about socialization experiences in sports. For example, Laura Robinson is a free-lance journalist, author, and a long-time campaigner for women's rights in sports (many of her magazine and newspaper articles are collected in *She Shoots, She Scores* [Robinson, 1997]). In *Crossing the Line: Violence and Sexual Assault in Canada's National Sport*, Robinson (1998) provides a searing exposé of junior hockey. She describes a sport system in which young male players (ages sixteen to twenty) are socialized in an abusive (not just harassment and hazing, but also sport practices that are injurious) and hypermasculine culture, often removed from family supports by the draft system. But these players are also highly rewarded and receive other support, in turn, for their own abusive behaviour.

Protected and pampered, as well as abused, in this sheltered world, the players sometimes behave in abusive ways in other settings. Robinson, through interviews and court records, notes a number of cases of rape and gang rape by junior hockey players. This book, together with a CBC television documentary in *the fifth estate* series called "Thin Ice" (1996) on which Robinson worked, and the late-1996 revelations regarding hockey coach, Graham James (see the Reflect on Sports box in chapter 7 on pages 202–203), has led to more sensitivity and concern about hazing and socialization practices in junior hockey. Some policy changes have made it somewhat more likely that, when players claim that they have been abused, or when fans claim that they have been sexually assaulted by players, they will now be believed.

In summary, these four examples of research on the social worlds of sports show that those worlds are *sites* for powerful forms of socialization. A full understanding of socialization processes and experiences requires knowledge of those worlds and the connection between them and the culture as a whole. Once we deeply understand a sport world, once we are able to delve into it through good research, the things that athletes think and do become meaningful and understandable to us, regardless of how they appear to those who are not part of those worlds.

Ideology: Sports as Sites for Struggling Over How We Think and What We Do

Socialization research has focused mostly on what occurs in the lives of individuals or small groups. However, as researchers have combined critical theories with cultural studies and post-structuralism,[3] they have carried out creative studies of *socialization as a community and cultural process*. Their research goes beyond looking at the experiences and characteristics of athletes. Instead, it focuses on sports as sites where people in society create and learn "stories," which they can use as they make sense out of the world and their lives. The stories that revolve around sports and athletes have their own vocabularies and images; their meanings shift, depending on the settings in which people tell them and hear them, and they often identify important cultural issues in people's lives. Researchers try to identify these stories and then determine how they fit into the culture and how people use them in connection with what they think and do.

Researchers also are concerned with whose stories about sports become dominant in the culture, since there are so many stories that could be told about sports. The dominant stories are culturally important because they identify what is natural, normal, and legitimate and therefore give priority to ideas and orientations that tend to privilege some people more than others, some interests more than other interests. For example, the stories and vocabulary frequently used in discourse about sports revolve around heroic figures who are big, strong, aggressive, record-setting champions. Canadian writer Varda Burstyn (1999, p. 23) says that these stories celebrate the notion of "higher, faster, stronger" that today serves the interests of capitalist expansion and traditional

---

[3]Poststructuralism is a theoretical and methodological perspective based on the assumption that culture today is constituted primarily through the production and consumption of symbols and rapidly changing media and computer images. Structuralists, including functionalists, conflict theorists, and some critical theorists consider material production and material reality to be the key dynamic around which culture is created and maintained. Those using a poststructuralist perspective focus on language, including both written and spoken discourse, because they assume that social life in today's postmodern culture is constantly negotiated, constructed, challenged, and changed through language and discourse. Much research done by poststructuralists deals with the media in their many forms and focuses on how images, identities, symbols, and meanings are fabricated through the media and then serve as the contexts for our lives. One of the goals of many poststructuralists is to do scholarly work that disrupts these media-generated discourses in ways that increase critical sensibilities in the culture as a whole.

manly values associated with conquest. This is an important way in which socialization occurs in connection with sports. Researchers are also concerned with whose stories are not told and with who is silenced or even "erased" from the stories that are told in the dominant culture. For example, researchers may study media coverage to learn what is *not* contained in narratives and images as much as what is contained in them. After all, we can learn as much about culture by seeing what *is not* represented in cultural discourses and images as we can by seeing what is represented.

Research on this form of socialization is difficult to do, because it requires a knowledge of history and a deep understanding of the settings in which sports and sport stories come to be a part of people's lives. But this research is important, because it deals with the influence of sports in the culture as a whole, rather than just in the lives of individuals and small groups.

Research on socialization as a community and cultural process is partly inspired by the ideas of Italian sociologist Antonio Gramsci. When fascists in 1930s Italy imprisoned Gramsci for speaking out against their political ideas, he spent time in prison thinking about why people had not revolted against repressive forms of capitalism in Western societies. Gramsci concluded that it was important to understand how people throughout a society form definitions of common sense and ideas about how society ought to be organized socially, politically, and economically. He thought that one of the most effective ways for powerful people to influence popular definitions and ideas, and thereby win support from the general population in a society, is to sponsor and control major sources of pleasure and joy in people's lives.

Gramsci suspected that most people use the cultural messages associated with everyday pleasure and joy in their lives to inform their ideas about the organization and operation of society as a whole. Therefore, if dominant groups in a society can influence the language, images, and messages tied to the fun and excitement in people's lives, they can encourage agreement with their ideas, or at least defuse the extent to which people might disagree with them. Therefore, the sponsorship and control of sports and other sources of pleasure is a useful strategy for maintaining power and privilege.

Gramsci's analysis helps us to understand why large corporations spend millions of dollars to sponsor sports and to advertise in connection with sports. For example, when eleven TOP (The Olympic Partners) sponsors[4] spent over US$550 million on Olympic promotion and sponsorship in the lead-up to the 2000 Sydney Games, is it only because the executives think that advertising in connection with sports will make them more money? Of course, this is an important consideration, but, more important for Coca-Cola, Panasonic, and other corporations is the fact that they can use the Olympics and other sports as vehicles for delivering cultural messages they want people in the world to hear. They want people watching the Olympics to agree that competition is the best way to allocate rewards in life and that successful and powerful people (and corporations) really deserve their money and power.

The people who run Coca-Cola and Panasonic want people to drink Coke and buy DVD players, but they also want them to develop an approach to life that associates pleasure with consumption, and social status with corporate logos. They want people to say, "These large companies are important in our lives, because without them we would not have the sports we love so dearly." They want people to think that enjoyment and pleasure in life depends on large corporations and their products. They want to establish consumption as a way of life, as the foundation for culture itself.

Their profits and power depend on it, and their marketing people know it. They are selling a whole way of life and an ideology in which people express their identities through competitive success and consumption. To the extent that people in society adopt this way of viewing the world and their relationship to it, corporate interests gain more power in society. Many sociologists refer to this process of forming consent around a particular ideology as the process of establishing **hegemony.**

The cultural messages associated with sports have become a part of our lives at the start of the twenty-first century. It is difficult to determine how these messages are heard around the world, but it is clear that major corporations see sports as important vehicles for delivering them. People in corporations know that their interests depend on establishing "ideological outposts" in people's heads. Sports, because they are pleasurable activities for so many people, are logical avenues through which these outposts can be built. Once established, these outposts are useful to corporations. In fact, they become terminals through which a range of corporate messages can be delivered effectively. To paraphrase Gramsci's conclusion about hegemony, it is difficult to fight an enemy that has outposts in your head.

This approach to socialization as a community and cultural process is difficult to understand unless we see it in action. The following examples of research highlight this informative approach to sports and socialization.

The Road to the Board Room U.S. sociologist David Riesman, an early supporter of the sociology of sport, commented: "The road to the board room leads through the locker room." In other words, characteristics of sports provide valuable socialization for the corporate world. Even before Riesman made this comment, a classic Canadian sociological study, *Crestwood Heights* (Seeley, Sim, and Loosley, 1956) had identified the importance of sports in an upper-middle-class community (now widely acknowledged to be Forest Hill in

---

[4] The TOP sponsors were Coca-Cola, IBM, John Hancock, Kodak, McDonald's, Panasonic, Samsung, Sports Illustrated/Time, UPS, Visa, and Xerox—nine U.S. corporations and one each from Japan and Korea.

Toronto). Their importance was in socializing boys into a career. "[E]ven in recreational activity, the youth of the community do not engage in sport or games as activities to be participated in for enjoyment only. Sport provides an enculturative [socializing] milieux that prepares boys to become executives, or more broadly, upwardly mobile *career competitors*" (Gruneau and Albinson, 1976, p. 298). The importance of sports, especially football, baseball, and hockey, was that they encouraged competition and teamwork, allowed stars to emerge, and created bonding and networking opportunities.

Although this idea seems to make sense for males from a particular social class—after all, most elite private schools require sport participation of their students—there are few studies in the sociology of sport that explore the socializing path from the locker room to the board room. Only Gai Berlage has focused on the issue, particularly with regard to the "glass ceiling" experienced by many women in business and politics: "Several organizational studies of women in corporations suggest . . . women's lack of experience with team sports as one reason they have not been more successful in the corporate world" (Berlage, 1982, p. 310; see also, Nelson, 1994). Harvard sociologist Orlando Patterson recently reiterated this idea in an essay on social inequality: ". . . women's exclusion from male bonding practices seriously impedes their access to vital tacit knowledge for successful entrepreneurial activity" (2002, p. 33). There are serious ideological implications of such socialization practices.

Lessons of the Anatomy Lab Brian Pronger's reflections on his undergraduate experiences in the anatomy laboratory studying human cadavers led him to sound some warnings about the type of education that physical educators and kinesiologists receive in Canada (Pronger, 1995). As with most physical education and kinesiology students in Canada, Pronger took a required course in anatomy as part of his physical education degree

at the University of Toronto (where he now teaches). The lab instructor told him: "The only way you really learn anatomy is to get your hands inside and manipulate the parts of the body." Given the amount of discussion that takes place among students afterwards, this is an extremely vivid experience; but it is also an experience that is controlled in a very precise way. Students "are told explicitly what to see and implicitly how to relate to it" (p. 441).

Pronger adapts and develops a critique that has been made more generally about medical education. Students are not encouraged to see the subjectivity and humanity of the human body; emotional responses such as joy, sadness, fear, and awe are strongly discouraged; and even an empirical sense of exploration and discovery is discouraged. Students are encouraged to see and experience the cadaver as a mechanical object, as a "technological body." This objectification and technological rendering of the body is also encouraged and developed in other required courses such as biomechanics and physiology, and just as in medicine (see the popularized version of critiques of objectification and technologization of the medical body in the Robin Williams film, *Patch Adams*), it has distinct consequences.

Pronger argues that the "objectification of the body in the gross anatomy lab is transposed into the practices of physical education which reproduce the body as an object: high performance sport, the fit body, and so on" (p. 442). Supposedly professional attitudes also encourage abuse of the body for the purposes of high-performance sports and physical appearance. How many times have you heard an athlete objectify his or her own injured body part—referring to "the ankle" or "the shoulder," rather than "my ankle" or "my shoulder"? Physical education and kinesiology students are socialized into this particular ideology of the body, and alternative views are not encouraged: "[s]tudents who would refuse to see the body technologically…would fail physical education" (p. 441). The hegemony

Nike-sponsored images are still used around the world in the post–Michael Jordan era. Just as Nike and other corporations worked hard to sever the Jordan persona from connections with African-American experiences, the search now continues for replacements—other visible minorities that allow people to comfortably ignore the legacies of colonialism and racism, while at the same time promoting corporate products. Here, NBA players Yao Ming and Vince Carter are on a Nike promotional tour of China. (CP/AP/Ng Han Guan)

of this ideology is extremely powerful, but, as with all hegemonies, it is vulnerable, and Pronger suggests some ways in which the objectification of the body may be resisted.

Diamonds Are Forever Susan Birrell and Diana Richter's (1994) observations of softball teams and in-depth interviews with players showed that the feminist consciousness of women can be used to alter the ways organized sports are played. The stories that emerged in

connection with the women's experiences came with vocabularies and images that empowered the players in their own feminist terms. This made their experiences very different from the experiences of most people who play power and performance sports. The study showed that sports do not always reproduce dominant ways of thinking and doing things. Sometimes sports can be played or organized in ways that clearly push the limits of what is traditionally accepted and acceptable in society. When this happens, socialization in sports may involve changes in how entire groups of people think about what is important in life and how social relationships can and should be organized.

Is Michael Jordan Black? Other studies also have focused on how popular images connected with sports become cultural symbols as they are represented in the media and everyday conversations. For example, David Andrews (1996b) has used a combination of critical theories to study the connection between racial ideology in the United States and the cultural stories created around Michael Jordan between 1982 and 1995. Andrews' analysis of commercials and other media coverage show how the "Jordan persona" was severed from African American experiences and culture, so that white America, seeking evidence that it was colour-blind and open to all, would identify with him.[5] Andrews uses historical information about race and depictions of the Jordan persona in media commercials to argue that, even though race and skin colour were erased from Jordan's public persona, we cannot understand Jordan's status

---

[5] David Shields (2000) provides a more popular version of Andrews' arguments when he explores "Vince Carter as African American"; and Brian Wilson (1997), a professor at the University of British Columbia, in his article, "Good blacks and bad blacks," deals with similar issues in an analysis of the media representations of African-American players in Canadian basketball.

and impact as a cultural icon without knowing how racism operates in the United States.

Andrews' research, as well as studies done by others using similar approaches, emphasizes that *none of us lives outside the influence of ideology* (Andrews, 1996a,b; Burstyn, 1999; Paraschak, 1997). This research is based on the premise that sports, because they are popular sources of pleasure in people's lives, are significant avenues through which people learn and possibly question ideology. Although this research is in its infancy, it holds the promise of showing us how sports influence collective consciousness in a culture and how people can disrupt that influence when it promotes stereotypes and exploitation.

WHAT SOCIALIZATION RESEARCH DOES NOT TELL US

Existing research does not tell us all we want to know about sports and socialization. We have many research snapshots and a few short videos, which enable us to describe and understand segments of the socialization processes that occur in connection with sports. We lack information on how these processes operate in the lives of people from various ethnic groups and social classes. In Canada, research on South and East Asians, First Nations Canadians, African Canadians, and French-Canadians in sports is especially needed. We also need studies of sport participation in high-income and low-income communities, as well as among wealthy and poor individuals and families.

There is a need for research on sport participation careers among young children and on how those careers are linked to overall social development, especially among girls and children from ethnic minority backgrounds. Similarly, we need research on older people, especially those considering or trying sports for the first time or the first time in a long while.

There is a need for research on how people make participation decisions about different types of sports. Sports come in many forms, and our guess is that socialization processes related to power and performance sports are different from experiences related to pleasure and participation sports (see pages 96–97).

If we knew more about each of these topics, we could provide sport participation opportunities that fit into the lives of a greater number of people, and we could make sports more democratic and less subject to the commercial forces that make them exclusive and elitist (Donnelly, 1993, 1996b).

We also need research on the emotional dimensions of socialization processes. Few sociologists have considered emotions in their research, but most of us know that decisions about sport participation are clearly connected with our feelings, fears, and anxieties. For example, decisions may be tied to what people in sports refer to as "psyching up": the emotional experience of forming expectations about what they will encounter in sports. These expectations are based on memories, as well as the images about sports that exist in the culture as a whole.

Stories about the emotional side of sports have been collected by social psychologists who have studied "flow experiences" among athletes (Jackson and Csikszentmihalyi, 1999). Flow occurs when we become so engrossed in what we are doing that we lose track of time and are carried along by the activity itself. The runner's high, peak experiences, and "that game when everything just seems to click" are examples of flow in action. Even though flow is a personal experience, it is tied to sociological issues such as how activities are organized and the amount of control participants have over their involvement in those activities.

Finally, we need more research on how the language used in certain sports influences sport participation decisions and the meanings given to sport experiences. When language hypes opposition, hostility, rivalries, confrontations, domination, and mastery over others, does it set the stage for memories, fantasies, and identifications that serve as powerful sources of personal identity and social dynamics? Our guess is that this type of language is at least indicative of how sports are organized and played. If so, it privileges some potential participants over others. For example, in the face of such language, are young women in high schools less likely than their male counterparts to try out for and stay on school teams because the language of sports in many schools is based on traditionally masculine images and orientations? What types of boys and men are likely to be attracted to sports described as forms of "warfare," requiring aggression, toughness, and the desire to dominate others? Are girls and women less likely to see sports as important in their lives after hearing a coach reprimand players by saying they played "like a bunch of girls"? Sociologists, especially those interested in gender equity and gender relations, would like to know answers to these questions. Research is needed to seek the answers.

On the practical side, when we learn more about sports and socialization, we can become wiser parents, coaches, teachers, managers, and sport administrators. Then we can create sports that offer a wider array of challenging and satisfying experiences.

SUMMARY

WHO PLAYS AND WHAT HAPPENS?

Socialization is a complex, interactive process through which people form ideas about who they are and how they are connected to the world around them. This process occurs in connection with sports as well as with other activities and experiences in people's lives. Research indicates that playing sports is a social experience as well as a physical one.

Becoming involved and staying involved in sports occur in connection with general socialization processes in people's lives. Decisions to play sports are influenced by the availability of opportunities, the existence of social support, the processes of identity formation, and the cultural context in which decisions are made. Studies of socialization into sports show that sport participation decisions are related to the processes of individual development, the organization of social life, and cultural ideology. People do not make decisions about sport participation once and for all time. They make them day by day as they set and revise priorities for their lives. Studies of socialization into sports have told us a few things about first experiences in sports and about who may have influenced and supported those experiences, but becoming involved and staying involved in sports is a long-term process. Influential factors and people change over time as people's lives change, and it is important to carry out studies that capture the complexities of these processes.

Changing or ending active sport participation also occurs in connection with general socialization processes. Again, these processes are interactive and are influenced by many personal, social, and cultural factors. Changes in sport participation are usually tied to a combination of identity, developmental, and life course issues. Ending sport participation usually involves transition processes, during which athletes redefine their identities, reconnect with friends and family members, and use available resources to become involved in other activities and careers. Just as people are not socialized into sports, they are not simply socialized out of sports. We have good information illustrating that changing and ending a career as a competitive athlete occurs over time and is often tied to events and life course issues outside of sports. These connections are best studied through methods that enable us to describe long-term transition processes.

Efforts to understand what happens to people when they play sports have been sidetracked by the popular belief that sports build character. This belief is grounded in faulty character logic and an oversimplified conception of sports and sport experiences. We know that, when people live much of their lives in and around sports, their characters and behaviours, positive or negative, are related to sport participation in some way.

When we consider sports and socialization, it is helpful to know that different sports involve different experiences and consequences. For example, what occurs in connection with power and performance sports is quite different from what occurs in connection with pleasure and participation sports. The visibility and popularity of power and performance sports today in many societies are related to issues of power and ideology: these sports fit the interests of people who have the power and wealth to sponsor and promote sports.

The most informative research on what happens in sports deals with (1) the everyday experiences of people who play sports, (2) the social worlds created around sports, and (3) community and cultural processes, especially in connection with the ideological messages associated with sports in society. As we listen to the voices of those who participate in sports, look in-depth at how they live their lives in connection with sports, and pay special attention to the ideological messages associated with sports, we learn more about sports and socialization.

Most scholars who study sports in society now see sports as sites for socialization experiences, rather than as causes of specific socialization outcomes. This distinction recognizes that powerful and memorable experiences may occur in connection with sports, and it recognizes that these experiences take on meaning only through social relationships that occur in particular social and cultural contexts. Therefore, the most useful research in the sociology of sport focuses on the social processes through which socialization occurs.

SUGGESTED READINGS

Note: In addition to the following references, we suggest that readers consult the studies summarized in this chapter; many have good discussions of socialization issues and bibliographies that identify other useful sources.

Coakley, J. 1996. Socialization through sports. In *The child and adolescent athlete* (pp. 353–63), edited by O. Bar-Or, Vol. 6 of *The Encyclopaedia of Sports Medicine*—a publication of the IOC Medical Commission. London: Blackwell Science (an overview of research on the impact of sport participation in people's lives; a focus on new research approaches to studying socialization).

Coakley, J., and P. Donnelly, eds. 1999. *Inside sports.* Routledge, London (twenty-two articles that summarize qualitative research projects on socialization and sports; written especially for beginning students, these original articles focus on the processes of becoming involved in sports, developing an identity as an athlete, doing sports, and then facing life beyond the playing field).

Donnelly, P. 2000. Interpretive approaches to the sociology of sport. In *Handbook of sports studies* (pp.77–91), edited by J. Coakley and E. Dunning. London: Sage (an overview of the emergence and development of interpretive sociology; examples of research using interpretive approaches and discussion of the impact of these approaches on research in the sociology of sport).

Dunk, T. 1991. *It's a working man's town: Male working class culture.* Montreal & Kingston: McGill-Queen's University Press (this study of the male working-class culture in Thunder Bay, Ontario, contains a great deal of information about leisure time and sports, and their meaning in this culture; Tuesday night softball (lob-ball) is a particular focus, and one chapter is devoted to this and weekend tournaments).

Lowes, M. 1999. *Inside the sports pages: Work routines, professional ideologies, and the manufacture of sports news.* Toronto: University of Toronto Press (Lowes spent time studying the sports department of a major city newspaper in Canada that he calls (anonymously) the *Big City Examiner*; he interviewed and hung out with the sportswriters and editor, talked to the people they talked to, and explored the ways in which sports news is produced each day).

Robidoux, M. 2001. *Men at play: A working understanding of professional hockey.* Montreal & Kingston: McGill-Queen's University Press (this book is, we believe, the first Canadian sociology of sport book to be nominated for a Governor General's Award; the nomination is well deserved for this insightful ethnography of the working lives of professional hockey players in the AHL).

Stebbins, R. 1987. *Canadian football: The view from the helmet.* London, ON: Centre for Social and Humanistic Studies, University of Western Ontario (explores Canadian football from the players' perspectives at the university, junior, and CFL [professional] levels, considering players' routines, the games, and careers, and placing analysis in the context of Canadian society).

Theberge, N. 2000. *Women's ice hockey and the politics of gender.* Albany, NY: State University of New York Press (this study of a leading women's hockey team in Ontario is the first of its kind; no previous research has explored women's experiences in team sports from the inside, and Theberge provides insights into various issues, especially the construction of community and experiences of physicality).

 WEBSITE RESOURCES

Note: Websites often change. The following URLs were current when this book was printed. Please check our Online Learning Centre website (www.mcgrawhill.ca/college/coakley) for updates, as well as for additional resources and study tools.

www.SportsEthicsInstitute.org (the Sports Ethics Institute is a nonprofit organization dedicated to promoting moral development in and through sports; associated with The Ethics Center at the University of South Florida)

www.sportinsociety.org/ (Center for the Study of Sport in Society; click on "Athletes in Service to America" and "Urban Youth Sports" to learn about how the CSSS is using sports to facilitate the development of young people in urban areas where resources are scarce and needs are great)

www.ausport.gov.au (the Australian Sports Commission outlines the goals of programmes for young people, mature people, people with disabilities, and others.

www.nd.edu/~cscc/ (the Mendelson Center for Sports, Character & Community, at the University of Notre Dame, provides reliable information about character and community development through sports)

(Ron Chapple/Taxi/Gettty Images)

Sports and Children

Are organized programmes worth the effort?

Somewhere along the way we developed a mistrust of idle time. Children became an investment; it cost money to join the classes and courses and sports that are supposed to turn them into well-rounded little human beings. It took adult time to drive and wait, and, well, if you have to be there anyway, you may as well get involved. Time is money, money is time. And if the child is the investment, what, then, is the return on that investment? Certificates, badges, trophies—perhaps even a professional career. There is simply no time for play in such a serious undertaking.

—**Roy MacGregor, author,** *The Seven AM Practice: Stories of Family Life* **(1996)**

Unless we pay attention to poverty-stricken children, our culture will fall apart. We already see the beginning of it. If we are not careful, the children who have never played games will inherit the earth, and that will be a joyless earth.

—**Les McDonald, president of the International Triathlon Union**

 Online Learning Centre Resources

Visit *Sports in Society's* Online Learning Centre at **www.mcgrawhill.ca/college/coakley** for additional information and study material for this chapter.

When, how, and to what end children play sports are issues that concern families, neighbourhoods, communities, and even national and international organizations. When sociologists study these issues, they focus on how children's experiences vary with the types of programmes or settings in which they play sports and with the cultural contexts in which they play. Since the early 1970s, the research done by sociologists and others has had a strong impact on the ways people think about and even organize youth sports. Parents, coaches, and programme administrators today are much more aware of the questions and issues that they must consider when evaluating organized youth sport programmes. Many of these people have used research findings to create and change organized programmes to better serve the interests of children.

This chapter deals with five major topics:

1. The origin and development of organized youth sports
2. Problems in adult-organized youth sports, and "made in Canada" solutions
3. Children in high-performance sports
4. Commonly asked sociological questions about youth sports, including
   - When are children ready to play organized competitive sports?
   - What are the dynamics of family relationships in connection with organized youth sports?
   - How do social factors influence youth sport experiences?
5. Trends in children's sports today, and recommendations for change

Throughout the chapter, the underlying question that guides our discussion is this: is there sufficent evidence to show that organized youth sports are worth all the time, money, and effort put into them? We asked this question as our children moved through childhood, and we continue to ask it as we talk with parents and work with coaches and policymakers who have made extensive commitments to youth sports.

ORIGIN AND DEVELOPMENT OF ORGANIZED YOUTH SPORTS

The way youth sports developed in anglophone Canada is quite similar to Britain and other countries in the Commonwealth (e.g., Australia), and to the United States. However, the development of youth sports in parts of Quebec was quite different. Also, ice hockey, particularly with the influence of the National Hockey League (NHL), has had a fairly distinct pattern of development. Canada has also led the way in efforts to resolve some widely recognized problems in adult-organized sports for children.

Modern organized sports emerged in British Public (private) Schools during the second quarter of the nineteenth century, where they became a mandatory aspect of character training (see chapter 14). By the last decade of the nineteenth century, organized sports and physical activity began to spread beyond the elite schools to inner-city children and youth. With no compulsory secondary education for poor children, this period of increasing urbanization and industrialization in Canadian cities led to the labelling of unemployed male working-class youth as a social problem. Working on the assumption that "the Devil makes work for idle hands," ministers, who had often been educated at private schools, began to establish programmes of sports and physical activity under the tenets of the "social gospel" (Howell and Lindsay, 1981).

Church leagues and the YMCA were followed by other organizations (the Boy Scouts, the Catholic Youth Organization, ethnic community clubs) that attempted to combine sports and physical activity with aspects of character and moral training. Unlike the upper-class youth who originally participated in school organized activities, and who were expected to be the future leaders in industry, the military, and the professions, character training for inner-city youth meant "respect for authority, punctuality, and the acceptance of external discipline. The virtues of following rules were explicitly emphasized, but there were few opportunities for the self-organization and leadership [as] in the private schools" (Hall, A., et al., 1991, p. 197). Critical sociologists refer to this as a social control response, since it was developed to deal with a perceived *social problem*; some still view aspects of organized youth sports (e.g., "midnight basketball") as a form of social control (Andrews and Pitter, 1997).

By World War II, adult-organized youth sports in the form of urban playground leagues and junior ice hockey were fairly well established in anglophone Canada. In more rural areas of Quebec, the influence of the Catholic clergy resulted in a different pattern of development. Anglophones ran most of the major sport organizations in Canada, and the francophone Quebec clergy felt that anglo-controlled sports could lead to assimilation for Quebec youth,[1] especially loss of language and religion. However, sports were much too attractive to young boys to be banned, so the clergy created a separate sport system with more emphasis on pleasure and participation than power and performance. The influence of the clergy was less pronounced in the larger urban areas of Quebec, and youth participation in power and performance sports was well established (Bellefleur, 1986, 1997; Harvey, 1988). This situation in rural Quebec lasted until the Quiet Revolution of the 1960s and 1970s.

There were exceptions to these patterns of development, but this was the general cultural context in which organized youth sport programmes were developed after World War II. As the first wave of the Baby Boom generation moved through childhood during the 1950s and 1960s, organized youth sports grew dramatically. Parents entered the scene, eager to have the characters of their sons built through organized competitive sports. Fathers became coaches, managers, and league administrators. Mothers did laundry and became chauffeurs and fast-food cooks, so that their sons were always ready for practices and games.

Most programmes were for boys eight to fourteen years old and emphasized competition as preparation for future occupational success. Until the 1970s, girls' interests in sports were largely ignored. Girls were relegated to arena seats and bleachers during their brothers' games. Then the women's movement, the fitness movement, and government legislation prohibiting sex discrimination all came together to stimulate the development of new sport programmes for girls (see chapter 8). During the 1980s, these programmes grew rapidly to the point that, in some sports, girls had nearly as many opportunities as boys. However, their participation rates have remained lower than rates for boys—for reasons we discuss later in this chapter (and in chapter 8).

Participation in organized youth sports is now an accepted part of the process of growing up in Canada, especially among the middle and upper classes, where family and community resources enable adults to sponsor, organize, and administer many programmes for their children. Parents now encourage both sons and daughters to participate in sports. Some parents may question the merits of programmes in which winning seems to be more important than overall child development, while other parents look for the win-oriented programmes, hoping their children will become the winners. Some parents also encourage their children to engage in noncompetitive physical activities outside of organized programmes, and many children participate in these activities as alternatives to adult-supervised organized sports. Social scientists have begun to study alternative sports, which have become increasingly popular in the lives of children in many countries around the world (Beal, 1999; Midol and Broyer, 1995; Rinehart, 1998).

---

[1] Assimilation and social control are also considered, by critical sociologists, to be a part of the motivation for introducing organized sports to youth in First Nations and immigrant communities (see chapter 9).

Organized Sports and Changes Related to Society, Family, and Childhood

Beginning in the 1950s, an increasing amount of children's free time and sport participation has occurred in organized programmes supervised by adults (Adler and Adler, 1998). This astonishing growth is related to a whole series of changes that have occurred in Canadian society, in Canadian families and relationships between parents and their children, and in Canadian sports since World War II. For example, in Canadian society:

- The return of troops from the various theatres of war led to the Baby Boom, and a large population of young people in Canada from the late 1940s through the 1960s. This was complemented by a significant increase in immigration during this period (Donnelly, 2000, p. 170);
- The housing needs of young families led to a massive growth in the development of suburbs, and suburbs—with their new sport and recreation facilities—became one of the major sites of adult-organized youth involvement (Donnelly, 2000, p. 170);
- There was a period "of unprecedented prosperity in Canada," and that prosperity was used in the provision of sport and recreation facilities in the new suburbs and in urban areas (Hall, A., et al., 1991, p. 198).

In terms of family life and parent-child relations, there were other significant changes that are especially relevant for the growth of adult-organized youth sports.

First, the return of (primarily male) troops led to restructuring of work, with jobs that had been carried out by women during the war being reclaimed by men. While this helped create what was considered the "typical" family (working father, stay-at-home mother, children), it was also connected with the new interest in child development (cf., Dr. Spock), and created, for middle-class and more affluent working-class families, available time for volunteer work, which often involved children's (especially boys') activities (Donnelly, 2000. p. 170).[2]

Second, the number of families with both parents working outside the home has increased dramatically, especially since the early 1970s. This created a growing demand for organized and adult-supervised after-school and summertime programmes.[3] Organized sports are especially popular among the activities provided in these programmes, because many parents think that sports offer their children opportunities to simultaneously have fun, learn adult values, and acquire skills valued in their peer groups. In many cases in Canada, parents were more involved in the lives of their children during this period because they were concerned about giving children opportunities that had not been available during their own childhoods—in Europe during the War, or in Canada during the Depression. They promoted social mobility for their children in various ways, from education to sports (Hall, A., et al., 1991, p. 198-99).

Third, since the early 1980s, there have been significant changes in what it means to be a "good parent." Good parents, in the minds of many people today, are those who can account for the whereabouts and behaviour of their children twenty-four hours a day. This expectation

---

[2] This 1950s–60s period of the "typical" family was short-lived for some, and non-existent for many others. However, it was enshrined by a number of U.S. television series (also seen in Canada). The growth of the women's movement in the late 1960s and 1970s, combined with changes in the economy that made it more difficult for families to thrive on a single income, led to the end of this era of the "typical" family. Note also that Spock's *Baby and Child Care* was first published in 1945 and, despite many imitators, had sold 28 million copies by 1977.

[3] In a recent trend in some communities, martial arts academies have made arrangements to pick up children directly from school and to drive them to the *dojo* for lessons. This service frees parents from an additional chauffeuring responsibility.

is a new component of parenting ideology. In recent years it has led many parents to seek organized, adult-supervised programmes for their children because they emphasize the control and leadership of adult coaches, have predictable schedules, and provide parents with measurable indicators of their children's accomplishments. When their children succeed, parents can make the claim that they are meeting their responsibilities.

Fourth, there has been a growing belief that informal, child-controlled activities often provide occasions for children to cause trouble. In its extreme form, this belief leads adults to view children as threats to social order. Many adults see organized sports as ideal activities for social control, keeping active children constructively occupied, out of trouble, and under the control of adults.

Fifth, many parents have come to see the world outside the home as a dangerous place for children. They regard organized sports as safe alternatives to hanging out or playing informal activities away from home. This belief is so strong that it often persists in the face of information about coercive coaching methods, the predatory behaviour of some coaches (Connelly, 1999; Donnelly and Sparks, 1997), and occasionally high injury rates in organized youth sports (Lyman et al., 1998; Micheli, 1990).

Sixth, an increasingly educated population of parents developed a growing belief in the value of sports for health and physical fitness, and adopted the elite private school belief that sports promoted the development of important values, attitudes, and habits that would carry over into other aspects of children's lives (Hall, A., et al., 1991, p. 188). Both parents and educators developed an increasing belief in the benefits of coaching and teaching for more rapid development of skill and for safety (and as a necessity to reach the high-performance or professional levels of sports). They were supported in this by "conventional wisdom in psychology, spread not only through schools but through the popular

media and self-help books, [which] emphasized the benefits of an early introduction to skill development and learning" (Hall, A., et al., 1991, p. 200).

Seventh, sports also changed during this period. High-performance sports became increasingly sophisticated and high profile, and professional sports became a major part of the entertainment industry.

The visibility of high-performance and professional sports increased people's awareness of organized sports as a part of culture. As children watch sports on television, listen to parents and friends talk about sports, and hear about the wealth and fame of popular athletes, they often become interested in playing the sports that others define as official and important. For this reason, organized sports with expert, adult coaches become attractive to many children. When children say they want to be gymnasts or soccer players, parents often look for the nearest organized programme. Therefore, organized youth sports are popular because children enjoy them and see them as activities that will gain them acceptance from peers and parents alike.

Taken together, these seven changes in society, in family and childhood, and in sports, account for much of the increased popularity of organized youth sports. Furthermore, these changes help us to understand why parents are willing to invest so many family resources into the organized sport participation of their children. Many of these programmes are quite expensive. The amount of money that parents spend on participation fees, equipment, and other things defined as necessary in many programmes has skyrocketed in recent years (Ferguson, 1999). For example, when Jay Coakley and his students interviewed the parents of elite youth hockey players who had traveled to Colorado for a major tournament in the late 1990s, they discovered that the families had spent at least US$5,000 and up to nearly US$20,000 per year to support their sons' hockey participation. As they discussed their expenses for fees, equipment, travel, and other things, many of them shook their heads and said, "I can't believe we're spending this much, but we are."

These seven changes also help us explain other forms of parental commitment to organized sports. When children participate in these programmes, parents often become personal chauffeurs and support personnel. They serve as coaches, referees, and umpires. They launder uniforms, keep track of equipment, prepare special meals, alter work and holiday schedules, and sit in bad weather and stuffy or cold sport facilities to watch their children.

One of the negative consequences of some of these changes is that parents in working-class and lower-income households may be defined as irresponsible or careless parents because they are unable to pay the financial price for controlling their children, as wealthier parents do. Furthermore, they are not as likely to have the time and other resources needed to participate in and provide the labour for organized sport programmes. (See chapter 10 for data on sport participation and social class.) In this way, organized sports for children become linked to ideological and political issues and to debates about "family values" in the society at large.

PROBLEMS IN ADULT-ORGANIZED YOUTH SPORTS AND "MADE IN CANADA" SOLUTIONS

The growth of adult-organized children's sports in Canada between the 1970s and the 1990s—estimated at approximately 2 million children in 1978 and 2.5 million in 1991—initially coincided with an important period of social criticism. Social movements such as the women's movement, the civil rights movement, and the anti-[Vietnam] war movement adopted an anti-authoritarian stance which involved critiques of the military, education, government, and even sports. Recognition that children's sports were being run by adults in a particularly joyless way, often in exactly the same authoritarian manner as adult high-performance

and professional sports, made children's sports a target of criticism. In democratic terms, there was also a recognition that if there were positive aspects of participation in sports—ranging from benefits to physical and mental health to the pleasures of participation—then such benefits should be available to all children.

Michael Smith, who taught at York University, identified four assumptions that appeared to dominate children's organized programmes in the early 1970s (1975, p. ix-x):

- Children play sports to entertain adults.
- Games and sports for kids must be organized and controlled by adults if they are to be of real value.
- Kids are miniature adults.
- The real value in sports lies in learning to be a winner, people can be divided into winners and losers, and sport[s are vehicles] to make sure you (or your kids) end up in the right group.

Each of these four assumptions is considered in more detail here, together with the steps taken in Canada in an attempt to solve the issues. It is striking, however, to note the extent to which many of these issues persist over a quarter of a century later.

Assumption 1: Children Play Sports to Entertain Adults

This is an ongoing issue and is clearly a double-edged sword. In our ongoing research, many young athletes that we have talked with expect their parents to attend every game or competition, and feel disappointed or neglected if they are not there. However, a few told us that they are sometimes embarrassed by one or both of their parents, who yell at them and at referees, coaches, and other players, especially when the parents say inappropriate things. A few others told us that the constant presence of one or more parents, even at practices, became a problem as they grew older and wanted to have time with

"Have you ever considered that maybe I'd like this to remain a repressed childhood memory?"
....

Many children who play sports do not enjoy videotapes of their games, meets, and matches. They would rather remember their experiences in their own terms. Too often, the tapes are used to identify mistakes and make youth sports more important than children want them to be.

friends away from their parents. And others noted that their parents (one or both) were hypercritical or judgmental, and used their presence at competitions, and sometimes practices, to generate a list of mistakes made by the athlete, which would all be pointed out to the athletes on their way home.

Why do parents attend their children's games? Certainly, practices are sometimes seen as a "babysitting" opportunity by parents, who may use them to carry out some errands or chores, but attendance at community and club-level games and competitions has become a ritual.[4] By attending, parents are able to demonstrate to other parents and to their children that

they are "good" parents (see preceding section on new demands on parents) who are prepared to support their children's activities and spend "quality time" with their children. They are also able to "look out" for their children, to ensure their safety and protect them from potential unfairness (see the section, "Major Trends in Youth Sports Today," later in this chapter). Most will cheer for their children and/or their child's team, and they have the opportunity to socialize with other parents. There is nothing wrong with this behaviour—it is a social occasion for parents who meet in the bleachers or the stands, or line their lawn chairs along the touch line, but it is not necessarily entertaining. There may be little pleasure or excitement in watching the ninth game of "beehive" soccer for the season, although most parents agree that the children "look cute."

But while there are positive and supportive aspects to the behaviour, there are also some mixed messages being sent, and some alternatives to consider.

First, in a society increasingly concerned about sedentary behaviour, the messages implicit in parents sitting down to watch their children play are significant. Is participation just for children? This is less an issue for parents who do participate in sports, and/or who spend time playing with their children. Parents' games, or parents' exercise programmes (e.g., a brisk hike around the playing fields) during the children's game may be healthy alternatives for organizers of children's sports to consider.

Second, watching your child is supportive, but it is not necessarily "quality time" since there is little time to interact. A recent report from the American Academy of Pediatrics provides an estimate that "by the time they are six years old, the average child will have spent more time watching television than they will talking to their fathers during their entire lifetimes" (Kesterton, 2002, p. A24). We have heard both positive and negative reports from young athletes about "quality time." Looking back, some see the time

---

[4] This is less the case for interschool sports, which are often played during working hours.

spent with one or both parents travelling to and from competitions, or in informal practices and pick-up games together, as enormously rich, fun, and rewarding time. Others grew to dread those times, which they remember as endlessly directive and judgmental.

Third, we wonder how children would feel if their parents were always present, sitting in lawn chairs around the school playground at recess, or standing at the back of the classroom. Time spent with children is extremely important; time spent watching children while they are doing something else may be less so, and some parents are now beginning to question whether they should be at every possible occasion in their children's lives.

Assumption 2: Games and Sports for Kids Must Be Organized and Controlled by Adults If They Are to Be of Real Value

Adults have a number of appropriate concerns about children's informal and/or unsupervised play. They are concerned about safety and want to protect children from bullying and accidents (see section, "Major Trends in Youth Sports Today," later in this chapter). They are concerned about instruction—that children will learn sport skills in an appropriate and safe manner. (After all, who would want their children to learn to swim without supervision and instruction?) And they hope that their children will receive messages about character development as a result of their participation.

> Sometimes I think that by being so involved in our kids' sports, we dilute their experience. After all, it's not *their* win, it's *our* win. Do all the valuable lessons—losing, striking out, missing the winning shot—have the same impact when Mom and Dad are there to immediately say it's okay?...As parents, we know that at some point we need to make it *their* game, *their* recital, *their* grades. If we share every element of their lives, we're cheating them out of part of it....As hard as it is to risk missing her first home run, or not being there to comfort him after the missed foul shot, at some point we need to take ourselves out of their ball game. Because that is what good parents do.
>
> —(Keri, 2000, p. 55)

However, since the early 1970s, many critics of adult-organized sports for children have agreed with Bill L'Heureux, then a professor at the University of Western Ontario: "The only problem with kids' sports is adults." Two major solutions to this problem have usually been offered: *ban the adults* or *educate the adults*, although other alternatives have also been recommended.

Proposals to *ban adults* from children's games may be traced to Devereaux (1976), and to a somewhat romanticized view of children's play that does not take into account the fact that supervision and guidance may sometimes be appropriate and necessary. Devereaux's film, *Two Ball Games* (1976), provides a direct and unfavourable comparison between an informal game of baseball in a public park and a Little League game. His argument, that adult involvement removes both fun and important educational experiences from children's play, was widely supported. Jay Coakley, who has carried out the most systematic comparison between the two variations of children's sports (see the Reflect on Sports box, "Different Experiences: Informal Player-Controlled Sports versus Organized, Adult-Controlled Sports," pp. 137–138) points out that each has advantages and disadvantages.

Apart from pick-up ball hockey and basketball games played in driveways and neighbourhood streets and playgrounds, there seem to be fewer and fewer opportunities for children to interact, learn, and play sports in contexts other than those directly supervised by adults. These opportunities have become increasingly rare, at least for middle-class children, since the 1970s (cf., Elkind, 1981), with one very obvious exception: so-called "alternative sports."

Alternative sports also trace their origins to the democratizing movements of the 1960s and 1970s. They emerged as "new games" (e.g., earth ball) in the U.S. (cf., Fluegelman, 1976) and as "cooperative games" (e.g., parachute games) in Canada (Orlick, 1978), countercultural alternatives to what were seen as the damaging effects of competition. Many of these activities have become a standard part of the physical education curriculum in elementary schools in Canada, and are often played in camps and daycare centres. Other alternative sports were adapted, created, or developed by teenagers and young adults: surfing, ultimate Frisbee, freestyle skiing, skateboarding, and, more recently, windsurfing, snowboarding, and mountain biking. "The playful and expressive qualities of these activities were accentuated precisely because the dominant sport forms lacked such characteristics and seemed overly rationalized, technologized, and bureaucratized" (Donnelly, 1988, p. 74). Of course, some of these activities have lost some of their original "alternative" meaning and have been incorporated, at least in part, by the dominant sport forms they originally opposed (e.g., snowboarding at the Olympic Games). But, for the most part, they retain the characteristics of informal, player-controlled games—action, personal involvement, and the opportunity to reaffirm friendships. (See the section on alternative sports in "Major Trends in Youth Sports Today," later in this chapter.)

The majority of children enjoy their participation in adult-organized sports, and proposals to ban adults were never pursued. However, the problems remained, and proposals to educate adults came to be seen as a more realistic alternative to banning adults. In addition to the points made above about when it is appropriate to have adult supervision and instruction, it also

became apparent that the structures of adult-organized children's sports were too well-established to dismantle them easily. Once this was recognized, academics, educators, and other policymakers set about devising ways of providing appropriate information to adults involved in youth sport programmes. It should be pointed out that Canada was among the first countries to formally recognize that problems existed, and to start to develop policies and procedures for their resolution. Several national conferences in the 1970s began to identify problems with adult-organized youth sports, and made a number of recommendations about adult involvement (Orlick and Botterill, 1975, pp. 161–63, 173–75).

One of the most significant "made in Canada" solutions was the development of coaching education. The Coaching Association of Canada (CAC) was formed in 1971 during a significant period of development in Canadian sports as the country geared up to host the 1976 Montreal Olympic Games. Its establishment coincided with the emerging critique of children's organized sport programmes, and the CAC, with its mission to "enhance the experiences of all Canadian athletes through quality coaching" (www.coach.ca), was seen as a key to resolving some of the problems. The National Coaching Certification Programme (NCCP), started by the CAC in 1974, established five levels of accomplishment in coaching—Level 1 (novice) to Level 5 (national)—and provided training programmes at each level based on theoretical, technical, and practical elements of coaching. For the purposes of children's sports, the parent volunteers who formed the backbone of children's organized sports programmes, were encouraged to achieve at least NCCP Level 1 certification. After struggling with a number of grandparenting issues (e.g., should a coach who has been coaching for fifteen years be obliged to take a novice coaching course), the certification became more and more accepted, recommendations to enrol for the courses became stronger, and holding NCCP Level 1 has now become mandatory for volunteer coaches in many youth sport organizations. Certification, especially if the course is well run, ensures that coaches have at least a minimal knowledge about medical, physiological, psychological, and social issues regarding child development and participation. Some coaches return to their old habits once they have achieved certification, and attempts to evaluate or mandate continuing education for coaches in a volunteer system are quite problematic. However, anecdotal reports suggest that the increasing numbers of women coaches in children's sport programmes are benefiting more than males from the certification programmes.

Various programmes and publications were developed to further the education of parents and coaches: for example, Taylor's *How to Be an Effective Coach* (1975); Orlick and Botterill's widely read *Every Kid Can Win* (1975); the Canadian Council on Children and Youth's extremely popular pamphlet and poster series, "Fair Play Codes for Children in Sport" (1979), which listed appropriate behaviour for all involved in children's sports—parents, coaches, officials, spectators, and players; Spink's *Give Your Kids a Sporting Chance* (1988); and the Bylsmas' *So Your Son Wants to Play in the NHL?* (1998), which attempted to bring a note of caution to parents with NHL ambitions for their sons. However, there have also been a number of books during this same period of time that have a somewhat different educational purpose: to teach parents how to turn their children into professional or Olympic athletes (e.g., Bompa, 2000; Duran, 2002; Petkevich, 1989).

The second most significant "made in Canada" solution to educating adults, and resolving some of the issues involved in adult-organized sports for children, was the re-invention of "house leagues." Although minor hockey had been organized before the 1970s into house leagues and the more elite "travel leagues," the house leagues became a target of criticism in the early 1970s. Conducting what was called

"change agent research," Dick Moriarty and Jim Duthie at the University of Windsor videotaped parents and coaches at house-league hockey games, then interviewed those parents and coaches about the values of youth sports and confronted them with the often contradictory videotape evidence. At the same time, they began to identify what we now call "best practices" to ensure that children have quality experiences in youth sports: making sure that teams were created with relatively equal levels of skill (i.e., make sure that one or two teams do not draft all the best players), ensuring that all players have approximately equal amounts of playing time (recognizing that all parents pay the same registration fee to have their children play in a league, and that children do not learn skills when they are sitting on the bench), and encouraging leagues to begin to emphasize skill development and to de-emphasize the outcome of games.

The Windsor and Essex County Leagues in southwestern Ontario began to introduce these changes in hockey, and the changes slowly began to spread across Canada and to other sports. Baseball, basketball, lacrosse, and soccer introduced this new concept of house leagues, emphasizing enjoyment and activity for young players. The change has not been a complete success. Anecdotal evidence suggests that some house-league coaches attempt to manipulate the player draft or give their best players more playing time (especially during playoffs and finals), and our observations of house-league parents suggests that some do not behave as well as might be expected. However, in general, the changes have greatly improved the involvement and experience of less-talented players, and the philosophy has even spread to individual sports. There are now many recreational programmes in swimming, skating, martial arts, gymnastics, and so on, which encourage skill learning and fun rather than competition.

Another "made in Canada" solution to educating adults emerged during the 1980s when there was a massive decline in participation by boys in hockey. Between 1983 and 1989, boys' registration declined 17.4 percent.[5] The decline was even more marked in Quebec where registrations dropped by 47 percent between 1974 and 1990, from a high of 111,960 to a low of 57,340 (Scanlan, 2002). While there were many reasons for the decline (e.g., the cost of hockey, demographic changes in Canadian society), a growing concern of parents was violence and the related fear of injury.[6] The response in Quebec was to begin to introduce "fair play" leagues (leagues that reward fair play, by awarding additional points for fewer penalties, and punish illegal play) and non-contact leagues. These forms of hockey have also spread across Canada. The solution to this issue started with "educated" parents, concerned about their children's safety, but led to the education of other parents and adults involved in organizing youth hockey. The safety issues have also led to concerns about skill development—especially recognition of the declining number of Canadian players in the NHL, and the fact that few Canadian players are among the scoring leaders in the NHL. The Open Ice Summit, chaired by Wayne Gretzky in Toronto in 1998, addressed the issue of practice time versus competition, and its recommendations are slowly leading to more emphasis on skill development in minor hockey.

Finally, and most recently, adults who organize sports in Canada (and especially hockey) have had to respond to two major child sexual

> Little leagues too often make little men out of little boys.
> —Dick Beddoes, sportswriter, TV Ontario's *Speaking Out* (1978)

abuse crises: the Graham James case and the Maple Leaf Gardens scandal (sexual abuse and sexual harassment in sports are discussed in more detail in chapter 7). Police checks and a number of educational programmes (e.g., STOP, "Speak Out," and "Respect" programmes) have been developed in response to this problem.

Educating the adults is an ongoing issue in children's sports programmes. The steps that have been taken in Canada have helped to ameliorate some of the problems, but anyone who follows children's sports is aware that we have a long way to go. A number of children's sport organizations have introduced parent education programmes, have encouraged parents to sign agreements and charters regarding their behaviour, and have even gone so far as to ban parents from hockey arenas, figure skating practices, and so on. But still there are problems. In hockey, 10,000 referees quit every year in Canada (one-third the total number of referees), partly as a result of the abuse received from parents, coaches, and players.[7]

Assumption 3: Kids Are Miniature Adults

Problems occur when adults fail to take into account that the athletes involved at this level of sports are children. Some problems are associated with the fact that children are smaller and not as strong as adults; others result when adults fail to consider children's stage of cognitive and physical development. Many of these problems are addressed in the upcoming section on "Children in High-Performance Sports," but two points are worth considering here.

---

[5] A small part of this loss was taken up by girls, whose registration in hockey increased 400 percent between 1989 and 1999 (from 10,000 to 40,000).

[6] The 1974 McMurtry Report in Ontario highlighted the growing concerns about violence in the game. As a result of all of these changes, and because of a massive increase in girls' participation, soccer passed hockey as the sport with the highest participation rate in Canada in 1990 (Scanlan, 2002).

[7] In Dartmouth, Nova Scotia, "[T]he dropout rate among officials is . . . one third of the national average," as a result of the introduction of a fair play league (Scanlan, 2002, p. 256).

First, how are children treated during their participation? Is there enough quality practice time to develop the skills necessary to participate? (Does hockey have too many competitions and too little practice? Does diving have too much practice and not enough competitions?) Do referees see educating children about the rules of the game (written and unwritten) as a part of their duties? Do league and sport administrators try to deal fairly with children with regard to transfers, sanctions, appeals, and so on, while also having to deal with their parents? Do coaches see it as their task to yell criticism about the mistakes young players invariably make, or to be supportive and explain how mistakes can be rectified? And do parents know that it is inappropriate to yell the same types of things at children's games as they do at Calgary Stampeders or Montreal Canadiens games?

Second, when children are playing, are the equipment and rules adapted to their age and ability levels? Are they playing with a small-size soccer ball or basketball? Is the net lower and the basket bigger than it is for adults in basketball? Are goalies in hockey and soccer expected to protect the same size goals as adults? Is the playing area smaller to encourage more action and involvement? Many creative changes in equipment and playing areas have been made for children, but more need to be made. With regard to rules, are children playing by the same rules as adults, and is this appropriate? The answer will vary depending on the sport and the level of competition, and some sports have been more creative than others here. For example, baseball created T-ball to overcome the problem of young children pitching and hitting pitched balls, introduced pitching machines into games, and is currently working on a number of modified and more active forms of baseball to attract participants at a time of declining registrations in the sport.[8]

---

[8] These issues of adaptation can be controversial, and some adults argue that children need to play with full-size equipment and formal rules in order to become used to them.

Assumption 4: The Real Value in Sports Lies in Learning to Be a Winner, People Can Be Divided into Winners and Losers, and Sport[s Are Vehicles] to Make Sure You (or Your Kids) End Up in the Right Group

Michael Smith's final assumption points to a struggle that is still alive in the field of children's sports and physical activity. On one side of the struggle, there are those, often educators, who advocate children's involvement in a variety of healthy forms of physical activity because of the established mental, physical, and social benefits that result. They advocate both competitive and non-competitive forms of activity, but sometimes emphasize the non-competitive and cooperative forms of activity because of the social benefits of cooperation (cf., Kohn, 1992). They also point out the "exclusive" nature of competition and the disturbing dropout rate in many competitive organized sports. As Canadian sport psychologists Terry Orlick of the University of Ottawa and Cal Botterill of the University of Winnipeg point out: "It's ridiculous to promote participation on the one hand, and then to cut interested individuals from the team, or to in any way limit their participation" (1975, p. 17). If children are being cut from programmes because of their lack of size or skills (instead of being taught those skills), and no alternatives are available, participation is reduced.

On the other side of the struggle, there are those who support the view that "people can be divided into winners and losers" and who want their children to participate in organized competitive sports because they believe it will give them a competitive advantage in life. Primary school teachers often hear from such parents advocating this view when they attempt to run cooperative educational programmes in their classrooms; and some analysts have argued that the growth in community sports, especially for younger males, occurred precisely because professional educators tended to discourage or de-emphasize competition in primary schools, and to play down the intensity of interschool competitions in high school.

Both sides in this struggle have seen some successes and failures. On the participation side, the development of house leagues and the widespread use of cooperative games have helped to promote participation; and interschool sports have, in general, managed to maintain an emphasis on participation and education rather than just competition. However, in the mid-1970s, many municipal Parks and Recreation Departments in Canada stopped organizing competitive sport programmes, ostensibly because of the criticism of and problems in such programmes, but cutting them was also a cost-saving move for municipalities. The loss of these low-cost opportunities to participate (which still exist in a number of U.S. cities) forced non-school-organized competitive sports for children into the non-profit and private sectors, where it became more difficult to control the problems that existed. Organized competitive sport programmes emphasizing competition are now an important part of most communities in Canada, and the introduction of house leagues has resulted in the provision of a wide range of participation and competition opportunities. But the problems outlined above still exist at the competitive levels—poor coaching, problem parents, high injury rates, and so on. As noted in the Reflect on Sports box, "Informal, Player-Controlled Sports versus Organized, Adult-Controlled Sports" on pp. 137–138, children themselves often de-emphasize competition, both in alternative sports and in other informal, player-controlled sports.

CHILDREN IN HIGH-PERFORMANCE SPORTS

At the Montreal Olympic Games in 1976, a tiny 14-year-old Romanian gymnast named Nadia Comaneci completed a number of amazing routines and was awarded the first ("perfect") scores of 10.0 ever recorded in the sport. She, and the large number of medals that were won by East German athletes, drew attention in the West to the sport system that had been developed in Eastern Europe and the Soviet Union. Doug Gilbert (1976), a sportswriter for the *Montreal Gazette*, described the system:

- Early exposure of children to physical education and a wide range of physical activities
- A broad base of participants in sports and physical activity
- Early identification of athletic talent
- Intensive and specialized training for those identified

East European and Cuban success in Montreal, combined with Canada's hurt pride as the first Olympic host not to win a gold medal and other political factors, triggered interest in the new system. Sport scientists began to conduct research into talent prediction and early specialization in sports, and sport organizations began to recruit younger and younger athletes. The early success of the female gymnasts, and victories for young female athletes in sports such as figure skating and swimming, provided an additional incentive for early involvement and specialization. Such a system was not completely new to Canada since it existed to some extent in hockey, but early intensive involvement was new to most other sports, and problems began to emerge.

By the early 1980s, commentators such as Hart Cantelon of Queen's University (1981) were beginning to identify the new participants as "child athletic workers," and their participation as "child labour," and as a social problem. Following Cantelon's lead, in 1985, Peter Donnelly began collecting data on these problems. He conducted a series of retrospective interviews with retired high-performance athletes in Canada. The 45 former athletes (16 male, 29 female) represented a variety of sports and claimed to have had successful careers; all had intensive involvement in the sport during their childhood and adolescence; all were given every opportunity to address both positive and negative aspects of their careers; and each spent approximately ten times more time on the negative than the positive.

They reported a variety of problems that they connected directly to their early intensive involvement and specialization. These included:

- Family concerns—problems such as sibling rivalry and parental pressure
- Social relationships—missed important occasions and experiences during childhood and adolescence
- Coach-athlete relationships—authoritarian and abusive (emotional, physical, sexual) relationships, especially in male coach/female athlete relationships
- Educational concerns—any achievements were earned in spite of the sport and school systems, not because of them
- Physical and psychological problems—injuries, stress, and burnout
- Drug and dietary problems— some experiences of drug use, widespread concern about eating disorders
- Retirement—widespread adjustment difficulties, especially when retirement was not voluntary

> **Last summer I was skating five hours a day, five days a week. I really wanted to try something else. I just . . . got sick of it. My parents . . . felt bad because I'd spent so much time and money on it.**
>
> —Megan, age 13, Grosse Point Woods, MI (1999)

These findings have been confirmed by additional informal interviews in Canada (including athletes who had heard or read about the research and approached Donnelly with their own stories) and other countries that adopted the early involvement and specialization model, and have been supplemented by reports in more popular sources (e.g., Ryan, 1995).

Donnelly also asked the former athletes whether they would repeat their careers (10 percent said no, and 65 percent gave a qualified yes—knowing what they know now) and whether they would permit their own children to become involved in intensive training in their sport (40 percent said no, and the 60 percent who said yes suggested that their experiences and knowledge would help them to protect their own children from the problems and provide them with a more positive experience).

As a result of these types of critiques, and especially following an intensive period of criticism about the U.S. women's gymnastics team (their youth, tiny bodies, and stress fractures gave rise to numerous concerns about eating disorders) following the 1992 Barcelona Olympic Games, three sport organizations made rule changes. The Women's Tennis Association (WTA) raised the age for turning professional to sixteen because of the well-publicized burnout of young players such as Tracy Austin, Jennifer Capriati, and Andrea Jaeger; and both women's gymnastics and women's figure skating organizations raised the minimum age for international competition to sixteen. However, we argue that the new age limits are only token changes, and, particularly in gymnastics and figure skating, they have done little to resolve the problems, and may even have made them worse. Extending the age of international competition without changing judging criteria, or introducing any regulations about health, nutrition, or bone density, just forces adolescent girls to attempt to maintain a pre-pubescent body type until they are even older.

Canadian children from all backgrounds, but now most commonly from the middle classes, who have shown talent in hockey, swimming, figure skating, tennis, gymnastics, and so on—all the sports that are invested in an early specialization developmental track—may experience the types of problems outlined above. Gabriela Tymowski, of the University of New Brunswick, has also begun to recognize these problems in recent research (2001a, 2001b). Solving the problems created by early intensive involvement and

REFLECT ON SPORTS

Solving the Problems in Children's High-Performance Sports

There are four possible resolutions to the challenges involved in nurturing the talent of highly talented children *and* assuring their all-round healthy development. Treat the problems as:

- An educational issue
- A children's rights issue
- A child labour issue
- A child welfare issue

Each of these has both advantages and disadvantages in attempting to resolve the problems for children in high-performance sports.

1. *Education:* This approach involves the education of all those adults involved in the lives of elite child athletes about child development issues and maintaining a balance in children's lives. Education is the approach most favoured by sport organizations: it is their response to the widespread criticism of problems in their sports (of which they are well aware), but education is also a response that they are able to control. It also slows the pace of any changes, thus allowing the status quo, with which all those involved (except the children and their parents) are familiar, to continue. Education is a slow process with which to affect social change. Thus, while education is necessary, it does not resolve the problems currently being experienced by many young people in the system. However, education has brought about some changes. For example, the Canadian women's gymnastics team now boasts that it is the oldest, tallest, and heaviest team in world competition, and that that is preferable to winning medals with "anorexic children."

2. *Children's rights:* The children's rights approach forms a bridge between the educational and the following legal responses to the problems. Pat Galasso, who was dean of physical education at the University of Windsor during the period of "change agent research" noted previously, produced one of the first children's rights charters in sports. He proposed (1988, pp. 334–36) that children in sports should have:

- The right to self-determination
- The right to knowledge
- The right to be protected from abuse
- The right to try out for a team or position
- The right to have properly qualified instruction and leadership
- The right to be involved in an environment where opportunity for the development of self-respect, and to be treated with respect, is imperative

While these rights are not exclusive to high-performance sports, enjoyment of these rights would mean a significant change in the structure of sports at that level. Charters only have moral rather than legal standing and therefore are related more to education and political will. However, the International Convention on the Rights of the Child (1989) does provide a legally binding constraint on signatory governments (including Canada and 187 other nations). At least eighteen of the forty-one articles in the convention touch on issues related to sport and physical activity participation, and identify rights that are occasionally or routinely violated in children's high-performance sports (Kidd and Donnelly, 1999). The convention provides a legal means to address violations, and convention challenges remain an unexplored approach in pursuing children's rights in sports.

3. *Child labour:* Several Canadian researchers have argued that children's involvement in high-performance sports is a child labour issue, and that the protections invoked by the laws governing workers and the workplace should be available to young athletes. For example, Beamish and Borowy (1988) argued that the agreement between athletes who qualify for the Athlete Assistance Programme and Sport Canada has all of the characteristics of a labour contract. Bart McGuire, CEO of the WTA, acknowledged the concerns about some young professionals: "If you have both parents who have given up their jobs and are living off the earnings of a player on the tour, the pressure gets

Continued

REFLECT ON SPORTS

Solving the Problems in Children's High-Performance Sports continued

to be a concern....Implicit in the relationship is the fact that if you don't practice for a few days, we don't eat" (cited by Brunt, 1999, p. S1). Since a number of adults (e.g., coaches, medical staff) may depend on the labour and income of young athletes for their livelihood, they may have more of a vested interest in the athlete's performance than in his/her healthy development. However, while children may be earning incomes, and playing in highly work-like environments, the legal system has been slow to adapt to the rapid changes that have occurred in sports, and this is still an area in which it is possible for authorities to deny that children are working. Thus, there are few protections in the form of limits on training time or the number of competitions, enforcement of the time that athletes devote to compulsory education, securing and investing their incomes, or access to health and safety regulations that govern workers and employers in the workplace.

4. *Child welfare:* Another possible legal avenue to pursue is child welfare laws, which have been described as more discretionary than child labour laws. As Tenebaum noted, "When we can reasonably foresee that others will be affected by our actions the law says that we owe them a "duty of care" in terms of how we ought to behave..." (1996, p. 25). This "duty of care" is considerably higher for children because of their special need

for attention and protection. Child welfare laws are intended to protect children from physical harm, negligence, sexual molestation, emotional harm, and abuse, and to ensure that they receive appropriate medical care. All of these protections have been violated in the case of children in high-performance sports. However, the agencies intended to ensure child welfare are usually so overworked with respect to, for example, child abuse, that they are not likely to be eager to investigate complaints involving sports.

From the four possible approaches to resolving the problems for children in high-performance sports, only the educational approach is currently in play—backed up to some extent by growing criticism of the problems and the moral force of children's rights. Perhaps the threat of legal action, internationally as a convention challenge, or provincially in terms of child labour or child welfare violations, would be enough to speed up the changes being brought about by education. However, that seems unlikely while adults continue to profit from child athletes, and more direct legal action may be necessary.

We think that it is probably best not to think of these as choices, but as a four-pronged attack on the problems. We also think that national sport organizations need to begin to make special provisions for children who are involved in high-performance sports. *What do you think?*

---

specialization raises a question of balance. (See the Reflect on Sports box, "Solving the Problems in Children's High-Performance Sports," above.) But that balance is difficult when we consider all of the adults who may have a vested interest in a child's success in sports—parents, coaches, sport administrators, educators, sport scientists, sports medicine staff, agents, and even media personnel (Donnelly, 1997). For some of these individuals, their careers and incomes may depend on a child's

success, and there are even cases of parents who have taken out a second mortgage in order to finance their talented child's sport development. Parents, coaches, and other interested parties are concerned that an overemphasis on the child having a "normal" life may lead to failure to fully develop his/her talent (and miss a chance at the Olympics and/or a career as a highly paid professional athlete), but it is apparent that an overemphasis on the talent can also lead to a variety of problems, from exploitation to burnout. It is precisely this lack of balance that led Donnelly (1993) to suggest that Canadian national team athletes were the survivors, rather than the products, of our high-performance development system, and that we had to find a way to stop "sacrific[ing] children on the altar of international and professional sport success" (p. 120).

SOCIOLOGICAL QUESTIONS ABOUT YOUTH SPORTS

When Are Children Ready to Play Organized Competitive Sports?

Parents ask readiness questions often. They wonder: should they sign their three-year-olds up for T-ball teams, put their five-year-olds on swim teams, and let their eight-year-olds participate in provincial skating competitions? Some want to give their children an early start on an imagined path to athletic glory; others do not want their children to fall behind peers in skills development; still others just want their children to have healthy fun and feel good about their bodies.

Answers to readiness questions are available in the various sub-disciplines of physical education and kinesiology, motor learning, exercise physiology, psychology, and sociology. When sociologists respond to readiness questions, their answers often reflect interactionist research carried out by those concerned with social development during childhood. This work suggests that at about eight years of age children begin to develop the cognitive and social abilities they need to fully understand the complex social relationships involved in most competitive sports. These abilities are not fully developed until about twelve years of age for most children.

Anyone who has ever watched two teams of seven-year-old soccer players knows about these developmental issues. Most children younger than twelve play what we call "beehive soccer": after the opening kick, there are twenty bodies and forty legs surrounding the ball, and they follow the ball around the playing field like a swarm of bees following its queen. Everyone is out of position, and all the players usually stay that way for the entire game. Meanwhile, the coaches and parents loudly plead with them to "Stay in position!" and "Get back where you belong!"

However, determining where you belong in most sports is difficult. Positions change, depending on the placement of teammates and opponents relative to the location of the ball. Understanding the concept of position requires the ability to do three things simultaneously: (1) mentally visualize the ever-changing placements of teammates and opponents over the entire field, (2) assess their relationships to each other and to the ball, and (3) then decide where you belong. The ability to think through these three things and accurately determine where you should be on the field develops gradually in connection with social experience and individual maturation.

Parents and coaches often are frustrated when children fail to understand positions and follow strategies. When adults do not know about cognitive and social development during childhood, they may accuse preteen children who are out of position of not thinking or trying hard enough, or of having a bad attitude. This frustrates children who *are* thinking and trying as best they can at their stage of development. Their attitude is *not* the issue.

"Beehive soccer" and its equivalents in other sports can be avoided in two ways. *First*, the actual games children play can be altered to focus on skills and expression, rather than competition and team strategies. In other words, games can be revised to fit the children's needs and abilities (Morris and Stiehl, 1989; Orlick, 1978; Torbert, 2000). This is a preferred strategy. *Second*, children can be systematically conditioned to respond in certain ways to certain situations during competitive games and matches. This requires practices during which coaches create various game situations and then have each player rehearse individual tactical responses to each situation. Doing this with every player for even a few basic strategies is very tedious. It may win games, but it is not a preferred strategy, because it often destroys much of the action and personal involvement that children value in sports. When action is destroyed, it causes some children to wonder if sports are worth their time and effort.

Children are not born with the ability to compete or cooperate with others, nor are they born able to mentally visualize complex sets of social relationships between teammates and opponents. They must learn these things, and the learning depends on a combination of social experience and the development of abstract thinking and interpersonal abilities. This learning cannot be forced. It occurs only as children move from a stage in which they see the world from their own limited viewpoint to a stage in which they can see the world from third-party perspectives. A third-party perspective is one that goes beyond their own views and the view of any other person they know (Donnelly, 2002). Third-party perspectives gradually emerge between the ages of eight and twelve years in most children. Therefore, organized sports for preteens should be controlled in ways that accommodate this gradually emerging ability; the highest emphasis should be on developing physical skills and basic cooperation. After all, children must learn to cooperate before they can compete with one another in positive ways. If they do not know how to cooperate, competitions can become nasty and brutish.

Finally, those of us who ask the question "When should children play organized competitive sports?" generally live in cultures in which scientific approaches to childhood development are popular, and people have the time and resources to organize children's activities. Youth sports are a luxury. They cost money and take time; therefore, many people cannot afford them. This is true even in wealthy countries among families with few resources. Many children around the world simply include movement and physical play in their lives as they learn how to be boys or girls in their cultures and learn to fit into class and occupational structures. When to begin organized sports is not an issue for them or their parents. How, where, when, and what they play are seriously constrained by the material conditions of their lives. As we think about organized youth sports, it is important to be aware of poverty within and between societies.

What Are the Dynamics of Family Relationships in Connection with Organized Youth Sports?

Organized youth sports require time, money, and organizational skills, and these usually come from parents. Therefore, playing organized sports is often a family affair; however, few sociologists have carried out research on how youth sport participation affects family relationships.

Anecdotal information indicates that youth sports serve as sites for bringing family members together in supportive ways. However, problems do occur. Parents may act in ways that damage their relationships with their children, and they may become so emotionally involved with sports that they put pressure on their children or fail to see that their children perceive their encouragement as pressure. When children feel pressure in either of these forms, they face a triple dilemma: (1) if they quit sports, they fear that the parents may withdraw support and attention; (2) if they play sports but do not perform well, they fear the parents will criticize them; (3) if they perform well, they fear they will be treated like "little pros" instead of children.

Studies by Coakley (2001), Donnelly (1993), and Kay (2000) all highlight the stresses experienced by parents and siblings in families where at least one of the children is involved in sports at a high-performance level. When a great deal of the family's time and resources are directed to the sport participation of one individual, it can become all-consuming, and Kay (2001) noted that, in the U.K., the divorce rate in such families was higher than the national average.

There is an interesting parental division of labour associated with youth sports. Mothers provide a wide range of off-the-field support, while fathers do the coaching and league administration. (M. MacNeill)

Organized youth sports have an impact on families and family relationships in other ways as well. Studies by Janet Chafetz and Joe Kotarba (1999) in the United States and Shona Thompson (1999a,b) in Australia highlight the fact that organized sport programmes for children could not exist without the volunteer labour of parents, especially mothers. Their research shows that mothers drive children to practices and games, fix meals at convenient times, launder dirty training clothes and uniforms, and make sure equipment is ready. Mothers raise funds for teams and leagues. They purchase, prepare, and serve food during road trips and at postgame get-togethers. They form and serve on committees that supervise off-the-field social activities and make phone calls about schedules and schedule changes. They manage the activities of brothers and sisters who do not play in the programmes, and they provide emotional support for their child-athletes when they play poorly or when coaches or fathers criticize how they play. Fathers also provide labour, but it is devoted primarily to on-the-field and administrative matters, such as coaching, field maintenance, and league administration (although mothers increasingly are taking on these tasks as well).

The analysis in both these studies focuses on the extent to which parent labour in organized youth sports reproduces a gendered division of labour in the family and the community, as well as in the minds of the children, especially the boys who play organized sports. The studies highlight the labour of mothers because this topic has been widely ignored by many who study sports in society. It is now important to build on this research and delve more deeply into the family dynamics that exist in connection with youth sports.

How Do Social Factors Influence Youth Sport Experiences?

Children make choices about playing sports, but they have little control over the context in which they make their choices. Many factors, including parents, peers, and the general social and cultural context in which they live, influence the alternatives from which they choose and how they define and give meaning to their choices. For example, children from low-income, inner-city backgrounds generally have fewer sport participation opportunities than other children have. Children with able bodies have more opportunities and receive more encouragement to play sports than do children with a disability. Choosing to play a contact sport, such as football, is seen by most people around the world to be more appropriate for boys than for girls. Boys who want to figure skate generally do not receive the same encouragement from peers as girls receive. When African Canadian boys choose to play certain sports, many people in Canada are more likely to identify them in terms of their sport participation than in terms of their other characteristics, such as academic achievements.

None of these statements is earthshaking. People know these things. They know that, as children make sport choices and give meaning to their sport experiences, they and the people around them are influenced by the prevailing cultural beliefs about age, gender, sexuality, race and ethnicity, ability and disability, and social class. This is how social forces influence youth sport experiences.

For example, research shows that sport choices and experiences are influenced by dominant definitions of gender in society. These definitions influence early childhood experiences when it comes to physical activities (White et al., 1992). In the United States, research has shown that fathers play with their sons more often and in more physically active ways than they play with their daughters. Furthermore, the physical activity messages that most young boys receive differ from the messages many young girls receive, both inside and outside family settings (Beal, 1994; Greendorfer, 1993; Hargreaves, 1994; Hasbrook, 1999; Lenskyj, 1986; Nelson, 1991).

One of the results of these messages is that, before most children take their first physical education class or play their first organized sport, they have clear ideas about their physical skills and potential. Boys are more likely to see themselves as being physically skilled than girls are, even though measurable gender differences in actual skill levels are small or nonexistent (Nelson, 1990, p. 9). Boys are more likely than girls to *think* they are better than they actually are when it comes to sport skills. This has an effect on their self-confidence and their willingness to use and test their bodies in active ways and voluntarily participate in physical activities. Girls learn to minimize the physical space they occupy, sexualize their bodies through modifying their appearance and movement, and accept the notion that boys are physically superior to them. At the same time, boys learn to present themselves as physically big and strong, to act in ways that claim physical space around them, and to expect to exert power and control over girls (Hasbrook, 1999; Hasbrook and Harris, 1999).

Physical self-concepts come to be connected with gender because many people expect different levels of sport-related skills from girls and boys. Gender-related expectations may be one of the reasons boys' ball games often dominate the space on elementary school playgrounds and in other public places. This pattern extends through the life course—just observe the extent to which young men appropriate space for themselves on the open playing fields of most Canadian campuses. Of course, many people actively discourage such gender-based patterns, but it is often difficult to change them, because they are deeply rooted in the culture as a whole.

The influence of social forces on youth sports has been identified in many studies. Research by Ingham and Dewar (1999) shows how dominant ideas about masculinity influence the meanings that boys give to their experiences in a youth hockey programme. Jay Coakley's research shows how dominant ideas about ethnicity and social class influence the funding and programme orientations of youth sport programmes in minority areas in inner cities and in white suburban areas in the U.S. (Coakley, 2002). Howard Nixon (2000) discusses the exclusion and the participation barriers faced by children with certain disabilities, and he outlines the complex and contentious issues surrounding the segregation and integration of people with disabilities in sport competitions. As we read these studies, it is important to focus on the experiences of children rather than simply look for differences by gender, ethnicity, ability, and social class. As we see how experiences vary, we learn how social forces interact with each other and influence children's lives on and off the playing field.

MAJOR TRENDS AND RECOMMENDATIONS

Major Trends in Youth Sports Today

In addition to their growing popularity, youth sports are changing in at least four other socially significant ways. *First*, organized programmes have become increasingly privatized. This means that more youth sports today are sponsored by private, non-profit, and commercial organizations, or are increasingly subject to user fees. *Second*, organized programmes are increasingly likely to emphasize the "performance ethic." This means that participants in youth sports, even in house leagues and low-key recreational programmes, are encouraged to evaluate their experiences in terms of developing technical skills and progressing to higher personal levels of achievement in one or more sports. *Third*, participation in so-called alternative sports has increased. This means that many young people prefer unstructured, participant-controlled sports, such as skateboarding, in-line skating, snowboarding, BMX biking, and various other physical activities that have local or regional relevance for children. *Fourth*, there seems to be an increasing culture of caution surrounding youth sports and physical activity, with increased supervision and surveillance, legislation in the face of concerns about injuries, sexual abuse, and other safety concerns.

These four trends have an impact on who participates in organized youth sports and what kinds of experiences children have when they do participate.

Privatization and User Fees in Organized Programmes Privatization, and the introduction of user fees, are interesting and sometimes alarming trends in youth sports today. While organized sports and physical activity have become more popular, there has been a decline in the number of publicly funded programmes with free and open participation policies. When local governments face budget crises, various social services, including recreation programmes, often are cut back. In the face of cutbacks, local parks and recreation departments and other public agencies sometimes have tried to maintain physical activity and instructional programmes by imposing participation fees to cover expenses. There are now user fees in interschool sport programmes as government cutbacks have also affected education budgets.

As noted previously, municipal Parks and Recreation Departments in Canada stopped organizing youth sport leagues in the mid-1970s, in part as a cost-saving measure. The remaining programmes of physical activity and instruction (e.g., skating and swimming) were increasingly subject to user fees, and there is now evidence of declining participation. For example, in a recent amalgamation of Toronto into a mega-city, the former city of Toronto, which had no user fees, joined with five municipalities that all had different user fees. This fee conflict was resolved into a single reduced-fee structure. The consequence was an increase in the number of participants in the other municipalities (indicating that there was probably a demand for the services, but that the higher user fees were preventing children and adults from participating) and a reduction in participants in the former city of Toronto (indicating that the introduction of user fees was a barrier to participation).

When children have schedules that are full of organized youth sports, they have little time to be with their parents. The irony is that many parents spend more time making it possible for their children to play sports than they spend with their children.

When municipalities no longer provided youth sport leagues, community non-profit organizations (e.g., the Burlington Youth Soccer Association) began to offer them. All involved fees, although commercial sponsors from the community and favourable public facility rental rates often helped to keep the fees fairly low. However, fees do depend on the cost of the activity, and how much travel and competition teams are involved in. Thus, a "travel team" in hockey usually involves significant costs for the parents of children involved—not just in terms of equipment and ice time but also with travel and tournament costs. In many parts of Canada, it appears that only middle-class children are now able to participate easily at the higher levels of hockey.

Commercial sport providers also have entered the youth sport scene in growing numbers. In Canada, these often take the form of private clubs for skiing, skating, golf, and other sports, or summer sport specialist camps providing intensive training in a sport. The camps are often owned by celebrity athletes and coaches, and are usually run on a commercial (for profit) basis. The private commercial programmes are usually selective and exclusive, and they provide few opportunities for children from low-income households. The technical instruction in these programmes is very good, and they provide children from wealthier families with many opportunities to develop skills. Through these commercial programmes, parents with enough money even hire private coaches for their children at rates of $35–$150 per hour.

At least two negative consequences are associated with this trend. *First*, privatized youth sports and recreation reproduce the economic and ethnic inequalities that exist in the larger society. Unlike public programmes, they depend on money paid by participants. Low-income and single-parent families often do not have the money to pay fees. This, in turn, accentuates various forms of ethnic segregation and exclusion, as well as social class divisions, in communities. *Second*, as public parks and recreation departments cease to offer programmes, they often become brokers of public parks for private, commercial, and non-profit, organized sport programmes. The private programmes that use public parks may not have commitments to gender equity and affirmative action, which are mandated in public programmes. If 83 percent of the participants in these programmes are boys, and 17 percent are girls, as was the case in Los Angeles in the late 1990s, what can be done to prevent the taxpayers from indirectly funding the perpetuation of gender inequity? (See the B.C. human rights case in chapter 8, p. 229). As you can see, there are a number of challenges associated with privatization.

Emphasis on the Performance Ethic The performance ethic has become increasingly important in many organized youth sport programmes. This means performance becomes a measured outcome and an indicator of the quality of the sport experience. *Fun* in these programmes comes to be defined in terms of becoming a better athlete, becoming more competitive, and being promoted into more highly skilled training categories. Often, the categories have names that identify skill levels, so there may be gold, silver, and bronze groups to indicate where a child is placed in the programme. Many parents find this attractive because it enables them to judge their child's progress and to feel that they are meeting their parental expectations (see the quote from MacGregor on the first page of this chapter).

Private programmes generally emphasize the performance ethic to a greater degree than do non-profit programmes, and they often market themselves as "centers of athletic excellence." Such an approach attracts parents willing to pay high membership, participation, and instructional fees. Another way to sell a private programme to

parents who can afford the cost is to highlight successful athletes and coaches who have trained or worked in the programme.

Parents of physically skilled children often are attracted to organized programmes emphasizing the performance ethic. They sometimes define fees and equipment expenses, which can be shockingly high, as *investments* in their children's future. They are concerned with skill development, and, as their children grow older, they use performance-oriented programmes as sources of information about scholarships, as well as networks for contacting coaches and sport organizations. They approach their children's sport participation in a rational manner and see clear connections between childhood sport participation and future development, educational opportunities, and success in adult life. Of course, the application of the performance ethic is not limited to organized sports; it exerts influence across a range of organized children's activities (Mannon, 1997). Childhood in some societies has been changed from an age of exploration and freedom to an age of preparation and controlled learning. Children's sports reflect this trend.

Increased Interest in Alternative Sports As organized programmes have become increasingly exclusive, structured, performance oriented, and elitist, some young people have sought alternatives, which allow them to engage freely in physical activities on their own terms. Because organized youth sports are the most visible settings for children's sport participation, these unstructured and participant-controlled activities are referred to as alternative sports—alternatives, that is, to organized sports. Alternative sports encompass an infinite array of physical activities done individually or with groups. Their popularity is based, in part, on children's reactions against the highly structured character of adult-controlled, organized sports (see Beal, 1995).

When we observe children in many of these activities, we are regularly amazed by the physical skills they have developed without adult coaches and scheduled practices and contests. Although we are concerned about injury rates and about the sexism so common in the social dynamics of these activities, we are impressed by the discipline and dedication of children who seek challenges apart from adult-controlled sport settings, and by the cooperation shown as they help each other, applaud each other's successes, and give advice to each other as they develop their skills.

This trend of participation in alternative sports is so widespread that media companies and other large corporations that sell things to children have invented competitive forms of these sports and present advertising images that highlight risk and the "extreme" challenges associated with some of the activities. They have sponsored events, such as the X Games, that provide exposure and material support for those who are willing to display their skills in a televised competitive format that is, or at least appears to be, highly organized and structured. Although the participants in these events are teens and young adults, many of the spectators are children. We suspect that children use the images from these media events to inform what they do when they play these sports, but we need research on this issue. So far, adult intervention in these activities has been limited to the provision of facilities such as skateboard parks and occasional words of advice regarding safety. Will the future bring adult skateboard coaches and organized programmes for participation? We would bet on it, but we are also sure that children will always seek opportunities to play sports on their own terms.

The Culture of Caution We often claim that play and sports are where children learn to take risks, have adventures, and generally prepare in a relatively safe way for the world that they will enter as adults. And, as we argue in subsequent chapters, those risks—particularly the risk of injury—are still there. But, in a rather contradictory way, there is growing evidence of increasing concern about safety of children, and a growing distrust of those whom parents pay and/or entrust to look after them. This involves growing surveillance—hidden cameras in children's nurseries to monitor the babysitter or nanny, "black boxes" in cars to check the location and driving behaviour of teenage children, webcams in nurseries and daycare centres to monitor child care, and parental presence at all games and practices to monitor children's safety and coaches' behaviours.

It also involves other concerns about safety, and about lawsuits. The Children's Society and the Children's Play Council in the U.K. recently surveyed children to find out what types of behaviour were being controlled in schools and playgrounds. Their findings (www.the-childrens-society.org.uk) were startling. For example:

- Yo-yos were banned from school playgrounds because they may cause injury.
- Tag and running games were banned in case children fell over.
- In one school, handstands were banned because one student had injured her elbow doing a handstand.
- Children were prevented from picking wild-flowers at a kindergarten because they may pick up germs from the ground.
- One school banned the use of a climbing frame in case children fell.

Playgrounds in Toronto, and in some British cities, have been closed because the equipment does not meet new safety standards, and, in this time of tax cuts and restricted municipal budgets, this equipment is not immediately replaced. A research report prepared by Professor David Ball for the Play Safety Forum in the U.K. ("Playgrounds: Risks, Benefits and Choices"—www.the-childrens-society.org.uk) calls for a balance between safety and some controlled risk and excitement: "Play provision is first and foremost for children and if it is not exciting and attractive to them, then it will fail, no matter how 'safe' it is."

REFLECT ON SPORTS

Different Experiences: Informal Player-Controlled Sports versus Organized, Adult-Controlled Sports

Jay Coakley and his students have observed children in sports, and interviewed the participants, since the 1970s. They found (Coakley, 1983) that the experiences are quite different depending on the type of organization:

- Sports informally organized and controlled by the players tend to be "action-centred."
- Sports formally organized and controlled by adults tend to be "rule-centred."

INFORMAL, PLAYER-CONTROLLED SPORTS

Players in informal and pick-up games of all kinds are interested in four things:

1. Action, especially action leading to scoring
2. Personal involvement in the action
3. A challenging and exciting experience (e.g., a close score in a competitive game)
4. Opportunities to reaffirm friendships during games

Games usually had two to twelve players who usually knew each other from previous games. Usually, they formed teams quickly using skill differences and friendship patterns. Starting games, and keeping them going and full of action, was a complex operation and depended on how good the players were at managing interpersonal relationships and making effective decisions.

While rules were similar to formal game rules, there were many modifications to maximize action, scoring, and personal involvement while keeping the scores close. For example, basketball free throws were eliminated, there were no yardage penalties in football, soccer throw-ins were limited, and pitchers moved close enough to batters for them to be able to hit the ball. The games usually had very high scores.

Personal involvement was maximized with clever rule qualifications, such as imposing handicaps on highly skilled players, permitting "do-overs" and other chances for less skilled players, and having every player eligible to receive a pass in football. Children almost always claimed that the biggest

source of fun in their games was hitting, catching, kicking, scoring, and any other form of action in which they were personally involved, and which kept the scores close.

Players tolerated a great variety of performance styles and moves, and even joking around and ignoring rules, so long as these did not interfere with the action. Older and more skilled players were involved in settling disputes, and arguments were usually handled in creative ways. Friendships were reaffirmed as children played together often, and they became more skilled at solving conflicts.

A word of caution: Problems in informal games do occur. Bigger and stronger children may exploit or even bully smaller and weaker ones, girls may be patronized or dismissed if they try to play with boys, and those excluded from games often feel rejected by their peers. Limited availability of play space or equipment can also cause problems.

FORMAL, ADULT-CONTROLLED SPORTS

Even though children still value action and personal involvement in formal sports, they are more likely to be serious and concerned with performance quality and game results. Action, personal involvement, and behaviour are strictly regulated by formal rules enforced by adults—coaches, managers, referees, scorekeepers, timekeepers, and so on. Children are also concerned with formal positions, and are likely to refer to themselves by their position—left winger, right fielder, goalie, and so on. Coaches and spectators continually emphasize the importance of these by encouraging children to "stay in position."

Playing time is often determined by a player's level of skill, and those spending more time on the bench may be bored or less interested in the game. Adult control also decreases the number of arguments and overt hostility between players, and more conflict has been observed between adults than between players on the same team. There were also fewer displays of affection among players, making it difficult to determine which players were friends.

Continued

REFLECT ON SPORTS

Different Experiences: Informal Player-Controlled Sports versus Organized, Adult-Controlled Sports continued

Rules standardize competition and control player behaviour. Their enforcement regularly causes breaks in the action that are not usually resented by the players (unless it is a penalty against their team). Adults usually apply the rules universally, seldom making exceptions even when there are differences in players' abilities and characteristics, and when the sanctions do not have an effect on game action or outcome. Games are played until the end regardless of quality of play or player satisfaction. Rules applied by coaches restrict players' freedom, but compliance is high.

Children in organized sports want to win, but are not usually obsessed by winning. Skilled players and those on successful teams are more concerned with winning. Most players want to have fun, but all know their win-loss records and league standings. Status on teams is largely based on coaches' assessments of players' skills. Status also leads to more playing time, which is highly valued, and more latitude during games.

ANALYZING THE DIFFERENCES

Which of these experiences is more valuable in the development of children? The answer is important to both the children involved and the adults who invest so much time, money, and energy into organized sports. Each experience makes different contributions to the lives of children, and people generally overrate the contributions of participation in organized sports and underrate the contributions of participation in informal sports (Schultz, 1999).

Informal sports clearly require creativity and interpersonal and decision-making skills. "The most important part of [informal sports] is learning how to set up the game, choose sides, agree with your peers, make compromises, figure out answers, [and] submit to self-directed rulings so that the game can continue" (Koppett, 1994, p. 294). They provide experiences involving cooperation, planning, organizing, negotiating, problem solving, flexibility, and improvisation (Adler and Adler, 1998). We do not know how much of this learning carries over to other settings, but we can assume that children are influenced by their experiences.

Organized sports demand that children be able to manage their relationships with adult authority figures. They learn the rules and strategies of culturally significant activities, and they may gain status that carries over to the rest of their lives. They see bureaucracy and hierarchy in action, and become acquainted with forms of rule-governed teamwork and adult models of work and achievement (Adler and Adler, 1998).

However, it is possible that too much participation in organized sports may lead children to view the world in passive terms, as something that is given rather than something people create. If this is true, we think that children may grow up thinking they are powerless to change the world in which they live. *What do you think?*

• •

Jay Teitel, a Toronto freelance writer, has pointed out some early indications of a culture of caution in youth sports. The unintended consequence of well-meaning parent and coach behaviour, according to Teitel, is a situation in which adults now play and children do not: "Abducting play is only the first part of our crime; holding play hostage, and then returning it to kids in adulterated form, is the second part"

(1999, p. 56). Teitel goes on to state: "We're so concerned about our children's emotional safety, their 'feeling good about themselves,' that on at least a certain middle-class level, we've gutted play by taking the risk out of it. We've created a vogue for games without winners, games closely supervised to make sure that there is no gloating or bullying—a moratorium on competition in general" (Teitel, 1999, p. 59).

When children are involved in informal, player-controlled sports and alternative sports, they take risks and create excitement, but adults often have legitimate concerns about safety. It will take some creative thinking, and perhaps a return to an old view that sometimes children hurt themselves during play, and it is often nobody's fault, in order to produce a balance between the culture of risk and the culture of caution.

Recommendations for Changing Children's Sports

In previous sections, we have examined how problems appear as adults become involved in organized sports for children, and how people in Canada have attempted to deal with the problems. We have also looked at the special problems presented by the early involvement and specialization model of involving children in high-performance sports, and outlined some possible solutions. In this final section, we return to the issue of resolving problems, making recommendations for both informal and adult-organized sports, and return to the issue of education with recommendations for coaching certification programmes.

Changing Informal and Alternative Sports Informal and participant-controlled alternative sports are unique because they are not controlled directly by adults. In fact, many children opt for such sports, because they want to avoid the organized structures of adult-controlled teams and programmes. However, it is possible for adults to become indirectly involved in ways that increase the safety of these sports and that maximize children's opportunities to participate in them.

This means that, instead of passing laws to suppress sports such as skateboarding or BMXing, adults should work with young people to provide safe settings for them to create their own activities. If adults do not become supportive of new informal and alternative sport forms, their children will use the extreme models of the X Games, Gravity Games, and other made-for-TV spectacles as primary sources of inspiration. The challenge for adults is to be supportive and to provide subtle guidance without being controlling. Children need their own space in which to be creative and expressive while they play sports. They show this all the time in their behaviour in informal, participant-controlled sports, and in alternative sports, where they engage in creative and cooperative ways. Adult guidance can be helpful in making that space as safe as possible and by making it open to as many children as possible, boys and girls as well as children from various ethnic and social class backgrounds.

We could call this the "life guard" model of supervision, or the "school recess" model of supervision. In both cases, a responsible adult is there to ensure safety, prevent bullying, and mediate disputes if called on, but not to direct the activity.[9] Competitive sports could be run on this model, which is, in many ways, a revival of a past model. In the 1920s, in the state of New York, Frederick Rand Rogers insisted that teachers and other adults should remain in the bleachers during school sports. He argued that the players could not learn to make decisions if adults always made them (Kidd, 1997, p. 128).

Changing Organized Sports There are a wide variety of organized sport programmes for children. This is especially true in countries that have no centralized state authority through which youth programmes are funded, controlled, and administered. Programmes vary

---

[9] Such activity can be very creative. At a primary school in southern Ontario recently, a teacher on recess duty noticed children playing an unusual new game. When she asked what it was, she was informed that they were playing Quidditch (a game from the Harry Potter stories). Although the original game involves broomsticks and flying, these children had created a terrestrial form of the game without adult involvement.

from one sport to another, from community to community, and from league to league. However, those in charge could improve conditions in most programmes, maximizing positive experiences and minimizing negative experiences for participants. This is true in other parts of the world as well as in North America.

In making recommendations for change, most people agree that organized programmes should meet the needs of the children who participate in them. This means that the children themselves are a valuable source of information, which adults can use as they organize and administer youth sports. If children seek fun in their own games by emphasizing action, involvement, close scores, and friendships, it makes sense that organized programmes also should emphasize them. The following recommendations are based on this assumption.

INCREASING ACTION Children emphasize *action* in their own games. Much activity occurs around the scoring area, and scoring is usually so frequent that it is difficult to keep personal performance statistics. Organized sports, although they do contain action, emphasize rules to promote order, standardized conditions, and predictability. The strategy of many organized teams is to prevent action, rather than stimulate it. Parents and coaches sometimes describe high-scoring games as undisciplined free-for-alls caused by poor defensive play. The desired strategy in the minds of many adults is to stop action: to strike out the batter (baseball and softball), to stall the game when you are in the lead (soccer and basketball), and to use a safe running play for a 4-yard gain (football). These tactics may win some games, but they limit the most exciting aspects of any game: action and scoring.

It is usually easy to increase action and scoring in organized sports, as long as adults do not view game models as sacred and unchangeable. Bigger baskets, goalies who are encouraged to play out, smaller playing areas, and fewer rules are ways to increase action. Why

not make all players eligible to receive passes and carry the ball in football, and use a 6-foot basket in a half-court basketball game? Many adults resist changes they think will alter game models—that is, the models used in elite, adult sports. They want children to play "the real thing," even though adults are prepared to make all kinds of modifications in their own recreational and pick-up games to achieve the following aspects of play. They forget that children are more interested in having fun than in playing as some adults do.

INCREASING   PERSONAL   INVOLVEMENT Children do not sit on the bench in informal games. They use rule qualifications and handicap systems to maximize their involvement and to promote action. Smaller or less skilled players may not contribute to the action as much as others do, but they play the whole game. If they are treated badly or excluded, they leave without being branded as quitters, or given lectures on commitment by their parents.

In organized games, playing time is often seriously limited for all but the most skilled players, and the substitution process is a constant source of problems for the coach and pressure for the players. Specialization by position further restricts the range of involvement. When ten-year-olds describe themselves as goalies, left defensive tackles, centre fielders, or left wingers, it is a sure sign that the range of personal involvement is limited.

Coaches and other leaders could extend personal involvement in organized sport programmes by rotating players to different positions and by coordinating group substitutions with opposing teams. They could alter team size to allow more players on the field, or they could reduce rosters so that there were more teams with fewer subs. Batting lineups for baseball and softball could include all team members, regardless of which ones were playing the nine or ten positions in the field. In ice hockey, the games could be played across the width of the rink and portable dividers and lightweight goals could be used; this would allow three times as many teams to compete at the same time. In basketball, the first-string teams could play a half-court game at one basket, while the second-string teams played each other at the other basket. A combined score could determine the winner. These and many other similar changes would increase personal involvement.

CREATING CLOSE SCORES "Good games" are those for which the outcomes are in doubt until the last play; double overtime games are the best. Lopsided scores destroy the excitement of competition. Children realize this, so they keep their informal games close.[10] Since motivation partially depends on how people perceive their chances for success, a close game usually keeps players motivated and satisfied. Just like adults who use handicaps to keep the competition interesting in bowling, golf, and other sports, children adjust their games to keep them close.

In organized games, lopsided scores are common and team records are often very uneven. Keeping players motivated under these circumstances is difficult. Coaches are forced to appeal to pride and respect to keep children motivated in the face of lopsided scores and long, losing seasons. Ironically, coaches also urge their teams and players to take big leads during games. This makes no sense.

Adults who control organized youth sports are usually hesitant to make changes affecting the outcomes of games, but they might consider some possibilities. For example, they could encourage close scores by altering team rosters or by using handicap systems during games. The underdog could be given an advantage, such as extra players or the right to use four downs, five

outs, or a bigger goal. Numerous changes could keep games close; however, when game models are viewed as unchangeable, possible changes are never even discussed.

MAINTAINING FRIENDSHIPS When children play informal and alternative sports, the reaffirmation of friendships is important. Friendships influence the ways in which teams are chosen and the dynamics of the problem-solving processes during games. Organized sports may provide useful contexts for making friends, but players need more opportunities to nurture relationships with teammates and with children on other teams.

Coaches and managers could ask groups of players in organized sports to plan game strategies or coach practice sessions. They could encourage players to talk with opponents, help them when they were knocked down, and congratulate them when they did something commendable. Too often, relationships between opposing players are cold and impersonal. Players should learn that games have a human component, which they can recognize during play. Most important, players should be expected to enforce most of the rules themselves during games. Through self-enforcement, they would learn why rules are necessary, how to take responsibility for their behaviour, and how collective action depends on taking other people and the expectations of others into consideration. Many people argue that self-enforcement would never work (although it does work in tennis)—however, if organized programmes do not teach young people how to cooperate to the extent needed to play games with their friends, then those programmes are not worth our time and effort.

Other changes are also needed. For example, Shane Murphy (1999), a psychologist who has worked with many athletes and families in his clinical practice, suggests that programmes include education for all participants, including parents, coaches, and players. The National Association for Youth Sports in the United States

---

[10]Close scores may be sacrificed when close friends want to be on the same team; playing with friends is sometimes more important than having evenly balanced teams.

also advocates and runs educational programmes for parents and coaches. Murphy also suggests involving children in decisions about youth sport programmes, designing programmes to teach life skills as well as sport skills, and using social goals to inform the philosophies of organized programmes. Finally, he suggests developing and enforcing codes of conduct for parents, coaches, and players. While codes of conduct have been introduced by a number of sport programmes in Canada, their enforcement is often inconsistent, or non-existent.

PROSPECTS FOR CHANGE Many organized youth sport programmes have made changes that reflect a concern for the needs and well-being of children. In fact, there are many excellent models for thinking about and making changes in youth sports (Chalip and Green, 1998; Morris and Stiehl, 1989; Murphy, 1999; Torbert, 2000). However, the approach most often used to guide changes in youth sport programmes is grounded in a functionalist theoretical perspective (see chapter 2). In other words, adults are most concerned with changes that will increase efficiency and organization in youth sports, and that will increase the skill levels of child-athletes. Thus, we see more training programmes for coaches, more formal rules regulating the behaviour of parents and spectators, and more rules for what is expected from players and coaches. There are more promotional brochures and advertising in the local media, more emphasis on the performance ethic, and more tournaments, playoffs, and championships.

As organized youth sports become increasingly affiliated with national organizations and sport governing bodies, the chance that these bodies will consider critical changes in game models and the structure of youth sports becomes increasingly remote. Changes occasionally may be considered at local levels, but even local sport programmes are not likely to change official game models or programme structures. Such changes would threaten the

"How many times have I told you to practise your basketball before you even think about homework?"
....

The fame and fortune of some professional athletes may encourage some parents to overemphasize youth sports in the lives of their children. Might this turn young athletes into "child workers"?

relationships of local programmes with the influential provincial and national organizations.

Changes are also slow to come because many adults who administer and support organized sport programmes have vested interests in keeping them as they are. They know the programmes are not perfect, but they are afraid changes in them will eliminate many of the good things they have accomplished in the past. In fact, one of the few triggers for progressive change seems to be a drastic decline in youth registrations in a sport, as noted previously with regard to hockey in Quebec, and as is currently occurring in youth baseball.

COACHING EDUCATION AS A MEANS OF PRODUCING CHANGES Earlier in this chapter, we wrote about the National Coaching Certification Programme as one of the "made in

Canada" solutions to the problems that were recognized in youth sports. The NCCP provides coaches with information on how to (1) deal with young people responsively and safely and (2) be more effective in organizing their practices and in teaching skills to young people. Most coaching education programmes emphasize putting athletes' needs ahead of winning, but none of them teaches coaches how to critically assess the sport programmes in which they work with young people. None presents information on how to make structural changes in the programmes themselves or on how to create alternatives to existing programmes. Even with two former NHL players as assistant coaches, Arnold (2002) notes the difficulties involved in introducing progressive changes to the way that they coached one minor hockey team in Peterborough, Ontario. Coaching education materials generally are based on the functionalist assumption that existing sport programmes are pretty good, but they could be better if coaches were to use more applied sport science as they work with child athletes.

Although coaching education is important, we worry that they foster what we might call a "technoscience approach" to youth sports. A technoscience approach emphasizes issues of control and skill development, rather than an overall understanding of young people as human beings. If this happens, coaches are defined as "sport efficiency experts," rather than teachers who provide young people with opportunities to become autonomous and responsible decision makers who control their own lives.

At this point, the NCCP has made a contribution to responsible coaching in youth sport programmes. But, as we examine coaching education and critically assess its place at all levels of sports, it would be good to remember that the former East Germany had one of the most efficient and highly respected coaching education programmes in the world. However, its programme was based on a technoscience approach, and did little to contribute to the overall development of young people as human beings. The East German

experience reminds us that, without critical self-reflection, the application of sport science knowledge to coaching will not necessarily make youth sports or the world any better. If coaching education were informed by critical self-reflection, it could lead to many positive changes in sport programmes for people of all ages.

SUMMARY

ARE ORGANIZED YOUTH SPORT PROGRAMMES WORTH THE EFFORT?

Children in all societies participate in various forms of movement and physical activity. For the most part, these activities take place in informal settings and are characterized by freedom and spontaneity. However, they do not occur in social and cultural vacuums. In fact, the forms and dynamics of children's physical activities are connected indirectly with larger socialization processes, through which participants learn how to be girls and boys and learn about the systems of social relations and cultural beliefs that exist in their families, communities, and nation-states. These processes vary from society to society and across cultural settings within societies.

While movement and physical activities exist in all cultures, organized youth sports are a luxury. They require resources and discretionary time among children and adults. They exist only when children are not required to work and only when there is a widespread belief in society that experiences during childhood influence a person's development and character. Youth sports have a unique history in every society where they exist. However, in all societies they have been constructed to emphasize experiences and to teach values defined as important in the society as a whole.

The growth of organized sports in North America and much of Europe is associated with the changes in the family that occurred during the last half of the twentieth century. Many parents now see organized sports as important extensions of their control over their children and as settings in which their children gain important developmental experiences.

In Canada, academics and some individuals involved in sports began to recognize quite early that adult-organized sport programmes for children leads to a number of problems resulting from the particular set of values that have come to be associated with them: that children's play is entertainment for adults, that only games organized and controlled by adults are of any value, that children are miniature adults, and that the real value of sport lies in learning to be a winner. We discuss a number of "made in Canada" attempts to resolve these problems: the development of house leagues, the introduction of a coaching education programme for volunteers in youth sports, the development of "fair play" leagues in hockey, and the introduction of child protection schemes. Developments in high-performance sports for children since the mid-1970s provide even more reason for concern, and, although there have been attempts to resolve some problems—for example, eating disorders—change has been very slow because some adults stand to profit from the status quo. Solutions in the form of education, children's rights, child labour laws, and child welfare laws are all examined.

Research in the sociology of sport can be used to answer many of the commonly asked questions about youth sports. Studies guided by symbolic interactionism help us understand that, prior to eight years old, children do not have the developmental abilities needed to understand the social dynamics of organized competitive sports, especially team sports in which complex strategies are used. Such abilities do not become fully developed until at least twelve years of age in most children. Studies guided primarily by feminist theories have begun to describe and explain some of the family dynamics associated with organized youth sports, especially in terms of

how they affect family relationships, family schedules, and the lives of mothers and fathers. Studies often guided by a range of critical theories illustrate how social factors influence youth sport experiences, including the participation choices available to children and the meanings given to various sport experiences.

Major trends in youth sports today include increased privatization of, and user fees for, organized programmes, a growing emphasis on the performance ethic in most programmes, and growing evidence of a culture of caution that limits the excitement and occasional risks associated with children's play and sport experiences. In response to these trends, some children have turned to informal and alternative sports, including the highly visible extreme versions of alternative sports.

Children's sport experiences vary with levels of formal organization and with the extent to which they are participant-controlled or adult-controlled. The dynamics of sport participation, as well as what children may learn from their experiences, are different in informal games than they are in organized youth sport programmes. It is likely that involvement across a range of participation settings is important in the developmental experiences of children.

Recommendations for changing children's sports can be formulated by using the characteristics of children's informal games as a guide. This would call for changes in the structure and organization of many youth sport programmes. These changes would emphasize increased action and involvement among all participants. They also would emphasize changes to keep game scores close and to give children opportunities to formulate and nurture friendships with teammates and opponents.

The prospects for change in organized youth sport programmes are inhibited by the vested interests of many adults in programmes as they are currently organized. Coaching education programmes could facilitate changes if they were to deal with youth sports in more critical terms.

Of course, no programme can guarantee that it will make children into models of virtue, but those who organize programmes can change them to minimize problems. This means that organized sport programmes for children *are* worth the effort—when the adults controlling them put the children's interests ahead of the programmes' organizational needs and their own needs to gain status through their association with child athletes.

 SUGGESTED READINGS

Adler, Patricia A., and Peter Adler. 1998. *Peer power: Preadolescent culture and identity.* New Brunswick, NJ: Rutgers University Press (the authors collected data over eight years on the lives of children in an upper-middle-class town; excellent information about how play, informal games, recreational activities, and organized sports fit into the social lives of children).

Arnold, E. 2002. *Whose puck is it anyway?: A season with a minor novice team.* Toronto: McClelland & Stewart (documents one season with the minor novice AAA Peterborough Petes, coached by the author and assisted by two former NHL players, Greg Millen and Steve Larmer; the coaches emphasized fun, equal ice time, and opportunities to play all positions; not all of the parents were happy, but the players and coaches had fun, and this is an entertaining account).

Bylsma, D., and J. Bylsma. 2000. *So you want to play in the NHL: A guide for young players.* Chicago: McGraw-Hill/Contemporary Books.

Bylsma, D., and J. Bylsma. 1998. *So your son wants to play in the NHL.* Toronto: McClelland & Stewart (these two books are by authors John Bylsma and his son Dan Bylsma, who plays for the Anaheim Mighty Ducks; one is directed at parents and the other at young players; while recognizing the dream of playing in the NHL, the authors also provide a great deal of useful advice about keeping ambition in proportion and emphasizing child and youth development rather than just developing a hockey player).

Cahill, B. R., and A. J. Pearl, eds. 1993. *Intensive participation in children's sports.* Champaign, IL: Human Kinetics (articles by Coakley and Donnelly provide sociological analyses of issues associated with children playing high-performance sports; articles by Gould and Weiss are also informative from a psychological perspective).

Coakley, J., and P. Donnelly, eds. 1999. *Inside sports.* London: Routledge (this collection includes accessible articles on sport experiences; articles by Hasbrook, Ingham and Dewar, and Chafetz and Kotarba deal directly with youth sports).

DeKnop, P., B. Skirstad, L.-M. Engstrom, and M. Weiss, eds. 1996. *Worldwide trends in youth sport.* Champaign, IL: Human Kinetics (background material on comparative research; excellent information about youth sports in twenty countries; summarizes research on youth sports in terms of global patterns, trends, problems, and policies).

Fine, G. A. 1987. *With the boys: Little League baseball and preadolescent culture.* Chicago: University of Chicago Press (a classic study of youth sports for boys; in-depth qualitative data on eleven-year-old boys illustrates how boys create their own ways of experiencing organized sports).

Rinehart, R., and S. Sydnor, eds. 2003. *To the Extreme: Alternative sports, inside and out.* Albany: State University of New York at Albany Press (twenty-five articles by scholars and noted athletes in alternative sports; articles do not focus on children, but they capture the spirit and experiences that attract many children to alternative, action, and extreme sports).

Ryan, J. 1995. *Little girls in pretty boxes: The making and breaking of elite gymnasts and figure skating.* New York: Doubleday (a timely, in-depth journalistic account and exposé of the lives of U.S. girls and young women in elite gymnastics and figure skating).

Thompson, S. 1999. *Mother's taxi: Sport and women's labor.* Albany, NY: State University of New York Press (deals with one of the more under-researched areas in the sociology of sport—the ways in which women's work and domestic labour facilitates their children's [and husbands'] sport participation).

WEBSITE RESOURCES

Note: Websites often change. The following URLs were current when this book was printed. Please check our website (www.mcgrawhill.ca/college/coakley) for updates and additions.

www.canadianhockey.ca (the official website of the Canadian Hockey Association includes the very insightful—and funny—"Relax, It's Just a Game" series of television and radio commercials)

www.lboro.ac.uk/departments/sses/institutes/iys/pages/about.html (site for the Institute of Youth Sport at Loughborough University in the U.K.; focuses on bringing together research from a variety of disciplines on issues related to youth participation and performance.

http://ed-web3.educ.msu.edu/ysi (site for The Institute for the Study of Youth Sports at Michigan State University; the institute sponsors research on the benefits and detriments of participation in youth sports, produces educational materials, and provides educational programmes for coaches, officials, administrators, and parents; useful links to other sites)

www.nays.org (site for the National Alliance for Youth Sports, a nonprofit organization with the goal of making sports safe and positive; links to other youth sport sites)

www.sportsparenting.org/csp (site for the Center for Sports Parenting, a Web-based program that offers immediate and practical guidance to parents, coaches, educators, administrators, officials, and others involved in youth sports)

www.momsteam.com (information at this parents' site is designed to create a safer, saner, less stressful, and more inclusive youth sports experience; it is directed at mothers of children in organized youth sport programmes)

www.sportinsociety.org/uys.html (site for the Urban Youth Sports Program of the Center for the Study of Sport in Society; focuses on issues in Boston, but it provides a useful conceptual model for what might be done in other cities to overcome barriers that limit youth sport participation and to increase opportunities for healthy development)

www.youth-sports.com (general site for information, advice, and instructional products for parents, coaches, and children involved in youth sports)

(CP/Jonathan Hayward)

"Deviance" in Sports

Is it out of control?

You don't go from 10.17 to 9.83 on Petro-Canada unleaded gas.

> —Jamie Astaphan, physician who provided steroids to Ben Johnson (1989)

You grow up getting special treatment because you're an athlete, then you get millions of dollars thrown at you. Shady people gravitate toward money.

> —Lew Lyons, sports psychologist (2000)

My definition of a pro is a guy who plays even when he's hurting.

> —attributed to Angelo Mosca, former Hamilton Ti-Cat football player

Note: This chapter was written with the assistance of Robert Hughes.

 Online Learning Centre Resources

Visit *Sports in Society's* Online Learning Centre at **www.mcgrawhill.ca/college/coakley** for additional information and study material for this chapter.

Despite the fact that this chapter is called "Deviance in Sports," using the sociological term "deviance" raises a number of problems for authors who have stated their preference for a sociological approach that combines interactionist and critical theories in order to study sports in society (for more about these theories see chapter 2). As we note below, the terms "norms" and "deviance" are derived from functionalist theory and are based on the assumption that there is a widespread consensus in society about what is "normal" behaviour (norms, normative), and therefore what is non-normative or "deviant." If we think of these concepts in terms of who has the *power* to define what is "normal" and what is "deviant," we can see how they raise concerns for critical theorists.[1]

Behaviour that is defined as "normal" at one time or in one place can be re-defined as "deviant" in another time and/or another place, and vice versa. Thus, for example, protests against injustice or inequality are often seen as "deviant" in this theoretical approach. In the nineteenth century, slaves escaping, and those helping them to escape, the United States to travel the underground railroad to Nova Scotia or southern Ontario were seen as "deviant" because slavery was normative in the U.S. In the early part of the twentieth century, women who engaged in passive resistance and other forms of protest in an attempt to win the right to vote were seen as "deviant" since it was not "normal" for women to have the right to vote. And, until Prime Minister Pierre Trudeau declared in the 1970s that "the state has no business in the bedrooms of the nation," there were laws against homosexuality in Canada. Nowadays, it is normal for the mayors of many major cities to march in annual "Gay Pride" parades. When Trudeau made his remarks he was giving voice to a changing attitude in society—there was no consensus, there was never a consensus, and, of course, there still is no consensus.[2] When a basketball player at Manhattan College turns her back on the U.S. flag during the pre-game national anthem to protest the impending invasion of Iraq, whether her behaviour is defined as "normal" or "deviant" depends on who is making the definition.

Using terms such as "norms" and "deviance" often proceeds from the assumption that "deviant" behaviour is always wrong, and that there is a consensus in society about what is "normal" and what is "deviant." We approach the issue from the position that there is often no such consensus in society; and this lack of consensus extends to the discipline of sociology. University courses on this topic may be called "social problems" or "social issues," the topic may be covered in "criminology," and courses that are called "Deviant Behaviour" or "Deviance" very often begin precisely with the qualification that we are making here about the socially constructed nature of "deviance." This chapter and the following chapter also make it quite clear that there is little consensus about social problems and social issues in sport.

We use the term "deviance" in this chapter, but to underline our point, and, to emphasize these qualifications, we use the term "deviance" in quotation marks. We intend the term to be understood with all of the cautions noted above, and the quotation marks are a reminder that "deviance" is a problematic term. This does not mean that we think that immoral or illegal behaviour, or behaviour that is designed to gain an unfair advantage over an opponent, or behaviour that is likely to lead to injuries to an athlete or his/her opponents, is acceptable. It means that we need to explore and

---

[1] In fact, one of the first theoretical attempts to combine interactionist and critical theories involved precisely this issue. Labelling theory argued that the power of an individual, or an institution such as the police, to label a person or behaviour as "deviant," and to have that label widely accepted, was as important as the behaviour itself.

[2] Of course, some Canadians still do not accept equal rights for women, and some Canadians still believe that homosexuality should be illegal.

understand such behaviour from the perspectives of, and in the context of, those involved; we do not need to accept mainstream definitions of what is "normal" and what is "deviant."

Cases of "deviance" among athletes, coaches, agents, and others connected with sports have attracted widespread attention in recent years. Pervasive media coverage of on-the-field rule violations and off-the-field criminal behaviour has led some people to conclude that such behaviour in sports is out of control.

Publicity given to criminal charges has come with continuing information about widespread behind-the-scenes drug and substance use among athletes. Disclosures of rampant drug use among elite cyclists in the Tour de France attracted worldwide attention in 1998. Statements by Olympic insiders claim that it is rare for anyone to win gold medals without taking performance-enhancing substances. Athletes avoid positive tests by using substances for which tests are not yet developed or approved. As the former director of drug testing for the United States Olympic Committee (USOC) has said, "Athletes are a walking lab, and the Olympics have become a proving ground for chemists" (Bamberber and Yaeger, 1997, p. 62).

Because popular beliefs have emphasized sport participation as a character-building experience, these highly publicized cases of "deviance" among athletes, coaches, and others in sports have shocked and disappointed many people. In their disappointment, some have concluded that the moral fabric of society itself is eroding. The mantra is nearly always the same: too much money and greed, too little discipline and self-control; the past purity of sports is gone.

In light of this conclusion, the purpose of this chapter is to look at the issue of whether such behaviour is, indeed, out of control in sports. We focus on four questions as we deal with this issue:

1. What problems do we face when we study "deviance" in sports?

2. What is the most useful way to define "deviance" when studying sports in society?
3. Are rates of "deviant" behaviours among athletes (on and off the field), coaches, and others connected with sports out of control?
4. Why do some athletes use performance-enhancing substances, and is it possible to control the use of these substances in sports?

These questions direct our attention to important issues in the study of sports in society.

PROBLEMS FACED WHEN STUDYING "DEVIANCE" IN SPORTS

Studying "illegal" or rule-violating behaviour in sports presents special problems for five reasons. First, *those involved in sports, especially the athletes, are governed by many different sets of regulations.* For example, there are the rules of the sport that determine actions and behaviours that are permitted and those that are not. These rules are enforced by the various governing bodies of the sport. Then there are the laws of the land, the criminal and civil codes of a country that also apply to athletes. Often there is confusion about who has jurisdiction in particular cases—is it the governing body of the sport, or is it the police?

However, there are two additional sets of rules that may be called on to determine the behaviour of those involved in sports. The first set is the particular rules that apply on a team, usually established by a coach and other team administrators. These rules may apply to dress codes, curfews, punctuality, diet, etc. Then there is a set of rules that are often called the "unwritten rules of sport" or the "spirit of the rules." These are supposed to govern the moral behaviour of athletes in terms of the codes of fair play, and include such elements as not running up the score on an opponent, or not taking advantage of an opponent's misfortune (e.g., a clearly erroneous call by an official). This last set of rules is most ambiguous, and the most frequently violated in modern sports.

It is difficult to study "deviance" in sports because athletes often engage in behaviours that would not be accepted in other settings. For example, behaviours that are acceptable in boxing, hockey, football, and other sports would get you arrested or sued if you were to use them off the field. (*Colorado Springs Gazette*)

For example, soccer and tennis have some clear examples of fair play, of playing by "the spirit of the rules." It is common and accepted (normal) behaviour in soccer that when a player on your team is injured, a player on the other team will kick the ball out of play in order to stop the game and allow the injured player to be treated. To resume play, a player on your team takes the throw in, but the ball is thrown to an opponent. These off-setting courtesies have become normal because referees are no longer permitted to stop play because of an injury—a consequence of actions that are the exact opposite of fair play (i.e., faking injuries). In tennis, it is not unusual, even in high level matches, for a player to recognize a line judge's mistaken call in his/her favour or against his/her opponent by deliberately giving the next point to his/her opponent. But what

if the fair play from tennis was applied to soccer—a mistaken call by a linesman means that you throw in the ball to your opponent; or that you refuse the goal kick and give your opponents a corner (or they refuse a corner and give you a goal kick)! Players attempting such actions would probably be defined as "deviant," and referees would probably not know how to respond. It is possible to think of many more examples to highlight the ambiguous and contested nature of such rules, and determining "deviant" behaviour depends both on context and on which set(s) of rules are being enforced.

Second, because of these different sets of rules, and associated with some of the confusion about jurisdiction, *what is accepted in sports may be unacceptable in other spheres of society*. Athletes are allowed and even encouraged to behave in ways that are prohibited or defined as criminal in other settings. For example, the behaviour of athletes in contact sports would be classified as felony assault if it were to occur on the streets; boxers would be criminals outside the ring. Ice hockey players would be arrested for behaviours they define as normal during their games. Racecar drivers would be ticketed for speeding and careless driving. Speed skiing and motocross racing would certainly be defined as a serious problem outside the sport setting. However, even when serious injuries or deaths occur in sports, criminal charges usually are not filed, and civil lawsuits asking for financial compensation are generally unsuccessful.

The use of hatred as a source of motivation in sports clearly deviates from the norms most people use to guide their behaviour in families, religious congregations, classrooms, and work settings. On the other hand, male teammates may embrace one another, touch each other supportively, hold hands, and cry with each other in sports, while the same behaviours in other settings would violate widely accepted traditional norms about masculinity.

Coaches treat players in ways that we would define as a major source for concern if teachers were to treat students, or managers were to treat employees, similarly. Team owners in North American professional sports clearly violate the combines laws that apply to other business owners. Fans act in ways that would quickly alienate friends and family members in other settings or lead people to define them as mentally distrusted.

Norms do exist in sport worlds but, when athletes and others push normative limits, responses are often different than they would be in other settings. Engaging in extreme behaviours that risk health and well-being and inflict pain and injury on others are not as quickly condemned in sports as they are in other activities. We tend to view the motives of people in sports, especially athletes, as positive, because their behaviours are directed toward the achievement of success for their team, school, commu-

nity, country, or corporate sponsor. Therefore, those behaviours, even when they clearly overstep accepted limits, may be tolerated or even praised, rather than condemned. Athletes and even coaches are seen as different in ways that evoke fascination and awe, rather than automatic condemnation. Most sociological theories about rule- and norm-violating behaviour have no way of explaining such a phenomenon.

Third, *the forms and causes of "illegal" behaviour in sports are so diverse that no single theory can explain all of them.* For example, consider the forms of "deviant" behaviour that have been engaged in by at least some male junior hockey players. The "letter" and the "spirit" of the rules of hockey may be routinely violated; players may break established curfews; they may use recreational and/or performance-enhancing drugs; they may accept illegal payments; they may engage in under-age drinking and get into fights in local bars; they may engage in the sexual harassment or sexual abuse of women; they may become involved in the abuse of rookie players at team initiations (hazing); they may ask others to do their high school homework; and they may engage in the vandalism of hotel or bus company property. This list only includes examples of the types of rule-violating behaviours recorded for one group of athletes at one level of competition. The list would be even longer if we attempted to produce a comprehensive list of rule violations, or if we include athletes at other levels of sports together with coaches, administrators, team owners, agents, and spectators.

Fourth, *training and performance in sports have become "medicalized."* Training and performance in sports are seen increasingly in medical and sport science terms. People now regard medical treatments previously reserved for those in poor health as tools for meeting the everyday challenges of training and competition in sports. Many people now believe that ingesting substances thought to enhance performance is a necessary part of being an athlete. Just go to a store that sells nutritional supplements to see all the products that can be purchased by anyone interested in improved sport performance. Count the ads for performance-enhancing substances in any recent issue of the magazines *Muscle Media* and *Muscle and Fitness.* The motto for these ads seems to be "strength and high performance are just a swallow away"! Of course, corporations encourage this approach when they use athletes' bodies to promote products and corporate profiles presented in terms of strength and efficiency (Hoberman, 1995). In the meantime, it has become much more difficult to determine just what behaviours are "deviant" and what behaviours are accepted parts of athletic training.

Fifth, *"deviant" behaviour in sports often involves an unquestioned acceptance of norms, rather than a rejection of norms.* This point is developed in detail in the following section. However, it is important to note, in terms of the problems faced when studying these types of behaviours in sports, that much of the "deviance" in sports does not involve a rejection of commonly accepted norms and expectations for behaviour. In the case of athletes, sports involve a combination of exciting experiences and powerful social processes, which encourage extreme behaviours. These behaviours are considered to be a problem when they fall outside of what most people would consider a normally accepted range, but they may not be punished because they reaffirm normative ideals in the society at large. In fact, this may even lead some athletes to define themselves as morally upstanding, and even righteous, as they push limits.

Problematic behaviour in sports, unlike in other settings, often involves an unquestioned acceptance of and extreme conformity to norms and expectations. For example, most Canadians see playing hockey as a positive activity. Young men, and increasingly young women, are encouraged to "be all they can be" as hockey players and to live by slogans such as "There is no *I* in t-e-a-m." They are often encouraged to increase their weight and strength, so that they

"I remember when none of this was reported in the paper. Those were the good old days."
....

Do the media give too much attention to the misbehaviour of athletes, or not enough? What is the point of the coverage, and what criteria should be used when deciding what to report and what not to report?

can play more effectively and contribute to the success of their teams. When young men go too far in their acceptance of these expectations for getting bigger and stronger, when they become so committed to playing hockey and improving their skills on the ice that they use muscle-building drugs, their behaviour is considered to be a social problem.

This type of "overdoing it" is dangerous, but it is grounded in completely different social dynamics from those operating in the "antisocial behaviour" of alienated young people who give up all hope for the future, reject commonly accepted rules and expectations, and use substances such as heroin to deaden their awareness of the world. Athletes accept without question the norms that define what it means to be an athlete, and it is overconformity to those norms, not a rejection of them, that often leads to extreme behaviours.

We must take into account this difference between a rejection of norms and an uncritical overconformity to norms when we study rule- and norm-violating behaviour in sports. Social processes in sports, especially high-performance sports, often encourage extreme forms of behaviour that represent normative overconformity. We must study these processes if we wish to understand the problematic behaviours of athletes today.

DEFINING AND STUDYING "DEVIANCE" IN SPORTS: THREE THEORETICAL APPROACHES

Using Functionalist Theory: "Deviance" Disrupts Shared Values

As noted above, "deviance" is a functionalist concept, and it is worth outlining in a little more detail how the concept fits the theory.

According to functionalist theory, social order is based on shared values. Shared values give rise to shared cultural goals and shared ideas about how to achieve those goals. "Deviance" occurs when people engage in behaviours that involve a rejection of cultural goals and/or the accepted means of achieving them. In other words, "deviance" involves a departure from cultural ideals: the greater the departure, the more disruptive the behaviour, the greater the "deviance." Conversely, the greater the conformity to cultural ideals, the greater the reaffirmation of the social order, the better the behaviour: in other words, conformity = morality.

Most functionalists see "deviance" as a result of faulty socialization or of inconsistencies that are a part of the social system itself. In other words, "deviance" occurs because people have not learned and internalized cultural values and norms or because there are conflicts and strains in society. Therefore, controlling "deviance" would call for more efficient socialization processes and an elimination of conflicts, strains, and inconsistencies in the social system.

In the case of sports, "deviance" would involve a rejection of cultural goals and/or a rejection of the approved means of attaining those goals. For example, "deviance" would occur if a person in sports were to reject the goal of improving one's skills and/or the notion that commitment and hard work are the means to achieve that goal.

One problem with this approach is that, if there is a lack of agreement about the importance of various goals, it becomes difficult to identify "deviance." For example, if we think the ideal in sports is to engage in fair play and you think the ideal is to win, then we will see any violation of the rules as "deviant," while you will see some violations as "good fouls" that contribute to winning. If we regard sports as a form of play in which intrinsic satisfaction is the primary reason for participation and you regard sports as "war without weapons" fought for external rewards such as trophies and cash prizes, then we will see aggressive behaviour as "deviant," while you will see it as a sign of courage and commitment. Because we do not see eye to eye on the ideals of sports, we will not define and identify "deviance" in the same way.

Another problem with this approach is that it leads many people to think that controlling "deviance" always calls for increasing conformity. The strategies for this are establishing more rules, making rules more strict and consistent, developing a more comprehensive system of detecting and punishing rule violators, and making everyone more aware of the rules and what happens to those who do not follow them. Of course, this subverts creativity and change, and it assumes that all conformity, even extreme conformity, is a cultural ideal. This assumption is questionable, because extreme conformity can lead to forms of fascism—certainly an undesirable outcome.

Despite these problems, many people (non-sociologists) use a framework based on functionalist theory when they discuss "deviance" in sports. Therefore, when they see behaviours that do not match their cultural ideals, they define the behaviours and those who engage in them as "deviant." Most often their recommendation is to "get tough," throw the "bad apples" out, and make the rules more strict and the punishments more severe. This approach also leads to the idea that people violate rules because they lack moral character, intelligence, or sanity and that good, normal, healthy people would not do such things.

This approach ignores the influence of powerful social processes in sports and leads people to unjustly label athletes as moral failures when, in fact, most athletes are "hyper-conformers" whose main fault is that they do not critically assess the norms that they have been taught in connection with sport participation. We will say more about this throughout the chapter.

Using Conflict Theory: "Deviance" Interferes with the Interests of Those with Economic Power

According to conflict theory, social order is based on economic interests and the use of economic power to exploit labour. Social norms reflect the interests of those with power and wealth, and any behaviour or person that violates those norms is defined as "deviant."

Those who use this theory assume that all people act in their own interests, and that people in power use their position and influence to make sure their definitions of what is good or bad become the official definitions of what is "normal" or "deviant" in the society as a whole. Those who lack power in society are at a real disadvantage, because they have nothing to say about the content or enforcement of rules. Therefore, the behaviour of people who lack power is labelled as "deviant" more often than the behaviour of people with power. To make matters worse, people who lack power do not have the resources to resist being labelled as "deviant" when their behaviour does not conform to the standards of the rule makers.

Conflict theorists assume that rules in sport organizations reflect the interests of owners and

sponsors and ignore the interests of athletes. Therefore, they see "deviance" among athletes as the result of rules that not only discriminate against athletes but also force them to deny their own interests and follow the expectations of those in power, even though their health and well-being may be harmed in the process. When this approach is used, athletes are viewed as victims of a profit-driven system, in which progressive change depends only on disrupting the rules and rebelling against them.

A problem with this approach is that it leads to the conclusion that all "deviance" in sports is the result of biased norms and the exploitive enforcement of those norms by those who have power. This conclusion is difficult to defend when many forms of "deviance" that exist in high-performance and professional sports also exist in lower levels of competitive sports, where the athletes themselves may be in more of a position of power and control. For example, the statement that the use of dangerous growth hormones in high-performance track and field is the result of rules through which athletes are forced to risk their health for clubs, countries, and corporate sponsors does not hold up, since similar forms of drug use exist among athletes who are not subject to the coercive tactics used by the economically powerful people who control revenue-producing sports.

In other words, it is unlikely that all bad things in sports today would disappear if athletes were in charge. This, however, does not mean that athletes should not have more control over the conditions of their sport participation; they should. But the point emphasized here is that, since much of the "deviance" in sports involves unquestioned acceptance of norms and extreme conformity to them, it is unrealistic to expect that most athletes have the critical consciousness needed to transform the meaning, organization, and purpose of sports in society today. Athletes certainly need to have their consciousness raised and to play a crucial role in transforming sports, but those using conflict theory are naïve when they assume that all the causes of "deviance" in sports would automatically disappear if the profit motive were to disappear and athletes were to have the power to make and enforce all rules in sports.

Those using conflict theory have another problem: they see all established forms of social control as oppressive, and they see no hope for change until social systems are radically restructured. Only then will athletes stop engaging in destructive and dehumanizing behaviours when they play sports. This is why those who use this theory have talked often about the need to change society as a whole in order to control "deviance" in sports. This may be an admirable long-term goal, but "deviance" is grounded in things other than profit-driven exploitation processes. Therefore, there are good reasons to explore other factors related to "deviance" and other means of controlling the behaviours that jeopardize the health and well-being of those who play sports.

Using Interactionist and Critical Theories: "Deviance" Is Based in Social Processes and Power Relations

Those who use functionalist theory define "deviance" as a failure to conform, and they see rule violators as disruptive and morally bankrupt; those who use conflict theory define "deviance" as behaviour that violates the interests of people with economic power, and they see rule violators as exploited victims. One of the main flaws in these approaches is that they ignore "deviance" that involves overconformity to rules and expectations. Another flaw is that neither takes into account the "norms"[3] used in sport cultures and the ways in which athletes use those "norms" to evaluate themselves and

others. It is clear that most people who violate rules in sports can not be classified either as morally bankrupt or as victims. For example, it is not accurate to say that young people lack moral character when they go overboard in accepting and overconforming to ideas about what it means to be an athlete. Nor is it accurate to define all athletes who engage in "deviance" as passive victims of an exploitative, profit-driven sport system. Of course, athletes do not control all the conditions of their sport participation, but they do play an important part in the creation and maintenance of the "norms" that guide their own decisions and behaviours in sports. According to critical theories, people make choices and can inspire change in their lives and in the cultures of which they are a part.

In light of these factors, Bob Hughes and Jay Coakley (1991) have suggested that our understanding of "deviance" in sports could be expanded if we were to assume two things:

1. Social norms emerge in connection with complex and powerful forms of social relations in sports and in society as a whole.
2. Behaviours, ideas, and characteristics usually fall into a normally accepted range, and those that do not fall into this range involve either overconformity or underconformity (including non-conformist behaviour).

The best way to illustrate these two points is by using a graph that depicts a normal bell-shaped curve (figure 6.1). The horizontal line below the curve—represents a continuum of behaviours, ideas, and characteristics, which ranges from cases of extreme underconformity on the left to cases of extreme overconformity on the right. Behaviours, ideas, and characteristics that fall into a normally accepted range are located in the middle of the bell curve to show that they occur with the most frequency. The height of the curve represents the frequency of behaviours, ideas, and characteristics along the continuum. The shaded areas at each end of the continuum represent "deviance"—that is, behaviours, ideas,

---

[3] We have referred to norms previously as normal or conformist behaviour at a societal level, but norms can also vary with the different groups and subcultures to which we belong. We are referring here to particular ways of behaving that are normal and acceptable in sport cultures (although these will vary markedly depending if they apply to, for example, skateboarders or lacrosse players).

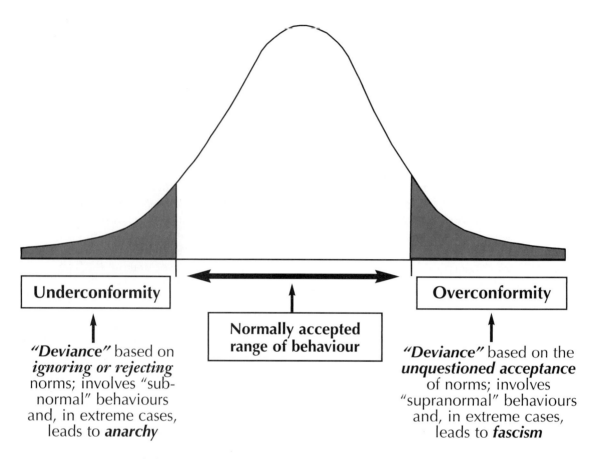

Underconformity

Overconformity

Normally accepted range of behaviour

"Deviance" based on
ignoring or rejecting
norms; involves "sub-
normal" behaviours
and, in extreme cases,
leads to *anarchy*

"Deviance" based on the
unquestioned acceptance
of norms; involves
"supranormal" behaviours
and, in extreme cases,
leads to *fascism*

FIGURE 6.1   Two types of "deviance" in sports. Most behaviour in sports falls within a normally accepted range in society. "Deviance" occurs on either side of this range. "Deviance" involving underconformity is grounded in different dynamics than "deviance" involving overconformity. Most people discuss "deviance" in sports in terms of athletes or coaches who ignore or reject norms; they do not identify "deviance" in terms of athletes and coaches who overconform to norms. In fact, "deviance" grounded in overconformity is often identified as an indication of commitment and dedication, even though it may be dangerous and have serious consequences for the health and well-being of self and others.

or characteristics that fall outside the boundaries of what is normally acceptable. In other words, "deviance" *consists of behaviours, ideas, or characteristics that fall outside a normally accepted range, because they involve extreme cases of overconformity or extreme cases of underconformity.*

"Deviant" underconformity is behaviour that involves a rejection or lack of awareness of norms, while **"deviant" overconformity** is

behaviour that involves an uncritical acceptance of rules. Both types of "deviance" can be dangerous.[4] For example, widespread underconformity pushed to an extreme would create conditions of anarchy or lawlessness in a group or society, while widespread overconformity pushed to an extreme would create conditions of fascism or blind faith in an ideal embodied in a rigid belief system or a charismatic leader.

Research shows that "deviant" overconformity occurs in sports. For example when Keith Ewald and Robert Jiobu (1985) studied adult men seriously involved in bodybuilding or competitive distance running, they concluded that some of the men displayed classic characteristics of "deviance" in the form of addictionlike overconformity to the norms in their sport. Many of the bodybuilders and distance runners followed training norms to such an extent that their family relationships, work responsibilities, and/or physical health were affected negatively, yet they never questioned what they were doing or why they were doing it.

This is not unique. Many elite athletes prepare so intensely for their sports that the needs of family members are ignored. Bette McKenzie (1999), a daughter of an NHL player and a former wife of an NFL player, notes that her ex-husband's "deviant" overconformity to the norms of professional football interfered with family relationships so much that it was a key factor in their divorce. Such overconformity may even become normalized for athletes' families. Thompson (1999) notes that there was a period of time when every spouse and partner of an NHL player that she interviewed, who had a baby during the playing season, had her labour induced. The date was determined by the playing schedule in order to facilitate the father's presence at the birth.

Other studies have identified other forms of "deviant" overconformity, such as self-injurious overtraining among distance runners (Nash, 1987); unhealthy eating behaviours and weight-control strategies among women athletes in elite amateur sports, and among men in

wrestling or those who work as jockeys;[5] extremely rigid and exclusive dedication to training and competition among ultra marathon bicyclists (Wasielewski, 1991) and triathletes (Hilliard and Hilliard, 1990); and uncritical commitment to playing sports with pain and injury.[6]

When we use this critical approach to define and study "deviance" in sports, we see how important it is to distinguish between behaviours that show indifference toward or a rejection of norms in sports, on the one hand, and behaviours that show an uncritical acceptance and overconformity to norms on the other hand. This approach also forces us to examine the value systems and social processes that exist in sport cultures. For example, the value system in high-performance sports often encourages overconformity to a set of norms or guidelines that athletes use to evaluate self and others as they train and compete (Donnelly, 1996b; Ingham et al., 1999; Johns, 1997). Because of this, much of the "deviance" among athletes (and coaches) involves *unquestioned acceptance of* and *conformity to* the value system embodied in what we have called the sport ethic.

The Sport Ethic and "Deviance" in Sports The **sport ethic** *is a cluster of norms that many people in power and performance sports have accepted and reaffirmed as the dominant criteria for defining what it means, in their social worlds, to be an athlete and to successfully claim an identity as an athlete.* The sport ethic constitutes the normative core of high-performance sport culture. Information from and about athletes and coaches has led us

---

[4]Some social scientists have used the terms *negative "deviance"* and *positive "deviance"* to refer to "deviant" underconformity and "deviant" overconformity, respectively. The term *positive "deviance"* is *not* used to imply that such "deviance" is good or beneficial to self or others. In fact, positive "deviance" involves extreme behaviours, ideas, or characteristics that can be very dangerous.

[5]See Davis, 1999; Donnelly, 1993; Franseen and McCann, 1996; Hawes, 1999b; Johns, 1992, 1996, 1997; Overdorf and Gill, 1994; Sundgot-Borgen, 1993a, b, 1994a, b; Thompson and Sherman, 1999; also see Wilmore, 1996, for a review of thirty-five studies.

[6]See Curry, 1993; Curry and Strauss, 1994; Nixon, 1993a, b, 1994a, b, 1996a, b; White and Young, 1997; Young et al., 1994; Young and White, 1995.

to conclude that the following four norms make up the sport ethic:

1. *An athlete makes sacrifices for "the game."* This norm stresses that athletes must love "the game" above all else and prove it by giving the game priority over other interests. To establish their identities as athletes, individuals must have the proper attitude, demonstrate unwavering commitment to their sports, live up to the expectations of fellow athletes, and make the sacrifices necessary to stay in the game. In other words, being an athlete involves meeting the demands of others in the sport and the demands of competition without question. This spirit emphasizes that athletes must make sacrifices and be willing to pay the price to play their sports. Coaches' pep talks and locker room slogans are full of references to this guideline.

   A U.S. college football player who had ten knee operations in six years and continued to play the game he loved between each operation explains this norm with these words: "I've told a hundred people that if I got a chance to play in the NFL, I'd play for free. It's never been about money. It's never been about anything but playing the game" (Wieberg, 1994, p. 8C). There are numerous examples of athletes who make sacrifices to continue playing the game because they love it; even retired athletes talk about giving back to the game because they care so much about it.

2. *An athlete strives for distinction.* The Olympic motto "Citius, Altius, Fortius" (swifter, higher, stronger) captures the meaning of this norm. Being an athlete means constantly seeking to improve. Winning symbolizes improvement and establishes distinction; losing is tolerated because it is part of learning how to win. Breaking records is the ultimate standard of achievement, because athletes are a special group dedicated to

climbing the pyramid, reaching for the top, pushing limits, excelling, exceeding others, and being the best they can be.

   This norm is highlighted by a Canadian university student who referred to striving for distinction despite pain and injury as "having an athlete mentality....Even if you know your limits as an athlete, oftentimes you'll push way past that, especially if you have a very short season....And you know if I play this game, I am going to die, and it's gonna hurt so much, but I'll have the whole year to rehab" (cited by Safai, 2001, p. 83).

3. *An athlete accepts risks and plays through pain.* According to this norm, an athlete does not give in to pressure, pain, or fear. The voluntary acceptance of risks is a sign of courage and dedication among athletes; playing under pressure is expected. The idea is that athletes do not back down from any challenge; standing up to challenges involves moral and physical courage. Being an athlete means that a person willingly confronts and overcomes the fear and the challenge of competition and accepts the increasing risk of failure and injury as he or she moves up the competitive pyramid.

   Sport discourse is full of references to this norm. Brian Burke, director of operations in the NHL, notes, "The code among our athletes is, if you have a pulse you play. There is no logical explanation for their pain threshold" (*Denver Post*, 1999: 7D). He also explains that coaches in hockey and other sports look for players willing to take risks and play through pain; they like injured players in the lineup because they inspire teammates to overconform to the norms of the sport ethic.

4. *An athlete accepts no limits in the pursuit of possibilities.* This norm stresses "the dream" and the obligation to pursue it without question. An athlete does not accept a situation without trying to change it, overcome it, and turn the scales. Those who successfully claim an identity as an athlete believe that participating

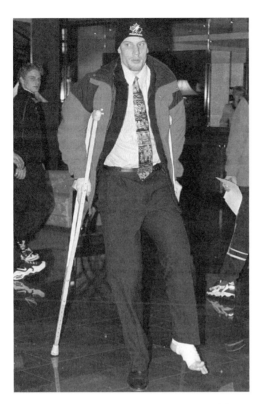

Athletes may overconform to the norms of the sport ethic to demonstrate their moral and physical courage. This often leads to high rates of injury in certain sports, as during the 1997 World Junior Hockey Championship, when Canadian team captain, Jesse Wallin, broke his foot during the preliminary round. Of course, these athletes do not see their overconforming behaviours as "deviant." Coaches and teammates praise their unquestioned acceptance of the norms of the sport ethic.
(CP/Jacques Boissinot)

in sports is a sphere of life in which anything is possible—if a person is dedicated enough. They feel obligated to pursue dreams without reservation; they ignore external limits as they attempt to achieve success. Of course, external rewards may influence athletes, but their pursuit of possibilities is driven primarily by what they believe they must do as athletes, apart from money.

This norm is clearly illustrated by a Canada West track and field athlete who, after injuring his shoulder, noted: "I got up and I jumped again and I actually jumped another six or so times and I recall afterwards basically being doubled over and not being able to do anything because it didn't hurt until I hit the mat" (cited by Young, White, and McTeer, 1994, p. 183). And a Canadian female athlete stated: "I never skated or played basketball without constant pain. However, this just made me push harder to beat it…The pain, while playing, was often enough to make me cry once I got home (never at the rink!). I dealt with it through the use of painkillers and denial" (cited by Young and White, 1995, p. 52).

These four norms, which make up the sport ethic, are deeply rooted in the culture of today's power and performance sports. At first glance, they call to mind slogans hanging on locker room walls and written in self-help and motivation books. By themselves, these norms call for behaviours that many people value: making commitments and sacrifices, striving for improvement, pushing yourself even when things are difficult or painful, and pursuing dreams. In fact, conformity to the sport ethic is what makes sport participation a unique and exciting activity for many people. However, "deviance" occurs when the norms of the sport ethic are accepted uncritically, without question and qualification, and then followed without limits, without setting boundaries.

Alberto Salazar, the retired marathon runner, discussed the dangerous consequences of "deviant" overconformity when he coached U.S. middle-distance runner Mary Decker Slaney during the mid-1990s. Slaney had undergone nineteen sport-related surgeries and was living in constant pain at the time. Salazar explained that

> [t]he greatest athletes want it so much, they run themselves to death. You've got to have an obsession, but if unchecked, it's destructive. That's what it is with [Slaney]. She'll kill herself unless you pull the reins back. (Longman, 1996, p. B11)

Salazar's warning shows that dangerous forms of "deviance" occur when athletes do not critically question the sport ethic and set boundaries that limit their conformity to its norms. Controlling these forms of "deviance" may be the biggest challenge facing sports today.

This is not to say that "deviant" underconformity is not a problem; however, when athletes reject norms or refuse to take them seriously, they are likely to be cut by coaches or others who control sports. When players are unwilling to make sacrifices for the game and refuse to strive for distinction, play through pain, and fight through limits as they pursue dreams, they do not last long in high-performance sports. Their underconformity is not tolerated, and their careers are terminated.

Reactions to "deviant" overconformity are different. When players go to extremes in conforming to the norms of the sport ethic, when they follow the norms to the point of risking their own safety and well-being, they are praised and hailed as heroes. Media commentators glorify athletes who overconform to the sport ethic; they praise athletes who play with broken bones and torn ligaments, have surgery after surgery to play the game, and request or submit to injections of huge doses of painkilling drugs to play through pain.

Spectators also glorify athletes who are willing to overconform to the sport ethic. In January 1999, Governor General Roméo LeBlanc even awarded the Meritorious Service Cross to Elvis Stojko for competing at the Nagano Olympics while injured. "'I salute your unbeatable spirit,' Leblanc told Stojko" (Stevens, 1999). (See quoted citation below.) Therefore, it is not surprising that many athletes go overboard in their acceptance of the sport ethic and overconform to its norms without question or qualification, even when overconformity creates problems, causes pain, disrupts family life, jeopardizes health and safety, or even shortens life itself. This type of "deviance" is dangerous, even though it is widely ignored.

The following is Mr. Stojko's citation:

**Elvis Stojko, M.S.C., M.S.M.
Richmond Hill, Ont.
Meritorious Service Cross (civil division)**

Despite a painful injury, Elvis Stojko, a three-time world champion, displayed an extremely high level of professionalism while competing in the Men's Figure Skating Singles at the Nagano Olympic Winter Games in 1998. His tremendous courage under such adversity won him a Silver Medal and demonstrated his indomitable spirit and dedication to the pursuit of excellence. This is the second award of a Meritorious Service Decoration to Mr. Stojko; he was awarded the Meritorious Service Medal in April 1995.

—(Press release, "Governor General to launch Canadian Figure Skating Championships and present Elvis Stojko with Meritorious Service Cross," issued by the Government House Press Office, January, 1999 [www.gg.ca])

Why Do Athletes Engage in "Deviant" Overconformity? Not all athletes overconform to the sport ethic, but many do. The following are three main reasons for overconformity:

1. Athletes find their experiences in sports so exhilarating that they want to continue participating as long as possible; they love their sports and will do almost anything to stay involved.
2. The likelihood of being chosen or sponsored for continued participation in sports increases when athletes overconform to the sport ethic. Coaches often praise athletes who engage in positive "deviance" and make them models on their teams.
3. Being a part of a team or a sport subculture involves having the respect of your peers. One of the best ways to do this is to overconform to the sport ethic, especially if your teammates expect such behaviour. (If such behaviour is not the norm on your team, they are likely to label you as "crazy.")

For these reasons, many athletes have come to use "deviant" overconformity to define and

REFLECT ON SPORTS

Just (Over) do It
The Sport Ethic in Nike Ads

Several years ago, Nike and other corporations adopted an advertising strategy in which they depicted and glorified "deviant" overconformity to the sport ethic. They assumed that this form of "deviance" would attract attention and sell products.

In 1996, during coverage of the Olympic Games in Atlanta, a Nike ad in *Sports Illustrated* asked boldly: "Who the Hell Do You Think You Are? Are You An Athlete?" The text in the ad answered this question with words that echo the norms of the sport ethic:

> Because if you are [an athlete], then you know what it means to want to be better, to want to be the best. And if you are [an athlete], then you understand it's not enough to just want to be the best. You can't just sit around and BS about how much you want it. Show me how much you want it. . . . Dare to do what it takes to be the best. And then, whether you win, lose, or collapse on the finish line, at worst you'll know exactly who you are.
>
> If You Can't Stand the Heat, Get Out of Atlanta!

In 1999, Nike ran ads showing the disfigured bodies of athletes who had pushed limits in their sports. The background tune, Joe Cocker's "You Are So Beautiful," was chosen to glorify these bodies, which were seriously injured and left permanently scarred or broken. Of course, the ad showed only the bodies of athletes who had recovered enough to play again. Erased from the images were athletes whose injuries had ended their careers and possibly left them so disabled that they cannot walk without pain or play actively with their friends and children. (In a recent Budweiser ad, athletes enumerated their injuries in terms of the number of black eyes, broken bones, etc.)

The images and narratives in these ads show that the advertising people at Nike understand the sport ethic and the tendency among athletes to overconform to its norms. We can not prove it, but we think that these ads and others like them encourage dangerous forms of "deviance." *What do you think?*

evaluate their sport experiences. Nike even has used it in TV commercials (see the Reflect on Sports box, "Just (Over) do It," above) by highlighting athletes who throw up, shed blood, collapse from exhaustion, and break bones as part of regular training and competition. "Just doing it" is fine, even commendable, but "just overdoing it" until you vomit, bleed, lose consciousness, or need surgery is "deviant." However, most athletes do not see overconformity to the sport ethic as "deviance." Instead, they see it as reaffirming their identities as athletes and their membership in select sport groups. This can be very important to them, especially when their continued participation and success in sports take on significant personal and social meanings.

Of course, not all athletes are equally likely to overconform to the sport ethic. We hypothesize that those most likely to do so include

1. Athletes who have low self-esteem or are so eager to be accepted by their peers in sports that they will make whatever sacrifices they think others want them to make
2. Athletes who see achievement in sports as their only way to get ahead, make themselves a name, and become important in the world

In other words, the athletes whose identities or future chances for success and significance are dependent on their sport participation are most likely to engage in "deviant" overconformity. In fact, they may use overconformity to the sport ethic to demonstrate their worthiness for continued membership and status within their sport groups. It is an athlete's vulnerability to group demands, combined with the desire to gain or reaffirm group membership, that is a critical factor in the incidence of "deviant" overconforming.

This may be why certain coaches create environments that keep athletes in a perpetual state of adolescence. Athletes are constrained to strive continually to confirm their identities and eliminate self-doubts by engaging in behaviours that please their coaches and teammate-peers. When this dependency-based commitment occurs, overconformity to the sport ethic becomes increasingly common, and many young people become willing to sacrifice their bodies and play with reckless abandon in the pursuit of affirmation and approval. When coaches encourage this, intentionally or naively, they promote dangerous forms of "deviance." If coaches were concerned with controlling "deviant" overconformity, they would help athletes set boundaries and limits when it comes to conformity to the sport ethic; they would encourage athletes to ask why they do what they do and how their lives as athletes are integrated into the rest of their lives.

"Deviant" Overconformity and Group Dynamics Being an athlete is a social as well as a physical experience. At elite levels of competition, there are special bonds that form between athletes as they follow the norms of the sport ethic—as they express their commitment to the game and make sacrifices, strive for success, play in pain, and pursue dreams together. These special bonds serve as a context in which extreme conformity to the norms of the sport ethic is encouraged and comes to be seen as an expected part of what a person does to reaffirm his or her identity as an athlete, as well as to be accepted by other athletes as "one of them."

In other words, the behaviours, ideas, and characteristics that demonstrate unqualified commitment to the sport ethic become "normalized." As athletes in high-performance sports collectively overconform to the norms of the sport ethic, the bonds between them become extraordinarily powerful, so powerful that they often separate athletes from the rest of the community. After all, "normal" people in the community cannot understand what it's really like to

be an elite athlete. They may view elite athletes with awe and admiration, but they do not really know what it takes to pay the price day after day, to face risk and pain, to subordinate one's body and being to the needs of the team, and to practise and sacrifice to improve skills and stay among a select few who can perform as no others in the world can when it comes to their sports. Only other athletes can understand this.

The group dynamics associated with participation in high-performance sports are very powerful. However, they are not unique. Other select groups, usually groups of men, experience similar dynamics. Examples can be found in the military, especially among Special Forces units. Former soldiers frequently talk about these dynamics and the powerful social bonds formed while they faced danger and death as members of groups that trained together as fighting teams. Examples also exist among test pilots and astronauts, as vividly described by journalist Tom Wolfe (1979) in his book *The Right Stuff*. He explains that pushing the envelope in a jet and trusting your life to fellow pilots as you do so is certain to create special bonds, along with feelings that you and the entire group are special. Similar bonds even exist in certain fraternities and sororities, where "pledges" voluntarily submit to systematic hazing processes designed to emphasize that all must pay the price to become members of such special groups of people. In fact, as a form of socialization, hazing rituals have long been a part of the identity formation and member selection that occur in many groups that are defined as special. Sport teams often have preseason hazing rituals, during which rookies are expected to follow the commands of team veterans, no matter how demeaning, sickening, painful, or illegal the commanded behaviours may be (Alfred University, 1999; Bryshun and Young, 1999; Johnson, 1999; Hawes, 1999a; Wieberg, 2000a, b).

As high-performance athletes endure the challenges of maintaining their membership in select groups and teams at the highest level of accomplishment in their sports, they develop not only extremely strong feelings of unity with other athletes but also the sense that they are unique and extraordinary people. After all, they are told this day after day by everyone from coaches to autograph seekers. They read it in newspapers and magazines, and they see in on TV and the Internet. When the sense of being unique and extraordinary becomes extreme, it may be expressed in terms of pride-driven arrogance, an inflated sense of power and importance, and a presentation of self that communicates superiority and even insolence. The Greeks used the word **hubris** to describe this expression of uniqueness and the accompanying sense of being separate from and above the rest of the community. We sense that many elite athletes today exhibit hubris. In fact, for some athletes it has become a key dimension of their public personas—they even market it and use it to attract attention and make people remember them.

The point in this section is that the social processes that exist in many sports, especially high-performance and professional (power and performance) sports, may do three things:

1. They may bond athletes together in ways that encourage and even normalize overconforming "deviance" in many of the social worlds created around sports.
2. They may separate athletes from the rest of the community while they inspire awe and admiration from those in the community.
3. They may lead athletes to develop hubris, which is expressed in ways that simultaneously bond athletes together and separate them from the rest of the community.

As we understand the impact of these social processes on athletes, we see that much of the "deviance" in sports is not motivated primarily by the desire to win or to make money. Instead, it is motivated by the desires to play the game, to be an athlete, and to maintain membership in an elite athletic in-group. This is not to say

that winning and money are irrelevant to athletes; they *are* important and powerful motivators. But we must remember that many athletes who know they will not win championships or make money from their athletic accomplishments frequently engage in "deviant" overconformity. These athletes, just like their more talented and money-making peers, are motivated by the belief that being a "real athlete" means taking risks, making sacrifices, and paying the price to develop skills and stay in the game. This means that the roots of "deviance" go deeper than individual desires to win or make money. In fact, these roots are grounded in the very values promoted through the sport ethic itself. Therefore, much of the "deviance" in sports is most accurately identified as a social issue rather than just a personal problem of individual athletes (cf., Mills, 1959). For this reason, it is especially difficult to control. Fines and jail sentences do little to slow it down. Throwing out the so-called bad apples may help in the short run, but the social processes that operate in the social world of many sports guarantee that there will be another crop of apples next season.

"Deviant" Overconformity and "Deviant" Underconformity: Is There a Connection? This analysis of "deviant" overconformity raises questions about other forms of "deviance" that exist in sports and among athletes, for example

- If the social bonds created in sports are powerful enough to normalize the forms of "deviant" overconformity that jeopardize health and well-being, are they also powerful enough to foster other forms of "deviance"?
- If the extreme behaviours, ideas, and characteristics of athletes separate them from the rest of the community, do athletes come to disdain nonathletes to the point that they might be likely to harass or assault them?
- If athletes develop extreme degrees of hubris, might they feel that they live their

REFLECT ON SPORTS   Hazing and University Policy

In this chapter, we have referred to the often demeaning, sickening, painful, or illegal nature of hazing activities. Initiation rituals on Canadian university sport teams have been described by Bryshun and Young (1999) and Johnson (1999). The forms of hazing activities vary by sport, by university (depending on traditions), and by gender. However, at the very least, hazing usually involves excessive drinking.

In the late 1990s, following a number of well-publicized incidents that involved student orientations and athletics teams (e.g., an incident at the University of Guelph in which a coach suspended two players for refusing to participate), many Canadian universities developed anti-hazing/initiation policies. These were zero tolerance policies imposed under the Code of Student Behaviour to deal with frosh week, fraternity, and sport team initiations, or specifically for athletes by athletics departments. Coaches were no longer permitted to sanction or participate in team hazing ceremonies, and athletes were supposed to be informed of their right to refuse to be coerced into excessive drinking.

The response of many university sports teams was to go underground; ceremonies were taken off campus to student houses, bars, and motels. Jay Johnson (1999) found evidence that the abuse of new team members on some teams escalated as the activities moved off campus. Students reported that this was because the previous limits established by the presence of coaches, and sometimes alumni, no longer existed, and that ceremonies were taking place beyond the reach of campus security.

Jay Johnson felt that universities and athletics departments may have made a bad situation even worse with their zero tolerance policies, and that they needed to take a little more responsibility for the behaviour of student athletes. With the support of the associate dean for athletics at the University of Toronto, Johnson received a grant from the university administration to develop alternative initiation ceremonies for athletics teams. These included outdoor activities such as ropes courses or short stays at a camp where athletes from several teams were involved in canoeing, rock climbing, and so on. They were held before the team's season started, coaches were also involved, and they sometimes brought their own children.

Recent evaluation research indicates that hazing has not been eliminated; there are still some underground initiations, and heavy drinking is still involved. However, some teams have reported that they are less degrading than in previous years because rookies and veterans had already bonded during the alternative initiations. The key seemed to be the inclusion of activities that are new to all players, both veterans and rookies, giving a sense of equality and cooperation from the start. When these are combined with good communications and clear athletics department policies regarding the rights and responsibilities of athletes, and with an increasing assertiveness on the part of some student-athletes who refuse, for example, to become involved in heavy drinking, it appears that some changes to long established traditions are possible.

We think that these are valuable policy alternatives. *What do you think?*

lives in a special zone, where normal community standards and rules do not apply to them or their friends?

• If people in the community view athletes with awe and admiration because of their extreme behaviours, ideas, and characteristics, might this view interfere with the enforcement of community standards and rules when athletes, especially high-profile athletes, violate them?

Research is needed on each of the issues raised in these questions. Our sense is that long-term overconformity to the sport ethic creates social conditions and group dynamics in sports that encourage notable forms of "deviant" underconformity, such as binge drinking, academic cheating, group theft and property destruction, drunken and careless driving, sexual harassment, physical assault, spouse abuse, and sexual assault.

This possible connection between these two types of "deviance" came to mind when an NFL football player said, "Hey, I have no problem sharing women with my teammates. These guys go to battle with me" (Nelson, 1994: 144).

This player's comment may be shocking, but it is consistent with other cases. For example, there are a number of cases where young male athletes did not break group silence after witnessing teammates gang rape a woman (Curry, 1991, 1998; Lefkowitz, 1997; Robinson, 1998; Safai, 2002). Hazing rituals have subjected prospective teammates to demeaning and even criminal treatment—coercing rookies to steal, drink to the point of passing out, harass others, urinate on each other, drink urine, hold each other's genitals, appear nude in public, and endure various forms of sodomy, beatings, and brandings (Bryshun and Young, 1999; Johnson, 1999).

The awe and admiration accorded to athletes who entertain as they push limits and engage in "deviant" overconformity on the field has clearly interfered with the enforcement of community standards and rules off the field. For example, there are cases when fans who normally preach a get tough on crime philosophy have threatened women who filed well-documented assault and rape charges against high-profile athletes (Benedict, 1997; Lipsyte, 1998; Robinson, 1998). There are cases where police officers have asked athletes who are being arrested to sign autographs for their children, and judges in the U.S. have made favourable decisions involving athletes who play on teams representing their alma mater or teams for which the judges have season tickets.

Controlling "Deviant" Overconformity in Sports "Deviant" overconformity presents special social control problems in sports. Coaches, managers, owners, and sponsors—people who exercise control of sports—often benefit when athletes blindly accept and overconform to the sport ethic. These people often see athletes who willingly engage in "deviant" overconformity as a blessing, not a curse. The fact that athletes often use their overconformity to the sport ethic as proof of their personal commitment and courage works to the advantage of all who benefit from winning records and high TV ratings. This is why those who control sports are unwilling to discourage this type of "deviance"—even when it involves using performance-enhancing substances, as explained later in this chapter.

The issue of social control is further complicated by the tendency to promote extreme overconformers to the sport ethic into positions of power and influence in sports. Because these people have proved they are willing to pay the price and use the sport ethic without reservation, they are seen as ideal candidates for certain jobs in sports, especially coaching jobs. For example, Bobby Clarke, currently general manager of the NHL's Philadelphia Flyers, was the player who reportedly deliberately slashed Valery Kharlamov during the famous 1972 series between Canada and the Soviet Union, resulting in a broken ankle. The attack was evidently carried out at the request of coach John Ferguson, and it had no real consequences for Clarke until the issue was raised recently at the thirtieth anniversary ceremonies by series star, Paul Henderson.[7] This creates a situation in which "deviance" and ethical problems among athletes are rooted in the organization of sport itself, in athletes' relationships with one another and with coaches and managers.

Everyone in sports must work together to discourage overconformity to the sport ethic. (See, for example, the Reflect on Sports box, "Hazing and University Policy," above.) This does not mean that we should ignore other forms of "deviance," or that underconformity

---

[7] This should be contrasted with the recent punishment of Roy Keane, the Manchester United soccer player who claimed, in his autobiography, to have deliberately injured an opponent in a game. His fine and suspension is the highest ever handed out by the British Football Association (FA)—a five-game suspension and a fine of £150,000 (over C$300,000).

and the rejection of rules and regulations is not a problem in sports. However, underconformity is regularly identified as a problem, and it is usually controlled effectively. Overconformity is more subversive, because it is widely ignored. For example, when a fourteen-year-old gymnast is late for practice, a coach immediately identifies this type of "deviance" and acts on the spot to eliminate it. However, when the same gymnast engages in unhealthy eating behaviours to lose weight as she strives for distinction and pursues her dream, many coaches, parents, and gym owners do not see this as "deviance," or they do not want to interfere with the mindset of a champion and the culture of the gym—until, of course, stress fractures interfere with competition and weight loss puts their athlete and daughter in a hospital.

The control of "deviant" overconformity demands that athletes, coaches, commentators, and fans raise critical questions about the meaning, organization, and purpose of sports, and about the sport ethic itself. In the absence of these questions, athletes will continue to think and act in ways that threaten the health and well-being of themselves and others. Furthermore, the common motivational strategy of convincing athletes that their teams are families, and that teammates must put their bodies on the line for each other because they go to battle together, clearly promotes the hubris and the athlete-community separation that perpetuate "deviant" overconformity. Athletes sometimes conclude that "outsiders are out to get us" and that "we have to stick together because nobody else understands us." They reaffirm their hubris in the process, and they further disconnect from the community whose standards apply to their lives. Of course, the price for this change is that we may limit the number of athlete/gladiators who entertain us as we sit safely in front of our TVs and interactive computers and watch people put their bodies on the line for our pleasure.

All social life contains tensions between overconformity and underconformity. In the case of sport, these tensions are especially evident because of the processes that encourage extreme conformity. This means that special efforts are needed to strike a balance between accepting rules and questioning rules. The more everyone in sports is involved in questioning and qualifying norms and rules, the more effective they will be in controlling "deviant" overconformity, although the control will never be perfect or permanent. Our sense is that controlling "deviant" overconformity is also an important step in controlling "deviant" underconformity. The ultimate goals are to diminish the separation between athletes and the rest of the community, to alter social processes so that athletes will be less likely to feel above the law, and to make the community aware of the need to deal with athletes without letting awe and admiration interfere. Athletes must be held accountable for their "deviance," regardless of their popularity in the community.

RESEARCH ON "DEVIANCE" AMONG ATHLETES

Headlines and media coverage of "deviance" among athletes are common, but systematic studies of "deviance" among athletes are rare. Publishing lists of arrest records and charges filed against athletes attracts attention, but it does not tell us much about whether "deviance" is out of control in sports, whether there is more "deviance" today than there was in the past, whether "deviance" involves overconformity or underconformity, or whether it is rooted in the characters of athletes, the culture and organization of sports, or factors that exist outside of sports. Most media reports conclude that "deviance" is caused by character weaknesses and a lack of discipline among athletes, or that it is the result of money and an overemphasis on winning. Few reports discuss the possibility that "deviance" is related to the culture and organization of sports or to social dynamics that exist in the social worlds created around sports.

When we review accounts of "deviance" among athletes, it is important to distinguish "deviance" that occurs on the field and in sport settings from "deviance" that occurs off the field and away from sports. They are related to different types of norms and rules, and they have different causes and consequences.

"Deviance" on the Field and in Sport Settings

Examples of "deviance" on the field and in sport settings include cheating (such as using the spitball or having an excessive curve on the blade of a hockey stick), gambling, shaving points, throwing games or matches, engaging in unsportsman-like conduct, fighting, taking performance-enhancing drugs, and generally finding ways to avoid rules. Some people claim that these types of "deviance" have become serious today, because the personal and financial stakes have become so great in sports.

Most long-term historical analyses, however, suggest that cheating, dirty play, fighting, and the use of violence are less common today than they were in the days before television coverage and high-stakes commercialization (Dunning, 1999; Maguire, 1988; Scheinin, 1994). These analyses make the case that sports today are more rule-governed than they were in the past and that instances of on-the-field "deviance" are more likely to be punished with formal sanctions within sports and criticized by observers outside sports. Therefore, it may be a mistake to blame "deviance" in sports today on money and TV.

Actually, it is very difficult to track and study rates of on-the-field "deviance" among athletes, because rules change over time and rules are enforced in different ways at different points in time. Research does suggest that athletes in most sports interpret rules very loosely during games and that they often create informal norms, which stretch official rules (Shields and Bredemeier, 1995). However, this is not new. Athletes have done this ever since umpires and referees have been enforcing rules. In fact, athletes in organized sports traditionally have played to the level permitted by umpires and referees—they adjust their behaviours according to how tightly the referees are calling a game (cf., Rains, 1984). But this does not mean that the players ignore rules or that "deviance" is out of hand. Nor does it mean that we ought to ignore identified forms of "deviance."

The perception that rates of on-the-field and sport-related "deviance" are increasing also may exist because there are more rules today than ever before, and sports are more rule-governed than they were in the past. A look at the rulebooks of sport organizations clearly shows that there are literally thousands of rules today that did not exist twenty years ago in sports, and every year more rules are added. WADA and international sport organizations now list thousands of banned substances. There are more ways than ever before of becoming "deviant" in sports! Furthermore, the forms of surveillance used today and the increased emphasis on rule enforcement means that more rule violators are caught today.

Finally, there is evidence that athletes in certain sports simply come to expect and engage in a certain amount of on-the-field intentional rule violation ("good fouls"), cheating, and aggression (Anonymous, 1999; Pilz, 1996; Shields et al., 1995). This approach seems to be more prevalent at higher levels of competition and to increase with time spent participating in a sport. It is also more common among men than women, and it is especially strong among members of winning teams and among non-starters. This finding is consistent with other research suggesting that playing most forms of power and performance sports does not promote moral development and moral decision making (Stoll and Beller, 1998).

However, in the absence of good historical data, our sense is that most on-the-field and sport-related rule violations are not more common today than they were in the past, and they are not out of control. "Deviance" does

SIDELINES

....

When winning becomes the sole measure of achievement, athletes may resort to "deviance" to keep opponents from the victory stand.

exist; *it is a problem.* It ought to be studied, and efforts should be made to control it without violating the principles of due process and justice. The form of sport-related "deviance" that may be more prevalent today is the use of banned performance-enhancing substances. This is clearly a serious problem, and it is discussed later in the chapter.

"Deviance" off the Field and Away from Sports

Off-the-field "deviance" receives widespread media attention. When athletes are arrested or linked to criminal activity, they make headlines and become lead stories on the evening news. Research on these forms of "deviance" has not provided clear conclusions about whether rates have gone up or down, or whether they are higher than rates among comparable segments of people in the general population. However, it is clear that felonies are a problem whenever they occur. They do harm that cannot be lessened by data showing that rates are lower today than yesterday or that rates among athletes are lower than rates for comparable people from similar backgrounds. Impaired driving is a potentially fatal act, and a sexual assault does extreme harm

to a person, regardless of who does it and how "the case" fits with rates for various groups and over history. Those who commit these crimes, athletes or not, must be held accountable—even if it means losing the big game next week.

At present, there are data from studies of delinquency and sport participation among U.S. high school students, from a few studies of excessive alcohol use among U.S. high school and university athletes, and from a very few studies of felony rates.

Delinquency Rates Current research on delinquency and sport participation is scarce, but past studies generally contradict attention-grabbing headlines about athletes. For example, when rates of off-the-field delinquent and "deviant" behaviour among U.S. high school athletes have been compared with rates among other students, the rates for athletes almost always have been found to be lower than those for other students from similar backgrounds. With a couple of exceptions, this general finding seems to hold for athletes in various sports, athletes in different societies, and both boys and girls from various racial and social class backgrounds (see Miracle and Rees, 1994, for a summary of these studies).

Of course, these findings may reflect the fact that students with histories of "deviant" behaviour do not usually try out for sport teams, that coaches cut them when they do try out, or that athletes receive preferential treatment, which keeps them out of court and jail when they are "deviant." It is also possible that forms of "deviance" among some athletes are obscured by a façade of conformity (Miracle and Rees, 1994); however, until we know more about off-the-field behaviours, it is difficult to argue that athletes have higher rates of delinquency than comparable nonathletes. Of course, as noted in chapter 4, sport experiences vary from programme to programme, and sport participation constitutes only a part of a person's experiences. Therefore, it is misleading to make generalizations about how sport participation affects behaviours. At present it seems safe to say that sport participation turns young people neither into models of virtue nor into delinquents in any systematic way.

Alcohol Use and Binge Drinking As most of us know from our own experience, underage and excessive alcohol consumption in high school and university is not limited to athletes. However, recent U.S. data indicate that male and female interuniversity athletes engage in more alcohol use, abuse, and binge drinking than other men and women students (Naughton, 1996b; Wechsler et al., 1997). Other data suggest that, among white, middle-class high school students, the young men on high school teams have higher rates of both regular alcohol use and total abstinence than other students; patterns among young women athletes are not significantly different from patterns among other female students (Carr et al., 1996).

These research findings are important because alcohol use and abuse may be related to other forms of "deviance." More studies are needed to see if the group dynamics of alcohol use and binge drinking are related to the dynamics underlying overconformity to other group norms among athletes. Getting drunk with fellow athletes may not be very different, sociologically speaking, from playing with pain to meet the expectations of teammates: "Have another five shots of tequila—it's what we teammates who make sacrifices and take risks together are doing tonight; are you a part of this special group or not?" Donnelly's (1993) research showed that binge drinking and other forms of excessive behaviour were common among the Canadian high-performance athletes that he interviewed at particular times in their careers (e.g., after major competitions, at the end of a season, or following retirement). (See the Reflect on Sports box, "Is Sport Participation a Cure for 'Deviant' Behaviour," pp. 171–172.) Again, research is needed to see if, why, when, and how often this occurs.

Felony Rates In North America, widely publicized cases of assault, hard drug use, and drug trafficking in which male athletes are the offenders have created a growing sense of urgency about the need for systematic studies of these forms of "deviance." Commentaries, theoretical analyses, and empirical studies have begun to focus on whether participation in certain sports goes hand in hand with high felony rates. However, systematic empirical research is scarce, and the studies that do exist report mixed findings (see Crossett, 1999, for a review and critique of research on sexual assault, in particular).

Another problem with studies of felony rates is that the data on the arrest rates for athletes are seldom compared with arrest rates in the general population and in populations comparable to the athletes in age and race. The incidence of assault and sexual assault among male athletes is an especially important topic and is discussed in more detail in the chapter on violence in sports (chapter 7).

In Summary The point of this section on off-the-field "deviance" among athletes is that athlete behaviour does not seem to be out of control. This does *not* mean that off-the-field "deviance" is not a problem; *it is a problem*, and both athletes and sport organizations must take responsibility for controlling it. Research suggests that the delinquency and crime rates of athletes may not be higher than they are for comparable peers. There are exceptions to this in the case of alcohol abuse and binge drinking and possibly in the case of other forms of "deviance," including certain forms of assault. However, research is needed to establish if and why athletes measure higher on various forms of "deviance" than other groups and individuals in society as a whole.

Finally, it is important to recognize that, while some people claim that off-the-field "deviance" among athletes is getting out of control, others claim that sport participation can be used to control "deviant" behaviour among young people. Although this latter claim also needs further testing, it is discussed in the Reflect on Sports box, "Is Sport Participation a Cure for 'Deviant' Behaviour," pp. 171–172.

Why Focus Only on "Deviance" among Athletes?

"Deviance" among athletes is an important issue, and it should be covered in some detail. However, athletes are not the only people in sports who violate norms. The following are a few other examples of "deviance" related to sports:

- Coaches who hit players, treat them inhumanely, use male players' insecurities about masculinity as a basis for motivating them, sexually harass women in and out of sports, subvert efforts to provide women with equal participation opportunities in sport, and violate organizational rules
- Coaches and sport administrators who ignore or try to subvert organization regulations about eligibility, gender and language equity, and so on
- Sport team owners who stretch or violate combines laws, collude with each other to hold down player salaries, and deliberately mislead city officials and voters in connection with stadium or arena funding issues
- Sport administrators (including those on the International Olympic Committee and related organizations) who take bribes and gifts in return for favours and who violate public trust and organizational principles by making decisions clearly based on their personal interests (see Jennings, 1996a,b; Jennings and Sambrook, 2000); since the 1999 revelations about corruption, the IOC no longer permits its members to visit cities that are bidding for future Olympic Games—perhaps they do not trust themselves to refuse offered bribes and gifts
- Team managers and player personnel staff who ignore the dynamics of race and ethnicity when they recruit, evaluate, hire, and promote administrative staff and coaches
- Media promoters and commentators who deliberately distort and misrepresent sport events, so that they can generate high television ratings or newspaper/magazine sales
- Agents who mislead athletes, misrepresent themselves, or violate rules as they solicit junior and student-athletes and represent professional athletes
- Parent/spectators who berate, taunt, and fight with each other, referees, and players as they watch their children in youth sports (the recent manslaughter case involving hockey fathers in Massachusetts has added a new level of significance to this issue)
- Spectators who endanger athletes by throwing objects onto the field of play, verbally attack athletes, fight with one another, destroy property in anger after losses and in "joy" after wins, place illegal bets on sports, and forge and sell autographs of athletes
- Judges who collude in order to ensure that certain athletes win medals, particularly evident in boxing (Jennings, 1996a) and in figure skating (for example, the case of Jamie Salé and David Pelletier at the 2002 Salt Lake City Olympics)

Some of these and other examples of "deviant" behaviours are discussed in other chapters. However, as we think about this list, we are reminded of the day in 1997 when Latrell Sprewell, then a player on the Golden State Warriors, choked his coach, P. J. Carlesimo. Sprewell was out of line, and he paid for it with fines and a suspension, which cost him one year of his career and over $6 million in salary and endorsements. As people debated whether Sprewell should have been punished even more severely, few asked why his coach had never been punished for regularly harassing and demeaning his players in ways that would have led him to be fired if he had been a supervisor or manager in most other U.S. organizations.

REFLECT ON SPORTS

Is Sport Participation a Cure for "Deviant" Behaviour?

We often hear that sports keep kids off the streets and out of trouble, and build character in the process, and then we hear about athletes who get into trouble and prove that years of playing sports have not kept them from being "deviant." How do we make sense out of this conflicting information? Fortunately, research can help.

A study by sociologist Michael Trulson (1986) suggests that *only certain types of sports and sport participation* can lower delinquency rates among young people. Trulson worked with thirty-four young men aged thirteen to seventeen who had been classified as delinquents, tested them for aggression and personality adjustment, and divided them into three groups matched on important background characteristics. For six months, each group met three times a week for training sessions with the same instructor. Group 1 received traditional Tae Kwon Do training, taught with a philosophy emphasizing respect for self and others, the importance of physical fitness, self-control, patience, perseverance, responsibility, and honour. Group 2 received "modern" martial arts training, emphasizing free-sparring and self-defence techniques; the coach provided no philosophy in connection with the physical training. Group 3 received no martial arts training but jogged and played basketball and football under the instructor's coaching and supervision.

Trulson's findings indicated clear changes in Group 1. After six months, the young men in this group had fewer delinquent tendencies, less anxiety and aggression, improved self-esteem and social skills, and more awareness of commonly held values. Those in Group 2 had increased delinquent tendencies and were more aggressive and less adjusted than when the study began. Those in Group 3 showed no change in delinquent tendencies or on most personality measures, but their scores on self-esteem and social skills improved over the six months.

THE MORAL OF THE STORY

Sport participation might keep kids out of trouble if it involves an explicit emphasis on (1) a philosophy of

Off-the-field "deviance" among athletes may decrease if athletes are taught a philosophy of nonviolence, respect for self and opponents, self-control, confidence in their abilities, and responsibility. This can happen in a variety of sports, even those involving heavy physical contact. (CP/Jacques Boissinot)

nonviolence, (2) respect for self and others, (3) the importance of fitness and control over self, (4) confidence in physical skills, and (5) a sense of responsibility. When these five things are absent, sport participation will seldom keep young people out of trouble. Simply taking kids off the streets is just the beginning. If they play sports with an emphasis on hostility,

Continued

REFLECT ON SPORTS

Is Sport Participation a Cure for "Deviant" Behaviour?
continued

dominating others, using their bodies as weapons, and defining masculinity in terms of conquest, we *cannot* expect rates of "deviance" to decrease.

Changing behaviour is a complex process, and to do it in connection with sport participation requires a clear programme of intervention in the lives of young people. This does not mean that all sports must be turned into treatment programmes, but it does mean that playing sports can not be expected to keep kids out of trouble unless participation connects them with other people in supportive and positive ways.

A WORD OF CAUTION

A study by sociologist Eldon Snyder (1994) suggests that, when athletes form special bonds with each other, become arrogant about their unity and uniqueness, and become subjectively separated from the rest of the community, their sport participation may foster "deviant" behaviours. Snyder did a qualitative analysis of a case in which nine U.S. university athletes were arrested after committing dozens of burglaries over two years. Seven of the athletes were on the men's swim team, one was on the track and field team, and one was a former member of the women's swim team (and currently dating one of the men); they all came from middle-class families.

Snyder examined records, testimony, and court documents in the case, including statements by athletes, parents, lawyers, and others. He did *not* conclude that sport participation had *caused* these young people to be "deviant." Instead, he concluded that playing sports had created the bonds and dynamics out of which the "deviance" of this group of student-athletes emerged. Snyder had no final explanation for why these young people did what they did, but he noted that sport participation certainly did not serve as a deterrent to "deviance."

This general conclusion is consistent with Peter Donnelly's (1993) research showing that certain forms of binge "deviance" are relatively common among elite athletes, especially after major competitions, at the end of their seasons, and following retirement. Donnelly interviewed recently retired national-level athletes in Canada and found that, when they had breaks in their training, they often felt, as one former athlete explained, that they "had to make the most of it. Go for it. Do everything to the max!" Another said that "when you partied, you just partied your face off [because] you knew that you would have to get into the grind tomorrow or the next day." Another explained that after the season they went on a binge by "eating, popping, drinking, injecting, and sniffing everything that wasn't nailed down."

A FINAL NOTE

These studies show that neither virtue nor "deviance" is *caused* by sports and sport participation. Sports are sites where young people often have powerful and exciting physical and social experiences. When they are organized so that young people can receive thoughtful guidance from adults who are sensitive to what young people need to develop self-respect and become connected to the rest of the community, good outcomes are likely (Coakley, 2002). However, when playing sports separates athletes from the rest of the community and fosters overconformity to the norms of the sport ethic, good outcomes are unlikely. The bonds formed among athletes can take them in many directions, including "deviant" ones. Sport programmes are effective only when they enable people to live more satisfying lives in the community; simply taking people off the streets for a few hours a week so they can bounce basketballs does little more than provide temporary shelter. *What do you think?*

• •

Some people said Carlesimo was a jerk, but there were no studies of how coaches harass and mistreat athletes and no discussions of whether they violate organizational or community rules

when they do so. Sprewell's actions were wrong, and they deserved to be punished, but he was not the only person who overstepped normative boundaries (see Walton, 2001).

PERFORMANCE-ENHANCING SUBSTANCES: A CASE OF "DEVIANT" OVERCONFORMITY IN SPORTS

Since the use of performance-enhancing drugs is widely considered to be cheating, and is against the rules of most sports, why do we not consider this as a case of underconformity to the sport ethic? Many people, including athletes such as British runner Paula Radcliffe, the new world record holder in the women's marathon, and Becky Scott, the Canadian cross-country ski Olympic medalist in Salt Lake City, are extremely concerned about athletes who cheat to win. Unfortunately, their particular sport ethic seems to be a minority view. As we demonstrate in this section, when the dominant sport ethic encourages doing whatever it takes to win, then the use of performance-enhancing substances becomes another case of overconformity.

Stories about athletes using performance-enhancing substances are no longer shocking; they appear regularly in the media. However, many people do not know that drug and substance use in sports has a long history.[8] Athletes have taken a wide variety of everyday and exotic substances over the years, and substance use has never been limited to elite athletes. Data suggest that, if today's drugs had been available in past centuries, athletes would have used them as frequently as athletes use them today (Hoberman, 1992; Todd, 1987). This makes it difficult to blame all drug use on the profit motive, commercial interests, television, and the erosion of traditional values.

Historical data also suggest that drug and substance use by athletes generally is not the result of defective socialization or lack of moral character. After all, users and abusers often are the most dedicated and committed athletes in sports! Nor are all substance users helpless victims of coaches and trainers who lack moral character, although coaches and trainers who push the sport ethic without question may directly or indirectly encourage the use of performance-enhancing substances. Instead, most substance use and abuse seem to be the same type of overconformity that occurs when injured distance runners continue training, even when training may cause serious injuries; when young female gymnasts control weight by cutting their food intake to dangerous levels; and when football players risk their already injured and surgically repaired bodies week after painful week in the CFL.

Apparently, many athletes enjoy playing their sports so much that they will do whatever it takes to stay involved and live up to the expectations of their fellow athletes. Of course, they seek on-the-field success, enabling them to avoid being cut or eliminated, but the desire to win is usually secondary to the desire to play and be accepted as an athlete. This means that, as long as some athletes are willing to take performance-enhancing substances to gain the edge they need to continue playing at the highest possible level of competence, others will conclude that they also must use similar substances to stay competitive at that level, even if it is against their better judgment. These dynamics, all connected with overconformity to the sport ethic, operate at various levels of sports—from local gyms, where high school athletes work out, to the locker rooms of professional sport teams—and among women and men across a wide variety of sport events, from the 100-metre sprint to the marathon and from hockey to football.

The important points are these: (1) performance-enhancing substance use and abuse are a form of "deviant" overconformity, and (2) substances believed by athletes to enhance performance will be used despite regulations that ban "doping." The usefulness of these points becomes clear when we examine efforts to define, ban, test for, and control the use of performance-enhancing substances.

---

[8]See the *Sports in Society* website (www.mcgrawhill.ca/college/coakley) for a summary of this history.

Defining and Banning Performance-Enhancing Substances

Defining "performance-enhancing substances" is difficult. They can include anything from aspirin to heroin; they may be legal or illegal, harmless or dangerous, natural or synthetic, socially acceptable or unacceptable, commonly used or exotic. Furthermore, they may produce real physical changes, psychological changes, or both.

Problems with definitions are faced whenever a sport organization develops an anti-drug or no-doping programme. For example, until 1999, the International Olympic Committee (IOC) defined doping in this way:

> [Doping is] the administration of or use by a competing athlete of any substance *foreign* to the body or any *physiological substance* taken in *abnormal quantity* or taken by an *abnormal route of entry* into the body with the *sole intention* of increasing in an *artificial* and *unfair* manner his/her performance in competition. When necessity demands *medical treatment* with any substance that, because of its nature, dosage, or application, is able to boost the athlete's performance in competition in an artificial and unfair manner, this too is regarded by the IOC as doping (USOC, 1992, p. 1 italics added to emphasize key terms).

This definition may sound good, but the IOC had difficulty defining all the terms in italics. For example, what is a substance "foreign" to the body, and why are the "foreign" substances of aspirin and ibuprofen not banned, while the "natural" hormone testosterone is banned? What is an "abnormal" quantity or an "abnormal" route of entry? Why are megadoses of vitamins not banned, while small amounts of many decongestants are banned? Why can athletes be stripped of medals when they swallow medications without intending to enhance performance, while other athletes are legally rehydrated with IV needles inserted into veins?

> **If the purpose of sport is personal growth and self-discovery, the athlete loses all in the Faustian pact with steroids.**
>
> —Bruce Kidd, *University of Toronto Magazine* (1989)

With new scientific discoveries being made every day and applied to sports, what is artificial and what is unfair? Why are needles permitted to inject certain painkillers but are considered dangerous and artificial when used to inject an athlete's own red blood cells into a vein (blood boosting)? Why is the electronic stimulation of muscles permitted? Is it fair to compete with knees that have surgically inserted synthetic ligaments because "natural" ligaments were destroyed? Why are biofeedback and other psychological technologies defined as "natural" and "fair," while certain forms of "natural" herbal tea are defined as "unnatural" and "unfair"? Are vitamins natural? amino acids? caffeine? human growth hormone? Gatorade? marijuana? How about so-called natural herbs, chemicals, and compounds now stacked floor to ceiling in stores that sell nutritional supplements with the promise of performance enhancement?

Is it natural to deprive yourself of food to make weight or meet the demands of a coach who measures body fat every week and punishes athletes who eat "normal" diets? Should athletes who "binge and purge" or become anorexic or exercise in rubber suits to lose weight be considered "normal"? In fact, what is normal about all of the social, psychological, biomechanical, environmental, and technological methods of manipulating athletes' bodies in today's high-performance sports? Are U.S. university football players "deviant" when saline solutions are dripped into their veins through intravenous needles in a pregame locker room to minimize the threat of dehydration on a hot playing field? Surely this is a performance-enhancing procedure. Is it normal, safe? How about twelve-year-old gymnasts who pop a dozen anti-inflammatory pills every day, so that they can train through pain? Are they "deviant"? Are they different from hockey players who pop a half-dozen

REFLECT ON SPORTS Ben Johnson, the Dubin Commission, and Drug Testing in Canada

The recent announcement that the U.S. Olympic Committee never declared a positive dope test for Carl Lewis before the 1988 Olympics in Seoul has reminded many Canadians of the Ben Johnson case.

Johnson, to the delight of Canadians, won the 100-metre gold medal in Seoul with a world-record performance. Later during the games, however, it was announced that he had tested positive for a banned steroid, stanozolol; his gold medal was taken away and awarded to the second-place American, Carl Lewis.

The response in Canada was mixed—people were stunned; some felt they knew that steroids were being used, and many were sympathetic and declared their support for Johnson. The federal government announced the formation of a commission to inquire into "the Use of Drugs and Banned Practices Intended to Increase Athletic Performance," under the leadership of Justice Charles Dubin (Dubin, 1990). The inquiry discovered widespread use of steroids among athletes at the Mazda Track Club based at York University, and Dubin recommended widespread changes in Canadian sport policy.

In response, a Sport Canada report titled, *Sport: The Way Ahead* (Best, Blackhurst, and Makosky, 1992), proposed that the Canadian sport system become a more open and athlete-centred system; and random, out-of-competition testing was introduced to ensure

that there would be no repeat of the Johnson affair. However, while the Canadian Centre for Ethics in Sport was established to provide doping information and education, and to administer testing, few of the expected changes in the sport system occurred. The resilience of the long-established power and performance system was only slightly challenged.

There were some powerful critiques of the Dubin Commission (e.g., Beauchesne, 1990; Burstyn, 2000; and MacAloon, 1990), pointing out the way in which the Commission was used to deflect blame from the government. The Commission, according to Burstyn:

• Minimized the importance of governmental policy and funding (e.g., the Athlete Assistance Programme that based its funding on athletes' world ranking) in promoting performance-enhancing drugs;
• Ignored the role of commercial and media interests in the evolution of an athletic drug culture; and
• Avoided examining the larger issues of drug use in elite and professional sports.

Some people think that Canada has gone too far, and that we have done a disservice to our athletes by implementing random out-of-competition testing when few of the countries we compete against, including the U.S., have gone as far. *What do you think?*

• •

Sudafed pills (containing pseudoephedrine) to get "up" for the game? How about NFL players who became addicted to painkillers after being regularly injected by physicians hired by team owners? Why do we call athletes heroes when they use an IV procedure to play in extreme heat or take large injections of painkilling drugs to keep them training and playing, and then condemn the same athletes when they take drugs to help them build muscles damaged by overtraining or other drugs to help them relax and recover after their bodies and minds have been

pushed beyond limits in the pursuit of dreams? Why do many athletes see the use of drugs as a noble act of commitment and dedication, while many spectators see it as a reprehensible act of "deviance" yet pay big money to watch athletes do superhuman things requiring extreme training regimes and strategies made possible by drugs? Why are spectators in some sports ambivalent about the whole issue, to the point where Mark McGwire's use of androstenedione (illegal in most sports, but not Major League Baseball at the time) during his home-run record season in 1998 was barely an issue for many people?

These and hundreds of other questions about what is artificial, natural, foreign, fair, and abnormal show that any definition of *doping* will lead to endless debates about the technical and legal meaning of terms. For this reason, by 1999 the IOC changed its definition of doping:

> Doping is: (1) the use of an expedient (substance or method) which is profoundly harmful to athletes' health and/or capable of enhancing their performance, or (2) the presence in the athlete's body of a Prohibited Substance or evidence of the use thereof or evidence of the use of a Prohibited Method.

Even this simplified definition, along with the eight single-spaced pages in which prohibited substances and prohibited methods are described, raises many questions. The establishment of the World Anti-Doping Agency (WADA), based in Montreal, is an attempt to put the IOC, the international sport federations, and as many countries as possible on the same page with regard to doping. However, the even more simplified definition in the World Anti-Doping Code (v. 3; WADA, 2003) is again subject to pages and pages of qualifications: "Doping is defined as the occurrence of one or more of the anti-doping rule violations set forth in Article 2.1 through 2.8 of the Code" (p. 10). Article 2.1 reads: "The presence of a *Prohibited Substance* or its *Metabolites* or *Markers* in an *Athlete's* bodily *Specimen*" (p. 10).

Meanwhile, physicians, pharmacists, chemists, inventors, and athletes continue to develop new and different aids to performance—chemical, "natural," and otherwise. This creates an endless game of scientific hide and seek, which shows no sign of letting up, regardless of definitions. In fact, we can expect it to become more heated and controversial as scientists manipulate the brain and nervous system and try to use genetic engineering to improve athletic performance. How will we define, identify, and

"Is this what those hormones are supposed to do, Carl?"

The negative side effects of various combinations of substances ("stacking and cycling") are difficult to identify. Controlled studies of banned substances are difficult to do, because it may not be ethical to experiment with the same dosages that athletes use. This means that the side effects of many substances are unknown.

deal with doping and drugs in light of all these possibilities? Drug use among athletes seems to be only one of many issues related to technology and the manipulation of athletes' bodies; soon we will be forced to deal with issues much more contentious than so-called doping.

Further complicating decisions about which substances to ban is confusion about their effects on athletic performance. Athletes learn things in locker rooms faster than scientists learn them in the lab, although the validity of locker room knowledge is frequently suspect. Furthermore, by the time researchers have good information about a substance, athletes have moved on to others, which have not been tested. This is why many athletes ignore "official statements" about the consequences and dangers of doping—the statements are about two to five years behind the "inventors" who supply new substances.

Sport organizations often withhold information about substances because they think that knowledge among athletes might encourage use. However, most athletes now obtain information in the locker room, at the local gym, and in both mainstream and underground publications that claim to provide a sound basis for making informed choices about substance use (see any issue of *Muscle Media*; Phillips, 1997; www.bigsport.com). Most athletes in international sports, such as the Olympics, also realize that the IOC and other sport organizations withhold information because they do not want to jeopardize the billions of dollars that corporate sponsors and TV networks pay for what they want to present to the world as a clean and wholesome event (Jennings, 1996a; Jennings and Sambrook, 2000).

Most antidoping policies are at least partially based on the belief that these substances are dangerous to the health of athletes. Although this is true in some cases, it is tough to argue this point to athletes who already make sacrifices, pay the price, and take many health risks as they strive for distinction and pursue dreams in their sports. For example, when athletes who have dedicated between four and fifteen years of their youth to make a national team or play a pro sport are told that taking certain hormones could shorten their lives by a few years or do damage to their livers or hearts, they do not listen very closely. Such messages do not scare many of them; they know that being an athlete means that you take risks and sometimes suffer in the process. Furthermore, when they are not encouraged to question the extreme commitment that promotes other dangerous forms of overconformity to the sport ethic, how can they be convinced to avoid substances that may negatively affect their health? After all, real athletes know that participation in power and performance sports is itself a threat to their health (Waddington, 2000)!

Finally, some people ask why drugs should be banned in sports when they are widely accepted in society and used to improve performance or treat conditions that interfere with performance at home or on the job. The majority of adults in most wealthy, high-tech societies use tranquilizers, pain controllers, mood controllers, antidepressants, decongestants, diet pills, birth control

pills, caffeine, nicotine, sleep aids, or alcohol. Doctors now prescribe or suggest for their patients various health-related hormone-drug-supplement therapies designed to improve strength and counteract the negative effects of aging; these include testosterone, various anabolic steroids, human growth hormone (HGH), HGH stimulants, androstenedione, DHEA, and creatine.[9] Every six months the list changes and grows longer as new discoveries are made and new supplements manufactured. In fact, if people really did say no to drugs, life in most Western societies would change dramatically. When a forty-five-year-old man takes HGH to maintain strength so he can perform on the job, why shouldn't his twenty-five-year-old son do the same thing in the CHL?

These facts give rise to an important question. Why bother to control athletes in ways that other people are not controlled? After all, do universities have rules banning caffeine used to enable students to study all night for a test? Do teachers make students sign an oath to avoid drugs that might enable them to do their coursework? Do employers tell executives not to use hormone therapies to keep them fit for work? Do wives tell their husbands not to take Viagra, the performance-enhancing drug that boosts sexual arousal? Why should athletes have to do these things when others competing for valued rewards do not? As these questions are asked, it remains difficult to define drugs, doping, and substance abuse in sports.

---

[9]Dehydroepiandrosterone (DHEA) is a hormone widely available over the counter in most countries (although not in Canada). It is a product of the adrenal glands, and it stimulates the production of testosterone. Some athletes and people over age forty take it to maintain lean body mass. At this time, it is not a banned substance for athletes. Creatine is a compound produced by the liver, kidneys, and pancreas. It may facilitate the renewal of anaerobic energy reserves, delay the onset of fatigue during intense exercise, and cut recovery time between workouts (Kearney, 1999).

As governing bodies add items to the banned substance list, some athletes use other substances to aid training and performance. During the late-1990s, the substances in this photo were a few of the ones preferred by some world-class athletes in the United States. By 2000, athletes had added androstenedione, tribulus terretris, creatine, and others to their "diets." Herbs and nutritional supplements are now being used instead of or in combination with various hormonal substances. (Jay Coakley)

Why Is the Challenge of Substance Control So Great in Sports Today?

In the final analysis, an athlete must make the decision to ingest or inject a performance-enhancing substance, but athletes do not live in a vacuum. They are a part of their particular sport subculture, a part of the larger sport culture, and members of the national and global society. As such, they are subject to a wide range of influences that are likely to influence their decision (Donnelly, 2003). Among the factors that contribute to the tendency among today's athletes to look to various substances for the edge they need to pursue their dreams and stay involved in the sports from which they derive enjoyment and other benefits, including material rewards, are the following:

1. *The visibility and resources associated with sports today have fueled massive research and development efforts devoted to performance-enhancing substances.* Numerous individual entrepreneurs and corporations have tied the development of performance-enhancing substances to the general realm of "alternative medicine" and have seen it as a way to make quick and substantial profits. The market for these substances is especially attractive because aging Baby Boomers (the massive population cohorts born between 1946 and 1964) see these substances as health aids. When these Baby Boomers are combined with athletes from all levels of competition, the potential for profits in the supplement industry is greater today than ever before. Therefore, the availability and diversity of substances are higher today than ever before.

2. *There is a deep fascination in most postindustrial cultures with technology and how it can be used to push or extend human limits.* This fascination has also been fostered by advertising slogans that promote the notion of uncritical hyperconsumption in society as a whole. Athletes, because they live in social worlds characterized by a "culture of excellence," hear those corporate messages more loudly than many others. They are dedicated to the notion that they should be the best they can be in a social world where they hear over and over that they can be anything they want to be—if they are dedicated enough.

3. *The rationalization of the body has influenced how people conceptualize the relationship between the body and mind.* People in most postindustrial

societies now see the body as a malleable tool serving the interests of the mind. Separating the body from the mind is common in cultures with Judeo-Christian religious beliefs, and it opens the door for people to seek substances to improve the body.

4. *There is a contemporary emphasis on self-medication.* People in postindustrial societies, where there is a growing distrust of established medical practices and an openness to new approaches to health, have intensified their search for new health-related and performance-enhancing substances. This has fuelled the production of substances that athletes now use on a regular basis.

5. *Gender relations are changing in contemporary society.* As traditional ideas about masculinity and femininity have been challenged, the threat of change has fueled a desire among some males to do whatever it takes to develop a physique that reaffirms an ideology of male strength and power. At the same time, the promise of change has fuelled a desire among many women to revise their notions of femininity and do whatever it takes to achieve forms of strength, power, and physical ability. Therefore, both men and women are likely to define performance-enhancing substances as valuable in their quests to preserve or challenge prevailing gender ideology.

6. *The organization of power and performance sports encourages athletes to overconform to the norms of the sport ethic.* Many contemporary sports are organized so that continued participation at the level needed to sustain an "athlete identity" requires winning in the form of outdoing others—making the cut, so to speak. The desire to maintain participation fuels the search for performance-enhancing substances.

7. *Coaches, sponsors, administrators, and fans clearly encourage most forms of "deviant" overconformity.* Athletes who pay the price, make sacrifices,

and put their bodies on the line for the sake of the team, the school, the community, the nation, and so on are held up as heroes. Athletes realize this, and many willingly take substances to "do their duty."

8. *The performance of athletes is closely monitored within the social structure of elite sports.* Elite sports today emphasize control, especially control over the body; conformity, especially to the demands of a coach; and guilt, especially when one does not meet the expectations of fellow athletes and those who sponsor participation (such as parents, sport clubs, and corporations).

When these eight factors are combined, it is easy to see why substance use is greater today than ever and why it is more difficult to control than ever.

Drug Testing as a Deterrent

Drug testing is controversial. One of the main arguments against testing is that it does not prevent athletes from using many performance-enhancing substances. In the face of testing, athletes use numerous evasive tactics. A practical argument against testing is that it cannot detect all the substances athletes use to enhance their performance. Athletes are often one step ahead of rule makers and testers. By the time the sport organizations ban substances and the testers calibrate tests to detect newly banned substances, the athletes have moved on to something else or have found new ways of masking the presence of banned substances in their systems. Meanwhile, the list of banned substances is growing to catalogue-length and athletes are overwhelmed with confusing rules.

Other arguments against drug testing are based on legal issues and social considerations. Mandatory testing and testing without cause violates a person's right to privacy and sets precedents for invasive testing programmes in other spheres of life. Privacy issues are very important, because future tests will require blood samples

"Don't worry, honey. Most of these are legal, some can't be tested for, others mask the ones they can test for, and some are too new for the tests!"

Some athletes take vast amounts of various substances in many combinations. The industries that produce performance-enhancing substances have stayed ahead of the testers in sports, and they will probably continue to stay ahead.

and DNA analysis as well as urine samples. Because sports are so visible, testing athletes could lead other people to consent to testing in their personal lives. Not only would this open the door to oppressive forms of social control in everyday life, but it also might encourage the use of social stigma to mark people whose bodies have been labeled as "impure" or "contaminated."

Arguments in favour of drug testing also reveal interesting dimensions of substance use in sports. Many people feel that performance-enhancing drugs should be banned from sports because they allow athletes to perform beyond their "natural" abilities and give them an unfair advantage over opponents. They say that this destroys the basis for competition and threatens the health of athletes. Others, using a hard-line law-and-order approach, favour testing because they define drug

use as immoral behaviour that "must be severely punished. Period. End of discussion."

When these people are told that current testing programmes are not effective, they call for more comprehensive tests, administered regularly without warning, mandatory for everyone (no excuses), and 100 percent effective and accurate (so that athletes have faith in them and will not think others are escaping detection). However, such a testing programme would be so expensive that it would bankrupt most sport organizations, and it would probably be illegal in certain countries. This is the financial challenge that now faces WADA and other sport organizations around the world. If they spend the money required for effective tests, they will have no money left to sponsor events!

Finally, many athletes have become skeptical about testing policies and programmes. They realize that political and economic interests can cloud the validity and reliability of testing programmes. They also know that drug testing is an enormously complicated bureaucratic process and that mistakes can occur at many points. This has already provoked legal challenges to test results. These challenges are complicated, because they often cross national borders, where judicial processes and definitions of individual rights and due process vary. In the meantime, athletes know that fellow athletes continue to be willing to overconform to the sport ethic and continue to seek creative ways to push their bodies to new limits in the pursuit of dreams.

Controlling Substance Use in Sports: Where to Start

Today's athletes, like their counterparts in the past, seek continued participation and excellence in sports. When they overconform to norms promoting sacrifice and risk in the pursuit of distinction and dreams, they are not likely to define the use of performance-enhancing substances as "deviant." Even Ben Johnson said: "You can never clean it up. People are always gonna be doing something. They feel good about themselves, and they feel it's right to do it" (Fish, 1993, p. A12). Johnson's point is made in another way by a physician who works with athletes; he observes that "athletes don't use drugs to escape reality—they use them to enforce the reality that surrounds them" (Di Pasquale, 1992, p. 2).

A central point in this chapter is that most athletes do not use performance-enhancing substances because they lack character, intelligence, or sanity, as might be concluded when using functionalist theory; nor do they use them because they are victims of biased and coercive rules, as might be concluded when using conflict theory. The solutions based in these theoretical approaches are also unsatisfactory. Tougher rules and increased testing have not and will not be effective; nor will changing the system so that athletes make all the rules.

As long as athletes accept without question or qualification the norms of the sport ethic, they will continue to voluntarily try or take anything to remain in sports. Moral panics over drug use and oversimplified solutions will not make athletes stop using substances they see as essential in maintaining their identities and their experience of participation. Because of the health dangers associated with a sport ethic that encourages doping, two Canadian researchers, Rob Beamish at Queen's University and Ian Ritchie at Brock University (2003, 2002), believe that athletes themselves, in a genuinely democratic process, should be able to decide, on a sport-by-sport basis, what performance-enhancing practices and substances should be permitted and which, if any, should be banned. In the case of banned practices and substances, athletes in the affected sport(s) should also determine how those banned practices will be monitored. Drug use can be controlled only when the people associated with sports critically assess the norms of the sport ethic in ways that lead them to set limits on conformity to those norms (Shogan and Ford, 2000).

In light of this approach, recommendations for controlling substance use in sport should begin with the following changes:

> Drug testing itself does not address the root problem. We must look beyond testing as the panacea that will cure this sickness in sport. While testing will always be necessary, we must ground the integrity of sport on the firmer base of fair play, ethics, and a sense of what is right.
>
> —Charles Dubin, Ontario Chief Justice (1990)

- *Critically examine the deep hypocrisy involved in elite power and performance sports.* How is it possible to encourage athletes to limit their use of performance-enhancing substances when federations and teams formally or informally approve the use of so-called legal performance-enhancing drugs and procedures? Using painkillers; using massive injections of vitamin B-12, artificial hydration, pure oxygen, and so on; playing with pins in broken bones or with high-tech "casts" to hold broken bones in place during competition; and using special harnesses to restrict the movement of injured joints all foster a sport culture in which the use of performance-enhancing substances is not only defined as logical but courageous.

- *Establish rules that clearly indicate that risks to health are undesirable and unnecessary in sports.* When fourteen-year-old girls in elite gymnastics who compete with training-induced stress fractures are turned into heroes and poster children for corporate sponsors, we all promote "deviant" overconformity in sports, and we set up athletes for permanent injuries and disabilities. Is this necessary for entertainment in our lives?

- *Establish rules stating that injured athletes should not be allowed to play until certified as "well" (not simply "able to compete") by an independent physician outside the team or programme in which the athlete is involved.* Too many team physicians have divided loyalties because they are paid by teams or by medical organizations that have contracted with teams or leagues (Pipe, 1998; Polsky, 1998). Trainers and physicians also need to be trained to realize how athletes often hide injuries in an effort to get back on the field.

- *Establish education programmes for young athletes.* Young people should learn to define *courage* in terms of recognizing limits and accepting the discipline necessary to accurately and responsibly acknowledge the consequences of sports injuries. They should also be taught to distinguish between the "pain of effort" and the "pain of injury." Learning to be in tune with one's body rather than to deny the body is important in controlling the use of potentially dangerous performance-enhancing substances.

- *Establish codes of ethics for sport scientists.* Too many sport scientists devote their professional attention to assisting athletes to overconform to the norms of the sport ethic, rather than helping them raise critical questions about how "deviant" overconformity is dangerous to the health and development of athletes. When they do this, they become high-tech panders. For example, sport psychology should be used to help athletes understand the consequences of their choices to play sports and to reduce the extent to which guilt, shame, and pathology influence participation and training decisions. This is the alternative to the technique of "psycho-doping," which encourages "deviant" overconformity by making athletes more likely to give body and soul to their sports without carefully answering critical questions about *why* they are doing what they are doing and what it means in their lives.

- *Make drug education part of larger "deviance" and health education programmes.* Parents, coaches, league administrators, managers,

trainers, and athletes should participate in formal educational programmes in which they consider and discuss the norms of the sport ethic and how to prevent "deviant" overconformity to those norms. Unless all these people understand their role in reproducing a culture supportive of substance abuse, the problems will continue. Such a programme would involve training to do the following:

- Create norms regulating the use of new and powerful technology and medical knowledge that go beyond the use of drugs.
- Question and critically examine prevailing values and norms in sports, as well as set limits on conformity to those values and norms.
- Redefine the meaning of achievement in sports in light of available new forms of performance-enhancing technologies.
- Teach athletes to think critically about sports, so that they understand that what happens in sports is a matter of choice and that changes in the current culture of sports are possible at all levels of competition.
- Provide parents, coaches, and athletes with the best and most recent information available on performance-enhancing technologies, so that they can make informed decisions about whether or not and how they will be used.

As it is now, we face a future without any clearly defined ideas about the meaning of achievement in sports in light of new financial incentives to set records and win events; the new importance of sport participation in the lives and identities of many young athletes; the new technologies, which clearly enhance performance; and the new forms of corporate sponsorship, which make image as important as ability. Therefore, we need *new* approaches and guidelines. Old approaches and guidelines combined with increasingly coercive enforcement methods will not work. Efforts to make sports into what we believe they were in the past are fruitless. We cannot go back to the past. We face new issues and challenges, which call for new responses. Widespread involvement in this process of facing new issues and challenges is needed, or else powerful entities, such as transnational corporations, will appropriate sport culture and the bodies of athletes as sites for delivering their messages about success, performance, efficiency, winning, and labouring in pain for the sake of achieving goals. We are already headed in that direction, and we are traveling at a rapid pace.

SUMMARY

IS "DEVIANCE" IN SPORTS OUT OF CONTROL?

The study of "deviance" in sports presents interesting challenges. This is due to four factors: (1) the forms and causes of "deviance" among those associated with sports are so diverse that no single theory can explain all of them, (2) what is accepted in sports may be "deviant" in the rest of society, (3) "deviance" in sports often involves an uncritical acceptance of norms, rather than a rejection of them, and (4) training in sports has become medicalized to the point that athletes use medical technology in ways that push normative limits.

Widely used conceptual frameworks in sociology do not offer useful explanations of the full range of "deviant" behaviour in sports, nor do they offer much help in devising ways to control it. Problems are encountered when functionalist theory is used—*"deviance"* is defined as failing to conform to ideals and "deviants" are seen as lacking moral character. Ideals are difficult to identify, and athletes may violate norms because they go overboard in their acceptance of them, not because they lack character.

Similarly, problems occur when conflict theory is used—*"deviance"* is defined as behaviours that violate the interests of those with money and power and "deviants" are seen as exploited victims

of economic power. People with power and money do not control all sports, and not all athletes can be described as exploited victims.

An approach using interactionist and critical theories seems to be most useful when explaining much of the "deviance" in sports today. Such an approach emphasizes that the dynamics of sport participation are grounded in the social worlds created around sports and that people in sports make choices and can act as agents of change in sports and the culture as a whole. Our use of interactionist and critical theories in this chapter highlights the distinctions between cases of "deviance" that involve extreme under-conformity and those that involve extreme over-conformity. Such distinctions are important because the most serious forms of "deviance" in sports occur when athletes, coaches, and others overconform to the norms of the sport ethic. The sport ethic is a cluster of norms that emphasizes making sacrifices, striving for distinction, taking risks, playing with pain, and pursuing dreams. When little concern is given to limiting conformity to these norms, "deviant" overconformity becomes a problem.

Research supports this explanation. Most on-the-field and sport-related behaviours among athletes fall within a normal range of acceptability; when they fall outside this range, they often involve overconformity to the norms of the sport ethic. Rates of off-the-field "deviance" among athletes are generally comparable with rates among peers in the general population; when rates are high, they often are connected with the dynamics and consequences of overconformity to the sport ethic.

The use of performance-enhancing substances is a form of "deviance" that is reportedly widespread among athletes, despite new rules, testing programmes, educational and treatment programmes, and strong punishments for violators. Historical evidence suggests that recent increases in rates of use are due primarily to increases in the supply and range of available substances, rather than to changes in the values and characters of athletes or increased exploitation of athletes. Most athletes through history have sought ways to improve their skills, maintain their athlete identity, and continue playing their sports, but today the search is more likely to involve the use of widely available performance-enhancing substances.

Despite expanding lists of banned substances, athletes have generally stayed one jump ahead of the rule makers and testers. When one drug is banned, athletes use another, even if it is more dangerous. If a new test is developed, athletes switch to an undetectable drug or use masking drugs to confuse testers. The use of HGH, blood doping, certain levels of testosterone, and many new substances still escape detection, and new testing programmes are problematic because they are so costly and many violate privacy rights or cultural norms in many societies.

Controlling "deviant" overconformity requires a critical assessment of norms in sports. A balance must be struck between accepting and questioning norms and rules; people in sports must critically qualify norms and rules and set limits on conformity, so that athletes who engage in self-destructive behaviours are not presented as heroes. Everyone in sports should question existing norms and create new norms related to the use of medical science and technology. The meaning of achievement in sports today must be revised if "deviant" overconformity is to be controlled. After all, what would happen if someone were to discover how to safely stimulate the brain so that the body produced hormones that would increase size and strength and dramatically change performance potential?

An effective transformation of sports also requires that all participants be involved in a continual process of critical reflection about the meaning, organization, and purpose of sports. Controlling "deviance" requires a critical examination of the values and norms in sports, as well as a restructuring of the organizations controlling and sponsoring sports. This critical examination should involve everyone, from athletes to fans.

SUGGESTED READINGS

Eitzen, D. S. 1999. *Fair and foul: Beyond the myths and paradoxes of sport.* Lanham, MD: Rowman & Littlefield (the theme of this book is that various forms of "deviance" exist in sports despite popular beliefs about sports building character and highlighting principles of fair play).

Eitzen, D. S. 2001. Sport and social control. In *Handbook of sports studies* (pp. 370–381), edited by J. Coakley and E. Dunning. London: Sage (although not dealing directly with "deviance," this article does outline useful information on the various ways sports are related to the dynamics of social control in society).

Hoberman, J. 1992. *Mortal engines: The science of performance and the dehumanization of sport.* New York: The Free Press (analysis of the use of sport science in the quest of extending human limits; raises questions about "deviance" and the medicalization of sport culture).

Houlihan, B. 1999. *Dying to win: Doping in sport and the development of anti doping policy.* Strasbourg: Council of Europe Publishing (a wide-ranging analysis of the prevalence of drug use in sports, and the development of anti-doping policies in various countries; this report anticipated the formation of WADA to develop a single international anti-doping policy).

Jennings, A., and C. Sambrook. 2000. *The great Olympic swindle: When the world wanted its games back.* London: Simon and Schuster International (the third book in a classic trilogy devoted to exposing forms of "deviance" among members of the IOC and others associated with elite amateur sports around the world; journalistic presentation based on meticulous investigative research).

Miracle, A. W., and C. R. Rees. 1994. *Lessons of the locker room: The myth of school sports.* Amherst, NY: Prometheus Books (chapter 5, pp. 101–25, "School Sports and Delinquency," summarizes research on sport participation in U.S. high schools and "deviant" behaviour).

Robinson, L. 1998. *Crossing the line: Violence and sexual assault in Canada's national sport.* Toronto: McClelland & Stewart (a journalistic exposé of the problems in minor and junior hockey in

Canada, ranging from hazing ceremonies to the sexual abuse of young women by players; the book also deals with the Graham James case of coach sexual abuse of players).

Yesalis, C. E., and V. E. Cowart. 1998. *The steroids game: An expert's inside look at anabolic steroid use in sports.* Champaign, IL: Human Kinetics (accessible discussion of how steroids are used in sports and how they are related to performance and health; explanation of testing issues and how steroid users have stayed ahead of the testers).

Young, K., ed. In press. *Sporting bodies, damaged selves: Sociological studies of sport-related injury.* Oxford: Elsevier Press (a collection of articles mostly dealing with the consequences of overconformity to the sport ethic in terms of risk taking and injury).

WEBSITE RESOURCES

Note: Websites often change. The following URLs were current when this book was printed. Please check our website (www.mcgrawhill.ca/college/coakley) for updates and additions.

www.mhhe.com/coakley8e (click on chapter 6 for information on the history of performance-enhancing drug use and drug testing in high-performance sports, information on recent cases of athletes testing positive for certain drugs)

www.wada-ama.org (site of the official worldwide drug- and substance-testing agency; online materials illustrate how the agency is presenting regulatory and educational materials)

www.bigsport.com (underground source of information about performance-enhancing substances, especially *anabolic* steroids)

www.espn.go.com/special/s/drugsandsports (provides basic information on a variety of drugs used by athletes; ESPN regularly includes on its site information about deviance in sports as it hits the news)

www.sportslaw.org (the Sports Lawyers Association often refers to "deviance" in sports in terms of the legal issues raised; this site lists articles and recent cases)

www.ajennings.8m.com/ (Jennings has exposed "deviance" in the IOC, and this site highlights his work and the work of others who have written articles on "deviance" in elite international sports)

www.alfred.edu/news/html/hazing_study.html (report of the National Survey of Initiation Rites and Athletics for NCAA Sports; excellent source of data from U.S. colleges and universities)

www.physsportsmed.com/issues/1998/06jun/pipe.htm (article calling for physicians to act assertively to control "deviance" in sports by reviving ethics in sports and encouraging athletes to minimize risk-taking behaviours on the field)

www.feminist.org/research/sports7.html (short summary of research dealing with contact sports and violence against women; the goal of this site is to empower women in sports)

www.ncava.org (National Coalition Against Violent Athletes; provides news, statistics, updates, and information about prevention programmes)

www.SportsEthicsInstitute.org (nonprofit corporation that fosters critical information and discussions about ethical issues in sports; site provides news, information, and links to online resources)

(Jay Coakley)

Violence in Sports

How does it affect our lives?

It's all bulls__t that you have to hate your
opponent. You can absolutely respect them and be
friends with them and then still absolutely die out
there on the court, trying to win.

> —**Martina Navratilova, pro tennis player (1999)**

Hockey is, by its nature, a physical game....But
we've crossed the line on some of the physical play
in recent years, putting our players in peril.

> —**Mario Lemieux, former NHL player (1999)**

Without violence, there would be no such thing as
hockey.

> —**Clarence Campbell, former NHL president
> (1975)**

 Online Learning Centre Resources

Visit *Sports in Society's* Online Learning Centre at
www.mcgrawhill.ca/college/coakley for additional
information and study material for this chapter.

Discussions of violence in sports, like discussions of "deviance," are often connected with people's ideas about the normative state of society as a whole. When violence occurs in sports, many people are quick to use it as an indicator that the moral foundation of society is eroding and that people, especially children, are learning a warped sense of morality as they watch athletes and use them as models for their own behaviour.

Many statements about violence in sports are contradictory. Some people think that violence is an inherent part of many games, while others think that violence in any form destroys the dynamics of games. Some people think that violence in sports reflects natural tendencies among males in society, while others feel that men use violence in sports to promote the idea that physical size and strength is a legitimate basis for maintaining power over others. Some say that violence in sports has increased to intolerable levels, while others say it is not as frequent or as brutal as it was in the past.

Contradictory statements and conclusions about violence in sports often occur for five reasons. First, many people do not define important terms in their discussions. They use words such as *physical, assertive, tough, rough, competitive, intense, intimidating, risky, aggressive, destructive,* and *violent* interchangeably. Second, they may not distinguish players from spectators, even though the dynamics of aggressive behaviour and violence in these two groups differ. Third, they may lump all sport forms together, regardless of differences in meaning, organization, purpose, and amount of physical contact involved. Fourth, they may not distinguish the immediate, short-term effects of playing or watching sports from the more permanent, long-term effects on patterns of violence among individuals and groups. Fifth, it is possible that we have actually underestimated the amount of violence associated with sports. Sociologist Kevin Young (2000), of the University of Calgary, has argued that we need to be concerned about all "sport-related violence," which

would include not only the issues addressed in this chapter but also forms of violence such as hazing (see chapter 6), terrorism and terrorist threats at sports events (Atkinson and Young, 2002), and forms of sexual harassment and abuse (see the Reflect on Sports box, "Sexual Harassment and Abuse" on pp. 201–202).

The goal of this chapter is to enable you to include information based on research and theories in your discussions of violence in sports. Chapter content focuses on five topics:

1. A practical definition of *violence* and related terms
2. A brief historical overview of violence in sports
3. On-the-field violence among players in various sports
4. Off-the-field violence involving players and others, and the impact of violence in sports on people's lives apart from sports
5. Violence among spectators who watch media coverage of sports or attend events in person

In connection with the last three topics, we make suggestions about how to control violence and limit its consequences on and off the field.

WHAT IS VIOLENCE?

Violence *is the use of excessive physical force, which causes intentional or has the potential to cause harm or destruction.* We often think of violence as actions that are illegal or unsanctioned, but there are situations in which the use of violence is encouraged or approved in a group or society. When violence occurs in connection with "deviant" underconformity or a rejection of norms in society, it is often classified as illegal and is sanctioned severely. When violence occurs in connection with the enforcement of norms, the protection of people and property, or "deviant" overconformity to widely accepted norms, it may be approved and even lauded as necessary for the preservation of order or the reaffirmation of important social norms. Therefore, violence is often, but not always, accepted and defined as legitimate, as when it is used by the military, police, or athletes in pursuit of victories representing communities or the ideals cherished by powerful people in those communities.

When violence occurs in connection with the widespread rejection of norms, it is often described as anarchy. When it occurs in connection with the use of extreme forms of social control or extreme overconformity to norms, it may be associated with a spirit of moral righteousness and the feeling that, even though violence produces harmful or destructive consequences, it is being done for the right reasons and should be rewarded. Under certain conditions, this type of violence is an expression of fascism.

In the case of sports, pushing a referee who has just penalized you or choking your coach in anger to express your defiance of his or her authority is violence based on a rejection of norms. These forms of violence would be defined as illegal and punished severely by teams and sport organizations, even if the referee or coach were not seriously injured. However, if a football player were to deliver a punishing tackle, which broke the ribs or destroyed the kidney of an opposing running back after his coach had told him to be aggressive and to put his body on the line for the team, the violence would be based on extreme conformity to norms. Such violence is "part of the job," and it would be seen as justified by most fans, highlighted on television replays, and respected by teammates and even many opponents. The player would feel righteous in his actions, despite their harmful consequences, and he would be prepared to do them again, even if it meant doing harm to his own body or the bodies of others. His violence would not be punished, because it conformed to current perceptions of how football should be played. Furthermore, it would be used to affirm his identity as an athlete and a football player.

The term **aggression** is used in this chapter to refer to *verbal or physical behaviour grounded in an intent to dominate, control, or do harm to another person.* Aggression is often involved in violence, but some violence may occur without aggressive intent. This definition allows us to distinguish aggressive behaviour from other behaviours we might describe as assertive, competitive, or achievement-oriented. For example, a very competitive person may use violence during a game without the intent to dominate, control, or do harm to others. However, there is often a difference between being aggressive and simply being assertive or trying hard to win or achieve other goals. The term **intimidation** is used to refer to *words, gestures, and actions that threaten violence or aggression.* Like aggression, intimidation is used as a means to dominate and control another person. These definitions help focus our discussion, but they do not eliminate all conceptual problems.

VIOLENCE IN SPORTS THROUGH HISTORY

Violence is certainly not new to physical activities and sports (Dunning, 1999; Guttmann, 1998). As noted in chapter 3, so-called blood sports were popular among the ancient Greeks and throughout the Roman Empire. Deaths occurred regularly in connection with ritual games among the Mayans and Aztecs. Tournaments during medieval and early modern Europe were designed as training for war and often had warlike consequences. Folk games were only loosely governed by rules, and they produced injuries and deaths at rates that would shock people today. Bearbaiting, cock fighting, dog fighting, and other "sporting" activities during those periods involved the treatment of animals that most people today would define as brutal and violent.

Research by figurational sociologists indicates that, as part of an overall civilizing process in Europe and North America, modern sports were developed as more rule-governed activities than the physical games in previous eras. As sports became formally organized, official rules prohibited certain forms of violence that had been common in many folk games. Bloodshed decreased, and there was a greater emphasis on self-control to restrict physical contact and the expression of aggressive impulses often inspired by the emotional heat of competition (Dunning, 1999).

As figurational theorists have studied these changes, they have noted that rates of sports violence do not automatically decrease over time. In fact, as overall behaviour and emotional expression in societies become more regulated and controlled, many players and spectators are more likely to experience violence and aggression in sports as pleasurable and exciting. Furthermore, the processes of commercialization, professionalization, and globalization have given rise to new forms of instrumental and "dramatic" violence in many sports. In other words, expressive violence has decreased over time, while goal-oriented and entertainment-directed violence has increased, at least temporarily, in many Western societies. Dunning (1999) notes that violence remains a crucial social issue in modern sports because sports are activities designed to create tension rather than relieve or discharge it, and sports continue to serve, in patriarchal societies, as an arena in which aggression is used to reproduce an ideology of male privilege. Finally, figurational sociologists point out that, when we study sports in society, we should remember that sports and sport behaviours are given different meanings by different groups and individuals and that issues of violence in sports can be understood only in relation to the social and cultural contexts in which it occurs. Of course, those using interactionist, critical, and feminist theories would agree with most of these points.

VIOLENCE ON THE FIELD

Types of Violence

The most frequently used typology of on-the-field violence among players is one developed by Mike Smith, a Canadian sociologist, who worked at York University until his untimely death in 1994 (1983; see Young, 2000). Smith identified four categories of violence associated with playing sports:

1. *Brutal body contact*. This includes physical practices that are common in certain sports and accepted by athletes as part of the action and risk in their sport participation. Examples are collisions, hits, tackles, blocks, body checks, and other forms of forceful physical contact that can produce injuries. Most people in society would define this forceful physical contact as extreme, although this form of violence is not punished or defined as illegal or criminal. Coaches often encourage this form of violence.

2. *Borderline violence*. This includes practices that violate the rules of the game but are accepted by most players and coaches as conforming to the norms of the sport ethic and to commonly used competitive strategies. Examples are the "brush back" pitch in baseball, the forcefully placed elbow in soccer and basketball, the strategic bump used by runners to put another runner off stride, the fist-fight in ice hockey, and the forearm to the ribs of a quarterback in football. Although these actions may be expected, they sometimes provoke retaliation by other players. Official sanctions and fines have not been severe for cases of borderline violence. However, public pressures to increase the severity of sanctions have grown in recent years, and the severity of punishments has increased in some cases.

3. *Quasi-criminal violence*. This includes practices that violate the formal rules of the game, public laws, and even the informal norms used by players. Examples are cheap shots, late hits, sucker punches, and flagrant fouls that endanger the players' bodies and reject the norm of respecting the game.

Fines and suspensions are usually imposed on players who engage in such violence. Players usually condemn this form of violence and see it as a rejection of the informal norms of the game and what it means to be an athlete.

4. *Criminal violence.* This includes practices that are clearly outside the law to the point that athletes condemn them without question and law enforcement officials may even prosecute them as crimes. Examples are assaults that occur after a game is over and assaults during a game that appear to be premeditated and violent enough to kill or seriously disable a player. These are relatively rare, and they are seldom prosecuted. However, there seems to be growing support for the notion that criminal charges are appropriate in some of these cases. This support grew in early 2000 when a hockey player intentionally slashed an opponent's head with his stick (see the Reflect on Sports box, "Brashear and McSorley: A Case of Criminal Violence?" on p. 191).

Kevin Young (2000) has noted that this is a useful general typology but that the lines separating the four types of violence tend to shift over time as norms change in sports and society at large. Furthermore, the typology says nothing about the origins of violence and how violent acts are related to the sport ethic, gender ideology, and the commercialization of sports. Acknowledging these weaknesses, we use this typology to make distinctions among various types of violence in sports as they are discussed through the chapter.

Violence as "Deviant" Overconformity to the Norms of the Sport Ethic

In Pat Conroy's novel *The Prince of Tides* (1986), there is a scene in which the coach uses words that many athletes in heavy contact sports have heard during their careers:

Now a real hitter is a headhunter who puts his head in the chest of his opponents and ain't happy if his opponent is still breathing after the play. A real hitter doesn't know what fear is except when he sees it in the eyes of a ball carrier he's about to split in half. A real hitter loves pain, loves the screaming and the sweating and the brawling and the hatred of life down in the trenches. He likes to be at the spot where the blood flows and the teeth get kicked out. That's what this sport's about, men. It's war, pure and simple. (p. 384)

Not all coaches use vocabulary that is so vividly descriptive, and some may avoid it because they know it might inspire dangerous forms of violent behaviour. However, there are many coaches, team administrators, and owners in contact sports who dream of having a team full of athletes who think this way.

When athletes do think this way, levels of violence in sports are generally high and they attract attention. In fact, journalists will describe it, sociologists and psychologists will try to explain it, and athletes will brag or complain about it. When an athlete dies or is paralyzed by this type of brutal body contact or borderline violence, the media usually present stories on violence in sports, asking if we have gone too far, if there is a need to pull in the reins, and if violence is rampant in sports and in society. Then they run multiple replays of violent acts and watch their ratings points and sales increase.

Although players do not always feel comfortable with the amount of brutal body contact and borderline violence in their sports, they generally accept these forms of violence, and even those who do not like them may use them to improve or maintain their status on teams and their popularity with spectators. Athletes whose violence involves overconformity to the sport ethic become legends on and off the field. Athletes who engage in quasi- and criminal violence often are marginalized in sports, and they may face criminal charges, although prosecuting such charges has been difficult and convictions are almost nonexistent (Young, 2000).

REFLECT ON SPORTS

Brashear and McSorley: A Case of Criminal Violence?

As we noted in the introduction to this chapter, there are always contradictory statements about violence in sports. One of the most striking contradictions concerns the place of the criminal law in sports. On the one hand is the view that the rules of sports do not trump the rule of law. This was first expressed in Britain, some 125 years ago, by Lord Justice Bramwell in the soccer manslaughter case of *Regina v. Bradshaw* (1878): "No rules or practice of any game can make that lawful which is unlawful by the law of the land; and the law of the land says you shall not do that which is likely to cause the death of another." On the other hand is the view that the criminal courts should stay out of sports. As Paul Kelly, Marty McSorley's lawyer, noted: "No legislative body has seen fit to . . . pass laws that specifically target violence in sports" (cited by Smith, 2002, p. S5).

While there are few cases of criminal assault charges being laid against athletes, the Marty McSorley–Donald Brashear incident is the most recent one in Canada, and it raises several interesting questions. On February 21, 2000, in an NHL game played in Vancouver between the Canucks and the Boston Bruins, Marty McSorley of the Bruins clubbed the Canucks' Donald Brashear on the head with his stick. The attack, which took place at the end of the game, knocked Brashear unconscious and bleeding from the nose; he was treated on the ice for ten minutes. Brashear was diagnosed with a grade 3 concussion; McSorley was given a match penalty and a game misconduct.

Following a public and media outcry, the NHL reviewed the incident and, on March 23, suspended McSorley for the remainder of that season (23 games, costing him C$100,000 in lost pay). Because this was the longest suspension ever given for a game incident, the NHL believed that the matter was settled. However, on March 7, a Vancouver Crown prosecutor filed charges of assault with a weapon against McSorley. Six months later, he was found guilty, and given a conditional discharge of eighteen months.

The event generated enormous media attention about whether the courts should have become involved. Coakley (2001) cites a fellow player as saying, "[McSorley's] lost the respect of every player in the league." However, Atkinson's (in press) systematic analysis shows that "players, league administrators, fans, and court officials [in general, framed] the event as both non-criminal and essentially victimless."

Hilary Findlay, of the Canadian Centre for Sport and Law, points out that "criminal assault is proved by showing an intent to inflict injury on another. While the Supreme Court of Canada ruled that you cannot consent to a fist fight, the sport arena is an exception. According to the law, players may consent to violent treatment, but the consent is limited" (cited by Smith, 2002, p. S5).

What are the limits of this consent? Do players consent to being clubbed unconscious by an opponent? We think that it is necessary to have clear limits regarding what is acceptable conduct on any sport playing surface. If sports will not bring charges against players who deliberately attempt to injure an opponent, then the courts need to step in. Does someone have to die before we establish limits? *What do you think?*

• •

Violence as "deviant" overconformity is also related to the insecurity of life in high-performance sports. Athletes learn that "you're only as good as your last game," and they know that their feelings of self-worth, their identities as athletes, and their status as team members are constantly under question. Therefore, many athletes are willing to take extreme measures to prove themselves, even if those measures involve violence. Violence becomes a means to prove self-worth and to reaffirm membership in the subcultural in-group of the select few who play the game at a high level. This is why athletes who do not play in pain are defined as failures and why those who do play in pain and with injuries are defined as courageous. After all, playing in pain and with injuries honours the importance of the game.

It is important to understand that violence grounded in overconformity to the sport ethic is not limited to men, although it is certainly more common in men's games than in women's games. Women also overconform to the norms of the sport ethic (Young and White, 1995), and, when they play contact sports, they face the challenge of drawing the line between physicality and violence. For example, when University of Waterloo sociologist Nancy Theberge (1999) spent two seasons studying the sport experiences of women on an elite ice hockey team in Canada, she discovered that the women loved the physicality of hockey and the body contact that occurred, even though body checking was not allowed. As one woman said,

> I like a physical game. You get more fired up. I think when you get hit…like when you're fighting for a puck in the corner, when you're both fighting so you're both working hard and maybe the elbows are flying, that just makes you put more effort into it. (p. 147)

The experience of dealing with the physicality of contact sports and facing its consequences creates drama and excitement, strong emotions, and special interpersonal bonds among women athletes, as it does among men. Despite the risk and reality of pain and injuries, many women in contact sports feel that the physical intensity and body contact in their sports make them feel alive and aware. Although many women currently are committed to controlling brutal body contact and other forms of violence in their sports, their love of the physicality of the game often makes this difficult to do. After all, they accept the sport ethic.

In the case of male athletes in contact sports, the love of physicality is connected with issues of masculinity in ways that lead overconformity to the norms of the sport ethic to be expressed through violence. Although elite women athletes who play contact sports do overconform to the norms of the sport ethic, their love of physicality is not connected with gender issues in ways that would encourage them to define violence in positive terms. Some women may do so, but they would not receive the same support and rewards that men receive when they do violence in sports.

Commercialization and Violence in Sports

There is no doubt that some athletes in power and performance sports are paid to do violence. Some are paid handsomely. However, many violent athletes in the past were not paid very well, and most athletes in high schools, universities, and sport clubs today are paid nothing to do violence, yet many of them have accepted on-the-field violence, despite what it has cost them in pain and injury.

Commercialization and money in sports have clearly expanded the opportunities to play certain contact sports in some societies, and sponsorship money attracts the media coverage that makes these sports and the violence they contain more visible to more people than ever before. Children watch this coverage, and they sometimes imitate violent athletes when they play informal games and organized youth sports. This is a problem, and it is related to commercialization and money, but it does not justify the conclusion that commercialization is the major cause of violence in sports.

We must remember that football players and other athletes in contact sports engaged in violence on the field long before television coverage and the promise of big salaries. In fact, players at all levels of organized football killed and maimed each other at *rates* that are higher than the death and injury rates in football today. There are more injuries today because there are more people playing football. Of course, this makes injuries and the violence that causes them very serious problems that must be dealt with, but to think that these problems are caused mainly by commercialization and money is a mistake.

The fighting that occurs in many men's sports is connected with issues of masculinity. In men's ice hockey, unless you throw down your gloves and fight in certain circumstances, your manhood is questioned. (CP/Jeff McIntosh)

This is an important point, because many people who criticize sports today blame all problems in sports, including violence, on money and greed. They state in one form or another that, if only athletes were true amateurs and played for their love of the game instead of money, they would be less violent. This conclusion is naive, and it distracts attention away from the deep cultural and ideological roots of violence in sports and in society as a whole. Taking money away from athletes would be relatively easy—amateur sports has done it for nearly a century! What is *not* easy is changing the culture in which athletes, especially male athletes, learn to value and use violence in sports.

> Hockey is the only team sport in the world that actually *encourages* fighting. I have no idea why we let it go on. The game itself is so fast, so exciting, so much fun to watch, why do we have to turn ice red so often?
>
> —Wayne Gretzky, hockey player (1990)

Suggesting that we must make changes in culture causes many people to be uncomfortable, because it places the responsibility for change on all of us. It is much easier to self-righteously blame "all those wealthy and greedy team owners, athletes, and TV people who destroy the purity and goodness of sports to make money." It is much more difficult for people to critically examine the culture of sports and the patterns of overconformity to the sport ethic, which many of them love to watch and discuss. Similarly, it is difficult for people to critically examine the definitions of *masculinity* and the structure of gender relations, which they have long accepted as a part of nature and goodness. But we must do these things if we want to understand violence in sports.

Commercialization, however, is not irrelevant when we consider violent discourse about sports. In fact, violence very often becomes part of the promotion of sport events, or a part of the entertainment industry. Consider, for example, Don Cherry's enormously popular "Rock 'em, Sock 'em" video series, which has been included on the Christmas list of many Canadian boys and some girls. The series—and its imitators—glorifies violence in the sport, or makes it humorous, and presents it for our entertainment. And what about the video clips that are very often assembled as a part of sport news broadcasting, often put together with funny music and amusing voiceovers. The clips involve people falling off horses, baseball fielders running into each other, gymnasts falling awkwardly, hockey players falling over the boards, and so on. These are real people (not cartoons) experiencing real pain and injury, and they are presented for our amusement. Does this become part of the desensitization-to-violence process that has been hypothesized to account for our experience of so much violence on news broadcasts and in the entertainment industry?

Commercialization clearly has inspired, at least in some cultures, a promotional and heroic discourse (see also chapter 11, pages 338–341) that presents images of revenge, retaliation, hate, hostility, intimidation, aggression, violence, domination, and destruction. It is obvious that such images attract attention and serve commercial purposes. The NFL, the NHL, and even the NBA have used these images for many years to promote their games. Of course, in true promotional fashion, the same media companies that sell these videos also publish articles that condemn violence and players who are "too violent." Violence sells, and antiviolence sells!

> **The Canadians were the inventors of the body check, the penalty bench, and the widespread view of fans that athletes who shirk bodily contact are pansies.**
> —Karl Adolph Scherer, hockey historian (1988)

Does this commercially inspired discourse represent the real on-the-field orientations of athletes, or does it represent efforts to create personas and attract attention, which have commercial value, even though most athletes do not really want to hurt opponents and make them bleed on the field? Research is needed on mainstream sports that sell violent images and narratives as a part of an entertainment package that also includes dramatic storylines delivered by paid announcers, sexy cheerleaders, and halftime dancers.

Violence and Masculinity

Violence in sports is not limited to men. However, critical and feminist research has shown clearly that, *if we want to understand violence in sports, we must understand gender ideology and issues of masculinity in culture.* Sociologist Mike Messner explains:

> Young males come to sport with identities that lead them to define their athletic experience differently than females do. Despite the fact that few males truly enjoy hitting and being hit, and that one has to be socialized into participating in much of the violence commonplace in sport, males often view aggression, within the rule-bound structure of sport, as legitimate and "natural." (1992: 67)

In fact, Messner explains that many male athletes learn to define injurious acts as "a necessary part of the game," rather than as violence, as long as they are within the rules of the game and within the informal norms the players use to judge and evaluate each other.

Across many cultures, playing power and performance sports has become an important way to prove masculinity. Boys discover that, if they play these sports and come to be seen as people who can do violence, they can avoid social labels such as "lady," "fag," "wimp," and "sissy"

"When are you gonna learn when it's necessary to use unnecessary roughness?"

In men's contact sports, players sometimes learn physical intimidation and violent behaviours as strategies. Both have been used to win games and build reputations.

(Ingham and Dewar, 1999). In fact, after reviewing a long history of research on this issue, Phil White of McMaster University and Kevin Young of the University of Calgary (1997) note that, if a boy or young man avoids these sports, he risks estrangement from his male peers.

Boys and men who play power and performance sports learn quickly that they are evaluated in terms of their ability to use violence in combination with physical skills. This learning begins in youth sports and, by the time young men have become immersed in the social world of most power and performance sports, brutal body contact and borderline violence are being encouraged by teammates and coaches, sometimes by parents (fathers more than mothers), and always by spectators. These young men learn that their status in the eyes of coaches and their identities as men in the eyes of their peers and the community at large often come to depend on their ability to do violence on the field (Weinstein et al., 1995).

The connection between violence and acceptance by peers in contact sports is illustrated in team rituals where established players subject rookies to various forms of violent and aggressive treatment. The goal of these rituals is to "see if a would-be player has what it takes to be one of us." Learning to "take it and give it back" is an expression of a player's manhood, as well as membership in a select fraternity of athletes. For example, when NHL player Bryan Marchment was asked how he felt about the consequences of his violence on the ice, he said, "Hey, it's a man's game. If you can't play, get out and play tennis." Of course, this orientation makes certain power and performance sports especially dangerous activities, but many men choose to play them because they have learned to define *masculinity* in terms of being tough enough to participate in the give-and-take of violent confrontations.

After reviewing dozens of studies on this topic, Phil White and Kevin Young (1997) concluded that power and performance sports emphasize an orientation that clearly "confirms and consolidates violent physicality as one of the cornerstones of masculinity" (p. 9).

Violence, Gender, Social Class, and Race

When it comes to understanding violence in sports, we must also understand the complex interconnections of gender, social class, and race. For example, when sociologist Mike Messner interviewed men who had been elite athletes in the U.S., he discovered that the men from lower-income families and minority-group backgrounds placed special importance on the *respect* they received when they played sports and when they used intimidation, aggression, and violence on the field. The men from these backgrounds were more likely than their white counterparts from middle- and upper-class families to encounter limited opportunities and to be channeled into sports where brutal body contact and borderline violence were a part of the game. As athletes in these sports, they sought respect by physically dominating others. This was an important part of establishing an identity as a man worthy of respect in the face of how people in society perceived the meaning of being minority men from poor families.

Messner also identified cases where some black male athletes had capitalized on the racist stereotypes held by whites. These men discovered that, by presenting a menacing and violent image on the field, they could intimidate competitors, especially those who thought black males were physically gifted and prone to violence by nature. One of the men Messner interviewed explained it this way:

> I'm tall, I'm thin, I'm a black person with a shaved head, and I'm fearful [looking]. You have to intimidate mentally....[Y]ou've got to talk shit in this game, you have to say, . . . "If you come close to me, I'm gonna hurt you!" (1992: 83)

This statement and other findings in Messner's study illustrate a few ways that gender, social class, and race have come to be linked in the experiences of athletes, and it shows that such links may be related to the incidence of violence in sports.

The Institutionalization of Violence in Sports

Learning to Use Violence as a Strategy: Noncontact Sports   In some noncontact sports, participants may try to intimidate opponents, but violence is rare. For example, tennis players have been fined for slamming a ball to the ground in protest or talking to an official or opponent in a menacing manner. Players in noncontact sports are seldom, if ever, rewarded for violent behaviours. Therefore, it is doubtful that playing or watching these sports teaches people to use violence as a strategy on the field.

Some athletes may use violent images as they describe competition, but they do not have actual opportunities to convert their words into deeds. For example, U.S. sprint cyclist and 1996 Olympic silver medalist Marty Nothstein used violent images as he described his approach to a race:

> I am really aggressive out there. I pretty much hate the guy I'm racing. It wouldn't matter if it were my brother....I want to destroy the guy. End it quick. Boom. One knockout punch.
> (Becker, 1996, p. 4E)

Of course, cycling does not allow him to physically destroy or punch a competitor, but sport discourse, even in noncontact sports, may have violence built right into it.

At this point, men who play noncontact sports use violent images in their descriptions of competition much more often than women athletes in those sports use them. The use of a language of violence is clearly linked to masculinity in most cultures. This does not mean that women do not use it, but it does mean that men use it more frequently. Apparently, many women realize that violent discourse reaffirms an ideology that works against their interests, as well as their health and well-being in society as a whole.

Learning to Use Violence as a Strategy: Men's Contact Sports   Athletes in power and performance sports involving heavy physical contact learn to use intimidation, aggression, and violence as on-the-field strategies. Success in these sports depends on the use of brutal body contact and borderline violence. Research shows that male athletes in contact sports readily accept certain forms of violence, even when they involve rule-violating behaviours, and that, as the amount of contact increases in a sport, so does this acceptance (Pilz, 1996; Shields and Bredemeier, 1995; Weinstein et al., 1995; White and Young, 1997). These athletes routinely disapprove of quasi-criminal and criminal violence, but they accept brutal body contact and borderline violence done within the rules of the game. They may not intend to hurt, but this does not prevent them from putting the bodies of opponents in jeopardy by doing what they feel they must do to "take the guy out," "break up the double play," "stop the drive to the basket," and so on.

In heavy contact sports (boxing, football, ice hockey, rugby, etc.), intimidation and violence have become widely used as strategies for winning games, promoting individual careers, increasing drama for spectators, and making money for athletes and sponsors. Athletes in these sports are quick to say that they do whatever it takes, whatever it takes to stop the other guy, whatever it takes to win. They realize that they are paid to do this, even if it causes harm to themselves and others. This was illustrated when highly successful NBA coach Pat Riley fined his players $1,500 if they did not give a hard foul to an opponent driving to the basket, or if they helped an opponent up after knocking him to the floor. His message was clear: be violent or be punished. Back in 1995, his message caused considerable controversy among people in the United States, but he continues to demand brutal body contact and borderline violence from his players. When one of his players crosses the line and uses quasi-criminal violence, the player may be fined by the NBA, but not by Riley.

ENFORCERS AND GOONS: BEING PAID FOR PUSH-ING THE LIMIT AND CROSSING THE LINE Violence also has been incorporated into game strategies in certain heavy contact sports by using players as designated agents of intimidation and violence for their teams. In hockey, these players have been called "enforcers," "goons," and "hit men."[1] They are expected to protect teammates and strategically assist their teams by intimidating, provoking, fighting with, and even disabling opponents. In fact, they are paid to do these things.

The violence of these enforcers and goons is well known to other players. For example, one hockey player described such a player this way: "His job is to hurt people. He goes for the knees a lot. He takes runs at you, and really all he's trying to do is hurt you and knock you out of the game" (Scher, 1993). For many years, the violence of enforcers and goons was

accepted widely. Many people associated with hockey even claimed that this violence limited other forms of violence that might be even more dangerous. However, the absurdity of this argument has been challenged more often in recent years, as highly paid superstars such as Mario Lemieux and Paul Kariya, with entertaining and nonviolent physical skills, have been sidelined by injuries caused by attacks by enforcers on opposing teams. Some players continue to act as enforcers and goons, and they are still paid for doing violence; however, every time they injure someone, many people raise questions about the wisdom of institutionalizing violence in sports in this manner. Hockey has gradually taken action to control the violence used by enforcers and the fighting that is usually a part of their violence. However, the use of enforcers is so deeply institutionalized as part of the strategy of hockey that change has been slow.

Learning to Use Violence as a Strategy: Women's Contact Sports Information on violence among girls and women in contact sports remains scarce. It seems that there are more cases of violence in some women's sports than there were in the past, but there are few studies that tell us if this is true and why it has happened.

Women's programmes have undergone many changes over the past twenty-five years. They have become more competitive, they are more likely to involve an emphasis on power and performance, and the stakes associated with success have increased considerably. Today, as the level of competition rises, and as women become increasingly immersed in the social world of elite sports, they become more tolerant of rule violations and aggressive behaviours on the playing field, but this pattern is less clear among women than it is among men (Nixon, 1996a,b; Shields and Bredemeier, 1995; Shields et al., 1995).

Some women use intimidation and violence in sports, and "there is no known biological reason that women cannot be as physically aggressive as

---

[1] It is interesting to note that many "enforcers" in the NHL refer to themselves as "policemen."

Lacrosse Women's World Cup in Tokyo, 1997

Both men and women are capable of aggressive behaviours. However, they may not link those behaviours to their identities in the same ways. What vocabulary and discourse do women in contact sports use to explain their involvement and achievements in sports? Do they use references to domination and control to the same extent that men do? (CP/Itsou Inouye/AP)

men" (Dunn, 1994), but most girls and women become involved in and learn to play sports in ways that differ from the ways in which most boys and men become involved in and learn to play sports. As women compete at higher and higher levels, they often become similar to men in the way they embrace the sport ethic and use it to frame their self-definitions as athletes. Like men, they are willing to take risks, make sacrifices, pay the price, and play with pain and injury; however, unlike men, they do not link toughness, physicality, and aggression to their gender identities: women do not link violence to definitions of what it means to be a woman in society. Coaches do not try to motivate women athletes by urging them to "go out and prove who the better woman is" on the field. Therefore, at this point in time, women are less likely than men to do violence on the field.

Do elite women athletes develop the same form of hubris (pride-based arrogance) that many elite male athletes develop? If so, how is it linked to their identities, and how do they express it in sports? Do women athletes use discourse containing a language of violence about sports? Research suggests that they do not (Nelson, 1994, 1998; Theberge, 1999, 2000a; Young and White, 1995), but more information is needed.

Pain and Injury as the Price of Violence

Many people today think about sports in a paradoxical way: they accept violence as a part of sports while they are concerned about the injuries caused by that violence. They seem to want violence without consequences—like the fictionalized violence they see in the media, in which people are hit but not really injured. However, sports violence is real, and it does cause pain, injury, disability, and even death.

Research on pain and injury among athletes has increased in recent years. Sociologists Howard Nixon (2000) in the United States, Kevin Young and his colleagues in Canada (White and Young, 1997, 1999; Young, 2000), and Ivan Waddington in England (2001) have studied pain, injury, and health issues in sports. Nixon's research suggests that over 80 percent of the men and women in top-level interuniversity sports in the United States sustain at least one serious injury while playing their sport, and nearly 70 percent are disabled for two or more weeks. Nearly all players, both men and women, say that they play while they are hurt, and many experience chronic pain. Nixon notes that the rate of disabling injuries in the NFL is over three times greater than the rate among workers in high-risk construction jobs. The rates of disabling injuries vary from sport to sport, but they are high enough in many sports to constitute a medical problem as well as a social issue.

Young's research focuses on professional sport participation as work, and his data indicate that pro sports involving brutal body contact are the most violent and dangerous workplaces in the occupational world (Young, 1993). The "normal" experiences of elite male athletes in sports such as football, rugby, soccer, and ice hockey regularly lead to arthritis, concussions, bone fractures, torn ligaments, partial blindness, partial and full paralysis, and even death. Men and women athletes conform to norms about playing with pain and injury, but prevailing ideas about masculinity in many cultures create an emphasis on violence and risk taking that makes men more vulnerable to serious injuries in sports (White and Young, 1997, 1999).

Waddington's research shows that the health benefits of playing sports are highest when participation involves rhythmic movements under conditions that can be controlled by the athletes themselves. The health costs are highest when participation occurs in highly competitive contact sports played under conditions that are outside the athletes' control. In other words, the violence inherent in power and performance sports takes a definite toll on the health of athletes.

Much of this research shows a close connection between dominant ideas about masculinity and the high rate of injuries in many sports. As one NHL coach explains, playing with pain and injuries is not only part of the ethos of power and performance sports but "at times your manhood is up for grabs. Playing hurt is a status thing. It's the simplest way of getting the respect of teammates, opponents, coaches" (Farber, 1998b, p. 94). Furthermore, when the give-and-take of violence leads to injury and pain, some men learn to "suck it up" and stay in the game—partly because of what it means to be an athlete and partly because of what it means to be a man in their social world. Men who have learned to define *masculinity* in terms that lead them to fear weakness and avoid emotional concerns for others often use violence to avoid labels that challenge their masculinity. In fact, they sacrifice their bodies to live by this code of manhood. As long as some athletes continue to uncritically accept the norms of the sport ethic combined

with dominance-based notions of masculinity, they will continue to define *violence* as behaviour that adds to their lives, rather than restricting, limiting, and sometimes ending their lives.

Controlling on-the-Field Violence

The roots of violence on the field are deep. They are grounded in overconformity to the sport ethic, processes of commercialization, and definitions of *masculinity*. Therefore, many men in power and performance sports resist efforts to control violence. They have come to think that their identities as athletes and as men depend on doing violence and that success and financial rewards on the field depend on strategic violence.

The most difficult type of violence to control is brutal body contact. It is grounded deep in power and performance sport culture and is tied strongly to a gender logic that emphasizes physical dominance over others as important to manhood. Unfortunately, about 90 percent of the serious injuries in power and performance sports occur *within the rules* of those sports. Men pay the price for their destructive definitions of *sports* and *masculinity*. As U.S. sociologist Mike Messner (1990) has noted, when players use their bodies as weapons, players' bodies are also the targets of those weapons. In this sense, it is possible to see expressed in sports a type of "dangerous masculinity" that, in fact, victimizes many young men (Young and White, 1999).

Efforts to control brutal body contact require changes in the culture of power and performance sports and the gender logic that supports that culture. At this time, the best strategy to do this is to be relentless in calling attention to the dangers and absurdity of the behaviours and the discourse that men and women use to reproduce that culture. We need to count and publish information on injuries and then tell parents about them before they enlist their children in the service of reproducing patriarchy and a gender logic that jeopardizes health and development. We need to calculate the cost of injuries due to brutal body contact and other types of violence in terms of medical expenses, lost work time and wages, days missed in classes, disability payments, family problems, and even loss in life expectancy.[2]

It is easier to control borderline, quasi-criminal, and criminal violence, although people continue to resist taking necessary actions. Enforcers should be eliminated. How? Suspend them (and cut salaries) for at least three games for borderline violence and at least half the season for more serious types. Have the suspensions carry over into the next season if necessary, prevent teams from replacing suspended players on their rosters, and fine team owners and put the money into research on sports violence and injuries. Unless owners are fined and teams punished, they will simply replace one "headhunter" with another. Owners and coaches know that some people will pay to see violence—and they are not sure if fans will pay to see non-violent play—so what is their incentive for controlling it unless they lose money when their players cross the line?

Assessing fines for violent players are generally ineffective. Fines of $5,000 mean nothing to players who make $1 million a year. They spend that much on phone calls telling their buddies about who their latest victims have been. Rather than fines, use unpaid suspensions. Suspensions prevent players from doing what they love to do, separate them from the game that sustains their identities as athletes, and cause their salaries to decline.

---

[2] Canadian data are rare. Using 1995 data, the Institute for Social Research (1996) at York University calculated the annual cost of sport and physical recreation injury in Ontario as C$637 million (health care costs, 42 percent; lost productivity/earnings, 46 percent; costs borne by individual and/or family, 12 percent).

VIOLENCE OFF THE FIELD

Do Violent Strategies Learned in Sports Carry Over to the Rest of Life?

When athletes in contact sports are arrested for violent crimes, many people assume that their violence off the field is related to the violent strategies they have learned and are rewarded for on the field.

Even some athletes are persuaded by this view. For example, John Niland, a former NFL player, stated:

> Any athlete who thinks he can be as violent as you can be playing football, and leave it all on the field is kidding himself. (Falk, 1995, p. 12)

However, research on the carryover issue is difficult to do, and studies are rare. Even if data in a study show a high rate of off-the-field violence among athletes, this does not prove that carryover has occurred. It is possible that people inclined to use violence in their lives choose to play power and performance sports more than other people do, or that certain athletes have had nonsport experiences emphasizing violence as a way to cope with problems and conflicts. In other words, an inclination to use violence to solve problems may have been high among certain people, even if they had not played contact sports.

Off-the-field violence among athletes also may be due to unique situational factors encountered by some athletes. For example, athletes with reputations for being tough might receive encouragement from others to be tough on the streets. They may even be challenged to fights in bars because of their reputations in sports. Athletes who grew up in neighbourhoods with high crime rates may find that when they return home they are identified as "marks" by locals who push drugs or run scams to make money. If they hang out in those neighbourhoods, they may attract locals who define them as "sell-outs" to big money and corporate sponsors. Some of these locals would like nothing better than to take the athletes down a notch or two. If trouble occurs and an athlete is arrested for fighting in these circumstances, it is not accurate to say that it is due to carryover.

Research on male hockey players in Canada suggests that those who have many years of experience in power and performance sports are more likely than recreational players or nonplayers to approve of off-the-field violence and use violence when they play other sports (Bloom and Smith, 1996). These results are helpful, but they still do not say whether violence in hockey is a cause or an effect of violence that occurs in other spheres of the players' lives. (see the Reflect on Sports box, "Sexual Harassment and Abuse," on pp. 202–203, for other aspects of sexual violence in sports.)

Assaults and Sexual Assaults by Athletes
Highly publicized cases of assaults, sexual assaults, rapes, gang rapes, and even murders that involve athletes who play power and performance sports have led many people to think that the violence in those sports carries over to personal relationships off the field, especially relationships with women. Information about the cases, including reliable statements made by assault and rape victims, often contains references to the athletic status and sport participation of the perpetrators (Benedict, 1997, 1998; Lefkowitz, 1997; Robinson, 1998). Furthermore, research on the conversations and biographies of athletes has presented powerful and shocking information suggesting that the social worlds created around men's power and performance sports subvert respect for women and promote the image of women as "game" to be pursued and conquered (Curry, 1991, 1996, 1998; Lefkowitz, 1997; Loy, 1995; Nack and Munson, 1995; Reid, 1997; Robinson, 1998). However, data on the arrest records of NFL players do not support the carryover hypothesis (Blumstein and Benedict, 1999).

How do we make sense of this? In a critical assessment of the debate about male athletes' violence against women, sport sociologist Todd Crosset (1999) reviewed all the published, primarily U.S. research on the issue. His review indicated that male interuniversity athletes, in particular, seem to be involved in more sexual assaults than other male students, but the differences are not significant in any study, and they are often related to other factors, which make differences difficult to interpret. Crosset concludes that trying to explain the violence of male athletes against women in terms of carryover from the violent, hyper-masculine world of men's power and performance sports leads us to miss important points as we study the problem of sexual assault. He also concludes that comparing assault rates of athletes with those of nonathletes distracts us from the following important points: violence against women does occur, it is a serious problem, male athletes are among the perpetrators of this violence, and we must understand the problem within the context of sports if we wish to deter assaults perpetrated by athletes.

Building on the framework developed by Crosset, and combining it with other research on patterns of violence in all-male groups, we hypothesize that a combination of the following factors accounts for male athletes' violence against women:

1. Support from teammates and fellow athletes for the use of force as a strategy for "doing" masculinity in their lives and being a man in their relationships with women
2. Perceived cultural support for an emphasis on physical domination as a source of status in the community and as a basis for identity as a man and an athlete
3. "Deviant" overconformity to the norms of the sport ethic, to the point that it creates strong social bonds among teammates, strong feelings that others cannot understand them or their experiences in sports, and a strong sense of hubris
4. Collective hubris among team members supporting the notions that those outside the

REFLECT ON SPORTS

Sexual Harassment and Abuse

Sexual harassment and abuse may be considered a type of sports-related violence. In addition to the type of sexual abuse by athletes described in this section, there is also the issue of sexual harassment and abuse of athletes and other young people by coaches and others in sport settings. Three major cases in Canada in 1997 created significant concerns about sexual abuse in sports (see Donnelly, 1999; Kirby, et al., 2000):

- Graham James pleaded guilty to the sexual abuse of two players while he was coach of the Western Hockey League's Swift Current Broncos. Several days later, Sheldon Kennedy—then a player with the NHL's Boston Bruins—held a press conference to announce that he was one of the victims.

- The arrest of Graham Stuckless, an equipment manager at Maple Leaf Gardens in Toronto, led to revelations about the existence of a "pedophile ring" at the Gardens during the 1970s and 1980s. Boys (primarily), lured by tickets to games, visits to locker rooms to meet players, and gifts of equipment, had been coerced into sexual acts (Vine and Challen, 2002).

- Liam Donnelly, the swim coach at Simon Fraser University, was fired following charges of sexual harassment by Rachel Marsden, a former student-athlete on his team. He was reinstated three months later after additional evidence seemed to suggest that the coach had himself been the victim of sexual harassment by Marsden.

These cases involved child sexual abuse (mostly boys), and one apparent false accusation; none involved the most widely reported form of sexual abuse in sports: that by a male coach against a female athlete. The publicity associated with these cases left many young women shaking their heads that it had taken the abuse of a high-profile male, Sheldon Kennedy, to provoke any real action. However, the cases served as a reminder of a number of incidents of abuse against female athletes that had passed with little attention; and they pro-

voked a great many calls about abuse in sports to sexual harassment counselors and to the Kids Help Phone telephone hotline from both boys and girls.

We have no good data on the prevalence of sexual harassment and abuse in sports. Studies have used different definitions of harassment and abuse, making it very difficult to compare results; and there is every reason to suspect that many incidents are unreported. The best Canadian data on child sexual abuse comes from a retrospective study with 10,000 adults in Ontario (MacMillan, et al., 1997). Some 12.8 percent of females and 4.3 percent of males reported childhood sexual abuse; 11.9 percent of females and 3.9 percent of males reported severe sexual abuse. The results also suggested, contrary to prevailing beliefs, that abuse was most often perpetrated by non-relatives (e.g., neighbours, babysitters, coaches). Thus, a small proportion of those reporting sexual abuse as a child are likely to have been abused by a coach.

The response in Canada to the three incidents outlined above, and to the 1993 and 1996 reports on the issue by the CBC television series, *the fifth estate*, has been among the most comprehensive in the world. Gordon Kirke's "Players First" report for the Canadian Hockey League (CHL) established some guidelines for major junior hockey; Sport Canada developed a policy for high-performance sports that linked funding for national sport federations to having a sexual harassment policy in place and an independent sexual harassment officer for each sport; the Canadian Hockey Association (CHA) developed "Speak Out" and "Fair Play" programmes, which they made available to hockey associations and other minor sports associations across Canada; and many local minor sport leagues instituted police checks for all children's sport coaches.

We feel that these "made in Canada" solutions are necessary albeit insufficient steps to deal with the issue of sexual harassment and sexual abuse in sports. It is important not to exaggerate the prevalence of sexual

Continued

harassment and abuse in sports. However, it is also important to recognize that many of the practices that have come to be accepted in sports—e.g., travel and transport arrangements, billeting and hotel plans, closed door meetings, one-on-one practice sessions, massage and medical examinations, hands-on guidance and spotting, etc.—need to be reconsidered. Best-practice strategies need to be developed, borrowing from contexts such as education where this issue has often been treated more seriously. *What do you think?*

fraternity of elite athletes do not deserve respect, that elite athletes can expect outsiders to defer to their wishes and demands, and that elite athletes live outside the norms of the general community

5. Support within their social world for the belief that women (apart from their own mothers and sisters) are "groupies" seeking status through relationships with elite athletes and that athletes need not take responsibility for the consequences of relationships with women

6. Institutional (team, athletic department, club, community) support for elite athletes, regardless of their behaviour

7. Institutional failure to hold elite athletes accountable when they violate community norms and rules

Research is needed on the relevance of these factors in an overall theory of assault and sexual assault perpetrated by male athletes. It is clear that male athletes do not target political leaders, corporate executives, and team owners in their off-the-field violence. With rare exceptions, they do not target mothers, coaches, or one another. Most often, the targets of violence are the people whom athletes define as unworthy of their respect, the people who athletes think cannot understand the meaning of their lives in elite sports, and the people who have characteristics directly opposed to the athletes' definitions of their own worth as athletes and as men. Therefore, common targets include many women, gay men, and cocky "straight" men in the community who publicly challenge an athlete's assumed status and privilege. Athletes' rates of violence may or may not be higher than those of other men, but our goal should be to understand violence *in the full social and cultural contexts in which it occurs.*

As noted in chapter 6, the norms and group dynamics in certain all-male sport groups encourage athletes to demean and humiliate those who do not come close to matching what they see as their own unique, elite status. In other words, off-the-field violence is not simply on-the-field violence that carries over to the rest of life. Instead, it is behaviour grounded in complex social processes related to the social worlds in which athletes live, define their identities as athletes and as men, and deal with their social relationships. As athletes are increasingly being separated from the rest of the community, these processes become more important, and assault rates among athletes go up. Until this separation is eliminated, assault will continue to be a problem, even if teams hire psychologists to assist athletes. This is a social issue as much as it is a personal problem.

Control Versus Carryover What about the possibility that athletes in power and performance sports will learn to control expressions of -

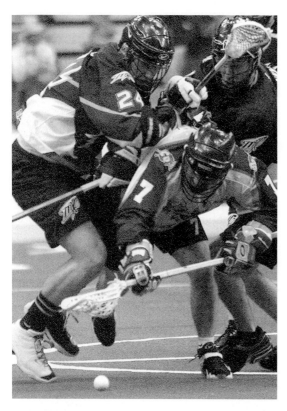

Establishing an identity as an athlete may involve being willing to take risks and to do violence to others. (CP/Ted Jacob)

actually measured higher on aggressive tendencies after a training period, and young men who participated in running, basketball, and football with standard adult supervision did not change at all in terms of their aggressive tendencies.

French sociologist Loic Wacquant did one of the most provocative studies on this topic. For over three years, Wacquant trained and "hung out" at a traditional, highly structured, and reputable boxing gym in a black ghetto area in Chicago. During that time, he observed, interviewed, and documented the experiences and lives of more than fifty men who trained as professional boxers at the gym. He not only learned the craft of boxing but also became immersed in the social world in which the boxers trained. He found that the social world formed around this gym was one in which the boxers learned to value their craft and to become dedicated to the idea of being a professional boxer; they also learned to respect their fellow boxers and to accept the rules of sportsmanship that governed boxing as a profession. In a neighbourhood where poverty and hopelessness promoted intimidation and violence all around them, these boxers accepted taboos on fighting outside the ring, avoided street fights, and internalized the controls necessary to follow a highly disciplined daily training schedule.

Trulson and Wacquant's findings, suggest that participation in sports, even martial arts and boxing, can encourage individuals to control violence. However, this control depends greatly on the conditions under which sport participation occurs. *If* the social world formed around a sport promotes a mind-set and norms emphasizing nonviolence, self-control, respect for self and others, physical fitness, patience, responsibility, and humility (the opposite of hubris), then athletes *may* learn to control violent behaviour off the field. Those most likely to benefit seem to be young men who need structured challenges and firm guidance dedicated to making them respect themselves when they do avoid violence (see the Reflect on Sports box, "Fair Play Leagues," below).

off-the-field violence? Could it be that sport participation teaches people to control violent responses to stress, defeat, hardship, and pain and enables them to avoid being violent off the field when they face adversity?

This possibility was explored in research that found a decrease in aggressive tendencies among male juvenile delinquents who received training in the philosophy and techniques of Tae Kwon Do (Trulson, 1986; summarized in chapter 6, pp. 171–172). The philosophy emphasized respect for self and others, confidence, physical fitness, self-control, honour, patience, and responsibility. Similar young men who received training in Tae Kwon Do *without* the philosophy

REFLECT ON SPORTS

Fair Play Leagues[1]

While sports are often extremely slow to make changes that may make them more safe (e.g., eliminating violence) or fair (e.g., eliminating doping), they tend to respond more quickly to declining participation (cf., the changes being made in baseball noted in chapter 5). During the 1980s, the Canadian Hockey Association (CHA) saw a sharp decline in the number of boys participating in hockey; between 1983 and 1989, there was a 17.4 percent drop in registration across Canada. The situation was particularly marked in Quebec, which went from a high of 111,960 in 1974 to a low of 57,340 in 1990—a drop of 47 percent.

There were various reasons for the decline—increasing costs, new ethnic communities with less interest in hockey, the massive growth of soccer (soccer became the most popular participation sport in Canada in 1990)—but one of the reasons was violence and concern about injuries. Hockey Québec introduced "Franc Jeu," a fair play system, in 1988. An earlier version had been tried in intramural hockey at Laval University, and a simplified version was tried out in the Quebec City area in 1987.

Franc Jeu involves setting a limit (agreed upon) for the permitted number of penalties in a game—for example, six penalties for each team in bantam and peewee (Scanlan, 2002). In addition to the two points a team is awarded for a win, an extra point is awarded for teams with six or fewer penalties; a point is lost for more than six penalties. Since research showed that approximately three players per team accounted for 50 percent of the penalties, more severe suspensions were introduced for players reaching a certain number of penalties and for coaches of teams with a high number of penalties. The rule changes seem to have stemmed the decline, and the Hockey Québec website (www.hockey.qc.ca) now claims 100,000 players in the province.

Some other leagues across Canada were concerned about violence and injuries, but they were reluctant to introduce rule changes. In 1994, the Dartmouth Whalers Minor Hockey Association (www.whalers.org) introduced a "Fair Play" programme into its league, based on the following five principles:

- Respect the rules
- Respect the opponents
- Respect the officials and their decisions
- Have everyone participate
- Maintain your self-control at all times

Some parents were reluctant, feeling that the teams would be less competitive. They were proven wrong, as Dartmouth teams went on to win four provincial championships in the next few years, and the number of injuries, penalties, and referees who quit dropped significantly. Fair play principles have been introduced in a number of leagues across the country, and there are other variations such as the "Turning Point" programme in Calgary, and "Team First" in British Columbia. Gaston Marcotte, a physical educator at Laval University, is "not aware of any league that has abandoned the fair play system once they've tried it" (cited by Scanlan, 2002, p. 255).

Some people think that Fair Play and Franc Jeu leagues take away from the essence of hockey. We think that they are an important "made in Canada" solution—both as a response to concerns about injuries and declining registrations, and as an example to reluctant league officials that positive changes are possible. *What do you think?*

---

[1] Confusingly, the CHA refers to its anti-sexual abuse initiatives as "Fair Play."

Unfortunately, these conditions are rare in many sports. Instead, most sport cultures emphasize hostility, physical domination, and a willingness to sacrifice one's body and being for the sake of competitive success. They also are organized to produce hubris, to separate athletes from the community, and to encourage athletes to think that others do not deserve their respect.

More studies are needed, especially those that dig into the social worlds of athletes in particular sports and outline the meanings athletes attach to their behaviours and to the place of violence in their worlds. Studies should also focus on issues of identity, group dynamics among athletes, ideological issues, and social factors associated with the incidence of violence. The aggression and violence learned in certain sports do not inevitably carry over to other relationships and settings, nor does sport participation automatically teach people to control violence. Instead of looking for examples of carryover or control, perhaps we should be looking for "cultural connections" between sports and ideologies associated with high rates of violence. This is discussed below.

Impact of Violence in Sports on Gender Ideology: Reproducing the Connection between Masculinity and Physical Domination

"Men are naturally superior to women": this statement arouses anger among many people today. However, many others still believe it. Furthermore, the hierarchical structure of gender relations in many cultures depends on this belief.

Power and performance sports emphasize *difference* in terms of power and strength, they emphasize *control* through domination of others, and they emphasize *status* as dependent on victories over others. In fact, in the minds of many people, power and performance sports "naturalize" differences, which take the form of rankings, and present difference as inevitable—as the way things are and should be in the world.

Power and performance sports, celebrate, among other things, the use of strength and violence in a quest for victory over others. At the same time, they reproduce an ideology of masculinity stressing the same factors. The irony in this approach is that, if gender were really grounded in biology and nature, there would be no need for such ideas about males and females to be taught and preserved through sports; they would just come naturally to boys and girls without our having to paint their bedrooms different colours when they were born. But the behaviours of males and females do not

come naturally, so those whose privilege depends on maintaining a gender ideology that emphasizes difference see power and performance sports as consistent with their interests.

This is the reason some men celebrate sports in which aggression is commonplace. They want to keep alive the notion of difference because it privileges them in the gender order. These are usually the same people who reject rules against fighting. For example, when rules were passed in the early 1990s to partially limit fighting in hockey, Tie Domi, a player with a reputation for doing violence complained:

> If you take out fighting, what comes next? Do we eliminate checking? Pretty soon, we will all be out there in dresses and skirts.
> (Domi, 1992, p. C3)

Domi's point is that, unless men can do violence in hockey, there will be nothing that makes them different from women, and the perception is that nothing is worse for a man than being like women—except, perhaps, being gay.

What happens to gender ideology when women play power and performance sports and use violence on the field? On the one hand, this contradicts the gender logic that women are frail and vulnerable. On the other hand, it reaffirms values and experiences that have worked to the disadvantage of many women. This means that women should be careful not to buy into the same emphasis on physical domination used by some men in sports. It is important for women to find ways to be strong and tough without being aggressive and violent.

The social impact of the ideology reproduced in connection with sports goes far beyond the off-the-field behaviour of the athletes themselves. It affects the cultural context in which we all live.

VIOLENCE AMONG SPECTATORS

Do sports incite violence among spectators? This question is important, because sports and sport events capture considerable public attention in

"Hey, watch it, pal! You stepped on my foot."

The language used in association with sports often refers to violence, but it is not known if such language actually incites violent behaviour.

communities around the world. Spectators number in the billions. To answer this question, we must distinguish between watching sports on television and attending events in person.

Violence among Television Viewers

Most sport watching occurs in front of the television. Television viewers may be emotionally expressive during games and matches. They may even become angry, but we know little about whether their anger is expressed through violence directed at friends and family members at home.

We also do not know much about violence among those who watch sports in more public settings, such as bars or pubs. Our sense is that most viewers are supportive of one another and restrict their emotional expressions to verbal comments. When they do express anger, they nearly always direct it at the characters in the mediated event, rather than at fellow viewers. Even when fellow viewers define outbursts of emotions as too loud or inappropriate, their efforts to settle a fan down are supportive rather than aggressive. When fans from opposing teams are in the same bar, there are usually other sources of mutual identification, which

keep them from identifying each other as targets of aggression, and they tend to confine expressions of their differences to verbal comments.

There have been cases when people, usually men, watching sports in a bar or other public place join in celebratory violence following victories in championship games. However, there are no studies of this phenomenon or of how watching the event on television may influence what happens.

Violence at Sport Events

Spectators attending noncontact sport events seldom engage in violence. They may be emotionally expressive, but violence directed at fellow fans, players, coaches, referees, ushers, or police are very rare. The attack and wounding of Monica Seles in 1993 stands out as one of the few violent incidents at a noncontact sport event, and that had more to do with celebrity stalking than with sport itself. Of course, there are occasions when fans use hostile words or engage in minor skirmishes when a drink is dropped onto another's head, but such cases of violence are often controlled quickly by the fans themselves.

Spectators attending contact sports tend to be vocal and emotional, but most of them have not been involved in violent behaviour. However, crowd violence does occur, and it has occurred with enough regularity and seriousness in certain sports to be defined as a problem for law enforcement, as well as a social problem involving personal injuries, deaths, and property destruction. This is true for Canada and the United States, as well as for other parts of the world.

Historical Background Media reports of violent behaviour at sport events around the world, especially at soccer matches, have increased our awareness of crowd violence. However, crowd violence is not new. Although data documenting the behaviour of sport spectators through the ages is scarce, research does suggest that spectator violence did occur in the past and that much of it would make crowd violence today seem rare and tame in comparison (Dunning, 1999; Guttmann, 1986, 1998; Scheinin, 1994; Young, 2000). Roman events during the first five centuries of the Common Era contained especially brutal examples of crowd violence (Guttmann, 1986, 1998). Spectators during the medieval period were not much better, although levels of violence decreased in the late medieval period. With the emergence of modern sports, violence among sport spectators decreased further, but it remained common by today's standards. For example, a baseball game in 1900 was described in this way:

> Thousands of gunslinging Chicago Cubs fans turned a Fourth of July doubleheader into a shoot-out at the OK Corral, endangering the lives of players and fellow spectators. Bullets sang, darted, and whizzed over players' heads as the rambunctious fans fired round after round whenever the Cubs scored against the gun-shy Philadelphia Phillies. The visiting team was so intimidated it lost both games . . . at Chicago's West Side Grounds. (Nash and Zullo, 1986: 133)

The account continues to explain that, when the Cubs scored six runs in the sixth inning of the first game, guns were fired around the stadium to the point that gunsmoke made it difficult to see the field. When the Cubs tied the score in the ninth inning, fans again fired guns, and hundreds of them shot holes in the roof of the grandstand, causing splinters to fly on to their heads. As the game remained tied during three extra innings, fans pounded the seats with the butts of their guns and fired in unison every time the Phillies' pitcher began his wind up to throw a pitch. It rattled him so much that the Cubs scored on a wild pitch. After the score, a vocal and heavily armed Cub fan stood up and shouted, "Load! Load at will! Fire!" Fans around the stadium emptied the rest of their ammunition in a final explosive volley.

Between 1900 and the early 1940s, baseball crowd violence was common in the U.S.:

bottles and other objects were thrown at players and umpires. Players feared being injured by spectators as much as they feared the "bean balls" thrown regularly at their heads by opposing pitchers.

These examples are not meant to minimize the existence or seriousness of current cases of crowd violence. They are intended to counter the argument that violence is a bigger problem today than it was in the past and that coercive social control tactics are needed to prevent what some people see as a growing decline of civility among fans. There are obnoxious and violent fans today, and they present problems, but they should not be viewed as new and unprecedented threats to the social order.

Celebratory Violence Oddly enough, some of the most serious forms of crowd violence associated with sports occur in connection with the celebrations that follow victories in important games. When these occur inside stadiums, they often are defined as displays of youthful exuberance and loyalty to the team or community. However, as property destruction moves outside the stadium into the surrounding community and involves large crowds of people, including those who did not attend the games, violence becomes more serious and is defined as a major law enforcement problem. Post-event riots in Canada have taken place in Toronto in 1983; Montreal in 1986; Hamilton, Ontario, in 1986; Montreal in 1993; and, the most violent of all, Vancouver in 1994 (Young, 2002). Unfortunately, there are few sociological studies of this type of violence. Lang (1981) included it in her typology of sport riots, referring to those involved in "victory" riots as "the licentious (or exuberant) crowd," but there has been no systematic data collection or attempts to understand the social dynamics of celebratory violence. However, incidents following some recent university football games in the United States have prompted a renewed interest in the topic.

Research and Theories about Crowd Violence
Researchers in North America have generally ignored violence at sport events. Apparently, violence at sport events has not been seen as significant enough, relative to other forms of violence, to attract research attention. The research that does exist has focused primarily on issues of race relations, and little attention has been given to other issues (Young, 2000). Kevin Young (2002), of the University of Calgary, has been almost a lone voice in attempting to draw attention to the very real issues of spectator violence at North American sport events. His most recent analysis is yet another reminder of the extent the problem. He begins with these scenarios:

> …officials clear the playing area and delay the game for eight minutes when missiles are thrown at players by irate fans; a riot involving approximately 2,000 fans results in parts of the stadium being vandalized, several fans being seriously injured, and the arena being evacuated; home fans are threatened with a game forfeit, 15 fans are arrested and 175 ejected for pelting players and officials with missiles; a city council intervenes following stabbings, repeated episodes of assault, and mass fighting involving players and fans; hundreds of police dressed in riot gear use tear gas to disperse 70,000 fans in a downtown area. A man is shot dead by a police officer, hundreds of people are injured, and over 50 arrests are made; vandalism, arson, and fighting provoke police into using rubber bullets and batons as players are detained inside the stadium until the rioting quells. (Young, 2002, p. 237)

Readers are then reminded that this is not European soccer hooliganism, but all actual events that have taken place at North American sport events in recent years. Young then goes on to outline the nature and patterns of spectator violence, which involve seven characteristics all seen at North American sport events—(1) missile throwing (coins, bottles, batteries, etc.), (2) use of firearms and other weapons, (3) field invasions, (4) property destruction and vandalism, (5) fighting among fans, (6) disorder primarily occurring at the games themselves (unlike soccer

hooliganism) with the exception of, (7) post-event riots (following both victories and defeats).

Young raises the troubling question of why spectator violence in North America has not received nearly the same amount of media and police/security attention that soccer hooliganism has in Europe, and outlines some important directions for research.

British and other European scholars have done most of the research on crowd violence, and most of their studies have focused on soccer and "soccer hooliganism." Studies grounded in social psychological theories have emphasized that displays of intimidation and aggression at soccer matches have involved ritual violence, consisting of fantasy-driven status posturing by young males who want to be defined as tough and manly (Marsh, 1982; Marsh and Campbell, 1982). These studies are interesting, and they describe classic examples of ritualistic forms of "aggro," but they ignore the serious and sometimes deadly violence perpetrated by soccer fans, especially during pre- and postgame activities.

Research inspired by various forms of conflict theory has emphasized that violence at soccer matches is an expression of the alienation of disenfranchised working-class men (Taylor, 1982a, b, 1987). In addition to losing control over the conditions of their work lives, these men also feel they have lost control of the recently commercialized clubs that sponsor top-level professional soccer in England. This research helps us understand that violence may be associated with class conflict in society, but it does not explain why violence at soccer matches has not increased proportionately in connection with the declining power of the working class in England.

Research inspired by interactionist and critical theories has emphasized a variety of factors, including the importance of understanding the history and dynamics of the working-class and youth subcultures in British society and how those subcultures have been influenced by the professionalization and commercialization of society as a whole, and soccer in particular

Two fans pretend to fight. Crowd violence has not been a major problem at most sport events, but, when it happens, there is a need for controlled intervention to prevent serious injuries. (CP/Ryan Remiorz)

(Giulianotti, et al., 1994; Giulianotti, 1995). More work is needed to develop critical analyses of crowd violence across various situations.

Figurational theory has inspired the most research on crowd violence. The work of those using a figurational approach represents a synthesis of approaches grounded in biology, psychology, sociology, and history. Much of this work, summarized by Dunning (1999) and Young (2000) emphasizes that soccer hooliganism is grounded in long-term historical changes, which have affected working-class men; their relationships with each other and their families; and their definitions of community, violence, and masculinity. Taken together, these changes have created a context in which soccer has come to represent the collective turf

and identity of people in local communities and the identity of British people as a whole. In either case, soccer becomes a site for defending and/or asserting community and identity through violence. Figurational research has provided valuable historical information and thoughtful analyses of the complex social processes of which soccer hooliganism is a part. It has also been used as a reference for those who have formulated some of the recent policies of social control related to soccer crowds in England and around Europe.[3]

General Factors Related to Violence at Sport Events   Crowd violence at sport events is a complex social phenomenon related to three factors:

1. The action in the sport event itself
2. The crowd dynamics and the situation in which the spectators watch the event
3. The historical, social, economic, and political contexts in which the event is planned and played

VIOLENCE AND ACTION IN THE EVENT   If spectators perceive players' action on the field as violent, they are more likely to engage in violent acts during and after games (Smith, 1983). This point is important, because spectators' perceptions often are influenced by the way in which events are promoted. If an event is hyped in terms of violent images, spectators are more likely to perceive violence during the event itself, and then they are more likely to be violent themselves. This leads some people to argue that promoters and the media have a responsibility to

---

[3]The causes of crowd violence at British soccer games, and at games in Europe and South America, are far too complex to explain in this chapter. Those interested in this phenomenon should consult the following: Adang, 1993; Armstrong, 1994; Dunning, 1999; Giulianotti, 1994; Giulianotti et al., 1994; Haynes, 1993; Murphy et al., 1990; Pilz, 1996; Roversi, 1994; Taylor, 1982a, b, 1987.

advertise events in terms of the action and drama expected, not the blood and violence.

Another important factor in the event is the action of the officials. Research on this issue is needed, but data suggest that, when fans believe that a crucial goal or a victory has been "stolen" by an unfair or apparently incompetent decision made by a referee or an umpire, the likelihood of violence during and following the event increases (Murphy et al., 1990). This is why it is important to have competent officials at crucial games and matches and why it is important for them to control game events, so that actions perceived as violent are held to a minimum. The knowledge that fan aggression may be precipitated by a crucial call late in a close, important contest puts heavy responsibility on the officials' shoulders.

VIOLENCE, CROWD DYNAMICS, AND SITUATIONAL FACTORS   The characteristics of a crowd and the immediate situation associated with a sport event also influence behaviour patterns among spectators. Spectator violence is likely to vary with one or more of the following factors:

- Crowd size and the standing or seating patterns among spectators
- Composition of the crowd in terms of age, sex, social class, and racial/ethnic mix
- Meaning and importance of the event for spectators
- History of the relationship between the teams and between spectators
- Crowd-control strategies used at the event (police, attack dogs, or other security measures)
- Alcohol consumption by the spectators
- Location of the event (neutral site or home site of one of the opponents)
- Motivations for spectators attending the event
- Importance of the team as a source of identity for spectators (class identity, ethnic or national identity, regional or local identity, club or gang identity, etc.)

The following comparison of game situations illustrates how many of these factors might be related to spectator violence.

The *location of an event* is important because it influences who attends and how they travel. If the stadium is generally accessed by car, if spectators for the visiting team are limited due to travel expense, and if tickets are expensive, it is likely that people attending the game have a vested interest in maintaining order and avoiding violence. On the other hand, if large groups of people travel to the game in buses or trains, and if tickets are relatively cheap and many of the spectators are young people more interested in having a memorable experience than in maintaining the status quo, confrontations between people looking for exciting action increase, and so does the possibility of violence. If groups of fans looking for excitement have consumed large amounts of alcohol, the possibility of violence increases greatly.

If spectators are treated as patrons rather than as bodies to be controlled, and if stadium norms emphasize service as opposed to social control, people are less likely to engage in defensive and confrontational actions, which could lead to violence. If the stadium or arena is crowded and if the crowd itself is comprised mostly of young men rather than couples and families, there is a greater chance for confrontations and violence, especially if the event is seen as a special rivalry whose outcome has status implications for the communities or nations represented by the teams.

Violence could take the form of celebratory riots among the fans of the winning team, fights between fans of opposing teams, random property destruction carried out by fans of the losing team as they leave town, panics incited by a perceived threat unrelated to the contest itself, or planned confrontations between groups using the event as a convenient place to face off with each other as they seek to enhance their status and reputations or as they reaffirm their ethnic, political, class, national, local, or gang identities.

Whenever thousands of people get together for an occasion intended to generate collective emotions and excitement, it is not surprising that crowd dynamics and circumstances influence the actions of individuals and groups. This is especially true at sport events where collective action is easily fuelled by what social psychologists call *emotional contagion*. Under conditions of emotional contagion, norms are formed rapidly and may be followed in a near spontaneous manner by large numbers of people. Although this does not always lead to violence, it increases the possibility of potentially violent confrontations between groups of fans and between fans and agents of social control, such as the police.

VIOLENCE AND THE OVERALL CONTEXT IN WHICH THE EVENT OCCURS   Sport events do not occur in social vacuums. When spectators attend events, they bring with them the histories, issues, controversies, and ideologies of the communities and cultures in which they live. They may be racists who want to harass those they identify as targets for discrimination. They may come from ethnic neighbourhoods and want to express and reaffirm their ethnicity. They may resent negative circumstances in their lives and want to express their bitterness. They may be members of groups or gangs in which status is gained partly through fighting. They may be powerless and alienated and looking for ways to be noticed and defined as socially important. They may be young men who believe that manhood is achieved through violence and domination over others. Or they may be living lives so devoid of significance and excitement that they want to create a memorable occasion they can discuss boastfully with friends for years to come. In other words, when thousands of spectators attend a sport event, their behaviours are grounded in factors far beyond the event and the stadium.

When tension and conflict are intense and widespread in a community or society, sport events may become sites for confrontations that cannot be considered as sport violence, but as sport-related violence (Young, 2000). For example, in 1955, francophone Maurice "Rocket" Richard, the star player of the Montreal Canadiens, was suspended by the anglophone NHL president Clarence Campbell. The suspension was the result of a stick-swinging incident, but it jeopardized both Richard's chance of achieving the single-season scoring record and the Canadiens' playoff chances. When Campbell showed up at the next Canadiens game, the resentment of the francophone fans spilled out into the streets of Montreal, resulting in a riot that lasted two days and caused dozens of injuries, thousands of dollars worth of property damage, and one hundred arrests. While the riot was triggered by the suspension of Richard, it came to express resistance to a long period of historical domination of Quebec politics and economy by an anglophone elite, and some have interpreted it as an action that anticipated "La Révolution tranquille."

In his classic book *Power and Innocence: A Search for the Sources of Violence*, Rollo May (1972) observed that all human beings need some means of achieving a sense of personal significance. Significance, he says, is best achieved when people are in control of their lives, but, when people are powerless and without resources, "violence may be the only way [they] can achieve a sense of significance." This may partially explain the violent behaviour of young, predominantly male soccer fans around the world. At least some of these young spectators perceive violence as a means of achieving a sense of significance. After all, violence forces others to take notice and respond to the perpetrator's existence. This is certainly not the only factor underlying violence among fans, but it is part of an historical, social, political, and economic context that we must understand when explaining violence among spectators.

Finally, it must be noted that nearly all crowd violence involves men. This suggests that future research on the topic must consider the role of masculinity in crowd dynamics and the behaviour of particular segments of crowds (Hughson, 2000). Female fans generally do not tip over cars and set them on fire or throw chairs through windows during so-called celebratory riots. They may become involved in fights, but not nearly to the same extent as men do. Crowd violence may be as much a gender issue as it is a racial/ethnic or social class issue, and controlling it may involve changing notions of masculinity as much as hiring additional police to patrol the sidelines at the next game.

Control of Crowd Violence Effective efforts to control spectator violence are based on an awareness of each of the three factors previously listed. *First*, the fact that perceived violence on the field positively influences crowd violence indicates a need to minimize violence among players during events. If fans do not define the actions of players as violent, the likelihood of crowd violence decreases. Furthermore, fans' perceptions of violence are likely to decrease if events are not hyped as violent confrontations between hostile opponents. Players and coaches could be used to make public announcements that defuse hostility and emphasize the skills of the athletes involved in the event.[4] High-profile fans for each team could make similar announcements. The use of competent and professionally trained officials is also important. When officials maintain control of a game and make calls the spectators see as fair, they decrease the likelihood of spectator violence grounded in anger and perceived injustice. These referees also could meet with both teams before the event and calmly explain the need to leave hostilities in the locker rooms. Team officials could organize pregame unity rituals involving an exchange of team symbols and displays of respect between opponents. These rituals could be given

We need more research on so-called celebratory riots. Research on other forms of collective behaviour suggests that they may not be as spontaneous and unplanned as many people think. (CP/Ryan Remiorz)

media coverage, so that fans could see that athletes do not view opponents with hostility.

Second, an awareness of crowd dynamics and the conditions that can precipitate violence is critical. Preventive measures are important. The needs and rights of spectators must be known and respected. Crowd-control officials must be well trained, so that they know how to intervene in potentially disruptive situations without creating defensive reactions and increasing the chances of violence. Alcohol consumption should be regulated realistically, as has been done in many facilities throughout North America. Facilities should be safe and organized to enable spectators to move around while also limiting contact between hostile fans of opposing teams. Exits should be accessible and clearly marked, and spectators should not be herded like animals before or after games. Encouraging attendance by families is important in lowering the incidence of violence.

---

[4] This occurred in 2003, during a tense time in U.S./Canada relations, after the invasion of Iraq. After several incidents of booing national anthems at sport events, players made pre-game announcements to ask for respect for the opponents' anthem.

Third, an awareness of the historical, social, economic, and political issues that often underlie crowd violence is also important. Restrictive law-and-order responses to crowd violence may be temporarily effective, but they will not eliminate the underlying tensions and conflicts that often fuel violence. Policies dealing with oppressive forms of inequality, economic problems, unemployment, a lack of political representation, racism, and distorted definitions of *masculinity* in the community and in society as a whole are needed. These are the factors often at the root of tensions, conflicts, and violence.

Also needed are efforts to establish connections between teams and the communities in which they are located. These connections can be used to defuse potentially dangerous feelings or plans among groups of spectators or community residents. This does not mean that teams merely need better public relations. There must be *actual* connections between the teams, the facilities, and the communities in which they exist. Players and coaches need to be engaged in community service. Owners must be visible supporters of community events and programmes. Teams must develop programmes to assist in the development of local neighborhoods, especially those around the stadium or arena.

The goal of these guidelines is to assist in the creation of antiviolence norms among spectators. This is difficult to do, but not impossible. Over the long run, it will be more effective than using metal detectors, moving games to distant locations away from either team's home, hiring scores of police, patrolling the stands, using video cameras for surveillance, and scheduling games in the early morning on Saturdays so that crowds will be sparse. Of course, some of these tactics can be effective, but they destroy part of the enjoyment of attending events, and they restrict attendance access for many people. We see them as last resorts or temporary measures taken only to provide time to promote the development of new spectator norms.

SUMMARY

DOES VIOLENCE IN SPORTS AFFECT OUR LIVES?

Violence in sports is an important and highly publicized topic. Violence in the form of excessive physical force that causes or has the potential to cause harm or destruction is not new to sports; however, as people see it as something that can be controlled, they deal with it as a problem. Violence among athletes ranges from brutal body contact to criminal violence, and it is linked with "deviant" overconformity to the sport ethic, money and commercialization, and cultural definitions of *masculinity*. It has become institutionalized in most contact sports for both men and women as a strategy for competitive success, despite the fact that it causes considerable pain and injury among athletes. The use of enforcers and goons is an example of the extreme form of this institutionalization. Controlling on-the-field violence has been difficult, especially in men's contact sports, because it is often tied to the way athletes see themselves as athletes and as men.

Male athletes in contact sports learn to use violence and intimidation as strategic tools, but it is not known if they carry over these strategies into off-the-field settings and relationships. Among males, learning to use violence as a tool within a sport is frequently tied to the reaffirmation of a form of masculinity that emphasizes a willingness to risk personal safety and a desire to intimidate others. If males who participate in certain sports learn to perceive this orientation as natural or appropriate, then sports may intensify serious forms of off-the-field violence, including assault and sexual assault. However, such learning is not automatic, and men may, under certain circumstances, even learn to control violence as they play sports. The most important impact of violence in sports may be how people use it to reaffirm an ideology of the "natural superiority of men," based in the belief that an ability to engage in violence is part of the essence of being a man.

Female athletes in contact sports also engage in aggressive acts, but little is known about how those acts and the willingness to engage in them are linked to the identities of women athletes at different levels of competition. At this time, many women seem to prefer an emphasis on supportive connections between teammates and opponents, as well as on pleasure and participation in sports. Therefore, aggression and violence do not occur as often or in connection with the same dynamics in their sports as in men's sports.

Violence among spectators is influenced by violence on the field of play, crowd dynamics, the situation at the event itself, and the overall historical and cultural contexts in which spectators live. Isolated cases of violence probably are best controlled by improved crowd management, but chronic violence among spectators usually signals that something needs to be changed in the way certain sports are defined and played or in the actual social, economic, or political structures of the community or society.

 SUGGESTED READINGS

Burstyn, V. 1999. *The rites of men: Manhood, politics, and the culture of sport*. Toronto: University of Toronto Press (chapter 4, "Organized Violence and Men's Sport" and chapter 5, "The Reproduction of Hypermasculinity" represent a feminist discussion of why many sports are violent and how violent sports affect the lives of both men and women).

Crosset, T. W., J. R. Benedict, and M. A. McDonald. 1995. Male student-athletes reported for sexual assault: Survey of campus police departments and judicial affairs offices. *Journal of Sport and Social Issues* 19 (2): 126–40 (contains original data from U.S. universities and provides an overview and critique of published accounts of sexual assault and sports; very helpful in discussions of this topic).

Dunning, E. 1999. *Sport matters: Sociological studies of sport, violence, and civilization*. London:

Routledge (in chapters 6 and 7, figurational theory is used to guide an analysis of soccer hooliganism around the world and sports crowd violence in North America).

Kirby, S., L. Greaves, and O. Hankivsky. 2000. *The dome of silence: Sexual harassment and abuse in sport*. Halifax, NS: Fernwood Publishing (a detailed analysis of a survey of two hundred sixty-six Canadian athletes with regard to sexual harassment and abuse; examines the values of sports and the Canadian sport community's policy response to recent revelations of sexual violence in sports; and provides important suggestions for future changes).

Robinson, L. 1998. *Crossing the line: Violence and sexual assault in Canada's national sport*. Toronto: McClelland & Stewart (a journalistic exposé of the forms of violence that exist on and off the ice in Canadian hockey; general critique of the rape culture of the hockey locker room and a hockey culture that supports expressions of violence by players and coaches).

Scanlan, L. 2002. *Grace under fire: The state of our sweet and savage game*. Toronto: Penguin Canada (a journalistic and insightful analysis of fighting in hockey, combining interviews with players and data from historical, sport sciences, and sport studies sources in a work that manages to condemn what is wrong with the game without condemning the game).

Sugden, J. 1996. *Boxing and society: An international analysis*. Manchester, NH: University of Manchester Press (detailed, insightful analysis of boxing as an element of cultures around the world; the analysis puts the violence of boxing into context as it focuses on the sport's social, economic, and historical roots and the moral, ethical, and political debates that it has evoked).

Vine, C., and P. Challen. 2002. *Gardens of shame: The tragedy of Martin Kruze and the sexual abuse at Maple Leaf Gardens*. Vancouver: Douglas and McIntyre (uses the tragedy of Martin Kruze—his coming forward in 1997 to blow the whistle on the Maple Leaf Gardens sex scandal, and his suicide later in the year—to explore the scandal, and the consequences of childhood sexual abuse).

Young, K. 2001. *Sport and violence. In Handbook of sports studies*, (pp. 382–407) edited by J. Coakley and E. Dunning. London: Sage (an overview of manifestations and explanations of sports violence among spectators and players; excellent analysis of issues related to policing sports violence).

Young, K. 2002. From "sports violence" to "sports crime": Aspects of violence, law, and gender in the sports process. In *Paradoxes of youth and sport* (pp. 207–24), edited by M. Gatz, M.A. Messner, and S.J. Ball-Rokeach. Albany, NY: State University of New York Press (comprehensive yet concise review of cases and studies of athlete/participant violence in North America; references to nearly all major work on this topic).

Young, K. 2002. Standard deviations: An update on North American crowd disorder. *Sociology of sport journal* 19 (3): 237–75 (comprehensive yet concise review of cases and studies of spectator violence in North America; references to nearly all major work on this topic).

WEBSITE RESOURCES

Note: Websites often change. The following URLs were current when this book was printed. Please check our website (www.mcgrawhill.ca/college/coakley) for updates and additions.

www.canadianhockey.ca (the Canadian Hockey Association's website includes information on anti-harassment and anti-violence initiatives)

www.whalers.org (the Dartmouth Whalers Minor Hockey Association website has comprehensive information about fair play leagues and anti-violence initiatives)

www.sportinsociety.org/mvp.html (the Mentors in Violence Prevention—MVP—programme is a gender violence prevention and education programme based at Northeastern University's Center for the Study of Sport in Society; it is designed to enlist high school, university, and professional athletes in the effort to prevent all forms of men's violence against women)

www.ed.gov/databases/ERIC_Digests/ed316547.html (summary of basic information about violence in sports; created by ERIC, the Educational Resources Information Center)

www.ncava.org (National Coalition Against Violent Athletes; news, statistics, updates, and information about prevention programmes)

www.silent-edge.org (a site dealing with harassment and abuse against figure skaters, with good links to other harassment-in-sports sites)

http://conventions.coe.int/Treaty/EN/cadreprincipal.htm (site for the Council of Europe; Document 120 contains the council's official position on "spectator violence and misbehaviour at sports events and in particular at football matches")

www.noviolence.com (presents a campaign to curb fan violence in soccer stadiums; links to other useful sites, as well as information about the campaign)

www.footballhooligans.org.uk (links and commentary discussing the myths and the reality of disruptive and violent behaviour in connection with soccer around the world, especially in Europe)

(M. MacNeill)

Gender and Sports

Does equity require ideological changes?

People used to ask me, "Aren't you worried it's going to mess up your reproductive organs?" Now they say: "You go, girl! Don't let anyone tell you no."

—Stacy Dragila, pole vault champion (1999)

[I]t's both demeaning and infantilizing to assign women's sports the chore of cleaning up the industry....[W]omen shouldn't be relegated to the ladies' auxiliary of men's sports—making less money and getting less attention, but proud in the knowledge that their play is uncorrupt.

—Rachel Giese, columnist (1998)

[The] little sister principle: Like the legions of girls who have played in goal for their brothers when an extra player was needed...[f]emale players are still largely looked upon as the little sisters who don't really belong in hockey.

—Elizabeth Etuc and Megan Williams, authors (1996)

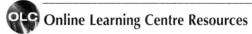

OLC Online Learning Centre Resources

Visit *Sports in Society's* Online Learning Centre at **www.mcgrawhill.ca/college/coakley** for additional information and study material for this chapter.

...ant to explain why most sports ... world have been defined as men's acti... hy half the world's population generally has been excluded or discouraged from participating in many sports through most of the twentieth century, and why there have been such major changes in women's participation since the mid-1970s. We also want to explain the relationship between sports and popular beliefs about masculinity and femininity and homosexuality and heterosexuality. Thus, gender and gender relations are central topics for those of us who study sports in society. Gender issues underlie many of the topics discussed in this book, and it has been impossible for us even to write the previous chapters without raising the issue. However, a separate chapter is necessary to identify the full significance of gender relations in sports. In the past, it was usual in sociology of sport textbooks and courses to deal with the issue of "women in sports." Those days are long gone as we have come to realize that it is not very realistic to study women, or men, in isolation from one another. If all humans were hermaphrodites, gender would not be an issue. Since the concept of gender implies that women must be studied "in relation to" men, and men must be studied "in relation to" women, gender relations are a key area of study.

When people discuss gender relations and sports, they usually focus on issues related to fairness and equity, as well as to ideology and culture. *Fairness and equity issues* revolve around topics such as

- Sport participation patterns among women
- Gender inequities in participation opportunities, support for athletes, and jobs in coaching and administration
- Strategies for achieving equal opportunities for girls and women

Ideological and cultural issues revolve around topics such as

- The production and reproduction of gender logic in connection with sports

- The ways in which prevailing gender logic constrains the lives of women and men and subverts the achievement of gender equity
- The cultural changes required to achieve gender equity and democratic access to participation in sports

The goal of this chapter is to discuss these two sets of issues and to show that, even though many people deal with them separately, they go hand in hand in real life. We cannot ignore either one if we are seeking fairness as we interact with others and as we participate in sports.

PARTICIPATION AND EQUITY ISSUES

The single most dramatic change in the world of sports over the past generation has been the increased participation of girls and women. This has occurred mostly in wealthy postindustrial nations. Changes have occurred in traditional, labour-intensive, poor nations as well, but many factors have kept such changes from being revolutionary in scope. Despite resistance in some countries, girls and women around the world now participate in a variety of school, community, and club programmes, which did not exist thirty years ago.

Reasons for Increased Participation

Five major factors account for recent increases in sport participation among girls and women:

1. New opportunities
2. Government equal rights legislation
3. The global women's rights movement
4. An expanding health and fitness movement
5. Increased media coverage of women in sports

New Opportunities New opportunities account for most of the increased sport participation among girls and women today. Prior to the mid-1970s, many girls and women did not play sports for one simple reason: teams and programmes

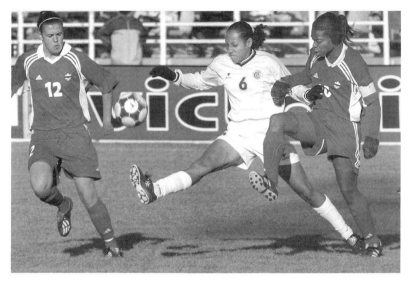

Due to a combination of factors, girls and women today see a wider range of sport participation images than they saw in the past. This has encouraged dramatic increases in sport participation. (CP/Rob Kruyt)

did not exist. Young women today may not realize it, but opportunities they enjoy in their schools and communities were not available to their mothers. Teams and programmes developed since the late 1970s have uncovered and cultivated interests ignored in the past. Girls and women still do not receive an equal share of sport resources in most organizations and communities, but increased participation clearly has gone hand in hand with the development of new opportunities. Most of these new opportunities owe their existence to some form of political pressure or government legislation.

Government Equal Rights Legislation Literally millions of girls and women would not be playing sports today if it were not for local and national legislation mandating equal rights. Many policies and rules exist today because of concerted efforts to raise legal issues and to pressure political representatives. The individuals and groups making these efforts have been committed to the struggle to achieve fairness in sports. In Canada, legal concerns about gender equity in sports coincide with the "official" start of the so-called "second wave" of feminism in Canada, the 1970 *Report of the Royal Commission on the Status of Women*. Two recommendations directly addressed the issue:

> **Recommendation 77:** We recommend that the provinces and territories (a) review their policies and practices to ensure that school programmes provide girls with equal opportunities with boys to engage in athletic and sports activities, and (b) establish policies and practices that will motivate and encourage girls to engage in athletic and sports activities.
>
> **Recommendation 78:** We recommend that, pursuant to Section 3(d) of the federal Fitness and Amateur Sport Act, a research project be undertaken to (a) determine why fewer girls than boys participate in sports programmes at the school level and (b) recommend remedial action.

The process of working toward achieving these, and other aspects of gender equity in Canadian sports has been long and slow, and, of course, we still have "fewer girls than boys participat[ing] in sport programmes at the school level," although

...s the case in 1970. In 1980, ...rogramme of the Fitness and ...port Branch was formed in Ottawa ...nic, 2000), showing some level of federal commitment to gender equity. However, the main tools for equity arrived with the repatriation of the Constitution in 1982. Schedule B of the Constitution Act, the Charter of Rights and Freedoms, gave all Canadians equal rights under the law. The 1985 Canadian Human Rights Act (together with various provincial Human Rights Acts) sharpened the tools, and women and men who had been lobbying for gender equity in sports were now in a position to press their claims. As a consequence, in 1986, Sport Canada published the *Sport Canada Policy on Women in Sport*, and steps have been gradually taken to implement that policy of equal opportunity at all levels of the Canadian sport system.

Governments in various countries also have passed laws and formulated policies promoting equal rights for girls and women in sports (e.g., Title IX, the Educational Amendments to the Civil Rights Act, in the United States). Women around the world have formed the International Working Group on Women and Sport (the IWG; see www.iwg-gti.org) to promote the enforcement of these laws and policies and to pressure resistant governments and international groups to pass equal rights legislation of their own (from 1998 to 2002, the IWG Secretariat was located in Hull, Quebec). Official power in these nations and organizations rests in the hands of men, and they often see women's sport participation as disruptive of the social or moral order. The women and men striving to produce changes in these settings have had to be persistent and politically creative to produce even minor changes.

The Global Women's Rights Movement The global women's movement over the past thirty years has emphasized that females are enhanced as human beings when they develop their intellectual *and* physical abilities. This idea has encouraged women of all ages to pursue their interests in sports, and it has led to the creation of new interests among those who, in the past, never would have thought of playing sports (Fasting, 1996). The women's movement also has helped redefine occupational and family roles for women, and this has provided more women the time and resources they need to play sports. As the ideals of the women's movement have become more widely accepted, and as male control over the lives and bodies of women has weakened, more women have chosen to play sports. More changes are needed, however, especially in poor nations and in the living conditions of low-income women in wealthy nations, but the choices now available to women are less restricted than they once were.

The global women's movement has fuelled both national and international political action. Many politically influential women's sport organizations have emerged in connection with the women's movement. For example, the Canadian Association for the Advancement of Women and Sport and Physical Activity (CAAWS) and similar groups in other nations have become important lobbying groups for change. The IWG emerged out of a 1994 conference, which brought women delegates from eighty countries to Brighton, England, to discuss "women, sport, and the challenge of change." After three days of discussion and debate, the delegates unanimously passed a set of global gender equity principles now known as the "Brighton Declaration." This document in revised form continues to be used by people as they apply pressure on governments and sport organizations to make new spaces for girls and women in sports. Follow-up conferences were held in Windhoek, Namibia, in 1998, and in Montreal in 2002.

Lobbying efforts by representatives from these and other groups led to the inclusion of an article (10g) specifically related to women's participation in sports and physical activity in the United Nations' Convention on the Elimination of All Forms of Discrimination against Women (CEDAW; www.unhchr.ch.html/menu3/b/e1cedaw.htm), and to statements related to sports and physical education in the official Platform for Action of the U.N.'s Fourth World Conference on Women, held in Beijing, China, in 1996. These statements called for new efforts to provide sport and physical education opportunities to promote the education, health, and human rights of girls and women in countries around the world. Canadians have been particularly active in these initiatives. What began as inspiration based in the women's movement has become a widely accepted global effort to promote and guarantee sport participation opportunities for girls and women.

The Expanding Health and Fitness Movement

Since the mid-1970s, research has made many people around the world more aware of the health benefits of physical activities. This awareness has encouraged women to seek opportunities to play sports. Although much of the publicity associated with this movement has been influenced by traditional gender logic and has been tied to the prevailing feminine ideal of being thin and sexually attractive to men, there also has been an emphasis on the *development of physical strength and competence*. Muscles have become more widely accepted as desirable attributes among women of all ages. Traditional standards remain, as illustrated by the clothing fashions and marketing strategies associated with women's fitness, but many women have moved beyond those standards and have focused on physical competence and the good feelings that go with it, rather than trying to look like anorexic models in fashion magazines.

Furthermore, many companies that produce sporting goods and apparel have jumped from the women's *fitness and appearance* bandwagon to the *fitness and sports* bandwagon. Even though their ads are designed to sell clothes, shoes, and even sweat-proof makeup, they present strong messages intended to "appeal to women's enthusiasm for sports as a symbol of female liberation and power" (Conniff, 1996), and they have encouraged and supported sport participation in the process.

Increased Media Coverage of Women in Sport.

Even though women's sports are not covered as often or in the same detail as men's sports (see chapter 12), girls and women now can see and read about the achievements of women athletes in a wider range of sports than ever before. Seeing women athletes on television and reading about them in newspapers and magazines encourage girls and women to be active as athletes themselves. This was clearly evident in Canada, as the Canadian national women's ice hockey team has won every World Championship competition that has been held, and particularly after the team's gold medal Olympic victory in Salt Lake City in 2002. The media images in the coverage of those events were very powerful and inspirational to girls and women.

As girls grow up, they often want to see what is possible before they experiment with and develop their own athletic skills. This is the case because many of them still receive mixed messages about becoming serious athletes. For example, girls' visions of being an athlete can be clouded by powerful images connecting thinness and vulnerability with sex appeal, and by homophobic fears about becoming too strong and too "malelike." Despite mixed messages, the media coverage of everything from professional women's basketball to synchronized swimming helps girls and young women conclude that sports are human activities, not male activities.

Media companies, like their corporate counterparts that sell sporting goods, have begun to realize that women make up over half the world's population and, therefore, half the world's consumers. In Canada, the CBC has made a conscious effort in recent years to provide equal coverage of men's and women's sports at the Olympics. Production and on-camera staff received media training with regard to equity issues, and one formal analysis of CBC television coverage of the Sydney Olympics (Cluer, et al., 2001) indicates that both the quantity and quality of men's and women's coverage was similar. Also, the recently launched digital

...men's Sports Network ...ates that commercial media in ...e beginning to take women's sports ...ously. Women's sports will continue to be covered in the media, and that coverage will change the images that all of us associate with sports and athletic achievement.

In summary, these factors collectively have fostered increased sport participation among girls and women, and the awareness that gender equity in sports is a worthwhile goal. Gender equity is far from being achieved, but there is no turning back to the days of excluding girls and women.

Reasons to Be Cautious When Predicting Future Participation Increases

Increases in the sport participation rates of girls and women have not come easily. They are clearly the result of the dedicated efforts of many individuals and groups. Progress has been remarkable, but gender equity does not exist yet in most sport programmes, and there are seven reasons to be cautious about the pace and extent of future sport participation increases:

1. Budget cutbacks and the privatization of sport programmes
2. Resistance to government regulations
3. Backlash among those who resent changes favouring strong women
4. Underrepresentation of women in decision-making positions in sports
5. Continued emphasis on "cosmetic fitness"
6. Trivialization of women's sports
7. Homophobia and the threat of being labelled "lesbian"

Budget Cutbacks and the Privatization of Sport Programmes Efforts to achieve gender equity are often subverted by budget cutbacks. Sometimes these are direct cuts to programmes; there is evidence of this in, for example, U.S. universities and, recently, some Canadian universities. More often, budget cutbacks have resulted in

the implementation of user fees, or a failure to implement planned programmes (sometimes planned to meet equity requirements). Programmes for girls and women may be vulnerable to budget cuts if they are less well established than boys' programmes, or if they have less administrative and community support. New programmes for girls and women have start-up costs that long-standing and well-established programmes for boys and men do not have. Therefore, budget cuts may cause women's programmes to fail at a faster pace than men's programmes, if they never have the chance to develop name recognition and market presence. Many programmes for boys and men are less vulnerable, because they have enjoyed decades of support and development and are now in a position to raise funds to keep them going. It should be pointed out, however, that cuts to, or non-implementation of, programmes for girls and women rarely happens without a fight in Canada. Equity legislation has provided the tools for those with the energy to resist a situation where access to sports and physical activity returns to the bad old days of provision for boys but not girls.

As public, tax-supported programmes are cut, and user fees are introduced or increased, sport participation becomes increasingly dependent on private support and sponsorship. This trend often has a negative impact on the provision of sport participation opportunities for girls and women, especially those who live in low-income households. Public programmes are accountable to voters, and they are regulated by government rules related to equal rights and opportunities. Private and non-profit programmes are accountable to the needs of their members or market forces, and they may not be expected or mandated to provide equal rights or opportunities.

This is often not a problem for females from wealthy backgrounds: they just buy what they want. In fact, private providers seek their business and make efforts to attract it. "Free enterprise sports" are great things for people with money, but not very good for those on tight budgets; nor are they good for women, who generally have lower salaries and less discretionary money than men. Private providers do not serve those who can not buy what they sell. When money talks, poor people are able only to whisper, and poor women often are silenced. Therefore, future participation increases may be unevenly distributed among girls and women; in fact, those who lack resources will probably suffer participation setbacks in the future.

Resistance to Government Legislation Those who benefit from the status quo often resist government legislation that mandates changes. This is certainly true in the case of legislation calling for gender equity in sports. They may claim that there is too much government interference in everyday life. Of course, they have operated programmes for boys and men for over a century without ever considering the needs and interests of girls and women, so it is easy to see why they would resist "government interference" demanding that they open their eyes. These people cannot turn back the clock when it comes to changes already made, but they can slow future changes.

Backlash among Those Who Resent Changes Favouring Strong Women When women play certain sports, they become strong. Strong women challenge the gender logic that underlies the norms, legal definitions, and opportunity structures that define and describe the conditions under which men and women form identities, live their lives, and relate to each other. The people who are privileged by the prevailing gender logic in society see strong women as a threat. They do all they can to discredit most women's sports and strong women athletes, and they call for a return to the "good old days," when men played sports and women watched and cheered.

The effects of this backlash on sport participation among girls and women are not completely clear. However, our guess is that it contributes to the mixed messages girls and women receive and even give to one another about

sports, and it fuels the trivialization of women's sports and the marginalization of strong women athletes. If this is occurring, future increases in sport participation rates will be slowed.

Underrepresentation of Women in Decision-Making Positions in Sports Despite radical increases in the number of sport participation opportunities for girls and women since the mid-1970s, women have not seen the same increases in the ranks of coaching and sport administration (McKay, 1997).

Of course, it is possible for men to do a good job in these positions; however, unless girls and young women see women in decision-making positions in their programmes, and perhaps even in men's programmes, they will be reluctant to define sports and sport participation as important in their futures. If women are not visible as leaders in sport programmes, some people conclude that women's abilities and contributions in sports are less valued than men's. This conclusion certainly limits progress toward gender equity in sports (Ligutom-Kimura, 1995).

Continued Emphasis on "Cosmetic Fitness" There are competing images of female bodies in many cultures today. Many girls and women hear confusing cultural messages that they should be "firm but shapely, fit but sexy, strong but thin" (Markula, 1995; see also, MacNeill, 1998; Smith, 2002). Although they do see images of powerful women athletes, they cannot escape the images of fashion models whose reputations depend on a body shape that women can match only by depriving themselves of the nourishment they need to be strong. These fashion images highlight thinness, bust size, waist size, lip shape, hairstyles, body hair removal, complexion, allure, and the clothes and accessories that together "make" the woman. Girls and women also hear that physical power and competence are important, but they see disproportionate rewards going to women who look young and vulnerable. They are advised to "get strong but lose weight." They

that muscles are good, but
...nfeminine. They are told
...ke competent women, but they
...tracted to the Dallas Cowgirls cheer-
...ders and the latest celebrity models with
breast implants and workout videos, rather than
to accomplished women athletes.

Despite cultural messages that promote
athletic images for females, powerful cultural messages also promote the "beauty myth" (Friedman,
2002; Hargreaves, 1994; Heywood, 1998; Wolf,
1991). Effective commercial messages for everything from makeup to clothing are premised on
the assumption that, if women have positive body
images, they will not spend as much money on
products whose sales depend on insecurities about
appearance. The ads are clear: "heterosexualized
hard bodies" are valued, especially when they are
displayed in the latest leotards and high-fashion
sport gear (MacNeill, 1998).

In sports, Brandi Chastain's removal of her
shirt after the U.S. national women's team won
the first Women's World Cup in soccer received
a great deal of media attention in many countries. In Canada and internationally, we have the
case of women's beach volleyball where, in a
stunning attempt to attract media attention to
the sport, the international volleyball federation
(Fédération Internationale de Volleyball, or
FIVB) required women players to wear revealing outfits. Of course, some women were comfortable with such outfits, but others were not.
Those who tried to refuse to wear the new uniforms were told that they would not be allowed
to participate (Drakich, 2002).

These messages about heterosexualized hard
bodies are so powerful that some women do not
want to play sports until they are thin enough to
look "right" and to wear the "right" clothes;
other girls and women combine participation
with pathogenic weight-control strategies. For
example, studies show that an alarming number
of women athletes use laxatives, diet pills,
diuretics, self-induced vomiting, binges, and
starvation diets in conjunction with their training

(Johns, 1996, 1997; Ryan, 1995; Tofler et al.,
1996; Wilmore, 1996). This increases the proba-
bility of injuries, jeopardizes health, and keeps
alive the idea that women must either conform to
the beauty myth or be rejected by men and by
women who subscribe to the myth and use it to
evaluate other females of all ages.

Finally, when the goal of playing sports is
cosmetic fitness rather than physical competence, there is a tendency to drop out of sport
programmes if weight is gained or when weight-
loss goals are achieved.

Trivialization of Women's Sports "Okay, women
play sports, but they are not as good as men and
people won't pay to watch them." Statements like
this are based on the assumptions that "real"
sports involve "manly" things, such as intimidation, violence, and physically dominating others
and that the measure of a sport is determined by
spectator appeal. Therefore, if sports involve
grace, balance, and coordination or do not attract
spectators, they are second-rate. This orientation
is widespread enough that it continues to interfere with the achievement of gender equity in
sports. It was also evident in the widespread
debate about, and media attention devoted to,
Annika Sorenstam's participation in a men's professional golf event (the Colonial Invitational).

Power and performance sports are grounded
in the values and experiences of men, and they
imply evaluative standards that work to the disadvantage of women. Of course, highly accomplished women athletes are challenging these
standards and establishing new ways to be excellent on the playing field without being violent or
physically overpowering opponents. They have
shown that basketball can be played with finesse
and passing and does not have to involve monster dunks and heavy body contact. They have
shown that exciting hockey can be played without bone-jarring body checks, and exciting soccer can be played without macho posturing on
the field. These new ways to play sports are
beginning to make sense for many people, but

others continue to insist that, as long as women can not outplay men, they do not deserve the same support that men receive to play sports.

Homophobia and the Threat of Being Labelled "Lesbian" Homophobia is a generalized fear or intolerance of lesbians, gay men, and bisexual people (Griffin, 1998). It may be expressed in terms of prejudice, discrimination, harassment, and violence toward those identified or believed to be homosexual or bisexual. It is a powerful cultural factor that has, among other things, discouraged many girls and women, and "out" gay men, from playing sports or making sports an important part of their lives.

Homophobia may cause parents to steer their daughters away from sports they believe attract lesbians, and away from teams or programmes where lesbians are believed to play or coach. Homophobia and public expressions of homophobic discourse influence and often limit the sport participation choices available to women (Veri, 1999). When women fear the label of "lesbian," or fear being associated with lesbians, they may avoid certain sports or limit their commitment to playing sports. These fears may be grounded in personal homophobia or in an awareness of homophobia among others and how others express it. These fears influence both heterosexual women and lesbians.

Some women athletes find that peers accuse them of being lesbians when they play certain sports or take sports very seriously. Some heterosexual women fear these accusations, and they may become defensive or even hide their athletic identities when they interact with homophobic others (Blinde and Taub, 1992). Closeted lesbians may fear the loss of secrecy, limit their relationships with others, and become lonely and isolated in the process (Bredemeier et al., 1999). Heterosexual and lesbian athletes often fear harassment and discrimination motivated by the homophobia of others. Heterosexual men may use homophobic discourse to tease women athletes and control all women who are intimidated by it. This continues to occur in

high schools and universities in Canada. Wh, women become defensive and give sport participation a lower profile in their lives, homophobia subverts gender equity. Challenging homophobic discourse and forcing others to confront their homophobia is a daunting task. Some open lesbians have become effective at doing this, but most other women lack the experience to do it effectively. Helen Lenskyj, of the Ontario Institute for Studies in Education at the University of Toronto, has provided some useful strategies (e.g., Lenskyj, 1991).

In the meantime, many women athletes go out of their way to emphasize traditional feminine attributes and even say in interviews that being an athlete is not nearly as important as eventually getting married, settling down, having children, and becoming a nurturing homemaker. Homophobia affects all women, lesbian and straight alike; it creates fears, it pressures women to conform to traditional gender roles, and it silences and makes invisible the lesbians who manage, coach, and play sports (Griffin, 1998; Lenskyj, 1999; Nelson, 1998). All of these could limit increases in sport participation among girls and women.

In summary, sport participation rates among girls and women will not continue to increase automatically. Just as the participation of men has been nurtured and developed through support and clear popular images of men in sports, so must it be for women. Without continued support and encouragement, without powerful new images, some of the progress of the past could be jeopardized. However, we will never backslide to the extreme inequality that existed before 1970.

Gender and Fairness Issues in Sports

We explore fairness issues by looking at (1) participation opportunities for girls and women, also focusing on the definition of equity; (2) the type of material and other forms of support that have been received by female athletes in comparison to male athletes; and (3) the availability of positions for women in coaching and sport administration.

225

tunities The history of sports was illustrated in late 1999, when news and ...iications presented their lists of top ...letes of the twentieth century. Some lists had no women on them; others had a few, but we saw no list with more than 5 percent women athletes. Of course, men developed these lists, and they used their memories and experiences to identify and rank athletes. They undoubtedly had less knowledge of the accomplishments of women athletes, but they had few women from which to choose. Women had few opportunities to play sports for the first eighty years of the century. Those who had noteworthy accomplishments often were "activists," known as much for breaking barriers as for setting records. Apparently, breaking the barriers that privileged men did not count for much among those who cast votes for athletes of the century; they defined *excellence* in other ways.

The types of sport participation opportunities available for girls and women always are related to dominant definitions of *femininity* in a culture. Prior to the early 1970s, many people believed that females were naturally frail and inclined toward graceful movements. When girls and women were encouraged to play sports, they were steered into figure skating, gymnastics, swimming, tennis, and other sports that people thought were unrelated to strength, power, and speed—the traits associated with masculinity. Some girls and women ignored barriers; played sports involving strength, power, and speed; and lived with the consequences. However, opportunities for sport participation were limited.

Over the past fifty years, some women athletes have demonstrated clearly that notions of female frailty were grounded in ideology, rather than nature. This has led to gradual changes in popular ideas about what girls and women could and should do in sports. Today, the vast majority of people in North America and many other regions agree that women should have the same participation opportunities as men. However, some people

continue to argue that women should not wrestle, box, play on men's contact sport teams, or ask men to share the resources that fund their sports.

Inequities in participation opportunities continue to exist in international sports. For example, there are still fewer sports for women than for men in the Olympics and other international events. Although important changes have occurred since the early 1980s, women athletes remain underrepresented in international competitions. The data in figure 8.1 and table 8.1 illustrate that women in the modern Summer Olympic Games always have had fewer events than men, and there always have been fewer women participants than men. The International Olympic Committee (IOC), which from 1894 to 1981 had no women members, did not approve a women's 1500-metre race until the 1972 Games in Munich. It was not until the 1984 Games in Los Angeles that women had the opportunity to run the marathon. Women waited until 1988 to run the Olympic 10,000-metre race and until 1996 to run the 5,000-metre race. The men on the IOC have justified these restrictions by claiming that "women need to be protected from such demanding events." Opportunities have increased over the past century, but gender equity has not been achieved. In fact, twenty-six countries, about 13 percent of all participating nations, sent only male athletes to the Atlanta Games in 1996. In 2000, the French Minister of Sports noted that, "Women's involvement in sports [around the world] is characterized by deep inequalities."

Equity sometimes is difficult to achieve because of fundamentalist religious beliefs in certain cultures. For example, strict Islamic beliefs forbid women from publicly exposing any surface of their bodies to the sight of men. Women in some traditionally Catholic nations have not faced moral restrictions, but they have lacked power and resources to make choices to play sports, and they have had far fewer participation opportunities than men. Women in traditional and poor societies often face barriers that preclude or

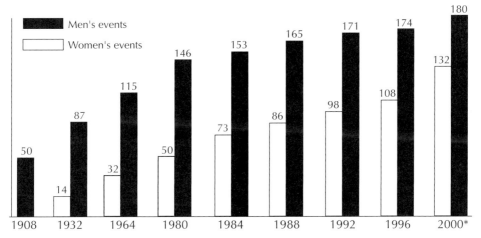

*Twelve events in 2000 were mixed, or open to both men and women. These twelve have been added to both totals for men and women. This procedure of adding mixed events to the total events for women and men was also used for each of the other Olympics in this graph.

FIGURE 8.1   Number of Summer Olympic events open to women and to men.

discourage sport participation, as well as limit the extent to which any woman could take sport seriously enough to train at an elite level. These barriers are both ideological and structural. In other words, they are related to *ideas* about what is and is not appropriate (ideology) and to the availability of *opportunities* and *resources* to take advantage of them (social structure).

Opportunities to play professional sports always have been scarce for women. Until recently, many people did not believe that spectators would pay to watch women play anything but "ladylike" sports, in which they competed alone (golf) or with nets separating the opponents and preventing physical contact (tennis). Norms in some countries began to change in the 1980s, but many people still doubted that spectators would pay to watch women play sports that went beyond the limits of dominant definitions of *femininity*. Although these limits have been pushed and broken, there remains "cultural encouragement" to highlight traditional notions of femininity. Therefore, many women athletes are still referred to as "ladies," and any

recognition of the participation of lesbians has been carefully erased in the media profiles of teams and leagues. The media emphasis is on heterosexual habits, lifestyles, and "looks"; children and husbands are made visible and discussed often. Homophobia has shaped the public image of women's sports, and lesbians have been made invisible, despite their strong presence in many sports. Participation opportunities for women will never match those enjoyed by men until ideological and cultural factors such as these are challenged and changed.

LEGAL DEFINITIONS OF EQUITY   Legal definitions of *equity* vary from one nation and community to another. In Canada, the Charter of Rights and Freedoms provides useful definitions of both equality and equity. Under Equality Rights, Subsection 15(1) defines equality:

> Every individual is equal before and under the law and has the right to the equal protection and equal benefit of the law without discrimination based on race, national or ethnic origin, colour, religion, sex, age or mental or physical disability.

Table 8.1   Male and female athletes in the modern Summer Olympic Games, 1896–2000

Year	Place	Countries Represented	Male Athletes	Female Athletes	Percent Female
1896	Athens	13	311	0	0.00
1900	Paris	22	1,319	11	0.01
1904	St. Louis	12	617	8	1.30
1908	London	22	1,999	36	1.80
1912	Stockholm	28	2,490	57	2.20
1916	Olympics scheduled for Berlin cancelled (World War I)				
1920	Antwerp	29	2,543	64	2.50
1924	Paris	44	2,956	136	4.40
1928	Amsterdam	46	2,724	290	9.60
1932	Los Angeles	47	1,281	127	9.00
1936	Berlin	49	3,738	328	8.10
1940	Olympics scheduled for Tokyo cancelled (World War II)				
1944	Olympics cancelled (World War II)				
1948	London	59	3,714	385	9.40
1952	Helsinki	69	4,407	518	10.50
1956	Melbourne	71	2,958	384	11.50
1960	Rome	83	4,738	610	11.40
1964	Tokyo	93	4,457	683	13.30
1968	Mexico City	112	4,750	781	14.10
1972	Munich	122	6,077	1,070	17.60
1976	Montreal	88	4,915	1,274	20.60
1980	Moscow	81	4,238	1,088	20.40
1984	Los Angeles	140	5,458	1,620	22.80
1988	Seoul	160	7,105	2,476	25.80
1992	Barcelona	170	7,555	3,008	28.50
1996	Atlanta	197	7,059	3,684	34.00+
2000	Sydney	199	6,582	4,069	38.20+

+ In 1996 and 2000, Canada sent approximately equal numbers of male and female athletes to the Olympics, primarily because several male team sports failed to qualify.

Note: These data show one hundred years of gradual progress toward the goal of gender equity. If this progress continues at past rates, one-half the participants will be women at the 2012 Summer Games. The number of athletes in 1976, 1980, and 1984 were lower than expected, due to boycotts.

Subsection 15(2) deals with *equity*:

> Subsection (1) does not preclude any law, program, or activity that has as its object the amelioration of conditions of disadvantaged individuals or groups including those that are disadvantaged because of race, national or ethnic origin, colour, religion, sex, age or mental or physical disability.

The difference between equality and equity has frequently been expressed in the form of a sporting analogy. U.S. President Lyndon Johnson first used it with regard to race relations in the United States, but it was refined by then Federal Minister for Health and Welfare in Canada, John Munro, in his 1970, *A Proposed Sport Policy for Canadians:*

We must face the fact that the opportunity for involvement in sports and recreation is extremely unequal between the socio-economic classes within our population….It's only fair, just as a dash [sprint] in a track meet is only fair, that everyone has the same starting line, and the same distance to run. Unfortunately, in terms of facilities, coaching, promotion and programming, the sports scene today resembles a track on which some people have twenty-five yards to run, some fifty, some one-hundred, and some as much as a mile or more (pp. 4–5).

Providing everyone with an equal starting line (i.e., an opportunity) is now considered to be *equality*. However, not everyone comes to that starting line with the same experiences and having had the same opportunities—so equality is not very meaningful if you announce that the recreational swim programme is open to everyone, or that everyone may try out for the swim team. People come to that opportunity having had a pool at home, having had public or private swimming lessons, or never having had the opportunity to swim or to learn to swim. Access to the opportunity is open and equal, but the opportunity itself is not the same for everyone. Bruce Kidd proposes that, "Equality focuses on creating the same starting line for everyone; equity has the goal of providing everyone with the opportunity to reach the finish line." A more programme-specific example of gender equity notes that: "An athletics program is gender equitable when the men's program would be pleased to accept as its own the overall participation, opportunities and resources currently allocated to the women's program and vice versa" (*Athletics Administration*, 1993, p. 22).

Both equality and equity are important, and the following examples show how each has been addressed (see also the Reflect on Sports box, "Girls Playing on Boys' Teams: The Justine Blainey Case," p. 231). In Coquitlam, B.C. in 1999, David Morrison won a sex discrimination case at the B.C. Human Rights Commission on behalf of his daughter Katie, a gymnast. He argued that the municipality did not give boys and girls equal access to sport and recreation facilities in that it subsidized male-only sports, especially hockey, but not his daughter's non-profit gymnastics club. As a result of losing the case, the city introduced what they called a Gender Equity Fund (C$50,000 a year for at least five years) and a Gender Equity Programme. In the initial monitoring steps introduced by the programme, Coquitlam found, for example, that at one arena, of the 207 hours of available ice time, 200 hours went to boys. Although these solutions were called an "equity" fund and programme, they were really about taking some steps towards equality in provision—about helping girls to reach the starting line.

Equity would involve additional steps to make up for the years of underfunding and underservicing experienced by girls' sports. Equity steps introduced at some programmes (e.g., the University of Toronto in 1994) include establishing some women-only hours for a pool and a weight room. These meet the requirements of some religions (e.g., Islam, in which women are expected to exercise out of the sight of men), but they also create a comfort level for many women who are not experienced at swimming or weight training, or who have had negative experiences exercising in male-dominated facilities. The University of Toronto also offers the START programme to women, providing initial instruction in a number of activities such as swimming and skating to women who have not had the opportunity to learn these skills before. In other words, the university is practising what has been negatively called "reverse discrimination"—it is offering services to women that are not currently available to men. In this way, it is attempting to meet the requirements of Subsection 15(2) of the Charter of Rights and Freedoms: "the amelioration of conditions of disadvantaged individuals or groups." The university recognizes that services and opportunities to participate in physical activity have not been available to all men, but that such opportunities have, historically, been far more available to men than to women.

Equity is difficult and controversial, but it is an important step towards equality.

Support for Athletes Female athletes in most North American high schools and universities seldom receive the same support enjoyed by the boys and men. This is also the case in sport-sponsoring organizations around the world. Historically, there have been serious inequities in the following areas:

- Access to facilities
- Quality of facilities (playing surfaces, locker rooms, showers, etc.)
- Availability of scholarships[1]
- Programme operating expenses
- Provision and maintenance of equipment and supplies
- Recruiting budgets
- Scheduling of games and practice times
- Travel and per diem expenses
- Numbers of coaches assigned to teams
- Salaries for administrators, coaches, trainers, and so on
- Provision of medical and training services and facilities
- Publicity for individuals, teams, and events

Inequities in some of these areas remain a problem at all levels of education, but they also are a problem in many community programmes. When they exist in community programmes, they often go undetected unless someone digs through data from public, nonprofit, and private programmes. Access to facilities, the number of programmes available, and the staff assigned to programmes are the most likely

---

[1]This applies primarily to U.S. colleges and universities, but scholarships are increasingly available in Canada. See chapter 14.

areas of inequity in community-based sports in North America and around the world.

Most people today realize that a lack of support for women athletes subverts sport participation among girls and women. For well over a century, men have built their programmes, shaped them to fit their interests and values, generated interest in participation, sold them to sponsors, and marketed them to potential spectators. Public funds and student fees have been used to start and maintain programmes for boys and men. As CAAWS recently noted:

> Many fitness, recreation and sport organizations across Canada do not allocate their resources, programs and decision-making fairly to both females and males without bias. As a result, the demographic profile of the people who use the organization's facilities does not match the demographic profile of the community. (2002, p. 6)

Girls and women only want the same treatment. Mary Jo Kane, director of the University of Minnesota's Tucker Center for Research on Girls and Women, says,

> Women are not asking for a handout, we're just asking for an investment. Just put the same investment in us that you put into men. Then we'll see what happens. (Lamb, 2000, p. 57)

For those who believe in fairness, it is difficult to argue with this position.

Jobs for Women in Coaching and Administration Most sport programmes are controlled by men. While women's sport programmes have increased in number and importance around the globe, women have not advanced to nearly the same extent in leadership positions. Data at all levels of competition show that women do not have equal opportunities when it comes to jobs in coaching and administration. Women are especially underrepresented at the highest levels of power in sports. For example, in Canada, only 17 percent of the national team coaches are women, while 47 percent of national team athletes are women (CAAWS, 2002).

Girls Playing on Boys' Teams: The Justine Blainey Case

One of the key gender equity issues involves girls and women playing on a team that is appropriate to their talents. When there are fewer opportunities for female athletes, one of the only solutions may involve playing on a boys'/men's team. While there were previous examples (e.g., Gail Cummings in Huntsville, Ontario), the Justine Blainey case was a landmark in terms of gender equity.

In 1984, twelve-year-old Justine Blainey and her brother David (to the relief of their mother who was driving them to practices and games) both made the Toronto Olympics peewee hockey team. When the Metro Toronto Hockey League discovered that a girl was playing on a boys' team, they immediately barred her from play (Robinson, 2002).

Blainey decided to challenge the ruling, and the case had important legal and human rights implications. The Ontario Court, in 1985, ruled that, although it violated the Canadian Charter of Rights and Freedoms, the Ontario Human Rights Code (OHRC) supported the right of the Ontario Hockey Association to prevent a girl from playing on a boys' team. In 1986, the Ontario Court of Appeal changed the OHRC on a majority decision. Justice Charles Dubin (who was later to lead the Inquiry on doping in sport; see chapter 6) pointed out that, in its present form, the OHRC "permits the posting of a 'no females allowed' sign by every athletic organization in this province" (cited by Hall, 2002, p. 181).

The cases produced a number of bizarre arguments for the Ontario Hockey Association, from the view that integrated hockey would damage girls both physiologically and morally, to the view that losing to a girl would damage a boy psychologically. With appeals, the case was not resolved finally until 1988, and effectively prevented Blainey from playing top-level hockey for a number of years (she eventually played university hockey at the University of Toronto). Perhaps even more damaging were the death threats, hate mail, and accusations (from men) that she was "that girl who wanted to destroy hockey" (cited by Robinson, 2002, p. 196).

The Blainey case also caused a split in women's sports, with some supporting her right to play on the best team available, and others arguing that it was a precedent that would damage women's sports by taking away all the best players.

In a strange case of history repeating itself, Canadian national team captain Hayley Wickenheiser was, in early 2003, denied by the Italian Ice Hockey Federation an opportunity to play professional hockey on a men's team in the Italian league. The ban was supported by the president of the International Ice Hockey Federation. Despite this, she eventually found a place on a men's professional team in Finland.

Should girls be allowed to play on boys' teams if they have the talent and there is no comparable opportunity for girls? We think so. Until there are equitable opportunities for girls, girls should be allowed to play up, but boys should not be allowed to play down. *What do you think?*

If we take the extreme case of U.S. universities and reverse it, what would men say if over 50 percent of the coaches and 82 percent of the administrators in men's programmes were women, while men held only 2 percent of the jobs in women's programmes?[2] They would be outraged! They would certainly call for major affirmative action programmes to achieve fairness, and they would be justified in doing so.

The coaching and administration situation is much the same on a global level (see McKay, 1997, for Australia, Canada, and New Zealand). Systematic data on coaches are not easy to collect from nation to nation, but over 90 percent of all

[2] The situation may be even worse internationally. For example, at the Salt Lake City Olympics, only the Canadian women's hockey team had a female coach.

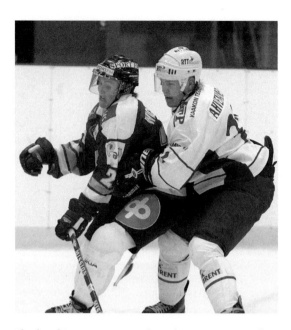

The legal interpretations of gender equity generally have supported girls who have wanted to play in sports traditionally reserved only for boys. But there is still resistance from some sport organizations, which is why Hayley Wickenheiser (above, left) played in Finland rather than Italy.
(CP/Lehtikuva, Jussi Nukari/AP)

national team coaches are men. The International Olympic Committee (IOC), probably the most powerful administrative body in global sports, has a membership of ninety-nine men and fourteen women. There were *no* women on the IOC from 1896 until the 1980s. Between 1990 and 1996, forty of forty-two new appointments went to men. Since 1996, the IOC has added enough women to meet its goal of 10 percent women in the IOC by the year 2000, but many national Olympic committees and international and national sport federations have not matched the IOC's progress. The goal of having women in 20 percent of the top decision-making positions in sport organizations around the world by 2005 may not be reached at the current rate of progress. It is clear that job equality in most sport organizations will not come until today's twenty-year-olds are grandparents.

The reasons for the underrepresentation of women in coaching and administrative positions in women's sports have been widely debated and studied (McKay, 1997, 1999; Pastore et al., 1996; Theberge, 1988, 1992; Wilkerson, 1996). The major reasons for this underrepresentation appear to include the following:

- Men have used well-established connections with other men in sport organizations to help them during the job search and hiring process.
- Compared with men, most women applicants for coaching and administrative jobs do not have the strategic professional connections and networks that they need to compete with male candidates.
- Job search committees often use subjective evaluative criteria, making it more likely that women applicants for coaching and administrative jobs will be seen as less qualified than men applicants.
- Support systems and professional development opportunities continue to be scarce for women who want to be coaches or administrators, as well as for women already in coaching and administrative jobs.[3]
- Many women have the perception that most athletic departments and sport organizations have corporate cultures that do not provide much space for those who see and think about sports differently than men do.[4]
- Sport organizations are seldom organized to be sensitive to the family responsibilities of coaches and administrators.
- Sexual harassment is more likely to be anticipated and experienced by women than by men, and women coaches and

---

[3] The Coaching Association of Canada sponsors a National Team Coaching Apprenticeship Program for women, providing a three-year national team experience for eighteen women in fourteen sports (www.coach.ca/women/). The only female on Canada's coaching staff at the World Track and Field Championships held in Edmonton in 2001 was an apprentice in the programme.

administrators often feel they are judged by more demanding standards than men.

These factors affect aspirations and opportunities, who applies for jobs, how applicants fare during the selection process, how coaches and administrators are evaluated after they obtain jobs, who enjoys his or her job, and who is promoted into a higher-paying job with more responsibility.

People on job search committees seek, evaluate, and hire candidates they think will be successful as coaches and administrators in sport organizations emphasizing power and performance. After looking at all the objectively measurable qualifications, such as years of experience and win-loss records, the search committee members try to subjectively assess such things as a candidate's abilities to recruit and motivate players, to command respect on the team and in the surrounding community, to build toughness and character among players, to maintain team discipline, and to interact effectively with others in the athletic department or sport organization.

Of course, none of these subjective assessments occur in a vacuum. They are influenced by ideas about men and women and about the goals and organization of sport programmes. Although people on search committees do not agree on all things, most think in subjective terms that favour men over women (Hovden, 2000; McKay, 1997). This is because coaching and other forms of leadership in sports often are seen in terms that are consistent with traditional ideas about masculinity: if you "coach like a girl," you are doing it wrong; if you "coach like a man," you are doing it right. Under these conditions, women get jobs only when they present compelling objective evidence of their qualifications, combined with other

---

[4] There is evidence of an increasing corporate culture in Canada, especially as the media begins to pay more attention to women's sports. Two recent women-in-sports conferences (Montreal, 2002; Hamilton, 2002) provided ample evidence of increased corporate culture, as does the sponsorship agreement between Nike and the Canadian Association for the Advancement of Women and Sport and Physical Activity.

SIDELINES

Women traditionally have been expected to play support roles for men in sports, as well as in society at large. This is changing, but these roles are still present in the gender logic grounded in the cultural ideology of many societies.

evidence that they can do things the way successful men have done them in the past. Of course, women also are considered for jobs when there are so few women coaches in a sport or athletic department that administrators feel that they may be accused of discrimination if they do not hire a woman. Sometimes, because of the conditions outlined above, there are so few qualified or experienced women coaches that even when a hiring committee has every intention of hiring a woman for a coaching position, there are no candidates.

When women are hired, they are less likely than men to feel that the sport organizations in which they are working are organized to be open and inclusive, and this has a negative impact on their job satisfaction (McKay, 1997; Pastore et al., 1996). In other words, women often feel that the culture of most sport organizations leaves little space and provides little support for those who see the world from different vantage points than those of the white men who have shaped that culture over many years. This is one reason that turnover among women in sport organizations is higher than among men.

Also important is the fact that the roles of coach and athletic administrator have been developed over the years by men, most of whom have had wives, who raised their children, provided them and their teams with emotional support, hosted social events for their teams and sponsors, coordinated their social schedules, handled household finances and maintenance, made sure they were not distracted by nonsport family and household issues, and faithfully attended games season after season. Of course, not all the men had such wives, but many of the successful coaches and administrators did. Women coaches and administrators seldom have husbands willing to do what wives have done to advance the coaching and administrative careers of their husbands. Furthermore, sport organizations are not family-friendly; child care is not provided for coaches' children, and schedules are not designed to accommodate responsibilities away from sports (McKay, 1999).

Finally, sport organizations have been notoriously negligent in controlling sexual harassment and responding to complaints from women coaches and administrators who have expectations that are different from the expectations of the men who have shaped organizational cultures. This means that, unless there are changes in the cultures of sport organizations, gender equity will never be achieved in the ranks of coaching and administration.

Strategies to Achieve Equity and Fairness

Equity is about who gets what. Appeals to fairness have not been very effective in bringing about gender equity in sports. Everyone supports fairness, but many do not want to give up what they already have to achieve it. This certainly has been the pattern in sport programmes in which men control most of the power and resources. Most men support the idea of gender equity, but few of them are willing to achieve it by sacrificing their privileges related to participation, support, or jobs.

This resistance has forced equity proponents to ask governments for assistance or to file lawsuits or human rights actions. Governments have been helpful, but they often are slow to respond. Legal actions have been effective, but they may involve costly legal fees and/or long-term commitments (see the Reflect on Sports box, "Girls Playing on Boys' Teams: The Justine Blainey Case," p. 231).

According to Donna Lopiano, executive director of the Women's Sport Foundation (WSF), equity can be achieved only through strategic political organization and pressure. She has called for the development of grass-roots organizations to systematically support and publicize sport programmes for girls and women. As these organizations publicly recognize the achievements of female athletes and their sponsors, more people will see the value of women's sports and join their efforts to achieve equity. The WSF and other organizations have facilitated this process with its resources, and they have been effective in bringing about progressive changes.

Lopiano (1991) also has urged people in sport organizations to use the following strategies to promote gender equity:

- Confront discriminatory practices in your organization and become an advocate for women athletes and women coaches and administrators.
- Be an advocate and a watchdog and insist on fair and open employment practices in your organization.
- Keep track of data in your organization and have an independent group issue a "gender equity report card" every year to the media.
- Learn and educate others about the history of discrimination in sports and how to recognize the subtle forms of discrimination that operate in sports today.
- Object to and alert the media to any policies that would result in a decrease in women's sport participation or participation opportunities.

- Package and promote women's sports as revenue producers, so there will be financial incentives to increase participation opportunities for women.
- Recruit women athletes into coaching and establish internships and other programmes to recruit and train women to enter jobs at all levels in your organization.
- Use women's hiring networks when looking for coaches and administrators in all sport programmes.
- Create a supportive work climate for women in your organization and establish policies to eliminate sexual harassment.

CAAWS has been taking similar steps in Canada, and has been actively lobbying the federal government in an attempt to ensure that gender equity is an important part of the new legislation governing sports in Canada (see chapter 13).

These are useful suggestions. They emphasize a combination of public relations, political lobbying, pressure, education, and advocacy. They are based on the assumption that increased participation and opportunities for women will not come without struggle and that favourable outcomes depend on organization and persistence.

However, it is important that those who struggle for gender equity understand the origins of inequities and critically assess the ideology that has shaped dominant forms of sport in their society. If women participate in existing sports and sport organizations without understanding the connections among sports, gender relations, and dominant definitions of *masculinity* in society, they often reproduce ideas about social life that privilege men, guaranteeing that women will never achieve full equity in sports. Striving for equity in activities and organizations that have been shaped over the years by the values and experiences of men *will not* eliminate the most important problems women face as they play and work in sports.

Equity is an important goal, but participation in sports based on a commercialized, media-driven version of the power and performance model should be critically assessed. Those who use critical and feminist theories to study sports in society have argued that real gender equity can never be achieved in sport activities and organizations shaped exclusively by the values and experiences of men interested in control and domination. They say that real equity requires the development of new models of sport participation, and new organizations shaped by the values and experiences of women and of men who do not see themselves in terms of dominant definitions of *masculinity* (Birrell, 2000; Nelson, 1998; Theberge, 2000a).

Girls and Women as Agents of Change Some people have assumed that women are empowered when they play sports and that empowered women are effective agents of fairness and equity in sports and in society as a whole. For example, author and former pro basketball player Mariah Burton Nelson says, "Sport is a women's issue because female sport participation empowers women, thereby inexorably changing everything" (1994, p. 9). Research supports Nelson's claim, but only to a point.

Sport participation does provide girls and women with opportunities to connect and reconnect with the power of their own bodies. This is important, because social life often is organized to encourage girls and women to see themselves as weak, dependent, and powerless. Many images of women in society present the female body as an object to be viewed, evaluated, and consumed, and many girls and women even learn to objectify their own bodies as they apply these images to themselves. Because physical identity and sense of power are grounded in a person's body and body image, sport participation can help women overcome the feeling that their bodies are objects. Developing physical skills can give women the confidence that comes from knowing that their bodies can perform with physical competence and power (Theberge, 1987). Furthermore, the physical strength often gained through sport participation goes beyond simply helping a woman feel fit; it also can make her feel less vulnerable, more independent, and more in control of her physical safety and psychological well-being (see Birrell and Richter, 1994; Blinde et al., 1993, 1994; Nelson, 1994, 1998; Theberge, 2000a; Young and White, 1995).

Playing sports also can change how girls and women relate to males. For example, when Fabiola, a standout aggressive in-line skater, was asked how men viewed her, she said, "Men say, 'Oh, girls suck,' and I hate that. I want to show them that girls are really strong" (Berger, 1999, p. 129). Fabiola does just that, and she is proud of being able to out-skate most men in the world. A seventeen-year-old working-class woman interviewed in England expressed similar feelings about her own weight training:

> I think mainly I want to be…equal with the blokes because I think too many girls get pushed around by blokes. They get called names and things. I think that's wrong. They say "a girl can't do this, a girl can't do that," and I don't like it at all. I'd rather be, you know, equal. (Coakley and White, 1999, p. 80)

These women and many others have used their competence in sports to express a sense of personal empowerment relative to men. However, this sense of empowerment does not occur automatically, nor is it always associated with a form of consciousness that would lead a girl or woman to actively promote fairness and equity issues in sport or any other sphere of life. Feeling competence as an athlete does not guarantee that women will critically assess gender ideology and gender relations, or work for fairness and equity in sport or anywhere else. For example, after interviewing women intercollegiate athletes in U.S. universities, Elaine Blinde and her colleagues (1994) reached this conclusion:

> Women's participation in sport may challenge traditional notions of women's capabilities and provide positive role models for girls and women. However, sport does not appear to be an effective vehicle for developing the athlete's consciousness as a woman or encouraging activism regarding the concerns of women.

In fact, some women athletes express negative attitudes toward the idea of feminism, and they make a point to distance themselves from social activism related to women's issues. In other words, those who play elite-level sports are not likely to be "boat rockers" critical of the gender order (McClung and Blinde, 1998; Young and White, 1995). There are four possible reasons for this:

1. Women athletes may feel they have much to lose if they are associated with civil and human rights issues for women, because others might identify them as ungrateful or marginalize them by tagging them with labels such as "feminist," "man-hater" or "lesbian" (Crosset, 1995).
2. The corporation-driven "celebrity feminism" promoted through highly visible women's sports today focuses on individualism and consumption, rather than everyday struggles faced by ordinary girls and women who want to play pleasure and participation sports, as well as ordinary women in need of child care, health care, and a decent job (Cole, 2000a).
3. The "empowerment discourses" associated with fitness and sports tend to emphasize self-empowerment through physical changes that improve heterosexual attractiveness (Eskes et al., 1998; MacNeill, 1999; Smith, 2002).
4. Women athletes, even those with high media profiles and powerful bodies, have little control over their own sport participation and little political voice in their sports or in society as a whole (Lowe, 1998).

Similarly, women hired and promoted into leadership positions in major sport organizations are expected to advance the status of power and performance sports in society. The men who control many sport organizations usually are not eager to hire women who put women's issues on the same level as sport issues. Of course, not all women in these positions become uncritical cheerleaders for power and performance approaches to sports, and to life in general. However, it takes effort

Playing sports and engaging in challenging physical activities give girls and women opportunities to connect with the power of their bodies.
(CP/Aaron Harris)

and courage to engage in a critical analysis of sports and then use the power of those positions to actually change the structure and organization of sports. Without this effort and courage, gender equity comes more slowly.

Boys and Men as Agents of Change Gender equity is not just a women's issue; equity also involves creating options for men to play sports that are not based on an extreme power and performance model. Sports that emphasize aggression and domination often lead to self-destructive orientations in the forms of chronic injuries, an inability to relate to women, fears of intimacy with other men, homophobia, and a compulsive concern with comparing oneself with other men in terms of what might be called "life success scores" (Burstyn, 1999; White and Young, 1997).

Some men understand that, when they seek status and rewards in sports and sport organizations in which success is defined in terms of dominating other men, ultimately their relationships with each other as well as with women become constrained and distorted. Bruce Kidd (1987), a former Olympic runner and now a physical educator and social scientist at the University of Toronto, has pointed this out:

> Through sports, men learn to cooperate with, care for, and love other men, in [many] ways, but they rarely learn to be intimate with each other or emotionally honest. On the contrary, the only way many of us express fondness for other men is by teasing or mock fighting. (p. 259)

Men who want to get beyond an expression of fondness based on teasing and mock fighting have good reason to join with those women concerned with critically assessing dominant sport forms in their society (Pronger, 1999).

In conclusion, some men and women realize that achieving gender equity in a full sense requires fundamental changes in how we think about gender and how we play sports. This brings us to the topic of ideological and cultural issues.

IDEOLOGICAL AND CULTURAL ISSUES

Cultural ideology refers to sets of interrelated ideas that people use to explain behaviour and social life. Ideology is so deeply rooted in our cultural being that we seldom think about it and almost never raise questions about it. We just take it for granted and use it as a form of "cultural logic" to make sense of the world. This is especially the case with gender ideology. Gender is one of the fundamental organizing principles of social life, and gender logic influences how we think of ourselves and others, how we relate to others, and how social life is organized at all levels, from families to societies. It influences what we wear, how we walk, how we present ourselves to others, and how we think about and plan for our future. Most people take gender logic as a "given" in their lives; they do not question it because it is so deeply rooted in their psyches and the way they live their lives.

The tendency to ignore our ideology and its impact on how we see and think about sports is a problem when we deal with fairness and equity issues. This is because complete fairness and equity cannot be achieved in sports unless we change the gender logic that has been used in the past to organize, play, and make sense of sports. Therefore, it is important to critically examine the prevailing gender logic in society, its affects on our lives, its connection with sports, and some strategies for changing it.

Gender Logic in Society

Gender logic varies from culture to culture. In most societies where men have been privileged in terms of legal status, formal authority, political and economic power, and access to resources, gender logic is based on a *simple binary classification system*. According to this system, all people are classified into one of two **sex** categories: male or female (see figure 8.2). These categories are seen in biological terms, and they are conceptualized to highlight difference and opposition; in fact, they are called "opposite sexes." Those in one category are believed to be naturally different from those in the other category, and they are held to different normative expectations when it comes to feelings, thoughts, and behaviours; these expectations outline the basis for how people define and identify **gender**—that is, what is masculine and

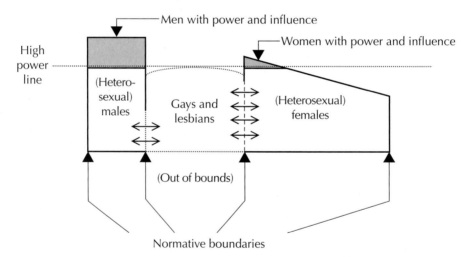

Note: The short double arrows (◄─►) indicate two processes: (1) movement into and out of the categories of heterosexual male and female and gay/lesbian, and (2) efforts to push normative boundaries to make more space for different ways of "doing" masculinity and femininity.

The "high power line" indicates that in society as a whole, men occupy a greater number of high power and influence positions such as heads of state, members of the senate/parliament, CEOs, and top-level leaders and decision-makers in religious organizations, education, sports, and the media. A few women in many societies have pushed the upper limits of gender categories to enter top power positions. However, the "glass ceiling" remains, even though it has been cracked.

FIGURE 8.2   The two-category gender classification system: a representation of gender construction in patriarchal cultures.

what is feminine. This classification and interpretation system is so central to the way many people see the world that they feel they cannot change or abandon it.

It takes dedication and hard work to maintain a simple binary classification system, because it is inconsistent with evidence showing that anatomy, hormones, chromosomes, and secondary sex characteristics vary in complex ways and cannot simply be divided into two sex categories, one male and one female. As biologist Anne Fausto-Sterling (2000) explains, "A body's sex is simply too complex. There is no either/or. Rather, there are shades of difference" (p. 3). Real bodies have physiological and biological traits, which are distributed along continua related to these dimensions of physiology.

Of course, this variation does not fit with a binary classification system, so, when people are born with physical traits that do not fit our definitions of *male* and *female*, genitals and reproductive organs usually are surgically "fixed" to make them fit (Fausto-Sterling, 2000). Hormones vary from one person to the next, and both men and women have testosterone and estrogen present in their bodies. However, testosterone is identified as a "male hormone" and estrogen as a "female hormone." Even chromosomal patterns do not always fit neatly into two distinct categories. Secondary sex characteristics also vary greatly, but we do our best to cover the variations with sex-appropriate clothes and various forms of body management emphasizing characteristics that identify us as male or female. Physical variation is real; however, to say that all variation can be reduced to two separate and "opposite" categories forces biology to fit popular social definitions of what males and females are supposed to be in physical terms.[5]

Another problem with a binary classification system is that it comes with relatively fixed ideas and expectations about how men and women are each supposed to feel, think, and act. These ideas and expectations emphasize difference, and they are the foundation for what is called *gender*. A binary gender classification system is based on the assumption that heterosexuality is natural and normal and that those who express feelings, thoughts, and behaviours that do not fit neatly into the two socially constructed categories of masculine and feminine are "out of bounds" when it comes to gender (review figure 8.2). When gender logic is based on this classification system, many people, including gay men, lesbians, and bisexuals, do not fit comfortably into either of the two categories, so they usually are defined as "deviant." A two-category system provides no social space or recognition for those who are neither heterosexual males nor heterosexual females. This, in turn, serves as a foundation for homophobia, a general fear and/or intolerance felt for those who are "out of bounds" in the classification system.

Another important aspect of a binary classification system is that the two categories are seldom equal. As represented in figure 8.2, males have access to higher levels of privilege, power, and influence than females, and men occupy the highest levels of power and influence in greater numbers than women. However, there is a social and personal cost with this access to and possession of power. When a two-category gender classification system exists in cultures where there is an emphasis on equal rights and freedom of expression, the accepted range of feelings, thoughts, and behaviours for men often is more restricted

---

[5]This created a dilemma for the International Olympic Committee and other sport governing bodies that used a two-category system. "Sex tests" have shown that some people who have the external physical genitalia of women, and have been raised as women and define themselves as women, do not "pass" the tests. Many women called for the tests to be dropped, and the IOC finally acceded to that pressure. Mandatory "sex testing" for female athletes was stopped in time for the Sydney Olympics (although the IOC maintained its right to impose "random" tests).

than it is for women. This means that the normative boundaries associated with masculinity and being a man are more restrictive and more closely regulated than the normative boundaries associated with femininity and being a woman. Because masculinity comes with greater chances of reaching a high level of power and influence, men have more to lose collectively if they do not conform to gender expectations. Therefore, they strictly patrol and police their boundaries and sanction those who do not stay within them. Women, on the other hand, have less to lose and more to gain if they push boundaries, although they must do so carefully. What this means in everyday life is that men have less social permission to express the feelings, attitudes, and behaviours associated with femininity than women have to express the feelings, thoughts, and behaviours associated with masculinity. This is why boys are teased for being "sissies," while girls are praised for being "tomboys"; it's also why men ballet dancers and interior designers are less likely to be socially accepted in society than are women wrestlers and women in Parliament (Laberge and Albert, 1999).

To demonstrate this point, ask yourself why it is easier to give construction kits and toy trucks as gifts to girls than it is to give dolls to boys. Ask the women in a gender-mixed group how many of them have bought clothing for themselves in the men's department of a store; most will say they have done so. Then ask the men how many of them have bought clothing for themselves in the women's department, and listen to the laughter caused by the tension of even thinking about the question! The responses illustrate that men face more restrictive normative boundaries related to gender than women face. However, the payoff for men is that they have more access to power (although not many men gain high levels of power).

Finally, one of the characteristics of a binary classification system is that normative boundaries are socially constructed, but not everyone accepts or conforms to them. The double arrows in figure 8.2 represent efforts by men and women to push and revise normative boundaries. Of course, women do more pushing than men, although there are potential costs associated with boundary pushing (and "gender bending"). However, normative boundaries often shift over time as the boundary pushers raise issues that lead to revised definitions of *masculinity* and *femininity*. Revisions come slowly, because so many people have vested interests and identities based in the two-category gender classification system; they use the system as their guide for perceiving and making sense of the social world.

Gender Logic in Sports

Gender logic is expressed in sports in a number of ways. In this section, we consider (1) the ways in which sports are used to celebrate a particular form of masculinity; (2) the ways in which girls and women who become involved in sports are seen as "invaders" of male terrain, with particular focus on the case of women's bodybuilding; and (3) the particular challenges faced by gay men and lesbians in sports.

Celebrating Masculinity Gender is not fixed in nature. Therefore, gender logic grounded in a binary classification system can be preserved only if people work hard to police gender boundaries and maintain them through myths, rituals, and everyday cultural practices. People must "practise" gender to keep the system viable. Kane (1995) and Theberge (1993, 2000) have shown that the binary classification system is so embedded in our consciousness that even many feminist critiques of sports and gender inequality tend to reinforce the system. The system is most effectively maintained when gender categories become embodied dimensions of people's lives—that is, they are built right into the way people move and experience the world with and through their bodies. This is how and why sports become important in connection with gender.

Sports have been important sites and activities for preserving gender logic in many cultures. The meaning of gender and its application in people's lives have been symbolized and powerfully presented in the bodily performances that occur in sports. Men's achievements in power and performance sports have been used as evidence of men's aggressive nature, their superiority over women, and their rights to claim social and physical space as their own. Big, tough, and powerful male athletes are symbolic proof of traditional gender logic.

When we take a critical look at dominant sport forms in many societies around the world, we see that they often involve actions highlighting masculine virility, power, and toughness—the attributes associated with dominant ideas about masculinity in those societies (Burstyn, 1999). Sport spectacles often celebrate an interpretation of the world that privileges men and perpetuates their power to organize social life to fit their interests. This is why Bruce Kidd (1987) has described sports stadiums, particularly the SkyDome, as "men's cultural centres." These facilities, often built with public funds, cater to the interests of men, and they host sports in which men "kill," "whip," "roll over," "punish," and "annihilate" other men while others, both men and women, cheer them on. (People often cheer when they see their binary classification system being reaffirmed in such powerful terms!) The images associated with these sports are images of a manhood based on aggression, physical power, and the ability to intimidate and dominate others; they emphasize a concern with ranking people in terms of their ability to dominate. As a major league baseball coach noted when asked about hitting strategies used by many players, he noted, "The bottom line is…you're dealing with the male ego. It's not just about winning…It's about dominating" (Armstrong, 2000, p. 3D). In this way,

> I shudder to think what would have happened to the Canadian World War II effort if we had depended on track and swimming participants instead of mannish hockey players.
>
> —Stan Obodiac, in *Toronto Telegram*, June 7, 1970

sports reinforce and perpetuate a gender logic that favours the interests of men over the interests of women.

Furthermore, the masculinized culture of sports takes on serious political implications, because it celebrates values that privilege men and marginalize women. After all, being tough, disciplined, and physically strong enough to dominate others often are the central criteria for evaluating everyone from coaches to business executives: "doing it like a man" is usually the way to gain power and influence.

Girls and Women as Invaders

The participation of girls and women in sports has always presented a threat to the preservation of traditional gender logic. This is why girls and women have been excluded from playing many sports (Theberge, 2002), or why they have been encouraged to play only sports that emphasized grace, beauty, and coordination. Through 60 percent of the twentieth century, this exclusion was rationalized by physicians and educators, who told women that they would damage their uteruses and breasts and would experience other physical problems endangering their abilities to have children if they were to play sports. Today's students laugh at these myths from the past, because young women now have access to information that refutes them. However, it has taken many years to destroy the myths and challenge traditional gender logic; in fact, myths continue to exist in cultures where literacy rates are low and men control the production and distribution of knowledge.

Revised forms of traditional gender logic still remain in postindustrial societies. Children learn it in their families, play groups, and schools (Harrison et al., 1999; Hasbrook and Harris, 1999). U.S. journalist Joan Ryan (1995) writes about traditional gender logic in women's gymnastics and figure skating:

Talent counts, but so do beauty, class, weight, clothes and politics. The anachronistic lack of am-bivalence about femininity in both sports is part of their attraction, harkening back to a simpler time when girls were girls, when women were girls for that matter: coquettish, malleable, eager to please. In figure skating especially, we want our athletes thin, graceful, deferential and cover-girl pretty. We want eyeliner, lipstick and hair ribbons....[We want athletes presented to us] free of the sticky issues of power, sexual orientation and aggression that encumber female athletes in sports [other than figure skating and gymnastics]. (pp. 5, 68)

Living with this gender logic is not easy. When U.S. women's figure skating champion Tara Lipinski was fifteen years old and training for the 1998 Nagano Olympics, she said that her most dif-ficult challenge was maintaining the strength and power needed to do seven triple jumps in a routine while still looking cute, soft, and feminine.

Many girls and women have challenged tradi-tional gender logic, and gender boundaries for females have been revised as a result. However, remnants of old boundaries continue to exist. For example, as girls enter their teens and their bod-ies are sexualized in terms of traditional gender logic, they still hear powerful cultural messages that being a tomboy may interfere with meeting expectations for heterosexual attractiveness, lifestyles, and the presentation of themselves. Playing sports is accepted, but the cuteness of being a tomboy usually disappears during adoles-cence. If young women do not conform to domi-nant definitions of *femininity* as they play sports, especially contact and power sports, they may still be socially marginalized and face homophobia in their social lives. Of course, if they have just won a world championship, this may not matter.

Women athletes deal with the consequences of traditional gender logic in various ways (Cox and Thompson, 2000). For example, those who play contact and power sports sometimes discover that, unless they are careful to act in "ladylike" ways (sometimes referred to as "emphasized feminini-ty," cf., Theberge, 2000), the label "tomboy" may change to "lesbian." Therefore, they sometimes try

Traditional gender logic is reproduced in many men's sports. Some of those sports inspire fantasies and symbols of a heroic manhood, in which playing the role of warrior becomes the substance of being a man. Do these fantasies and symbols influence how boys define *masculinity?* (CP/Jacques Boissinot)

to be more feminine by wearing bows, ribbons, ponytails, makeup, dresses, tights, heels, or engage-ment or wedding rings; by saying how they like to party (with heterosexuals in heterosexual clubs); and by making statements about boyfriends or hus-bands and their desire to eventually settle down and have children (Mennesson, 2000). If women ath-letes in contact and power sports do not do these things, some people define them as threats to the ideas about "nature" and morality that are based on the two-category gender classification system. This is one of the ways that homophobia enters sports and the lives of women athletes (Griffin, 1998;

REFLECT ON SPORTS

Women Bodybuilders
Expanding Definitions of Femininity?

Women bodybuilders have been described as power-ful women, unfeminine freaks, the ultimate sexualized hard bodies, new women, gender benders, entertain-ers, and sideshows for real sports. Descriptions have varied over time and from one group to another as gender ideology has changed.

Until the late 1970s, there was no such thing as competitive women's bodybuilding. It did not exist, because it so totally contradicted dominant defini-tions of *femininity* and what people saw as natural muscular development for women. The first body-builders challenged those definitions of *femininity*, pushed the boundaries of social acceptance, and raised questions about what is natural when it comes to the bodies of women.

Many people continue to see women bodybuilders as rebels or "deviants", as freaks of nature. According to the gender logic used by most people, all humans can and should be classified into two distinct and mutually exclusive categories: females and males. People using this logic assume that females and males have different qualities and characteristics, that these differences are grounded in nature, and that females are the "weaker sex" when it comes to muscles and strength.

According to Leslie Heywood, a lifelong athlete and currently a professor of English (at the State University of New York at Binghamton) and a body-builder, women bodybuilders have challenged this gender logic and threatened dominant ideas about men and women and about what is natural (see also Hall, 1996, pp. 59–63). She explains that women's bodybuilding is

> an in-your-face confrontation with traditional roles, an unavoidable assertion of . . . unequivocal self-expression, an indication of women's right to *be*, for themselves . . . not for anyone else. In a culture that still mostly defines women's purpose as service for others, no wonder female bodybuilding is so controversial. (1998: 171)

Therefore, bodybuilders have been accused of being unfeminine, because they are "too muscular," too like men. Of course, not everyone accepts this gender

logic, and, for those seeking new or expanded defini-tions of *femininity*, women's bodybuilding has provid-ed exciting new images. These images challenge notions of "female frailty" and raise questions about the biology of gender difference.

Like others who challenge the prevailing gender logic, women bodybuilders often face the constraints of dominant definitions of *femininity*. The first women bodybuilders were careful not to be too good at build-ing muscles. They emphasized a toned, symmetrical body displayed through carefully choreographed graceful moves. Their goal was to stay within the boundaries of femininity as determined and required by mostly male contest judges. However, even this presented problems, because definitions of *femininity* have never been set permanently. Definitions change, and judges could not provide unchanging guidelines for what was too muscular or how much body sym-metry was needed to look feminine.

Many women bodybuilders are frustrated as they try to anticipate changing guidelines. For example, one bodybuilder observed,

> When you compete, your muscularity is all, but the judges insist on [our] looking womanly. They try to fudge the issue with garbage about symmetry, propor-tion and definition. What they really want is tits and ass. (Cammie Lusko, cited in Bolin, 1992a)

Some bodybuilders try to live with the confusion caused by prevailing gender logic by making clear dis-tinctions between how they present themselves dur-ing competitive posing and what they do in their workouts (Bolin, 1992b, 1998). In the gym, they focus on bodywork and muscle building. As Heywood notes, "The gym remains a place where the female body, unlike other places, can, by getting strong, earn a little respect" (1998: 187). Serious training over-rides concerns about how *gender* is defined outside the gym. Workouts are not "gendered," and body-builders, both women and men, train in similar ways.

The public arena of competitive posing is different, and the women try to neutralize the socially imposed

Continued

Women Bodybuilders continued

stigma of having "too many" muscles. They use "femininity insignias" to carefully construct a presentation of self that highlights the "look" of dominant femininity as it is defined today. They may dye their hair blonde; wear it in a long, fluffy style; and adorn it with a ribbon. They manicure and polish fingernails or glue on false fingernails. They employ makeup artists, carefully choose posing bikinis for color and material, wear earring studs and an engagement or wedding ring, shave all body hair, and perhaps use plastic surgery to soften the contours of their faces or enhance their breasts. When they pose, they may walk on their toes, use graceful dance moves, and smile incessantly. They try to be seen with husbands or male friends, and they cautiously flirt with male judges. They do all this to appear "natural" according to dominant definitions of *femininity* (this process is described in Bolin, 1998).

Of course, none of this is natural. When women bodybuilders walk on stage, the femininity insignias they inscribe on their bodies contrast with their muscularity to such an extent that it is difficult for anyone who sees them not to realize that femininity is a social construction rather than a biological fact. As Schulze noted:

> A female body displaying "extreme" muscle mass, separation and definition, yet oiled up, clad in a bikini, marked with conventionally "feminine"–styled hair and carefully applied cosmetics juxtaposes heterogeneous elements in a way that frustrates ideological unity and confounds common sense. (1990, p. 68)

The contestants in women's events today are clearly more muscled than 99 percent of the men in the

world, and they challenge the notions that women are the "weaker sex" and that femininity implies frailty and vulnerability.

Those who benefit from traditional gender logic and definitions of *femininity* have tried to erase images of heavily muscled women and present images of "heterosexualized hard bodies"—bodies desired by men and dependent on men for sexual satisfaction. They use airbrushed photos of bodybuilders in soft-porn poses that highlight vulnerability and accessibility (Heywood, 1998). Muscles are softened or the women are photographed leaning on or looking up to even more muscular men. Women often go along with this heterosexualized image, so that they can obtain publicity, endorsement contracts, and appearance fees. Back at the gym, however, they train in ways that contradict the photos. And, as Leslie Miller, a sociologist at the University of Calgary, and Otto Penz (1991) have shown, women bodybuilders have invaded male space and redefined it for themselves.

Even though the public part of women's bodybuilding has been commercially manipulated to fit with traditional gender logic, women bodybuilders have made it possible for women to view the development of muscles and strength as a source of personal empowerment. This empowerment focuses on personal change, rather than the development of progressive and collective politics among women, but those personal changes challenge dominant definitions of *femininity*. Is this one of the things that sports should do? *What do you think?*

· ·

Krane, 1996). The dynamics of this process are discussed in the Reflect on Sports box, "Women Bodybuilders," above.

Another manifestation of traditional gender logic is the existence of gender-based double standards for evaluating the behaviour of athletes. For example, what would people say if hockey star Hayley Wickenheiser were to beat

up a man or a couple of women in a bar fight? What if a women's rugby team were to drop their shorts and "moon" some tourists in a public setting? What if (hypothetically) Canadian WNBA players Tammy Sutton-Brown or Stacey Dales-Schuman were to talk about how they had "accommodated" over 2,000 men during the past few years (as Magic Johnson did, with reference to women, in the early 1990s)? Or what if one of them had had four children with four different fathers? What if players on a women's university basketball team were to have prominent tattoos or brands on their arms (and they were not butterflies and flowers)? What if the *Sun* newspapers were to publish photographs of Anna Kournikova surrounded by men wearing skimpy swimsuits and looking at her lustfully? Would these women athletes be judged more harshly than male athletes behaving or represented in the same way? We hypothesize that they would be.

This hypothesis does not contradict the points made in the previous discussion of normative boundaries for men and women. When male athletes have bar fights, "flash a moon" in public, admit numerous sexual relationships with women, display macho tattoos, and are pictured in magazines with "available" women draped all over them, they are defined by many people as "tough studs" acting as men act, and acting within traditional normative boundaries for men. However, if the men were to say they were gay or were to talk about their intimate relationship with a male partner, they would be judged more harshly than women who have done the same. For example, when NBA star Magic Johnson said he was HIV positive in 1991, most sport fans were upset, but they expressed great relief when Johnson said he had contracted the virus in one or more of his 2,000 sexual relationships with women. As long as he did not contract it with a man, people saw him and his behaviour within the bounds of traditional masculinity. Similarly, if a female athlete were to say she wears men's boxer shorts around the house and under her street clothes, nobody would define this as "out of bounds," but, if a male athlete were to say he wears women's underwear, he would face serious social sanctions, and jokes about his identity would be made in the media.

While women athletes still live with the consequences of traditional gender logic, the growing achievements of many women in sports have challenged that logic and forced many people to think in new ways about masculinity, femininity, and gender relations (Theberge, 2000a). In fact, some women's sports have been important sites for pushing the normative boundaries for girls and women and questioning definitions of *femininity*. In some cases, women athletes have even encouraged people to raise questions about the validity of the two-category gender classification system and to rethink the meaning of gender in society.

Homophobia and Challenges Faced by Gay Men and Lesbians in Sports When a two-category gender classification system based on heterosexuality is the foundation for defining *gender* in a society, gay men, lesbians, bisexuals, and transgendered people are seen as being outside of normative boundaries. Therefore, they are feared, ignored, or marginalized, and they may be harassed and, in extreme cases, physically attacked. Discussions about the identities and lives of those who live outside traditional gender boundaries often evoke strong emotions, defensive reactions, and moral judgments. Exceptions to this exist among people who have questioned the use of a two-category gender classification system and have defined *gender* in more open and flexible ways.

The same is true in sports: gay men and lesbians are not accepted, homophobia is widespread, and people in sports avoid the topic of homosexuality for fear that the walls of their two-category gender classification system might crumble if they were to acknowledge and talk about it. The silence about gays and lesbians in sports is deafening (Etue and Williams, 1996; Lenskyj, 1999; Nelson, 1991; Pronger, 1999; Theberge, 2000, Ch. 6). People know that gay men and lesbians play sports, but discussions that acknowledge this are avoided. The exceptions to this exist among openly gay men and lesbians who play and watch sports, as well as

Traditional gender logic is changing. However, when men or women become seriously involved in sports that challenge the two-category gender classification system, some people may tease or discourage them.

among women and men who play on teams and in programmes that have developed an open and inclusive culture in which lesbian and gay coaches and teammates are accepted. The irony of the silence about sexuality and sports is that sport is a highly sexualized arena, even though it is presented in cultural mythology as asexual or nonsexual; the sexuality of sports is denied because homophobia will not let it be recognized (Burstyn, 1999; Pronger, 1999).

LESBIANS IN SPORTS   Pat Griffin's groundbreaking book *Strong Women, Deep Closets: Lesbians and Homophobia in Sports* (1998), provides clear evidence that "sports and lesbians have always gone together" (p. ix). She notes that this evidence has been ignored and that widespread homophobia has led to the creation of many myths about lesbians. In fact, the myth that all female athletes are lesbians has been used for nearly a century to exclude and discourage all women from playing sports. Today, lesbians play sports, but their identities have been erased as much as possible in the publicity and media coverage of women's sports.

Myths about lesbians have a range of consequences in sports. They have created among many lesbian athletes a sense of loneliness and isolation, combined with fears about being outed. They have created forms of discrimination experienced by lesbians seeking jobs or promotions as coaches and administrators. They have created fears among heterosexual women about relating to lesbian teammates and coaches. There were some rumours in the Canadian media before the Nagano Winter Olympics in 1998 of friction on the women's hockey team between coaches and players of different sexualities. After the team won a silver medal, these same rumours were sometimes used to account for why the team had not won gold. Finally, they have created a situation in which lesbians must carefully choose and use one of the following six identity-management strategies: being completely closeted; passing as heterosexual; covering lesbian identity; being "out" by not covering identity in all situations; being "out" by revealing identity only to trusted others; or being an open lesbian in sports and the rest of their lives (Griffin, 1998).

In general, women's sports are characterized by a "don't ask, don't tell" atmosphere. Many heterosexuals are uncomfortable dealing with the idea and reality of lesbians in sports, and lesbians often choose a "don't rock the boat" strategy, which enables them to play the sports they love to play without being harassed. However, such a strategy has its costs, and it does not encourage changes that might defuse and even eliminate homophobia in women's sports. Educator Pat Griffin makes a good case for being open and truthful about sexual identity, but she also notes that open lesbians must be prepared to handle everything from angry hostility to cautious acceptance. For example, when tennis star Martina Navratilova publicly revealed her lesbian identity, she faced various forms of hostility and lost many millions of dollars in endorsements, according to most estimates. Griffin (1998) notes that handling challenges is made easier when there are friends, teammates, and coaches who provide support; when organizations exist to challenge expressions of homophobia and advocate tolerance; and when there is institutionalized legal protection for gays and lesbians in organizations, communities, and society. In Theberge's study of an elite hockey team, both heterosexual and lesbian players agreed that "in the dressing room, we're all hockey players" (2000, p. 93).

GAY MEN IN SPORTS   Men's sports have always been key sites for reproducing dominant forms of masculinity. Playing sports has been a rite of passage for boys to become men, and many people define male athletes in contact and power sports as the epitome of what it means to be a heterosexual man in society. Therefore, there is much at stake in maintaining the silence about gay men in sports and in discouraging gay male athletes from revealing their identities. This is clearly explained by University of Toronto physical educator Brian Pronger:

> Sport practice is…an important expression of orthodox masculinity. Because homosexuality is a departure from sexual orthodoxy, homosexual

athletes tend to be feared, mistrusted, and stigmatized. They are perceived as "letting down the team" by sabotaging the types of masculinity that sport tends to celebrate. (1999: 187)

This is why the normative boundaries of gender are actively patrolled and strictly policed in men's sports. Transgressions of those boundaries jeopardize the cultural legitimacy of the two-category gender classification system and the access to power and influence that men have in connection with that system. The message to boys and men in sports is loud and clear: "don't be a fag and don't play like a girl." The message to gay men of all ages is also clear: "don't challenge the two-category gender classification system; it works for us men and has given us gender-based privileges and power in sports and in society."

These messages have created deep fears of homosexuality in men's sports. Heterosexual men have developed threatening antigay locker room discourse—forms of verbal gay bashing that would keep gay men in the closet forever and keep heterosexual men silent about homosexuality and fearful of doing anything that could be labelled "gay." Of course, this is the goal, and it has been achieved with frightening efficiency. Stories about gay male athletes are nearly nonexistent; Canadian gay athletes such as Mark Tewksbury (Olympic gold medalist in swimming) and Mark Leduc (Olympic silver medalist in boxing) waited until their competitive careers were over before they "came out." Heterosexual men have kept quiet, even when male coaches have sexually abused them (Donnelly and Sparks, 1997; Nack and Yaeger, 1999; Robinson, 1998); and most men will sacrifice their bodies to maintain the myth that real men are tough, no matter what the consequences (White and Young, 1997).

The silence creates a context in which boys and men feel ashamed about feelings of affection toward other men and feel that they must mimic violent caricatures of masculinity to avoid being accused of being "fags" (Messner, 1996). After all, real men play with pain and injuries; they do not admit they are afraid; and they do not confide affectionately in other men, even the teammates they care about deeply. Instead, connections between men in football are expressed through bell-ringing head-butts, belly bashers, shoulder pad slams, arm punches, posttouchdown tackles in the end zone, military-like salutes, and other ritualistic behaviours. Fists are clenched and forearms bumped after home runs in baseball. Other men's sports have their own masculinity rituals. In some cases, these rituals would be funny if they did not symbolize an approach to manhood that can make sports a dangerous place to be. Furthermore, coaches know athletes fear any association with homosexuality, and some coaches even call male athletes "ladies" or "fags" to take advantage of institutionalized homophobia and turn it into a willingness to be aggressive and violent on the playing field.

A significant effort to break the silence about gay men in sports is the book *Jocks: True stories of America's Gay Male Athletes*. Written by gay journalist and former coach Dan Woog (1998), the book tells the stories of twenty-eight gay men who play, coach, or work in sports. All the men are out to some degree, and Woog tells their stories in a deeply personal, informative, and emotionally moving way. Some of the stories are positive and hopeful, while others are sad and depressing.

Eric Anderson (2000), an openly gay track coach in a California high school has followed Woog's lead and interviewed eighteen self-identified gay male high school and college athletes in the United States. His data support a statement made by one of Woog's interviewees:

> It's not that people in athletics are innately more homophobic than others. But athletics is an area in which they're given permission to dislike and exclude gays. (Woog, 1998: 231)

This point is important, because heterosexual male athletes should *not* be defined as the cause of problems for gay athletes. Problems are caused by definitions of *gender* grounded in a two-category gender classification system. Solutions rest in finding new ways to view gender and gender relations.

Strategies for Changing Ideology and Culture

The major point of this section is that fairness and gender equity in sports require a complete rethinking of our definitions of *masculinity* and *femininity*, as well as our ideas about the purposes and goals of sports and sport organizations. This is a complex and challenging task; the following sections offer a few suggestions for how it might be undertaken.

Alternative Definitions of Masculinity   We need new definitions of *masculinity* in society. Dominant forms of sport tend to normalize the idea that masculinity involves aggressiveness and a desire to physically dominate others. In fact, some people associate men's behaviour in sports with biological nature and conclude that traditional definitions of *masculinity* are "natural." Strong and aggressive men are lionized and made into heroes in sports, while weak or passive men are marginalized and emasculated.

As boys and men apply this ideology to their lives, they learn to view manhood in terms of things that jeopardize the safety and well-being of themselves and others. They may ride the tops of elevators, drive cars at breakneck speeds, play various forms of "chicken," drink each other under the table, get into fights, use violence in sports as indicators of manhood, use dangerous substances to build muscles, avoid interacting with women as equals, keep sexual scores in heterosexual relationships, rough up girlfriends or wives, rape, or kill "unfaithful" women. Some men learn that size and toughness allow them to get away with violating norms and that status depends on making others fear or depend on them. If men take this ideology far enough, they may get in the habit of "forcing their way" on others through physical intimidation or coercion.

Even though this ideology of masculinity can be dangerous and socially isolating, male athletes are seldom criticized for using it to guide their behaviour in sports. For example, we have never heard coaches scold athletes for hitting someone too hard or showing no feeling when they have blown out someone's knee, have knocked someone unconscious, or have paralyzed or even killed an opponent (as in boxing). Is it dangerous to teach young men not to hesitate to hurt people or not to express remorse when they do? Does this destroy their ability to empathize with others and feel their pain? If boys are taught to be tough and to dominate others, will they be able to develop intimate and supportive relationships with other men or with women? How will they handle their relationships with women? Will their rates of assault and sexual assault be high?

The frightening record of men's violent and destructive behaviour suggests that there is a need to develop additional and alternative definitions of *masculinity*. The dominant definition of *masculinity* and the idea that "boys will be boys" are closely associated with serious problem behaviours in many societies around the world—in other spheres of everyday life as well as sports (Loy, 1995). However, the dominant forms of sports seem to prevent people from raising questions about gender ideology. The study of sports in society has an important role to play in raising these questions.

Alternative Definitions of Femininity The experiences of many women athletes also suggest a need to develop additional definitions of *femininity*. This process has already begun; however, until there is widespread acceptance of alternatives to dominant definitions of *femininity*, women will continue to face problems in connection with playing certain sports. These problems can take many forms, and they often begin early in life. For example, some girls still do not receive the same kind of encouragement as their brothers to be socially independent and physically active in play activities and sports. As

The legacy of the two-category gender classification system remains strong in many cultures. Pairs figure skating is one example that emphasizes the differences in strength and appearance between men and women. But which athlete in this photo is taking the risks? (CP/Frank Gunn)

infants, they are handled more gently and protectively than boys. Boys are thrown into the air more often, given more toys requiring active play and the use of motor skills, and allowed to explore more of their physical environments before being cautioned and constrained by their parents. Girls are watched over more closely, even before they start to walk. This pattern of protectiveness and constraint continues through childhood and limits girls' participation in sport activities.

The need for alternative definitions of *femininity* should not be taken to mean that girls and women should adopt behaviours that express traditional ideas about masculinity. It is important for girls and women to explore and connect with the power of their bodies and to do so in competitive sports as well as other physical activities. Therefore, there is a need for definitions of *femininity* that embrace the notions of competing with other women in sports, competing with men, and striving for victories while respecting opponents (Nelson, 1998). Finally, there is a need for definitions of *femininity* that include and support visibly strong women. There are still people who see strong women and say, "Do you think she is really female?" (Caudwell, 1999); apparently, they have no space in their categorization system to handle a woman who is strong.

This is the same orientation that for many years sustained gender testing in sports. Strong women always challenged that practice, and have now been successful. New spaces must also be created to recognize and support lesbian identities in sports and in society.

Changing the Way We "Do" Sports Gender equity involves more than inventing new ways to "do" masculinity and femininity. It also depends on changes in how sports are organized, promoted, played, and portrayed. We need new types of programmes, new vocabularies to describe those programmes, new images that people can associate with sports, and new ways to evaluate success and the enjoyment of sport experiences (Burstyn, 1999; Nelson, 1998). At the same time, we need women and men who are able to critically assess sports to become a part of existing programmes and work to change sports from inside. (See chapter 15, pp. 489–490.)

One strategy for achieving fairness and gender equity is to develop new sport programmes that change how we "do" sports. Some of the possibilities include the following:

1. Programmes promoting lifetime sport participation and emphasizing combinations of competition and partnership, individual expression and teamwork, and health and skill development

2. Programmes reflecting an ethic of care and connection between teammates and opponents (Duquin, 1993)
3. Programmes providing coaching and administrative opportunities for women, thereby creating more experiences that generate feelings of empowerment among women and the opportunities to put those feelings into action, just as men have had for many years in sports
4. Programmes bringing boys and girls and men and women together in shared sport experiences that break down traditional gender logic

The creation of new sport programmes should not be the only strategy used to achieve equity. New programmes are useful, but they may present political problems when it comes to gender equity issues. Following are some examples:

1. When women's sport programmes are structured differently from men's programmes, it can be difficult to determine if there are equal opportunities for girls and women.
2. New sport programmes that are different from those already in existence run the risk of being perceived as "second class," thereby perpetuating the gender logic of female inferiority.
3. New sport programmes are more difficult to promote than programmes based on existing models, and it is much easier to apply pressure for equal resources within schools, universities, and other organizations when asking for comparable programmes than when asking for new programmes.
4. Sports that cannot be used to reproduce masculinity often are devalued and defined as "not real" and are treated accordingly.

The point here is that efforts to create new sport programmes run the risk of inadequate funding and the loss of some community support. On the other hand, the approach in which girls and women simply participate in dominant sport forms has risks as well: girls could be discouraged from playing sports, ideals could be compromised, and problems tied to beliefs about male superiority could be reproduced.

In the long run, it may be most effective for those interested in promoting fairness and gender equity to maintain both approaches simultaneously. This means that those who strive to participate in existing sports should continue to be aware of alternatives for the future. Then, as they gain power in sports, they will have a vision of how participation opportunities might be maximized for all people. Likewise, those who envision new sport forms should recognize that women could use their participation in existing sports and sport organizations to establish credibility and gain access to the power and resources needed to make changes.

All of us can encourage ideological and cultural change by critically assessing how we talk about sports. We could eliminate the language of difference and domination associated with sports and sport participation. Labels such as "sissy," "tomboy," "fag," and "wimp" inscribe gender into sports in ways that interfere with gender equity. Motivating young men by telling them to go out and prove their masculinity on the playing field has similar consequences. Locker-room language that bashes gays and demeans women also subverts the achievement of gender equity; the listener who stands by and says nothing in response to this language perpetuates inequities. The use of military metaphors to describe what happens in sports is another way that sports are masculinized: "throwing long bombs" and "killing the opposition" are just two examples of metaphors that are based primarily on the experiences of men, not women (Segrave, 1994; Trujillo, 1995).

Structural and ideological changes promoting gender equity also could be encouraged through rule changes in sports. For example, there is a need for rules to eliminate violence in such sports as hockey, football, and rugby. Men will object to such rules by saying they make sports into "girls' games," but such comments only prove that the rules are necessary. Sports also need more rituals that bring opponents together in ways that emphasize partnership rather than hostility and rivalry. As one of the ads in the IOC's Celebrate Humanity series states:

> You are my adversary, but you are not my enemy.
> For your resistance gives me strength, your will
>   gives me courage, your
> Spirit ennobles me.
> And though I aim to defeat you, should I succeed
>   I will not humiliate you.
> Instead, I will honour you, for without you I am a
>   lesser man (sic).

Gender equity depends on redesigning sports from both the outside and the inside, as well as developing new sports that reflect the values and experiences of women and of men who do not identify themselves in terms of the dominant definition of *masculinity*.

SUMMARY

DOES EQUITY REQUIRE IDEOLOGICAL CHANGES?

Sport participation among females has increased dramatically since the late 1970s. This has been primarily the result of a growth in opportunities fuelled by equal rights legislation, the women's movement, the health and fitness movement, and increased publicity given to women athletes.

Despite this trend of increased participation, future increases in sport participation among girls and women will not be automatic. In fact, there are reasons to be cautious when we predict increases. These reasons include budget cuts and privatization of sports, resistance to government policies and legislation, backlash in response to changes favouring strong women, a relative lack of women coaches and administrators, a cultural emphasis on cosmetic fitness among women, the trivialization of women's sports, and the existence of homophobia.

More women than ever are playing sports and working in sport organizations, but gender inequities continue to exist in participation opportunities, support for athletes, and jobs for women in coaching and administration. Even when sport participation leads to feelings of personal empowerment among women, the achievement of full gender equity is impossible without a critical analysis of gender logic in sports and society as a whole. This critical analysis is important, because it not only gives direction to women's efforts to achieve fairness and equity but also shows that there are reasons for men to join women who are trying to achieve equity.

The major point of this chapter is that gender equity in sports is integrally tied to ideological and cultural issues. Gender equity will never be complete or permanent without changes in the gender logic that people use to think about masculinity and femininity and without changes in how sports are organized and played. Dominant sport forms in society are currently based on a two-category gender classification system, which leads to the conclusion that girls and women are, by definition, inferior to boys and men. The gender logic based on this classification system includes beliefs about male-female differences that "naturalize" the superiority of men over women and erase the existence of gay men and lesbians from cultural images about sports and athletes. Therefore, sports celebrate a form of masculinity that leads to the social marginalization of many men and women. As this form of masculinity is celebrated through sports, homophobia and misogyny are built right into the structure of sports and sport organizations.

Because of prevailing gender logic and the fact that sports have been shaped by the values and experiences of men, real and lasting gender equity depends on changing dominant definitions of *masculinity* and *femininity* and on changing the way we "do" sports. New sports and sport organizations need to be created, while existing ones need to be changed both from the inside and through outside pressure. Change in sports may be accomplished through a combination of strategies: using new ways to talk about sports; developing new rules to control violence and injuries and to foster safety for all players; and creating new rituals and orientations based on the pleasure and participation approach to sports, rather than the power and performance approach. Unless ideology changes, fairness and gender equity will never be completely and permanently achieved. This is the reason those interested in gender equity in sports should be interested also in gender and gender relations issues outside of sports.

 SUGGESTED READINGS

Birrell, S. 2000. Feminist theories for sport. In *Handbook of sports studies* (pp. 61–76), edited by J. Coakley and E. Dunning. London: Sage (provides a detailed and insightful account of how feminist theories have been informed by, and developed in, the sociology of sport).

Burstyn, V. 1999. *The rites of men: Manhood, politics, and the culture of sport.* Toronto: University of Toronto Press (an insightful feminist analysis of gender ideology, masculinity, and sports; focus on history, media, commercialization, violence, drugs, and social change).

Fausto-Sterling, A. 2000. *Sexing the body: Gender politics and the construction of sexuality.* New York: Basic Books (a thoroughly researched analysis of the "science of the body," showing how and why two-sex/gender classifications systems are neither natural nor cultural universals; written by a biologist who knows the history and sociology of sex and gender).

Griffin, P. 1998. *Strong women, deep closets: Lesbians and homophobia in sports.* Champaign, IL: Human Kinetics (the first book to explore the experiences of lesbians in sports; written by an educator with personal, professional concerns about ethics and equity in sports).

Hall, A. 2002. *The girl and the game: A history of women's sport in Canada.* Peterborough, ON: Broadview Press (this detailed account of the struggles for women's sports in Canada goes from the cycling craze of the 1890s to the fitness boom of the 1990s).

McKay, J. 1997. *Managing gender: Affirmative action and organizational power in Australian, Canadian, and New Zealand sport.* Albany: State University of New York Press (data from in-depth interviews and the media coverage of sports are used to show how affirmative action policies are subverted in sport cultures dominated by corporate interests and men protecting their power and influence; based on critical and feminist theories).

Messner, M.A. 2002. *Taking the field: Women, men, and sports.* Minneapolis: University of Minnesota Press (analysis of gender as it is incorporated into the everyday lives of sport participants, the structures of sport organizations, and the ideologies and belief systems transmitted through the media).

Robinson, L. 2002. *Black tights: Women, sport and sexuality.* Toronto: HarperCollins (explores many of the current issues regarding women's involvement in sports: financing, sex testing, lesbian athletes, sweatshop labour, checking in hockey, sexual abuse, eating disorders, media coverage, bikinis in beach volleyball, and playing on the same team with men).

Theberge, N. 2000. *Gender and sport. In Handbook of sports studies* (pp. 322–33), edited by J. Coakley and E. Dunning. London: Sage (despite its brevity, this is a thorough analysis of gender relations in sports, focusing on the ways in which sports have been used to construct and emphasize the differences between masculinity and femininity, and the challenges to that construction).

Theberge, N. 2000. *Higher goals: Women's ice hockey and the politics of gender.* Albany: State University of New York Press (research based on two seasons of observations and interviews with the members of an elite women's hockey team; the author provides a valuable inside-the-locker-room look at how women define and give meaning to their sport experiences.)

Thompson, S. 1999. *Mother's taxi: Sport and women's labor.* Albany: State University of New York Press (research on how sports in many situations depend on behind-the-scenes free work done by mothers, wives, and girlfriends; data were gathered in Australia, but the analysis is relevant for other postindustrial countries where adult leagues and youth sports are a prominent part of community life).

White, P., and K. Young, eds. 1999. *Sport and gender in Canada.* Don Mills, Ontario: Oxford University Press (the sixteen chapters in this collection provide insightful analyses of current issues; discussions of gender relations and power, sexuality, homophobia, harassment and abuse, aging, disabilities, race and ethnicity, and the organization of sports).

Woog, D. 1998. *Jocks: The true story of America's gay male athletes.* Los Angeles: Alyson Books (twenty-eight stories that give voice to and represent the experiences of gay men who play, coach, referee, and work in sports; written by a journalist sensitive to the need to break the silence about gay men in sports).

 **WEBSITE RESOURCES**

Note: Websites often change. The following URLs were current when this book was printed. Please check our website www.mcgrawhill.ca/college/coakley) for updates and additions.

www.mhhe.com/coakley8e (discussion of cheerleaders and gender issues)

www.caaws.ca (the Canadian Association for the Advancement of Women and Sport and Physical Activity maintains this comprehensive and up-to-date website outlining programmes, research, and lobbying efforts related to women and sports in Canada)

http://raw.rutgers.edu/womenandsports (valuable gateway site for women in sports links)

http://education.umn.edu/tuckercenter/default.html (site of the Tucker Center for Research on Girls and Women in Sports, directed by Mary Jo Kane; describes the centre and provides numerous links to women in sports sites)

www.de.psu.edu/wsi/contacts.htm (site for WomenSports International; provides links to sites about women's sports in Australia, Canada, Japan, United Kingdom, and the United States) www.de.psu.edu/wsi/wsweb.htm (site for Women's Sports on the web; links to sites about women's sports around the world; see especially the link to *Women in the Olympic Movement*)

www.feminist.org/research/sports2.html (special coverage of "empowering women in sports"; this site has useful links and information about issues related to gender relations and women in sports)

www.feminist.org/gateway/sp_exec2.html (numerous links to sites dealing with girls and women in sports; links include many sites related to gender equity)

www.iwg-gti.org (site of the International Working Group on Women and Sport; contains information on programs, policy issues, and problems faced by girls and women in more than 100 nations)

(Arthur Tilley/Taxi/Getty Images)

Race and Ethnicity

Are they important in sports?

The challenge in sports in the 21st century is going to be diversity.

      —Harry Edwards, sociologist/activist (2000)

What if Wayne Gretzky's grandfather had decided not to emigrate from Russia?

      —Paul Quarrington, author (1988)

Canadian Wins Gold Medal.
Jamaican-Canadian Accused of Steroid Use.
Jamaican Stripped of Gold Medal.

      **—Frank Edwards, cartoonist, captioning
Ben Johnson controversy (1988)**

It's a vast country, so that inspires you. It's also the greatest hotel on earth: It welcomes people from everywhere. It's a good country to write from because in many ways Canada is the world.

      —Yann Martel, author (2002)

Canada is today the most successful pluralist society on the face of the globe, without any doubt in my mind. . . . That is something unique to Canada. It is an amazing global asset.

      **—Aga Khan IV, Imam of the Shia Ismaili
Muslims (2002)**

 Online Learning Centre Resources

Visit *Sports in Society's* Online Learning Centre at **www.mcgrawhill.ca/college/coakley** for additional information and study material for this chapter.

Ethnicity and race are characteristics of every person, and sports involve complex issues related to them. These issues have increasing social relevance as global migration and political changes bring together people from different racial and ethnic backgrounds and create new challenges for living, working, and playing together. The challenges created by racial and ethnic diversity are among the most important ones we will face in the twenty-first century (Edwards, 2000).

Cultural beliefs about race and ethnicity influence social relationships and the organization of social life. Sports not only reflect this influence but also are sites, and may even be tools, whereby people challenge or reproduce dominant beliefs and forms of racial and ethnic relations in a society. As people make sense of sports and give meaning to their experiences as athletes and spectators, and the experiences of others, they often take into account ideas about skin colour and ethnicity.

Not surprisingly, the social meanings and the experiences associated with skin colour and ethnic background influence access to sport participation, decisions about playing sports, and the ways in which sports are integrated into everyday life. People in some racial and ethnic groups use sport participation to express their cultural identity and even their sense of biological and cultural destiny. In some cases, people may be identified and evaluated as athletes, or non-athletes, because of the meanings given to their skin colour or ethnic background.

Thus, sports also are cultural sites where people formulate or change their ideas about skin colour and ethnic heritage. These ideas often are carried over and used in other parts of people's lives. This is why sports are more than mere reflections of racial and ethnic relations in society and why it is important to study them if we want to understand the dynamics of racial and ethnic relations in society.

In light of these factors, this chapter focuses on the following topics:

1. Definitions of *race*, *ethnicity*, and *minority group*, as well as the origins of ideas about race in culture
2. The use of race logic in sports
3. Racial and ethnic relations in Canada
4. The dynamics of racial and ethnic relations[1] in Canadian sports
5. The challenges of racial and ethnic relations in Canadian sports

DEFINITIONS OF *RACE, ETHNICITY,* AND *MINORITY GROUP*

Discussions about race and ethnicity can be confusing when people do not define their terms, and terminology is constantly changing, connecting issues of power and identity with various systems of classification. In other words, who has the power to define and classify groups of people? Also, this dynamic area of study offers little consistency in the use of racial and ethnic terminology. For example, although we use the terms *black* and *white* to highlight the significance of skin colour, we do not normally use the terms *yellow* and *brown*. If we use terminology that suggests a person's heritage (e.g., African, Asian, European), we lose sight of the diversity associated with each of those heritages, and we lose the powerful implications of skin colour. The shifting and sensitive nature of this terminology is evident with reference to Aboriginal Canadians, who may also be referred to (and identify themselves) as *Indians, First Nations,* and *Native Canadians.*[2] The dynamic nature of this

---

[1] The term "relations" is not used here in the organizational sense of promoting good relations between groups, but in the sociological sense of exploring the ways in which groups stand in relation to one another, especially in terms of power.

[2] Of course, even the designation "Native Canadian" is full of complications, because, even in the simplest of terms, this designation refers to status and non-status Indians, and Inuit and Métis peoples.

aspect of social life is evident in this chapter, but it is important to begin with shared definitions of important terms.

In this chapter, **race** refers to a category of people regarded as socially distinct because they share genetically transmitted traits believed to be important by people with power and influence in a society. When people identify a racial group, they use or infer a classification system that divides all human beings into distinct categories, which share physical traits passed from one generation to the next through genes. Therefore, race involves a reference to physical traits, but it is ultimately based on a socially constructed classification system developed around the meanings that people have given to particular physical traits (see the next section for further explanation).

Racism involves discrimination or unequal treatment on the basis of those physical traits. It is "the uncritical acceptance of a negative social definition of…'racialized groups.'" Such groups "are believed to lack certain abilities or characteristics, which in turn characterizes them as culturally and biologically inferior" (James, 1999, p. 133). Because racism is such a complex phenomenon with various manifestations, it is more common to refer to **racisms**. Racism may be deliberate, or may be more indirect and unintentional— what Essed (2002) refers to as "everyday racism." It also exists at different levels in society—that is, individual, institutional, or systemic racism that exists at an organizational level, and structural or cultural racism that exists in the whole society.

Ethnicity is different from race in that it refers to the cultural heritage of a particular group of people. Ethnicity is *not* based on biology or genetically determined traits; instead, it is based on characteristics associated with cultural traditions and background. An **ethnic group** is a category of people regarded as socially distinct because they share a way of life and a commitment to the ideas, norms, and material things that constitute that way of life. In an immigrant society such as Canada, ethnicity is also related to a person's national origin such that very often

people are seen as, for example, "Italians," ignoring both their diversity and the fact that they may have been born in Canada.

Confusion is created when people use *race* and *ethnicity* interchangeably as they deal with social and behavioural issues. One reason some people use these terms interchangeably is that most racial and ethnic groups are assumed to be "minority groups." However, this is not always accurate. **Minority group** is a sociological term used to refer to a socially identified collection of people who may experience discrimination and suffer social disadvantages because of discrimination. Of course, this collection of people does not have to be a racial or an ethnic group, or even a numerical minority, *and* not all racial or ethnic groups are minority groups. The terms *minority* and *majority* refer more to relative power. For example, whites in Canada are a racial group, but they would not be a minority group unless another racial group had the power to subject them to systematic discrimination, which would put them at a collective disadvantage in the social, economic, and political life of Canadian society. The term **visible minority** is used to refer to racial minority groups who are identifiably different, often by skin colour, from the racial *majority* group.

Further complicating the issues of race and ethnicity is that, in terms of people's identities, (1) many people share more than one racial and/or ethnic heritage; (2) a person's racial and/or ethnic identity is not a stable characteristic, changing depending on one's context and particular circumstances of life (e.g., a person of mixed Irish and Ukrainian heritage may emphasize different aspects of that identity depending on which grandparents are being visited, whom she marries, etc.); and (3) sometimes ethnic and racial identities are imposed when, for example, a visible minority Canadian is asked where he is from, and "St. Johns" or "Regina" or "Timmins" is not accepted as the answer.

In summary, it is important to remember that the definition of *race* focuses on the interpretation given to biologically based traits and characteristics, while the definition of *ethnicity* focuses on culturally and nationally based orientations and behaviours. The definition of *minority group* focuses on an identifiable collection of people who suffer disadvantages at the hands of a majority who define them as inferior or unworthy and have the power to negatively affect their lives.

Origins and Implications of the Concept of Race

When people divide human beings into racial categories, they use classification systems based on social meanings given to particular biological traits. The racial categories that people use today are cultural creations, and they are not indicators of deep underlying biological truths about human beings and their similarities and differences. The physical traits that people use to identify races are traits that have been given special meaning among a particular group of people. This meaning often is tied to complex beliefs about the deep importance and implications of a particular trait. In other words, the trait comes to symbolize something about the "biology" and genetic ancestry of the person who has it.

Over the past three centuries, there have been numerous attempts to develop a valid biological classification system that can be used to divide humans into distinct racial groups. Scientists have used classifications based on many factors, including mental characteristics, brain size, skin colour, and many combinations of head shape, hair texture, stature, and nose shape, along with skin colour. In the process, they have "discovered" dozens of races, subraces, collateral races, and collateral subraces—as they have been labelled in various racial classification systems. In fact, they have found that differences between people were so numerous and overlapping that it is impossible to fit humans into distinct biological categories that do not overlap in many ways; instead, dozens of categories are needed and, even then, many collections of people fall between or around categories.

Popularly used racial classification systems are confusing, because they are based on *continuous traits*, such as skin colour or other biological characteristics that exist to some degree in everyone. Height is a good example of a continuous trait: everyone has some height, people vary from short to tall, and it is impossible to use biological criteria for separating people into distinct "height groups." Height falls along a continuum, with the shortest person in the world on one end of the continuum, the tallest person on the other, and everyone else in between. If we want to divide people into height groups, we have to come to some type of social agreement about where one group ends and the next begins. Therefore, height groups would be based on social agreement, rather than biological fact.

The same is true for skin colour, which also is a continuous trait. Skin colour varies from *white* to *black*, with an infinite array of colour shades in between. Where should lines be drawn to distinguish one racial group from others? There are no biological rules for where to draw lines or how many to draw. Even after lines are drawn at particular points along the continuum, someone else can decide to draw them in other places! Where to draw the lines, and how many lines to draw, are based on social decisions about biological characteristics. This is why many scientists have abandoned the search for a biology-based racial classification system.[3]

---

[3] This conclusion needs to be qualified. Using genetics to identify and understand disease patterns in certain human populations has been successful. However, the "races" identified through these attempts do not correspond even closely to the racial definitions and classifications popularly used by Europeans and North Americans today and in the past. In fact, these new, medically useful "genetic populations" often group blacks and whites together. For example, there is evidence of a "sickle cell race," but it includes Greeks, Italians, and Africans living close to the equator (see Begley, 1995).

Racial classification systems have little biological utility because

> …the characteristics we see with the naked eye that help us distinguish individuals from different continents are, in reality, skin-deep. Whenever we look under the veneer, we find that the differences that seem so conspicuous to us are really trivial. (Boyd, 1996: A14; see also Cavalli-Sforza and Cavalli-Sforza, 1995, chapter 9)

This view received even greater support with the completion of the Human Genome Project, and evidence showed that only a tiny fraction of human genetic differences was accounted for by differences in race. However, people around the world continue to use racial classification systems to identify and mark themselves and others in social relationships and everyday life. And they continue to do so because marking people by race is always a political act. It is a statement about relative power, and the systems of classification are invariably developed by the more powerful in order to mark out the less powerful, and, as a consequence, mark themselves in relation to the powerless.

These systems vary from one culture to another, because different cultures use different definitions of *race*. Thus, a person might be classified as "black" in Canada, but not in Brazil, Haiti, or Egypt, where the meanings and uses of race are different. For example, former tennis player Yannick Noah explains that in his native France he is considered black, but in Africa he is considered white. In Brazil, he would be classified in yet another way, because people there use up to 135 terms when asked to classify their race. Only 4 percent of Brazilians classify themselves as black, even though half of all Brazilians would be "black" according to prevailing racial definitions in North America. Also confusing is that not all racial classification systems use skin colour as the primary distinguishing trait.

Biological variations do exist among certain human populations, but traditional racial classification systems distort and oversimplify those variations. The racial classification system used by many people in Canadian and U.S. culture is based on widely shared and culturally unique social meanings associated with skin colour. Historically, the key principle underlying this classification system has been the "one drop rule," or the rule of *hypo-descent*. This rule was developed in the U.S. by white men to ensure that the "white race" would remain "pure" and that property ownership would remain in the hands of white males, even when children were born to one black and one white parent. As long as a person had "one drop of black blood," he or she was defined as black. There was no social recognition of racially mixed parentage in the United States (although in Canada, there is self definition and some social recognition of Métis people), and people were classified as black even though they had white ancestry. This helped preserve the institution of slavery in the U.S., it kept assets and estates in the hands of white men, and it discouraged white women from having sexual relationships with black men because the children born of those relationships would be considered black, and the women would face discrimination and the prospect of being socially separated from their children.

Definitions of *race* have changed over the past three hundred years, but the legacy of the "one drop rule" still creates confusing social and identity issues. For example, Tiger Woods identifies himself as "Cablinasian"—a term he invented to accurately describe the fact that he is one-fourth Thai, one-fourth Chinese, one-fourth African American, one-eighth Native American, and one-eighth white European (Ca-bl-in-asian = *Ca*ucasian + *Bl*ack + *In*dian + *Asian*). Despite this, he and other mixed-race persons in sports, such as Jarome Iginla, are constantly referred to as black, even though one of their parents or grandparents is white.

As a *cultural creation*, race has been and continues to be a powerful force around the world. Race is not a valid biological concept, but it continues to have life-and-death implications for

An increasing number of people around the world claim a mixed biological heritage. Tiger Woods is a good example of a person with a diverse ancestry with roots on four continents. The racial classification systems that traditionally have been used do not take this into account. (Lennox McClendon, AP/Wide World Photos)

many people, and it is tied to systems of privilege and discrimination that affect all people. This makes race and race theories important topics for study if we want to understand behaviour and social relationships. However, when it comes to using racial classifications in our personal lives, we should recognize that the human race contains many combinations of changing physical similarities and differences and that *traditional racial categories are based on social meanings given to those similarities and differences, not on biology.*

RACE LOGIC

This section briefly considers the origins of **race logic**: the way that it is reproduced and

challenged in sports, and its relationship to gender and social class. A more extended analysis, focusing primarily on race logic in the United States, is featured on the Online Learning Centre. The feature includes a Reflect on Sports Box called "'Jumping Genes' in Black Bodies," which critically examines the assumption that athletic ability is related to racial biology.

Origins of Race Logic

Racial classification systems and ideas about the meaning of race developed during the period of European colonization between the sixteenth and nineteenth centuries. In an attempt to explain why everyone did not look and behave as they did, Europeans started with the assumption

Race logic operates in many ways. In some cases it influences white athletes to avoid the sports in which black athletes have a record of excellence. This race logic did not influence Nicholas Macrozanaris on the Canadian 4 x 100m relay team. (CP/Paul Chiasson)

that they were normal, and that anyone who did not look and behave as they did was "deviant" (see chapter 6) and inferior.

Whiteness became the standard against which others were evaluated, and whites developed theories that interpreted physicality and physical skills among non-whites as signs of intellectual inferiority. By the nineteenth century, these ideas fit neatly with the ideology of "social Darwinism," a deliberate distortion of the Darwinian notion of "survival of the fittest," which led to the conclusion that whites were superior beings who deserved to be in positions of power and control around the world. This race logic made sense to whites because they had the "facts" to support it.

Such race logic proved to be very convenient to colonizers, who used it to justify the ill-treatment and enslavement of native peoples, and the forcible imposition of "superior" European religions and cultures on colonized peoples.

Because it was so convenient, race logic eventually became institutionalized in the form of a complex racial ideology about skin colour, intelligence, character, and physical characteristics and skills.[4] This race logic or ideology has been revised continually over the years to fit new circumstances, explain contradictions, and justify new forms of racial discrimination.

Race Logic in Sports

Skiers from Austria and Switzerland (countries that together are a little smaller than New Brunswick and Nova Scotia, with populations that together are about half the size of the

---

[4] We use *race logic* and *racial ideology* to mean the same thing—that is, a complex set of beliefs shared by many people and used to describe and interpret people, behaviours, and events in racial terms.

Canadian population) have won many more World Cup championships than Canadian skiers. Despite this, people do not look at race-based genetic ancestry to discover why Austrians and Swiss are such good skiers. We already know why: they live close to the Alps, some learn to ski before they go to school, they live in cultures in which skiing is highly valued, many of their friends ski and talk about skiing, they see Austrian and Swiss skiers winning and making money in highly publicized World Cup competitions, and some of their cultural heroes are skiers. Race logic focuses on these *cultural* factors when athletes are white; no scientists are searching for a "ski gene."

Similarly, no one has claimed that white Canadians owe their success in hockey to naturally strong ankle joints, instinctive eye-hand-foot coordination, or an innate tendency not to sweat so that they retain body heat in cold weather. When Olympic swimming finals in all events involve white men and women, no thought is given to explaining performance success in terms of race-related genetic ancestry. The "fact" of white success in these sports is not studied from a racial perspective; whiteness is invisible because race logic has made it the taken-for-granted standard from which everything else is viewed.

Research and arguments using race logic have focused almost exclusively on black males, seeking to explain their successes and failures in terms of natural or instinctive qualities or weaknesses, rather than experience, strategy, motivation, and intelligence. When black males dominate two or three highly visible spectator sports, it is an issue that, according to race logic, must be studied and explained. The search for racial differences begins, and if differences are found they are assumed to be the cause of the success. However, when race logic influences the identification of facts, the classification of the facts identified, or the interpretations of the relationships among the facts, science reproduces a view of the world that emphasizes racial differences

rather than shared humanity (see the Reflect on Sports box, "'Jumping Genes' in Black Bodies," on the Online Learning Centre).

Of course, race logic does not only affect white people. This is a controversial issue, but we suspect that many young black men and women in Canada and the United States grow up believing that the black body is special and superior when it comes to physical abilities in certain sports. If life chances are perceived to be limited, this could lead to a single-minded focus on becoming a professional athlete (see the Reflect on Sports box, "The Odds of Becoming a Professional Athlete," in chapter 10), to the detriment of pursuing education and other career possibilities. While this ambition may be more prevalent in the U.S., the evidence suggests that similar ambitions are encouraged among young African-Canadian males, particularly given the pervasiveness of U.S. media and popular culture icons, and access to U.S. athletic scholarships and professional leagues (cf., Joyce, 1997; Spence, 1999; Wilson, 1999).

Race logic becomes difficult to escape. Research in the U.S. (Godley, 1999b) found that when black student athletes excelled in academic work and were placed in honours classes, their identity in the culture of the school and their interactions with teachers and fellow students focused on their athlete status. White and Asian student-athletes were identified as honours students rather than athletes. Research on African-Canadian students both supports and contradicts these U.S. findings. Christopher Spence, a former CFL player, and a middle-school principal in Toronto at the time he wrote *The Skin I'm In* (1999), described the experiences of young African-Canadian males in terms of pressure and encouragement to focus on sports. However, research by Carl James (1995, 2003), a professor at York University, illustrates that among some African-Canadian high school students, high school sport participation can provide exactly the experiences that are usually claimed for all students: opportunities to extend one's circle of friends and interact with teachers in non-classroom settings, and increased desire and confidence to achieve academically.

Finally, and again there is no systematic research on this, we suspect that race logic may influence sport choices among some whites, or lead them to have less confidence in their abilities in certain sports. This may be why the times of white runners in certain sprints and long-distance road races have actually become slower over the years; their genes have not changed, but their choices and motivation have changed (Bloom, 1998; George, 1994; Merron, 1999; Weir, 2000). Informal observations at several Ontario Federation of School Athletic Associations (OFSAA) track and field championships and basketball playoff games reveal similar characteristics in white Ontario high school students. White sprinters on 4 x 100 relay teams often assumed that they were going to lose when competing against relay teams with black sprinters. This assumption was reinforced by coaches who, in pre-race talks, sometimes tried to prepare the students for the fact that they may not win. Similar conversations were heard at basketball tournaments when predominantly white teams were about to face predominantly black teams. This reinforced race logic and any beliefs that the black students may have had that they were superior athletes.

Race Logic, Gender, and Social Class

There are complex interconnections between race logic and gender logic in the world of sports. However, it is worth restating that the vast majority of research in the area of race and ethnicity concerns African-American males; there is far less research on African-American females, and none that we are aware of on African-Canadian females. Again, to the extent that views of African-American males have a cross-border influence in Canada[5]—an influence that has been detected by, among others,

Brian Wilson at the University of British Columbia and Gamal Abdel-Shehid at the University of Alberta—we conclude this section by examining the ways in which race, masculinity, and social class have come together in both Canada and the United States.

Richard Majors (1998) suggests that as African-American males from low-income families faced limited life chances, they experienced a combination of frustration, self-doubt, anger, and emotional withdrawal from schools, families, and the mainstream economy. They coped "by channeling their creative energies into the construction of unique, expressive, and conspicuous styles of demeanor, speech, gesture, clothing, hairstyle, walk, stance, and handshake" (Majors, 1998, p. 17). Majors calls this strategy "cool pose." It has become part of the public personas of many black males in the U.S., and an integral part of some sports, especially basketball and football.

Brian Wilson (Wilson and Sparks, 1996) and Patrick Solomon of York University have both discovered evidence of "cool pose" in Canada (specifically in Toronto). However, as Wilson (1999) points out, while their "findings cannot be directly paralleled to the 'cool pose' of inner-city America because of Canada's distinct racial context, there is still a symbolic resistance against systemic and structural racism" (p. 242). This distinct racial, and ethnic, context is discussed in the next section.

RACIAL AND ETHNIC RELATIONS IN CANADA

As we have noted previously, Canada is such an unlikely country. Unlike most other countries,

---

[5] Because of travel, education, and widespread exposure to, and enjoyment of, U.S. media and sports, Canadians enjoy a great deal of knowledge of the U.S.—a level of knowledge that is not generally reciprocated. This is a result primarily of the relative power of the two countries.

the population does not share an ethnicity, or even have a common language. It is complicated in terms of climate, size, geography, population, and the distribution of that population. It has two or three founding nations (depending on who is counting); two official languages; a complex sharing of governmental power between the federal government, ten provinces, and three territories; and more spiritual, ethnic, and racial diversity, as well as a higher rate of immigration, than any country in the world. When Toronto was bidding to host the 1996 Olympics, one of the slogans was: "Everyone in the world has a relative in Toronto." With more than 180 recognizable racial/ethnic groups in the city, the statement has a reasonable degree of accuracy.

The "elephant in the room" for Canada is the United States—continually there just south of the border, the world's most prolific manufacturer and exporter of cultural products (films, television programmes, magazines, books, music, sports, etc.) that are readily available to Canadians. Even before the signing of the 1988 Free Trade Agreement, and the subsequent signing of NAFTA, Canada's politics and economy were often developed in relation to the U.S. Since the late 1980s, that relationship has intensified, and it has had an ongoing effect on Canadian political and economic decisions. The proximity of the U.S. is so pervasive that Canadians love to celebrate their differences—delighting, for example, in Joe, from the "I Am Canadian" Molson beer commercials, and Rick Mercer's "Talking to Americans." The Canadian team hockey victories in the 2002 Winter Olympic Games had a special significance because both teams beat U.S. teams in the gold medal games—in the United States.

For the purposes of this chapter, the most striking characterization of "difference" between the two countries is the widely held belief that, with regard to immigration, the United States is a "melting pot," while Canada is a "cultural mosaic." This belief is grounded in two theories of the way colonial and immigrant societies are, or ought to be, organized.

Assimilation, or the "melting pot" view, sees a society constructed of different ethnicities and races; a society in which immigrants (and colonized native peoples) are to abandon their traditional identities and cultures and become "American." The process(es) by which assimilation occurred were widely explored by U.S. sociologists in the middle of the last century. Park (1950) proposed four stages of assimilation: initial contact between immigrants (or natives) and members of the core society (or colonizers); a period of *competition* between their respective cultures; a period of *accommodation* in which immigrants (or natives) learned to adapt to the new culture while the members of the new culture perhaps accommodated or even incorporated some aspects of the traditional cultures; followed finally by *assimilation* of the immigrants (or natives) into the new culture. Gordon (1964) developed a rather more complicated model, involving seven stages of assimilation.

The theories were based primarily in the idea that immigrants were Europeans rather than from other parts of the world, and did not really take account of their different cultures or religions or reasons for coming to North America. These ranged from the voluntary "seeking a better life" to the involuntary fleeing from war or persecution. The circumstances of immigration and the culture of origin both influence the inclination to assimilate, and attempts to preserve aspects of traditional culture. Canada (until the 1970s) and the United States both practised assimilation, but in neither country was it official policy. Adult immigrants were frequently left to their own devices, with assimilation occurring to differing degrees. Both countries had forms of cultural pluralism, with communities and populations readily identifying themselves, for example, as Italian-Canadians or Irish-Americans.

The real focus of assimilation was the children of immigrants, and schools and sports and recreation became significant mechanisms by which people were incorporated into Canadian and U.S. society (Loy and Booth, 2001).

Children are often the first to learn the language of their new society, and they often become the language bridge for contact between their parents and the new society. School curricula directly and indirectly teach children how to be Canadian or American, and their exposure to media and cultural practices such as sports and games also involves assimilation. LaFlamme's (1977) study of cricket in Buffalo, New York, provides an ideal example of this process. A significant number of West Indian immigrants settled in Buffalo in the 1950s and 1960s, and developed an active cricket league. However, despite encouragement from their parents to play cricket, the children of these immigrants were exposed to North American games and U.S. "black" culture, both in school and in their social lives—they began to play the games of their new society (football, baseball, and basketball). As their parents grew older and no longer played, cricket died out in the community.

Multiculturalism (cultural plurality), or the "cultural mosaic" view, began to emerge in Canada in the 1960s. Following on the heels of the Royal Commission on Bilingualism and Biculturalism, Canada began to formally recognize two official languages and two distinct cultures deriving from the original French and English immigrants to Canada. It was a short step to recognize that if a country whose primary source of population growth was immigration was enriched by having two cultures, it would be even more enriched by recognizing and supporting the distinct cultures of the immigrant communities. In 1971, Prime Minister Pierre Trudeau stated:

> Every ethnic group has the right to preserve and develop its own culture and values within the Canadian context. To say that we have two official languages is not to say that we have two official cultures and no particular culture is more "official" than another. A policy of multiculturalism must be a policy for all Canadians. (*House of Commons Debates*, October 8, 1971; cited by Hall, et al., 1991, p. 174)

Assimilation and multiculturalism are not, in practice, opposite or conflicting theories or policies, and "melting pot" and "cultural mosaic" are not strictly accurate characterizations of the United States or Canada respectively. A number of jurisdictions in the United States, usually in large cities, practise multiculturalism policies and even bilingualism (English and Spanish), although there are occasional backlash responses such as attempts to declare English as the official language of the United States. However, in many places, there is little attempt to accommodate immigrants, an observation outlined clearly by Mark Grey (1999) in his study of sports in Garden City (Kansas) High School.

The important point to recognize here is that no immigrants are permitted to incorporate their entire culture of origin into the multicultural society. For example, all immigrants are assimilated with regard to the laws and political system of Canada, and many embrace assimilation—wanting to become Canadian and wanting their children to be Canadian. The multicultural society in Canada offers the possibility of multiple identities—it is possible to be Canadian *and* also to be Korean, Serbian, or Chilean. Under Canadian policies, it is not necessary to deny or abandon one's, or one's parents', culture of origin. In fact, that culture is considered to enrich Canadian culture, and is celebrated with festivals, religious and cultural celebrations, dances, cuisines, sports, and the opportunity to maintain and pass on language. However, it is precisely these aspects of multiculturalism that have led some to criticize the way the policies are implemented as being superficial and apolitical.

The sporting manifestations of multiculturalism are fascinating and sometimes unexpected. Peter Donnelly's students at the University of Toronto are encouraged in one assignment to seek an aspect of physical culture (sports, exercise system, or dance) associated with particular ethnocultural communities in Ontario, and to examine them in terms of multiculturalism and assimilation. They have found that, in general, there is a rather slow assimilation of sports and games, with increased evidence of traditional physical cultural practices among more recent immigrant communities than among more established communities. For example, people actively involved in kabbadi (Indian), cricket (various Commonwealth countries), capoeira (Brazil), tinikling (Philippine dance), and the raffia ball games (e.g., sepak takraw) of Southeast Asia can all be found in the Toronto region. However, Gaelic football and hurling (Irish), eisstock (Austrian, German, Swiss), and pesapallo (Finnish) have far fewer participants than in the past, though they are still in evidence.

Soccer provided some unexpected results with regard to multiculturalism and assimilation. In an early study, John Pooley (1981), who went on to teach for many years at Dalhousie University, studied ethnic soccer clubs in Milwaukee. He had expected to find that, in the melting pot society, soccer would be one of the ways in which assimilation was encouraged. He found precisely the opposite. All of the players on teams run by, for example, the German, Polish, and Hungarian clubs were from those ethnic groups, and they spoke their language rather than English. Donnelly and Day (Day, 1981) replicated Pooley's study in London, Ontario, expecting to find similar results precisely because of multiculturalism policies. However, in the various soccer and social clubs they studied (e.g., Portuguese, German, Polish, Italian, etc.), soccer seemed to be promoting assimilation! The club officials explained it in this way: Through the 1960s, when immigration to Canada from Europe was quite easy, the clubs only had players from their country of origin, and they spoke their original language on the field and at social events at the clubs. If a club needed a new striker, they would recruit one from the "old country." ("We'd just get on the phone to Portugal and say, 'We need a striker,' and he'd be there in a couple of weeks.") As immigration policies tightened, the clubs began

to recruit players from other communities, with, for example, Scottish players on the Italian team and even Serbian players on the Croatian team. With the new multi-ethnic teams, a common language was needed on the field of play and in the social club, and that language was invariably English. Jim McKay, a Canadian sport sociologist now working at the University of Queensland, carried out a similar study among Italian soccer clubs in metro Toronto. He also found that "the necessity of recruiting from outside the Italian community promoted assimilation and inter-ethnic contact rather than the preservation of ethnic identity and solidarity" (Hall, et al., 1991, p. 178).

In a sense, this blending of assimilation and multiculturalism produces many of the better features of multiculturalism. Rather than a distinct "mosaic" of ethnic communities, the communities come together socially and through intermarriage, not as something that is homogenized as "Canadian," but as new and distinct possibilities. Sports have an interesting place in these processes, sometimes becoming a part of the process of assimilation, and sometimes a part of the process of resisting assimilation and reproducing a cultural community (e.g., Dallaire, 2000, 2000; Dyck, 2001). Research is needed to better understand the contexts in which these processes occur.

The possibility of assimilation, both to the degree necessary and to the degree preferred, together with the option of retaining some aspects of a traditional culture, has many interesting manifestations. For example, the Toronto Parks and Recreation department was recently approached by a group of Muslim women who had emigrated from Somalia. They had decided that, in order to become Canadian, they had to become involved in sports—they had recognized sports as a distinct feature of "Canadian" life. With the support of the Toronto Maple Leafs, Toronto Parks and Recreation established a ball hockey programme under the conditions necessary for practicing Muslims (Berck, 2003). Involvement in ball hockey is a step in assimilation, but it does not mean that other aspects of Somali culture and identity, including games, have to be abandoned. Immigrants to Canada seem to be quite capable, to varying degrees, of maintaining multiple aspects of identities. They are Somali, for example, and are able to pass on aspects of being Somali to their children, while at the same time becoming Canadian. It is the success of these policies that attracts researchers and policymakers from immigrant countries in Europe, the U.S., and Australia and New Zealand to study Canadian multiculturalism with a view to developing and fine-tuning their own policies. This does not mean that there are *no* tensions between ethnic and racial groups, or that there are *no* inequalities in access to power, but there seem to be less than in other diverse societies.

A Snapshot of the Canadian Population, 2001

Data from the 2001 Census released by Statistics Canada (www.statcan.ca)[6] provide a thorough picture of the racial and ethnic structure of Canada. This structure has important implications for the distribution and meaning of sports and physical activity in the country. The population of Canada is a little over 30 million. Definitions of "visible minority" and "ethnicity," which have been operationalized in order to determine measurement, are, as a consequence, somewhat different from those given at the beginning of the chapter, and the definitions show the complexity of such measurements. The definition of visible minority is taken from the Employment Equity Act: "persons, other than Aboriginal peoples, who are non-Caucasian in race or non-white in colour." Ethnic origin, which is also self-reported in the census, is defined as

"the ethnic or cultural group(s) to which an individual's ancestors belonged." Statistics Canada notes that:

> The reporting of ethnic origin, and subsequent interpretation of the results, has become increasingly complex due to a number of factors. The concept of ethnicity is fluid and is probably the *most complex concept measured in the census*. Respondents' understanding or views about ethnicity, awareness of their family background, number of generations in Canada, and the length of time since immigration can affect the reporting of ethnicity from one census to another. Increasing intermarriage among various groups has led to an increase in the reporting of multiple origins, which has added to the complexity of the ethnic data. ("Increasing complexity of ethnic reporting" in Statistics Canada "Canada's Ethnocultural Portrait"; emphasis added.)

The following provides some highlights of the ethnic and racial structure of Canada in 2001:

- Respondents listed more than 200 ethnic origins.
- 5.4 million people (18.5 percent) were born outside Canada. (Only Australia has a higher proportion of its population born outside the country.)
- Immigration continues at a rate of less than 1 percent of the population each year (ranging between 0.6 and 0.9 percent in the 1990s). There were 1.8 million immigrants between 1991 and 2001: 58 percent from Asia (including Middle East); 20 percent from Europe; 11 percent from the Caribbean and Latin America; 8 percent from Africa; and 3 percent from the U.S.
- Before 1961, 90 percent of all immigrants came from Europe.
- Between 1991 and 2001, almost three-quarters of all immigrants settled in three major cities: Toronto (43 percent), Vancouver (18 percent), and Montreal (12 percent).
- Almost 4 million (non-Aboriginal) Canadians identified themselves as visible minorities (13.5 percent), an increase from 4.7 percent

---

[6] All data in this section are from the 2001 Census, and can be found at this web site.

Table 9.1   Canadians Self-Identifying as Visible Minorities, 2001 Census

Visible Minority Group	Population	Percentage of Visible Minority Population	Percentage of Canadian Population
Chinese	1 million	26%	3.5%
South Asian	.92 million	23%	3.1%
Black	.66 million	17%	2.2%
Filipino		8%	
Arabs and West Asian		8%	
Latin American		5%	
Southeast Asian		5%	
Korean		3%	
Japanese		2%	
Other		3%	

Source: Data from Statistics Canada "Canada's Ethnocultural Portrait" accessed via
www12.statcan.ca/english/census01/products/analytic/companion/etoimm/canada.cfm

Table 9.2   Most Frequently Reported Ethnic Origins, 2001 Census

Reported Ethnic Origin	Population	Percentage of Canadian Population
Canadian	11.7 million	39.4%
English	6.0 million	20.2%
French	4.7 million	15.8%
Scottish	4.2 million	14.0%
Irish	3.8 million	12.9%
German	2.7 million	9.3%
Italian	1.3 million	4.3%
Chinese	1.1 million	3.7%
Ukrainian	1.1 million	3.6%
Aboriginal	1.0 million	3.4%

Source: Data from Table "Top 10 Ethnic Origins" in Statistics Canada "Canada's Ethnocultural Portrait" accessed via
www12.statcan.ca/english/census01/products/analytic/companion/etoimm/canada.cfm

in 1981; these include those shown in table 9.1 (as a proportion of the total visible minority population and, for the first three, a proportion of the national population; the remaining seven account for 34 percent of the visible minority population and some 4 percent of the national population).

- There are approximately 1 million Aboriginal people (North American Indian, Inuit, and Métis).
- Intermarriage (primarily) resulted in 11.3 million (38 percent) reporting multiple ethnicities in 2001 (an increase from 7.8 million in 1991).

Table 9.2 shows the most frequently reported ethnic origins (the total exceeds 100 percent because of the reporting of multiple ethnicities).

In table 9.2, the fact that over 39 percent of the population identified their ethnicity as "Canadian" is intriguing, and it causes complexity for Statistics Canada. Some 23 percent (6.7 million people) claim Canadian as their only ethnic origin; 16 percent (about 5 million people) claim Canadian in addition to other ethnic origins (e.g., Chilean and Canadian; Sri Lankan and Canadian; French, Irish, and Canadian). Most non-Aboriginal Canadians are aware that their ancestors came from another country sometime in the last 400 years. As Statistics Canada notes, a combination of political views (in an immigrant society, to identify one's ancestry is a political act), a person's awareness of his or her ancestors, and the number of generations one's ancestors have been in Canada, all have an effect on this claim of ethnicity. Thus, all Canadians have one or more ethnicities, but some of that record is being lost as Canada becomes more secure in its identity.

Related to the ethnic and racial structure of Canada is its language structure. As noted above, the country is officially multicultural and bilingual, and government resources are sometimes available to assist in the maintenance of heritage languages and Aboriginal languages in addition to the two official languages. In the 2001 census, some 87 percent of the population (approximately 26 million people) gave a single language response—61.5 percent (18.25 million) English, 20 percent (5.9 million) French, and 5.5 percent (1.7 million) another language. In addition, 13 percent of the population listed more than one language—3.5 percent (over 1 million) both English and French, and 9.5 percent listed English and/or French and another language.

Canadian and U.S. Differences in Racial and Ethnic Logic

The racial and ethnic structure of Canada outlined above is quite different from that of the United States. German is now the most frequently cited ethnic heritage in the U.S., and a dominant European-heritage, English-speaking majority ranks ahead of Latin American and African-American minorities. As in Canada, there are growing South Asian and East Asian populations. In Canada, the most frequently cited ethnic heritage (after Canadian) is English; the dominant European-heritage majority is divided linguistically, and ranks ahead of Aboriginal, Chinese and South Asian minorities. Visible minorities in Canada, although a rapidly increasing segment of the population, constitute some

13.5 percent of the total population—a smaller proportion than in the United States. Thus, while both populations are characterized by diversity, Canada's population is rather more diverse and, because of a higher rate of immigration, is growing increasingly diverse. Many urban and suburban Canadians regularly negotiate a set of racial, ethnic, and language relations, in their neighbourhoods and workplaces. Racism is considered to be a U.S. problem, and the commitment to multiculturalism often results in an incorrect assumption that racism does not exist in Canada.

The primary focus of race/ethnicity issues and research in the United States concerns "black" and "white" relations. The long history of slavery, which, in part, resulted in a Civil War; the re-victimization of African Americans through the "Jim Crow laws" following the abolition of slavery; and the Civil Rights movement of the 1960s, have made these relations a central focus of U.S. consciousness. The Canadian experience of this particular axis of racial relations is rather different. While slavery was practised in Canada from the seventeenth to the nineteenth centuries, it began to decline after 1793 when John Graves Simcoe, the Lieutenant Governor of Upper Canada, sponsored "a bill...passed by the Legislature of Upper Canada making it illegal to bring a person into the colony to be enslaved" (see "The Anti-Slavery Movement in Canada" Exhibition on the National Archives of Canada website, www.archives.ca). Following the success of William Wilberforce's campaign to abolish slavery in the United Kingdom, the practice formally ended in Canada in 1834.

The end of slavery in Canada, and its continuing practice in the southern U.S., led to the formation of a number of anti-slavery societies, the last and most successful of which was the Anti-Slavery Society of Canada founded in 1851 by the Hon. George Brown, owner of *The Globe* newspaper and a Father of Confederation, and Rev. Dr. Michael Willis, Principal of Knox College at the University of Toronto (www.archives.ca). The Anti-Slavery Society of Canada was active in the

"Underground Railroad" that brought many escaped slaves to Canada.

These differences do not mean that African Canadians were exempt from discrimination in Canada, or that Canada was immune to continuing U.S. influences with regard to race logic. The segregation of U.S. professional baseball as a result of the "Jim Crow laws" in the 1890s had its counterpart in Canada with the removal of African-Canadian players from teams (Humber, 1983), and there were even some African-Canadian hockey teams formed after hockey began to practise segregation.[7] African Canadians were not the only group to suffer from intolerance, as the following examples indicate:

- The use of Chinese immigrants to construct the railroad was followed by the imposition of a Head Tax to discourage further immigration from China.
- The anti-Semitic, "one is too many" policy, which denied access to Jewish immigrants trying to escape Nazi Germany before World War II, ended too late to save many from the concentration camps.
- Relations with Aboriginal peoples resulted in many children suffering in the residential school system, and in the traumatic forced resettlement of some Inuit peoples.
- The imprisonment of German immigrants in internment camps during World War I was repeated during World War II with Germans, Italians, and Japanese.

After World War II, racial and ethnic relations slowly began to settle in Canada. The Brooklyn Dodgers signed African-American baseball player Jackie Robinson to their Montreal farm team in 1946 before bringing him to Brooklyn to break the U.S. colour barrier in baseball in 1947.

---

[7] Morton (1983) notes that, in the 1920s, "nothing could hide the raw racial intolerance that had flourished since the [First World] war" (p. 170), and the Ku Klux Klan even made an appearance in western Canada in 1928.

And Willie O'Ree became the first African Canadian to play in the NHL (with the Boston Bruins) in 1958. However, as noted in the following section, African Canadians constitute only a little over 2 percent of the Canadian population, and while "black" and "white" relations in Canada demonstrate some ongoing problems (related, in part, to Canadian consciousness about this set of racial relations in the United States), other axes of racial and ethnic relations figure rather more prominently in Canada.

THE DYNAMICS OF ETHNIC AND RACIAL RELATIONS IN CANADIAN SPORTS

Sports have been significant sites of cultural, political, linguistic, and nationalistic struggles in Canada since 1970, when Pierre Trudeau began to see sports as one of the vehicles for the development of pan-Canadian unity. These struggles were first played out when, in an assertion of Canadian sovereignty, federal funding suddenly became available for the proposed Arctic Games (for Inuit and Dene peoples) after a U.S. oil-tanker (the *Manhattan*), accompanied by a U.S. icebreaker sailed, without Canadian permission, through territorial waters in the Northwest Passage in 1969. They continued in the lead-up to and during the Montreal Olympics in 1976 (Kidd, 1992), and leaped onto the front pages during the 1984 Sarajevo Winter Olympics when, following Gaétan Boucher's gold medals in two speed-skating events, Quebec Premier René Lévesque was reported to have said, "Quebec 2, Canada 0." They were still evident in 1994 when the then leader of the Parti Québécois, Jacques Parizeau, pointed out that athletes from Quebec had won nine of the thirteen Canadian medals at the Lillehammer Winter Olympics (Laberge, 1995); in 1995, when Quebec City was bidding for the 2002 Winter Olympics (Rail, et al., 1995); in 1998, when the Bloc Québécois published a Dissenting Report on the Mills Report

(Mills, 1998); and in 2002, when Swim Canada head coach Dave Johnson made some unfortunate remarks concerning Quebec swimmers.[8]

It should be evident from this that the major axis of racial/ethnic relations in Canadian sports is that concerning francophone and anglophone relations. However, Hall, et al. (1991, p. 179), pointed out that there are two other important axes of racial and ethnic relations evident in Canadian sports: relations between natives and non-natives, and relations between the two principal colonizing groups (French and English) and other immigrants and their descendants. In the following sections, we draw on these three axes, while also extending the latter category to consider relations between whites and visible minorities in Canada.

Francophone and Anglophone Relations

Under federal jurisdiction, Canada is officially a bilingual country. Francophones live in every province and territory of Canada; however, New Brunswick is the only officially bilingual province, and Quebec is the only French-language province and has the largest francophone population. Bilingual federal services are often available across the country, but provincial and territorial bilingual services vary significantly, with Quebec making many more accommodations for anglophones living in the province than are made for francophones living in the predominantly anglophone provinces.

After 1759, when the English forces defeated the French forces at Quebec City, there was a long period of discrimination—economic, political, and cultural/linguistic—against francophone Canadians that is well-documented in Canadian history. In many ways, the twentieth century was characterized by a long slow struggle against this discrimination, culminating in the *la révolution tranquille* of the 1960s and early 1970s. Shifts in Canadian federal policy towards official bilingualism, bi- and multi-culturalism, and asymmetrical federalism have modified, but not ended, discrimination; and the formation of the Parti Québecois, and its electoral successes in Quebec, have maintained the idea that Quebec may change the terms of its relationship with Canada.

The Montreal anglophone community figures prominently in Canadian sport history, and anglophones dominated the development of sports and sport organizations in Quebec.[9] While sports remained a major interest of francophones in larger communities, where there was a significant level of participation in organized sports, several researchers have pointed out that the major influence of the Catholic Church (especially in smaller communities) resulted in a somewhat different pattern of sport development in francophone Quebec (Bellefleur, 1986, 1997; Harvey, 1988). Indeed, for the francophone Catholic hierarchy in the first half of the twentieth century in Quebec, sports under the control of anglophones (including professional hockey) posed a danger of assimilation. Unable to prevent the growing interest of francophones in sports, the clergy took the initiative to create a separate sport system with a less competitive set of values (Meisel and Lemieux, 1972). For example, in hockey, the Confédération des Loisirs du Québec established a "section hockey" separate from the anglophone-dominated Quebec Amateur Hockey Association. The hockey section had the aim of opposing the commercialization and

---

[8] The remarks followed an incident when a Quebec swimmer had been reprimanded for carrying her provincial flag to a medal ceremony at the 2002 Commonwealth Games. The incident led to an outcry in Quebec media and in Parliament, with commentators pointing out, for example, that Catriona LeMay Doan had not received a similar reprimand for carrying the Saskatchewan flag to a medal ceremony.

---

[9] Parts of the following discussions of francophone/anglophone relations in sports are drawn from Donnelly, et al. (2001).

professionalization of amateur hockey, with the following goal: "replacer le hockey dans sa perspective d'activité physique salutaire, hygiénique et éducative."[10] Less explicit goals involved the maintenance of Quebec culture and language under clerical influence, and the maintenance of nationalist sentiments.

The long period of discrimination had certain characteristics that led some, by the 1960s, to equate the anti-discrimination struggles of francophones with those of African Americans (and the Civil Rights movement) in the United States. The two situations were so different that the analogy is a stretch—the primary similarity being that both were self-assertive movements against a long history of discrimination. However, in terms of the sociology of sport, the types of research that were initially carried out on the francophone/anglophone situation in Canada was quite similar to that carried out on the "black" and "white" situation in the United States. This was "distributive" research, designed to determine, and to offer explanations of, the ways that sports were distributed in the population—the proportions of "blacks" and "whites," anglophones and francophones in different sports. These distributions were then compared to the proportion of "blacks" and francophones in the population in order to determine if the population was fairly represented, underrepresented, or overrepresented in the sport.

Distributive Research Just a few weeks after the publication of John Munro's *A Proposed Sport Policy for Canadians* (1970), the document that proved to be the real turning point in the transformation of Canada's sport system, it was announced that Montreal had been awarded the 1976 Summer Olympic Games. Bruce Kidd (1992) has outlined the way in which francophone/anglophone politics were played out in the context of hosting the

Olympics in Quebec. These politics were fuelled, in part, by a series of studies outlining the underrepresentation of francophone athletes on Canadian national teams and in the NHL (e.g., Boileau, et al., 1976; Landry, et al., 1966, 1972; Marple, 1975). For example, Roger Boileau, Fernand Landry, and Yves Trempe (1976) studied francophone representation on Canadian national teams for the years 1908 to 1974. During this period of time, when the proportion of francophones in Canada varied between 25 and 30 percent, francophone representation on Canadian national teams at Summer Olympics, Winter Olympics, Pan-Am Games, and Commonwealth Games rarely exceeded 10 percent. In only one sport (haltérophilie/weightlifting) were francophones overrepresented (43 percent).

Following the earlier work of David Marple (1975) and others, Marc Lavoie of the University of Ottawa reviewed the research to 1989, and carried out a series of studies that showed underrepresentation of francophone athletes in the NHL. However, in another parallel to research on African Americans in the United States, Lavoie (1989) showed that francophones were also "stacked"[11] in certain playing positions—goalies mostly, followed by forwards, and very few defencemen. Grenier and Lavoie (1992) also showed that while anglophone and francophone goalies and forwards had similar levels of pay in the NHL, francophone defenders were paid 10 to 15 percent less than anglophones. Lavoie (1998) has recently updated this research.

In its planning and athlete development programmes for the 1976 Olympics, the Quebec government set a target of 30 percent francophones on the Canadian team, and funded the development of Québecois athletes. The goal was almost achieved, and the percentage of francophones on the Canadian team (28 percent)

---

[10] Translation: "return hockey to its place as beneficial, hygienic, and educational physical activity."

[11] "Stacking" is discussed in detail in a feature on the Online Learning Centre.

was just about exactly representative of the francophone proportion of the Canadian population (although there were no francophones in a number of sports). The national team studies continued after the 1976 Olympics (e.g., Haut Commissariat à la Jeunesse, aux Loisirs et aux Sports, 1978), and showed a decline in the proportion of francophone athletes. In the most striking parallel between U.S. and Canadian research, Kjeldsen (1984) compared francophone representation on Canadian Olympic teams and African-American representation of U.S. Olympic teams. Although Canada followed the U.S. boycott and did not send athletes to the Moscow Olympics in 1980, a team was announced, and Kjeldsen found that less than 15 percent of the athletes and almost 8 percent of the coaches were francophone. For the 1980 Winter Olympics in Lake Placid, francophone representation on the Canadian team was 17.6 percent for athletes and 3.6 percent for coaches. Research by Hall, et al. (1991), on Canadian teams at the 1984 Los Angeles Olympics (12 percent of the athletes) and the 1988 Seoul Olympics (12.7 percent of the athletes) showed that the decline continued. There was similar underrepresentation at the executive level of sport organizations. Hall, et al., pointed out that "in 1955, 8.6 percent of the executive positions were filled by francophones; 7.8 percent in 1975; and approximately 10 percent in 1980" (1991, p. 177).

Recently, the proportion of francophone athletes on national teams has increased. There are some clear specialties—short track speed skating, freestyle skiing, diving, women's water polo, synchronized swimming, etc.—although there are still a number of teams with no francophone athletes. Sport development has maintained a high priority in Quebec, and the situation for francophone athletes on national teams has improved since the 1980s. However, although the proportions of athletes may be more representative, there are still problems of concern—the number of coaching and executive positions

occupied by francophones, language issues (see the next section), etc. The history of distributive issues outlined above is important because of the sociological issues it highlights. How do we account for these differences in the distribution of francophone and anglophone athletes on Canadian national teams and in the NHL?

Two clear approaches have emerged as sociologists have attempted to explain their data—**cultural** explanations and **structural** explanations. Gruneau and Albinson describe the cultural interpretation of national team data given by Boileau, et al. (1976):

> They note that Québec was largely a rural and "traditional" society until the early 1960s. Intensely competitive urges and a need for achievement in sport were not a part of the dominant value system. At the same time, Boileau et al. argue that the lack of involvement in sports was also contingent upon a rejection of the personal values of anglophones— many of which were thought to be reflected in the structure and organization of sport. (1976, p.104)

In other words, sports were not important in francophone culture in Quebec, and maintaining a francophone culture in Quebec was associated with rejecting the type of power and performance sports associated with anglophones. Lavoie (1989) reviewed, and rejected, similar cultural explanations for the underrepresentation of francophones in the NHL: the francophone style of play (characterized as too much offence and too little aggression and work ethic), the belief that it was necessary to pay francophone players more to induce them to leave Quebec, and the language problems associated with having a non-English-speaking player on the team. Thus, Quebec culture and the (anglophone) culture of the NHL clashed to the disadvantage of non-star francophone players.

Structural explanations take into account the differences in power (political, economic, etc.) between anglophones and francophones, and argue quite distinctly that underrepresentation was a result of discrimination. Talented

Gold medal-winning biathlete, Myriam Bédard, signalled the recent struggles over language in Canadian sports when she refused to accept the unilingual (English) services, including coaching, provided by Biathlon Canada. (CP Frank Gunn)

francophone athletes were often not selected for national teams because of discrimination on the part of the anglophone sport executives making the selections. Coulombe and Lavoie (1985) argue that francophone players reached the NHL primarily in those positions where there were objective measures of performance—the statistics indicate clearly that one goalie is better than another and, almost with the same degree of clarity, that one forward is better than another. Assessing the play of defencemen is more subjective. Where a francophone player was objectively the better player, he would be selected; more

subjective assessments opened the door to stereotypes and discrimination.

The clash between cultural and structural explanations came to a head in an academic debate in the *Sociology of Sport Journal* in 1992. The debate was sparked by the publication of two articles, by Phil White of McMaster University and Jim Curtis of the University of Waterloo (White and Curtis, 1990a; 1990b), which advocated a cultural explanation of francophone/anglophone differences in sport participation. The articles reviewed 1976 national survey data in Canada showing that francophones had a lower rate of participation in competitive sports (and a higher rate of participation in recreational sports) than anglophones. Both articles indicate that the data support a "values-differences" interpretation—that there are differences in the orientation to achievement between anglophones and francophones (with anglophones being more achievement-oriented), which explain the differences in involvement in competitive sports. White and Curtis (1990b) also focus on the differences in school socialization for francophones and anglophones in Canada to account, in part, for the values differences (i.e., that before the Quiet Revolution it was not common for francophone schools to be involved in interschool sports). Critical commentaries on the articles by researchers from the Université de Montréal (Laberge and Girardin, 1992; McAll, 1992) advocated a structural interpretation, pointing to a long history of structural inequality between francophones and anglophones in Quebec that was reflected in discrimination in many aspects of life including sports. Curtis and White (1992) replied by re-advocating their cultural explanation and providing additional data.

Academic debates such as this are often presented as an either/or situation—you must accept either a cultural explanation or a structural explanation of the differences in sport participation, and the underrepresentation of francophones on national teams and in the NHL. However, explanations of social life are often far more complex and nuanced. There is clear evidence of cultural differences between anglophones and francophones in Canada; and there is clear evidence of a long history of structural inequality and discrimination. The question that remains, and is suggested by Laberge and Girardin (1992), is to what extent cultural differences are a result of structural inequality—of being subject to, and resisting, discrimination?

By 1986, research in Quebec was shifting from a singular focus on underrepresentation to what was now being termed, le "fait français" ("si le fait d'être francophone pouvait nuire aux athlètes québécois dans la réalisation de leur performance sportive"[12]). Suzanne Laberge (1986) of the Université of Montréal was pointing to both the underrepresentation of, and subtle discrimination against, francophone high-performance athletes, and she produced a short statement of the ongoing problems in 1988. The most recent analysis, the report of the Comité sur la place du Québec dans le système sportif Canadien (2001) also shows ongoing problems, the most significant of which is the issue of language.

Language Issues in Canadian Sports Language issues in Canadian sports have received a great deal of attention in the last few years. Three events in particular seem to have sparked this interest. The first was the case of Myriam Bédard, "which made it possible to publicly denounce the kind of discrimination experienced by a number of athletes. Ms. Bédard won medals in the most prestigious international competitions after refusing to accept the unilingual English services provided to her by Biathlon Canada" (Sports Québec, 1998, p. 22). In the second, the Canadian Olympic Association (COA/AOC) was accused of making little provision for the use of French at an athletes' reception before the 1998 Nagano Olympics. A representative of the COA/AOC was called before the parliamentary committee on official languages to explain and apologize (Feschuk, 1998). Just six months later, at a ceremony held at the CBC in Toronto to announce the Canadian flag-bearer at the forthcoming Commonwealth Games in Kuala Lumpur, it quickly became apparent to the media present that the Canadian Commonwealth Games Association/l'Association Canadienne des Jeux de Commonwealth had made no provision for statements/announcements or interviews in French. The proceedings were saved when the flag-bearer, New Brunswick swimmer Marianne Limpert, stepped forward to translate and answer questions in both English and French (Christie, 1998). Sport Canada increased its efforts to address the issue of bilingualism in Canadian sports, and, in November, 1999, the newly appointed Secretary of State for Amateur Sport, Denis Coderre, following a letter of complaint from Bloc Québécois MP Caroline St-Hilaire, initiated a study by the Commissioner for Official Languages (Office of the Commissioner of Official Languages [OCOL], 2000).

Sports became a distinct part of Canadian language politics in 1982 when the issue of official languages was first added to the issue of underrepresentation. Max Yalden, then Commissioner of Official Languages, presented a report to the Ministry of Fitness and Amateur Sport that noted: "In our opinion, it is unacceptable that [federal] taxpayers' money be used to support such national bodies [sport organizations] if adequate services are not provided in both official languages." Federal and provincial study groups were formed, and while the federal study group noted a "real determination" on the part of the Ministry/Sport Canada to encourage national sport organizations (NSOs) to offer their services in both French and English, the Quebec inquiry press release noted:

---

[12] Translation: "if the fact of being francophone could be a disadvantage to Québécois athletes in realizing their goals in sport."

...97.5 percent of the respondents estimate they have some trouble to obtain information in French from the Canadian Sport Associations. The problems they face are numerous and vary from one federation to another. Officer training, clinics, meetings and general information are all scarcely available in French.

Following the upheaval associated with the Ben Johnson affair at the 1988 Seoul Olympics, Sport Canada set about transforming national sport policy, including the poor state of language relations reported by the Federal-Provincial Advisory Committee on Equal Linguistic Access to Services in Sport.

Despite these policy initiatives, very little changed, and embarrassing incidents continued. For example, the case of Myriam Bédard refusing to work with Biathlon Canada (noted above), and the accusations of discrimination voiced by Bloc Québécois members of parliament in the House of Commons when it became apparent that the hockey team Canada sent to the 1994 Lillehammer Olympics included only one francophone player (Canadian Press, 1994). Only recently, since federal funding has been linked specifically to pressure to establish services in both official languages, and as sport organizations are beginning to show a greater sensitivity to equity issues, are there any real signs of change.

The Official Languages Act only applies to Sport Canada (now part of the Department of Canadian Heritage), rather than the NSOs. However, the Sport Canada website includes the Treasury Board Policy on Official Languages, indicating that French and English have equal status in Canada and that the policy applies to NSOs receiving federal funds:

> ...federal institutions providing grants or contributions to voluntary non-governmental organizations for activities, projects or programmes involving service to a public composed of members of both official language communities must take the necessary measures to ensure that the recipients of public funds respect the spirit and intent

of the Official Languages Act when serving the public. (www.pch.gc.ca/progs/sc/pol/lang/index_e.cfm)

This commitment from Sport Canada was specified most recently in the Sport Funding and Accountability Framework (SFAF), introduced in 1995–96 (see the Reflect on Sports box, "Sports and Bilingualism," pp. 278–279).

Native and Non-Native Relations

With a population of about one million—over 3 percent of Canada's population—Aboriginal Canadians represent one of the most rapidly growing segments of the population. Although officially classified as one minority group in Canada, First Nations peoples comprise many dozens of diverse cultural groups—the usual Canadian designation of "Indian and Inuit" does not capture this diversity. Popular ideas about Aboriginal Canadians have their own history and have grown out of different forms of ethnic relations. Furthermore, Native Canadian lifestyles and sport participation patterns are diverse and vary depending on social class and whether people reside on or off reserves. The diverse cultures are also characterized by diversity in physical culture, with many different sports and games, for men and women, a part of native cultures. Many sports in traditional Native Canadian cultures have combined physical activities with ritual and ceremony.

For example, in perhaps the most intriguing tradition, "Running is said to bring myths to life, and to create a link between runners and the universe" (Unwin, 2001, p. 21). Native lore in North and Central America is full of stories about feats of speed and endurance in running, and a number of well-known runners (in the European sport tradition) have emerged from Aboriginal cultures. Lacrosse (tewaarathon, to the Iroquois) is perhaps the best known of the originally native sports in Canada, and is now officially designated Canada's national summer sport.

Although there is quite a lot of research on anglophone/francophone relations in sports in Canada, quite the reverse is the case with regard to native and non-native relations. There is a fairly substantial body of descriptive historical research on Aboriginal sports and physical activities, but only three researchers appear to have carried out any consistent social scientific research on the issue: Gerry Glassford, formerly of the University of Alberta; Michael Heine, now at the University of Manitoba; and Vicky Paraschak at the University of Windsor. Paraschak's (1989) review of the history of native sports in Canada indicates that relations between non-natives and natives were characterized by *exploitation*, *racism*, and *ethnocentric distortion*. To these, we can add *assimilation* and *resistance* as characteristics of the relationship.

Exploitation Exploitation is evident in numerous examples of the use of native athletes and their sports. For example, when George Beers, a Montreal dentist, "Europeanized" the game of lacrosse and formed the Lacrosse Club of Montreal in 1860, he effectively ended traditional ways of playing the game and made continued native participation in their own game problematic. Natives were used, because of the novelty value of their "Indianness," on international tours to promote the game, but were often excluded from play in Canada because of the strict amateur rules and the inability of native players to afford travel and membership fees without compensation. In fact, some amateur rules (e.g., the Montreal Pedestrian Club) specifically precluded native athletes from participation (Kidd, 1988). As the sport began to professionalize by the end of the nineteenth century, clubs again turned to native players because of their skills at the game, and paid them to play.

Similar examples of exploitation are evident in distance running, which was an extremely important, often professional, sport in the early years of the twentieth century. Bruce Kidd

(1980), of the University of Toronto, has painstakingly detailed the exploitation of one of the best-known native runners, Tom Longboat, an Onondagan from the Six Nations reserve in Ontario. As noted below, such examples of overt exploitation would nowadays meet with a great deal more *resistance*.

Racism In partnership with *exploitation*, native athletes also met with a great deal of racism in the nineteenth and twentieth centuries. For example, native athletes were often excluded from participation in organized sports, especially those in which they had skill and experience (e.g., lacrosse, running, snowshoeing). As noted above, this was sometimes a result of the enforcement of strict amateur rules, which were associated with a European distaste at possibly being defeated by individuals who they considered to be socially inferior and of a lower social class (similar motives were evident in the segregation of black athletes from participation at this time). Eddington (2000) points out that, "Not until twenty years after it became Canada's national game were the Iroquois Nationals allowed to join the International Lacrosse Federation" (p. 14), as the first native team in the league in 1887.

Racism also had vicious personal effects, with racist slurs aimed at native athletes by spectators; slurs were even considered legitimate expression in the media. For example, Lou Marsh, a sportswriter for the *Toronto Star*, and the individual after whom the Canadian Athlete of the Year trophy is named, "carried on a bizarre campaign against [Tom] Longboat…describ[ing] him as 'the original dummy.…Wily…unreliable…as hard to train as a leopard'" (Unwin, 2001, p. 23). Bruce Kidd's research effectively challenged the traditional characterizations of Longboat as "unmanageable" and "obstinate." While this type of casual racism is no longer unchallenged, native athletes still report negative experiences with non-native athletes and spectators. For example, in major junior and NHL hockey, there are reports of incidents

REFLECT ON SPORTS

Sports and Bilingualism

The Sport Funding and Accountability Framework (1995–96) introduced a series of five-year funding plans to support thirty-eight of the approximately sixty Canadian national sport organizations (NSOs). Funding was linked to government social and sport policy objectives, including "minimum expectations in five areas of social policy: official languages, athlete-centredness, women in sport, harassment and abuse in sport, and athletes with a disability" (OCOL, 2000, p. 19). The agreement between Sport Canada and the NSOs stated: "The Recipient agrees... to take into account official languages considerations when providing services to the public or members" (OCOL, 2000, p. 18).

A series of steps were outlined for the NSOs, as well as for the national sport centres and multi-sport organizations (e.g., the Canadian Olympic Committee and Canadian Interuniversity Sport) that receive federal funding. The steps required that written materials (rules, policies, etc.), websites, and services to athletes and the public be available in both official languages by March, 1999. Very few of those receiving federal funds have met the expectations, and it seems that ongoing funding has not been tied to meeting the minimum expectations.

What difference does it make if we have a primarily unilingual sport system in a bilingual society? In her review of the high-performance sport system (2000), Official Languages Commissioner Dyanne Adam stated:

> [T]he Canadian sport system does not meet the needs of francophone [high performance] athletes, and does not provide them equal access... In a system that boasts that it is centred around the athlete, francophone athletes should not have to overcome the double challenge of mastering English in addition to their sport in order to succeed at a high level. (Clark, 2000, p. S2)

In addition to having to learn a second language, OCOL (2000) found many examples of unequal treatment of francophone national team athletes. For example, at one national team selection camp, all the coaches were unilingual (English); a bilingual athlete who had been selected to the team had to accompany a coach to translate as the coach informed a francophone athlete that he had not made the team.

Of course, anglophones in the sport community, as the linguistic majority, also view bilingualism as a burden. They complain about translation costs and delays—"why should we have to wait for documents to be translated so that everyone may receive them at the same time?" They also point out that they are in a "no win" situation—"even when we spend money on translation, we get into trouble because it's not accurate." However, in a study of language relations in CIS and the CHA (Donnelly, et al., 2001), the real consequences of translation problems were evident. For example, there was a difference in the interpretation of the Canadian Interuniversity Athletic Union (now CIS) eligibility rule, which was not quite the same in English and French. Because the English version stands in case of a dispute, there was a possibility that francophone athletes and teams could be disadvantaged. In other examples, Hockey Québec had numerous translation problems with CHA materials. For example:

- Delays in the receipt of translated documents were sometimes so long that when the French text arrived it was outdated. Staff received translated invitations to events that had already occurred. One staff member said, "Often, the French version of the administrative regulations was received months after they had been distributed in English. When the updated rule book is not in the hands of the coaches and referees by August or September, it is too late. They already are in the arenas working with the kids; they have to know about the rule changes and the new rules...." CHA programmes that were supposed to be implemented immediately, were also delayed.

- Translations carried out by the CHA have been full of errors, sometimes to the point of being unintelligible. All translated materials sent from the CHA had to be carefully proofread, and thousands of books or documents had to be destroyed because of translation errors.

• The potentially serious consequences of translation errors were evident when an English document on concussions stated that, following a violent blow to the head, a player should be prevented from playing for the rest of the *game*; the French version provided by the CHA stated that a player should be prevented from playing for the rest of the *period*.

All of the above examples,[1] and even some of the solutions proposed by anglophones, involve extra time and work for francophones. For example, in an attempt to avoid the financial cost of providing bilingual services, some anglophone sport executives suggested that francophone and bilingual volunteers should do translation and interpretation work.

The Office of the Commissioner of Official Languages (OCOL) regularly heard arguments about the cost of translation and interpretation services and demands that the federal government meet these costs because they were incurred as a result of federal regulations. They responded: "We do not believe that the federal government alone should bear the cost of enabling national organizations to function in both languages: providing services to members in both English and French represents a benefit to the organization and should be considered a normal cost of doing business in Canada" (2000, p. 26). One benefit is that the existence of bilingual services attracts francophones and builds membership. In turn, this creates a larger selection pool for representation on national teams. Some of the predominantly anglophone NSOs have followed precisely this pattern, either to increase their francophone representation or because a large pool of talented francophone athletes already existed (e.g., Skate Canada); it is surprising that others have been so slow to follow. An additional benefit lies in the legitimacy achieved by an organization that is seen to be bilingual. However, while some level of bilingualism is necessary for funding, for membership and representation, and perhaps for legitimacy, these factors are also associated with a quite widespread belief that Canada is a better place because of bilingualism and multiculturalism.

What do you think?

_____

[1] The CIS, CHA, and several other NSOs have made efforts to become more bilingual in the last few years. Others stubbornly remain unilingual English, to the distinct disadvantage of over 20 percent of the Canadian population.

•••

between players and with spectators, and Mann Cup and Minto Cup games between native and non-native lacrosse teams are sometimes characterized by brutality (Campbell, 1995).

Other recent incidents give pause because, while they may seem to be racist, no evidence is available. For example, Ted Nolan, a former NHL player who became the first Native Canadian head coach of an NHL team, was fired by the Buffalo Sabres shortly after he was named as NHL Coach of the Year in 1997. There was no explanation, and, unlike most head coaches who lose their jobs, he has not worked in the NHL since. Brenda Zeman's (1988) book on native athletes, and a series of articles by Laura Robinson (e.g., 1995, 1997, 2000, 2002) dramatically outline continuing difficulties and discrimination experienced by Native Canadian athletes.

Ethnocentric Distortion Paraschak (1989) points out that most of our knowledge about Native Canadians is distorted because the experience is presented from a Euro-Canadian perspective rather than from the standpoint of native peoples. This has resulted in certain native practices (e.g., gambling) being condemned; in athletic ability being defined as "natural" rather than as a result of training and skill development, as in the experience of black athletes (Heine, 1991); and in ethnocentric assumptions about the character of native peoples (e.g., they are "less civilized"). In a subtle and complex analysis, Paraschak (1999) brings together race and gender to explore the differences between the meaning of gendered action in Native Canadian sports and physical activities from the standpoint of Native Canadians and Euro-Canadians. Take, for example, the different views of masculinity evident in native (Inuit) and non-native styles of play in hockey, which has resulted in non-native complaints about the Inuit style of play:

> [The] Inuit style of play fits with traditional Native methods of violence expression, which rarely involve face-to-face confrontation [in hockey, for example, taking the form of hitting people from behind and skating away]. Non-Inuit players, however, adhere to different norms [dropping gloves and fighting face-to-face] which is perceived to be more manly....Inuit athletes construct different norms of masculinity...in which Native male athletes see themselves as being more athletically talented [skating faster, shooting harder] than White athletes. (Paraschak, 1999, pp. 158–9)

These differences can only be resolved with greater knowledge and understanding of each other's perspectives. At the present time, Native Canadian athletes have far more knowledge of the non-native sport perspective than vice versa.

Assimilation and Resistance Among the civil and equal rights movements that started in the 1960s was a native rights movement in North America that began to challenge (resist) discrimination and attempts to assimilate (annihilate) native cultures. A part of this movement involved, first, a self-conscious attempt to maintain and restore traditional native sports and physical activities, such as pow-wows, snow-snake competitions, the

Northern Games, and Dene Games; and second, to establish native-only sporting events in which native solidarity and self-determination could be developed during participation in non-native sports, such as the North American Indigenous Games, and native hockey tournaments (Paraschak, 1996). These became necessary because of legal actions by colonists banning traditional native activities (e.g., Potlatch, Sun Dance), because of the activities of Christian missionaries that also led to the loss of traditional cultures, and because of government action in mandating education in residential schools. These various actions had the effect of assimilation and the loss of native languages and cultures. Cultural loss meant that many natives were more familiar with hockey, baseball, and other Euro-Canadian sports than they were with traditional sports. The establishment of two forms of games (traditional and native-only) recognized this reality.

Assimilation also takes more subtle forms. Paraschak (1982) pointed out that the only television available in the Arctic was from southern Canada and the United States, showing only mainstream sports; young physical education teachers from southern Canada, usually spending only one or two years in the Arctic, would teach Euro-Canadian sports and physical activities rather than learning native activities. The combined effect of these is additional loss of traditional sporting cultures. The forms of resistance outlined above—organizing traditional and native-only events—create an additional problem. As Hall, et al., note, the actual organization of such activities "seems so removed from the spontaneous play and games of a traditional culture" (1991, p. 181). And, despite attempts to recreate "bush consciousness" (Heine, 1995), "Native time" (Paraschak, 1996), and traditional ways of organizing activities (e.g., choosing judges at the last minute who then determine the rules for that event), as Mrozek (1987) pointed out, "the consciousness of having to preserve the culture fundamentally alters what is preserved—turning it into a museum piece" (p. 38).

Lacrosse has an interesting history: the traditional native game was Europeanized, native players were then excluded from play, and now, native players are actively involved in the Europeanized version of their game. Here, the Six Nations Arrows celebrate their Ontario Lacrosse Association major junior A championship in 1998.
(CP/Brian Thompson/*Brantford Expositor*)

Perhaps the most striking symbolic piece of Native Canadian resistance occurred at the 1984 Los Angeles Olympics when Alwyn Morris, a gold medalist in canoeing, held up an eagle feather on the podium during the medal ceremony. The action was carried out with the permission of the IOC (who have strong rules against political protests or statements at the Games), since it was presented to them as a spiritual and traditional aboriginal action. However, the action combined the traditional with the modern—a Native Canadian medalist in a traditional Canadian activity which had been Europeanized and modernized for the Olympics, holding aloft an eagle feather. It sent a powerful symbolic and political message to Native Canadians. Morris has since been involved in founding the North American Indigenous Games and the Aboriginal Sport Circle in Canada.

Colonizing Nations and Immigrant Relations

While there is little research on native and non-native relations in Canada, there is even less on this final axis of racial and ethnic relations. Indeed, apart from the study by Donnelly and Day (Day, 1981) of ethnic soccer clubs in London, Ontario, noted previously, and master's theses written by McKay at the University of Waterloo and Chamberlain at the University of Alberta, there is very little on this particular set of relations. The editor of a special ethnic sports issue of *Polyphony* (1985, p. 10) noted:

> [The] study of sports organizations and their sponsors could enrich our understanding of the problems of immigrant integration in Canadian society and of the constant encounter of immigrants and their values with the host society and its ways.…In fact the formation of any sports team, or the events and rituals surrounding any organized game, contain those elements of a cultural artifact…which show ethnicity to be a complex process and a negotiation, not just a hard fact acquired from the census or from looking at someone's surname.

In the three examples that follow, we consider Canadians and Americans as national groups in Canadian sports, and examine European-Canadian relations with Asian- and African-Canadian visible minorities.

Canadian/American Relations Major U.S. professional sports leagues have sought to expand internationally in recent years. Part of the process of preparing for such expansion has been the introduction of NBA basketball players and NHL hockey players into Olympic competition, and all four major sport leagues playing international exhibition games and even some regular season games (e.g., the Montreal Expos starting its 2003 Major League Baseball season in Puerto Rico). However, three of the leagues (baseball, basketball, and hockey) already have international teams—in Canada—and the fourth enjoys a reciprocal relationship with a Canadian league (NFL/CFL); all the leagues have U.S. and Canadian players playing in both countries. These relationships produce different tensions that point to an analysis of Canadians and Americans as national groups. This has been the case particularly with the CFL.

The ongoing reliance of the CFL on U.S. players was formalized in 1965 when players were first designated as "imports" (usually Americans) and nonimports (usually Canadians).[13] In 1970, the controversial "designated import" rule was introduced, allowing two U.S. quarterbacks on each team, ensuring that Russ Jackson was the last Canadian to play quarterback in the CFL. In 1996, CFL rosters were set at 36 players, 17 nonimports, 17 imports, and two quarterbacks (essentially 19 American players, one of whom was the "designated import," and 17 Canadians).

Imports included both black and white players (as did the nonimports), and some elements of Canadian and U.S. race relations were played out in the CFL. Smith and Grindstaff (1972) found that, although the status of black athletes in the league improved during the 1950s and 1960s, black players were, in general, not treated equally. During the early 1970s, U.S. research began to show that African Americans in the NFL and in MLB were "stacked" in noncentral positions (see the Online Learning Centre feature on "Stacking"), and Donald Ball (1973), a sociologist at the University of Victoria, carried out a study to determine if the stacking of black players was also evident in the CFL.

When Ball adjusted the centrality model slightly to designate "primary" and "supporting"

positions in the game, he found that it was not African-American players but white Canadian players who were "stacked" in the supporting positions. They were also unlikely to play in the central and primary positions, and they earned lower salaries than the Americans. Cantelon's (2001) update on this research suggests that little has changed in the last 30 years. Just as we have discussed Canada as a "cultural mosaic," it was also common in the early 1970s (as it is even more so today) to criticize Canadian dependency on U.S. corporations by referring to Canada as a "branch plant" (of the U.S.) economy. Ball (1973) concluded his study by pointing out that the "lack of expectations about Canadian players" could be taken to mean that the CFL "is just one more tile in the mosaic of the branch plant economy" (p. 110).

The "designated import" rule, which virtually rules out a career in professional football for Canadian university quarterbacks (as quarterbacks), has received only one serious challenge. In 1979, Jamie Bone, who had been a star quarterback with the University of Western Ontario Mustangs, was cut from the Hamilton Tiger-Cats tryout camp. Hall, et al. (1991), describe his response, and the result:

> [Bone] complained to the Canadian Human Rights Commission that the CFL's designated import rule discriminated against him on the grounds of national or ethnic origin because it prevented Canadians from being hired to play quarterback. The Commission...concluded that it was always in a team's best interest to select the most talented quarterback regardless of his national origin, and that although a particular CFL coach may mistakenly perceive the designated import rule to favour hiring imports to play that position, the rule itself does not. (p.178)

Since the majority of coaches and general managers in the CFL are Americans, or have U.S. football experience, it is generally assumed that they will look first to the United States for their key (skill, primary, and central)

---

[13] The rule is rather more complicated than place of birth since it defines imports as those who played football outside Canada before their seventeenth birthday. The nonimports (sometimes referred to by those analyzing the CFL as "nonimportant") did not play outside Canada as youngsters, but the age designation permits those Canadians whose university football careers were in the U.S. to be counted as nonimports, even if they became naturalized Americans.

Canadians know a great deal about the U.S.—and U.S. sports—but that knowledge is not reciprocated. We wonder what the response might have been if the Blue Jays had flown the U.S. flag upside-down in Toronto during the 1992 World Series? (CP/Hans Deryk)

players, and fill up the remainder of their roster with the required 17 Canadians. In both the Ball study and the Bone case, Canadians appear to have become a minority group in their own country, a group that seems to be subject to unequal treatment. However, the treatment of black players has improved markedly in the last 30 years, to a point where there are now several African Americans in leadership positions in the CFL.

More recently, nationalistic tensions have taken a different form that sometimes leaves Canadians shaking their heads, or smiling wryly at international misunderstanding. For example, the issue of booing national anthems at NHL games has become the basis for tension. Some people in the crowd booed the U.S. national anthem before a game in Montreal in March, 2003, an action that was interpreted as a protest against the U.S. invasion of Iraq and was given widespread negative publicity in both the United States and Canada (where it became the subject of a Don Cherry anti-francophone rant). However, U.S. fans booing the Canadian national anthem before a 2002 Stanley Cup playoff game on Long Island, just a few days after four Canadians were killed and eight were injured when they were victims of U.S. "friendly fire" during the invasion of Afghanistan, only generated a small amount of negative publicity in Canada, and very little in the U.S. Major League Baseball has been particularly insensitive about national differences, with incidents ranging from the flying of the Canadian flag upside down at a World Series game in Atlanta (against Toronto) in 1992, to a directive from the Commissioner's office that "God Bless America" be played during the seventh inning stretch at all home openers, and Sunday and holiday games, to honour U.S. military involved in the invasion of Iraq. The Commissioner's office clearly had not given any thought about how this was to be carried out, or received, in Montreal and Toronto; or to the fact that the Canadian government has determined that, without United Nations sanction, the invasion is an illegal action and that Canada will not participate. If the four U.S. major professional sport leagues show similar insensitivity to national feelings in countries other than Canada, it does not bode well for international expansion.

Americans are not the only "imports" to play in Canada. Canadian sport teams also have, for example, Latino baseball players and European hockey players. The experiences of sporting migrants in the new global economy of sports is only now beginning to be explored. Alan Klein (1991, 1999) has focused on the experiences of Dominican baseball players in Canada and the United States, and Joe Maguire (1995) has studied Canadian hockey players in the U.K. But hockey has the largest number of imports in Canada, and research on the experiences of European players is only just beginning as Kristi Allayne, a Master's student at Queen's University, is collecting extremely interesting interview data with eastern European players in major junior hockey.

Asian-Canadian/European-Canadian Relations   A small amount of research has focused on European-Canadian relations with Asian visible minorities in Canada. British and Australian research has shown lower participation levels in sports and physical activities among Muslim girls and women (immigrants and children of immigrants from South and West Asia), and interpretations suggested that such girls were constrained by parental rules about activities outside the home and that their time was devoted to domestic and familial duties. These interpretations suggested that sports and physical activity are not valued in Muslim cultures, especially for girls.

However, Canadian research, while showing some similar results, reached a different interpretation because it involved interviews directly with Muslims and South Asians. This research suggests that it is not sports and physical activity itself, but sports and physical activity structured in Western ways that has less value. For example, Nakamura (2002) found that some Muslim women prefer to participate under specific conditions, such as with a modest and flexible dress code and/or in segregated spaces. Islam is not monolithic. It can be expressed in varying ways and does not preclude physical activity for men or women. Many of Nakamura's subjects were interested

In Canada, there have been few studies of Asian Canadians in sports. Like other young people who seek alternatives to organized competitive sports, this young Asian Canadian has taken up snowboarding. (John Terence Turner/Taxi/Getty Images)

in participating in sports and physical activity, and some had been active in their country of birth. However, they had specific needs related to Islam that affected when and how they could participate, needs that illustrate how activities themselves can have religious connotations. For some, the needs are simple—young women played basketball or soccer in high school while wearing track pants and/or the hijab. High schools and interschool leagues that were flexible permitted this, and it was only at the higher levels—when international rules were enforced—that participation was considered to be impossible (e.g., international soccer federation [FIFA] rules require that shorts be worn). For others, the needs are more complex and involve segregated spaces that cannot be observed by men. Some schools and universities have taped windows, and have scheduled women-only hours to accommodate such needs. However, when such accommodations in rules or scheduling are not available, the young women interviewed preferred not to participate.

In studies on South Asians in Canada carried out by Susan Tirone at Memorial University of Newfoundland, Tirone and Pedlar (2000) found that the South Asian teens and young adults they interviewed were more likely to participate in leisure activities with family and with members of their ethnic group. Such activities are less likely to register in surveys of physical activity. Tirone (1999–2000) also found that some South Asian teens experienced racism and indifference towards their culture when they participated in community recreation programmes and competitive sports. As a way of coping with such experiences, they would either withdraw from participation altogether, or overcompensate, feeling the need to excel precisely because they were visible minorities. Tirone found that many of the South Asian young adults felt hurt at the indifference "Canadians" showed toward their culture; they felt that the people around them had little interest in learning more about their country of origin or their traditions, despite Canada's policy of multiculturalism. This feeling of disenchantment with multiculturalism could lead to isolation—to the sense that one's ethnic identity and community are a haven where one feels welcome.

Canadian research has only scratched the surface of analysis of these complex racial and ethnic relations, and we have found no research on the largest visible minority groups in Canada: East Asians.

African-Canadian/European-Canadian Relations Recently, Giller Prize–winning author Austin Clarke wrote:

For years, television did not show the faces of black hockey players—even though there were a few. And I remember that during an international tournament of junior world hockey played in some European country, that the Canadian television media went to Herculean lengths not to show the face of a black player! (2003, p. 10)

The vast majority of research on race and ethnicity, and on race and ethnicity in sports, has been carried out in the United States. By far the majority of that research concerns one particular set of racial relations—that between people of sub-Saharan African heritage and people of European heritage. As noted previously, this particular set of relations has a history in the United States that is rather different from the overall development of racial and ethnic relations in Canada, and different issues must be discussed in Canada. However, because of the complex, interdependent, and often dependent relations between Canada and the United States—for example, economic ties; the widespread exposure of Canadians to U.S. media; and, in sports, the interconnection of players between the two countries in all major team sports—many Canadians have absorbed U.S. ideas about the "black and white" issue of race relations. Wilson (1997, 1999), Wilson and Sparks (1996, 2001), and Shehid (2000, 2002) have pointed to the ways in which American "blackness" has been appropriated into understanding Canadian "blackness" in sports.

And while this has often been the case, there are other connections to explore than that between African Americans and African Canadians. For example, there is a long history of African-Canadian participation in hockey and, despite the cruelty of racism, the long-delayed entry of African-Canadian players into the NHL. Also, there is a strong connection between African Canadians and the Caribbean (particularly Jamaican) rather than the African-American sprinting tradition. However, this paved the way for what Henry and Tator (2002) term "the discourse of Canada's national identity," which they characterize as being "marked by erasures, omissions, and silences" (p. 232). For example, Jackson (1998) has examined the celebration of Ben Johnson as a Canadian hero at the 1988 Olympics. That Canadian identity was withdrawn by the media after the positive steroid test, and Johnson was then referred to as an immigrant, or Jamaican, rather than "Canadian." In terms of Henry and Tator's *Discourses of Domination*, this overlaps with the discourse of otherness, in that it created a distance between "us" ("white" Canadians) and "them" (Jamaicans), despite the fact that Johnson was a Canadian citizen. Jackson (1998) cites a 1988 newspaper article that captures ironically the patronizing tone of the discourses: "But then why would anyone expect an immigrant boy from rural Jamaica to be able to handle the pressure and temptations of such success."

A great deal of research remains to be done on African-Canadian experiences and relations with European-Canadians in sports. Several researchers have made a valuable start: Carl James of York University on the experiences of black high school athletes, and Gamal Abdel-Shehid (University of Alberta) and Brian Wilson (University of British Columbia) on black youth, sports, and identity. As with all other aspects of racial and ethnic relations in Canadian sports, we need a great deal more information. All kinds of other relations are possible in addition to the ones discussed here, and, in a country as diverse as Canada, it will become increasingly important to understand these sets of relations. For example, Margaret MacNeill (University of Toronto) is beginning to explore the meaning of, and positive reaction to, Daniel Igali's wrestling gold medal on the final day of the 2000 Sydney Olympics. His Nigerian background, Canadian citizenship, and embrace of the Canadian flag following his victory raise all kinds of questions

about skin colour, immigration, and identity; and his more recent participation in kabbadi with South Asian Canadians highlights the complexity and diversity of racial and ethnic relations in Canada.

THE CHALLENGES OF RACIAL AND ETHNIC RELATIONS IN CANADIAN SPORTS

Many people have concluded that racial and ethnic issues are irrelevant in sports today. They think that playing fields are generally level, barriers to participation have been removed, personal prejudices and stereotypes have been controlled, and long-time patterns of discrimination have been eliminated or are disappearing with each passing year.

This conclusion reflects the positive changes that have occurred over the past fifty years in Canada, but it ignores the challenges that are faced now that some sports are becoming more multiracial and multi-ethnic in terms of participation. It also overlooks the legacy of past problems and how that legacy still influences what happens in sports today. Overall, race and ethnic relations have improved in many sport settings, but sports are far from being a paradise of established racial and ethnic harmony.

Today's challenges related to race and ethnic relations are not the same ones that people faced twenty years ago in sports. Experience has taught us that challenges associated with racial and ethnic relations never disappear once and for all time; they simply change as circumstances change. When one set of problems is solved, the solutions create new situations, which contain new challenges. For example, once racial and ethnic segregation is eliminated, people face the challenge of living, working, and playing together with those who have different experiences and cultures. Meeting this challenge requires more than enforcing rules of fairness and promoting affirmative action. In addition, it involves learning about the perspectives of other people, understanding how they perceive things, and then determining how relationships can be formed and maintained while respecting differences, making compromises, and supporting each other in the pursuit of common goals.

Too many people think in fairy tale terms when it comes to racial and ethnic relations: they believe that, once everyone comes together on the same team, in the same classroom, or the same organization, they will live happily ever after. However, coming together is just the first step in a never-ending process of relationship building. Racial and ethnic diversity brings potential vitality and creativity to a team or group, but this potential does not automatically become reality. It takes awareness, commitment, and work to bring it about.

The following sections deal with three of the major challenges related to racial and ethnic relations in sports today: (1) eliminating racial and ethnic exclusion in sport participation, (2) dealing with and managing racial and ethnic diversity in sports, and (3) integrating positions of power in sport organizations. A final section deals with the prospects for successfully meeting these challenges.

Eliminating Racial and Ethnic Exclusion in Sport Participation

Why are some sports characterized by disproportionately high rates of participation by racial and ethnic minorities, while others have little or no racial or ethnic diversity? One answer to this question is that some teams and leagues have commercial incentives to recruit the best players regardless of race or ethnicity, and they are organized so that diversity does not disrupt existing power relationships or require people in the organization to change their lives in significant ways. For example, forms of discrimination and exclusion in sports are most likely to be challenged and eliminated under the following six conditions (Edwards, 1973):

1. When people with power and control benefit financially if discrimination and exclusion are eliminated
2. When individual performances can be measured precisely and objectively and do not depend primarily on the subjective assessments of scouts and coaches
3. When members of an entire team benefit from the achievements of teammates
4. When superior performances by athletes do not lead to promotions in the organization or control over fellow players
5. When team success does not depend on friendships and off-the-field social relationships between teammates
6. When athletes have little power or authority in the organizational structure of a sport or sport team

Under these six conditions, those who control sport teams can recruit racially and ethnically diverse players without feeling threatened, giving up power and control, or upsetting the existing structure and relationships within the team. Of course, there is no guarantee that policies of discrimination and exclusion will always be eliminated when these conditions exist. Through history, racism and bigotry have been so strong that racial and ethnic barriers were maintained, even when games could be won and money could be made if they were eliminated. Some of these barriers still exist today, although they are more difficult to maintain in the face of increasing concerns about civil rights.

The forms of racial and ethnic exclusion that are most important today occur at the community level, where they are hidden behind policies that tie participation to fees and access to transportation. Some communities claim to have open sport and recreation programmes, when there are few or no facilities in areas where racial and ethnic minorities live and when fees and ready access to transportation are required for participation. This is exacerbated in isolated Northern communities where there may be no facilities and where transportation may mean expensive air fares. Furthermore, as sports are organized by nonprofit and private organizations, there is a tendency for class-based patterns of exclusion to have an impact on some racial and ethnic groups more than others. Even though this form of exclusion is not grounded directly in racial and ethnic discrimination, its effects are much the same as those of past forms of exclusion, and they are more difficult to attack on the grounds that they violate civil rights. Eliminating these forms of exclusion will be one of the most difficult racial and ethnic challenges of this century (Donnelly and Coakley, 2002).

Dealing With and Managing Racial and Ethnic Diversity in Sports

As sports become more global, as teams recruit players from around the world, and as global migration creates pressures to develop racially and ethnically sensitive policies related to all aspects of sports, there will be many new racial and ethnic challenges faced by players, coaches, team administrators, and even spectators. It is naïve to think that the racial and ethnic issues that exist around the world today have no impact on sports or that sports can deal with these issues in ways that eliminate them once and for all time. Sport history in Canada and the United States shows that a host of new challenges were encountered when Jackie Robinson signed with the Brooklyn Dodgers in 1946 and Willie O'Ree signed with the Boston Bruins in 1958.[14] As the first black players in their respective leagues, they faced enormous challenges, but so did their teammates, other players in the leagues, coaches, and fans. Both Robinson and O'Ree had to endure incident after incident of unspeakable racism by opponents, spectators, and racists in the general population. Teammates had to make decisions about if and

how they would support their new teammate. Coaches had to manage a new set of racial dynamics that they had not previously experienced, such as who would be the black players' roommates on road trips and how to deal with players who made racist remarks that could destroy team morale. Fans who had never socialized across racial lines had to deal with supporting an integrated team, and perhaps sitting next to someone from a different race—something they had never done before. Announcers and reporters had to decide how they would report on the black players' experiences—whether they would report on the racism of other players who were fan favourites, or whether they would pretend that race was not a major issue, even though it was.

The outcomes in MLB and the NHL were quite different. Baseball continued to integrate; black (13 percent), Latino (26 percent), and now Japanese (1 percent) players are now well represented in the league (Lapchick and Matthews, 2002), and while racism has not disappeared (e.g., in terms of management opportunities), there has been clear progress. In the NHL, progress has been much slower. Willie O'Ree played in only two games for the Bruins in 1958, and 43 more during the 1960–61 season. In 1977, Tony McKegney was cut by the Birmingham Bulls of the World Hockey Association after season ticket holders complained about having a black player on the team. And in 2003, former NHL goalie John Vanbiesbrouck resigned in disgrace from his position as coach and general manager of the Sault Ste. Marie Greyhounds of the Ontario Hockey League after using the "N" word

---

[14] In the late 1940s, Conn Smythe, owner of the Toronto Maple Leafs, epitomized the casual racism and explicit barriers to black athletes when he was reported to have said, "I would give $10,000 to anyone who could turn Herb Carnegie white." The highly talented Carnegie never had a chance to play in the NHL.

to refer to the nineteen-year-old team captain, Trevor Daley. Black and native players report racist comments at all levels of hockey, and even European players find that they are subject to ethnic abuse. But there are some signs of progress. Although the NHL is still 98 percent white, there are now 14 black players, and several of East Asian heritage; Jarome Iginla was a star at the 2002 men's Olympic hockey tournament; and Anson Carter scored the gold medal winning goal at the 2003 World Hockey Championships. Perhaps Willie O'Ree's current position as Director of Youth Development on the NHL's Diversity Task Force is beginning to have an impact.

This example of just one professional sport is intended to illustrate how racial and ethnic issues are never settled permanently. Issues faced today present new challenges. For example, some NHL hockey coaches have players on their teams from six different national and cultural backgrounds. Many of these players bring potentially disruptive racial and ethnic stereotypes with them, they may speak different languages, and they have different experiences and customs that may be defined as strange by teammates, team staff, and spectators. Translators are now needed on hockey and baseball teams, many players need cultural diversity training, coaches must learn new ways to communicate effectively, and the marketing departments for teams must learn how they can take advantage of racial and ethnic diversity as they market the teams to new groups of potential fans. Ethnic and cultural issues enter into sponsorship considerations and the products sold at games, and cultural and ethnic awareness is an important qualification for employees who handle team advertising and sponsorship deals.

Many sport teams in western Europe also have dealt with diversity issues over the years, but the racial and ethnic tensions that have accompanied high rates of migration from Africa and eastern Europe have recently created new challenges for teams, players, coaches,

and sport organizations. Racial and ethnic issues vary from sport to sport, and they often are connected with related issues of national identity, labour migration, and citizenship status. Populist leaders in some nations have raised questions about allowing immigrants to play on national teams, and some fans have associated players from Africa with social and economic problems in their lives. These issues are not likely to go away anytime soon in Europe, North America, or other parts of the world. Challenges related to managing racial and ethnic relations are here to stay, and they will change over time.

Integrating Positions of Power in Sport Organizations

Despite progressive changes in many sports, the major positions of power and control continue, with a few exceptions, to be held by white men. No racial report card (Lapchick and Matthews, 2002) is available specifically for Canada, so only anecdotal evidence is available.

It seems that U.S. leagues have sometimes found leadership positions for visible minorities in their Canadian branch plants. For example, Cito Gaston managed the Toronto Blue Jays to consecutive World Series wins in the 1990s, and the Montreal Expos had a long-term, and highly respected, Latino manager with Felipe Alou. The short-lived Vancouver Grizzlies of the NBA had African Americans as coach (Sidney Lowe) and President/General Manager (Stu Jackson). The Toronto Raptors also had African Americans in leadership positions— Isiah Thomas was Vice President and General Manager, and Lenny Wilkens was recently the team's coach. In the CFL, African Americans are coaching the Toronto Argonauts (Mike "Pinball" Clemons) and the Saskatchewan Roughriders (Danny Barrett), and another visible minority, Joe Paopao (Samoan heritage), coaches the Ottawa Renegades.

We have noted the ongoing underrepresentation of francophone Canadians in leadership positions in Canadian sports, but there are signs of change in, for example, the NHL, where a number of coaching positions have been taken by francophones in recent years. Of course, francophone Danielle Sauvageau held the highest profile women's leadership position in Canada when she coached the national hockey team to Olympic gold in 2002. However, there has only been one non-white NHL coach: Ted Nolan, a Native Canadian (Ojibway) coached the Buffalo Sabres, and was named Coach of the Year for the 1996–97 season. While opportunities have increased, there are still barriers to be overcome.

Prospects for Change

It is clear that people do not give up racial and ethnic beliefs easily, especially when they come in the form of well-established ideologies rooted deeply in their cultures. Those who have benefited from those ideologies will resist changes in the relationships and social structures that are built on and reinforce their beliefs. This is why certain expressions of racism and ethnic bigotry have remained a part of sports in Canada and other societies.

Sports may bring people together, but they do not automatically lead people to question the way they think about race or ethnicity or the way they relate to those from other racial or ethnic groups. For example, white team owners, general managers, and athletic directors in the United States worked with black athletes for years before they ever hired black coaches, and it took concerted social and legal pressures to force those in power positions to act more affirmatively when it came to their hiring procedures. Blacks are still underrepresented in coaching and administration, because people in power do not easily change the ideologies and social structures that support their power (Shropshire, 1996). Our

purpose here is not to argue that sports are unique when it comes to resistance to progressive changes. In fact, many sport organizations are more progressive than other organizations when it comes to racial and ethnic relations. However, these good things do not happen automatically or as often as many think; nor do changes on the personal level automatically lead to changes on an organizational or institutional level. Challenging the negative personal beliefs of other people is one thing; changing the relationships and social structures that have been built on those beliefs is another thing. Both forms of change are needed, and neither occurs automatically just because sports bring people together in the same locker rooms and stadiums.

For racial and ethnic relations to be improved through sports, those who control sport teams and sport events must make organized, concerted efforts to bring people together in ways that will encourage them to confront and challenge racial and ethnic issues. These efforts must be initiated and supported by all racial and ethnic groups, or else they will fail (Oglesby and Schrader, 2000). Of course, it has never been easy for people to deal with racial and ethnic issues. However, if it could be done in connection with sports, it would be significant, because sports attract so much public attention in societies today.

We need a new vocabulary to deal with the existence of racial and ethnic diversity in social life and to promote affirmative action on both personal and organizational levels. We must get away from the notion that skin colour or ethnicity signifies some sort of biological essence that shapes character and physical abilities. In connection with sports, we must realize that, when we ask questions about so-called racial performance differences, we are merely reproducing a racial ideology that has caused hatred, turmoil, and confusion in much of the world for over two hundred years. Now we must ask questions about how people give meaning to physical and cultural characteristics and then use those meanings as a basis for their thoughts and their relations with others. However, even framing questions this way requires a big shift in the way many people view the world.

Sport leaders at all levels of competition should be encouraged to sponsor training sessions on racial and ethnic diversity. Everyone from team owners and athletic directors to the people in training rooms should attend these sessions. Coaches need them, and so do athletes. Even those who are already sensitive to diversity issues should be made aware that there is a formal commitment in their organizations to acting on those sensitivities. Furthermore, there are always new things to learn about the perspectives of those whose experiences and cultures are different from our own. In fact, when the perspectives of racial and ethnic minorities are not used to guide efforts to make things better in society as a whole, those efforts often fail. When making things better means doing things to fit the interests of those with power and influence, real change is unlikely.

SUMMARY

ARE RACE AND ETHNICITY IMPORTANT IN SPORTS?

Racial and ethnic issues exist in sports, just as they exist in most other spheres of social life. As people watch, play, and talk about sports, they often take into account ideas about skin colour and ethnicity. The meanings that are given to skin colour and ethnic background have an impact on access to sport participation and the decisions that people make about sports in their lives.

Race refers to a category of people identified through a classification system based on meanings given to physical traits among humans; *ethnicity* refers to collections of people identified in terms of their shared cultural heritage. Racial and ethnic minorities are populations that have endured sys-

tematic forms of discrimination in a society. The concept of race has a complex history.

Racism, which involves discrimination or unequal treatment on the basis of physical traits, takes different forms and exists at different levels in society: individual, institutional, and structural. Ideas about race often take the form of race logic, which people use to identify and make sense of racial differences. Race logic, like other social constructions, changes over time as ideas and relationships change. However, over the past century, race logic has led many people to assume that there are important biological and even cognitive differences between the races and that these differences explain the success, or lack of success, of non-whites in sports.

To some degree, race logic has influenced how African Americans and many blacks around the world view their own physical abilities, how people identify black males who excel in sports, and how some whites make sport participation decisions. Race, gender, and class relations in American society have combined to create a context in which black males emphasize a personal presentation of self that has been described as "cool pose," or a stylized persona that has not only added to the commodity value of the black male body in sports but also enabled some black athletes to use race logic to intimidate opponents, especially white opponents, in sports.

The sport participation patterns among francophones, Native Canadians, and other ethnic and visible minority peoples have their own histories. Combinations of various ideological, historical, economic, and political factors have influenced those histories. However, the sport participation of any minority group usually occurs under terms set by the dominant group in a community or society. Minority groups seldom have been able to use sports to challenge the power and privilege of the dominant group, even though individual minority-group members may experience great personal success in sports.

The fact that some sports have histories of racially and ethnically mixed participation does not mean that racial and ethnic problems have been eliminated in those sports. In fact, harmonious racial and ethnic relations never occur automatically in any setting. Furthermore, harmony is never established once and for all time. As current problems are confronted and solved, new relationships and new challenges develop. This means that racial and ethnic issues must be given regular attention in order to anticipate and meet challenges successfully. Success also depends largely on whether members of the dominant group see the value in racial and ethnic diversity and are committed to facing diversity issues alongside those who are different from them.

Sports certainly are not free of problems related to racial and ethnic relations. However, it is important to acknowledge that, despite problems, sports can be sites for challenging race logic and transforming racial and ethnic relations. This happens only if people in sports plan strategies to encourage critical awareness of race logic and ethnic prejudices. This awareness is required to eliminate forms of racial and ethnic exclusion in sports, deal with and manage racial and ethnic diversity in sports, and integrate racial and ethnic minorities into the power structures of sport organizations. Without this awareness, these and other problems will cause conflict in the future.

SUGGESTED READINGS

Bale, J., and J. Sang, eds. 1996. *Kenyan running: Movement culture, geography, and global change.* London: Frank Cass (uses a combination of philosophy, history, sociology, and geography to examine myths around Kenyan running; views running as a body culture that is best understood in the context of colonialism, modern globalized sports, and the Kenyan nation-state).

Bretón, M., and J. L. Villegas. 1999. *Away games: The life and times of a Latin American baseball player.* Albuquerque: University of New Mexico Press (two journalists tell the story of a young player from the Dominican Republic; they provide detailed information about the experiences of Latino athletes who dream of playing big-time sports, are hired by U.S. sport organizations, deal with the challenges of working in U.S. culture, and then face the harsh realities of life after sports).

Carnegie, H. 1997. *A fly in a pail of milk: The Herb Carnegie story.* Oakville, ON: Mosaic Press; O'Ree, W. 2002. *The autobiography of Willie O'Ree: Hockey's black pioneer.* Toronto: Key Porter Books (Herb Carnegie was called "the best that never played" in the NHL, and Willie O'Ree broke the colour bar in the NHL; at one level, these are standard autobiographies of hockey players, but, at another level, they present disturbing stories of the racism experienced by Carnegie and O'Ree).

Kidd, B. 1980. *Tom Longboat.* Toronto: Fitzhenry & Whiteside (a short, illustrated, and accessible biography of Longboat that should be read in conjunction with Kidd's [1983] article in order to understand the achievements of this Onondagan athlete, and the racist context in which they were accomplished).

Lavoie, M. (1998). *Désavantage numérique: Les Francophones dans la LNH.* Hull: Vent D'Ouest (explores in detail the underrepresentation of francophones in the NHL, providing excellent data and convincing analyses).

Paraschak, V. 1997. Variations in race relations: Sporting events for native peoples in Canada. *Sociology of Sport Journal* 14 (1): 1–21 (analysis of native sporting practices in four parts of Canada; results show that these practices cannot be understood apart from the patterns of race relations that frame the everyday lives of native peoples).

Zeman, B. 1988. *To run with Longboat: Twelve stories of Indian athletes in Canada.* Edmonton: GMS Ventures (these stories of Native Canadian athletes, in sports ranging from running to ski jumping, give a vivid accounts of successes experienced and problems encountered as athletes from a minority culture participate in the dominant culture's power and performance sports).

WEBSITE RESOURCES

Note: Websites often change. The following URLs were current when this book was printed. Please check our website (www.mcgrawhill.ca/college/coakley) for updates and additions.

www.aboriginalsportscircle.ca (covers most issues related to First Nations, Inuit, and Métis sports in Canada; the Aboriginal Sport Circle links native sport associations and also promotes sports for native peoples)

www.sportinsociety.org/rgrc.html (see the *Racial and Gender Report Card*—a comprehensive research document that analyzes hiring practices in the NBA, the NFL, Major League Baseball, the NHL, Major League Soccer, the Women's NBA, the NCAA and its member institutions, and major Olympic sports organizations in the United States)

www.sportinsociety.org/ptw.html (Project TEAMWORK encourages sensitivity to racial, ethnic, and gender issues, it is a diversity awareness and conflict resolution program composed of a multiracial, mixed-gender team of former professional and collegiate athletes trained to work with middle and high school students to combat all forms of discrimination and teach practical conflict resolution skills)

http://racerelations.about.com/cs/raceandsports (a general site with links to articles on diversity and other sources that cover race and ethnicity-related issues in sports)

(Laura Robinson)

Social Class

Do money and power matter in sports?

Cost restricts access to recreational activities for low-income families. Less than half of low-income families with children spend money on user fees for recreational activities, compared to 72% of high-income families.

—**The Progress of Canada's Children,** *Canadian Council on Social Development* **(1998)**

High performance sport is a demanding undertaking in a ruthlessly competitive international environment....It involves...a more than full-time commitment without ever guaranteeing a payoff in the end. It is not a job that just anyone can do; there are few jobs that are more demanding.

—**Rob Beamish and Jan Borowy, authors (1988)**

We are already in a situation where we are expecting children to play games they cannot afford to watch.

—**Harry Edwards, sociologist/social activist (2000)**

 Online Learning Centre Resources

Visit *Sports in Society's* Online Learning Centre at **www.mcgrawhill.ca/college/coakley** for additional information and study material for this chapter.

People like to think that sports transcend issues of money, power, and economic inequalities. They see sports as open to everyone, watch many sports on "free" television, and define success on the field in terms of ability and hard work. However, formally organized sports depend on material resources. The fates of teams, events, and media coverage rest in the hands of wealthy and powerful individuals and corporations. More than ever before, it takes money to play sports and receive the coaching needed to develop sport skills. Ticket prices are expensive, and spectators often are segregated by social class in the stadium: the wealthy and well-connected sit in club seats and luxury boxes, while others are seated in various sections, depending on their ability to pay for premium tickets or buy season tickets. It even takes money to watch sports on television when events air on subscriber cable (the way most Canadians receive their TV signals), digital, satellite, or pay-per-view formats. This means that sports and sport participation are connected with the distribution of economic, political, and social resources in society. Money and power do matter in sports.

Many people also believe that sports are avenues for economic success for people from all social classes. Rags-to-riches stories frequently are told in sport discourse. However, these beliefs and stories detract from how sports can and sometimes do subvert economic success, and how sports perpetuate existing economic inequalities in society.

This chapter deals with matters of money and wealth, as well as with issues related to social class and socioeconomic mobility. Our discussion focuses on the following questions:

1. What is meant by *social class* and *class relations*?
2. How do social class and class relations influence sports and sport participation?
3. Are sports open and democratic in the provision of economic and career opportunities?
4. Does playing sports contribute to occupational success and social mobility among former athletes?

SOCIAL CLASS AND CLASS RELATIONS

Social class and the related concepts of social stratification, socioeconomic status, and life chances are important concepts in the study of society and social life. They are important because economic resources are related to power in society, and economic inequalities influence nearly all aspects of people's lives.

Social class refers to categories of people who share a position in society based on a combination of their income, wealth, education, occupation, and social connections. People in a particular social class also share similar **life chances**—that is, they share opportunities to achieve success and gain economic power. Social classes exist in all industrial societies, because there are economic inequalities and differences in life chances among people in those societies.

Social stratification is the concept used to refer to structured forms of economic inequalities that are part of the organization of everyday social life. In other words, people from lower-social-class backgrounds have fewer opportunities to achieve success and gain economic power than people from upper social classes. Children born into wealthy, powerful, and well-connected families are in better positions to become wealthy, powerful, and well-connected adults than children born into poor families that lack influence and social networks connecting them with educational and career opportunities.

Most of us are very aware of economic inequalities in society, but there are few public discussions about the impact of social class on our views of ourselves and others, our social relationships, and our everyday lives (Perrucci and Wysong, 1999). In other words, we do not often discuss **class relations**—that is, we do not discuss the many ways that social class is incorporated into social processes in society. In schools and the media, we hear about the importance of equal opportunities, but we learn little about how people in upper socioeconomic classes use their income, wealth, and power to maintain privileged positions in society and pass that privilege from one generation to the next. We hear about those who have moved up and out of the lower socioeconomic classes through hard work and strong character, and about new millionaires, but we learn little about the oppressive effects of poverty and the limited opportunities available to those who lack economic resources, access to good education, and well-placed social connections.

People in many postindustrial societies are often uncomfortable with critical discussions of social class and class relations (Sage, 1998b). The myth of equality in many democratic societies (the idea that "we are all middle class now") discourages such discussions, even though we may be aware of class and class relations in our lives. This is especially true when it comes to sports and sport participation.

The discussion of social class and class relations in this chapter is grounded in critical theories. The focus is on how economic inequality is maintained in society, how it serves the interests of those with wealth and economic power, and how it affects what happens in sports and the lives of people associated with sports.[1]

SPORTS AND ECONOMIC INEQUALITY

Money and economic power exert significant influence on the meaning, organization, and purpose of sports in society (Gruneau, 1999). Many people believe that sports and sport participation are open to all people and that inequalities related to money, position, and influence do not spill over into the organized games we play and watch. Although this may be true in a few informally organized sports, it is *not true* in the case of most formally organized sports.

Formally organized sports could not be developed, scheduled, or maintained without economic resources (see chapters 1 and 3). Those who control money and economic power use their financial clout to organize and sponsor sports. As they do so, they give preference to sport forms that reflect and maintain their own values and interests. For example, the wealthy aristocrats who organized the Olympic Movement and sponsored the modern Olympic Games established a definition of *amateur* that privileged athletes from wealthy backgrounds around the world. This definition excluded athletes from working-class backgrounds,[2] who could afford to train only if they used their sport skills to help them earn a living. The definition of *amateur* has been revised over the years, so that more people are able to participate in sports. However, money and economic power now operate in different ways as powerful corporations use the Olympics to expand profits and market share by linking their logos and products to athletes and global sport images. Social class and class relations have been expressed in sports in many ways during the past century.

Elite and powerful groups in society always have had considerable influence over what types of activities will be organized as sports and how those sports will be defined, organized, and played. Even when grass-roots games and physical activities have become formally organized as sports, they have not been widely sponsored or promoted unless they could be used to promote the interests and ideology of those with money and economic power in society. This is why it is

---

[1]For informative discussions of social theories and the analysis of class and class relations in society, see Gruneau (1999) and Sugden and Tomlinson (2000).

[2] In Canada, the definition extended to Native Canadians when, in the late nineteenth century, native lacrosse players were arbitrarily designated as professionals.

(Jay Coakley)

(CP/Jonathan Hayward)

The inequality of social classes is often reflected in sports. Upper-income groups have used certain sports to maintain exclusive lifestyles emphasizing consumption and competition. When sports are connected to the lifestyles of particular status groups, they reproduce social class differences rather than equal opportunities.

important that we understand the dynamics of class relations when we study sports.

The Dynamics of Class Relations

One way to understand the dynamics of class relations in connection with sports is to think about how age relations are involved in sports and sport participation. Consider this: even though children are capable of creating their own games, adults have intervened and developed youth sport programmes. These programmes are organized around the ideas and

orientations that adults think should be emphasized in the lives of children and in social life generally. As noted in chapter 5, adults possess the *resources* to develop, schedule, and maintain organized youth programmes that reflect what they think children should be doing and learning as they play. This does not mean that children do not enjoy adult-controlled sports, but it does mean that their enjoyment occurs in a framework that legitimizes and reproduces the power of adults over the lives of children.

When children's behaviour in organized sports deviates from adult expectations, adults use their power to force compliance or convince children that it is in their best interest to play "the right way." When children comply and meet adult expectations, the adults say they possess "character" and reward them accordingly. This is why many people perceive autocratic coaches as heroes; these coaches reaffirm the cultural belief that the world is a better place when adults have full control over young people and when young people consent to that control. In this way, sport reproduces a hierarchical form of age relations, in which adult power and privilege are defined as natural and necessary aspects of social life.

Class relations work in similar ways. People in the upper social classes have the resources to organize and promote sports that support their ideas about how social life should be organized. For example, they are able to play sports in exclusive clubs to emphasize the idea that wealthy and influential people are special in society and deserve special places to play sports. They also are able to create and sponsor forms of organized sports that reinforce ideologies supportive of existing economic relationships and organization in society. For example, popular spectator sports around the world now are presented in ways that emphasize competition, individualism, highly specialized skills, the use of technology, and dominance over opponents; they are *not* presented in ways that emphasize partnership, sharing, open participation, nurturance, and mutual support. This ties sports to an ideology that stresses individual achievement through competition, in which participants use technology and equipment to outscore and dominate others.

This ideology gives rise to a form of **class logic** in which economic success (winning) becomes proof of individual ability, worth, and character. People who use this class logic to interpret their own lives often set out on an endless quest for individual economic achievement. They measure success in terms of how many "things" they can acquire and how they rank relative to their peers when it comes to economic worth. Things and wealth become symbols of their identity, status,

and moral worth. A key component of this class logic is illustrated by a popular locker-room slogan often repeated by coaches in their pep talks: "When you're satisfied with your performance, you're finished." This privileges high-performance athletes *and* renders all claims about achieving "excellence" problematic. Since there is no set measure of excellence, it can never be achieved; anyone who thinks they have achieved excellence in sports is soon reminded that they have not when someone comes along who is more "excellent" (Kidd, 1988). Class logic stresses that achievement is measured in terms of a never-ending quest to improve the "bottom line." This way of thinking drives market economies and enables people with wealth and power in those economies to preserve and extend their resources.

When people in a society adopt a class logic that says "You get what you deserve, and you deserve what you get," wealthy and powerful people tend to be defined as worthy winners, while the poor and powerless tend to be defined as lazy losers. This clearly works to the advantage of those who have more wealth and economic power than others, and it promotes the idea that economic inequality in society is necessary for society to operate efficiently (an idea that is fundamental to functionalist theory; see chapter 2). This idea is promoted even further when those with resources sponsor sports. People in society learn that, if they want the enjoyment of playing and watching sports, they must look to the wealthy and powerful, and to various levels of government, for support and sponsorship. When support and sponsorship comes, people tend to accept the ideological strings attached to it. This, of course, is part of the process of how sports are tied to class relations in society.

Class Relations and Those Who Have the Power in Sports

Sport decisions are made at many levels, from neighbourhood youth sport programmes to the International Olympic Committee. Although scholars who study sports in society are concerned with identifying those who exercise power in various settings, they usually do not develop lists that rank powerful people in sports. But such lists do exist. For example, the *Globe and Mail*, often considered to be Canada's national newspaper, has published an annual list of Canada's sports leaders for several years. The list appears at the end of the calendar year, and is based on several sportswriters' assessments of which people during the year have been the leading figures in Canadian sports (based on factors such as influence and newsworthiness). Non-Canadians are sometimes included (e.g., NHL Commissioner Gary Bettman), but they are included because of their influence on Canadian sports.

Table 10.1 identifies the twenty-five people for 2002, along with their ranking in 2001. Because the list usually includes people who have been in the news, the list varies quite a lot from year to year; in 2002, only six were also ranked in 2001. (Those from the 2001 list not ranked in 2002 are footnoted in the table.) The 2002 list includes twenty-seven people (twenty-six in 2001) because some are ranked together as partners. The list includes four women (four in 2001), two persons of colour (one in 2001), three francophone Canadians (four in 2001), one corporation (zero in 2001), and twenty white men (twenty in 2001). All four women on the list, and both persons of colour (both men), are active athletes (in 2001, one of the women was a coach, another a media executive); four of the white males are active athletes, although one is also part-owner of a team. Of the remaining seventeen white males (Mario Lemieux counts as both owner and player), three are owners or part-owners of professional sport franchises (five in 2001), one is the largest owner of thoroughbred race tracks in North America, four are executives or management at professional sport franchises (two in 2001), three are NHL executives (including the commissioner) and one is head of the NHL Players' Association (just Bettman and Goodenow in 2001). The list is

completed with the CEO of the Canadian Olympic Committee, the CEO of the Vancouver/Whistler 2010 Winter Olympics bid, an NHL players' agent, the CEO of cable sports network TSN, and a hockey broadcaster. The list is most striking for who is absent—who is not newsworthy, or does not have power and influence in Canadian sports.

If this list is compared with the annual *Sporting News* list, in the U.S., of the 100 most powerful people in sports (www.sportingnews.com), there are some important differences. The U.S. list focuses more on power and influence than on newsworthiness, so fewer athletes are in the top 25. The U.S. list is also a sobering reminder of the power and influence of U.S. and international corporations on the world of sports. However, there are also some striking similarities between the U.S. and Canadian lists (see the Online Learning Centre for Jay Coakley's analysis of the *Sporting News* list). It is clear that, in addition to wealth and control of the resources of major corporations, leagues, and franchises, dominant forms of gender logic and race logic also have an effect on who has power in sports.

Those who control economic resources in Canada and around the world make decisions that influence the visibility of sports, the ways in which they are organized, and the images and meanings associated with them. While these decisions do not ignore the interests of people in Canada and around the world, their main purpose is to establish and expand the power and profitability of the organizations represented by the decision makers. Therefore, sports tend to revolve around the meanings and orientations valued by those with economic resources and power while providing enjoyable and entertaining experiences to people around the world.

This is why some critical theorists have described sports as cultural vehicles for developing ideological "outposts" in the minds of people around the world: when transnational corporations become the primary providers of popular pleasure and entertainment, they are able to

Table 10.1   The *Globe and Mail's* 25 leading figures in Canadian sports, 2002 (6 December)

Rank/Name	Position/Organization	2001 Rank[a]
1 Wayne Gretzky	Part-Owner, Phoenix Coyotes, NHL;	
	Executive Director, Canadian Olympic men's hockey team	1
2 Jamie Salé and David Pelletier	Pairs skaters, Canadian Olympic team	
	Skate/Patinage Canada	3
3 Skip Prince	President, Montreal Alouettes, CFL	NR
4 Andy Van Hellemond		
and Colin Campbell	Executives, National Hockey League, Toronto office	NR
5 Beckie Scott	Cross-country skier, Canadian Olympic team, Ski Canada	NR
6 Hayley Wickenheiser	Hockey player, Canadian Olympic team,	
	Hockey Canada	NR
7 Gary Bettman	Commissioner, National Hockey League	7
8 Hugh Campbell	President and CEO, Edmonton Eskimos, CFL	NR
9 Steve Nash	Basketball player, Dallas Mavericks,	
	NBA/Canadian Olympic team	NR
10 Jarome Iginla	Hockey player, Calgary Flames, NHL/Canadian Olympic team	NR
11 Frank Stronach	Race horse and race track owner, Magna International	22
12 Brad Watters	Owner, Toronto Rock/Ottawa Rebel, NLL;	
	Ottawa Renegades, CFL	NR
13 Dan Thompson (deceased)	CEO, Canadian Olympic Committee	NR
14 Bob Goodenow	Executive Director, NHL Players' Association	15
15 J.P. Ricciardi	General Manager, Toronto Blue Jays, MLB	NR
16 Keith Pelley	President, TSN	NR
17 Mario Lemieux	Owner and player, Pittsburgh Penguins,	
	NHL/Canadian Olympic team	9
18 Jack Poole	CEO, Vancouver/Whistler 2010 Winter Olympics bid	NR
19 Don Meehan	Agent, NHL players and Ron MacLean	NR
20 Lennox Lewis	Professional boxer	NR
21 Jose Theodore	Hockey player, Montreal Canadiens, NHL	NR
22 Patrick LaForge	President and CEO, Edmonton Oilers, NHL	NR
23 Christine Sinclair	Soccer player, Canadian Soccer Association/	
	Under-19 national team	NR
24 Ron MacLean	Broadcaster, CBC *Hockey Night in Canada*	NR
25 Roots Canada	Clothing manufacturer and Olympic team outfitter	NR

[a] Ranked in 2001 list, but not 2002:

Players (rank)	Organization	Owners/Executives (rank)	Organization
Vince Carter (2)	Toronto Raptors	Richard Peddie (10)	Maple Leafs Sports
Larry Walker (5)	Colorado Rockies		and Entertainment
Mike Weir (13)	PGA	Mike Lysko (11)	CFL Commissioner
Patrick Roy (19)	Colorado Avalanche	George Gillett, Jr. (16)	Montreal Canadiens
Lori Kane (20)	LPGA	Paul Godfrey (23)	Toronto Blue Jays
Coaches (rank)	**Organization**	Glen Grunwald (24)	Toronto Raptors
Pat Quinn (14)	Toronto Maple Leafs/		
	Canadian Olympic team	**Media (rank)**	**Organization**
Lori Nichol (17)	Figure skating	Ted Rogers (6)	Rogers Cable
Wally Buono (21)	Calgary Stampeders	Rick Brace (8)	CTV Netstar
			Communications
Owners/Executives (rank)	**Organization**	Nancy Lee (12)	CBC Sports
Larry Tannenbaum (4)	Maple Leafs Sports		
	and Entertainment	**Agent (rank)**	
Ted Rogers (6)	Toronto Blue Jays	Gordon Kirke (25)	
		Politician (rank)	
		Denis Coderre, Secretary of State for Amateur Sport (18)	

Source: "The Top 25—Canada's Sports Leaders 2002" December 6, 2002 by James Christie and William Houston. Reprinted with permission from *The Globe and Mail*.

use pleasure and entertainment to deliver many other messages about what should be important in people's lives. This is a clear manifestation of class relations at work.

Sports as a Vehicle for Transferring Public Money to Wealthy Individuals and Private Corporations

The dynamics of class relations sometimes have ironic twists. This is certainly true in connection with the ways in which sports have been used as vehicles for transferring public monies collected through taxes into the hands of wealthy individuals and corporations in the private sector. For example, Andrew Zimbalist, a sports economist at Smith College in the U.S., points out that, since 1990, the four major sport leagues in North America have built seventy-two new stadiums and arenas costing US$19.4 billion. He also notes that 66 percent of this cost was paid from public funds (cited by McGregor, 2003). Most of this construction has taken place in the United States, although there is evidence that U.S. cities are beginning to learn the lesson that Canada learned in the 1970s and 1980s. The enormous cost overruns associated with construction of the Montreal Olympic Stadium and Toronto SkyDome led to the end of significant corporate welfare for professional sport arena and stadium construction. While governments have shown an inclination to use public funds to support professional sports, public opinion has been dead set against it, as then Industry Minister John Manley discovered in 2000. He first acceded to Canadian NHL teams' requests for public subsidies, and then withdrew the offer within a few days because of the public outcry. The majority of the professional sport arenas built in Canada since 1990 (e.g., the Corel Centre in Ottawa, GM Place in Vancouver, the Air Canada Centre in Toronto) were, for the most part, financed privately.

However, in Canada, there are a number of other ways of transferring public money into private hands in professional sports, including the following:

- *National unity subsidies:* After the nearly successful separation referendum in Quebec in 1995, the federal government established a national unity programme in 1997 that involved, in part, displaying the Canada wordmark and the Maple Leaf flag in as many public places as possible. Events that received federal funding were required to display the Canada wordmark, and subsidies were offered to events for patriotic displays. Among the beneficiaries of this C$40 million per year programme, run by the Ministry of Public Works, were the Canadian NHL teams, which received approximately C$1 million a year to show the Canada wordmark at games, and the CFL which received C$1 million to have Maple Leaf flags displayed on football players' helmets. Funds were also paid to auto races, such as the Formula 1 Grand Prix in Montreal. The terms of the programme were changed in December 2002, following evidence of misuse of funds. The Ministry will now only finance non-commercial events.
- *Tax breaks:* The federal and provincial governments have devised various ways to benefit professional sports through tax breaks. For example, in the last days of Mike Harris's premiership in Ontario, he secretly signed a C$10 million tax break for each of the two NHL teams in the province. Rod Bryden's attempt to create a tax relief form of ownership for the NHL Ottawa Senators in 2002, which received approval from the Canada Customs and Revenue Agency, would have meant the withdrawal of C$100 million from federal income (which means either cuts to federal programmes, or an increase in other forms of taxes). Fortunately, the deal fell through at the last minute. Professional sports also benefit from the much abused entertainment tax write-off—businesses and corporations receive a 50 percent tax break on

season tickets and luxury boxes, which means that they are more likely to lease luxury boxes and pay the ticket prices being charged by the leagues and events. Alberta's plan to use provincial lottery funds to support the province's two NHL teams, while not a tax break, removes money from public revenue to support wealthy owners and well-paid players.

- *Hosting major events:* Perhaps the most significant public subsidy to professional sports occurs as a result of hosting major events such as the Olympics, Commonwealth Games, Pan American Games, Jeux de la Francophonie, the World Track and Field Championships, the World Junior Hockey Championships, other world championships, FISU Games, and even Canada Games. It is now widely recognized that hosting a Summer or Winter Olympics is very popular with the construction and development industries in the city and country where the Games are held. For example, when Atlanta hosted the Olympics in 1996, the major payoffs associated with the new construction and increased property values went directly to a small group of real estate developers and major corporations, which were in a position to use the millions of dollars of public money invested in the Atlanta area to their benefit. At the conclusion of the Games, major new facilities were turned over to the owners of professional sport franchises in Atlanta. The lesson of Atlanta was, perhaps, first learned in North America at the Montreal Olympics in 1976, when an enormously expensive Olympic Stadium came to be used by the Expos of MLB and the Alouettes of the CFL—the owners only responsible for rent, not construction costs. Two years later, the Commonwealth Games in Edmonton resulted in the construction of Commonwealth Stadium (to be used subsequently by the Eskimos of the CFL) and the arena now known as the Skyreach Centre, where the NHL Oilers play (it is not clear

why a hockey arena was built for the Commonwealth Games other than to take advantage of public funds available for a Commonwealth Games to support an NHL team). The Calgary Saddledome (now called the Pengrowth Centre), built for Olympic ice hockey, was used by the Calgary Flames of the NHL even before the 1988 Olympics. Stadium and arena upgrades are also publicly funded for hosting events, but provide a long-term, low-cost benefit to professional sports. For example, Winnipeg hosted the Pan Am Games in 1999, and Edmonton hosted the World Championships in Athletics (track and field) in 2001. In both cases, the stadia primarily used by the local CFL teams—the Blue Bombers and the Eskimos respectively—were upgraded at public cost.[3] The upgrades included construction of a Jumbotron in each stadium which, in the case of Edmonton, was one of the first major expenditures of the World Championship organizing committee, and was being used by the Eskimos two years before the event. Hamilton is currently bidding to host the Commonwealth Games in 2010, and Vancouver/Whistler will host the Winter Olympic Games in 2010. Hamilton is expecting to receive C$80 million in federal funds if the bid is successful (money that will certainly be used to help upgrade or replace Ivor Wynne Stadium, home of the Tiger-Cats of the CFL). Vancouver/Whistler expects to receive C$600 million in federal and provincial funds now that its bid is successful (some of which is likely to be used to support the upgrading of Vancouver's professional sport facilities).

---

[3] In the case of Edmonton, the federal (C$40 million), provincial (Alberta, C$40 million), and municipal (Edmonton, C$6 million) governments contributed C$86 million toward the cost of hosting the World Championships in Athletics. The annual budget for Sport Canada, supporting all "amateur" high-performance sports in Canada, is currently some C$77 million.

"Oh sure, they told us that 'sports unite ALL the classes,' when they wanted us to PAY for this place!"

As they sit in the distant bleachers and spot wealthy people in luxury boxes and club seats, these fans discover that the dynamics of social class operate in ways that privilege some people more than others. To say that "sports unite the social classes" is to ignore these dynamics that often separate people from different social class backgrounds.

Studies indicate that middle- and lower-income individuals pay disproportionately more to support these various subsidies, and, for the last decade, this corporate welfare has been occurring at a time when there have been numerous cuts to health care, education, and the social services relied on by low-income and unemployed individuals. Of course, there is a small trickle-down benefit to the community in terms of jobs (often part-time and/or low-paying; see the Online Learning Centre for a feature on jobs created by sports) and trade for local businesses. But the average taxpayers who help to fund the Olympics and other events will never see the benefits enjoyed by those whose power and wealth gave them the ability to take advantage of public investments. Even the facilities that are constructed are of much more benefit to professional and high-performance sports than they are to the community in terms of public access. The highly touted Calgary Olympic Park (C$9 admission fee even to go jogging or cross-country skiing) and Calgary Olympic Oval, while open for public recreation, are not easily accessible to low-income people.

As journalist Andrew Jennings has noted, the emerging pattern in connection with hosting the Olympics is that "the IOC will take its profits, the sponsors and television networks will make theirs and the local taxpayers will foot the bill" (1996a, p. 293). Helen Lenskyj (2000, 2002), of the Ontario Institute for Studies in Education, has addressed these issues specifically with regard to the Sydney Olympics and the two Toronto Olympic bids. And the Toronto-based anti-Olympic bid group, Bread not Circuses, has compiled an impressive list of the financial and other problems associated with hosting major games. This method of transferring public money to powerful individuals and corporations in the private sector is another clear manifestation of class relations at work in connection with sports.

SOCIAL CLASS AND SPORT PARTICIPATION PATTERNS

In all societies, social class and class relations influence who plays, who watches, who consumes information about sports, and what information is available in the mainstream media. Involvement with sports goes hand in hand with money, power, and privilege. Organized sports are a luxury item in the economies of many nations, and they are most prevalent in wealthy nations where people have discretionary money and time (see chapter 11).

In all societies, it is people in high-income, high-education, and high-status occupational groups who have the highest rates of active sport participation, attendance at sport events, and even watching of sports on television

(Donnelly and Harvey, 1999). This also has an effect on who becomes a high-performance athlete. Bruce Kidd (1995) notes that Olympic athletes and officials have always come from the most privileged groups in society.

The social class limitations on involvement were recognized early in the direct involvement of the federal government in Canadian sports. John Munro's *A Proposed Sport Policy for Canadians* (1970) was one of the first statements to use the sporting analogy that later came to characterize the difference between equality and equity:

> We must face the fact that the opportunity for involvement in sports and recreation is extremely unequal between the socio-economic classes within our population....It's only fair, just as a dash [sprint] in a track meet is only fair, that everyone has the same starting line, and the same distance to run. Unfortunately, in terms of facilities, coaching, promotion and programming, the sports scene today resembles a track on which some people have 25 yards to run, some 50, some 100, and some as much as a mile or more. (Munro, 1970, pp. 4–5)

Unfortunately, little has changed in Canadian sports, and two studies, some fifteen years apart, of high-performance athletes show this. A study of Canada Winter Games athletes in 1971 (Gruneau and Albinson, 1976), and a study of Canadian national team athletes in 1986 (Beamish, 1990), showed that access to high-performance sports had become even more limited by social class. Rick Gruneau of Simon Fraser University found that, in 1971, 42 percent of the fathers of Winter Games athletes came from the highest occupational levels in Canada (compared to 17 percent of the total population). By 1986, Rob Beamish of Queen's University found that 68 percent of the fathers of national team athletes came from the highest occupational categories. This pattern also exists in high-performance sports in countries around the world, except for those where there is direct state support of national team athletes (e.g., China and Cuba).

Even the health and fitness movement, which often has been described as a grass-roots phenomenon in Canada and the U.S., is confined primarily to people who have higher-than-average incomes and educations and work in professional or managerial occupations. People in lower-income groups may do physical labour, but they do not run, bicycle, or swim as often as their high-income counterparts. Nor do they play as many organized sports on their lunch hours, after work, on weekends, or during vacations. This pattern holds true throughout the life course, for younger and older age groups, among men and women, among various racial and ethnic groups, and among people with disabilities: social class is related strongly to participation, regardless of the category of people in question (see Donnelly and Harvey, 1999).

The Canadian evidence in support of this is overwhelming. For example, table 10.2 shows the Canadian Council on Social Development's (2001) analyses of the Statistics Canada National Longitudinal Survey of Children and Youth (NLSCY for 1994 and 1996), which reported the relationship between children's recreation participation and family income of those above and below the low-income cut-off (LICO).

When the data are analyzed by family income quintiles (separating families into five equal groups from the lowest 20 percent family income to the highest 20 percent), in all cases, the relationships are linear: the more a family earns, the more likely its children are to participate in sports and physical activity. Preliminary analyses of the 1998 NLSCY (Statistics Canada, 2001) show no significant change in these findings:

- Children who were least likely to participate in organized activities were those in lower-income families, those with very young parents, those whose primary caregiver had less than a high school education, and those in single-parent families.
- Younger children in the lowest-income quintile were three times more likely to have never participated in organized activities (sports, music, art, or clubs) than children in the highest quintile.

Table 10.2   Recreation participation for children from families above and below the poverty line

Participation	Above LICO[a]%	Below LICO%
Participation in sports with a coach one or more times a week	59.1%	37.1%
Participation in dance/gymnastics one or more times a week	31.5%	21.1%
Participation in community clubs (e.g., Guides/Scouts, Boys and Girls, 4H)	26.0%	22.0%
Attendance at overnight camp	22.8%	17.6%
Attendance at day camp	34.5%	21.8%

[a] The LICO is not strictly a poverty line, but it is often taken as a measure to indicate level of disposable income; the cut-off is based on individuals or families who spend 20% or more than the Canadian average of their income on food shelter and clothing.

Source: Statistics Canada National Longitudinal Survey of Children and Youth (NLSCY) for 1994 and 1996.

- Younger children whose parents had less than a high school education were more than twice as likely to have never participated in organized activities than those children whose parents had higher education.

These general survey findings are confirmed by more focused community studies (e.g., Hughes and Griffiths, 1992; Offord, Lipman, and Duku, 1998).

Participation patterns also may be explained in terms of class relations. The long-term impact of economic inequality on people's lives has led to connections between certain sports and the lifestyles of people with differing amounts of wealth and power (Bourdieu, 1986; Laberge and Sankoff, 1988). For the most part, these connections reflect patterns of sponsorship and access to opportunities for involvement. For example, wealthy people have lifestyles that routinely include participation in golf, tennis, skiing, sailing, and other sports that are self-funded and played at exclusive clubs and resorts. These sports often involve the use of expensive facilities, equipment, and/or clothing, and they have come to be associated with "class" as people with money and power define it. The people who engage in these sports usually have considerable control over their work lives, so they have the freedom to take the time needed to participate, or they can combine participation with their work and even have someone else pay for it, in some cases!

The lifestyles of middle-income and working-class people, on the other hand, tend to include sports that by tradition are free and open to the public, sponsored by public funds, or available through public schools. When these sports involve the use of expensive equipment or clothing, participation occurs in connection with some form of financial sacrifice: buying a motocross bike means not taking a vacation this year and working overtime for a couple of months.

The lifestyles of low-income people and those living in poverty seldom involve regular forms of sport participation. This is exacerbated by the fact that the majority of people living below the poverty line are women, who have not had the same level of access to sports as men. Life chances vary by social class, and, when people spend much of their time and energy coping with the challenges of everyday life, they have few resources left to develop sport participation traditions as part of their lifestyles. Spending money to play or watch sports is a luxury few can afford. Furthermore, when hard work has not made them winners in the economy, they may have little interest in playing or watching sports popularly associated with an ideology claiming that poverty is associated with laziness and a lack of character. At the same time, those

Children in suburban areas often have safe streets on which they can play. The boys in this cul-de-sac have access to many portable basketball goals, and they often recruit friends to play full court games in the street. Of course, they also play roller hockey, soccer, baseball, and football, and they water ski behind one of the boats owned by families in the neighbourhood. They grow up with opportunities to play many different sports. (Jay Coakley)

who are successful in the economy are so supportive of that ideology that they are willing to spend thousands of dollars each year to keep their club memberships, season tickets, and luxury boxes, so that they can reaffirm the cultural ideas that work to their advantage.

It should come as no surprise, given these relationships between social class and participation in sports and physical activity, that there is also a striking relationship between social class and population health:

> Working class people have on average lower birth weight and higher rates of infant mortality, are smaller at maturity, less healthy, and die at a younger age than those in higher class categories.

Major types of mental disorder and physical illness including heart disease, cancer, diabetes, pneumonia and bronchitis are all more common at lower levels of the class structure….(Giddens, 1989, p. 215)

It is often assumed that these findings are a result of lower levels of physical activity among people in a lower social class, but there is no evidence to support this assumption. Surveys of population physical activity are usually based on middle-class assumptions about white-collar sedentary jobs, and are likely to presume that individuals who do not go to the gym, jog, or take other forms of recreational exercise are "inactive." However, "housework, child care, manual labour, work that involves being on your feet, and [other activities] . . . account for the majority of energy expenditure of Canadians [and] remain unrecorded in most surveys" (Donnelly and Harvey, 1996). Since lower-income people are more likely to be occupied in manual work, to take public transport, and to have limited access to services for child care and house cleaning, it would be inaccurate to assume "inactivity" because of a lack of involvement in recreational activity.

Despite this, "top people live longer" (Evans, et al., 1994), and they do so despite various statistical controls for smoking and physical inactivity (i.e., if you smoke twenty cigarettes and day and you are rich, you are likely to live longer than someone who smokes twenty cigarettes a day and is poor). Canada's National Forum on Health attributes these differences not to "lifestyle choices," or to more participation in fitness activities, better knowledge of health among the better educated, or greater ability to purchase health care among the wealthy, but to the sense of being in control of one's life (National Forum on Health, 1997). As noted above, higher-income people have considerable control over their work lives, so they have the freedom to take time to participate in healthy recreational activities, or even combine such activity with their work.

Homemaking, Child Rearing, and Earning a Living: What Happens When Class and Gender Relations Come Together in Women's Lives

The impact of social class on everyday lives often varies by age, gender, race and ethnicity, and geographical location. For example, women in family situations have been less likely than their male counterparts to be able to negotiate the time and resources needed to maintain sport participation (Thompson, 1999a,b). When a married woman with children decides to join a soccer team that schedules practices late in the afternoon, she may encounter resistance from members of her family. Resistance is certain if she traditionally has served her family as chef, chauffeur, and tutor. "Time off for good behaviour" is not a principle that applies to married women with children. On the other hand, married men with children may not face the same resistance within their families. In fact, when they play softball or soccer after work, their spouses may delay family dinners, keep dinners warm until they arrive home, or even go to the games and watch them play.

Women in middle- and lower-income families most often feel the constraints of homemaking and child rearing. Women sociologists in Canada began to focus on these issues in the 1980s, combining gender and social class (socialist feminism) in order to examine the implications for the lives and leisure of working-class women (e.g., Armstrong and Armstrong, 1984; Bray, 1983, 1984; and Luxton, 1980). Without money to pay for child care, domestic help, and sport participation expenses, these women simply do not have many opportunities to play sports. Nor do they have time to spare, a car to get them to where sports are played, access to gyms and playing fields in their neighbourhoods, or the sense of physical safety they need to leave home and travel to where they can play sports. Furthermore, sports often are social activities occurring among friends, and, if a woman's friends do not have resources enabling them to play, she will have even fewer opportunities and less motivation for involvement (Gems, 1993). Of course, this is also true for men, but women from middle- and lower-income families are more likely than their male counterparts to lack the network of relationships out of which sport interests and participation emerge.

In a striking "made in Canada" solution, Wendy Frisby of the University of British Columbia started a fitness programme called Women Organizing Activities for Women for low-income single mothers in several communities in British Columbia (Frisby, et al., 1997). The targeted population was involved in the planning process, which resulted in the provision of child care—something that the professionals involved in the process had not anticipated. Without involvement of the "clients" in the planning, they would not have been able to participate ("Who would look after our children?"), the programme would have failed, and the targeted population would have been blamed for lack of interest. "[T]he women felt ownership for the programs because they had the freedom to choose whether to get involved and their voices were taken into account during the project" (1997, p. 20).

Women from upper-income families often face a different situation. They have the resources to pay for child care, domestic help, carryout dinners, and sport participation, and they are more likely to have husbands who share domestic duties. They often participate in sport activities by themselves, with friends, or with family members. They have social networks made up of other women who also have the resources to maintain high levels of sport participation. Women who have grown up in these families often have played sports during and since their childhoods and have attended schools with good sport programmes. They seldom have experienced the same constraints as their lower-income counterparts. While this is not to say they do not have any problems negotiating time for sport involvement, their rates of successful negotiation are relatively high. Their opportunities are much greater than those of lower-income women, even though they may not be equal to those of upper-income men.

The sport participation of girls and young women also may be limited when they are asked to shoulder adult responsibilities at home. For example, in low-income families, especially single-parent families, teenage daughters often are expected to care for younger siblings after school until after dinner, when their mothers get home from work. According to one girls' team coach in a New York City high school, "It's not at all unusual that on a given day there may be two or three girls who aren't [at practice] because of responsibilities at home" (Dobie, 1987). The coach also explained that child-care duties keep many girls from coming out for teams. His solution was to coordinate a cooperative child-care programme at practices and games, so that girls from low-income families could meet family expectations *and* play sports. However, when coaches are not so creative or accommodating, some girls drop out of sports to meet responsibilities at home. Boys and girls from higher-income families seldom have household responsibilities that force them to drop out of sports. Instead, their parents drive them to practices, lessons, and games; make sure they have all the equipment they need to play well; and then give them cars, so they can drive themselves to practices and games.

Getting Respect and Becoming a Man: What Happens When Class and Gender Relations Come Together in Men's Lives

Boys and young men learn to see and use sport participation as a special and legitimate means of establishing a masculine identity, but specific views and strategies vary by social class. For example, in a qualitative analysis of essays written about sports by fifteen- to sixteen-year-old francophone boys in the Montreal area, Suzanne Laberge, of the Université de Montréal and

Mathieu Albert (1999) discovered that ideas about sports and masculinity varied among upper-class, middle-class, and working-class boys. The upper-class boys connected sport participation to masculinity because they saw sports as an arena in which they could learn to be leaders, and leadership was a key dimension of masculinity as they defined it. The middle-class boys connected sport participation to masculinity because they saw sports as an arena for sociability and opportunities to gain acceptance in male groups, thereby confirming their manhood. The working-class boys connected sport participation to masculinity because they saw sports as an arena for displaying tough, hypermasculine behaviours, which represented their conception of manhood.

Sociologist Mike Messner has noted that, in U.S. culture, "the more limited a boy's options appear to be, and the more insecure his family situation, the more likely he is to make an early commitment to an athletic career" (1992: 40). However, this was not so much the case among males from middle-class backgrounds. One former athlete who later became a junior high school coach explained this in the following way:

> For…the poorer kids, [sports are] their major measuring stick….They constantly remind each other what they can't do in the sports arena. It's definitely peer-acceptable if they are good at sports—although they maybe can't read, you know—if they are good at sports, they're one of the boys. Now I know the middle- and upper-class boys, they do sports and they do their books. …But as a whole, [they put] less effort into [sports]. (quoted in Messner, 1992: 57–58)

This coach was suggesting that social class factors create social conditions under which young men from lower-income backgrounds often have more at stake when it comes to sport participation. What this coach did not point out is that the development of sport skills often requires material resources that do not exist in low-income families. Thus, unless equipment

Professional boxing has long been a sport for men from low-income groups in Canada and the United States, one of the few avenues of achievement and success available. While most professional boxers start as amateurs, amateur boxing is a sport in its own right, drawing from both middle- and low-income populations. Damien Roach of Manitoba and Francois Maltais of New Brunswick are participating in the 54 kg event at the 2003 Canada Winter Games in Dalhousie, NB. (CP/Andrew Vaughan)

and training are provided in public school athletic programmes, young men from low-income groups stand little chance of competing against upper-income peers, who are able to buy equipment and training if they want to develop skills.

In fact, young people from upper-income backgrounds often have so many opportunities to do different things that they may not focus attention on one sport to the exclusion of other sports and other activities. For someone who has a car, nice clothes, money for university education, and good career contacts for the future, playing sports may be good for bolstering popularity among peers, but it is not perceived as a necessary foundation for an entire identity (Messner, 1992). This often leads young men from middle- and upper-income backgrounds to disengage gradually from exclusive commitments to playing particular sports and striving for careers as athletes. When these young men move through adolescence and into adulthood, opportunities may take them in a variety of directions; playing sports may be important, but not usually in the same ways that it is for young men from working-class and low-income families. (See, for example, the feature, "Fighting to Survive," on the Online Learning Centre.)

Class Relations in Action: The Decline of School Sports and Physical Education, and the Increase of User Fees

In a 2003 speech, Chris Rudge, CEO of the Canadian Olympic Committee, criticized Ontario (while praising Alberta, British Columbia, and Quebec) for its commitment to athlete development at both the high-performance and grass-roots levels. He pointed out that, because of cuts to the public sector and its tax-reduction policies, Canada's wealthiest and most populous province, whose athletes used to comprise 40 percent of Canada's Olympic teams, now provides only 30 percent (Christie, 2003). The provincial government now contributes approximately $1 per person to athlete development (about $12 million with a population of 12 million), and a series of cuts to education, recreation, and municipalities has made participation too expensive for many.

The public sector cuts interconnect in ways that have a cumulative effect on who is able to participate:

- Cuts to education, combined with a new academic curriculum, mean that there are fewer physical education specialist teachers, and fewer physical education classes being taught. When this is combined with teacher burnout and alienated teachers, fewer extracurricular activities/interschool sports are available; and cutbacks mean user fees for almost all activities (Donnelly, et al., 2001).
- Cuts to the budget of the Ministry responsible for sports and recreation mean that less money is available for sport organizations.
- Cuts and downloading to municipal budgets mean that all Parks and Recreation Departments now have user fees, and that, in many cases, they provide fewer services for more money.
- Sports and recreation organizations often relied on low-cost rental of school facilities. In order to make up for budget cuts, schools have increased rental fees, increasing the difficulties for those organizations. For example, a basketball club in Collingwood used to charge $50 per player and now charges up to $400. Increasing costs of up to 2,000 percent have been recorded (Campbell, 2003; Picard, 2003).

- Many swimming pools in Toronto are located in schools, but are available for joint school and community use with the costs shared by the municipality and the Board of Education. Cutbacks have created a crisis whereby many pools may close.

In every case, public sector cutbacks have increased the costs of participation in sports, and reduced the numbers of participants at the grass-roots level. With fewer athletes to draw from, those cuts are now being felt at the high-performance level. These concerns are also being related to increasing childhood obesity, a condition that is likely to lead to significantly higher costs to the public sector (medical care) in the future than investment in sports and physical activity would cost today.

Class Relations in Action: The Cost of Attending Sport Events

It is still possible to attend recreational, high school, and university sports for free or at little cost, and, in some communities, the tickets for minor league sports are reasonably priced. But tickets to most professional events are now beyond the means of many people, even those whose taxes may be being used to pay for the facilities in which the events are played. The cost of attending these events has increased far beyond the rate of inflation over the past decade.

The average ticket price for attending games at the four major sport leagues in North America increased significantly between 1991 and 2001: MLB, 119 percent; NFL, 98 percent; NBA, 121 percent; and NHL, 99 percent. These increases are more than five times the rate of inflation in Canada (18 percent, as measured by the Consumer Price Index) for that decade. Table 10.3 shows the league average Fan Cost Index (Team Marketing Report, 2003: www.teammarketing.com) and the Fan Cost Index for Canadian teams in those leagues:[4]

Table 10.3   Fan Cost Index for Canadian teams in North American Leagues, 2002–03

League/Team	Increase/Decrease from Previous Season	Fan Cost Index[a] (US$)
MLB average (2003)	+3.29%	$148.66
Toronto Blue Jays	+8.22%	$134.05
Montreal Expos	+11.46%	$94.62
NFL average (2002)	+4.2%	$290.41
NBA average (2002–03)	+3.8%	$254.88
Toronto Raptors	+10.6%	$193.90
NHL average (2002–03)	+0.5%	$240.43
Toronto Maple Leafs	+7.6%	$263.28[b]
Vancouver Canucks	+0.6%	$211.89
Ottawa Senators	-2.0%	$204.41[c]
Montreal Canadiens	+11.1%	$192.81
Calgary Flames	+5.9%	$178.87
Edmonton Oilers	+8.9%	$176.52

[a] The Team Marketing Report's Fan Cost Index is based on the cost for two adults and two children to attend a game (average price tickets, parking, drinks and hot dogs, 2 hats),
[b] Only Canadian team to cost more than the league average.
[c] Only Canadian team to cost less than previous season.

Source: Team Marketing Report Inc., 2003 (www.teammarketing.com)

New stadiums include expensive luxury boxes and sections of club seating where upper-income spectators have special services available to them: wait staff, special food menus, private restrooms, televisions, telephones, refrigerators, lounge chairs, temperature controls, private entrances with no waiting lines or turnstiles, special parking areas, and other things to make attendance at a game resemble going to a private club. For example, when Detroit's new Comerica Park opened in 2000, ticket prices increased 103 percent from what they were in Tiger Stadium in 1999. This is typical of what happens when the taxpayers build a stadium: the owner jacks up prices to attract relatively wealthy fans to the games. Similarly, in the privately built Air Canada Centre, ticket prices increased significantly in comparison to the Maple Leaf Gardens, and they have increased each year (to sell-out crowds in basketball and hockey) despite the size of the payroll or the performance of the team.

As ticket prices increase and as spectators are increasingly segregated by their ability to pay, social class and class relations become more evident in the stands. Everyone at the games may cheer at the same times and experience similar emotions, but social class differences in society are not transcended at the events; in fact, they are reaffirmed and are becoming more apparent.

An interesting fact is that class relations partially account for the failure to organize fans so that they can collectively have more influence over ticket and concession costs at games. People in luxury boxes, club seats, and other exclusive seats are not eager to align themselves with those who cannot attend games or afford the high-priced tickets. In fact, they have used expensive tickets as status symbols with their

[4] The Fan Cost Index has not been applied to teams in Canadian leagues. However, data from the CFL for 2003 indicate that the average ticket price is approximately C$30, and the range of average ticket prices in the league is approximately C$26 (Calgary, Toronto, Winnipeg) to approximately C$35 (Montreal, Ottawa).

friends and business associates. They *want* class distinctions to be preserved in connection with attending games, and they are willing to pay, for example, over US$1,500 per ticket for NBA courtside seats in New York and Los Angeles to conspicuously display their status. Attendance and seating at many events, from the opening ceremonies at the Olympics to the Stanley Cup Finals, also are tied to conspicuous displays of wealth, status, and influence. As long as this is the case, efforts to organize fans will fail.

In summary, sports, sport participation, and sport spectatorship are closely tied to social class and class relations in societies. Organized sports require material resources, and sport programmes and events usually depend on the approval and support of those with power and influence. This creates a tendency for sport programmes and events to be organized in ways that recreate and perpetuate existing forms of class relations in a society. Furthermore, patterns of sport participation and spectatorship clearly reflect the distribution of resources and opportunities in a society.

ECONOMIC AND CAREER OPPORTUNITIES IN SPORTS

Do sports and sport organizations provide opportunities for upward social class mobility[5] in society? The general answer to this question is yes, but it must be qualified in light of the following:

1. The number of career opportunities in sports is limited and, for athletes, opportunities are short term.
2. Opportunities for women are growing but they remain limited.
3. Opportunities for blacks, Aboriginals, and other minorities are growing but they remain limited.

We discuss each of these qualifications in the following sections.

"Ah, the glamorous life of a spoiled, overpaid professional athlete!"
....

Only a few professional athletes achieve fame and fortune. Thousands of them play in minor and semipro leagues, where salaries are low and working conditions are poor.

Career Opportunities Are Limited

Young athletes often have visions of becoming professional athletes or going to the Olympics; their parents may have similar visions for them. But the chances of turning these visions into reality are very low regardless of social class. (See the Reflect on Sports box, "The Odds of Becoming a Professional Athlete," pp. 313–314.)

Most professional sport opportunities are short term, averaging three to seven years in team sports and three to twelve years in individual sports. This means that, after a playing career ends, there are about *forty additional years* in a person's work life. Unfortunately, many people, including athletes, coaches, and parents, ignore this fact.

Ideas about careers in professional sports often are distorted by misinterpretations in media coverage. The media focus on the best athletes in the most popular sports. The best athletes tend to have longer playing careers than

---

[5]**Social mobility** refers to changes in wealth, education, and occupation over a person's lifetime or from one generation to the next in families. Social mobility can occur in either a downward direction or an upward direction.

REFLECT ON SPORTS   The Odds of Becoming a Professional Athlete

In the United States, the athlete development system to most professional team sports is relatively straightforward—high school team to university team to professional team. Therefore, it is relatively straightforward to calculate the chances of high school and university players making it to the professional level (see the Online Learning Centre feature, "Career Opportunities are Limited"). These odds are not good in the U.S., ranging from 993:1, for a high school baseball player ever playing in Major League Baseball, to 4,562:1, for a female high school basketball player ever playing in the WNBA.

In Canada, the development system is not nearly so straightforward. Student-athletes play basketball in high school and university in Canada, but that is not usually considered to be a track to a top-level professional career—some of the better players may play professional basketball in a men's or women's league in Europe. A scholarship to a U.S. university provides one of the only routes to the NBA or WNBA. Football provides similar opportunities for Canadian students, with chances to play at Canadian universities, win a scholarship to a U.S. university, and play in the CFL or occasionally the NFL. However, there is a parallel junior football system that also makes tracking from high school to university to professional football problematic. In the case of baseball, while many high schools and some universities have teams in Canada, serious young players are usually involved in youth baseball leagues. The case is similar for hockey, with few considering high school or even university hockey as a potential route to the NHL.

Given these various routes—high school, youth leagues, junior leagues, Canadian university, U.S. university—is it possible to calculate the odds of Canadian players becoming professional athletes? There are no academic studies of this topic, but two Canadians have collected data that are comparable, and which give a sense of the odds of becoming a professional player in hockey and golf:

- Jim Parcels (2000), who worked for the Ontario Minor Hockey Association, wrote a research paper entitled, "The chances of making it in pro hockey for Ontario minor hockey players." Since the competitive structure of minor hockey is based on a player's age, Parcels used players born in 1975 as his sample. Of all the boys born in Ontario in 1975, 30,000 played minor hockey at one time or another. By 1991, 22,000 were still registered as players. Here's what happened to them:
  - 22,000 were eligible for the Ontario Hockey League Junior draft in 1991 (underage Bantam) and 1992 (open Midget)
  - 232 were drafted by (then) sixteen major junior teams[1] (only 105 played at least one game in the OHL)
  - 90 completed three to four years of OHL eligibility
  - 41 opted to play NCAA Division I hockey[2]
  - 48 were drafted from OHL and NCAA to NHL
  - 4 signed NHL free agent contracts
  - 35 signed contracts with NHL teams
  - 26 played at least one NHL game by April 2000
  - 16 were active in the NHL in April 2000

Thus, of the 30,000 original players from 1975, sixteen remained active in 2000, giving odds of 1875:1; if only those 22,000 who participated in minor hockey long enough to be eligible for the junior draft are counted, the odds are 1375:1. The odds are also becoming longer as each of the major leagues further globalizes its search for players—the proportion of Canadian players in the NHL is down to a little over 50 percent.

- Henry Brunton, the national coach for the Royal Canadian Golf Association, has been tracking Canadian male golfers who accept scholarships at U.S. universities (considered to be one of the main routes to the PGA Tour). In 2002, he calculated that there were 3,000 varsity golfers at U.S. universities,

Continued

REFLECT ON SPORTS   The Odds of Becoming a Professional Athlete continued

and 227 of them were Canadian. Assuming that 750 (25 percent) of those players were in their fourth year of university and were eligible, "only three made it to the finals of the PGA Tour's qualifying school. Not one got his tour card" (Brunton, cited by Rubenstein, 2003, p. S5). Brunton argues that U.S. golf scholarships are not a good idea for most talented young golfers in Canada (see next section for problems with scholarships for Canadian student-athletes in the U.S.).

We admire the ambition and drive of talented young athletes who dream of becoming professionals, but we are also concerned that they may not leave themselves

alternatives if their dream does not work out. Given these odds, we think that young players, and their parents, should always give themselves alternatives (e.g., in terms of education and other interests). *What do you think?*

———

[1] 1975 was the best draft year ever in Ontario; for the 1971 cohort, only 11 played at least one NHL game, and for 1976, only 9 had played by April 2000.

[2] Very few completed a degree; meanwhile, 60 of the former major junior players went on to play CIS hockey at Canadian universities, and data indicate that 50 percent to 60 percent graduate.

• •

others in their sports. Little coverage is given to those who play for one or two seasons before being cut or forced to quit for other reasons, especially injuries. For example, we hear about the long football careers of popular quarterbacks, but little or no coverage is given to the numerous players whose one-year contracts are not renewed after their first season. The average age of players on the *oldest* NFL team in 2000 was less than twenty-eight. This means that only a few players older than thirty-five are still in the league. Much more typical than thirty-three-year-olds contemplating another season are twenty-four-year-olds trying to deal with the end of their careers as paid athletes.

Opportunities for Women Are Growing but Limited

Career opportunities for women athletes are growing, but they are still scarce relative to opportunities for men. Tennis and golf have provided some opportunities for women during the past fifty years. However, the professional

tours for these sports now draw athletes from around the world, rather than from North America, Australia, and a few European nations. This means that the competition to make a living in these sports is greater than it has ever been. There are expanding opportunities in professional figure skating, volleyball, basketball, soccer, curling, show jumping, bowling, skiing, bicycling, track and field, and rodeo, but the number of professional women athletes remains very low, and only a few women make large amounts of money.

Pro volleyball and basketball leagues were established in the United States during the 1990s, but they provide opportunities for fewer than 250 athletes, and the pay is low. For example, many rookies in the WNBA make the US$30,000 minimum salary, and the average salary was US$58,000 during the 1999 season. Furthermore, the future of the leagues is tenuous; volleyball loses money, and the future of the WNBA depends on the men who control the NBA. Opportunities exist to play in Europe, but, again, they are limited and salaries are low.

Overall, the advice for women who aspire to make a living as professional athletes is "don't quit your day job."

What about other careers in sports? There are jobs for women in coaching, training, officiating, sport medicine, sports information, public relations, marketing, personal training, and administration. As noted in chapter 8, most of the jobs in women's sports continue to be held by men, and women seldom have been hired for jobs in men's programmes, except in support positions. Women in most postindustrial nations have challenged the legacy of traditional gender logic, and some progress has been made in various administrative positions in some sport organizations (Lapchick and Matthews, 2000). For example, in Canadian and U.S. universities where men's and women's athletics have been run from the same department, a man invariably served as athletic director while a woman was often an assistant athletic director (with responsibility for women's sports). In recent years in Canada, there have been a small, but growing, number of women athletic directors, with overall responsibility for both men's and women's sports.[6] However, there is a need for systematic data in Canada on positions held by men and women, and some comparative data on salaries. A heavily gendered division of labour continues to exist in nearly all organizations (McKay, 1997, 1999). In traditional and developing nations, the record of progress is negligible, and very few women hold positions of power in any sport organizations (Rintala and Bischoff, 1997).

For a number of reasons, including the persistence of traditional gender logic, job opportunities for women have not increased as rapidly as women's programmes have grown. This pattern exists in nearly all job categories and nearly all sport organizations.

We can expect that patterns will continue to shift toward equity, but many men will resist real transformation and will impede the deep ideological changes that would open the door to full equity. Job opportunities for women will grow, and we will see more women coaches, sports broadcasters, athletic trainers, administrators, and referees. Changes will occur more rapidly in community-based recreation and fitness programmes where financial rewards are low, and in certain sport industries that target women as consumers and need women employees to make more money. But the gender logic used *inside* many sport organizations will continue to privilege those perceived as tough, strong, and aggressive—and men are more likely to be perceived in such terms; women with these attributes sometimes have their sexuality questioned.

As it is now, many women who work in sport organizations face the burden of dealing with an organizational culture that they have had little or no role in shaping. This contributes to high turnover among women. Professional development programmes, workshops, and coaching clinics have not been widely sponsored for women employees, although some women's organizations, such as the Canadian Association for the Advancement of Women and Sport (CAAWS), have stepped in to provide assistance and guidance for women working in sports. Barriers to career opportunities for women in sports are being hurdled and knocked over, but the forces that have limited opportunities in the past still exist. As noted in chapter 8, equity issues and ideological issues are tied together. Hiring more women is only one aspect of the changes needed to achieve real equity; another is changing the cultures of sports and sport organizations and the ideas about masculinity that shaped them. This suggests that real transformation will come when enough men in sports and sport organizations change how they see themselves, how they

---

[6] It is interesting to note that there have been a few significant administrative opportunities in Canada for women: the first Minister of Sport, Iona Campagnolo; the first Director General of Sport Canada, Abbie Hoffman; a General Manager of the former Ottawa Rough Riders, Susan Pollack; and the CEO of CIS, Marg McGregor.

relate to others, and how they define the terms of their manhood (McKay, 1997).

Opportunities for Racial and Ethnic Minorities Are Growing but Limited

The dynamics of racial and ethnic relations in any culture are unique, and they vary from one group to another (see chapter 9). Making generalizations about racial and ethnic relations and how they are related to opportunities in sports is difficult. However, it is important to remember that dominant sport forms in any culture tend to reproduce dominant cultural values and the social structures supported by those values. This means two things: (1) members of the dominant culture may exclude or define as unqualified those who come from different cultural backgrounds, and (2) racial and ethnic minorities often face the challenge of taking on the values and orientations of the dominant culture if they want to become a part of sports and sport organizations.

Of course, some members of the dominant culture have valued cultural diversity and have made cultural spaces for racial and ethnic minorities in sport organizations. For example, this has occurred in baseball and soccer in the U.S. as Latinos have been hired for management and administrative jobs. Also, some members of ethnic groups assimilate and willingly accept the "cultural terms" on which dominant sports are based. However, those who give priority to their culture in their identities may not be willing to assign secondary importance to their own cultural values and orientations to play sports or work in sport organizations in which their culture is not valued or even acknowledged by other employees, or respected within organizational rules and practices.

As we noted in chapter 9, racial and ethnic relations are significantly different in Canada than in the U.S. There are intersections between visible minorities and social class, as in the U.S., but these

As we noted in chapter 9, there has been only one non-white coach in the NHL. Ted Nolan, an Ojibway from Northern Ontario, coached the Buffalo Sabres, and was named NHL Coach of the Year for the 1996-97 season. He was fired before the following season, without any public explanation, and has not coached in the NHL since. (CP/Bill Sikes/AP)

have not been examined systematically in sports in Canada, except in the case of francophones and anglophones. Thus, we have no data at this time with which to explore careers in sports for visible minorities, either as athletes or in management and administrative positions. It is probably safe to speculate that, in Canada, visible minorities are underrepresented in many sports and sport organizations. There are various reasons for this, but at least part of this underrepresentation is related to racism, as well as to fears of diversity and a lack of understanding of how diversity can contribute in a positive way to the operation and overall culture of an organization. However, given the policies of multiculturalism, and recognition of equity issues and ethnic diversity, there has been some sensitivity in Canada to recognizing and responding to issues of diversity in sports. Given that the best evidence available at this time is anecdotal, to what extent this has been successful we cannot say until relevant research is available.

In summary, sports are becoming increasingly open and democratic in the provision of economic and career opportunities, but they are far from ideal in this respect. White men hold most of the power in sports and sport organizations, and they have used their power to maximize economic returns and opportunities for themselves. With a few exceptions, data show that women and racial/ethnic minorities have been left out of or excluded from opportunities at the level of ownership and corporate control. In the case of other career opportunities in sport organizations, there has been more openness in recent years. Women and racial/ethnic minorities have made their way into staff and middle-management jobs, but they remain seriously underrepresented in head coach and top-level administrative jobs in most sport organizations. Changes in this pattern will occur as the white men who currently hold positions of power in these organizations become more aware of the skills of minority and women candidates, the advantages of diversity in sport organizations, and the possibility of working effectively with people who are different from them. If this does not occur fast enough, then legal and political pressures will be used to bring about needed changes (Shropshire, 1996).

SPORT PARTICIPATION AND OCCUPATIONAL CAREERS AMONG FORMER ATHLETES

What happens in the occupational careers of former athletes? Do they have career patterns that are different from the patterns of those who have never played competitive sports? Is sport participation a stepping stone to future occupational success and upward social mobility? Does playing sports have economic payoffs after active participation is over?

These are difficult questions, and there are only a few studies that have compared former athletes with others on issues related to social class and social mobility. These studies usually suggest that, as a group, the young people who had played sports on high school, community, and university teams experienced no more or less occupational success than others from comparable backgrounds. However, two Canadian studies carried out twenty years apart suggest that there may be some career or social mobility advantages to early sport participation. Norman Okihiro (1984), of Mount Saint Vincent University, found that involvement in extracurricular activities did not lead to more prestigious jobs, but it was associated with a "facility for dealing with people" that could have a long-term career benefit in the new economy. Curtis, et al. (2003), found that those who participated in organized youth sports tend to have higher incomes as adults (a finding that was stronger for males than females). Interestingly, both studies suggest similar explanations for their results—youth sport participation produces net gains in social, cultural, and physical capital, which are assets in the job market. The meaning and cultural significance of sport participation changes over time, and those changes may be related to career processes in some way.

Research suggests that, *if* playing sports is connected to processes of career success, it occurs in one or more of the following ways:

- Playing sports, under certain circumstances (see list on next page), may teach young people interpersonal skills, which carry over into various jobs and enable them to be successful.
- Some people with power and influence may define former athletes as good job prospects

and give them opportunities to develop and demonstrate work-related abilities, which serve as the basis for career success.

- Individuals who were very high-profile athletes may be able to use their reputations to obtain and succeed at certain types of jobs.
- Playing sports, under certain circumstances (see list below), may connect athletes with others who can help them obtain good jobs after they retire from sports.

After reading this research, our view is that playing sports is most likely to be positively related to occupational success and upward mobility when it does the following things:

1. Increases opportunities to complete academic degrees, develop job-related skills, and/or extend knowledge about the organization and operation of the world outside of sports
2. Increases support from significant others for *overall* growth and development (not just sport development)
3. Provides opportunities to make friends and develop social contacts with people outside of sports and sport organizations
4. Provides material resources and the guidance needed to use those resources to create or nurture career opportunities
5. Expands experiences fostering the development of identities and abilities unrelated to sports
6. Minimizes risks of serious injuries that restrict physical movement or require extensive and expensive medical treatment

These are not surprising hypotheses. Taken together, they emphasize that playing sports can either constrict or expand a person's overall development (see chapter 4). When expansion occurs, athletes often develop work-related abilities and connections with career opportunities. When constriction occurs, the development of work-related abilities and career opportunities are likely to be limited.

Highly Paid Professional Athletes and Career Success after Playing Sports

Conclusions about the connections among sport participation, career success, and social mobility must be qualified in light of the dramatic increases in the salaries of some professional athletes over the past twenty to thirty years (see chapter 11). Before the late 1970s, few athletes made enough money in sports to pave their ways into other careers after they retired. However, some top athletes today make enough money in a few years to finance any one of a range of career alternatives after they retire from sports—if they do not throw their money away or hire irresponsible agents to manage their money.

Of course, many professional athletes have short careers or play at levels at which they do not make much money. When they retire, they must deal with the challenge of entering another career and making a living. Many experience patterns of success and failure similar to the patterns experienced by comparable others, who did not play sports. Their post-sport careers may not enable them to drive new cars, travel to exciting places, or read their names in newspapers every week, but this does not mean they should be seen as failures or victims of sports.

As noted in chapter 4, retirement from sports is best described as a process rather than a single event, and most athletes do not retire from sports on a moment's notice—they gradually disengage from sports and shift their personal priorities in the process. Although many athletes smoothly disengage from sports, develop other interests, and move into relatively satisfying occupational careers, some do encounter varying degrees of adjustment problems that interfere with occupational success and overall life satisfaction. For example, when sociologist Mike Messner interviewed former elite athletes, he found that many of the men who had been heavily involved in sports since childhood encountered serious adjustment problems as they tried to make the transition out of sports. A former NFL player explained:

> You miss the camaraderie of the fellas. There's an empty feeling....The one thing that has been the major part of your life is gone....You don't know how people are going to react to you....You wonder and question. (Messner, 1992: 121)

Anecdotal evidence from other team sports suggests that these feelings are common to many athletes. Bette McKenzie (1999) makes this point with regard to both her father (former NHL player) and her husband (former NFL player).

Messner's research led him to suggest that retiring athletes, especially those who had dedicated themselves to playing sports ever since they were children, face two major challenges:

1. Reconstructing their identities in terms of activities, abilities, and relationships unrelated to sport participation
2. Renegotiating relationships with family members and close friends, so that they receive feedback and support for identities having little or nothing to do with playing sports

Messner also noted that young men from low-income families were more likely to have problems when retiring from sports, because they had fewer material resources to aid them in the transition process and because they were more likely to have identities deeply rooted in playing sports. The men from middle-class backgrounds, on the other hand, seemed more likely to benefit from the doors opened by sports and the social connections related to sport participation; they also had greater access to material support and were less likely to have identities exclusively rooted in playing sports.

Studies also have shown that adjustment problems are more likely when an injury forces retirement from sports. Injuries often complicate retirement and tie it to other problems related to self-esteem or health; injuries disrupt "life plans"

SIDELINES

....

Only a small proportion of former athletes are able to cash in on their athletic reputations. The rest must seek opportunities and work just like the rest of us. Those opportunities vary, depending on qualifications, experience, contacts and connections, and a bit of luck.

by throwing off the timing of retirement and forcing a person into life decisions before they are expected. This is not surprising, and athletes often need career-related assistance when this occurs.

When athletes have problems making the transition out of sports into careers and other activities, it seems that sport organizations have some responsibility to offer assistance, especially in amateur and minor league sports, where athletes earn little or no money for playing sports (Dacyshyn, 1999). Some sport organizations, including Sport Canada and AthletesCAN, are beginning to do this through forms of career transition programmes. Many of these programmes involve workshops dealing with career self-assessments, life skills training, career planning, résumé writing, job search strategies, interviewing skills, career placement contacts, and psychological counselling.

Of course, some organizations do not see the issue of career transition as a high priority, and some do not have the resources to initiate and conduct transition programmes or hire others to do so. But there is a growing belief that, after young men and women are expected to train full time, the organizations that benefit from their dedication have an obligation to help them make a successful transition into life after sports.

Athletic Grants and Occupational Success

Discussions about playing sports and upward social mobility in the United States, and increasingly in Canada, include references to athletic scholarships. Most people believe that these scholarships are valuable mobility vehicles for many young people. This belief raises many questions. How many students receive athletic scholarships as opposed to other forms of financial assistance? How much are athletic scholarships worth to those who receive them? Who receives them, and how many recipients would not attend university without them?

Surprisingly, these questions remain unanswered. U.S. universities do not report the amount of athletic aid that goes to particular student-athletes. Therefore, it is unknown which individual athletes receive scholarships, how much the scholarships are worth, or how important they are in the educational lives of the recipients.

It is known that the actual number of *full* athletic scholarships in the U.S. is often exaggerated. High school students who receive standard recruiting letters from university coaches often tell people they are anticipating *full* scholarships, when, in fact, they may receive only partial aid or no aid at all. Students receiving tuition waivers or other forms of partial athletic aid often lead people to believe they have full scholarships. Athletic scholarships are awarded one year at a time and may not be renewed for certain athletes, who may continue their education while people believe they have scholarships. Finally, many people simply assume that student-athletes, especially at big U.S. universities, all have scholarships. Of course, such exaggerations are misleading, causing people to think that sport participation has more relevance for upward mobility than it actually does.

According to NCAA data, there were 4.6 million students in NCAA institutions in 1999. Of these, about 103,000 students had some form of athletic aid, although for all three NCAA divisions fewer than 16,000 students had full scholarships (room, food, and full tuition). The other 85 percent were receiving aid covering a portion of total expenses. This means that in 1,027 NCAA universities, one-third of 1 percent (0.34 percent) of all students received full scholarships, and about 2.2 percent of all students received some form of athletic aid. Clearly, far fewer students receive full athletic scholarships than is commonly believed. In fact, academic scholarships are many times more plentiful than athletic scholarships, even though most high school students think otherwise.

This information is especially relevant for Canadian students who often see (as do their parents) particular status associated with achieving an athletic scholarship to a U.S. university. Some Canadian student-athletes have extremely rewarding experiences. A few gain the opportunity for a university education that may not have been available to them in Canada because of somewhat lower and more flexible admission standards at many U.S. universities. Some Canadian student-athletes enjoy sport training opportunities that may not have been available to them in Canada—high-level coaching, opportunities that result from the climate in the southern U.S. (e.g., year-round outdoor track season, year-round swimming training and competitions in outdoor pools), and the opportunity to be drafted into professional sports. For example, Canadian track athletes Graham Hood and Charmaine Crooks both had successful scholarship experiences in the U.S.

But many Canadian student-athletes are disappointed by their U.S. university athletic scholarship experiences. They may find themselves involved in a much more intense level of competition and training than they have previously experienced, often resulting in burnout and over-use injuries. To many, it is made clear that a

The sports played by young people from low-income households often occur in public spaces, such as this public school playground. Young people from upper-income backgrounds usually have the resources to purchase access to privately owned sport facilities and spaces. This results in different sport experiences and different sport participation patterns from one social class to another. (Tini Campbell)

scholarship puts them in the employ of the Athletics Department, and that the requirements of their sport participation must be given priority over any other aspects of their lives as students if they wish to keep their scholarship. Many do not achieve the education that they expected, are unable to take the degree programme or courses of their choice, and may not graduate (e.g., because the scholarship ends before they have enough courses to complete their degree). And the majority of Canadian student-athletes find that the financial costs of attending a U.S. university are significant, despite the scholarship.

Parcels (2000) and Brunton (Rubenstein, 2003), whose work on tracking Canadian athletes to professional careers was noted in the Reflect on Sports box, "The Odds of Becoming a Professional Athlete," pp. 313–314, have

reservations about U.S. scholarships. For example, many NCAA hockey teams carry a roster of thirty players, but only have seventeen scholarships available. Parcels notes that the number of Ontario players receiving a *full* scholarship declined 63 percent between 1990 and 2000. Because coaches are likely to spread scholarships among the team, most Canadians find they receive 40 to 60 percent of a full scholarship. Given that they are classed as "out of state" for the purposes of tuition, and that they may incur greater travel expenses than a U.S. player, Canadians are likely to end up paying a great deal more than they may have at a Canadian university (Parcels estimates that students could end up with US$50,000–$75,000 of debt). NCAA Division I golf teams carry ten to twelve players, but are only allocated four or five scholarships. A highly ranked Canadian player may receive 50 to 75 percent of a scholarship, but is also likely to end up incurring more costs than expected, and therefore debt or significant expenses for parents. Golfers on a U.S. university team may miss five weeks of classes each year because of travel and competition obligations, and also find it difficult to graduate in four years.

Many Canadian students who receive a U.S. athletic scholarship claim that they have received a *full* scholarship, thus increasing the motivation of others to aspire to the athletic scholarship route. In reality, they are likely to be incurring a great deal of unexpected expenses and debt, and earning a less-than-complete education. Athletes in nonrevenue sports at U.S. universities often come from wealthier backgrounds than those in revenue-producing sports. Ironically, football and basketball players may be more isolated from campus and community life than athletes in swimming, tennis, soccer, volleyball, rowing, lacrosse, field hockey, and other sports in which white students predominate. If isolation subverts the opportunities that expand experiences and contacts, then playing sports is more likely to contribute to career success for students who already come from successful backgrounds, thereby reproducing existing forms of economic inequality in society. Of course, the few football and basketball players who sign big contracts distract attention away from this more important aspect of class relations.

When athletic aid goes to financially needy young people who focus on learning and earning their degrees, sport participation certainly increases their chances for career success. But how many of those athletic scholarships, full and partial, go to young people who could not or would not attend university without them? A portion of those who receive athletic scholarships could and would attend university without them. This does not mean we should do away with scholarships, but it does mean that links among playing sports, receiving athletic scholarships, achieving career success, and experiencing upward social mobility must be carefully qualified.

SUMMARY

DO MONEY AND POWER MATTER IN SPORTS?

Social class and class relations are integrally involved in sports. Organized sports depend on those with money and economic power. In the process of sponsoring the sports that provide entertainment and participation opportunities, those with money and power fund and promote sport forms that fit their own interests and foster ideas supportive of economic arrangements that work to their advantage. This is why the dominant sport forms in North America promote an ideology of competition and achievement that stresses the notion that "you always get what you deserve, and you always deserve what you get." This ideology constitutes a class logic that drives a combination of individual achievement and consumption, along with corporate expansion, in society. The use of this logic leads to favourable conclusions about the character and qualifications of those who are

wealthy and powerful in society, while it disadvantages those who are poor and powerless. Furthermore, it leads to the conclusion that economic inequality in society is not only good but also natural.

Class relations also are connected with the ways in which wealthy and powerful people around the world have become involved in sport team ownership, event sponsorship and organization, and the media coverage of sports. In fact, sport events seem to be one of the vehicles these people can use to transfer public money into their own hands. As public funds support major forms of sport entertainment in their cities and regions, those with wealth and power receive subsidies and income, which they use to maintain their privilege.

Sport participation patterns in society and around the world reflect the impact of material resources and social class on the ways in which people live their lives. Organized sports are a luxury that many people around the world cannot afford. Even in wealthy societies, sport participation is most common among those in the middle and upper classes. Patterns of sport participation throughout a society reflect class-based lifestyles, which emerge as people make decisions about how they will use the resources they do have.

Sport participation patterns also reflect the combination of class and gender relations. We see this in the case of lower-income girls and women who have low participation rates, as well as in the case of lower-income men who see sports in terms that have unique identity implications in their lives. Public sector cutbacks are having an increasing impact, limiting sport participation for those from low-income families. That impact is now beginning to be felt at the high-performance level as the pool of talented athletes declines.

Patterns of watching sports also are connected with social class and class relations. This is demonstrated by the increased segregation of fans in stadiums and arenas. Luxury boxes, club seating, and patterns of season ticket allocations separate people by a combination of wealth and power, so that social class often is reaffirmed when people attend sport events.

Opportunities for careers that hold the hope of upward social mobility do exist for some people in sports. For athletes, these opportunities often are scarce and short-lived, and they reflect patterns of gender and ethnic relations in society. These patterns take various forms in the case of careers in sport organizations. Although opportunities in these jobs have become increasingly open over the past decade, white men still widely hold the top positions in sport organizations. This will change only when the organizational cultures of sport teams and athletic departments become more inclusive and provide new ways for women and visible minorities to participate fully in shaping the policies and norms used to determine qualifications in sports and to organize social relations at the workplace.

Research on sport participation and career development generally indicates that, when young people use sport participation to expand their social worlds and personal experiences, they have an advantage when seeking occupational careers. However, when sport participation constricts social worlds and personal experiences, it is likely to have a negative effect on later career success. The existence of these patterns varies by sport. Of course, the extremely high incomes of a few athletes today almost guarantee their future career success and economic security.

Retirement from athletic careers often creates stress and personal challenges, but most athletes move through the retirement process without experiencing *excessive* trauma or difficulty. Those who do experience difficulties are usually those whose identities and relationships have been built exclusively on sports. These people may need outside assistance as they move into the rest of their lives and face the challenge of seeking jobs, maintaining satisfying careers, and nurturing mutually supportive and intimate social relationships.

Athletic scholarships help some young people further their educations and possibly achieve career success, but these scholarships are few. Furthermore, they do not always change the future career patterns of young people, because many scholarship recipients have the motivation and resources to attend university without sport-related financial assistance.

In conclusion, sports clearly are tied to patterns of class, class relations, and social inequality in society. Money and economic power do matter, and they matter in ways that reproduce economic inequality in society.

SUGGESTED READINGS

Coakley, J., and P. Donnelly, eds. 1999. *Inside sports.* London: Routledge (many of the chapters in this collection contain clear examples of how class intersects with gender and race in everyday sport experiences; articles in Part 4 deal with the transitions associated with retirement from high-performance sports).

Curtis, J., W. McTeer, and P. White. 2003. Do high school athletes earn more pay?: Youth sport participation and earnings as an adult. *Sociology of Sport Journal* 20 (1): 60–76 (the authors use Canadian survey data to compare later life earnings, and find that those who were involved in sports when they were young earn more than those who were not; they examine several alternative explanations of the data, and suggest that the social, cultural and physical benefits of sports have important effects on occupations).

Gruneau, R. 1999. *Class, sports, and social development.* Champaign, IL: Human Kinetics (a new foreword and postscript accompany this reprinting of a classic analysis of how the meaning, organization, and purpose of sports are closely tied to the struggles between social classes and the processes of domination and subordination in society as a whole; excellent information on theories used to study class and class relations).

Joravsky, B. 1995. *Hoop dreams: A true story of hardship and triumph*. New York: Harper Perennial (text adaptation of the documentary film; provides some details missed in the film).

McKay, J. 1997. *Managing gender: Affirmative action and organizational power in Australian, Canadian, and New Zealand sport*. Albany: State University of New York Press (data from in-depth interviews and the media coverage of sports are used to show how affirmative action policies are subverted in sport cultures by a combination of class-based and gender relations).

Robidoux, M. 2001. *Men at play: A working understanding of professional hockey*. Montreal & Kingston: McGill-Queen's University Press (an insightful ethnography of the working lives of professional hockey players in the AHL, the working-class level of hockey, it shows in graphic terms the less-than-luxurious working conditions, and the highly uncertain and extremely controlling working environment at this level of hockey).

Sugden, J., and A. Tomlinson. 2000. Theorizing sport, social class, and status. In *Handbook of sports studies* (pp. 309–321), edited by E. Dunning and J. Coakley. London: Sage (an overview of the theoretical perspectives sociologists have used to understand economic inequality and class-based lifestyles in society; describes how the concept of hegemony can be used to understand complex power relations between social classes and other status groups in connection with sports).

Thompson, S. 1999. *Mother's Taxi: Sport and women's labor*. Albany: State University of New York Press (research on how sports in many situations depend on behind-the-scenes free work done by mothers, wives, and girlfriends; data were gathered in Australia, but the analysis is relevant for other postindustrial countries where adult leagues and youth sports are a prominent part of community life).

www.sportingnews.com/features/powerful (*The Sporting News*, a U.S. weekly, presents annual lists of the 100 most powerful people in sports, often in the first or last issue of the calendar year; the lists are intended to be international, but they focus primarily on power in sports from a U.S. perspective, and they are only one picture of power in the world of sports)

www.finelinefeatures.com/hoop (site for *Hoop Dreams*, a classic documentary film that provides a personalized look at social class and class relations issues in the lives of two young men living in a Chicago neighbourhood in the U.S.)

www.sportinsociety.org (the Center for the Study of Sport in Society often posts its most recent *Race and Gender Report Card*; this provides valuable information about patterns of fairness and discrimination in major sport organizations in the United States)

www.sportinsociety.org/sportscap.html (designed to provide women, people of colour, and people with disabilities with improved access to the sporting industry ranging from internships to high-level management, legal, and medical positions)

WEBSITE RESOURCES

Note: Websites often change. The following URLs were current when this book was printed. Please check our website (www.mcgrawhill.ca/college/coakley) for updates and additions.

(Alison Derry)

Sports and the Economy

What are the characteristics of commercial sports?

The National Hockey League is a business. Its business is entertainment. The entertainment it presents is sport.

—**John Ziegler, former NHL Commissioner (1978)**

When I started in track and field, there was no confusion about goals, no lure of money. I didn't think of money, because nobody did then. You did track and field because it was wonderful to do. It was something very deep inside you, something very personal. It was not something to barter.

—**Debbie Brill, Canadian high jumper (1986)**

We played hockey because we loved it. Anything we got paid was a bonus.

—**Maurice "Rocket" Richard (n.d.)**

I don't see myself as a hockey team owner. I see myself as a sports/entertainment/media brand manager.

—**Ted Leonsis, owner, Washington Capitals (2000)**

What corrupts an athletic performance…is…the presence of an unappreciative, ignorant audience and the need to divert it with sensations extrinsic to the performance. It is at this point that…sports …degenerate into spectacle.

—**Christopher Lasch, social critic (1977)**

 Online Learning Centre Resources

Visit *Sports in Society's* Online Learning Centre at **www.mcgrawhill.ca/college/coakley** for additional information and study material for this chapter.

Sports have been used through history as forms of public entertainment. However, sports never have been so thoroughly commercialized as they are today. Never before have economic factors so totally dominated decisions about sports, and never before have economic organizations and large corporate interests had so much power and control over the meaning, organization, and purpose of sports. The economic stakes for athletes and sponsors have never been higher than they are today. The bottom line has replaced the goal line for many people associated with sports. For example, shares in the Manchester United soccer club rose on the London (England) stock market after David Beckham was sold to the Real Madrid club.

Sports today are evaluated in terms of gate receipts and revenues from the sale of concessions, licensing fees, merchandise, media rights, and Internet hits. Games and events are evaluated in terms of market shares, ratings points, and advertising potential. Athletes are evaluated in terms of endorsement potential and media personas; their popularity and celebrity often depend on their ties to corporate names and logos. Stadiums, teams, and athletic events are named after large corporations rather than historical figures and places with local meaning. Corporate interests influence team colours, uniform designs, the scheduling of events, how the media will cover events, and even what announcers will say during the coverage. In fact, media/entertainment companies own a growing number of sport teams; they sponsor and even own events in the new "sportainment industry." Sports are now corporate enterprises, integrally tied to marketing concerns and processes of global capitalist expansion. The mergers of major corporate conglomerates during the 1990s have connected sports teams, sport events, media companies, entertainment industries, and the Internet. The names of transnational corporations have become synonymous with the athletes, events, and sports that provide pleasure in people's lives.

Because of the importance of economic factors in sports, this chapter focuses on the following questions:

1. Under what conditions do commercial sports emerge and prosper?
2. How does commercialization influence the meaning, organization, and purpose of sports?
3. Who are the people who own, sponsor, and promote sports, and what are their interests?
4. How much money do athletes make, and what is their legal status in various sports?

Because of the overwhelming presence of male professional team sports, and the availability of economic data, this chapter tends to focus on those forms of sports. Also, because of the globalized nature of economies and sports, it is difficult to take a particularly Canadian approach to this chapter on sports and the economy. Many of Canada's sports are shared with the U.S., or even more internationally in the case of, for example, golf and hockey. Canada's economy is integrated with the U.S. to a very great extent, and some of our major sport teams and leagues are "branch plants" of U.S. leagues.[1] Players and coaches are highly mobile, crossing borders with little difficulty, and Canada has seen three major teams (Vancouver Grizzlies of the NBA and the Quebec Nordiques and Winnipeg Jets of the NHL) move to the United States in recent years. Even those most Canadian of sports, curling and lacrosse, are influenced—the National Lacrosse League is a cross-border league, and curling is not only international, it is also produced and mediated as a part of the international sportainment industry. Thus, these interconnections are reflected in this chapter.

---

[1] Cantelon (2001) has argued that even the CFL is Americanized to a disturbing extent. *Note:* The term North American is used in this chapter to refer to Canada and the United States, and excludes Mexico.

THE EMERGENCE AND GROWTH OF COMMERCIAL SPORTS

General Conditions

Commercial sports are organized and played to make money as entertainment events. They depend on a combination of gate receipts, concessions, sponsorships, and the sale of media broadcasting rights. Therefore, commercial sports grow and prosper best under certain social and economic conditions.

First, they are most prevalent in market economies, where material rewards are highly valued by those connected with sports, including athletes, team owners, event sponsors, and spectators.

Second, commercial sports usually exist in societies with large, densely populated cities, because they require large concentrations of potential spectators. Although some forms of commercial sports can be maintained in rural, agricultural societies, revenues would support neither full-time professional athletes nor full-time sport promoters. Thus, only four provinces in Canada have NHL teams, and only six provinces have CFL teams.

Third, commercial sports require that people in a society have time, money, transportation, and media connections to attend or to use the media to tune into sport events. Commercial sports are a luxury, and they prosper only in societies where the standard of living is high enough that people can afford to use resources playing and watching events that have no tangible products. Commercial sports require sophisticated transportation and communication systems, so that sponsors can make money. Therefore, they are most commonly found in relatively wealthy, urban, and industrial or postindustrial societies; they are found less often in labour-intensive, poor societies where people focus their energy and resources on staying alive rather than paying to be entertained by athletes.

Fourth, commercial sports require *large amounts of capital* to build and maintain stadiums and arenas in which events can be played and watched. Capital funds can be accumulated in either the public or the private sector, but, in either case, the willingness to invest in sports depends on anticipated payoffs in the form of publicity, profits, or power. Private investment in sports is motivated primarily by expected financial profits; public investment is motivated primarily by a belief by those in power that commercial sports will serve their own interests, the interests of "the public," or a combination of both (see chapter 13).

Fifth, commercial cross-border sports depend, to a certain extent, on a favourable exchange rate. The artificially low Canadian dollar of the 1990s and early 2000s created difficulties for some Canadian teams competing in leagues where they are obliged to make payments in U.S. dollars.

Sixth, commercial sports are most likely to flourish in cultures where lifestyles involve high rates of consumption and emphasize material status symbols. This enables everything associated with sports to be marketed and sold: athletes (including their names, autographs, and images), merchandise, even team names and logos. When people express their identities through possessions such as clothing or equipment, and through associations with visible representatives of the community, they are likely to buy sport tickets and other possessions that associate them with sports, teams, and athletes. Passions and states of mind are sold to audiences, and then audiences are sold to sponsors and the media (Burstyn, 1999).

Class Relations and Commercial Sports

Which sports become commercialized in a society? As noted in chapter 10, priority is usually given to the sports that are followed and watched by people who possess or control economic resources in society. For example, golf has become a major commercial sport, even though it does not lend itself to commercial presentation. It is inconvenient to stage a golf event for a live audience, and it is difficult to cover golf on television. Camera placements and media commentary are difficult to arrange, and live spectators see only a small portion of the action. Golf does not involve vigorous action or head-to-head competition, except in rare cases of match play. Basically, if you do not play golf, you have little or no reason to watch it.

But a high proportion of those who *do* play golf are relatively wealthy and powerful people. These people are important to sponsors and advertisers, because they make consumption decisions for themselves and their families, as well as for their businesses and thousands of employees. They buy luxury cars or computers for themselves, but, what is more important to advertisers, they buy thousands of company cars and computers for employees. Furthermore, they make investment decisions involving money from a variety of sources, and they buy high-ticket items that other people can not afford. Golfers as a group have economic clout that goes far beyond their personal and family lives.

This makes golf an attractive sport for advertisers, who sell images and products to consumers with money and influence. This is why auto companies with high-priced cars sponsor and advertise on the PGA, LPGA, and Champions PGA tours. This is also the reason major television companies cover golf tournaments: they can sell commercial time at a high rate per minute, because those watching golf have money to spend—their money and the money of the companies, large and small, that they control. The converse of this is also true: sports attracting low- and middle-income audiences often are ignored by television or covered only under special circumstances.

Market economies always privilege the interests of those who have the power and resources to influence which sports are selected for promotion and coverage. Unless people with power and resources are interested in playing, sponsoring, or watching a sport, it is not likely to be commercialized on a large scale. When wealthy and powerful people are interested in a sport, it will be covered, promoted, and presented as if it had cultural significance in society. The sport may even be described as a "national pastime" and come to be associated with the development of ideal personal character, community spirit, civic unity, and political loyalty. Furthermore, it may be supported with public money allocated for the construction of stadiums and arenas, even if this directly subsidizes and benefits wealthy team owners, sponsors, and promoters.

This is one reason hockey has become "Canada's game." Hockey celebrates and privileges the values and experiences of the men who control and benefit from corporate wealth and power in North America. This explains why men pay thousands of dollars to buy expensive season tickets to professional hockey games, why male executives use corporate credit cards to buy blocks of "company tickets" to hockey games, and why corporation presidents write hundred-thousand-dollar cheques to pay for luxury boxes and club seats for themselves, friends, and clients. Hockey is entertaining for these spectators, but, more important, it also reproduces a way of viewing the world that fosters their interests. These arguments apply even more to the case of football in the U.S.

Of course, women who want to be a part of the power structure often discover it is wise to do what the men do. If women executives do not play golf, or go to the next big game, and take clients with them, they may be cut out of the "masculinity loop" that is the core of corporate culture.

The Creation of Spectator Interest in Sports

How do so many people become sport spectators in certain societies? Why do they look to sports for entertainment? Although these are complex questions with many answers, in many societies, spectator interest is related to a quest for excitement, a cultural emphasis on material success, personal experiences in sports, and easy access to sports through the media.

The Quest for Excitement What happens when social life becomes highly controlled and organized? Can we become stuck in everyday routines to the point that we become emotionally stale and seek activities that offer tension-excitement and emotional arousal? According to figurational sociologists Eric Dunning and Norbert Elias, historical evidence suggests that this has occurred in modern societies. Sports, they argue, offer contexts in which rules and norms can be defined and interpreted to allow forms of emotional arousal and exciting behaviours that eliminate boredom without disrupting social order (Dunning, 1999; Elias and Dunning, 1986). In fact, sports generally are characterized by a tension between boredom and social disruption. Managing this tension involves a challenge: norms and rules must be loose enough to break boredom, but not so loose that they permit violence or other forms of dangerous or disruptive deviance. When norms and rules become too controlling, sports become boring and people lose interest; when they are too loose, sports become sites for reckless and dangerous behaviours, which can jeopardize health as well as social order. Finding the balance and maintaining it is the trick.

This explanation of spectator interest in sports raises other questions. Why do many people give priority to sports over other activities in their quest for excitement? Critical theorists suggest that answers can be found by looking at the connection between ideology and cultural practices. This leads us to consider three other factors.

Success Ideology and Spectator Interest Many people watch games or read about them now and then, but spectator involvement is highest among those who are committed to the twin ideas that success is always based on hard work and that hard work always leads to success.

These people often use sports as a model for how the social world *should* operate. When sports promote the idea that success is achieved only through hard work and dedication to efficiency, these people have their beliefs and expectations reaffirmed, and they are willing to pay for that reaffirmation. This is why sport media commentators emphasize that athletes and teams make their own breaks and that luck comes to those who work hard. This is why large corporations use the bodies of elite athletes to represent their public relations and marketing images, emphasizing efficiency, power, the use of technology, and the achievement of success (Hoberman, 1994). And this is why athletes make so much money today—they reaffirm a success ideology, which reproduces privilege among powerful people around the globe.

Youth Sport Programmes and Spectator Interest Spectator interest often is created and nurtured during childhood sport participation. When organized youth sport programmes are publicized and made available to many young people in a society, commercial sports have a better chance to grow and prosper. With some exceptions, sport participation during childhood leads to spectator interests during adulthood. Children who learn to value sport skills and emphasize competitive success in their personal experiences generally grow up wanting to watch the "experts" compete with one another. For those who continue to participate actively in sports, watching the experts provides models for improving skills and motives for playing sports as well as they can. For those who no longer play sports, watching the experts maintains connections with the images and experiences of success learned in organized competitive youth sports.

Media Coverage and Spectator Interest The media promote the commercialization of sports (see chapter 12). They provide needed publicity and create and sustain spectator interest among large numbers of people. In the past, newspapers and radio did this job; today television has the greatest effect on spectator involvement; tomorrow it may well be the Internet.

Television has increased spectator access to events and athletes all over the world, and it provides a unique "re-presentation" of sports. It lets viewers see close-up camera shots of the action on the field/court/ice, and the athletes and coaches on the sidelines/benches/dugouts. It replays crucial plays and shows them in slow motion, helping viewers imagine that even they could do what elite athletes do. It even brings viewers into the locker rooms of championship teams.

On-air commentators serve as fellow spectators for the media audience, including those "interactive" spectators watching television while they are online with sports websites. These commentators heighten identification with athletes and dramatize and embellish the action in an event. They supply inside stories, analyze strategies, describe athletes as personalities, and glorify the event, magnifying its importance.

Television can be especially effective in recruiting new spectators. People who have not played a sport themselves must learn the rules and strategies used in a sport before they become faithful spectators. This learning occurs easily through television. No tickets need be purchased, and questions that may sound stupid in front of strangers can be asked without embarrassment in the family living room. In other words, television provides a painless way to become a spectator, and it increases the number of people who will buy tickets, regularly watch televised games, and even become pay-per-view customers in the future.

Economic Motives and the Globalization of Commercial Sports

Commercial sports have become global in scope for two reasons. *First*, those who control, sponsor, and promote sports are looking constantly for new ways to expand their markets and maximize profits. *Second*, transnational corporations with production and distribution operations in many countries can use sports as vehicles for introducing their products and services all around the world. The following recent examples illustrate these two reasons.

Sport Organizations Look for Global Markets

Sport organizations, like other businesses, wish to expand their operations into as many markets as possible around the world. For example, team and league profits would increase significantly if the U.S.–based NFL and the North American–based NBA, NHL, and Major League Baseball (MLB) were able to sell broadcasting rights to television companies in countries around the world and were able to sell licensed merchandise (hats, shirts, jackets, etc.) to people around the world. This is already occurring, but the continued success of many major sport organizations requires that they create spectator interest outside the boundaries of their home nations. Success also depends on using the media to export a combination of game knowledge and athlete-identification. In this way, sport organizations become exporters of culture as well as products to be consumed. The complex export-import processes that occur in connection with sports were studied by sociologists in the past and are attracting more attention today (Donnelly, 1996a; Klein, 1991, 1997; Maguire, 1999).

The desire for global expansion was the main reason the NBA was happy to let its players represent their national teams in the Olympics starting in 1992, even though the players risked injury and fatigue, which could have jeopardized their participation in the following NBA season (and did, in a few cases). The worldwide coverage of Olympic basketball provided the NBA with publicity worth many millions of dollars. This publicity has helped market NBA broadcasting rights and official NBA products all over the world, including China. High-profile NBA players have been introduced to hundreds of millions of people, and many of these people have become more interested in seeing these players in action.

Therefore, the NBA finals and All-Star games are now televised in over one hundred countries every year.

NHL hockey followed the NBA's lead in 1998, entering national "dream teams" in the Olympics. Major League Baseball has even organized The Envoy Program, which sends the best high school and university baseball coaches in North America to work with federations and young players in other countries (Johnson, 2000). This programme has targeted twenty-nine countries, and now MLB merchandise is distributed in nineteen countries outside North America, and nearly one in four players on major league teams were born outside the United States.

The recruitment of international players also has an impact on expanding markets. Interest in the NHL has grown significantly in Europe with the increase in the number of European players. Star players can also have a surprising impact. Ichiro Suzuki and several other Japanese players have not only increased interest in MLB in Japan, but also attracted Japanese tourists and Japanese-Canadian and Japanese-American fans to baseball games. Similarly, Yao Ming's success with the Houston Rockets of the NBA has greatly increased interest in the NBA in China, and attracted Chinese-Canadian fans to games when Houston plays in Toronto. International interest also expands the market for league products.

The spirit of global expansion has led NFL, NBA, NHL, and MLB teams to play games in Mexico, Japan, England, France, Germany, Australia, and other countries. The NHL always has been a Canadian–U.S. league; MLB and the NBA have franchises in large Canadian cities; the NFL, which has a relationship with the CFL, assisted in the formation of the World Football League and even subsidized the formation of a football league in Europe (Maguire, 1990). So far, American football has not been very successful in Europe, although it has been a little more successful than the attempt by the CFL to expand into the U.S. market.

This spirit of global capitalist expansion is not new; nor is it limited to North American sport organizations. Sports such as soccer and tennis already enjoy a global market, and sports such as rugby and cricket are seeking more global markets. The International Olympic Committee (IOC) gradually has incorporated national Olympic committees from over two hundred nations and has turned the Olympic games into the most successful and financially lucrative media sport events in human history. Soccer's FIFA (Fédération Internationale de Football Association) has a long history of global expansion, which predates the global expansion of any North American sports (Sugden and Tomlinson, 1998, 1999). When the 1994 Soccer World Cup for men and the 1999 World Cup for women were hosted in the U.S.A., the people in charge of FIFA clearly realized they had much to gain if they could create spectator interest in soccer among Americans. Soccer exceeds hockey in youth participation in Canada, and is second only to basketball in youth participation in the United States. Media companies in Canada and the United States have discovered that traditional and new ethnic populations in many cities are eager to see soccer teams representing their nations of origin or the nations of their parents or grandparents (Donnelly, et al., 2002).

Corporations Use Sports as Vehicles for Global Expansion The fact that sports, sporting events, sport teams, and athletes can be used to capture the attention and emotions of millions of people has not gone unnoticed in the world of business. Corporations need symbols of success, excellence, and productivity that they can use to create "marketing handles" for their products and services and to create public good will for their policies and practices. This is why corporations have invested so much money into associating their names and logos with athletes, teams, events, and sport facilities.

"Winning at sports isn't so hard. It's all in the uniform."

The expansion and growth of commercial sports around the world have little to do with the players' interests. Owners and executives from the media and other corporations are making many of the decisions about sports today.

People around the world still associate Michael Jordan with the "Air Jordan" trademark copyrighted by Nike. They frequently associate the Olympics with Coca-Cola. In Canada and the United States, the crowning Olympic achievement is to have your image on a cereal box. Status among many children depends on wearing expensive shoes and clothing with official logos and other sport images on them. The Canadian-based athletic clothing company, Roots, which first came to international attention when it outfitted the Canadian team at the Nagano Olympics in 1998, achieved a marketing coup when it won the rights to clothe both the Canadian and U.S. (and several other) teams at the Salt Lake City Olympics in 2002—enjoying huge sales of replica items in both Canada and the U.S. Companies whose profits depend on the sales of alcohol, tobacco, fast food, and candy are eager to have their products associated with the healthy image of athletes and sports; this enables them to respond to those who would challenge the wholesomeness of their products. After all, if beer, cigarettes, beef burgers, deep fried foods, and candy bars bring us the sports we love, how can they be bad for our health?

Sportswriter Jay Weiner has argued that Michael Jordan was a key figure in the process of corporations' using sports to boost bottom lines. He explains that Jordan "commercialized his sport and himself, turning both into brands for an emerging legion of sports marketers....In his own way, Jordan did spread an ideology. It was that sports are not just games but tools for advertisers. It was that basketball isn't a playground thing, but a corporate thing" (1999: 77).

We now live in an era of the transnational corporation. Of the one hundred largest economies in the world in terms of revenues, one-half are corporations, not nations (Anderson and Cavanagh, 1996). General Motors, Exxon, Mobil, Mitsubishi, Mitsui, and Ford Motor Company each have an economy greater than that of over 80 percent of the nations around the world. The two hundred largest corporations in the world control over one-third of the economic activity around the globe. The decisions made by executives in these corporations influence the economies of entire nations and even regions of the world: they affect which people have jobs, what they do in those jobs, how much they make, what the working conditions are, what products will be available for purchase, and how much they will cost.

When these corporations enter the world of sports, they negotiate deals that promote their interests and increase their power in the realm of transnational relations. At this point, their power is largely unchecked; the so-called free trade initiatives of the 1990s, such as the World Trade Organization and the North American Free Trade Agreement, enable many organizations to operate largely outside the laws of any single nation. Capitalist expansion in the past was at least partly regulated, and its negative consequences were partly softened by the laws of nation-states. Today, however, capital flows with few restrictions, often outside the control of nation-states. As corporations and the multibillionaires who own or control them continue to do business around the world, they need to create global images of themselves as positive cultural, political, and economic forces.

This is partly why corporations pay billions of dollars every year to sponsor sports and why, in the U.S., for example, they spend three times as much sponsoring sports as they do sponsoring the arts, festivals and fairs, and attractions. General Motors and Coca-Cola will combine to spend nearly $2 billion to sponsor Olympic sports between 1998 and 2008. Like other transnational corporations, they want to promote the belief that enjoyment and pleasure in people's everyday lives depend on corporations and their products. Their goal is to use this belief as the foundation for *ideological outposts* in the minds of people around the world (see chapter 4). Corporate executives realize that they can use such outposts to defuse opposition to corporate policies, and they can use them as transmission points through which to deliver a wide range of ideological messages about what is and should be happening in the world. This is an especially useful strategy for global corporations that want to defuse resistance to products that may not be compatible with local cultural values, such as Coca-Cola and Kentucky Fried Chicken in Islamic Pakistan.

For example, when a Coca-Cola executive gave a presentation to IOC officials before the 1996 Games, he assumed that, after nearly eighty years of sponsoring the Olympics, Coca-Cola had established outposts he could use to transmit messages that the officials would accept, so he told the officials the following:

> Just as sponsors have the responsibility to preserve the integrity of the sport, enhance its image, help grow its prestige and its attendance, so too, do you [in sports] have responsibility and accountability to the sponsor. (Reid, 1996: 4BB)

Of course, in the face of millions of sponsorship dollars, these officials were not likely to oppose the interests of Coca-Cola or to resist the notion that they were responsible for promoting Coca-Cola's interests around the world and would be

held accountable for doing so. The fact that drinking cola was not consistent with the nutritional profile of elite athletes or the worldwide health goals of the Olympic Movement no longer mattered to the sports officials; their minds had been colonized by Coca-Cola.

Outposts in Action: Branding Sports Ranchers sear their logos (brands) onto the hide of the animals, so there is no doubt about ownership or control. Corporations have done the same things with sports (Bellamy, 1998).

Sport venues have been branded by airlines, such as the Air Canada Centre (Toronto) and the United Center (Chicago); communications and high-tech corporations, such as the Corel Centre (Ottawa), Bell Centre (Montreal), and the MCI Center (Washington); and automobile corporations, such as General Motors Place (Vancouver) and Ford Stadium (Detroit). There are dozens of additional stadiums named after other corporations in finance and oil (Pengrowth Centre) banking, real estate, retailing, and even lifting equipment (Skyreach Centre). In fact, North American stadiums without corporate names are becoming rare. Local traditions, used as the basis for naming sport places in the past, are being abandoned for the benefit of corporations that own the teams that use them.[2]

The branding of sport places also exists inside the stadiums, arenas, and gymnasia, where every available surface is sold to corporate sponsors. Surfaces without corporate messages are now defined as wasted space, even in publicly owned facilities. As corporations brand public spaces, community identities are transformed into brand identities, and the physical embodiments of local traditions and histories are transformed into corporate embodiments of messages to

---

[2]Each paragraph in this section could have been extended to a full page of examples of how corporations have branded sports. The examples here are a small sample of what could have been included.

The corporate branding of sport events, facilities, and participants is widespread today. Corporations whose profits come from the sale of alcohol, tobacco, fast food, and candy are especially eager to sponsor sports. They want their products associated with activities defined as healthy or deeply connected with important cultural values, such as those related to the auto-mobile and individualism, power, and speed. Canadian government legislation to end tobacco sponsorship takes full effect in October, 2003, which will mean the removal of Players sponsorship on cars such as this one at the 2002 Montreal Indy, and may mean the end of Canada's most lucrative tourist event, the Formula 1 Grand Prix of Montreal. (CP/Ryan Remiorz)

consume and enjoy the place, compliments of corporations that bring pleasure into our lives.

Sport events have been branded. Auto racing has the Air Canada Formula 1 Grand Prix in Montreal, and the Molson Indy Champ Car races in Montreal, Vancouver, and Toronto. Tennis has the Rogers AT&T Cup for women (there is no name sponsor for the men's Tennis Masters Series tournament in Canada at the time of writing). Golf has the Bell Canadian Open, the Telus Skins Game, and the BMO Financial Group Canadian Women's Open. Curling has the Nokia Brier, the Scott Tournament of Hearts, and the Ford World Curling Championships. Skiing has the Pontiac GMC Cup Alpine races, the Mars Canadian Juvenile Championships, and the CIBC Coupe Nor-Am Cup Series. Skating has MasterCard Skate Canada, and the BMO Financial Group

Canadian Championships. And Subaru is the name sponsor on an adventure racing series.

Corporate branders have missed very few sports. In 2001, Export A was sponsoring extreme sports events in defiance of the tobacco ban (discussed later in this chapter), promoting cigarettes to adolescents. Molson's Sno-Jam was one of the sites where Export A distributed trin-kets such as key chains and screensavers. Mountain, road, and track cycling national championships in Canada are all sponsored by Tim Hortons. And equestrian events at Spruce Meadows have such illustrious sponsors as the BMO Financial Group (again), Shell, BP, Chrysler, and Direct Energy.

Corporations brand teams around the world in cycling, soccer, rugby, and most other sports. Teams in Japan are named after corporations, not just cities. Players and even referees in most sports wear corporate logos on their uniforms. Soccer teams often are known for their "colours," and corporations have made it a point to incorporate their logos and names onto the jerseys associated with teams. Many soccer teams wear the logo of a sport manufacturer endorsed by the league, along with the logo of the team sponsor. Manchester United, the most famous team in the world, wears the logos of Nike and Vodaphone on its uniforms.

Agents today tell their athletes that they are brands and that their goal is to merge with other commercial entities. We now know "Air Jordan" (Michael Jordan and Nike), "Air Canada" (Vince Carter and Air Canada), "Shaq Attaq" (Shaquille O'Neal and Reebok), and other athletes through their mergers with corporations. We think of them in terms of their endorsement identities as well as their play on the field. In fact, Michael Jordan, Wayne Gretzky, and John Elway established mvp.com, a website enabling them to present themselves as brands and to offer site visitors opportunities to "Shop by Sport," "Shop by Brand," and "Shop by Department." If you cannot shop and consume by yourself, they will advise you on what to buy and how it will make your game better and give you pleasure. These athletes, whose celebrity is so great that it potentially transcends corporate branding, are realizing that they can make more money if they turn themselves into brands than if they simply endorse corporate products.

The NFL's Super Bowl, too expensive for a large corporation to brand on its own, has become known as much for its television commercials as for the game. The game generates much interest in Canada, though Canadians rarely see the ads that cost so much money—US$2.2 million for 30 seconds in 2003.

The future of corporate branding is difficult to predict. A cellphone company paid Joseph Chebet to take a portable phone and pretend he was calling long distance to Kenya after he crossed the finish line as the winner of the 1999 "long-distance" Boston Marathon. The call was bogus, but the race and the finish line were branded through a covert strategy. New technologies will be used in future branding strategies. Ads during television coverage are being inserted digitally on the field, court, and other surfaces of arenas and stadiums. Virtual advertising will become standard as people buy video recorders that edit out commercials. Corporations will stop buying commercial time and start buying "brand placement rights," so that their names, logos, and products will appear directly in the content of the games and matches. This makes it possible for athletes' uniforms and bodies to be branded and for the brand to be changed whenever a new corporation pays higher rights fees.

Can corporations go too far in their branding of sports? There seems to be little resistance to corporate branding; however, Nike apparently went too far when it attempted to brand the clothing worn by the journalists covering the 1998 Nagano Games. It seems that athletes, teams, events, and places are for sale, but the journalists who report the news about sports are not for sale, yet.

It is obvious that sports are for sale, and corporations are the buyers. Corporate executives realize that sports produce enjoyable and emotional identifications with athletes, teams, events, and places; therefore, corporations have branded them to associate their products and services with sources of pleasure in people's lives. In less than a generation, sports have been so thoroughly branded that many people accept it as inevitable—just the way it is, and the way it should be. This is how ideologies are formed and how hegemony occurs in the process (see chapter 4).

In summary, commercial sports grow and prosper best in urban, industrial societies with relatively efficient transportation and communications systems, combined with a standard of living that allows people the time and money to play and watch sports. Class relations are involved in the process through which sports become commercialized. Spectator interest is grounded in a combination of a quest for excitement, ideologies emphasizing success, the existence of youth sport programmes, and media coverage that introduces people to the rules of sports and the athletes who play them. Sport organizations and powerful transnational corporations have fostered the global expansion of commercial sports that can be marketed profitably. This expansion seems likely to continue into the foreseeable future as corporations continue to brand athletes, teams, events, and sport places. The next question to ask is whether commercialization changes the games themselves.

COMMERCIALIZATION AND CHANGES IN SPORTS

What happens to sports when they become commercialized and dependent on revenues? Do they change, and, if so, in what ways?

Whenever a sport is converted into commercial entertainment, its success depends on spectator appeal. Although spectators have a variety of motives underlying their attachment to sports, their interest in sport events usually is related to a combination of three factors:

- The uncertainty of an event's outcome ("Is it going to be a close contest?")
- The risk or financial rewards associated with participating in an event ("How much is at stake in the contest?"; "How much money is involved, or pride, ego, and physical well-being?")
- The anticipated display of excellence, heroics, or dramatic display by the athletes ("Who is playing, and how good or flashy is the person?")

When spectators say they saw a "good game," they usually are talking about one in which (1) the outcome was in doubt until the last minutes or seconds, (2) the stakes were so high that the athletes were totally committed to and engrossed in the action, or (3) there were a number of excellent, heroic, or dramatic performances. Games or matches that contain all three factors are remembered and discussed for a long time.

Because uncertainty, high stakes, and excellent/heroic/dramatic performances attract spectators, commercial sports emphasize these things to attract large audiences. To understand the changes associated with commercialization, we must look at three aspects of sports:

1. The structure and goals of sports
2. The orientations of the athletes, coaches, and sponsors
3. The organizations that control sports

Structure and Goals of Sports

Commercialization influences the structure and goals of most newly developed sports, but it has not produced dramatic changes in most long-established sports. Among the new sports developed for commercial purposes, it is clear that rules have been designed to promote on-the-field action that a targeted audience will see as entertaining. Entertainment is *not* the only issue considered in connection with the structure and goals of these sports, but it is a primary issue. This is apparent in the case of sports such as indoor soccer, indoor football, beach volleyball, roller hockey, and certain forms of extreme games. For example, the rules in the X Games are designed to attract the attention of younger viewers who have less interest in football and tennis than in skateboarding, in-line skating, and BMX cycling; the rules emphasize dangerous and spectacular moves as well as the use of technical equipment manufactured by event sponsors.

Established sports have undergone rule changes to make the action more exciting and understandable for spectators, but the changes have not altered the basic designs and rule structures of the games themselves. For example, the commercialization of the Olympic Games has led to minor rule changes in certain events, such as the introduction of rally scoring in volleyball and the cutting of compulsory routines from gymnastics and figure skating, but the basic structure of the typical event has remained much as it was before the days of corporate endorsements and the sale of television rights. Of course, there is ongoing talk about some events with little spectator appeal being dropped from the Olympics (e.g., fencing, modern pentathlon). The Olympic Programme Commission, which develops and presents recommendations on sports and Olympic events to the IOC Executive Board, has media interest as a primary mandate for admitting or retaining a sport in the Games. Thus, new sports have been added to attract new viewers (e.g., beach volleyball, snowboarding), especially younger viewers from wealthy countries where people have money to spend on sponsors' products.

The enormous television audiences in North America for Olympic ice hockey at the 2002 Salt Lake City Olympics—in Canada, over ten million for the men's final and some seven million for the women's final—have caused the NHL to look more seriously at the international rules for the game. It is clear that the audiences found the large ice surfaces (leading to a more open passing game and less obstruction), the restrictions against fighting, and the hurry-up face-off rule extremely attractive in leading to a faster-paced, more exciting game. Given the NHL Governors' conservative reluctance to tamper with any of the rules of hockey lest some parts of the audience become displeased (e.g., slow change and inconsistent enforcement of the obstruction rule, reluctance to outlaw fighting), and their outright refusal to adopt a larger ice surface because it would mean removal of some of the highest priced seats at their arenas, they adopted the hurry-up face-off with surprising speed. The result was faster games during the 2002–03 season, often lasting only two-and-a-half hours instead of the usual three hours. However, an unintended consequence has been the need for television broadcasters to review their schedule for commercials since there are fewer game breaks in which to show them. Also, there is a great deal more time between the first and second games on *Hockey Night in Canada*, which broadcasters are learning how to fill.

Rule development and rule changes associated with commercialization usually are intended to do a combination of five things: (1) speed up the action, so that fans will not become bored; (2) increase scoring to generate excitement; (3) balance competition, so that events will have uncertain outcomes; (4) maximize the dramatic moments in the competition; and (5) provide commercial breaks in the action, so that sponsors can advertise products.[3]

A review of rule changes in many sports shows the importance of these five factors. For example, the designated hitter position in baseball's American League was added to increase scoring opportunities and heighten the dramatic action. Soccer and hockey rules were changed in an attempt to prevent matches from ending in ties. Tennis scoring was changed to meet the time requirements of television schedules. The four-rock rule was introduced to encourage more offensive play in curling. Golf tournaments now involve total stroke counts, rather than match play, so that big-name players will not be eliminated in the early rounds of televised events. Free throws were minimized in basketball to speed up action. Sudden-death overtime periods were added to many sports, so that spectators can determine the winner easily, without having to assess the overall quality of play in an event.

Even though many of the changes have been prompted by commercial concerns, they have not altered the basic structure and goals of most long-established sports. Furthermore, changes also reflect the concerns of athletes, who have more fun when there is more action,

---

[3] Rule changes such as those concerning women's uniforms imposed by the international volleyball federation also seem to be designed to draw audiences by selling sex appeal.

"Our football league will give the people what they **REALLY** want—substance-enhanced brutes maiming each other without the restrictions of 'sissy rules.' God bless America."

When Vince McMahon, majority owner of World Wrestling Entertainment, announced his proposed football league, the XFL, he clearly indicated that the new league would be based on what he learned as he turned pro wrestling into a major entertainment form. NBC liked what he said and signed a TV contract with the league. But the league failed after just one season.

more scoring, and a closer contest. Players may object to TV time-outs, but they and their coaches now anticipate them and use them in their overall game strategies.

Because sports are social constructions, they change in connection with social relationships and shifts in social conditions and power relations in the society as a whole. Some people regard the structure and goals of sports as sacred and unchangeable, but they overlook the fact that people established the rules for all sports, and the orientations of those people were influenced by their relationships and the cultural conditions prevalent at the time the rules were made. Of course, it is important to

acknowledge that economic relations and conditions are carefully considered today as changes are discussed and made.

People may voice complaints about changes in the structure and goals of sports when they attend events that have been organized intentionally as *total entertainment experiences*, complete with loud rock and rap music, video displays designed to provide entertainment having little to do with sports, paid cheerleaders and mascots who direct crowd behaviour, fireworks displays, and on-site announcers who manage spectator emotions with their own excited verbal descriptions of and responses to the action. As dedicated, long-time sports fans sit through this "total entertainment experience," in which others do the wave, watch cartoon characters on the video display, and respond to the antics of paid mascots dressed in cartoon-like costumes, they complain that the game has changed. But, on the field of play, the rules and structure of the game probably have changed little; the biggest changes are in the context surrounding the game and in the orientations of the athletes, coaches, and sponsors.

Orientations of the Athletes, Coaches, and Sponsors

When sports are commercialized, they usually come to be characterized by a "promotional culture" (Gruneau and Whitson, 1993). Like other entertainment industries, commercial sports are geared to selling public performances to audiences and selling audiences to sponsors. Sports are promoted through marketing hype based on myths and images created around players and team identities. Athletes become entertainers, and some even become celebrities. In connection with the promotional culture of commercial sports, the orientations of those connected with the sport tend to emphasize heroic actions in addition to aesthetic actions.

This means that, when sports become entertainment, it is necessary to attract a mass audience to buy tickets or watch events on television.

Attracting and entertaining a *mass* audience is not easy. Such an audience consists of many people who lack technical knowledge about the complex physical skills and strategies used by athletes and coaches. Without this technical knowledge, hype and drama become primary sources of entertainment. Hype and drama are easily understood, so these spectators enjoy situations when athletes take risks and face clear physical danger; they are impressed by the dramatic expressions of athletes; and they are entertained by athletes dedicated to the game and to victory, regardless of personal cost. For example, when people lack technical knowledge about football, they are more likely to be entertained by a running back's end-zone dance after a touchdown than by the lineman's block that enabled the running back to score the touchdown. Those who know little about the technical aspects of ice skating are more entertained by triple and quadruple jumps than by difficult routines carefully choreographed and practised until they are smooth and flawless. Without dangerous jumps, naïve spectators quickly become bored. Those who lack technical knowledge about basketball are more likely to talk about a single slam dunk than about the well-coordinated defence that enabled the team to win a game. Karl Malone of the NBA Utah Jazz explains that players know this, and in the NBA they "are more concerned about dunking [than other aspects of the game, because] that's how you get on TV" (in Latimer, 2000: 28C). Thus, dunkmania rules, and players are booed if they "just" shoot a layup and ignored if they hit a 15-foot jump shot.

Spectators without technical knowledge about a sport tend to enjoy watching athletes project exciting or controversial personas, and they often rate performances in terms of dramatic expression leading to dramatic results. They are impressed by style as well as skills. They are thrilled by long touchdown passes, not 5-minute touchdown drives made up of 4- to 6-yard runs. They call for home runs, not sacrifice flies. They are more impressed by athletes who collapse as they surpass physical limits than by athletes who know their limits so well they can play for years without going beyond them.

Sports are not the only activities affected by commercialization in this way. For example, popular music has been developed as a form of mass entertainment, so that *style* (that is, the ability to project a distinct and dramatic persona) often supersedes musical ability as a basis for popularity and commercial success. Some popular music stars are great musicians, others are average, and some are lousy. When audiences lack technical knowledge about music, significant differences in musical ability can be buried under large amounts of style. It is style that sells; musical ability may be important, but it will not take a person to the top of the promotional culture of the popular music world.

After observing many athletes in all the major sports in the United States, commentator Bob Costas noted the following:

> The players have caught on to what the cameras want. They know what postures and noises will get them on air. [NBA players] know that cameras are under the basket. So a guy dunks the ball, looks right at the camera and screams. (Pluto, 1995: 275)

Costas knows that the players look at things differently when they are entertainers; in fact, after they do something entertaining, they even look at the replay screens from the field of play to view their actions as spectators.

Thus, when a sport depends on the entertainment of mass audiences, those who play and coach often revise their ideas about what is important in athletic performances. The danger of movement becomes important in addition to the beauty of movement; style and dramatic expression become important in addition to fundamental skills; pushing beyond limits becomes important in addition to exploring limits; and commitment to victory for the team and sponsor becomes important in addition to active participation. When sports become commercialized, most people associated with them develop *heroic orientations* in addition to *aesthetic orientations*.

Figure 11.1 explains these terms and outlines how athletes, coaches, and others associated with a sport might alter how they assess on-the-field performances as a sport becomes increasingly commercialized. It shows that, when there is a need to entertain a mass audience, orientations change. In fact, games or matches may be described as "showtime," the major leagues are often referred to as "the show," and athletes describe themselves as entertainers. This does *not* mean that aesthetic orientations cease to be important or that people are no longer impressed by beauty and skills in sports, but it does mean that heroic orientations enter into the mix of what constitutes a good sport performance. The heroic is what attracts a mass audience.

Some athletes, however, realize the dangers associated with heroic orientations and try to limit the emphasis on heroic actions in their sports. For example, some former figure skaters have called for restrictions on the number of triple and quadruple jumps that can be included in skating programmes. These skaters are worried that the commercial success of their sport is com-

ing to rely on the danger, rather than the beauty, of movement. Other skaters, however, seem to be willing to adopt heroic orientations in an effort to please audiences and meet the expectations of many athlete-peers in skating. The dynamics of this process are complex. We explored this in chapter 6, in our discussion of the way athletes come to use the norms of the sport ethic to evaluate themselves and others in their sports. Michelle Kwan won her third world skating championship in 2000, as she came from behind by landing seven triple jumps in her routine, while the leaders missed their triple-triple combinations.

Another indicator of the emphasis on heroic orientations and actions in commercialized sports appeared during the 1996 Olympics. *USA Today* rated Olympic athletes on an "Olympic Advertising Index" (7 August 1996: 3B). The index consisted of four 10-point scales: (1) Pizzazz Factor (flair, warmth, and charm), (2) On-Camera Appeal (poise, ability to project a positive and intelligent image), (3) Athletic Ability (medals won, records set), and (4) Rodman Potential (a negative scale related to marketing risk factors,

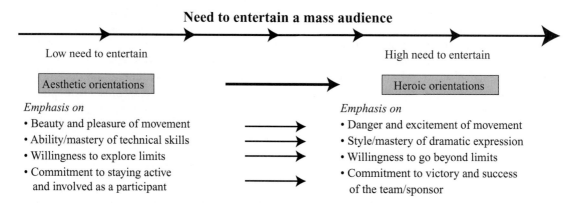

Note: The orientations associated with many spectator sports today have shifted from the aesthetic to the heroic. Many people in a mass audience do not have the technical knowledge about a sport to be entertained by aesthetic action; instead, they seek and focus on heroic action. Therefore, athletes, coaches, and others associated with the game put more emphasis on heroic orientations in their own approaches to action in the game.

FIGURE 11.1   Shifting orientations: what happens when there is a need to entertain a mass audience.

unpredictability). Scores on the four scales were totalled, and athletes were assessed in terms of their commodity value for sponsors. Scores such as these are used for endorsement purposes, but might they also be used to evaluate the revenue-generating potential of athletes as they are recruited and signed to contracts? This would be a logical extension of the commercial logic of today's spectator sports.

Organizations That Control Sports

Commercialization also leads to changes in the organizations that control sports. When sports depend on the revenues they generate, the control centre in sport organizations usually shifts further from the players. In fact, the players in heavily commercialized sports often lose effective control over the conditions of their own sport participation. These conditions come under the control of general managers, team owners, corporate sponsors, advertisers, media personnel, marketing and publicity staff, professional management staff, image consultants, accountants, and agents. The organizations that control commercial sports are intended to coordinate the interests of all these people, but their primary goal is to maximize revenues. This means that organizational decisions generally reflect the combined economic interests of many people having no direct personal connection with a sport or the athletes involved in it. The power to affect these decisions is grounded in resources that may not be connected with sports. Therefore, athletes in many commercial sports find themselves cut out of decision-making processes, even when the decisions affect their health and the rewards they receive for playing.

As decision making in sport organizations moves further away from athletes, there is a tendency to hire employees, develop policies, and negotiate deals that give a low priority to the interests of athletes. These organizational changes have important implications for what happens in sports. They also make it necessary for athletes to seek new tactics for promoting their own interests, financial and otherwise.

As corporate interests come to dominate sports, athletes often defer to the policy recommendations of team owners, agents, advertising executives, media people, and corporate sponsors. This was vividly illustrated by NBA player Scottie Pippen, who was asked why he was playing in the 1996 Olympics despite a bad ankle, which would interfere with his ability to play for the Chicago Bulls if he did not give it rest. Pippen said, "I made a commitment to a lot of companies, and I'm sticking with it." After he realized he had spoken too truthfully, he added, "But endorsements aren't the focal point. To play in an Olympics in my own country is something I've always wanted to do" (Michaelis, 1996: 8D). Despite his quick cover-up, it was clear that Pippen had accepted that the interests of his corporate sponsors were primary in his life. He knew he was dependent on corporations, and he answered to them first.

Commercialization has created a situation in which corporations define the conditions of sport participation. This is not especially new in North America, where people have accepted corporate branding of professional and other sports, but this shift is occurring more and more in other countries, where corporate interests promote the use of the North American commercial model for their sports, or where transnational corporations take the corporate model wherever they think money or publicity is to be gained by owning and sponsoring sports.

OWNERS, SPONSORS, AND PROMOTERS IN COMMERCIAL SPORTS

Professional Sports in North America

Professional sports are privately owned. The owners of most teams and franchises at all levels of professional sports, from the smallest minor league teams to the top franchises in the NFL, NBA, NHL, and MLB, are individuals or small partnerships. Large corporations, especially entertainment and real estate companies, own a growing proportion of the top teams and franchises. Similarly, sponsors and event promoters range from individuals and small businesses to large transnational corporations.

The ownership model established in North American professional team sports is by no means normal, or natural, or universal. The private ownership model is one choice out of several possible forms of ownership, one of which is the more public form of ownership uniquely exemplified in North America by the Green Bay Packers of the NFL. The team has 1,800 shareholders (90 percent of whom live in the Green Bay, Wisconsin, area), who own 4,700 shares in the team—no individual may own more than 200 shares.[4] In Europe and Australia, there are examples of teams owned by membership-based clubs. Club members democratically elect a board, which employs professional managers and coaches to run the team. These models allow shareholders and members to have some control on major decisions, and ensure accountability on the part of board members and employees. In a very real sense, it permits a community to share in, and enjoy a sense of ownership of, the team that claims to represent that community. Corporate laws also ensure that there is some transparency with regard to the team's accounts.

The private ownership model ensures that each of the major leagues functions as a private men's club for the owners (the vast majority of the owners are male), who are able to control the terms of their business in private, away from the eyes of the communities they supposedly represent and the fans of the teams. When funds are needed, these owners seek help from the taxpayer (through government subsidies or local government assistance in stadium rent relief or construction), rather than offering local people

an opportunity to own part of "their" team through a sale of shares. The private ownership model benefits team owners far more than fans.

Most people who own the hundreds of minor league teams around North America do not make much money. In fact, most are happy to break even and avoid the losses that are commonplace at this level of professional sports ownership. Also, many teams, leagues, and events have been financial disasters over the past forty years. Four football leagues, a hockey league, a few soccer leagues, a volleyball league, two men's and four women's basketball leagues, a team tennis league, and a number of basketball and soccer teams have all gone out of business, leaving many owners, sponsors, and promoters in debt. This list does not include all those who have lost money on tournaments and special events.

Ownership of the top professional franchises in North America is very different from ownership at other levels of professional sports. Franchise values ranged from about US$80 million to US$800 million in early 2003. Owners are large corporations, partnerships of wealthy individuals, or very wealthy individuals who have millions and even billions of dollars in personal assets. Leagues are organized as monopolies, teams often play in publicly subsidized facilities, owners make good to excellent returns on their investments, or realize other benefits. For example, media corporations that own teams are able to show the games on their networks, and use the broadcasts to advertise their other programmes. Owners of other businesses are able to use their ownership of professional sport teams to show their clients special and attractive forms of hospitality (such as the opportunity to meet the players, visit the locker room, and watch the game from the owner's box), which assists their other businesses. Support from media companies and corporate sponsors almost guarantees continued financial success at this level of ownership. The recent financial losses experienced by some owners in MLB and the NHL suggest that some owners may have damaged this "goose that laid the golden egg."

---

[4] The Green Bay Packers are an anomaly that reportedly makes the NFL and other major leagues quite uncomfortable. The NFL would much prefer that the team be sold to private owners; public ownership keeps alive the idea that other teams could be owned in this way.

Similarly, the large corporations that sponsor particular events, from major golf and tennis tournaments to Champ Car and Grand Prix races, know the costs and benefits associated with the events. Their association with top events not only provides them advertising platforms but also connects them with clearly identified categories of consumers. Television companies sponsor events, so that they can control their own programming. Entertainment companies own teams and sponsor events, so that they can control multiple aspects of the entertainment marketplace and link them together in mutually supportive ways—in the U.S., for example, from Disneyland to ABC television to ESPN to the Anaheim Mighty Ducks to nationwide promotions at fast-food restaurants, where action figures of sport celebrities can be sold with meals for children.

As previously noted, sport sponsorship enables companies that sell tobacco, alcohol, and various forms of food with questionable nutritional value to link their products and logos to popular activities. Because people associate sports with physical performance and strong bodies instead of cancer, heart disease, obesity, and other forms of poor health, these companies are eager to be sponsors. It increases their legitimacy in society and defuses resistance to corporate policies and practices. However, government concerns about the costs of health care resulting from the ongoing use of tobacco products led, in Canada and other countries, to regulations against tobacco sponsorship and advertising. Bill C-71, the Tobacco Act, was passed in 1997. The bill specifies a "phasing out" period, to be completed in 2003, for tobacco sponsorship of sports and cultural events. Event organizers have been busily seeking replacement sponsors for events ranging from tennis and golf to auto racing and equestrian. Grand Prix auto racing, which has relied heavily on tobacco sponsorship, is threatening to withdraw races from countries (including Canada) that no longer permit tobacco companies to advertise or sponsor events.

"This is Pepsi McDonald announcing live from L.A.'s Windows 2004 Stadium, where the Microsoft Raiders are set to meet the Boeing Seahawks. Team captains Nike Jones and Budweiser Williams prepare for the Franklin Mint Coin Toss, right after these words from our sponsors."

The branding of sports has become pervasive. Will it ever be this extreme? What will stop it from becoming like this?

Investments in sports and sport events are motivated by many factors. In some cases, investors are sports fans with money; they invest to satisfy life-long fantasies, to build their egos, or to experience vicariously the achievements of athletes. Sports ownership and sport sponsorship gain them more prestige than other business ventures, often making them instant celebrities in their cities; they are famous all over town, from the mayor's office and the Chamber of Commerce to neighbourhood bars and local elementary schools. Commercial sports enable these wealthy people to combine business and power seeking with fun.

However, those who invest in sports seldom get so carried away with fun and fantasy that they forget business or what it takes to promote capitalist expansion. They do not enjoy losing money or sharing power. They may look at their athletes as heroes and may even treat them as their children, but they want to control their athletes to maximize returns on their investments. They may be civic boosters and supporters of public projects, but they see the public good in terms that emphasize capitalist expansion and their business interests (Schimmel et al., 1993). Their goals are to generate revenues and to establish a firm basis for continued financial success. They may not agree with fellow owners and sponsors on all issues, but they do agree on the need to protect their investments and maximize profits.

Team Owners and Sport Leagues as Monopolies

The tendency to think alike has been especially strong among the team owners in the major North American sport leagues. In fact, unity among these owners has led to the formation of some of the most effective monopolies in the history of North American business. Even though each sport franchise in these leagues is a separate business, the franchise owners in each sport have come together to form organizations representing their collective interests. They traditionally have used these organizations to limit the extent to which teams compete against each other for players, fans, media revenues, and sales of licensed merchandise; they also have used the organizations to eliminate competition from those who might try to form other teams and leagues in their sports.

For example, each league (the NBA, the NFL, the NHL, and MLB) has developed a system to force new players to negotiate contracts only with the team that drafted them; this enables owners to sign new players to contracts without bidding against other teams, which might be willing to pay the players more money.[5] Owners also have

agreed to prevent new teams from being added to their leagues without their collective permission; when permission is given, the new team owner is charged an entry fee to become a part of the league. Since the 1960s, when these fees were first assessed, they have escalated from the US$600,000 paid by the Dallas Cowboys to join the NFL in 1960 to the US$700 million paid by Houston's NFL team in 1999 (the team's first season was in 2002). Between 1991 and 1994, four teams (including the Ottawa Senators) were added to the NHL, each paying expansion fees of US$50 million; between 1998 and 2001, four more teams were added, each paying expansion fees of US$80 million. These are just *entry fees*, divided among the existing owners. They do not include other start-up expenses, player salaries, or operating costs, which may amount to about US$90 million to US$140 million per year, depending on the sport. Nor do these fees include "infringement payments" made to existing teams in the same TV markets or the forfeiture of TV revenues during the first year(s) of operation (a US$5–US$20-million annual loss, depending on the sport). Furthermore, a new owner can locate only in a city approved by current owners, and existing owners usually cannot move their teams to other cities unless all owners collectively approve of the move.

These policies do two things: (1) they regulate and limit competition between owners, and (2) they prevent new teams from competing with established teams for players, fans, and television rights. Team owners in each league do not allow changes that could threaten their collective interest, their control over the sport, or their ability to make money. This is how monopolies operate (Eitzen, 2000, 2003).

The owners in each sport league also have agreed to sell the national broadcasting rights to their games as a group and then share the revenues from national media contracts. This limits the number of games available to the viewing public, and it even prevents some people from seeing their home teams play in the stadiums built by

---

[5] This system has been successfully challenged only once, by Eric Lindros, who refused his draft by the Quebec Nordiques of the NHL, successfully arguing that he could only realize his economic potential by playing in a larger media market where more sponsorships and endorsements would be available (he went on to play for the Philadelphia Flyers). The challenge was also complicated by language and regional politics in Canada, with some distasteful remarks being made about playing in Quebec. Ironically, the Nordiques were shortly thereafter sold to Denver (to become the Colorado Avalanche), where they went on to win several Stanley Cups.

public money. But it enables team owners to make huge sums of money in their media contracts while forcing people to buy tickets to games.[6] The Canadian and U.S. governments have approved this monopolistic method of doing business, which guarantees relatively predictable revenues for team owners and gives them the power to influence television companies and the commentators working for those companies. This is why announcers often sound like cheerleaders for the sports their companies pay to broadcast.

Furthermore, team owners have combined their monopolistic media tactics with exclusive-use clauses in their contracts with the stadiums or arenas they use. This has been an effective tool for preventing other leagues from capturing the spectator interest they need to make a profit. Other leagues in each sport have been driven out of business, because existing owners have been allowed to operate as cartels.

Being a part of a legal monopoly has enabled most team owners to make massive sums of money over the past four decades. For example, in the mid-1960s, NFL teams were bought and sold for about US$10 million; in 2003, the average franchise value was nearly US$531 million. That's an average capital gain of US$521 million over thirty-five years.[7] This is what a monopoly does: it limits the supply of teams and drives up the value of existing teams. Of course, team owners do not count capital gains in their discussions of expenses and revenues, and they usually argue that they must constantly raise ticket prices to meet expenses. When you are part of a monopoly, you can get away with this.

Even though the NBA, the NFL, the NHL, and MLB are grouped together in this section, these leagues differ from one another in many important ways. These differences are complicated, and they change from year to year as each league encounters new and unique challenges and opportunities. For example, contracts with networks and major cable television companies vary from one league to another. The NHL has been the least successful in negotiating big-money contracts due to the low viewer/spectator value of ice hockey in most of the U.S., while the NBA and the NFL have been the most successful in recent years (see chapter 12).

Each league also has unique internal agreements regulating how teams can negotiate the sale of *local* broadcasting rights to their games. The NFL does not allow teams to sign independent television contracts for local broadcasts of their games, but MLB does. This has created great disparities in the incomes of baseball teams. For example, the New York Yankees sell their local rights for about US$60 million per year, while the Montreal Expos sold theirs for about US$500,000 (Kaplan, 2002).[8] Despite a 1996 labour agreement that enables small-market teams to share a few revenues earned by big-market teams, significant disparities still exist. In fact, the gap between the highest-revenue-generating team (Yankees) in Major League Baseball and the lowest (Montreal) was US$200 million per year in 2002. This is why some teams can hire the best players but others must hire low-cost players unlikely to win a championship.

The biggest differences among the NBA, the NFL, the NHL, and MLB are related to their contractual agreements with players' associations in each league. Although each league traditionally has tried to give athletes as few rights as possible, athletes have fought for

---

[6] It should be noted that the media revenue bonanza has not been as readily available to the NHL as it has to the other three major leagues. Also, the CFL has been criticized severely by the Canadian public in recent years for its local media blackout.

[7] This is an average. Franchise values range from a low of about US$80 million for small-market NHL teams to an estimated US$800 million for teams such as baseball's New York Yankees and the NFL's Washington Redskins.

[8] Uncertainty about the future of the Expos in Montreal (still there at the time of writing) has reduced the Expos broadcast rights significantly in the last few years.

nearly forty years to gain control over important parts of their careers and to increase their
salaries in the process. We discuss this later in
the chapter.

Team Owners and Forms of Public Assistance

The belief that cities must have professional
sport teams and must provide big sport events in
order to be "world-class" has led to many forms
of public support for sport owners and sport
organizations. The most common form of support is the use of public funds to construct,
maintain, and do business in arenas and stadiums. As noted in chapter 10, this type of "stadium socialism" has enabled wealthy and powerful
capitalists to use public money for their personal gain. Of course, capitalists are not opposed to
welfare when it comes to them, and, in fact, the
New Democratic Party in Canada has regularly
referred to public subsidies to wealthy corporations as "corporate welfare."

Owners have justified stadium subsidies and
other forms of public support for professional
sport teams using five major arguments
(Lavoie, 2000):

1. A stadium and a pro team create jobs; those
   who hold the jobs spend money in the city
   and pay taxes in the process.
2. Stadium construction infuses money into
   the local economy; this money is spent over
   and over as it circulates through the city;
   and the sales of construction materials generate tax revenues.
3. The team will attract other businesses to the
   city and will bring visitors from outside the
   area to spend money in the city.
4. The team will attract regional and national
   media attention, which will boost tourism,
   enable local firms to sell their products
   outside the city, and contribute to overall
   regional economic development.
5. The team will create positive psychic and
   social benefits, making people feel better
   about themselves as individuals and about

the city as a whole; pride and social
solidarity will be increased in connection
with the team's identity.

These arguments sound good, and they often are
supported by studies commissioned by team
owners and others who want public money to be
used to subsidize teams. But dozens of studies
done by *independent* economists, both social
democratic and conservative, do *not* support these
arguments (Cagan and deMause, 1998; Noll and
Zimbalist, 1997; Palmer, 2000, 2001; Rosentraub,
1997). The social democratic economists tend to
argue that there are far more important things
(health, education, housing, etc.) on which taxpayers' money should be spent; the conservative
economists often point to what they consider to
be inappropriate spending of taxpayers' money, in
this case on corporate welfare that is not likely to
produce any major returns. These studies highlight the following issues:

1. Teams and stadiums do create jobs;
   however, apart from highly paid jobs for a
   handful of athletes, stadium jobs are low-
   paying and seasonal. Football stadiums may
   be used fewer than fifteen days per year, and
   the ushers, parking lot attendants, ticket
   agents, and concessions workers do not
   make full-time living wages. Furthermore,
   the vast majority of players' salaries are not
   spent in the cities where they play; in fact,
   players may not even live in those cities, or
   the country.
2. Construction materials often are brought in
   from other locations, as are specialized
   construction workers. The companies that
   design and build stadiums are seldom local,
   and they spend their consulting dollars in
   other cities.
3. Stadiums do attract other businesses, but
   these are often restaurant and entertainment franchises with headquarters in other
   cities. These franchised businesses often
   drive out locally owned businesses.
   Spectators do come from out of town, but

What defines a world-class city? Powerful local businesspeople and their political allies often believe that sports and sport facilities are needed to stimulate the economy and attract people to their cities. Therefore, they lobby for new stadiums and other sport-related facilities. (CP/Frank Gunn)

the vast majority of these people live close enough that they do not spend the night in connection with attendance at a game, and they spend a limited amount of money on food and other forms of entertainment outside the stadium.

4. Stadiums and the teams that use them do generate public relations for the city and for tourism, but tourists who visit the city for other reasons may stay away when big sport events are in town or when games are scheduled. Regional economic development is limited, because local people who spend money at and around the stadium have fewer dollars to spend in their own neighbourhoods. A stadium may help businesses in the immediate area, but it often hurts other businesses, because discretionary money is limited in any population. Spending $4,000 on a pair of season tickets to NBA games often means that one will

spend less money on going out to dinner and buying entertainment close to home.

5. A pro sport team may make some people feel better, but the macho orientations that accompany the games of most men's pro teams actually may make some people feel uncomfortable. Also, when teams have losing records or lose big games, there is evidence that fans do not feel better about their lives.

These counterarguments are supported by research, but most economists make them with one qualification: whenever a city spends $100–$500 million on a public project, there are bound to be some positive benefits. However, the issue is whether the public good could be better served if the money were spent on something other than a stadium used by wealthy owners and players to increase their already sizable assets (see the Reflect on Sports box, "Stadium Construction: A Tale of Two Cities," pp. 348–349).

REFLECT ON SPORTS

Stadium Construction: A Tale of Two Cities

Two cities, one on the north shore of Lake Ontario, the other on the south shore of Lake Erie, each built new stadiums in the last fifteen years. Toronto built the SkyDome; Cleveland built stadiums for football and baseball, and an arena for basketball. They all cost taxpayers a great deal of money.

TORONTO

When Toronto decided to build a downtown, multi-sport, domed stadium, city planners decided that they had learned the lesson from Montreal's Olympic Stadium—the stadium would have a roof that worked, and a financial plan that worked. The prime tenant was to be the Toronto Blue Jays, which played in the not-very-glamorous Exhibition Stadium. A public-private partnership was developed in which twenty-eight companies each paid C$5 million (totalling C$140 million). Ontario Premier David Peterson guaranteed the remainder of the costs from Ontario taxpayers. The SkyDome was supposed to cost C$180million, and it was supposed to make a profit.

During construction, the scope of the project mysteriously expanded—a major hotel and a health club added C$112 million to the stadium's cost. Restaurants, Skyboxes (luxury boxes), and the Jumbotron were also added, although no one is able to say who approved these expenditures. With "rush charges" imposed in an attempt to meet "opening day" (two months later than MLB's official opening day of the 1989 season), the final cost of the SkyDome was C$600 million.

For their $5 million investment, the twenty-eight companies received a Skybox, and those who sold applicable products received vending rights. Thus, McDonald's became famous for its $7 hot dogs, and Labatt, which owned the main tenant, the Blue Jays, saw the team increase in value to about C$180 million while winning back-to-back World Series in 1992 and 1993. In the meantime, the province and its taxpayers became responsible for the debt.

The SkyDome made C$17 million profit (before debt payments) in its first year and owed C$40 million for the year in debt payments, so the debt con-

(CP/Scott MacDonald)

tinually increased. The provincial Liberals lost the 1990 election, leaving the newly elected provincial New Democrats with the responsibility for paying for the SkyDome. By 1993, that debt had risen to C$400 million, and the government decided to cut its losses, paid off the debt, and sold the SkyDome to a group of private investors (including Labatt) for C$151 million in 1994.

The Blue Jays were transferred to Interbrew (makers of Stella Artois) when Labatt was sold, and are now owned by Rogers (the cable and telecommunications company). The Toronto Raptors played in the SkyDome while they waited for the Air Canada Centre to be built, and the Toronto Argonauts still play in the SkyDome, albeit to small crowds. Ownership of the SkyDome has also changed hands several times, and it is still reportedly not making money.

The Blue Jays' ten-year lease ended in 1999, and, as the team was losing money, the club attempted to negotiate a reduced rent. The SkyDome, which was also losing money, refused. In a move that is striking for its irony, and circularity, the Blue Jays declared that they would return to Exhibition Stadium, which was scheduled for demolition, and they paid the City of Toronto C$50,000 to delay the demolition. Fearful of losing its only major tenant, the SkyDome signed a new ten-year lease with the Blue Jays that is estimated to be C$72 million less that its first lease. At least the roof works.

CLEVELAND

During the 1990s, about US$1 billion of mostly public money was spent to build three sport facilities and related infrastructure in Cleveland. Inner-city residents during the same time had to fight the city to fund a drinking fountain in a park in a working-class area of the city, and teachers were holding classes in renovated shower rooms in the public schools. The owners of the sport teams enjoyed profits, because they received a fifty-year exemption on taxes related to their teams and facilities, as well as the equivalent of US$120 million in tax abatements on other real estate development in the areas around the stadiums (Bartimole, 1999). This meant that, in 1998, the city lost nearly US$50 million in city and county tax revenues.

Cleveland decided to publicly fund a football stadium to replace the team that Art Modell, the owner of the Cleveland Browns, had moved to Baltimore in 1995, because Maryland had given him a rent-free US$200 million stadium, all its revenue-generating potential, and a US$50 million bonus for moving. Maryland spent this money because in 1984 Robert Irsay had moved his Baltimore Colts to Indianapolis because the city offered him better facilities and more money. When many people in Maryland complained about such a large public subsidy to a wealthy man while schools in Baltimore were rationing toilet paper and chalk and students were wearing coats to class because the schools could not pay their heating

bills, Modell responded to the critics by saying the following:

> I feel for the schools. I feel for welfare. But look at the positive effects of pro football on a community, the emotional investment of people at large. You can't equate that with fixing up the schools. (Brady, 1996: 19C)

Meanwhile, back in Cleveland, Richard Jacobs, who had bought the Cleveland Indians for US$45 million in late 1986, saw the value of his team skyrocket, and he sold it for US$323 million to Larry Dolan, whose two brothers control the massive media company Cablevision. This gave Jacobs capital gains amounting to US$21.4 million per year for the time he owned the team. The new stadium built by the taxpayers certainly contributed greatly to this gain.

Of course, there are people who object to this form of public stadium subsidy, but they do not have the resources needed to oppose well-financed, professionally packaged plans developed by political advisors hired by team owners. Furthermore, most of the social activists who might lead the opposition are already busy dealing full-time with problems related to drugs, education, homelessness, poor schools, and the overall shortage of social services in cities. They cannot take leave from these urgent tasks to lobby full-time against the use of public money to benefit millionaire team owners and millionaire celebrity athletes.

We think that cities need to hold referenda on construction projects such as these; and that municipal governments should be obliged to fund social impact studies (carried out by independent agencies) and citizens' information meetings before committing to such projects. *What do you think?*

The stories in the box have been repeated many times in cities around Canada and the United States (Eitzen, 2000; Shropshire, 1999). Team owners enlist the services of large architectural firms, which provide them with lobbyists,

political advisors, and public relations people, who make sure the local media cover the campaign for a new stadium from a positive angle. The lobbyists focus on gaining support from politicians and members of committees formed to study the feasibility of building a stadium. Public relations people devise ads that subtly threaten that teams will move unless public money is used in their interest. This tactic of threatening to move teams unless facilities are built is a form of blackmail used by sport team owners to "encourage" public support. Team owners and advisors try to have votes on bond issues held in political off years, so that voter turnout will be light. They recommend the formation of stadium taxing districts that encompass white suburbs, where they can count on support at the polls, even if voters in the inner city are opposed to subsidizing the wealthy. They set up "public" support groups, to which they donate large amounts of money, usually one hundred times more than opponents can raise, to fund massive advertising campaigns. Meanwhile, sportswriters run supportive stories in major newspapers, sports anchors on the local news talk about the benefits of the new team or new stadium, and sports radio talk show hosts hype the subsidies, even though they are usually supporters of right-wing politics (after all, their jobs often depend on the vote).

Once a stadium is built, franchises increase in value about 25 percent, and team owners are in a powerful negotiating position to get what they want when it comes to using the stadium for their own benefit. Their success has been so complete that *Financial World* magazine noted that "virtually every stadium [in the U.S.] is a money pit for taxpayers by any normal measure of return on investment" (Osterland, 1995: 107). Of course, the final irony is that many taxpayers cannot afford to buy tickets to see games in the stadiums their money has built.

The enormous public costs associated with Olympic Stadium in Montreal and the SkyDome in Toronto eventually became a lesson for Canada, and no major stadiums have been constructed since the SkyDome; new arenas that are used for professional sports (e.g., the Air Canada Centre in Toronto, Corel Centre in Ottawa, and the Bell Centre in Montreal) have

been built by the owners of the teams that use them. Some public concessions have been made in terms of taxes, planning and zoning permission, and other rights, but these have not been cases of public investment for private profit in the way that has been so evident in the U.S. However, as we pointed out in chapter 10, both Canada and the U.S. take advantage of hosting major international sports events to construct and upgrade sports facilities that are often then made available to professional sports teams.

In addition to facility subsidies, team owners receive other forms of public support. The federal governments in Canada and the U.S. allow businesses to deduct 50 percent of the cost of game tickets and luxury box leases as business expenses on their federal tax returns. For example, a company in Denver spends $100,000 on pro sport tickets; $50,000 is deductible; and this saves between $18,000 and $22,000 on company federal and state taxes, so the ticket cost is about $78,000, with indirect government subsidies covering the rest. This is why businesses buy about 75 percent of all season tickets sold by top sport teams. Not only do companies save on taxes while their executives and clients use company tickets to attend games, but they also help teams sell out their seats. This in turn drives up ticket prices for the average fan, whose taxes are, in some cases, paying off the bonds for the stadium. Meanwhile, wealthy people sit in luxury skyboxes that may have been built with public money, and deduct the leases as business expenses for their corporations. This lowers tax revenues, which could be used for needed public programmes.

Meanwhile, it has regularly been pointed out in Canada that such use of business-expense tax deductions constitutes an important site of tax fraud, since many of the users of season tickets or luxury boxes are not business clients but family members and friends or other employees in the business. Atkinson (2000) points out that many of the unused tickets, for which a tax reduction has been received, are sold to scalpers.

When thinking about public subsidies to sport teams, it is useful to consider alternative uses of public funds. For example, in the U.S., Colorado Springs used US$6 million of public money in 2000 to construct a youth sport complex consisting of 12 baseball, softball, and T-ball fields of various sizes with bleacher seating; 10 soccer/football fields; 6 volleyball courts; an in-line skating rink; a batting cage (for baseball hitting practice); and a number of basketball courts. Meanwhile, nearly $300 million of tax money from Denver and five surrounding counties was used to build the Denver Broncos and wealthy owner Pat Bowlen a new stadium. Instead of the stadium, the US$300 million could have been used to build 600 baseball, softball, and T-ball fields; 500 soccer/football fields; 300 volleyball courts; 50 in-line skating rinks; 50 batting cages; and 250 basketball courts around the metro area. Which of these two alternatives would improve the overall quality of life in the Denver metro area more? The youth facilities would be open seven days a week to everyone in the community for nominal fees; the new stadium will host 72,000 people nine times a year at a cost of at least US$60 a seat, and people at home will be able to watch the team on TV nine times a year.

According to urban politics professor Charles Euchner, "Cities have two choices. Forget about major league sports. Or feed the monster" (Brady and Howlett, 1996: 13C). Unfortunately, people in the media and local politics often support feeding the monster, because they benefit from the monster's existence. Do sport reporters make their reputations covering youth sports? Do politicians raise money and attract votes by taking big campaign donors to a local soccer field to watch a pickup game? In the last major campaign to use public money to support a professional team in Canada, the failed 1995 "Save the [Winnipeg] Jets" campaign, there were some disturbing examples of the ways in which local people could be encouraged to feed the monster—more donations were received in one week than the Winnipeg United Way receives in a year. Also, the provincial and municipal governments were prepared to make major donations of taxpayers' money towards the construction of a new arena at a time when the provincial government was laying off teachers and nurses, and the city was closing libraries and swimming pools (Silver, 1996; Smith, 1997). Feeding the monster raises serious public policy questions about who should receive public subsidies, and what activities and facilities should be supported by public funds.

Sources of Income for Team Owners The owners of top pro teams in the major men's sports make money from the following sources: (1) ticket sales; (2) sale of media rights (radio, and national, local, and pay-per-view television); (3) league expansion and mergers (share of expansion fees); (4) tax shelters; (5) increase in franchise value (difference between the price paid for a team and its current worth); (6) revenue through sale of stocks (as in the Toronto Maple Leafs in the 1970s and early 1980s and the proposed stock sale of the Ottawa Senators in 2002—such sales rarely offer any ownership or control) (Beamish, 1988, pp. 144–48); (7) stadium revenue, including leases on club seats and luxury suites, concessions and parking, and the sale of stadium advertising and naming rights; and (8) licensing fees and merchandise sales. The amounts and proportions of each of these sources of revenue vary from league to league, and they are difficult to track because team owners try to shelter them, so they will not be counted as part of "league revenues" and included in the total amounts to compute salary caps and player salaries. The majority of revenue for NFL owners comes from television—over 60 percent of all their revenues—while TV revenues for NHL owners are less than 20 percent of their total revenues. Stadium revenues have become increasingly important in all leagues, and it should be noted that naming rights for some of the newer stadiums and arenas have been sold for as much as US$195 million for twenty years (for example, the American Airlines Center in Dallas).

The recent wave of new stadiums in the U.S. is the result of owners' demanding venues that can generate new revenue streams. This is why new stadiums in both Canada and the U.S. resemble shopping malls with a playing field, ice, or court in the middle. Owners want to capture as much of the entertainment dollar as they can inside the stadium itself, and do it with tax-payer money in the U.S., so that they can avoid debt payments. The stadium now is considered to have so much revenue-generating potential that the value of a franchise with a new stadium increases about 25 percent.

Of course, owners realize that many people may not feel comfortable with the idea of putting public money into the pockets of the wealthy, so they make sure that when their teams take the field, court, or ice announcers describe them as "your" B.C. Lions, Calgary Stampeders, Toronto Rock, or Montreal Expos (Sage, 1996). The owners are happy to have people feel as if the teams belong to them, as long as these people let the owners collect all the revenues and keep all the capital gains when they sell the teams.

Amateur Sports in North America

Amateur sports do not have owners, but they do have commercial sponsors and governing bodies, which promote and sanction events and control athletes. Generally, the sponsors are large corporations, which support amateur sports for advertising purposes. The governing bodies of amateur sports operate on a nonprofit basis, although they do use revenues from events to maintain their organizations and their power over amateur sports.

Centralized sport authorities administer amateur sports in most countries. They work with the national sport organizations (NSOs) of individual sports, and together they have control over events, athletes, and revenues. Sport Canada, C.I.S., and the Canadian Olympic Committee are

Recently built stadiums resemble shopping malls, and some fans define their attendance as a shopping opportunity. The people who attend games are a captive audience, and team owners want to capture as many of their entertainment dollars as possible. This fan has fallen for the lure of consumption to the point that he is less interested in the game than he is in buying products to prove he was at the game.

examples of such centralized authorities; they develop the policies that govern the various national sport organizations in Canada.

All amateur sport organizations share an interest in two things: (1) *power* and (2) the *money* generated through sponsorships and revenue-producing events. Sponsorship patterns in amateur sports also take many forms. Intercollegiate sport programmes seek various forms of corporate support. Some universities have, in effect, sold their athletic departments, consisting of all athletic teams and the bodies of athletes, to corporate sponsors in exchange for money, scholarships, and equipment. Universities in Canada are seeking all kinds of alternative sources of funding for their athletics teams, ranging from the private sector funding of football teams at Laval University and the University of Regina, to the attempt by the University of Toronto to raise an endowment fund for each of its interuniversity teams. At this time, a growing number of university athletic departments have contracts with either Nike or Reebok. Others have signed contracts with Adidas and Converse, even with Pepsi-Cola, Coca-Cola, or MARS. Contracts may require athletes and other students to drink only certain soft drinks or eat certain candy bars on campus or in the locker room at halftime. Of course, this form of sponsorship is a clever way for private corporations to use tax-supported institutions as vehicles for their own profit making, while being hailed on campus as the saviours of sport teams. Corporations and universities enter these agreements outside of any democratic processes, which might involve votes on the part of students, athletes, or the taxpayers whose money funds the universities. The only significant democratic intervention so far by students at major Canadian and U.S. universities has been to ensure that items carrying the university logo sold at campus stores (e.g., sweat shirts) are made by companies that are subject to fair labour agreements.

Although Sport Canada provides some base funding to fifty-one NSOs and another thirty multi-sport/service organizations, the NSOs of amateur sports long have depended on corporate sponsorship money, and they continue to seek those sponsorships to pay for athlete training, operating expenses, and the staging of events. Designated corporate logos now appear on most of the clothing worn and equipment used by amateur athletes. In some cases, individual athletes seek corporate sponsorships on their own, hoping to remain free to train and compete without having to be completely dependent on their NSOs. However, they remain under the control of their NSO in a contractual agreement (Beamish and Borowy, 1988) that nowadays may require personal appearances at events involving the NSO's major sponsors. Athletes may gain more money with their own sponsors, but they rarely gain more control of their lives because their personal sponsors also require appearances by the athletes. Some athletes find it difficult to maintain an appropriate training regimen

because of these obligations. Many NSOs now hold media training sessions for their athletes, who are told that they must thank their sponsors during any press conference or interview.

As this model of corporate sponsorship is used more and more around the world, the economics of sports increasingly becomes tied to the fortunes and fluctuations of market economies and large corporations. Corporations seek out only those sports and athletes that give them the visibility they desire, and economic recessions could mean the end of sponsorships. Future agreements will require athletes and coaches to be spokespersons and cheerleaders for the interests of international corporate capitalism in the world, although this has already happened to a significant degree.

THE LEGAL STATUS AND INCOMES OF ATHLETES IN COMMERCIAL SPORTS

When sports are commercialized, athletes become entertainers. This is obvious at the professional level, but it is true in other commercial sports, such as junior hockey and highly sponsored sports such as figure skating and equestrian. Professional athletes are usually paid for their efforts, while amateur athletes receive rewards within limits set by the organizations that govern their sport participation. This raises three questions: (1) what is the legal status of the athlete-entertainers who work in these sports? (2) how are athlete-entertainers rewarded for their work? and (3) how might underage elite athletes (in sports ranging from hockey to tennis) in this system be protected from exploitation?

Many people have a difficult time thinking of athletes as workers, and they hesitate to consider owner-player relations in professional sports as a form of labour relations. This is because people usually associate sports with play in their own lives, and they see sports as fun rather than work. However, when sports are organized to make money, players are workers, even though they may have fun on the job. Of course, this is not unique; many workers enjoy their jobs and have fun doing them; however, regardless of how much they enjoy their work, issues of legal status and rewards for work are important.

This section focuses on commercial sports in North America. We will not consider the sports that may collect a few gate receipts but never make enough money to pay for anything beyond basic expenses for the events.

Professional Athletes

Legal Status: Team Sports The legal status of athletes always has been the most controversial issue in professional team sports in North America. Until the mid-1970s, professional athletes in the major sport leagues had little or no legal power to control their own careers. They could play only for the team that drafted and owned them. They could not control when and to whom they might be traded during their careers, even when their contracts expired. To make matters worse, they were obliged to sign standard contracts forcing them to agree to forfeit all rights over their careers to team owners. Basically, they were bought and sold like property and were seldom consulted about their own wishes. They were hired labour at the mercy of team owners and officials hired by team owners.

In all sports, this system of employee restriction has been called the **reserve system.** Although the dynamics of this system varied from one league to another, it enabled team owners to restrict the movement of athlete-employees from one team to another. As long as owners were able to do this, salaries remained low, and athletes had no power to control the conditions under which they played their sports. Parts of the reserve system continue to exist in professional sports, but various players' associations have challenged the system in court and forced significant changes that increase the labour rights of many professional athletes.

In any other business, a reserve system of this sort would violate combines laws. For example, it is illegal for the owners of all computer software firms to form relationships and decide among themselves whom they want to hire next year among all people with degrees in information systems. It also would be illegal for them to agree not to hire graduates who were "reserved" by another company. This use of employee restrictions would destroy the freedom of professionals in information systems to choose where, and with whom, they wanted to work. Furthermore, if these workers could not take jobs with other companies without permission from their current employers, even after their employment contracts had expired, their salaries would be kept low, because companies would not have to compete with each other to hire the people with the best skills. And, if these workers could be sold or traded to other companies without being consulted, they would have no real control over their own careers.

But this type of reserve system was defined as legal in sports, and owners used it for many years with minimal interference from any government agency. Team owners justified this form of control over athletes' careers by saying it was needed to maintain a competitive balance among the teams in their leagues. They argued that, if players were free to work for anyone they wanted to, the wealthiest owners in the biggest cities and TV markets would buy up all the good athletes and prevent teams in smaller cities and TV markets from maintaining competitive teams. The irony of this argument has been that team owners have all been wealthy capitalists who praised the free market, while maintaining that the free market would destroy the business of sports. In other words, these capitalists became "sport socialists" to protect their power and wealth under the umbrella of a monopoly inconsistent with the principles of free enterprise.

Many professional athletes objected to the reserve system, but they could not mount an effective legal challenge of the system until the 1970s. Then, in 1976, U.S. courts ruled that, under certain conditions, professional athletes had the right to become *free agents*. This right was important, because it allowed players whose contracts had expired to seek contracts with other teams that might bid for their services. This legal change had a dramatic effect on the salaries of NBA and MLB players beginning in the late 1970s (see table 11.1). For about fifteen years, team owners in the NFL and the NHL avoided much of the effect of this legal change by negotiating restrictions on free agency with players' associations. But, in 1992, after players in both leagues mounted challenges, these restrictions were partially lifted. The hockey players went on a ten-day strike during the Stanley Cup playoffs and forced owners to sign a short-term contract, in which the players obtained slightly more control over their careers. The football players, after challenging the NFL for about five years in a series of court cases, won an antitrust suit, which forced team owners to agree to let NFL players become free agents after being in the league for five years.

It would take many pages to explain the full implications of court decisions and labour negotiations on the legal status and rights of players in each professional team sport. Conditions change every time a new case is resolved or a new labour agreement is made. In part, it was this complexity that kept most players from challenging the restrictions of the reserve system over the years. It was not until the formation of players' associations and unions in the 1960s and 1970s that they had the support and organization they needed to push for changes. Each players' association used the collective strength of all the players in its league to bargain against the collective strength of all the owners in that league.

Although the players' associations often have been unpopular with many sport fans and detested by team owners and league officials, they have enabled players to gain more and more control over their salaries and working conditions since the late 1970s. Labour negotiations, players' strikes, and owner lock-outs of players in all professional team sports always have focused on issues of freedom and control over careers, even though money issues have attracted most of the attention in the media coverage. Players always have known that, when they were free agents and had the freedom to sell their skills to the highest bidder, salaries would increase to the highest level that the owners could afford to pay.[9]

Free agency now exists for veteran players in all leagues. The drafting of rookies still occurs, but the number of rookies reserved through the draft gradually has been cut back, allowing more players to try out with teams they think offer them the best chances of getting contracts. Definitions of who qualifies as a veteran and the amount of freedom enjoyed by free agents vary from league to league.

Although players' organizations and unions have done much to change the legal status of athletes in various professional sports, it has not been easy to keep players organized. Owners do not look kindly on players who have served as representatives in unions or players' associations. Athletes are often hesitant to join any organization that may ask them to strike for an entire season, especially since their careers seldom last more than four to seven years in team sports. Therefore, a season-long strike for the average player means sacrificing 15 to 25 percent of lifetime income as a professional athlete. Strikes are also risky because they alienate fans and because team owners may hire nonunion players. Finally, the highest-paid players in certain leagues are now so wealthy and in such good positions to negotiate contracts on their own that they do not identify with other players,

---

[9] Present-day players may have forgotten that salaries increase significantly when two rival leagues are bidding for their services, as was last the case when the World Hockey Association challenged the NHL in the 1970s. Leagues make major efforts to maintain their **monopoly** status as the only league selling the highest levels of their sport, and their **monopsony** status as the only league buying the services of the best players (Beamish, 1988). Both of these statuses help to keep player salaries lower than they might otherwise be.

Table 11.1   Average salaries in major North American professional leagues, compared with median family income, 1950–2002[a]

| Year | NFL | SPORT LEAGUE | | | | | Median U.S. Family Income[c] | Median Canadian Family Income[d] |
		NBA	WNBA	NHL	MLB	CFL		
1950	15,000	5,100		5,000	13,300	NA	4,000	NA
1960	17,100	13,000		14,100	19,000	NA	5,620	NA
1970	23,000	40,000		25,000	29,300	NA	9,867	NA
1980	79,000	190,000		110,000	143,000	NA	21,023	C51,698
1990	395,400	824,000		247,000	598,000	NA	35,353	C54,560
2000	1,116,100	3,600,000	60,000	1,050,000	1,988,034	C45,900[b]	50,732	C55,161
2002	1,316,625	4,500,000	60,000	1,500,000	2,383,300	NA	51,500	NA

All figures are in US$, except were noted.

[a]Data on players' salaries come from many sources. All NFL salaries are from the NFL Players Association (Duberstein, 2002). Average salaries before the mid-1970s are estimates, because players' associations did not exist, and teams were notorious for their inconsistent and creative bookkeeping practices. Average salaries often differ from one source to another, because some are based on rosters at the beginning of the season, whereas others are based on rosters at the end of the season. Differences also reflect whether signing bonuses, prorated portions of those bonuses, and salary deferrals are included with or without interest adjustments.

[b] Although CFL teams have a C$2.44 million salary cap, it is widely believed that the cap is not enforced. CFL salaries have varied widely over time and are also secret. This figure is based on a player salary survey carried out by the CFL Players' Association in April 2001.

[c]This represents total family income—parents and children in the same household. Half the families fall above the median, and half fall below. Data are from the U.S. Census; figures for 1950 and 2002 are estimates.

[d] Data are from Canadian census figures. They are not easily comparable with the U.S. figures because (1) Statistics Canada reports figures that are controlled for inflation, so these are in constant 2000 C$, and (2) the exchange rate varied during this time.

Note: Players' salaries increased slowly from after World War II through the mid-1970s. During those years, pro athletes made from two to four times the median family income in the United States. After free agency was put in place in the 1970s, salaries began to skyrocket. As teams made more revenues from gate receipts and television rights and were forced to compete for players, and as players' unions provided support for players' rights, salaries increased dramatically. Although caution should always be used in comparing average (mean) incomes with median incomes (which, as we note on p. 358 are usually lower), in 2002, the ratios between salaries in the major men's professional sports and the median family income No wonder people identify with the women in the WNBA and why people have so little sympathy for male athletes in labour disputes with team owners, even though many of the owners are billionaires or multibillion-dollar corporations.

about 15 to 25 percent of whom make the minimum salaries in the leagues, or close to the minimum. Although the unions and players' associations created the conditions for the current good fortune of these superstars, some of them no longer see these organizations as useful to them. The superstars depend on their agents, not on athlete-worker organizations. All these factors make it very difficult to keep players organized.

Finally, professional athletes in most minor leagues have few rights and little control over their careers. For the pros at this level—who are more numerous than those working at the top levels of professional sports—the pay is low, careers are uncertain, rights are few, and owners have the last word (cf., Robidoux, 2001). Parcels (2000) reports that minor pro hockey players are traded, on average, three-and-a-half times during a five-year career, and notes that one player was traded twenty-six times in five years. In fact, the average high school teacher in Canada has a higher salary and more rights as a worker than nearly all the pro athletes in the minor leagues.

Legal Status: Individual Sports The legal status of professional athletes in individual sports varies greatly from sport to sport and even from one athlete to another. Although there are important differences among boxing, bowling, golf, tennis, auto racing, rodeo, horse racing, track and field, skiing, and other sports, a few generalizations are possible.

The legal status of athletes in individual sports largely depends on what athletes must do to train and qualify for competition in their sports. For example, few athletes can afford to pay for all the training needed to develop professional-level skills in a sport. Few athletes are in a position to meet the other requirements associated with official participation in sport competitions, which may include having a recognized agent or manager (as in boxing), being formally recognized by other participants (as in most auto racing), obtaining membership in a professional organization (as in most bowling, golf, and tennis tournaments), or gaining a special invitation through an official selection group (as in track and field meets).

Whenever athletes need sponsors to pay for their training and whenever contractual arrangements with other persons or groups are required for their participation, the legal status of athletes is shaped by their agreements with sponsors and sanctioning groups. This is why the legal status of athletes in individual sports varies so much. Take boxing as an example. Because many boxers come from low-income backgrounds, they cannot develop on their own the skills they need to become recognized competitors. They need trainers, managers, and sponsors of their training. After their skills are developed, it takes money and carefully nurtured business connections to arrange and promote bouts.

Relationships with trainers, managers, and sponsors come with conditions attached for the boxers. These conditions may be written in formal contracts or based in informal agreements. In either case, they require the boxers to forfeit control of their lives and a portion of the rewards they may earn in bouts in return for the help they need to become professionals. Unless boxers have good legal experience or win a few big-money fights, they seldom have control over their careers. They are forced to trade control over their bodies and careers for the opportunity to continue boxing. This is a classic example of how class relations operate in sports: when people lack resources, they cannot negotiate the conditions under which their sport careers develop.[10]

The legal status of athletes in individual sports is defined in the bylaws of some professional organizations, such as the Professional Golf Association (PGA), the Ladies' Professional Golf Association (LPGA), the Association of Tennis Professionals (ATP), and the Professional Rodeo Cowboys Association (PRCA). Because athletes control many of these organizations, their policies support athletes' rights and enable athletes to control the conditions under which they compete. Without these organizations, athletes in these sports would have few guaranteed rights.

Income: Team Sports Despite the publicity given to the super-contracts of some athletes in the NBA, the NFL, the NHL, MLB, and premier soccer leagues in Europe, salaries vary widely across the levels and divisions in professional team sports. For example, many players at the minor league level in baseball, hockey, and other team sports make less than social workers, teachers, and other nonsport workers. U.S. census data for 2000 shows that the median annual

---

[10] This also applies to team sports, where only Eric Lindros—who comes from a well-off middle-class family—was able to negotiate the conditions of his draft.

salary for professional athletes was US$32,700 (half of all professional athletes made less than this amount, and half made more).

The average annual salary in the National Basketball Developmental League is US$30,000, and, in the NBA Rookie League, it is US$25,000. Salaries for more than 3,000 players on 160 minor league baseball teams and a similar number of minor league hockey players range from US$100 a game, at the lowest levels, to a high of about US$60,000 at the top minor league level (Renck, 2002). These are basically seasonal jobs with few benefits. However, we hear only about salaries among top players in the top leagues.

To understand the range of income in pro sports, consider that, during the 2002 Major League Baseball season, 10 percent of the players made 40 percent of all the salary money paid. The US$70 million they earned was more than all the salary money paid to 80 percent of all major league players (Kaplan, 2002). Unequal distributions like this distort average (mean) incomes—the MLB average is about US$2.4 million a year, while the median salary is less than US$900,000 a year. Similarly, in the NHL, average salary for 1999–2000 was US$1,136,375, but the median salary was US$700,000 (Robidoux, 2001). The following breaks down the salary distribution of the 900 players in the NHL:

- Twenty players (2 percent) earned US$5.4–US$10.3 million.
- One hundred sixty players (18 percent) earned US$1.5–US$5.4 million.
- Three hundred twenty-nine players (37 percent) earned US$600,000–US$1.5 million.
- Three hundred ninety-one players (43 percent) earned US$150,000–US$600,000.

The big salaries for a few players drive up the averages for entire leagues.

Putting growing salary inequality in sports into more personal terms, the US$23.6 million earned by Shaquille O'Neal during the NBA's 2002–03 season was nearly US$5 million more

SIDELINES

©1982 M.T.F.-T.W.S.-Lakewood. CO

"I make $6 million a year, and I don't feel guilty!"
....

Most athletes generate revenues that match their salaries or prize money. Like other entertainers, a few of them have benefited from national and international media exposure. Sport events are now marketed in connection with the celebrity status and lifestyles of high-profile athlete-entertainers.

than all 200 WNBA players made during their 2001 and 2002 seasons. According to his current contract, O'Neal will earn more than US$32 million for the 2005–06 season. Meanwhile, half of the NBA players make less than US$2 million a year, and many make between US$350,000 and US$400,000 a year. O'Neal makes more than the combined salaries for the 70 lowest-paid players in the NBA.

As top stars' salaries are increasing at rapid rates, most of the hockey and baseball players on more than 300 minor league teams across North America would love to make US$20,000 per season, and they only dream of making the US$400,000 minimum salary in the NHL or the US$300,000 minimum in MLB. So would CFL players who have not kept pace at all with rising salaries in other leagues: "25 years ago, the average CFL salary was about half of that in the [NFL]. Today's average salary (C$45,900) is less than 2 percent" (Naylor, 2002a). On the 2000 Players' Association survey, annual salaries ranged from C$28,000 to C$150,000, although, in 2002, Joe Montford of the Toronto Argonauts was believed to be earning C$200,000 a season. The median salary in the CFL is probably much lower than C$45,900.

The data in table 11.1 indicate that players' average salaries have grown far beyond median family income in the United States and in Canada. For example, players in 1950 made average salaries that were not much different than median family income. In 2000, players' salaries were up to forty-four times greater than median family income. This disparity between players' salaries and general family income is the reason so many fans no longer see the players as "workers" and why they may not side with the players during strikes and lockouts. Of course, siding with owners is also difficult, because most of them make more than even the highest paid players when you add their salaries and capital gains on franchise values. It is important to remember that, as of 2002, the estimated percentage of league revenues received by players ranged from 52 percent to 70 percent. The owners used the rest to cover other expenses and to pay themselves. Each league, except the NHL, has a salary cap, and owners pay athletes only what they must to sign them to contracts; contract amounts are shaped by the economics of the league and the labour agreements that players' associations have with leagues.

The dramatic increase in salaries at the top level of pro sports is due to two factors: (1) changes in the legal status and rights of players, which have led to free agency and the use of a salary arbitration process, and (2) increased revenues flowing to leagues and owners. Salaries for every year in each major team sport since 1970 show that large increases in salary levels have corresponded closely to court decisions and other events changing the legal status of athletes and giving them bargaining power in their contract negotiations with team owners. Unions and lawsuits have worked for some athletes, as they have for many workers in other industries.

Income: Individual Sports As with team sports, publicity is given to the highest-paid athletes in individual sports. However, not all players of these sports make enough money from tournament winnings to support themselves comfortably. In fact, many golfers, tennis players, bowlers, curlers, track and field athletes, auto and motorcycle racers, rodeo riders, figure skaters, and others must carefully manage their money so they do not spend more than they win as they travel from event to event. When tournament winnings are listed in the newspaper, nothing is said about the expenses for airfares, hotels, food, and transportation or about competition expenses for coaches, agents, managers, and other support people. The top money winners do not worry too much about these expenses, but most athletes in individual sports are not big money winners.

In recent years, the disparity between the top money winners and others has increased considerably on the men's and women's golf and tennis tours. Many people are surprised to learn that 90 percent of the 1,921 players registered on the Sanex Women's Tennis Association Tour made less than US$40,000 in prize money during the 2002 season, and over half made less than US$1,000 for the year. In comparison, Venus and Serena Williams won more than US$6 million in the same year.

The vast majority of the men and women playing professional tennis, golf, and other individual sports do not make enough money to pay their competition expenses each year, although a lucky few have sponsors who pick up training and travel expenses. But some athletes in individual sports may be under contract to share their winnings with the investors who sponsor them. The investors cover expenses during the lean years but then take a percentage of winnings when the athletes win matches or tournaments. For example, boxers traditionally have received very little of the prize money from their bouts; even today, much goes to promoters, managers, trainers, and sponsors.

Sponsorship agreements sometimes have caused problems for professional athletes in individual sports. Being contractually tied, for example, to an equipment manufacturer or another sponsor often puts athletes in a state of dependency. They may not have the freedom to choose when or how often they will compete, and sponsors may require them to attend social functions, at which they talk with fan-consumers, sign autographs, and promote products. This may interfere with training/resting periods, and make maintaining high-level skills difficult.

The money is very good for a few athletes in individual sports, while most others struggle to cover expenses. Only when sport events are broadcast on television can athletes expect to compete for major prize money and earn large incomes.

Amateur Athletes in Commercial Sports

Legal Status of Amateur Athletes The primary goals of amateur athletes always have been simple: to train and to compete. However, the achievement of those goals has not always been easy, because amateur athletes have not had significant control over the conditions of their sport participation. Instead, control has rested in the hands of amateur sport organizations, each setting rules that specify the conditions under which training and competition can occur. Although these rules usually are intended to ensure fairness in competition, they sometimes have been used to protect the power and interests of the organizations, rather than the athletes they are supposed to serve. When this has happened, amateur athletes have not been able to participate when and where they would prefer to.

The rights of amateur athletes in Canada were first given voice by Bruce Kidd and Mary Eberts (1988), and were taken over by athletes themselves with the formation of AthletesCAN in 1994. AthletesCAN was not a union (although many have felt the rights of amateur athletes are so routinely violated that a union would be beneficial, e.g., Beamish and Borowy, 1988), or even

a professional association, but it did provide a forum for athletes to exchange information, and a voice for athletes. However, careers are so short and ephemeral for amateur athletes, and so full of training and competitions, that athletes usually have no time for, and give no thought to, political action. Their NSOs are also likely to discourage such thoughts and actions. AthletesCAN still provides a forum for the exchange of information, but that information is more likely to involve sponsorship and self-marketing opportunities than it is with protecting the rights of athletes. The introduction of the Sport Funding and Accountability Framework by Sport Canada in 1995 linked NSO funding to the introduction of certain equity issues—gender, language, disability—but enforcement has been limited. The Alternative Dispute Resolution (ADR) mechanism introduced in Bill C-12 (see chapter 13) provides another forum for the insurance of athletes' rights in certain disputes with their NSOs, but a clear statement of, and policy to ensure, athletes' rights is still absent in Canadian amateur sports.

The continued lack of power among U.S., Canadian, and international amateur athletes is especially evident in U.S. inter-university sports. Even in revenue-producing sports, athletes have few rights and no formal means of filing complaints when they have been treated unfairly or denied the right to play their sports. The athletes are not allowed to share the revenues they generate and have no control over how their skills and their names and images can be used by the university or the NCAA. For example, when the athletes become local or national celebrities, they have no "right of publicity" enabling them to benefit from their celebrity status. They cannot endorse products or be paid when universities use their identities and images to promote events or sell merchandise.

Although many amateur athletes recognize the problems associated with their lack of rights, it has been difficult for them to lobby for changes. Challenging the NSO and the COC in court is expensive, and would take years of a young person's life. Forming an athletes' organization, as noted above, would make it possible to bargain for rights, but bringing together athletes from various sports would require many resources, and convincing athletes, many of whom have adjusted to their dependency and powerlessness, to take assertive and progressive action would be a major challenge. Furthermore, the prospect of amateur athletes' engaging in collective bargaining to gain rights and benefits would be seen as a serious threat to the whole structure of amateur sports. Athletes may be treated as employees by coaches and NSOs, but there is a fear that, if they were legally defined as employees, they would be eligible for the same considerations granted to other workers in Canada. This makes everyone from coaches to NSOs nervous (Beamish and Borowy, 1988).

Although recent changes have called for the appointment of athletes to NSO boards, the likelihood of significantly increasing athletes' rights is not great. There are no formal structures for effectively gaining more control over the conditions of training and competition. In the meantime, athlete advocacy groups outside sports are needed; athletes need support in gaining at least some control over their sport lives and the revenues created by their skills.

Although amateur athletes in Olympic sports have made some strides to gain control over their training and competition, it has been difficult for them to make an impact on the organizations that control their sports. In fact, as sports become more commercialized, the centres of power in sports move further and further away from athletes. Now that athletes are included on the boards of NSOs, sponsors and media people who operate outside the NSOs are making many of the decisions about training and competition. The paradox for athletes is that, as they gain more resources to train and compete, the control of their training and competition moves further away from them. The exceptions, of course, are those athletes with national visibility and the individual power to negotiate support that meets their interests.

Income of Amateur Athletes Amateur athletes in commercial sports face another paradox: they generate money through their performances, but they often face limitations in sharing that money with sponsors and sport organizations. Although Canadian and U.S. national team athletes may receive small stipends for living expenses while they train, many amateur athletes receive no compensation at all for their involvement in events generating gate receipts and media rights payments.

Intercollegiate athletes playing big-time university football and basketball in the U.S., including some Canadian students on scholarships, who must also pay significant travel expenses, may generate hundreds of thousands of dollars for their universities, but NCAA rules prohibit them from receiving anything more than renewable one-year scholarships, and those scholarships may not cover anything more than tuition, room, meals, and books. This means that a basketball player from a low-income family, such as Toronto's Jamaal Magloire (who now plays for the New Orleans Hornets of the NBA) can bring fame and fortune to a university for three or four years and never legally receive a penny for expenses outside the classroom—no money for clothes, a personal computer, academic photocopying, school supplies, laundry, transportation around town, dates, travel home for vacations, non-sport-related medical or dental bills, phone calls home, and so on.

It is the unfairness of this situation that has led to many of the under-the-table cash payments to university athletes. These payments and other illegal gifts have become so commonplace in the U.S. that many leaders in university sports have suggested that the NCAA revise its policies on compensation for athletes. However, it is not easy to develop a fair method of compensation.

Therefore, some top-level athletes leave university long before graduation as they attempt to play professional sports.

Other amateur athletes in both university and Olympic sports face similar difficulties in capitalizing on their commercial value. However, changes in eligibility rules now permit some athletes to earn money without jeopardizing their participation status in amateur sports. Rules are less restrictive than they have been in the past. However, many athletes still cannot make money *beyond* an approved basic cost-of-living stipend and travel expenses related to training and competition in their sport. Therefore, if a sixteen-year-old gymnast on the Canadian national team takes money to be a part of an exhibition tour after the Olympics, she is not eligible to participate in NCAA gymnastics. This also means she may not receive an athletic grant to attend university. Furthermore, if an Olympic figure skater participates in a professional skating competition, her amateur status may be revoked (although there is now a re-application process).

Even though some of the restrictions of amateurism have been lifted in Olympic sports, many athletes do not share in the revenues generated by the events in which they participate. For example, the Olympic Games generate hundreds of millions of dollars in gate receipts and sponsorships, but the athletes who make the games possible receive none of that money, apart from training support through the sport organizations they are affiliated with and the cash awards medal winners *sometimes* receive from those organizations (e.g., the recently introduced awards by the COC) or their governments.

Questions about the fairness of this situation have been raised by an increasing number of athletes. University of Ottawa economist Mark Lavoie (2000) has noted that "the day cannot be too far off when the so-called amateur athletes will threaten to go on strike in order to get their share of the huge revenues generated by worldwide mega-events such as the Olympic Games" (p. 167).

SUMMARY

WHAT ARE THE CHARACTERISTICS OF COMMERCIAL SPORTS?

Commercial sports are visible parts of many contemporary societies. Their growth is associated with urbanization, industrialization, improvements in transportation and communications technology, the availability of capital resources, and class relations. People's interest in paying to watch sports is encouraged by a quest for excitement in highly organized and controlled societies, a cultural emphasis on individual success, widely available youth sport programmes, and extensive media coverage of sports. The recent expansion of commercial sports also has been fuelled by sport organizations seeking global markets, as well as transnational corporations using sports as vehicles for global expansion. The global expansion of commercial sports will continue as long as it serves the interests of transnational corporations.

Commercialization has influenced changes in the structure and goals of certain sports, the orientations of people involved in sports, and the organizations that control sports. Those connected with commercial sports tend to emphasize heroic orientations over aesthetic orientations. Style and dramatic expression impress mass audiences, while fine distinctions in ability often are overlooked, except by those who have deep knowledge about a particular sport. Overall, commercial sports have been packaged as total entertainment experiences for spectators, even spectators who know little about the games they are watching.

Commercial sports are unique businesses. At the minor league level, most of them do not generate substantial revenues for owners and sponsors; in fact, they are risky businesses. However, team owners at the top levels of professional sports have worked together to make their leagues into effective entertainment monopolies. Along with event sponsors and promoters, these owners are involved with commercial sports to make money while having fun and establishing good public images for themselves or their corporations and its products, policies, and practices. Owners in the major team sports have used monopolistic business practices to keep costs down and revenues up, especially through their collective sale of broadcasting rights to media companies. Profits also have been enhanced by public support and subsidies, often associated with the construction and operation of stadiums and arenas. It is ironic that North American professional sports often are used as models of competition, when, in fact, they have been built through a system of autocratic control and monopolistic organization. As NFL team owner Art Modell once said about himself and his fellow owners in the NFL, "We're twenty-eight Republicans who vote socialist." What he meant was that NFL owners are conservative individuals and corporations that have eliminated much free market competition in their sport businesses and have used public money and facilities to increase their wealth and power.

The administration and control of amateur commercial sports rest in the hands of numerous sport organizations. Although these organizations exist to support amateur athletes as they train and compete, major goals within the organizations have been to maintain power and control and to maximize revenue generation. Those with the most money and influence usually win the power struggles in amateur sports, and athletes seldom have had the resources to promote their own interests in these struggles. Corporate sponsors have become a major force in amateur sports, and their interests have a major impact on what happens in these sports.

Commercialization has made athletes entertainers. Athletes generate revenues through their performances. Therefore, issues related to players' rights and the sharing of the revenues generated by their performances have become very important. As rights and revenues have increased, so have players' incomes. Media money has been key in this process.

Not all athletes in professional sports make vast sums of money. Players outside the top men's sports, and golf and tennis for women, have incomes that are surprisingly low. Income among amateur athletes is limited by rules set by governing bodies in particular sports. In amateur sports, athletes may receive direct cash payments for performances and endorsements, and some receive support from the organizations to which they belong, but relatively few make large amounts of money.

The structure and dynamics of commercial sports vary from nation to nation. Commercial sports in most of the world have not generated the massive amounts of revenues associated with a few high-profile, heavily televised sports in North America, Japan, and western Europe. Profits for owners and sponsors in Canada and the U.S. depend on supportive relationships with the media and government. These arrangements have done much to shape the character of all sports in North America, professional and amateur.

Of course, the commercial model of sport is not the only one that might provide athletes and spectators with enjoyable and satisfying experiences. However, because most people are unaware of alternative models, they simply continue to express a desire for what they already receive, and their desires are based on limited information influenced by people with commercial and corporate interests (Sewart, 1987). Therefore, changes will occur only when people connected with sports are able to develop visions for what sports could and should look like if they were not shaped so overwhelmingly by economic factors.

SUGGESTED READINGS

Cagan, J., and N. deMause. 1998. *Field of schemes: How the great stadium swindle turns public money into private profit.* Monroe, ME: Common Courage Press (two journalists use a critical approach to outline the strategies used by various professional team owners in the United States to use public money to establish and promote their business operations; discussion of how these strategies might be undermined or resisted).

Lavoie, M. 2000. Economics and sport. In *Handbook of sports studies* (pp. 157–170) edited by J. Coakley and E. Dunning. London: Sage (overview of research on labour economics and the economics of professional sports; issues receiving special attention are salary determination, free agency, salary caps, profit maximization, and franchise location).

Sage, G. H. 1998. *Power and ideology in American sport: A critical perspective.* 2d ed. Champaign, IL: Human Kinetics (chapters 6–9 provide overviews of commercialization and the political economy of sports in the United States).

Stein, G. 1997. *Power play: An inside look at the big business of the National Hockey League.* Secaucus, NJ: Carol Publishing Group (the former president of the NHL provides information about the NHL as a business organization).

Wetzel, D., and D. Yaeger. 2000. *Sole influence: Basketball, corporate greed, and the corruption of America's youth.* New York: Warner Books (two journalists give a behind-the-scenes look at how sneaker companies develop connections and brand loyalty among young athletes; shows how black market professionalism exists among high school and college athletes and how young athletes are misled and exploited by large corporations).

Wilson, J. 1994. *Playing by the rules: Sport, society, and the state.* Detroit: Wayne State University Press (an insightful social political analysis of how the relationship between sport and the state in the United States has developed to enable the commercialization of sports to occur; deals with economic issues as they are connected with public policy and law through recent history and with emerging global issues).

WEBSITE RESOURCES

Note: Websites often change. The following URLs were current when this book was printed. Please check our website (www.mcgrawhill.ca/college/coakley) for updates and additions.

www.fieldofschemes.com (representing the book of the same name by Joanna Cagan and Neil deMause; site contains information from the book as well as key links to recent articles and related sites)

www.sportslaw.org/slapubs.htm (the Sports Lawyers Association publishes the *Sports Lawyers Journal;* this site lists articles, many of which are devoted to the legal issues associated with the special legal context in which professional sport teams operate)

www.HockeyZonePlus.com (data on the business and economics of hockey in Canada and around the world; salary information for teams, NHL players, and players in nine leagues around the world, including the professional hockey league in Russia; information on the values of franchises, team ownership, attendance, and coaches' salaries, as well as much additional financial information)

www.cfl.ca (any of the sites for professional sport leagues provide a picture of how they present themselves for commercial purposes; don't expect to find any critical information at these sites)

www.cflpa.com (any of the sites for professional sport players' associations provide more interesting, and sometimes critical, information about the leagues, and about the struggles that have occurred—and in the case of labour disputes, are occurring—in relations between players and owners)

www.wwe.com (illustrates extreme example of "entertainment sport")

(Photographs by M. MacNeill)

Sports and the Media

Could they survive without each other?

We see precious little in the sports pages that corporate entertainment does not want us to see.

—**Geoffrey Smith, professor, Queen's University (1999)**

[I]t's clear to me that few sports reporters or editors think they have any duty to make Canadians better informed about the accomplishments of their countrymen. They obviously feel that most Canadians are uninterested in non-professional athletic competition. But I think they're wrong. Given a fair chance, Canadians are.

Ken Read, Canadian skier (1987)

I'll tell you what Canadians do better than anyone else in the world—that's produce hockey games. *Hockey Night in Canada* does a hockey game better than ABC, NBC or CBS ever could.

—**Dan Matheson, TV announcer (1993)**

Hockey has been the source of community pride and national unity; if the CPR held the country together during the early years of Confederation, certainly *Hockey Night in Canada* has done so in recent years.

—**Bruce Kidd, author (1969)**

 Online Learning Centre Resources

Visit *Sports in Society's* Online Learning Centre at **www.mcgrawhill.ca/college/coakley** for additional information and study material for this chapter.

The media, including newspapers, magazines, books, movies, radio, television, video games, and the Internet, pervade human culture. Although we all incorporate the media into our lives in different ways, the things we read, hear, and see in the media are important parts of our experience. They frame and influence how we think about the world; we use media images and messages as we evaluate social events and envision the future. We also use them as we form ideas about everything from personal relationships and consumer products to political candidates and international affairs. This does not mean that we are slaves to the media or that we are passive dupes of those who control the media. The messages presented by media institutions continually attempt to tell us what to think (direct political statements and more indirect ideological messages), do (public service announcements), and buy (commercials, advertising, and consumer "news" items), and the information and messages are then subject to our interpretation and comparison with our other sources of information (often other media sources). However, by setting the agenda so successfully, the media greatly influence what we think about. Our lives and our social worlds are clearly informed by media content, and, if the media did not exist, our lives would be different.

Sports and the media are interconnected parts of our lives. Sport programming is an important segment of media content, and many sports depend on the media for publicity and revenues. In light of these interconnections, this chapter considers four general questions:

1. What are the characteristics of the media?
2. How are sports and the media interconnected?
3. What images and messages are emphasized in the media coverage of sports in Canada and the U.S.?
4. What are the characteristics of sports journalism?

CHARACTERISTICS OF THE MEDIA

Revolutionary changes are occurring in the media. The personal computer and the emergence of the Internet have propelled us into a transition between an era of sponsored and programmed media for mass consumption, and an era of personally generated and constructed media content and experiences. The pace and specific implications of this transition are unknown, but university students are among those whose experiences are on the cutting edge of this media revolution. Although it is important to discuss new trends associated with this transition, and to develop frameworks for describing and explaining them, it is also important to understand the traditional media and their connections with sports.

In this chapter, we distinguish between print media and electronic media. **Print media** include newspapers, magazines and fanzines, books, catalogues, event programmes, and even trading cards: words and images printed on paper and available to many readers. **Electronic media** include radio, television, film, video games, the Internet, and computer publications of many types: words, commentary, and images we receive through audio and video devices. Computers and the Internet have blurred traditional lines separating print media from electronic media, because they present virtually unlimited online combinations of the printed word and audio/video content.

Taken together, the media provide *information*, *interpretation*, and *entertainment*. Sometimes they provide two or three of these things simultaneously, although, when they do, entertainment goals are likely to skew the provision of information and interpretation. The media connect us with parts of the world and construct a version of that world. They bring us information, experiences, people, images, and ideas that would not otherwise be part of our everyday lives. However, they connect us with *selected* information experiences, people, images, and ideas. Therefore, as we experience these connections, our reality is constructed in the process.

Media content—what we do and do not read, hear, and see—is always edited and "re-presented" by those who control them: the producers, editors, programme directors, technicians, programmers, camerapersons, writers, commentators, sponsors, and Internet site providers.[1] These people provide information, interpretation, and entertainment based on their interest in one or more of five goals: (1) making profits, (2) shaping values, (3) providing a public service, (4) building their own reputations, and (5) expressing themselves in technical, artistic, or personal ways.

In nations where most of the media are privately owned and operated, the dominant interest is profit making. This is not the only interest, but often it is the most influential. For example, media expert Michael Real explains that there has been no greater force in the construction of media sport reality around the world than "commercial television and its institutionalized value system [emphasizing] profit making, sponsorship, expanded markets, commodification, and competition" (1998: 17). The Internet will be the major force influencing media reality in the future, and it is likely that commercial interests will influence the value system that emerges in connection with the Internet.

In nations where the popular media are controlled and operated by the state, the dominant interests are shaping values, providing a public service, and, to a lesser extent, providing entertainment. However, state control of the media has been eroded by the emergence of the Internet and the access to information, interpretation, and entertainment it provides to those who have computers and modems. There have been various efforts to block access to the Internet in nations that control media, and various filtering systems have been introduced in libraries and schools in many countries. And some governments and corporations have introduced Internet surveillance systems.

The particular nature of electronic media available to Canadians is distinct from the U.S., combining both private/commercial forms with a modified form of state-funded media, and providing ready access to U.S. commercial and public television through cable, satellite, and digital access. Because of Canadian geography and population distribution, the first electronic linking of the country coast-to-coast by radio (in the 1930s) and television (in the 1950s) were considered to be as significant as the completion of the CN and CP railroad links across the country in the latter part of the nineteenth century. They provided the possibility of common communication across the country and were significant in developing a sense of national identity.

Canadians now have several French and English private networks on television and radio, and CBC/SRC as state-supported networks that are also partially privatized, showing commercials on television and producing some programmes. (CBC/SRC radio is not commercial.) Given the recent misinformation propagated by Don Cherry about the "government owning the CBC," it is important to understand the control of media in Canada. All media, private and public, are regulated by a government agency, the Canadian Radio-television and Telecommunications Commission (CRTC), which grants and renews licences, and sets standards for (and monitors) Canadian content. The CBC/SRC is a Crown Corporation (cf., Canada Post, etc.) that receives partial support for its budget from Parliament through the Ministry of Canadian Heritage. The remainder of its budget is derived from selling commercial time on television, as well as from other sources such as selling productions internationally. Thus, the CBC is not completely private but has to compete with private media corporations for the sale of commercial time; nor is it

---

[1]Personal e-mail communication is not included in this discussion of the media.

completely public- or state-owned because, as a Crown Corporation, it has an arms-length relationship with the government and is often critical of the government.[2]

Since most Canadians receive their television signals via cable, their basic cable packages usually also provide the four major U.S. networks and U.S. public television. Canadians also have access to a range of specialty channels, including sport specialty channels such as TSN/RDS, WTSN (digital), Sportsnet, and the Outdoor Life Network. In some areas, it is also possible to see French (TV5) and Italian (Telelatino) league soccer games, and to keep up with British and other international sports through a variety of digital channels. Given that three of the four major leagues in North America have teams in both Canada and the U.S., and the fourth (the NFL) enjoys a relationship with and trades players with the CFL, and given that all four major professional sports (except the CFL) are covered by both Canadian and U.S. commercial network television, often with the Canadian network showing the U.S. coverage, we often refer to "North American" media in this chapter to indicate Canadian and U.S. (but not Mexican) media. Differences between Canada and the U.S. begin to emerge in the coverage of sports that may be shown in one country but not in the other (e.g., curling), occasionally in the quality of coverage (e.g., Canadian expertise at hockey coverage, U.S. expertise at football coverage), and regularly in the coverage of events such as the Olympics.

As a consequence of this broad range of coverage, many Canadians enjoy the possibility of comparing coverage. In the case of the

Olympics, for example, Canadians have been able to follow the last four Olympics (Atlanta, Nagano, Sydney, and Salt Lake City) by comparing and contrasting CBC and NBC English-language coverage of the Games, and they have been able to supplement their viewing with SRC French language broadcasts, TSN/RDS commercial supplementary coverage, and CBC/SRC radio hourly updates. However, the flow of U.S. media into Canada, together with the various ideologies discussed later in this chapter, is often considered to be overpowering, and some have argued that we may be losing a distinctively Canadian culture (including sports) as a result. The relationship is not completely one way though, and many in the U.S. (and other countries) follow CBC radio through the Internet. Also, during the Olympics, many Americans in border states have taken to watching live Canadian coverage rather than pre-packaged, prime-time coverage from NBC.

Returning to the five goals that drive media content, power relations in society influence the priority that is given to them. Those who make content and programming decisions act as filters as they select and create the images and messages re-presented by the media. In the filtering, or re-presentation, process, these people usually emphasize images and messages consistent with the dominant ideologies in the society as a whole. Thus, the media often serve the interests of those who have power and wealth in society. As corporate control of commercial media has increased and such media have become hyper-commercialized, media content has emphasized consumerism, individualism, competition, and class inequality as natural and necessary in society, while it marginalizes any emphasis on civic values, anticommercial activities, and political activity (McChesney, 1999).

Of course, there are some exceptions to this pattern of promoting corporate interests in capital expansion, but, whenever media content effectively challenges dominant ideologies, those responsible for that content can expect to

[2] Public broadcasting in other countries may take other forms: in countries where total funding is received directly from the government (e.g., the People's Republic of China), the government often enjoys a great deal of control and is never criticized by the public broadcaster; other countries may fund their public broadcasters by charging viewers a licence fee (e.g., the BBC in the U.K.).

face struggles associated with their place in the media. This is a problem when it banishes someone from a media career, subverts particular types of programming, or leads to self-censorship that defers to the interests of those with power and money. Even when there is legal protection for freedom of speech, those who work in the media often think carefully before presenting images and messages that challenge the interests of those who have power and influence in society, especially when those powerful people own or control the media and sign the paycheques of those who work for them. As the old expression says, "the freedom of the press belongs to those who own one."

This does not mean that we in media audiences are forced to read, hear, and see things we are not interested in or that those who control the media ignore what we think. But it does mean that, apart from the Internet sites we create and control, we seldom have direct control over the content of what we read, listen to, and see in the media. The media re-present to us edited versions of information, interpretation, and entertainment—versions that people who control the media think we want, or ought, to consume. For example, in the case of sports, those people not only select which sports and events will be covered but also decide what kinds of images and commentary will be emphasized in the coverage (Kinkema and Harris, 1998; Rowe, 1999). When they do this, they play an important role in constructing the overall frameworks that we in media audiences use to define and explain sports in our lives.

Those of us who have grown up with television seldom think about media content in this way. For example, when we watch sports on television, we do not often notice that the images and messages we see and hear have been carefully designed to heighten the dramatic content of the event and emphasize dominant ideologies in the society as a whole. The pregame analysis, the camera coverage, the camera angles, the close-ups, the slow-motion shots, the attention given

to particular athletes, the announcer's play-by-play descriptions, the colour commentary, the quotes from athletes, and the postgame summary and analysis are all presented to entertain the media audience and keep sponsors happy.

Television commentary and images tend to highlight action, competition, aggression, hard work, individual heroism and achievement, play through pain, teamwork, and competitive outcomes. Television coverage has become so seamless in its re-presentations of sports that we often define televised games as "real" games, more real even than the game seen in person at the stadium. Magazine editor Kerry Temple explains:

> It's not just games you're watching. It's soap operas, complete with story lines and plots and plot twists. And good guys and villains, heroes and underdogs. And all this gets scripted into cliffhanger morality plays....And you get all caught up in this until you begin to believe it really matters. (1992: 29)

Even though the media content of sports programming is carefully edited and re-presented in a total entertainment package, most of us believe that, when we see a sport event on television, we are seeing it "the way it is." We also think that, when we hear the commentary or read the report on the event, the commentators and journalists are "telling it like it is." We do not usually think that what we are seeing, hearing, and reading is a series of commentaries and images selected for particular reasons and grounded in the social worlds and interests of those producing the event, controlling the images, and making the commentary. After all, television coverage gives us only *one* of *many* possible sets of images and messages related to a sport event; there is a wide array of images and messages that we do *not* receive. For example, if we were to go to the event in person, we would see something quite different from the images represented on television, and we would come up with our own descriptions and interpretations, which might be completely unrelated to those provided by media commentators.

"Quick! Over here—I think we've got our next 'what I sacrificed for sports' spokesmodel!"

Media representations of sports highlight "the thrill of victory and the agony of defeat." They contain an abundance of spectacular plays and crashes. However, these are minor parts of the totality of experience in sport events.

This point was clearly illustrated in a comparison of CBC and NBC coverage of the Atlanta and Sydney Olympics. The CBC has a policy of extensive live coverage (regardless of the time of day in the six different time zones across Canada), focusing on all events that include Canadian competitors, and other major competitions. The live coverage is mixed with highlight packages, magazine pieces, and studio and on-site interviews. In contrast, NBC strategically created entertaining drama by re-presenting what media analysts have described as "plausible reality" in their broadcasts; to do this, they deliberately withheld information so they could frame events in their terms, even though they knew those terms to be contrary to what was expressed by the athletes and others involved. They gave priority to entertainment over news and information. Former U.S. Olympic swimmer Diana Nyad,

who was in Atlanta, observed, "Compared to the TV audience, the people in Atlanta have seen a completely different Olympics" (National Public Radio, 1996, 6 August broadcast). She also noted that television and other media coverage revolves around a focus on gold medals, which is a distortion of what the live events involve for most of the athletes and spectators. Both CBC and NBC represented the events to their viewers, and both had particular stories to tell, but the strategy of packaging events in U.S. prime time was quite distinct from the Canadian re-presentation. In other words, television constructs sports and viewer experiences in important ways. And it happens so smoothly that most people think that when they watch a game on television they are experiencing sports in a natural form.

What would people say if all television documentaries were sponsored by environmental organizations, by women's organizations, or by labour organizations? They would probably raise questions about the content of the documentaries, the interpretations of the announcers, and the political slant of coverage in the documentaries. They would look for ways in which the interests of the environmentalists, feminists, or labour organizers were shaping images and messages and influencing overall information, interpretation, and entertainment in the programmes. The sponsors of over 99 percent of all sports programming in the media are capitalist corporations, which succeed or fail depending on their ability to generate profits, so why do we not ask more questions about what this means? Why do we spend so little time thinking about *why* we see what we see in sports coverage, *why* we hear the things commentators say during the coverage, and what we do *not* read, see, and hear as we consume media sports? Whether we are aware of it or not, our experiences as spectators are heavily influenced by the decisions of those who control the media, and their decisions are influenced by social, political, and economic factors—including dominant ideologies related to gender, race, and class (see chapters 8 to 10). We explore this later in the chapter.

Characteristics of the Internet

The Internet extends and radically changes our media connections with the rest of the world, because it gives us virtual access to potentially unlimited and individually created and chosen information, interpretation, and entertainment. A simple way to explain this is to say that being online is partly like having open voice, video, and text connections with everyone in the world who also is online. Some of these connections permit real-time interaction, while others provide posted text and images, which we can access on our own terms and in our own time frame. For example, we can interact with fellow fans in chat rooms; ask questions of players and coaches; locate scores, statistics, and other sport-related materials others have displayed online; and play various online games associated with sport events around the world.

Unlike television, the Internet is not limited to sequential programming. Television may offer dozens and even hundreds of channels, but we are forced to watch programmes on schedules set by television companies, although we can record them and watch them on our own time as the television companies have presented them. The Internet is unique in that it offers the possibility of accessing variously created media content on our own time at our own pace. In fact, we can even create media content to match our interests and the interests of our friends. This gives us a form of control that radically alters media experiences and mediated realities.

In the case of sports, currently most people use the Internet as an extension of the existing media. They may link to team sites and listen to live game audio because local radio and television does not cover all games. However, the audio is from television broadcasts of games televised in other regions. They may go online and order tickets or make reservations for tee-times instead of using the phone to do so. They may go to a team's chat room for postgame discussions instead of joining game-related conversations on talk radio or initiating them by calling friends on the phone. They may use online sites to track game statistics and read posted commentary to complement the commentary and images in the games they watch on television or read about in the print media. They may join online fantasy leagues or playoff drafts and use the data summaries provided by an Internet site, so that they do not have to use newspapers' box scores as sources of information about the performance statistics of the players they have selected for their teams. They may place bets and check scores online instead of calling bookies and watching television to find scores.

The fact that heavily used Internet sites are sponsored and maintained by existing media companies means that the Internet, in some ways, extends the reach, influence, and power of existing media organizations. However, the Internet also provides virtual access to nearly unlimited information around the world and potentially frees people of the control of large media companies (McDaniel and Sullivan, 1998).

If we want real-time scores of major spectator sports in many postindustrial nations, we can obtain them through many online news sites. Of course, many of us also have access to numerous television channels and may obtain real-time scores through them. However, if we are online, we can go immediately to the sport and the score we are looking for without waiting for a commentator or television channel to provide information about the event.

If we want sports stories by journalists, we now have virtual access to stories written by newspaper, magazine, and online journalists around the world.[3] The material that many people write is not immediately accessible online, but we are moving in that direction. As this occurs, certain sources will require subscriptions for access. There will be registrations and subscriber fees, and we will make choices, just as we do today with our newspaper and magazine subscriptions. The difference will be that we will not be forced to wait for our paper or magazine to be delivered by surface mail, and there will be free sites offering many of the same things as the sites that require fees.

Information, interpretation, and entertainment from numerous sources will be available to us if the Internet remains open to all and people remain committed to public access to information and ideas, even if sites are maintained with ads paid for by sponsors. In the meantime, large corporations, especially media and entertainment companies, are working hard and investing massive amounts of money to frame and shape the Internet in terms that fit their interests. This means that the Internet is "contested terrain," and there will be important struggles over issues of access, ownership, and the rights of users to share information and ideas. Through 2003, these struggles have revolved around sharing music files. But in the longer term, they have important implications for the future of democracy and the dynamics of social life. If the interests of e-commerce suppress policies that guarantee a free and open Internet information highway, a key opportunity to revolutionize the media will have been undermined (N. Solomon, 2000).

Will the Internet primarily be a vehicle for democratizing social life and freely sharing ideas and information without constraints set by private interests? Or will the Internet primarily be a means of expanding capital, increasing productivity and consumption, reproducing the values that drive market economies, and maintaining the notion that corporations are *the* source of pleasure and excitement in our lives? The answers to these

questions will emerge as we struggle over how the Internet will be incorporated into our lives.

As more of us experience sports online, obtain the software needed for coordinated audio/video/data streaming, and gain access to broadband Internet connections, we will have more control over the conditions of media sport consumption. Theoretically, the Internet can provide each of us with the ability to create our own spectator sport realities and experiences. For example, people today can have interactive experiences through online connections during a game. In the future, they may use the Internet to make choices about camera angles during a game, follow athletes into locker rooms, listen to what coaches and players say, pull up data they wish to see during the game, and even select audio commentary or interactive commentary as they watch. If they subscribe to certain sites, they will watch players' home lives. This, of course, brings spectators closer and closer to the people, emotions, and actions in events.

As this occurs, being a spectator will become a more active and creative experience, and spectators will participate directly in the construction of media reality. In a sense, they will assume positions similar to those of journalists and announcers and will become part of the construction of events. How this will change the reality of mediated sports and our experience of them remains to be seen. In the future, we will be "players all," and performance will constitute our realities in new ways (Rinehart, 1998).

However, the future is difficult to predict. Will people choose 500-channel high-definition digital television over the medium of the Internet? Will the economics of technology and the "digital divide" between technology haves and have-nots segregate spectators even further by social class? Will the culture of the Internet favour men, or will it enable all spectators to create realities that fit interests related to gender, race and ethnicity, and social class? Answers to these and other questions will depend on the forces shaping the future of the Internet.

---

[3]Internet sports reporters often have difficulties obtaining "press passes and privileges" at traditional sport events. Although events such as the X Games issue over one-third of their press credentials to "dot.com" reporters, Internet sites were denied credentials at the 2000 Sydney Olympics. However, the IOC realizes that it has to resolve the potential conflict between the lucrative television rights holders and the Internet (see p. 375), and online journalists were accredited for the first time at the Salt Lake City Olympics in 2002.

Commercial forces guarantee that the first people to enjoy these new spectator experiences and realities will be those with the money or organizational connections to buy or gain access to the hardware, software, and bandwidth to move around the Internet as fast as they wish, to as many sites as they wish, and to whatever images they wish to view. Class relations will influence future Internet spectator experiences, but, depending on public policies and programmes,[4] the Internet could also blur class differences when it comes to future access to information, interpretation, and entertainment.

Characteristics of Video Games and Virtual Sports

Sports also come into our lives through video games and virtual experiences. Sport video games are popular in wealthy nations, and some people have even participated in virtual sports of various types, although most virtual sports are experimental and not available for general participation.

The images in video games have become increasingly lifelike in recent years, and those who play the games have uniquely active spectator experiences. Social science research on video games has focused on violence and gender issues in action games generally; it has not focused on games modelled after "real" sports. It is clear that people who play sport video games have different experiences than those who watch televised sport events. Golf fans may now match their video golf skills with the physical skills of pro golfers by going online and golfing on the same course as Tiger Woods or other high-profile players whose shots have been represented and archived

through digitized images. This changes watching a tournament into a participatory experience, unlike spectator experiences in the past. Research is needed to document, describe, and analyze these differences and the character of the experiences and realities of those who select video games, choose challenges, control action, and compete against other players or standards programmed into the game.

SPORTS AND THE MEDIA: A TWO-WAY RELATIONSHIP

The media and the commercialization of sports are closely related topics in the sociology of sport. In fact, the media intensify and extend the process and consequences of commercialization. For this reason, much attention has been given to how sports have been influenced by the media, while little attention has been given to how the media have been influenced by sports. However, there is actually a reciprocal relationship between these two important spheres of life: each has influenced the other, and each has grown to depend on the other for its popularity and commercial success. In fact, when Sut Jhally, the well-known popular media analyst at the University of Massachusetts, was a Ph.D. student at Simon Fraser University, he coined the term "sport-media complex" to characterize the symbiotic relationship between the two (Jhally, 1984).

Do Sports Depend on the Media?

The existence and success of commercial sports and sport organizations depend heavily on the media, but this is not true of all sport forms. People played sports long before the media began to cover and re-present the events. Even now, people participate in a variety of sports that receive no media coverage. When sports exist just for the participants, there is no urgent need to advertise games, publicize results, and interpret what happened. The players already know

---

[4] As a result of federal government policy, in 1999, Canada became the first country to have all schools and libraries connected to the Internet. Industry Canada's Community Access and Connecting Canadians programmes provide broadband access to remote and northern communities, attempting to ensure more democratic access to the Internet.

Commercial sports depend heavily on the media. All media hype events, and television pays rights fees, which have become increasingly important to the overall success of commercial sports. The payoff for corporations is that their logos are continually on camera and in newspaper photographs such as this one. The logo placement costs far less than television commercials and print advertisements. (CP/Chuck Stoody)

these things, and they are the only ones who matter. There is no need to attract and entertain ticket-buying spectators. It is only when sports become commercial entertainment that they depend on the media.

Sports are unique forms of entertainment, because they require the media to provide a combination of coverage *and* news. People attend plays, concerts, and films and engage in many leisure activities without needing regular media coverage to enhance enjoyment. However, with sports, this coverage is very important. When a stage play is over, it is over—except for a review

after opening night and the personal conversations of those who attended the play. However, when a sport event is over, many people wish to discuss statistics, important plays, records, standings, the overall performances of the players and teams, upcoming games or matches, the importance of the game or match in terms of the season as a whole, the postseason, the next season, and so on. The media are important vehicles for these discussions.

Without media coverage, the popularity and revenue-generating potential of commercial spectator sports would be seriously limited. Information about events generates interest, and interest generates revenues from the sale of tickets, luxury boxes, club seats, concessions, parking, team logo merchandise, and licensing rights. After games or matches have been played, the scores become news items, and the interpretations of the action become entertainment for fans, regardless of whether they attended the event in person or not. This seems to be the case globally—for bullfights in Mexico, cricket matches in South Africa, soccer matches in Brazil, and sumo bashos in Japan. Reporting often takes a different tone in international competitions or multi-sport events such as the Commonwealth Games. In these cases, information and interpretation of the action are supplemented with national comparisons and evaluations of national sport development systems.

Sports promoters and team owners, especially those in countries with market economies, are well aware of the need for the media coverage of sports. Therefore, they often go out of their way to accommodate reporters, commentators, and photographers (Koppett, 1994). Media personnel often are given comfortable seats in press boxes, access to the fields of play and the players' locker rooms, summaries of statistics and player information, and play-by-play information on what is happening during events. Providing these services costs money, but it guarantees media coverage, and it encourages those covering the events to be supportive and sympathetic in what they write and say. Sometimes, media interest is so overwhelming that reporters have to adopt the same strategy occasionally used by military and political reporters—forming pools in order to obtain information. This is currently the case with the large contingents of Japanese media who are following the careers of Ichiro Suzuki and Hideki Matsui in Major League Baseball. In the case of Ichiro, one reporter is designated to ask post-game questions in the locker room, and then shares that information with the hundred or so Japanese reporters waiting outside (Nakamura, 2003).

Although all commercial spectator sports depend on the media, some of them have a special dependence on television. Television is different from the other media in that television companies pay considerable amounts of money for broadcasting rights. Rights fees provide sports with predictable sources of income. Once contracts are signed, television money can be counted on, regardless of bad weather, injuries to key players, and the other factors that interfere with ticket sales and with other on-site revenue streams. Without television contracts, commercial success is unlikely, which is why the NHL has been so anxious to negotiate a full-coverage U.S. network contract.

Television revenues also have much greater growth potential than revenues from gate receipts. Only so many tickets can be sold to an event, and tickets can cost only so much without turning people off. But television audiences can include literally billions of viewers, now that satellite technology transmits signals to most locations around the globe. For example, Toohey and Veal (2000) estimate that a cumulative audience of over 25 billion viewers in over 200 countries watched television coverage of the Sydney Olympics. In 2002, it has been estimated that 1.1 billion people watched Brazil beat Germany in the men's World Cup soccer final, and that the cumulative audience for the tournament was approximately 30 billion in over 200 countries (making it the most viewed event in television history).

The size of the potential TV audience and the deregulation of the television industry are the two main reasons television rights have increased in value at phenomenal rates since the early 1970s (Bellamy, 1998). David Whitson (1998), of the University of Alberta, points out that television rights fees not only have made commercial sports more profitable for promoters and team owners but also have increased the attractiveness of sports as vehicles for advertising products nationally and internationally. This enables athletes to demand higher salaries and turns some of the athletes into national and international celebrities, who then use their celebrity status to endorse products sold around the world. For example, Tiger Woods' global popularity is due as much to the invention of the satellite dish as to his golf skills.

As it becomes realistic to broadcast games and events on the Internet, there will be interesting changes in how media rights are negotiated. The global reach of the Internet creates new possibilities for big companies, which want to reach relatively wealthy people worldwide; however, it also creates challenges, because it cuts into the television rights that have been negotiated within various regions around the world. This challenge has, for example, prevented the International Olympic Committee (IOC) from selling Internet rights to the Olympics. After all, what would CBC television say if canada.com, the Global television website, were to present the Olympics on the Internet and cut into CBC's audience in Canada. The CBC has already vigorously protected its exclusive rights against rebroadcast of Olympic coverage against other broadcasters such as Toronto's multicultural TV (CFMT, now Omni; Greenberg, et al., in press). They, and every other company that had bought television rights, would sue the IOC.

Have Commercial Sports Sold Out to the Media?
There is no question that some sports have become dependent on television for revenues and publicity. The NFL, for example, brings in

about 60 percent of its revenues from television contracts. However, television money comes with strings attached. Accommodating the interests of commercial television requires numerous changes in the ways sports are organized, packaged, scheduled, and presented. Some of these changes include the following:

- The schedules and starting times for many sport events have been altered to fit television's programming needs.
- Halftime periods in certain sports have been shortened, so that television audiences will be more likely to stay tuned to events.
- Prearranged schedules of time-outs have been added to football, basketball, and hockey games to make time for commercials.
- Teams, leagues, and championships/world cups have been formed or realigned to take advantage of regional media markets and to build national and even international fan bases for sports, leagues, and teams.

Many other changes associated with television coverage are not entirely due to the influence of television. For example, professional teams extended their seasons and the number of games played, a change that would have occurred even without television. Commercial sports would have added extra games simply to increase gate receipts. Extra games do make television contracts more lucrative, but the economic reasons for adding games include more than just the sale of television rights. The same is true for the additions of sudden death overtime periods in some sports, the tiebreaker scoring method in tennis, rally scoring in volleyball, the addition of medal play in golf, and the three-point shot in basketball. Each of these changes is grounded in general commercial interests independent from television coverage, but *television adds to the urgency and importance of these changes*.

Television *expands and intensifies* the commercial interests that are already an important part of spectator sports in many societies (Bellamy, 1998). Although some changes in sports result

from the requirements of television coverage, the real reason for most changes over the past three decades has been the desire to produce more marketable entertainment for all spectators and a more attractive commercial package for sponsors and advertisers. Furthermore, these changes have been made willingly in most cases. The trade-offs usually have been attractive for both players and sponsors. In fact, many of the sports and athletes not currently receiving television coverage gladly would make changes in the way their events are packaged, scheduled, and presented if they could reap the attention and money associated with television contracts. Are there limits to what they would change for television coverage? In many cases, yes; in a few cases, no. Selling out is not so much a matter of making changes; it is a matter of giving up control and autonomy while participating in sports.

Have the Media Corrupted Sports? When people discuss sports and the media, many voice the concern that dependence on the media, especially dependence on television, might corrupt sports. However, the notion that television is the root of all evil in sports fails to take into account two factors:

1. *Sports are not shaped primarily by the media in general, or by television in particular*. The idea that television by itself has somehow transformed sports does not hold up under careful examination. Sports are social constructions; as such, they have been created gradually through interactions among athletes, facility directors, sport team owners, event promoters, media representatives, sponsors, advertisers, agents, and spectators—all of whom have diverse interests. The dynamics of these interactions have been grounded in power relations and shaped by the resources held by different people at different times. Although not everyone has equal influence over changes occurring in sports, media interests are not

the only factors producing changes in sports or in the relationship between sports and the media. It is unrealistic to think that media people have been able to shape sports to fit their interests alone.

2. *The media, including television, do not operate in a political and economic vacuum.* The concerns of those connected with sports and the relationships they have with one another are heavily influenced by the social, political, and economic contexts in which they live. The media in most countries are regulated by government agencies and policies. Although these regulations have been loosened or lifted in recent years, the media must negotiate contracts with teams and leagues under legal constraints. Economic factors also constrain the media by setting limits on the value of sponsorships and advertising time and by shaping the climate in which types of programming, such as pay-per-view sports and cable and satellite subscriptions, might be profitable. Finally, the media also are constrained by social factors, which inform people's decisions on whether they will read about, listen to, or watch sports.

These two factors raise serious questions about whether the media corrupt sports. There are certainly important connections between these two spheres of life, but those connections are grounded in complex sets of social, economic, and political relationships, which change over time and vary from culture to culture. It is these relationships that we must understand if we are to understand the media's impact on sports. In other words, the conclusion that the media corrupt sports is based on an incomplete understanding of how the social world works and how sports are connected with social relations in society.

With that said, it is also important to remember that nearly all of the most powerful people in sports around the world are CEOs or owners of major, global corporations. Nearly all of them are

white men from English-speaking nations. Their corporations include U.S.-based AOL Time Warner and Disney, and Australian Rupert Murdoch's News Corporation International. Canadian multi-media corporations include Quebecor, CanWest Media Inc., Rogers Telecommunications Inc. (owners of the Toronto Blue Jays), and BCE Inc. (Bell Canada, CTV, the *Globe and Mail*, and part owners of the Toronto Maple Leafs and Toronto Raptors). Each wants to offer programming that people in their countries and around the globe will watch, and that transnational corporations will sponsor and use as advertising vehicles. The sports selected for national and global coverage have been and will continue to be dependent on the media for their commercial success, and the salaries and endorsement income of athletes also have been and will continue to be dependent on the media. However, in the symbiotic relationships of the sports-media complex, there are two sides to this process.

Do the Media Depend on Sports?

There is much more to the media than sports coverage. This is especially true for magazines, books, radio, movies, and the Internet, although it is less true for newspapers and television. The Internet does not depend on sports, but certain online services may make money from sports fans who use the Internet to obtain up-to-the-minute scores and information about particular events, and to enter online discussions about athletes, teams, and events.

Neither the book publishing nor the film industry depends on sports. Until recently, there have been few successful books and films about sports. The urgency and uncertainty that are so compelling in live sports are difficult to capture in these media; however, since the late 1980s, both publishers and film studios have produced projects with tragic, inspiring, and outrageous stories about sports figures.

Most radio stations give coverage to sports only in their news segments, although local

As the global media gain more influence in sports around the world, what will become of sports? This is being asked in England, as media organizations come to control more and more of elite professional soccer and as soccer teams at other levels lose the resources they need to exist.

football, baseball, hockey, and basketball games often are broadcast on local radio stations. However, some communities have talk radio stations that feature sports talk programmes that attract large audiences. These audiences have clear demographics: they are mostly young men with higher than average incomes, and this helps radio stations sell advertising.

Most magazines devote little or no attention to sports coverage, although the number of special interest sport magazines and fanzines in Canada and other countries is increasing.[5] A quick study of any local magazine rack shows that people who are interested in skiing, skateboarding, snowboarding, biking, moto-cross, car racing, and dozens of other sports now have magazines devoted to their interests.

The media most dependent on sports are newspapers and television. The companies that control these media are at least partially dependent on sports for their commercial success. This is especially true in the United States.

Newspapers Newspapers at the beginning of the twentieth century had a sports page, which consisted of a few notices about upcoming activities, a short story or two about races or university games, and possibly some scores of local games. By the late 1920s, the sports page had grown into the sports "section," which resembled the sports sections of today's newspapers. As sports have become a highly visible part of popular culture in many postindustrial societies, special daily and weekly sports newspapers have emerged, which are completely dependent on sports. Furthermore, sports coverage has gradually grown to account for up to 20 percent of the major newspapers in many cities.

---

[5] Interestingly, in English-speaking countries, only the U.S. has been able to produce a long-term, successful, general-interest sports magazine: *Sports Illustrated.*

In most major North American newspapers, more daily coverage is given to sports than to any other single topic of interest, including business or politics. The sports section is the most widely read section of the paper. It accounts for at least one-third of the total circulation and a significant amount of the advertising revenues for big-city newspapers. It attracts advertisers who might not put ads in other sections of the paper. Advertisers know that, if they want to reach young to middle-aged males with average or above-average incomes, they should place ads in the sports section. This is an attractive prospect for businesses that sell tires, automobile supplies, new cars, car leases, airline tickets for business travelers, alcoholic beverages, power tools, building supplies, sporting goods, hair growth products, and even escort services. Other advertisers are clinics and doctors specializing in treating impotence or providing testosterone and other hormone therapies, bars or clubs providing naked or near-naked female models and dancers, and organizations offering gambling opportunities (see a sample of major-city newspapers to confirm this). Ads for all these products and services generate considerable revenues for newspapers.

The future of newspapers' dependence on sports is difficult to predict. If the Internet becomes the main source of information about major sports nationally and around the world, then newspapers may return to emphasizing information and the interpretation of local sports, including high school teams, university teams, and youth sports. This can already be seen as more major-city newspapers publish sections on a weekly basis that highlight local athletes. They know that if people in Regina use the Internet to read about the Roughriders, they will still have to buy the local newspaper to read about Campbell Collegiate's football team.

Television Companies Some television companies in North America also have developed a dependence on sports for programming content and advertising revenues. For example, sport events are a major part of the programming schedules of national network stations in Canada and many cable and satellite-based stations. Some media companies even sponsor events or buy teams, which they then promote and televise (e.g., Rogers and the Blue Jays).

Sports account for a growing proportion of income made on the sales of commercial time by television companies. Many cable and satellite companies have used sport programmes to attract subscribers from particular segments of the viewing public, and then they have sold audiences to advertisers. For example, when TSN first started selling commercial time to businesses, it sent out a flyer stating, "We Deliver the Male" (Sparks, 1992). People in Canada and some other parts of the world can watch sport programmes nearly 24 hours a day, if they have the time, interest, and cable/satellite hook-ups.

An attractive feature of sport programmes for the major Canadian networks (CBC/SRC, CTV, TVA, and CanWest Global) is that they can be scheduled on Saturday and Sunday afternoons—the slowest time periods of the week for television viewing. Sport events are the most popular weekend television programmes, especially among viewers who may not watch much television at other times during the week. This means the networks are able to sell advertising time at relatively high rates during what normally would be dead time for programming.

The networks also use sport programmes to attract commercial sponsors that might take their advertising dollars elsewhere if television stations did not cover certain sports. For example, games in the major men's team sports are ideal for promoting the sales of beer, life insurance, trucks and cars, computers, investment services, credit cards, and air travel. The people in the advertising departments of major corporations realize that sports attract male viewers. They also realize that most business travelers are men and that many men make family decisions on the purchases of beer, cars, computers,

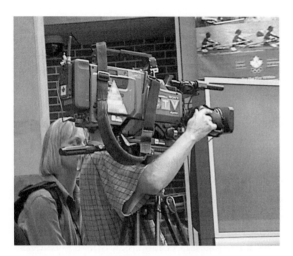

Major networks regard sports as attractive programming because they can schedule them on weekend afternoons, usually a slow time for television viewing. Coverage of sports also attracts male viewers, and male viewers attract corporate advertisers for many products. (M. MacNeill)

investments, and life insurance. Finally, advertisers also may be interested in associating their product or service with the culturally positive image of sport. This is especially important for a product such as beer, which may be a target for groups such as MADD, or those with concerns about alcoholism or tobacco, which is a frequent target of health advocates, among others.[6]

Golf and tennis are special cases for television programming. These sports attract few viewers, and the ratings are usually low. However, the audience for these sports is attractive to certain advertisers. It is made up of people from the highest income groups, including many professionals and business executives. This is the reason television coverage of golf and tennis is

sponsored by companies selling luxury cars and high-priced sports cars, business and personal computers, imported beers, investment opportunities with brokers and consultants, and trips to exclusive vacation areas. This is also the major reason the networks continue to carry these programmes: although few people watch them, they generate revenues from sponsors with products to sell to high-income consumers.

In the mid-1990s, television executives "discovered" women viewers of sports and women's sports. Data since the late 1980s has indicated that, in the U.S., women have made up more than half the viewing audiences for both winter and summer Olympic Games. This led NBC to hype women's sports, and to appeal to women viewers for the 1996 and 2000 telecasts of the games, and led CBC to emphasize gender equity in all aspects of Olympic coverage. Other women's sports have also attracted television coverage, although their coverage pales in comparison with the coverage received by certain men's sports. Women's events do not receive more coverage partly because women viewers of women's games have not been identified as a target audience by advertisers. Furthermore, men make up over half of the viewing audience for women's sports; they are often the same men who watch men's sports, and sponsors have already targeted them during the coverage of men's events.

Cable and satellite television companies also have found they can attract advertising money by televising sports that appeal to other clearly identified segments of consumers. For example, the X Games, which consist of sports appealing to young people, especially young males between twelve and twenty-five years old, attract advertisers selling soft drinks, beer, telecommunications products, and sport equipment such as helmets, shoes, and skateboards.

Over the past two decades, television companies have paid rapidly increasing amounts of money for the rights to televise certain sports. The contracts for these rights are negotiated every few years; some may be negotiated annually. In

[6] Although tobacco advertising is officially banned on Canadian television, and tobacco companies are no longer permitted to sponsor sports events, tobacco company logos still appear regularly on Canadian screens, especially in coverage of U.S. and international auto races.

the case of the major men's spectator sports in the United States and around the world, contracts may involve hundreds of millions of dollars, and more than a billion dollars (US), in the cases of the Olympics, the NFL, the NBA, soccer's World Cup, and premier-level soccer in England.

Table 12.1 illustrates the increases in media rights fees paid by U.S. media companies for the four major North American men's professional leagues. The dominance of the U.S. contracts is evident particularly in the NHL. The CBC pays substantially more (C$60 million) on a *per capita* basis (i.e., in terms of potential viewing audience—Canada's population is 10 percent of the U.S. population) than the ABC network in the U.S. (US$120 million). Despite this, because ABC pays more and because the New York–based NHL is desperately seeking a major U.S. network contract, the NHL allowed ABC/ESPN some say in scheduling 2003 play-off games, with an increased number of Saturday afternoon games as ABC filled that non-peak time in its schedule. For CBC/SRC, this meant that some Saturday nights had no game for *Hockey Night in Canada/La soirée du Hockey*, despite that traditional slot in the schedule. As a consequence, in part, of the loss of Saturday night games, by early May, playoff audience ratings in Canada had declined 11 percent over the previous year (Houston, 2003).

Table 12.2 illustrates the incredible increase in television rights fees paid for the Olympics by Canadian television (CBC and/or CTV), the European Broadcasting Union, and the U.S. networks over the last thirty years. The IOC receives rights fees from media companies around the world. Australia, Japan, and continental Asia are paying increasingly higher fees. The U.S. network NBC signed a US$3.55 billion deal with the IOC to ensure the rights to five Olympic Games between 2000 and 2008, and, in 2003, the network extended that deal to include the 2010 and 2012 Games for an additional US$2.2 billion. NBC paid about US$250 million more for Sydney than Atlanta to provide continuous coverage during the Sydney Games on their international cable channels, CNBC and MSNBC. The European Broadcasting Union (EBU), which is the umbrella organization for European radio and television corporations (both eastern and western Europe since 1993), negotiates Olympic rights fees with the IOC. Despite representing a significantly higher population that the United States, the EBU has traditionally paid lower fees—in part because many of the national broadcasters are non-commercial, but it has also been suggested that the EBU receives favourable deals because so many members of the IOC are European. Despite this, the EBU fees have

Table 12.1 Escalating U.S. annual media rights fees for major commercial sports in North America (US$millions)[a]

Sport	1986	1991	1996	2001	2005
NFL	400	900	1,100	2,200	2,200
MLB[b]	183	365	420	420	558
NBA	30	219	275	660	767
NHL[c]	22	38	77	120	120

[a]These amounts are not inflation adjusted. Most data come from *USA Today*.
[b]Amounts for baseball do not include local television or radio rights fees negotiated by individual teams or national radio rights fees; amount for 1996 includes national radio rights, and amount for 2001 is an estimate.
[c]Includes U.S. and Canadian rights; only U.S. rights for 2001 and 2005; CBC pays C$60m./year for NHL rights.

Table 12.2   Escalating media rights fees for the Olympics (in US$millions)

Summer Olympics	Canada (CBC/CTV)	EBU[b]	US Network
1976 Montreal	1.8[a]	6.55	25.0
1980 Moscow	1.044	7.15	87.0
1984 Los Angeles	3.0	22.0	225.0
1988 Seoul	4.17	30.24	300.0
1992 Barcelona	16.5	94.5	401.0
1996 Atlanta	22.0	247.0	456.0
2000 Sydney	28.0	350.0	705.0
2004 Athens	37.0	394.0	793.0
2008 Beijing	45.0	443.4	894.0
Winter Olympics	**Canada (CBC/CTV)**	**EBU**	**US Network**
1976 Innsbruck	0.36	1.2	10.0
1980 Lake Placid	0.907	3.855	15.5
1984 Sarajevo	1.8	5.6	91.5
1988 Calgary	3.4	6.9	309.0
1992 Albertville	10.1	20.3	243.0
1994 Lillehammer	12.0	26.3	300.0
1998 Nagano	17.0	72.0	375.0
2002 Salt Lake City	22.0	120.0	545.0
2006 Turin	28.0	135.0	613.0

[a]Estimated value
[b]Combines EBU and eastern European broadcasters (OIRT); the two merged in 1993

increased 4800 percent in the last thirty years, compared to 3600 percent for the U.S. fees and 2500 percent for the Canadian fees. Canadian broadcasters have received relatively favourable deals with the IOC in comparison with the U.S., paying approximately 5 percent of the U.S. rate (although they would have been much better off if they had been able to negotiate with the EBU).

The data indicate clearly that television companies want sports in their programming, and they think sports will increase their profits. They realize that the Olympics and the men's soccer World Cup have become the biggest world television events in human history, that the cost of advertising on the *top* sport events is generally much higher than it is for other types of programmes (US$2.2 million for a 30-second slot during the 2003 Super Bowl), that sports involve minimal production costs, and that sports have relatively predictable ratings. Even though there have been cases in which television companies have lost money on sports, profits are generally good, and sport programmes can be used as a basis for promoting other programmes and attracting hard-to-reach viewers.

Another trend is that, as televised sport events have increased, the ratings for many particular events have gone down. As people have more choices, the viewing audience becomes fragmented. More people are watching television sports, but there are more choices than ever before. This means that rights fees for the very large events will continue to increase, but fees for other events, including some "special interest" events (such as bowling, in-line skating championships, and international skiing races) will be limited. When interest among particular viewers is especially strong, as for championship boxing and certain other sport events, pay-per-view (PPV) sports programming will push rights fees to high levels. Television companies know that PPV sports can generate massive revenues, but they also know that pay-per-view events must be introduced cautiously and selectively. Many viewers are not willing to pay up front to see an event on television; nor are they accustomed to doing so. In the meantime, pay-TV has become an accepted part of people's lives in the form of subscription fees for cable and satellite sports channels.

The fragmentation of television sports audiences seems likely to continue. New technology may bring as many as five hundred channels into people's homes. Some of these channels will provide sports coverage and will come to depend on sports for their income. As new digital television technology is sold to consumers around the world, it is certain that television companies will use sport events strategically to encourage consumers to invest in the switch from their old analogue televisions to digital sets.

Regular sports programming provides opportunities for major television companies to promote their other programmes and boost ratings during the rest of the week. It also serves a public relations function, by enhancing the image and legitimacy of television among people who may watch very few programmes other than sports.

In 1994, Rupert Murdoch, owner of the Fox Television Network in the United States, paid the NFL US$1.58 billion and the NHL US$155 million in an attempt to use pro football and hockey coverage between 1995 and 1999 as the centrepiece of a global corporate expansion strategy. Murdoch's idea was to use

"Fox-televised athletes as a sort of human growth hormone for the network's other programming" (Knisley, 1996). He knew that North American television viewers were dedicated to watching NFL football and NHL hockey, and he used that knowledge to leverage his plan to acquire local television affiliates around the United States and thereby compete with the major television networks. He also planned to use sports coverage as part of a global expansion through his other media companies around the world. He even bought the Los Angeles Dodgers in 1998 for US$311 million (a record payment for a baseball franchise at the time) and tried to purchase the Manchester United Football Club in England in 1999 for $1 billion. Manchester United is the largest and most highly valued soccer club in the world, and the British government disallowed his takeover bid because it would have given him too much control over sports and the media through which they are seen. However, his overall strategy of acquiring sport teams and television rights to cover sports has worked, and his News Corp conglomerate is among the most powerful media organizations in the world. Although the NHL strategy was not very successful, and caused a great deal of amusement in Canada when Fox introduced the FoxTrak "glow puck" (Mason, 2002), which was designed to help U.S. viewers to see the puck, by late 1997, Murdoch's Fox Television, was able to pay US$17.6 billion for the rights to televise NFL games through 2005.

Other corporations have also used this strategy as they have initiated a series of vertical and horizontal mergers and acquisitions in the entertainment, news, sports, television, and Internet industries (known as convergence). As the twenty-first century began, there were eight major global corporate conglomerates, and four national media conglomerates in Canada (BCE, CanWest, Quebecor, and Rogers), controlling most of what we do and do not read, see, and hear in the media (McChesney, 1999). Harvey and Law (in press) have examined this process of convergence and its effects on sports in international and Canadian media; Field (2003) has provided a case study of media ownership of professional sport teams in Toronto. Of course, this has serious implications for the types of sports programmes we see and do not see, what we hear and do not hear in commentary, the sites we visit on the Internet, and the corporate messages that are presented in connection with athletes, teams, events, and sport places. More important, it has serious implications for the viability of democracy around the world. There are some preliminary indications that "convergence" has not been a very successful corporate strategy, and we may be witnessing some dismantling of sport-media conglomerates in the future (e.g., both of Disney's professional teams are for sale).

Sports and the Media: A Relationship Fuelled by Economics and Ideology

There is no question that commercial spectator sports depend heavily on the media, although noncommercial sports continue to exist and often thrive without media coverage. Similarly, some media companies that publish daily newspapers and produce television programmes in Canada depend on sports to generate circulation and viewer ratings.

In countries with market economies and privatized media, the interdependence of sports and the media is grounded primarily in concerns about money and profits. Sports can sell newspapers and attract television viewers. This helps sell advertising space and advertising time. In turn, the media generate revenues for sport organizations and create sport-related images, which can be sold in connection with everything from coffee mugs and jackets to shoes and baseball gloves. Sports and the media clearly have a relationship in which each depends on the other for its commercial success and its prominent place in popular culture in many societies around the world.

Since the 1970s, global economic factors have intensified the relationship between sports and the media. Major transnational corporations

needed vehicles for developing global name recognition, cultural legitimacy, and product familiarity. They were also eager to find ways to promote ideological support for a way of life based on consumption, competition, individual achievement, and comparisons of status and material possessions. Media sports clearly offered global corporations a means of meeting these needs: certain sport events attract worldwide attention; satellite technology takes television signals around the world; sport images are associated with recognizable symbols and pleasurable experiences by billions of people; and sports and athletes usually can be presented in politically safe ways by linking them with local identities and then using them to market products, values, and lifestyles that are related to local cultures or to accepted forms of cultural diffusion. Therefore, powerful global corporations have underwritten or sponsored the media coverage of sports, especially on television.[7]

An important source of corporate sponsorship money for sports comes from the alcohol and tobacco industries. For them, the sports media are key vehicles for presenting and promoting their products in connection with activities defined as healthy by most people around the world. This enables them to present positive corporate and brand images, which they hope will counteract negative images about their products. We find these images most frequently in print media and stadium signage. In fact, they regularly appear in the prime advertising space of sports magazines and on the surfaces of stadiums and other facilities that host car and horse races. Following the ban on tobacco advertising on television in Canada, tobacco companies turned their efforts to sponsoring tennis, golf, show jumping, and auto racing events. Data from Physicians for a Smoke-Free Canada indicate the success of this strategy: the tobacco logo

---

[7]See the *Sports in Society* Online Learning Centre for a discussion of how this has occurred with the Olympics.

often appeared on-screen for far more time than the total of paid advertising time; for example, during the du Maurier men's tennis finals in 1998, the paid advertising time was over twenty-seven minutes, and the du Maurier logo was on-screen for a total of thirty-four minutes (www.smoke-free.ca/filtertips02/Television.htm). Bill C-71, the Tobacco Act passed in 1997, phased out this type of sponsorship.

It is clear that the marriage of sports and the media has been held together and strengthened by the vast amounts of money coming from corporations whose executives see sports as tools for promoting profits and ideologies consistent with their interests. When profits are low, their shared interest in promoting ideologies supportive of general capitalist expansion keeps the partners together.

IMAGES AND MESSAGES IN MEDIA SPORTS

To say that sports are "mediated" is to say that they are re-presented to readers, listeners, and viewers through selected images and/or messages. A growing number of people who study sports in society do research that involves digging into these selected images and messages to identify the ideas or themes on which they are based. As they do their digging, they assume that media sports are symbolic constructions, much like action films, television soap operas, and cartoons (Rowe, 1999; Wenner, 1998). In other words, a telecast of a football game is a re-presentation of certain people's ideas about football, social life, human beings, what is important in the world, and what the viewing audience wants to see and hear. Although different people interpret media images and messages in different ways, many people use mediated sports as reference points as they form, revise, and extend their ideas about sports, social life, and social relations.

Because media sports are part of everyday experience in today's societies, it is important to consider the following questions:

1. How are sports constructed in and through the media?
2. What general ideas or themes underlie the images and messages re-presented in media sports?
3. Do reading about, listening to, and viewing sports have an effect on other types of behaviour, such as active sport participation, attendance at sport events, and sports gambling?

How the Media Construct Sports

In societies where the media are privately owned and are dependent on financial profits, sports are selected for coverage on the basis of their entertainment value. The images and messages are presented to provide as much of the event as possible and to fit the perceived interests of both the audience and the sponsors. Sports that are difficult to cover and present through a profitable entertainment package usually are ignored by the media, or they are covered only in terms of occasional highlights, emphasizing spectacular and heroic injuries or achievements (e.g., adventure racing).

The sports pages of most major newspapers and articles in sports magazines provide scores, statistics, accounts of big plays and individual heroics, and behind-the-scenes stories; they use photos to depict action. Television coverage focuses on the ball (puck, etc.) and individual athletes, especially those who are currently winning the game, match, meet, or race. Television announcers provide play-by-play analysis and narratives designed to entertain a mass audience. The major differences in how the traditional print media and electronic or broadcast media construct sports are summarized in table 12.3.

The sports media in general present images and commentary that "hype" sports by exaggerating the spectacular, inventing and

Table 12.3   Differences between newspaper/magazine and radio/television coverage of sports

Newspaper/Magazine Coverage	Commercial Radio/Television Coverage
• Emphasizes news and information • Offers summaries of past events • Provides concrete information and data • Bases success on maintaining credibility • Highlights behind-the-scenes stories • Is more likely to provide criticism of sports and sport personalities	• Emphasizes entertainment • Offers play-by-play images and narratives • Provides real-time representations of action • Bases success on generating hype • Highlights action and heroic plays • Is more likely to provide support for sports and sport personalities

Source: Based on material in Koppett, 1994.

focusing on rivalries, and manufacturing reasons that events are important and should be read about, listened to, or viewed. Mark Lowes (1999), of the University of Ottawa, points out that they also emphasize elite sport competition. For example, Canadian newspapers and commercial television (since the 1950s) have increased their coverage of professional sports and decreased coverage of amateur sports. This shift has been accompanied by a growing emphasis on the importance of winning and heroic actions instead of other factors associated with sports and sport participation. The result is that media audiences consume carefully "selected" versions of sports. These versions represent what corporate sponsors will fund with their advertising money and what media people think audiences want to consume. There is very little research on this process, but, what research there is, Canadian researchers led the way. The type of research is known as **production ethnographies**—researchers carry out detailed observations of the actual production process of sport broadcasts, at production meetings, control centres, editing suites, and commentary positions, taking detailed notes and conducting informal interviews during quiet moments. The first of these was carried out by Rick Gruneau, who is now in the Department of Communications at

Simon Fraser University. He studied the production, by CBC television, of a World Cup ski competition at Whistler (Gruneau, 1989), discovering in particular how broadcasters establish the "story line" even before the event takes place. This was followed by Margaret MacNeill's (University of Toronto) research on the CTV host broadcaster production of (men's) hockey at the 1988 Calgary Olympics (MacNeill, 1996), which focused on the ways in which the broadcaster produced different ideas of nationality for the various teams competing in the tournament. MacNeill is continuing this type of research in an extensive study (along with Graham Knight of McMaster University and Peter Donnelly) of the ways in which the CBC/SRC produced ideas of Canadian identity at the 2000 Sydney Olympics. Outside Canada, Silk and Amis (2000) conducted a production ethnography of coverage of the 1998 Commonwealth Games in Kuala Lumpur.

It is important to study this "production process" because popular ideas about sports are heavily informed by the images and messages represented in media sports. Furthermore, the themes underlying these images and messages influence our ideas about social relations and social life in general. In other words, cultural ideology is embedded in media coverage. We discuss this in the following sections.

Themes Underlying Media Images and Messages

Success Themes The images and messages represented in mediated sports emphasize themes that identify important issues and particular ways of looking at and interpreting the world. For example, television broadcasts of sports in Canada and the U.S. usually emphasize success through competition, hard work, assertiveness, domination over others, obedience to authority, and coming up with big plays such as home runs, long touchdown passes, and single-handed goals. The idea that success also can be based on empathy, support for others, the sharing of resources, autonomy, intrinsic satisfaction, personal growth, compromise, incremental changes, or the achievement of equality receives little attention.

Media representations of sports usually exaggerate the importance of competitive rivalries and winning and losing in athletes' lives. For example, media coverage of a sport such as snowboarding is organized around the competitive quest for medals, when, in fact, many of the athletes and the spectators at the events are not very concerned about competition or medals (Crissey, 1999; Florey, 1998). The athletes enjoy the external rewards that come with winning and they certainly want to demonstrate their competence, but they also emphasize expression and creativity apart from scores and competitive outcomes. Furthermore, they see friendships with other competitors as more important than media-hyped rivalries. However, media coverage highlights competitive success, because it is valued in the culture as a whole, and it is easy to use to attract sponsors and consumers.

The success theme underlying images and narratives in U.S. media sports is more apparent than in media sports in other cultures (see the Reflect on Sports box, "Sydney 2000: The Disappointment Games," pp. 388–389). Televised sports in the United States emphasize winners, losers, and final scores. Even silver and bronze medals are defined as consolation prizes at best; and games for third place in tournaments are now often not played. Writers and announcers focus on "shoot-outs" and sudden death play-offs instead of ties, they define *success* in terms of dominating others, and they praise those who make big plays or big hits and sacrifice their bodies for the sake of a win. Rare are references to learning, enjoyment, and competing *with* others, even if players see their participation in these terms. The media do not "tell it like it is"; rather, they tell it to support the interests of those who benefit from cultural commitments to competition, productivity, and material success.

Of course, this does not mean that people do not enjoy media sports. Enjoyment is central, and it drives media sport consumption. However, there are many ways to enjoy sports, and the media highlight the ways that fit popular and corporate interests simultaneously. Discovering other ways to enjoy sports is left to individuals and groups, who actively seek alternatives to commercialized media sports.

Masculinity and Femininity Themes There are both gender equity issues and ideological issues in the media coverage of sports. Even as we move into the twenty-first century, men's sports receive well over 80 percent of the coverage in all the media, and the images and narratives about gender tend to reproduce traditional gender ideology (Duncan and Messner, 1998).

Coverage of women's sports is not a priority in the media, except in the case of the Olympics, figure skating events, major tennis and golf tournaments, and hockey and soccer world championships. Overall, the coverage of women's sports in big-city newspapers has increased since the mid-1990s, but it remains less than 15 percent of the sports section. Sports magazines have been notoriously slow to cover women athletes and women's sports, although they frequently have images of women as sex objects in ads for cigarettes, liquor, and other

REFLECT ON SPORTS

Sydney 2000: The Disappointment Games?

"The 2000 Summer Olympics are quickly becoming the Disappointment Games for Canada."

—*Ottawa Citizen*, September 20, 2000

The *success* theme is evident to a lesser extent in Canada, where it also has its corollary—the *disappointment* theme. This theme is produced in the media when the performances of Canadian athletes at international events do not meet the predicted and hyped expectations. After only six days of Olympic competition, and despite an unexpected gold medal in the men's triathlon, the Canadian media began to characterize the Sydney Games as a failure for both Canada and Canadian athletes. Disappointment emerged in a relatively uniform and decisive way as the dominant theme in media coverage, and it persisted long after the Games ended. The theme emerged primarily in response to losses by four athletes—two swimmers, a kayaker, and a track cyclist—who had all been identified as medal prospects.

Predicting which athletes will win medals is standard media practice. However, it sets up expectations not only for athletes but also for the media themselves, whose credibility is put at stake. As a result, the media often interpret specific individual losses as a broader and more abstract issue or problem; in this case, disappointing results by the Canadian team and for Canada as a whole.

As opposed to failure, which is relatively objective (you win or you lose), disappointment is related emotionally to more subjective expectations and aspirations. Disappointment reflects the way that an event such as the Olympics joins individual athletic identities with collective national identities. So when an athlete who was expected to win fails to win, that is a problem for the athlete; but when we (and the media) have invested our emotions in success, disappointment extends to us, and increases the scope for allocating responsibility and blame.

The "Disappointment Games" story developed along a chain of blame and responsibility. This began with the athletes whose losses defined the theme's emergence. In media interviews, three of the four athletes assumed responsibility for their poor results. This allowed the media to absolve them personally, and to extend the chain of blame elsewhere. They had played their part by accepting personal responsibility

• •

products. However, some new women's sports magazines are now appearing, in contrast to the fitness magazines that were the only physical activity publications aimed at women.

The pattern of underrepresentation is well-established in Canada (cf., Urquhart and Crossman, 1999). During the early 1990s, CAAWS kept a scorecard of the volume of women's sports coverage in Canadian newspapers. In October 1994, CAAWS reasoned that, with a strike in MLB and a lock-out in the NHL, there would be a great deal more opportunity for newspapers to cover women's sports. They found that, for the week of

October 17–23, in thirteen of twenty Canadian newspapers, coverage of women's sports actually decreased over the previous year (CAAWS-ACAFS, 1997; McGregor, 1997). The newspapers were not happy about such a scorecard, and they rationalized the absence of women's sports in a number of (unsatisfactory) ways (Ormsby, 1997). The Toronto Metro Inter-school Athletic Association (1997) also found significant differences in the coverage of high school sports in Toronto newspapers, the vast majority of coverage going to men's sports. And projects carried out by third- and fourth-year students at Acadia University and third-year for failure, and the media was free to seek other causes for its, and our, disappointment.

Several possible explanations were examined including coaching and cycles of sport success and failure. However, what emerged as the principal explanation—initiated by voices in the sport community—was the lack of administrative support and the lack of sufficient government funding to win medals in the increasingly competitive world of international sports. Comparisons were continually made with Australia, which had made a major financial investment in achieving Olympic success. Analysts estimated that each of Australia's 16 gold medals cost C$20 million just on spending in the year before the Olympics—approximately five times Sport Canada's budget for that time.

In a striking parallel, New Zealand media also developed a disappointment theme, with exactly the opposite interpretation. New Zealand had also invested heavily in athlete development, and failure was interpreted in terms of a "sporting nation" that had gone soft from losing sight of its traditional values; the athletes had been spoiled by too much economic support!

Given the size of its population, and the fact that it sends full teams to both Summer and Winter Olympic Games, Canada is quite a successful

Olympic nation. Polls of the Canadian public showed that they were satisfied with athlete performances in Sydney, and that they believed more money should be invested in grass-roots sports rather than high-performance sports. Many Canadian high-performance athletes are seriously financially distressed, and many of them believe the high-performance sport system in Canada is seriously underfunded. We think that the *disappointment* theme is another version of the success theme; individuals take the blame for their performances, they promise to work harder, and we are encouraged to invest more in their training.[1] We also think that funding decisions should consider all aspects of sports. They should not be made in the light of media-generated stories of disappointment. *What do you think?*

_____

[1] It is interesting to note that many of the media sources advocating greater public investment in Canada's high-performance athletes had spent the previous decade calling for more and more cuts to government expenditures.

physical and health education students at the University of Toronto found consistent underrepresentation and trivialization of women's sports in many Canadian print and electronic media outlets, including the University of Toronto student newspaper.

Women's sports are televised more than they were in the early 1990s, especially on certain specialty channels, but the coverage given to women's sports is not much more than 15 percent of all television sports programming. The women's sports that have been covered regularly in the media are those emphasizing grace, balance, and aesthetics—attributes consistent with

traditional gender ideology and images of femininity (Duncan and Messner, 1998; Jones et al., 1999), or traditional Canadian activities such as curling's Scott Tournament of Hearts. Individual sports are usually given priority over team sports in the coverage (Tuggle and Owen, 1999), and women's figure skating is the most frequently televised women's sport event. But there is strong evidence of increasing coverage of women's soccer and hockey, culminating in the huge television audience in Canada (7.4 million) for the women's hockey final in Salt Lake City.

However, a sustained period of criticism from sport sociologists, organizations such as

Hockey is the most popular televised sport in Canada. The coverage of hockey tends to reflect the traditional gender values that are important to many people in the culture. On the "Coach's Corner" segment of the CBC's *Hockey Night in Canada*, Don Cherry (right) presents a stereotypical form of masculinity. (CP/*Maclean's*/Phill Snel)

CAAWS, and fans of women's sports appears to be having positive effects that may be more evident in Canada than in the United States. A recent student project at the University of Toronto showed that coverage of high school sports was now gender balanced in the *Toronto Star* in terms of quantity of coverage, although there were still some differences in quality of coverage. WTSN, although only available as a digital channel, has added a new dimension to the television coverage of women's sports. And new policies at CBC Sports seem to be ensuring much more equitable coverage of events such as the Olympics. Despite that fact that Billings and Eastman (2002a, b) were still showing significant gender differences in the NBC coverage of events at the Sydney Olympics, Cluer, et al. (2001), in a case study of CBC coverage of diving at the Sydney Olympics, found almost no differences in the way that men's and women's diving was re-presented for the television audience. The researchers pointed out that new equity policies introduced by Nancy Lee, the head of

CBC Sports, together with a determination to carry them out and a programme of education for production and commentary staff, led to a situation where men's and women's sports receive equal coverage.

The men's sports most often covered emphasize bulk, height, physical strength, and the use of physical force and intimidation to dominate opponents—all qualities consistent with traditional images of masculinity. For example, hockey is the most popular televised men's sport in Canada, and television coverage emphasizes traditional notions of masculinity.

Coverage of women sports through the 1980s and most of the 1990s contained commentaries that often highlighted the personal characteristics of the athletes, such as their attractiveness, their spouses and children, their domestic interests and skills, and their vulnerabilities and weaknesses (Eastman and Billings, 1999; Weiler and Higgs, 1999). Television commentators for women's sports have in the past referred to women athletes by their first names and as "girls" or "ladies," although this pattern has changed as researchers have called attention to its sexist implications. Commentators for men's sports have seldom referred to men athletes by their first names and almost never call them "boys" or "gentlemen." It is assumed that playing sports turns boys into men. Similarly, references to physical strength have been much more common in commentaries about men athletes, even though women clearly demonstrate strength and power, even in sports such as figure skating, golf, and tennis (Weiler and Higgs, 1999).

Men's sport events often are promoted or described as if they had some special historical importance, while women's sport events often are promoted in a lighter, less serious manner (Duncan and Messner, 1998). Men's events are unmarked by references to gender and represented as *the* ("real") events, while women's events almost always are referred to as *women's* events. For example, there is the NBA and the WNBA, the PGA and the LPGA, and, since the 1990s, the Women's World Cup of soccer has been added to *the* World Cup. This is called **gender marking**, and only women's events are so marked.

Homosexuality is ignored in nearly all media coverage, while heterosexuality is acknowledged directly and indirectly among men and women in sports (Duncan and Messner, 1998; Kane and Lenskyj, 1998; Pronger, 1999; Sabo and Jansen, 1998). Lesbian images are often carefully erased from coverage, even though the partners of players and coaches are known and visible among spectators. Men's physical connections with each other are noted when they hold hands in a huddle or pat one another on the buttocks, but similar connections among women athletes are usually ignored for fear that lesbian images might offend media audiences. Lesbian athletes in golf, tennis, and basketball are rarely profiled in ways that acknowledge partners or certain aspects of their lifestyles—those parts of their personal stories are not told. In media-constructed sport reality, lesbians and gay men in sports generally are invisible unless they make it a point to present themselves as "out." Even then, they are marginalized in

coverage. As media studies scholar Pam Creedon notes, "Homosexuality doesn't sell" (1998: 96). Meanwhile, heterosexual athletes and their partners are discussed and pictured regularly, and nobody accuses these heterosexual athletes of pushing their values and agendas on others.

These patterns associated with gender and sexuality have been slow to change partly because sports media organizations in all societies are "gendered institutions" (Creedon, 1998). Most of these organizations have been and continue to be structured and scheduled around men's sports. Because reporters' work schedules have been established around the coverage of men's sports, the regular coverage of women's sports has required changes in institutionalized patterns of sports media work. Furthermore, the *vast* majority of sports media personnel are men, and the highest-status assignments in sports media are those that deal with men's sports. Even women reporters and announcers know that their upward mobility in the sports media industry demands that they cover men's events in much the same ways that men cover them. If they insist on covering only women's events, or if they are assigned only to women's events, they will not advance up the career ladder in media organizations. Advancement also may be limited if they insist on covering men's sports in new ways that do not reaffirm the "correctness" of the coverage patterns and styles developed by men.

Although women in the print media now regularly cover men's sports, few women ever have provided regular commentary for men's sports in the electronic media. Women reporters who cover men's sports are more readily accepted in the locker rooms of men's teams than they were in the past, although male athletes and coaches have been very protective of this "masculinized space." Changes have occurred partly because men have discovered ways to maintain privacy, such as using towels and robes, and having designated interview times—just as women athletes have always done when male reporters cover their events. However, it took the men nearly two decades to make these discoveries, because deeply rooted gender ideology often impedes rational thought.

When it comes to issues of masculinity, most sports coverage uses images and narratives that reproduce dominant ideas about manhood. Most television sports can be characterized as soap operas for men. The serialized nature of the broadcasts and the storylines they represent facilitate the construction of a symbolic and an actual community of sport spectators that is as masculine as the culture represented by the players on the field (Rose and Friedman, 1997). Michael Messner and his colleagues (1999) report that the sports coverage most often consumed by boys in the United States depicts aggression and violence as normal and exciting behaviour, portrays athletes who play in pain as heroes, uses military metaphors and terminology related to war and weapons, and highlights conflict between individuals and teams. Furthermore, women are seldom seen in the sport programmes that boys watch most often and, when women do appear, they often are portrayed as sex objects, cheerleaders, spectators, and supportive spouses and mothers on the sidelines of the action.

Overall, gender themes related to masculinity and femininity remain central in media re-presentations of sports. However, it is important to note that viewers do not accept media re-presentations at face value. Instead, they make sense of them in their own terms; when they have special knowledge or a personal connection with the sport or the athletes involved, they are even likely to ignore or critique the re-presentations in the media (Bruce, 1998).

Race and Ethnicity Themes Just as media coverage of sports can influence ideas about gender and gender relations, it also can influence ideas about race and ethnicity and racial and ethnic relations. However, patterns related to the media representations of race and ethnicity in sports have not been as clear as they have been for gender.

Racial stereotypes have influenced coverage in the past, but in recent years those who produce media re-presentations of sports in North America seem to be sensitive to many racial issues and the general issue of cultural diversity (Sabo and Jensen, 1998). Indeed, it seems that policy and equity education in the sports media concerning issues of race and ethnicity has often outstripped similar changes that might occur with respect to gender and sexuality generally. Journalists are less likely to use descriptions of white or visible minority athletes that reproduce traditional, racist stereotypes. However, interviews with black sports journalists and announcers indicate that they remain wary of what they see as a disproportionate number of "poor boy makes good" stories written about black athletes and of coverage highlighting the material possessions of black athletes who have large pro contracts (Thomas, 1996).

Do some people see physically talented or angry black male athletes in different terms than physically talented or angry white male athletes? This issue is beginning to be explored by researchers in comparative studies of "whiteness" and "blackness"; and David Shields (2000) briefly explores this complex issue of perception using the example of Vince Carter of the Toronto Raptors. If they do, then media re-presentations influence people in racialized ways, even when media producers are sensitive to racial issues and do their best to avoid stereotypes (cf., Wilson, 1997). However, equal coverage sometimes does not lead to equal perceptions. This is a crucial and puzzling point that must be considered when we discuss racial themes in sports media coverage.

Equally important and sometimes puzzling is the fact that, when media coverage avoids stereotypes and re-presents successful images of black, Asian, or Aboriginal athletes, some whites then conclude that racism is no longer a problem in society. This is because the media do not re-present a full range of racial issues and perspectives in their content, and sports fans may not have enough information to put images of successful visible minority athletes into a fully realistic context. Of course, this is frustrating to those in the media who have made successful efforts to avoid stereotypes in their coverage, but it reminds us that simple "color adjustments" (Riggs, 1991) in the media do not change the context in which people make sense of media reality.

Stereotypes related to ethnicity and nationality are also evident in sports media coverage. Although media personnel in some nations have been alerted to how ethnic and national stereotypes may influence their representations of athletes and teams, evidence suggests that subtle stereotypes occasionally may be used in sports media coverage (Mayeda, 1999; Sabo and Jensen, 1998; Sabo et al., 1996). For example, the most frequent issue of stereotyping and ethnic misunderstanding in Canada concerns relationships between francophones and anglophones. While language and flag issues concerning French and English, Canada and Quebec, are most likely to be reported in both French and English media, ethnic stereotypes also occasionally appear in coverage. Commentators have occasionally portrayed Asian athletes as methodical, mechanical, machinelike, mysterious, industrious, self-disciplined, and intelligent. The achievements of Asian athletes may be attributed more to cognitive rather than physical abilities, and stereotypes about height and other physiological characteristics are sometimes used to explain success or failure in sports (cf., Nakamura, 2003). Latinos occasionally have been described as flamboyant, exotic, emotional, passionate, moody, and hot-blooded (Blain et al., 1993). Of course, it is important to acknowledge the existence and influence of cultural factors in sports, but it also is important for journalists to know enough about ethnicity and ethnic relations that they do not inadvertently use stereotypes instead of learning about the experiences and characteristics of the people they describe and discuss.

Stereotypes of people from different nations and cultures vary around the world. International political and economic relationships often influence stereotypes and how they are applied in the media coverage of sports. The sports journalists most likely to avoid the use of stereotypes are the ones that understand the history of those relationships and their implications for ethnic relations.

One way to reduce covert bias in the media is to hire more racial and ethnic minority reporters, editors, photographers, writers, producers, directors, camerapersons, and commentators (Rowe, 1999). Lip service has been paid to this goal, and progress has been made in certain media, but members of racial and ethnic minorities are still underrepresented in many sports newsrooms, press boxes, broadcast booths, and media executive offices (Lapchick, 1995; Thomas, 1996). This is unfortunate, because we all learn from colleagues from backgrounds different from our own. When we do not have the advantage of working in racially and ethnically diverse settings, another way to increase racial awareness is to provide all personnel with good training workshops on racial ideology and racial and ethnic relations. Where this has been done, as in the CBC equity training, it has been effective (Thomas, 1996).

Other Ideological Themes in Media Sports It is not easy to identify themes underlying the images and messages in media sports. Analyses using critical theories have focused on the extent to which images and narratives in sports media re-present dominant ideas about social life and social relations in society as a whole. These studies have identified the three themes we have already discussed (success, gender and sexuality, and race and ethnicity), as well as themes related to nationalism, competitive individualism, teamwork, aggression, and consumerism (Kinkema and Harris, 1998; MacNeill, 1996; Real, 1998; Rowe et al., 1998).

These themes should not surprise anyone who has read about, listened to, and viewed sports in Canada. The images and narratives in sports media clearly emphasize *nationalism and national unity*. In fact, the sports that we consider to be "Canadian"—hockey, our version of football, curling, and lacrosse—are, with the exception of lacrosse, the most widely televised sports in the country. When teams and athletes from Canada are competing against teams and athletes from other countries, the sport events are usually framed in an "us versus them" format. In ideological terms, at the height of the Cold War, the 1972 hockey series against the Soviet Union was the most dramatic event. However, it would have been difficult to imagine a more ideologically fitting and dramatic end to the 2002 Olympic men's and women's hockey tournaments. Both Canadian teams faced the host United States teams, and did so at a time when Canada was feeling particularly "dissed" by U.S. foreign, trade, and security policies. The huge television audiences for the two games highlight the nationalist feelings that were involved. Despite CBC media training that explicitly frames commentators as "objective" reporters, and precludes such statements, commentators are still heard to declare that "we won" (see chapter 13).

Media images and narratives also emphasize *individual efforts* to achieve competitive victories, even in the coverage of team sports. Games are promoted with announcements such as this: "It's Vince Carter versus Shaquille O'Neal as the Raptors face the Lakers." These promos emphasize the idea that individuals must take responsibility for what happens in their lives and that team failures can be traced to individual failures and flaws. This idea is central to the ideology of individualism, a key element of neo-liberalism, which influences everything from the structure of our welfare systems to the ways employees are evaluated and rewarded in the economy.

Apart from emphasizing individualism, media images and narratives also stress *teamwork*, in the form of obedience to authority, group loyalty, and the willingness to sacrifice for the good of the group (Kinkema and Harris, 1998). Media coverage clearly identifies coaches as the organizers and controllers of teams; commentators praise athletes for being team players and praise coaches for their ability to fit players

"Yes, I KNOW I let you watch Homicide and Cops with me, but I'm afraid this hockey game is MUCH too violent for children."

This father has distinguished between fictional violence and real-life violence on television. Does watching real-life violence in certain sports have an impact on viewers? If video games are rated for violent content, should sports also be rated?

into team roles that lead to victories. This teamwork theme clearly fits with the ideology underlying the market economy and most business organizations: teamwork means loyalty and productivity under the direction of a leader-coach. These are also traditional, perhaps even old-fashioned corporate values now. New economy companies are more likely to emphasize democratized workplaces, flexibility, and creativity, but these values have not yet found their way into the ideology of sport coverage.

The importance of *mental and physical aggression* is another theme underlying the images and narratives in media sports. Rough, aggressive play is described as a sign of commitment and skill (Messner et al., 1999). Checks in hockey may be described as bone-crushing hits, hard fouls in basketball are described as warnings to the opposition, and brush-back pitches in baseball are said to keep batters on their heels. Even the scores on the late-night news are full of violent images: the Raptors *annihilated* the Knicks, the Alouettes *destroyed* the Blue Bombers, the Flames *scorched* the Canucks, Williams *blew away* Jeyaseelan, and on and on. The scores sound like the results of military operations in a war. In fact, the language of sports media in North America is often a language of violence and warfare. Aggression is celebrated, while kindness and sensitivity may be dismissed as indications of weakness. In the U.S., this clearly fits with the ideology many Americans use to determine strategies in interpersonal, business, and international relations, especially in the highly charged and militarily aggressive early years of the twenty-first century: "kicking ass" is a celebrated goal, and failing to punish the opposition is a sign of weakness. Presenting games as personal confrontations and mean-spirited turf wars has long been a strategy in sports media.

Finally, the emphasis on *consumerism* is clear in the media coverage of sports: over 15 percent of televised sports consists of commercial time, ads fill newspapers and magazines, and Internet sites use multiple strategies to attract attention to ads located on screens containing scores, commentary, and links. "TV time-outs" are a standard feature of televised football, hockey, and basketball games, and announcers remind media spectators, "This game is being brought to you by...." The audiences in sports media are encouraged to express their connections to teams and athletes by purchasing shirts, shoes, jackets, official hats, official sweatpants, and team-branded coffee cups, among literally thousands of other branded products. This is clearly consistent with consumer ideology in North American society. "You are what you buy" is one of the tenets of a market economy.

Overall, the images and narratives in the media coverage of sports in North America stress themes representing dominant ideologies and widespread ideas about how the world does and

should work: order, control, and tough discipline are essential; gender differences are grounded in nature, not culture; the primacy of the nation must be preserved, unless capital expansion requires a blurring of national boundaries; individuals must be accountable, work in teams, and outproduce others; and consumption is essential to happiness and is the basis for identity.[8] These themes run through sports media. This is the reason media coverage of sports is heavily sponsored by people and corporations with power and influence in society—they favour these themes, and they sponsor images and narratives that infuse them into public consciousness.

Media Impact on Sport-Related Behaviours

Active Participation in Sports Do the media cause people to be more active sport participants, or do they turn people into couch potatoes? When children watch sports on television, some will copy what they see, if they have or can make opportunities to do so. Children are great imitators with active imaginations, so, when they see and identify with athletes, they may create informal activities or seek to join youth sport programmes to pursue television-inspired dreams. However, participation grounded in these dreams does not last long, especially after the young people and their parents discover that noteworthy accomplishments require years of dedication and expense. However, other motives may develop in the process and inspire healthy participation patterns.

Many adults who watch sports on television do not play anything they watch, while many others are active participants in one or more sports (Wenner and Gantz, 1998). As the television coverage of sports has increased since the early 1970s

---

[8] These dominant ideological themes are hegemonic, that is, they dominate and they have, in general, become consensual; but they are never completely consensual and they are continually subject to critical interpretation and re-analysis.

in North America, so, too, have levels of inactivity. It is important to be careful about these types of statistical relationships, and while some have speculated that the growth of television sports and the Internet have led to inactivity, there is no evidence that one caused the other. In fact, there is some evidence to suggest that the growth of sports on television may encourage participation. Media coverage reveals possibilities, and the rapid increases in girls' participation in gymnastics, soccer, and hockey have all been attributed to media exposure of these sports. MacNeill (in press) has also identified what she terms "active viewing"—not in sports, but in early teens who she found engaged in the vigorous physical activity of dancing along with music videos. There is a need to study cultural changes as they are related to the use of the media in people's lives. At this point, the safest conclusion is that the media probably have no major *net* effect one way or the other on active participation in sports and other physical activities.

Attendance at Sport Events Game attendance is related to many factors, and its relationship to the media is complex. On the one hand, the owners of many professional teams enforce a local television blackout rule based on the belief that television coverage hurts game attendance and ticket sales. In support of this belief, many people say that they would rather watch certain sport events on television than attend them in person. On the other hand, it is clear that the media publicize sports, promote interest in them, and provide the information people need to identify with athletes and teams and to become committed fans—and, therefore, game attenders (Weiss, 1996; Zhang et al., 1997).

The most logical conclusion is that the media and game attendance are positively related: people who watch more games on TV also attend more games (Zhang et al., 1996a). However, we must qualify this conclusion. First, as ticket prices increase, and as the numbers of local elite games increase across various sports, more people may limit attendance when there is the option of watching a local game on television. Second, because the media focus attention on elite sports such as NHL hockey, they may undermine attendance at less elite events such as local junior games. Thus, the media may be positively related to attendance at the top levels of competition but negatively related to attendance at lower levels of competition (Zhang et al., 1996b). Research is needed to explore this issue in more depth.

Gambling on Sports Betting on sports is widespread, but the only certain link between gambling and the media is an indirect one. The media, especially newspapers, television, and the Internet, make people aware of *point spreads* and *betting odds* for various events. Point spreads and betting odds are determined by bookies, who want to make sure they do not go broke by taking too many bets on a particular outcome in a sport event. When the media publicize point spreads and odds, and when bets can be placed online, the media certainly make it easier for people to bet on sports. However, the conclusion that the media or the Internet *causes* gambling is difficult to defend.

At this time, relatively few people see betting on sports as an important legal or moral issue, despite its destructive consequences for those who become dependent on the excitement of having money on a game. Many people are accustomed to buying lottery tickets and participating in government-sponsored gambling activities, such as SportSelect, so it is difficult to convince them to take seriously restrictions that limit or ban betting on sports. Gambling is also encouraged by a cultural emphasis on striking it rich and getting something for nothing. In the meantime, people use the media as vehicles to gain the information they need in the gambling process and, in some cases, to place their bets. However, to say that the media cause or even encourage gambling is to ignore the social and cultural context in which people choose to place bets on sports.

Audience Experiences with Media Sports

Media sports provide topics of conversation, sources of identity, feelings of success when favourite teams win, opportunities to express emotions, occasions for getting together with others, and a focus for those who are passing time alone (Wenner and Gantz, 1998).

A summary of audience research done by media studies experts Lawrence Wenner and Walter Gantz (1998) indicates that, in the U.S., adults integrate sports media into their lives in a variety of ways. Although studies have identified some adults, more men than women, who focus considerable attention on watching sports, over-all patterns indicate that watching television sports is not a major activity in the lives of most adults. Studies also have found that men and women who live together often share time watching sports and that this usually is a positive activity in their relationships. In other words, "stay-at-home armchair quarterbacks" and "football widows" are not as common as many people believe. Men do watch sports more than women watch, and men are more likely to be committed fans; however, when men and women are highly committed fans, they watch and respond to sports on television in very similar ways. In fact, data suggest that "fanship" is more important than gender or any other factor when it comes to people's viewing experiences. Scheduling and viewing conflicts occur for some couples, but most couples resolve conflicts without negative effects on their relationships. Partners usually learn to accommodate each other's viewing habits over time as they live together. In cases where differences in viewing habits and fanship are associated with problems, there usually is a history of relationship problems, and many factors other than watching sports on television are the causes of those problems.

Future studies along these lines will tell us more about how sports media experiences are integrated into our lives and how they become activities around which social life occurs. While there are no major reasons to expect that Canadian results regarding viewing sports on television would differ from those in the U.S., it would be useful to obtain comparative data. The use of the Internet and video games should be included in these studies.

THE PROFESSION OF SPORTS JOURNALISM

It has been suggested that one of the goals of sports journalism is "the generation of more and more entertaining material about something that doesn't *really* matter too much" (Koppett, 1994: 162–163). However, sports do matter—not because they produce a tangible product or make an essential contribution to our survival but because they re-present ideas about how the world works and what is important in life. Therefore, what sports journalists do matters very much when it comes to cultural ideology and the public consciousness. In fact, when comparing the four major roles in sports—fans, athletes, controllers (owners, coaches, referees, etc.), and interpreters (media and media relations personnel)—Edwards (1981) notes that journalists and public relations staff give meaning to what we are seeing, and supply the ideology: "For this reason, [journalists and media relations people] exercise the greatest power in sport" (p. 397).

In addition to constructing the meanings associated with people's experiences of sports, journalists also help people enjoy and understand sports. Furthermore, the coverage of sports often has an impact on sports and the athletes who are covered. As used in this section, *journalists* include writers in the print media and announcers in the electronic media.

Journalists on the Job: Relationships with Athletes

As the television coverage of sports has expanded, sportswriters for newspapers and magazines have had to produce stories that go beyond the action and scores in sports. This has forced them to seek information about the personal lives of the athletes fans have watched on television. As journalists sought this information, athletes discovered that they could no longer trust writers to hold information in confidence, even if it was disclosed in the privacy of the locker room: if sportswriters hear an athlete say something that might attract readers' attention, the statement is likely to be printed. This has prevented many athletes from saying the spontaneous things that would make good material for reporters, and it has created tension between players and sportswriters.

This tension has intensified as differences in their salaries and backgrounds have become more pronounced. For example, wealthy athletes from various racial and ethnic backgrounds without university degrees have little in common with middle-class, university-educated, white writers. In the face of these differences, journalists in the print media have felt less compelled to protect or glorify athletes in their stories, and athletes have become increasingly protective of their wealth and status and wary of the motives of writers.

One of the outcomes of this situation is that professional teams and even NSOs (since this has now extended even to national team athletes) have found it necessary to offer players training sessions on how to handle interviews without saying things that sound bad or can be misinterpreted. Research carried out on Canadian Olympic athletes by Margaret MacNeill (1998) in the 1990s showed that they were in a very difficult situation with the media. On the one hand, they were denied by their NSO the right to comment on their organization or coach to the media. On the other hand, they were not aware of their media rights. For example: "Athletes wrongly assume that communicating 'off-the-record' statements to the sports media will protect either their anonymity and/or the privacy of the person or organization they are commenting about" (MacNeill, 1998, p. 111). Resulting in part from this research,

"I may just be a rookie anchorman, but I know how to report violence, drug abuse, and corporate corruption—I used to do the sports."

"If it bleeds, it leads" has long been the motto of media news. The same approach is now used in media reports on sports. As critical users of the media, we should know that media coverage is not a good basis for making generalizations about the world or about sports.

CAAWS and the Coaching Association of Canada produced *A Media Guide for Athletes and their Coaches* (1998), and the Canadian Olympic Committee holds media training workshops and has a booklet available to athletes.

Tensions also have called attention to ethical issues in sports journalism. Responsible journalists, including writers and announcers, have become sensitive to the fact that they should not jeopardize people's reputations simply for the sake of entertainment. This does not mean that journalists should avoid criticism that might hurt someone, but it does mean that they should never hurt someone unintentionally or without good reason (Koppett, 1994). Otherwise, they are engaging in destructive, self-serving sensationalism, which raises ethical concerns about the invasion of privacy. Unfortunately, journalists constantly face "gray areas" in which ethical guidelines are not clear, and the need to present attractive stories often encourages them to push ethical limits.

Sportswriters and Sports Announcers: A Comparison

Not everyone who covers sports for the media has the same focus. In the print media, the focus is on entertaining people with information and in-depth analysis, while radio and television announcers entertain people with action and commentary, which create on-the-spot urgency. The implications of these differences are summarized in table 12.4.

According to sports journalist Leonard Koppett (1994), the main difference between sports coverage in the print media and sports coverage in radio or television broadcasts is this: the print media woo readers with reliable and thorough stories, while radio and television broadcasts try to dazzle and fascinate audiences enough to keep them glued to their sets. Therefore, the print media hire writers who can tell reliable and thorough stories, while broadcast companies hire announcers who can excite and entertain an audience with rapid commentary. This is why newspaper and magazine writers (especially the latter) often do the most thorough investigative reporting, and why the most popular media personalities sit in television broadcasting booths and talk with a sense of urgency about whatever is occurring in an event. This does not mean that there are no examples of investigative journalism in electronic media. *Sports Journal*, on CBC Newsworld, and the *Inside Track*, on CBC radio, regularly carry investigative pieces; and mainstream investigative journalists from programmes such as *the fifth estate*, *Disclosure* (both CBC), and *W5* (CTV) occasionally pay attention to sports, with pieces

Table 12.4 Sportswriters and sports announcers: a comparison of roles

Role Characteristics	Sportswriters[a]	Sports Announcers[b]
• Job security	High	Low
• Salary	Low	High
• Popularity/public recognition	Low	High
• Freedom of expression in job	Moderate to high	Low; heavily restricted
• Purpose of role	To give information about sport events	To "sell" sport events; to entertain
• Role expectations	To be objective investigators	To be personable entertainers
• Opportunities to do investigative reporting	Sometimes	Very rare
• On-the-job contacts	Copy desk editors and subeditors	Broadcast executives, team management, sponsors, advertising people
• Relationships with players	Sometimes tense and antagonistic	Friendly and supportive
• Level of response evoked from public	Low to moderate	Moderate to high

Source: Adapted from Koppett, 1994.

[a]The primary focus here is on newspaper reporters. Magazine writers have similar jobs, but they are different in that they often cover issues and topics in greater depth.

[b]The primary focus here is on television announcers. Radio announcers have similar jobs, but they are different in that they must focus more on description in their commentary and less on interpretation.

on such issues as sexual harassment in sports, violence and injury in sports, or the influence of the Russian "mafia" on the NHL.

While considering these differences and reviewing table 12.4, remember that there are exceptions to these role descriptions. Some writers go beyond information and analysis and write to be provocative or to shock and entertain. The successful ones have relatively high salaries and a reasonable amount of job security, especially those who are provocative. On the other hand, as noted above, some television announcers do investigative reporting in which information and analysis take priority over entertainment; and there is some cross-over, with sportswriters appearing regularly on sport discussion items on TSN/RDS and other programmes. Given these exceptions, the major differences between sportswriters and sports announcers are accurately represented in table 12.4.

The efforts of television companies to provide a combination of play-by-play commentary and entertainment lead them to hire popular retired athletes and coaches to be announcers. Some people complain that sports figures have few skills to make them successful broadcasters, but most television executives realize that media spectators identify with and define them as credible sources of information about sports, even when their journalistic skills are low.

Regardless of the specific characteristics of announcers and commentators, the content of the narrative stays within parameters set by teams and media companies. U.S. radio and television announcer Chip Caray, who has worked on broadcasts for the Atlanta Braves, the Seattle Mariners, and the Chicago Cubs, explains, "Our bosses expect us to broadcast a certain way. No one has ever told me how to broadcast. But I draw my paycheck from the same place as the players" (in Russo, 1999: 7D). This is why announcers seldom stray from a fairly standard entertainment approach and why we should never expect to hear critical comments about sports as social phenomena as we watch sports on television.

SUMMARY

COULD SPORTS AND THE MEDIA SURVIVE WITHOUT EACH OTHER?

It is difficult to understand social life today without paying serious attention to the media and media experiences. This is the major reason we study the relationship between sports and the media. There are some differences between Canada and the U.S. in this relationship, but also a number of distinct similarities.

Media sports, like other parts of culture, are social constructions. This means they are created, organized, and controlled by human beings, whose ideas are grounded in their experiences and ideologies. The media do not *reflect* reality as much as they provide *re-presentations* of selected versions of reality. These selected re-presentations are grounded in power relations in society, and the images and messages contained in the media are likely to represent dominant ideas and ideologies and to promote the interests of those who benefit most from those ideas and ideologies. The possible exception to this is the Internet, a medium that offers revolutionary potential in that it enables people to create their own media realities.

Sports and the media have grown to depend on each other as both have become more important parts of culture in many societies. They could survive without each other, but they would both be different than they are now. Commercial sports would not be so widespread, and there would be less emphasis on elitist forms of competitive sports, although active participation in sports would not automatically increase. Without exposure to sports through the media, people would probably give lower priority to organized competitive sports in their everyday lives.

The media also could survive without sports. But they, too, especially newspapers and television, would be different. Newspaper circulation probably would decrease, and television programming on weekends and holidays would be different and less profitable for television companies.

The strong symbiotic relationship between sports and the media suggests that none of us will live to see organized sports without media coverage or the media without sports programming. However, history also shows that this relationship in North America has developed within a larger cultural context, one in which high priority is given to commercial profits and the creation of attractive media events. Furthermore, the relationship between sports and the media has been and continues to be created through the ever changing interactions among athletes, agents, coaches, administrators, sport team owners, sponsors, advertisers, media representatives, and a diverse collection of spectators. Each group has tried to influence the relationship, and each has had a different amount of resources to use in the process.

Sports coverage in the electronic media are re-presented to audiences with dramatic, exciting, and stylized images and narratives designed to be entertaining for audiences and attractive to sponsors. The influence of these sports media in our lives depends on how many sources we have to experience sports. Direct experiences with sports influence how we interpret and use what we read, listen to, and view in the media. If we have little direct experience in and with sports, the media play a more central role in creating our sport realities and in influencing how those realities are integrated into the rest of our lives.

Research suggests that dominant ideologies related to success, gender, race, ethnicity, nationalism, competition, individualism, teamwork, violence, and consumerism are perpetuated through the images and narratives contained in the media coverage of sports in North America. Future research will tell us more about how people use media images and narratives as they form ideas about sports, their social relationships, and the social world. Especially important in the future will be research on how

people use the Internet and video games as sites for constructing their experiences in and with sports. We know thirteen-year-olds who would much rather play video sport games than watch games on television. In the future, many of them will do both at the same time. We know twenty-five-year-olds who enjoy the sport-related interactive experiences they have on the Internet more than the games themselves. Sports media and the experiences associated with them are changing rapidly, and it is important that we study them in ways that promote critical media literacy rather than the uncritical celebration of media culture (Kellner, 1995).

SUGGESTED READINGS

Andrews, D.L., and S.J. Jackson. 2001. *Sport stars: The cultural politics of sporting celebrity.* London/New York: Routledge (sixteen articles focusing on the cultural, political, economic, and technological factors that influence sport celebrity and how sport celebrities influence the everyday lives of people).

Kelly, M.C. 2001. *Hanging it out on Camera 3: Canadian sports in the media era.* Toronto: Prentice Hall Canada (journalist Malcolm Kelly interviewed Canadian journalists [in all media] and athletes for this popular book on Canadian sport media; the author takes interesting stances on a number of issues and controversies relating to Canadian sports and media coverage since the era of radio.).

Lowes, M. D. 1999. *Inside the sports pages: Work routines, professional ideologies, and the manufacture of sports news.* Toronto: University of Toronto Press (description and analysis of "newswork" and the production of sports news for daily newspapers; uses ethnographic research methods to study the everyday processes in the newsroom, on the beat, with information sources, and in the profession of sports journalism).

Messner, M., et al. 1999. *Boys to men: Sports media.* Oakland, CA: Children Now (www.children@childrennow.org) (an analysis of messages about masculinity contained in sports programming and commercials during sport programmes; based on data from a national U.S. poll of children, focus groups, and content analysis of sport programmes and commercials).

Rowe, D. 1999. *Sport, culture, and the media: The unholy trinity.* Buckingham and Philadelphia: Open University Press (clear analyses of the processes of "making media sports" and explanations of how media studies can be used to "unmake" and understand sports media texts, including commentating, writing, photography, filming, and Internet sites).

Wenner, L., ed. 1998. *MediaSport.* London and New York: Routledge (key source containing seventeen chapters written by recognized experts on the media and sport; emphasizes critical cultural studies approaches while providing citations to a range of research on media production, institutions, texts, and audiences; chapters emphasize issues related to gender, race and ethnicity, celebrity, globalization, and corporate influence).

Whannel, G. 2000. Sports and the media. In *Handbook of sports studies* (291–308), edited by J. Coakley and E. Dunning. London: Sage (an overview of the sports-media relationship and its implications for global social processes).

Whannel, G. 2002. *Media sport stars: Masculinities and moralities.* London/New York: Routledge (analysis of how the media have created sport stars around particular ideological themes—in this case, around prevailing notions of masculinity, goodness, and the importance of consumption in society).

WEBSITE RESOURCES

Note: Websites often change. The following URLs were current when this book was printed. Please check our website (www.mcgrawhill.ca/college/coakley) for updates and additions.

www.mhhe.com/coakley8e (essays on the ideology underlying media sports, the interdependence of the Olympics and the media, and the impact of watching violent sports on behaviour)

www.cbc.ca (the Canadian Broacasting Corporation website, for both French and English radio and television, has good material on sports, especially during the Olympics)

www.tsn.ca (TSN is part of the BCE/Bell Globemedia conglomerate; the site includes links to other parts of BCE's television holdings, such as RDS, WTSN, the Outdoor Life Network, the NHL Network, and ESPN Classic Canada)

www.aafla.org (amateur Athletic Foundation site; go to "AAF Research Reports" for sports media studies on children and sports media, gender issues, race and ethnicity issues)

www.real-sports.com (site for the magazine *real SPORTS*, dedicated to the coverage of women in sports; no ads for beauty products, as in "fitness and sports" magazines for women)

www.nfl.com/fans/forher/index.html (site designed to recruit women to watch NFL games and become NFL fans)

(Peter Donnelly)

Sports and Politics

How do governments and globalization influence sports?

Let us export our oarsmen, our fencers, our runners into other lands. That is the true free trade of the future.

—Pierre deCoubertin, founder of modern Olympics (1892)

I don't think sportsmen can use "sports and politics don't mix" as an excuse. I didn't want to represent 50 million English people touring a country where the regime was abhorrent.

—Stuart Barnes, British rugby player, on his refusal to tour South Africa in 1974 (1994)

The Montreal Olympics can no more have a deficit than a man can have a baby.

—Jean Drapeau, then Mayor of Montreal (1976)

No person shall play or take part in any game or sport upon a highway.

—City of Burlington, Uniform Traffic By-Law 1984-1

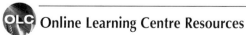

Online Learning Centre Resources

Visit *Sports in Society's* Online Learning Centre at **www.mcgrawhill.ca/college/coakley** for additional information and study material for this chapter.

Organized competitive sports long have been connected with politics, government, and the nation-state. **Politics** refers to power and how it is gained and used in social life, and **government** refers to formal organizations and agencies that have the authority to make rules regulating people's behaviour. Politics is involved in all social relationships and organizations, including those related to sports. Governments operate in connection with nation-states, and they influence sports in many ways. **Globalization** consists of the long-term processes of social change that involve relationships between nation-states and the use of power on an international level.

This chapter deals with sports and politics. The goal is to explain how sports are involved in politics on many levels and how politics are involved in sports. Chapter content focuses on three major issues:

1. The reasons governments become involved in sponsoring and controlling sports
2. The ways sports are connected with important political processes on local, national, and global levels, including the impact of the Olympic Games on global politics and relationships among nation-states
3. The frequently contentious political processes that occur in sports and sport organizations

When reading this chapter, remember that *power* is the key concept in politics. As used in this chapter, the term **power** refers to an ability to influence others and achieve goals, even in the face of opposition from others (Weber, 1968/1922). **Authority** is a form of power that comes with a recognized and legitimate status or office in an organization or set of relationships. For example, a large corporation has *power* if it can influence how people think about and play sports and if it can use sports to meet its corporate goals. Sport organizations such as the IOC, FIFA, the CIS, or a local parks and recreation department have *authority* over the sports they administer, as long as people associated with those sports accept the organizations as legitimate sources of control.

Most organized sports are controlled by at least three levels of authority (table 13.2 on p. 430 shows the levels of sport organizations in the Canadian amateur sport community):

- The various levels of government who have an interest in, and control of (through legislation and funding), sports and physical activity—in the Canadian confederation these include the municipal and regional levels, the provincial[1] and territorial levels, and the federal level (discussed in the first part of this chapter);
- Businesses and corporations who sponsor sports and athletes, ranging from a local real estate company who sponsors house league soccer to transnational corporations who are the major sponsors of the Olympic Games (referred to in the second part of this chapter);
- The various sport organizations that run sports at local, regional, provincial, national, and international levels (discussed in the last part of this chapter).

Thus, in this chapter, *politics* refers to more than issues concerning formal sport governing bodies; instead, it refers to all forms of power relations in sports.

THE SPORTS-GOVERNMENT CONNECTION

When sports become popular community activities, government involvement often increases. Many sports require sponsorship, organization, and facilities—all of which depend on resources that few individuals possess on their own. For example, sport facilities are often so expensive that

---

[1] Although the provincial level is extremely important in terms of sport participation and athlete development in Canada, there are very few studies of the provincial level of sport organization; see, for example, Harvey and Proulx (1988) on Quebec, and Rob Pitter (1996), of Acadia University, on Alberta. Therefore, the primary focus of this chapter is on the federal level.

regional and national governments may be the only community entities with the power and money to build and maintain them. For this reason, many people see government involvement in sports as a necessity. Government involvement also is tied to the belief that sport participation, sport organizations, and the people associated with sports often need to be regulated and controlled by an independent agency that represents the interests of all people in a community or society.

The nature and extent of government involvement in sports vary from one community and society to the next, and government involvement occurs for one or more of the following seven reasons (Allison, 1993; Houlihan, 1994; Wilson, 1994):

1. To safeguard the public order
2. To maintain health, fitness, and physical abilities among citizens
3. To promote the prestige and power of a group, community, or nation
4. To promote a sense of identity, belonging, and unity among citizens
5. To reproduce values consistent with the dominant ideology in a community or society
6. To increase support for political leaders and government
7. To promote economic development in the community or society

The Canadian government has been involved in sports and physical activity for all of these reasons since the 1943 National Fitness Act. However, most analysts trace the first formal involvement in sports to 1961, with the passage of Bill C-131, the Fitness and Amateur Sport Act. The reasons for involvement vary over time. The initial involvement was associated both with population health and with concerns about the declining fortunes of Canadian national hockey teams at the Olympics and World Championships. By the late 1960s, during Prime Minister Pierre Trudeau's first term of office, concerns about national unity (Quebec separatism, western alienation, northern isolation)

and national identity became more prominent. After failing to win any gold medals at the 1976 Montreal Olympics, there was a new emphasis on high performance and national prestige to the point where, by the end of the 1980s, a U.S. academic (MacAloon, 1990) was referring to the Canadian high-performance sport system as "the Big Red Machine."[2] By the 1990s, there was slightly less emphasis on high performance, a growing concern with equity and health issues, and increasing emphasis on hosting sport events for community and regional economic development and for national unity. Mick Green's useful chart (table 13.1) outlines this development in far more detail, pointing to key political moments since 1961, what was involved in terms of organization, administration and funding, and implications for high-performance sports.

The reasons for government involvement in sports are discussed in more detail below.

Safeguarding the Public Order

Governments often make rules about what types of sports are legal or illegal, how sports must be organized, who should have opportunities to play sports, where certain sports may be played, and who can use public sport facilities at certain times. Ideally, these rules protect individuals and groups as they pursue interests that may conflict with the interests of other individuals or groups. This is why a government might officially ban sports such as bullfighting, bare-fisted boxing, or even bungee jumping. In the case of commercial sports, governments may regulate the rights and duties of team owners, sponsors, promoters, and athletes.

Local governments may try to eliminate conflicts by requiring permits to use public facilities and playing fields. They may pass rules prohibiting potentially dangerous sport activities

---

[2] This was a comparison with the East German sport system—"Red" was a reference to both communism and the colour of the Maple Leaf.

Table 13.1 The development of federal policy for Canadian sports, 1961–2003 (adapted from Green, 2003)

Key political policy	Organization and administration	Funding	Effect on high-performance sports
1961: Bill C-131, *Fitness and Amateur Sport Act*	Fitness and Amateur Sport Directorate (FASD) established	C$5 million per annum allocated for national programme of fitness and amateur sports	First recognition of support for high-performance sport programmes
1967: Inaugural Canada Games	Major facilities programme; invoked "Unity through Sport" theme	Federal government shares costs with provinces and municipalities	All levels of government involved with facilities for high-performance sports
1969: *Report of the Task Force on Sport for Canadians*	Proposed independent body for elite sports (not realized); highlights inadequate coach training; elite focus led to Ross Report on mass participation programmes	Recommends public/private sector cooperation in creating a structure for sports	Legitimation of federal involvement; first indications of a rational approach to sport planning; "National Unity" theme again linked to high performance
1970: White Paper, *A Proposed Sports Policy for Canadians*	Sport Canada (elite) and Recreation Canada (mass) established in FASD; National Sports and Recreation Centre founded	Budget grows from approx. C$6 million in 1971 to C$25 million in 1976; COA's Game Plan '76 established in 1972; Athlete Assistance Programme (AAP) established in 1973	Mass participation rhetoric, but programmes focused on high-performance sports—key actors[a] played prominent role; "National Unity" theme prominent
1976: Iona Campagnolo, first Minister of State for Sport and Fitness; Montreal Olympics	Construction of elite facilities for Montreal Olympics	Further support promised for amateur sport and fitness programmes	Campagnolo states elite sports are priority; 11 medals won but no gold
1977: Green Paper, *Toward a National Policy on Amateur Sport*	Recreation Canada redesignated Fitness and Recreation Canada	Period of economic austerity in Canada; pressure on funding allocations for sports	Focus on elite sports and poor performances in international competitions
1978: Edmonton Commonwealth Games	Facilities constructed for Edmonton Games	Federal funding of C$21 million for Edmonton Games	Federal policy bears fruit, first in unofficial rankings
1979: White Paper, *Partners in Pursuit of Excellence: A National Policy on Amateur Sport*	Renewed calls for autonomous Sport Canada rejected; Fitness and Recreation Canada divided	NSO grants tied to specific goals to be achieved in elite sports; reliance on sport lottery monies	"National Unity" theme; key actors[b] crucial in technical and bureaucratic approach to high-performance sports
1981: White Paper, *A Challenge to the Nation: Fitness and Amateur Sport in the '80s*	Fitness and Recreation Canada amalgamated under Fitness Canada; recommends elite national training centres	Priority funding for sports committed to excellence; AAP consolidated	Elite sports remain in hands of federal government; funding for social-equity issues noted
1982: Approval of "Best Ever" programme for 1988 Calgary Winter Olympics	Four-year plans required from sports involved—the QPP	C$25 million budget for "Best Ever" programme	Confirmation of support for elite sports; strengthening of bureaucratic approach
1986: Women and Sport Policy	Sport Canada	No budget attached	First real step in introducing social-equity issues
1988: Calgary Winter Olympics; Ben Johnson drugs scandal at Seoul Summer Olympics	Major facilities constructed for Calgary but later criticized for high-performance focus	Approx. C$300 million overall federal commitment for Calgary, and "Best Ever" funding for both Games	Calgary a success; only ten medals from Seoul; calls for re-evaluation of elite sports after drug scandal

Key political policy	Organization and administration	Funding	Effect on high-performance sports
1988: Task Force Report, *Toward 2000: Building Canada's Sport System*	Need "coherent Canadian Sport System"; addressed elite *and* social-equity goals; skepticism regarding link between elite goals and education	Reiterated earlier goal for NSOs to contribute 50 percent of funding; goal, and threats to reduce funding, not realized	Further focus on elite sports; critiques regarding ignoring drugs/ethical issues; reaffirms professionalization at high-performance level
1990: Dubin Inquiry	Recommends a re-evaluation of sporting structures and processes, and anti-doping policy	Critical of federal funding controlling "the entire sports system"	Perceives a "moral crisis" in high-performance sports; critiques federal focus on high-performance sports
1992: Task Force Report on Federal Sport Policy–*Sport: The Way Ahead* (Best Report)	Broad recommendations (many ignored) relating to objectives in respect of wider social goals	Recommends reduction in sports funded; financial constraint in Canada; cut in NSO funding (~25 percent)	Recommends less focus on elite sports; medal targets should not be primary criterion of success
1993: Ministry of State for Fitness and Amateur Sport abolished by Progressive Conservatives	Fitness Canada moved to Health Canada, and Sport Canada to newly created Canadian Heritage	Sports fall victim to general cutbacks in government spending	Seen by some as decrease in importance of amateur sports; by others as less direct government involvement
1995: Sport Funding and Accountability Framework (SFAF) introduced	Attempt to encompass wider social goals in funding process to NSOs	Dependence on government direction reduced to dependency on federal funds	Rhetoric suggests move from QPP, Sport Recognition System, and elite focus
1998: Mills Sub-Committee Report, *Sport in Canada: Everybody's Business*	Examination of the "sport industry" in Canada; creation of Secretary of State (Amateur Sport) position	Recommends federal government continue policy and funding support for amateur sports generally	Recommends increase in number of NSOs to be funded; more funding for coach training; and "carded" athletes
2000: Response to the *Mills Report* (news release from Canadian Heritage)	Commitment to create "national policy on sport"; plans regional conferences	Additional C$7.5 million in funding for amateur sports	Beneficiaries: AAP, National Sports Centres, and agencies involved in fight against doping
2001: *Towards a Canadian Sport Policy: Report on the National Summit on Sport*	Three "priority actions"—Participation, Excellence, Building Capacity (the "3 Pillars")	Recommends additional C$650 million from 2001–08 for sports generally	Recommends funding excellence ("spending by result"); and public-private partnerships
2003: Bill C-12, *An Act to Promote Physical Activity & Sport*	Federal focus moves from high performance to integration of sport system under the "3 Pillars"	No specific policy guidelines with regard to future funding allocations	No initial extra funding for high-performance sports; focus at NSO level remains mainly on high performance

[a] John Munro, Minister of Health and Welfare, and Lou Lefaive, at this time Director of the Fitness and Amateur Sport Directorate (Macintosh et al., 1987: 57).
[b] Roger Jackson, former Director of Sport Canada; Lou Lefaive, Director of Sport Canada; Geoff Gowan, technical director of the Coaching Association of Canada; Marion Lay, a former Olympic swimmer and, at this time, a consultant with Sport Canada; and Dan Pugliese at the National Sport and Recreation Centre.

in public places. For example, skateboarding, in-line skating, and bicycling may be banned on city sidewalks or in certain public parks, or they may be confined to certain areas, so that pedestrians will feel safe. Likewise, local officials may close streets or parks to the general public, so that sport events can be held under controlled and safe conditions. For example, marathons in such places as Ottawa and Boston require the involvement of the government and government agencies, such as the city police.

Governments may pass laws or establish policies that safeguard the public order by guaranteeing that participation in publicly funded sports is open to everyone. The Canadian Charter of Rights and Freedoms (see chapter 8) is the constitutional tool of federal government regulation intended to promote fairness in access to all walks of life, including sports and physical activity. Sport Canada, the government agency that oversees high-performance sports, has established a nationwide policy on women in sports and, through the 1995 Sport Funding and Accountability Framework, has the opportunity to tie government funding to NSOs to implementation of gender-, language-, and disability-equity programmes. Governments around the world are enacting or considering similar laws to establish fairness in sport participation opportunities for men and women, and for persons with a disability.

Safeguarding the public order also involves policing sport events. Local police or even military forces may be called on to control crowds and individuals who threaten the safety of others. During the Olympics, for example, the host city and nation provide thousands of military and law enforcement officials to safeguard the public order. This was especially evident at the 2002 Salt Lake City Olympics. As the first major international sport event after the September 11, 2001, attacks in the United States, security at the Salt Lake City Games was more evident than at any other Olympics. At a cost of US$310 million (25 percent of the Games budget), some

Local governments often regulate where and when certain sports may be played, and these regulations often target street hockey and skateboarding. However, they are frequently ignored, and enforcement usually only follows a complaint. (Dick Hemingway Editorial Photographs)

16,000 security personnel were supplemented by continual aerial surveillance, a 45-mile no-fly zone, and sophisticated surveillance technology (Atkinson and Young, 2002).

Some governments have attempted to safeguard the public order by sponsoring sport events and programmes for at-risk youth, such as the NightHoops programme in several Canadian cities and a programme offered by the Vancouver Police Department. Sports, it is argued, can be used to keep them off the streets and thereby control crime rates, vandalism, loneliness, and alienation. However, many of these programmes fail, because they do not deal with the deprivation, racism, poverty, dislocation, community disintegration, and political powerlessness that cause social problems in communities and societies (cf., Coakley, 2002; Pitter and Andrews, 1997).

Finally, sports often have been used in military and police training, so that the soldiers and police will be more effective protectors of the public order. For example, military academies in the United States and other countries traditionally have sponsored numerous sports for their cadets, and the World Police and Fire Games are held every two years because people believe that sport participation keeps law enforcement officials and firefighters prepared to safeguard the public order.

Maintaining Health, Fitness, and Physical Abilities

Governments also have become involved in sports to promote fitness among citizens. For example, nations with government-funded health insurance programmes often promote and sponsor sports to improve physical health in the general population and thereby reduce the cost of health services. This was one of the major reasons the Canadian government promoted and funded fitness and sport programmes during the mid-1970s. The government was facing serious financial crises, and officials believed that sport participation among Canadians ultimately would increase fitness and cut health-care costs (Harvey and Proulx, 1988).

However, the Canadian government seems to have an ambivalent attitude towards fitness issues. While ParticipACTION enjoyed a significant period of support from the Ministry of State for Fitness and Amateur Sport, the Ministry was closed in 1993 by the Progressive Conservative government, and the responsibilities of Fitness Canada were transferred to Health Canada.[3] Since then, ParticipACTION

---

[3] While ParticipACTION had some success in drawing the attention of Canadians to the importance of physical activity, Margaret MacNeill (1999), of the University of Toronto, has pointed out that the public service announcements were not without problems. They were aimed at white, middle-class Canadians, not reflecting the diversity of the population, and were full of gender stereotypes.

went into a period of decline, and was closed down in 2001. While Health Canada currently has a C$175 million programme to prevent smoking (more than twice Sport Canada's annual budget), far less is invested in fitness. In response to growing concerns about obesity, especially among Canadian children, the Minister of Health introduced *Canada's Physical Activity Guide* in 2002; but there has been no corresponding campaign of public service announcements to publicize them, or any investment in creating new opportunities for physical activity. Most recently, the Romanow Report (2002) on health care in Canada drew attention to the need to "[i]ntegrate prevention and promotion initiatives as a central focus of primary health care targeted initially at reducing tobacco use and obesity, and increasing physical activity in Canada." Similarly, Bill C-12, the *Act to Promote Physical Activity and Sport* (2003), identifies physical activity as a determinant of health: "The government's policy on physical activity seeks to promote physical activity as a fundamental element of health and well-being of Canadians…and to help them reduce the barriers that prevent them from being active." However, knowledge of the benefits of physical activity and concerns about the detrimental effects of lack of physical activity, especially among young people, has not yet been translated into any tangible policies and actions.

Similar motives have led to government sponsorship and organization of fitness and sport programmes in other nations. Many people believe that sport participation improves fitness, fitness improves health, and good health reduces medical costs. This belief persists in the face of the following factors (Waddington, 2000; Wagner, 1987):

- Many of the illnesses that increase health-care costs are caused by environmental factors and living conditions, and they cannot be changed through any sport or fitness programme.

- Certain forms of sport participation do not lead to overall physical fitness or identifiable health benefits.
- The win-at-all-costs orientation, which sometimes develops in connection with sports, may actually contribute to injuries and increased health-care costs (for example, more than forty thousand knee injuries in U.S. football every year require costly care, surgery, and rehabilitation).
- The demand for health care sometimes increases when people become more concerned with fitness and the physical condition and appearance of their bodies. This is because people who participate in competitive sports can become so concerned with performance that they seek medical care designed for training and rehabilitation.

Because of these factors, governments become cautious and selective in their sponsorship of sports for health purposes. Today, governments are more likely to emphasize noncompetitive physical activities with clear aerobic benefits and less likely to sponsor highly competitive sports involving physical contact and norms promoting the physical domination of opponents.

In the past, government involvement in sports also was grounded in the belief that fitness and physical abilities are related to economic productivity. Although this relationship is hard to prove, some private corporations in countries with market economies fund their own fitness centres and sport programmes, thinking that it will make their employees more productive while improving employee health and controlling insurance costs. However, many are discovering that productivity and worker satisfaction are related to the overall quality of working conditions and workers' autonomy, not to employee fitness or opportunities to participate in sports. This is not to say that neither governments nor corporations should provide sport participation opportunities for people. Instead, it emphasizes that sport provision does not replace the need to provide overall living and working conditions that are safe, fair, and responsive to the lives of workers and citizens.

Promoting the Prestige and Power of a Group, Community, or Nation

Government involvement in sports frequently is motivated by a quest for recognition and prestige. This occurs on local, national, and even global levels. For example, a spokesperson for the South Korean government said that its sponsorship of the 1988 Summer Olympic Games was an announcement to the world of its emergence as a developed nation with a strong economy. Co-sponsorship of the 2002 World Cup of soccer (with Japan) was intended to reinforce the image of South Korea on the world's stage. The 1996 Summer Games provided an occasion for local boosters to present Atlanta as a world-class city symbolizing the "new South," now open to all people regardless of race or national background. Sydney, the host of the 2000 Summer Games, was presented to the world as a city with clean air in a country with a pleasant climate and vital business connections with emerging nations in Asia.

This quest for recognition and prestige also underlies government subsidies for national teams across a wide range of sports, usually those designated as Olympic sports. Government officials use international sports to establish their nation's legitimacy in the international sphere, and they believe that, when athletes from their nation win medals, their national image is enhanced around the world. This belief is so strong that many governments now offer their athletes financial rewards for winning medals in the Olympics. The importance of national success in sports is not new. Even in 1958, when Brazil won its first World Cup in soccer, there was a strong feeling among most Brazilians that they could now stand tall in the international arena and that their way of life was equal to or perhaps even better than those of the nations of Europe. They felt that Brazil now had to be recognized and dealt with as an equal in international relations (Humphrey, 1986). Similar feelings have been expressed more recently in connection with World Cup performances by soccer teams from such African nations as Cameroon and Nigeria.

In a similar manner, many people believe that a nation's failures in international sport events cause a loss of prestige in the global cultural arena. For example, when national teams from England lost in major international competitions to teams from countries that had learned to play sports invented in England, some people in England worried that the losses were symptoms of their nation's general decline in world affairs (Maguire, 1994, 1999).

The declining fortunes of Canadian teams in international hockey, especially the Olympics and World Championships, starting in the 1950s was, in part, responsible for federal government involvement in sports. The lack of hockey success was interpreted as a loss of international prestige by Prime Minister John Diefenbaker, who proposed government involvement to "assure hereafter that Canada's representation in the field of international competition, particularly in amateur sport, shall be of the very best" (cited by Macintosh, Bedecki, and Franks, 1987, p. 35). While Canadian performances in international sports improved, Canada did not win an Olympic gold medal in ice hockey for 50 years (1952–2002). That the success of Canadian women at consecutive World Championships throughout the 1990s did nothing to enhance assessments of national strength, strongly attests to the lack of status of women's sports.

Attempts to gain recognition and prestige also underlie local government involvement in sports. For example, cities may fund sport clubs and teams and then use those teams to promote

> Sports have been revered by fascists and communists, by free-marketers and filibusters. They have also been, paradoxically, reviled by all those political factions. Sports may be among the most powerful human expressions in all history.
> —Gerald Early, professor of modern letters, Washington University, St. Louis (1998)

themselves as good places to live, work, locate a business, or spend a vacation. In fact, some people in North America feel that, if their city does not have one or more major professional sport team franchises, it cannot claim world-class status (see Whitson and Macintosh, 1996). Because of the success of the Oilers in the 1980s, and the ongoing success of the Eskimos, Edmonton still declares itself to be the "City of Champions," much to the chagrin of people in Calgary.

During the "Save the [Winnipeg] Jets" campaign in 1995, when Winnipeg-born, Toronto-raised actor Keanu Reeves was booked to play Hamlet in a Winnipeg theatre, he noted that one of the only things he knew about Winnipeg was the Jets (Smith, 1997). The statement was used by those supporting the campaign to indicate that, without the Jets, the city would cease to be known (presumably in U.S. newspapers). In an insult to their prairie neighbour, some Winnipegers started to say that, if the Jets left, they would be just like Regina (see Nauright and White, 1996; Scherer, 2001; Silver, 1996). Of course, the city survived the loss and has experienced an economic boom in recent years. However, the strength of the campaign is a clear indication of how strong an outpost the NHL and other major league sports have in people's heads.

Promoting a Sense of Identity, Belonging, and Unity

Groups, organizations, towns, cities, and nations have used sports to express collective sentiments about themselves (Allison, 2000; Bairner, 1996; Houlihan, 2000; Maguire, 1994, 1998, 1999, 2000; Nauright, 1996a,b). Any team or athlete representing a specific group has the potential to bring people together and to create emotional unity among group members. For example, when a nation's soccer team plays in the World Cup, people across the nation are united, regardless of differences in race, religion, language, education, occupation, and income. This unity may be connected with their feelings of attachment to the nation as a whole and their convictions about the nation's history and traditions, even about its destiny in the world order.[4]

However, it is important to ask critical questions about the long-term consequences of this emotional unity and about whose interests are served by the images, traditions, and memories around which identities are expressed. When government involvement and sponsorship of a sport are designed to promote a sense of identity and unity among a collection of people, it is important to understand how that identity and unity are connected with patterns of power and social relations. For example, when men's sports are sponsored and women's sports are ignored, what does that say about a group's identity and the values around which the identity is created (cf., Robinson, 2000)? What if the sport involves participants from only one ethnic or language group, or from a particular social class? These questions show that identity itself is political, in the sense that it can be constructed around various ideas of what is important in a group.

Furthermore, the unity created by sports does not change the important social, political, and economic realities of life in any way. In fact, after games end, social distinctions quickly are reaffirmed as people go about their everyday lives (Arbena, 1988). Of course, the emotional

unity that sports sometimes create feels good, and it even may be associated with a spirit of possibility, but it can gloss over the need for social transformation, rather than inspiring collective action that might transform society and make it more fair and just.

Local government involvement in sports is also motivated by concerns to promote and express particular forms of identity. Club soccer teams in Europe often receive support from local governments, because the teams are major focal points for community attention and involvement. The teams not only reaffirm community identity among local citizens but also bring large numbers of community people together when games are played. In fact, the games often become important social occasions within towns or regions and provide opportunities for meeting new people, renewing old acquaintances, and maintaining a personal sense of belonging to a group. In this context, we can consider sports to be *invented traditions* used to remind people of what they share and how they are connected with one another.

When the population of a community or society is very diverse, or when social change is rapid and widespread, governments are even more likely to intervene in sports for the purpose of promoting a sense of identity and unity (Maguire and Stead, 1996). For example, as national boundaries have become less and less visible and relevant in people's lives, many national governments around the world have used sports to promote a sense of national identity (Houlihan, 1994; Maguire, 1999). Even though the long-term effectiveness of this strategy is difficult to assess, many government officials are convinced that sports create more than temporary good feelings of togetherness. Of course, it is important to remember that nearly all of these officials are men, and the sports they support often are tied to traditions that have privileged men in the past. As always, there are several layers to the politics associated with sports.

---

[4] The massive television audiences for the men's and women's hockey finals at the Salt Lake City (2002) Olympics—over 10 million for the men's game and some 7 million for the women's game—included many individuals who would not normally consider themselves to be "hockey fans."

Emphasizing Values Consistent with the Dominant Ideology

Governments also become involved in sports to promote certain values and ideas among citizens. For example, governments generally have strong vested interests in maintaining the idea that success is based on discipline, loyalty, determination, and the ability to keep working in the face of hardship and bad times. Sports, especially world-class and elite competitive sports, have been used in many nations to promote these values and to foster particular interpretations of how social life does and should work.

This was a major motive for the government sponsorship of sports in the former Soviet Union, as articulated by a prominent Soviet sociologist:

> Physical culture is an important means to educate…an active fighter for communism, and it is an effective social factor in the ideological education of the public.…When people engage in physical exercise their ideology and moral consciousness are shaped through acquiring information on sports ethics and its manifestation in the activities of Soviet athletes; this is assimilated through the practical mastery of communist standards of behaviour during training and competition. (Ponomaryov, 1981: 117–118)

However, because many people in the Soviet Union did not accept government-sponsored ideas, they attached their own meanings to Soviet sports. Instead of associating them with collectivism and comradeship, they saw them as symbols of government coercion, exploitation, and distorted national priorities (Riordan, 1993). Sports could not rescue the political ideology of Soviet communism.

In nations with market economies—such as Canada and the U.S., among others—sports often are associated with success and hard work, so, instead of references to collectivism and the common good, there are references to competition and individual achievement. Instead of an emphasis on comradeship, there are stories showing how individuals have reached personal goals and experienced self-fulfillment through sports. An emphasis on competition, personal achievement, and individual fulfillment pervades the media coverage of sports in nations with market economies. Although it is not known whether such an emphasis actually strengthens a popular commitment to dominant cultural ideology, it clearly provides people with a vocabulary and real-life examples that are consistent with that dominant ideology. In a sense, the vocabulary and stories that accompany sports in market economies tend to emphasize that using competition to achieve personal success and to allocate rewards to people is natural and normal, while alternative approaches to success and allocating rewards are inappropriate.

A classic example of a government's use of sports to promote its own political ideology occurred in Nazi Germany in 1936. Most countries hosting the Olympic Games have used the occasion to present themselves favourably to their own citizens and the rest of the world. However, Adolph Hitler was especially interested in using the games to promote the Nazi ideology of "Nordic supremacy" through the Berlin Games, which preceded World War II. The Nazi government devoted considerable resources to the training of German athletes, and those athletes won eighty-nine medals: twenty-three more than the second-ranked U.S. team, and over four times as many as any other country won during the Berlin Games. This is the reason the performance of Jesse Owens, an African American, was so important to countries not aligned with Germany at that point in history. Owens' four gold medals and world records challenged Hitler's ideology of Nordic supremacy, although it did not deter Nazi commitment to a destructive political and cultural ideology.

The Cold War era following World War II was also full of incidents in which countries, especially the United States, the USSR, and East Germany, used the Olympics and other international sport competitions to claim the superiority of their political and economic systems. Today,

Canadian prime ministers, such as Prime Minister Jean Chrétien here, use sports for political advantage. They seldom miss an opportunity to be seen or to be connected with championship teams and successful athletes. However, we should also recognize that athletes, such as Canada Games athletes Ryrie Brisco (left) and Samir Louati, often appreciate recognition by the country's leading politician. (CP/Fred Chartrand)

such claims are less apt to be associated with international sports; instead, there is a growing emphasis on the logos and products of international corporate capitalism.

Increasing Support for Political Leaders and Government

Government authority rests ultimately in legitimacy; if people do not perceive political leaders and the government as legitimate, trouble is inevitable. In the quest to maintain legitimacy, political officials and ruling government parties may use sports. The assumption is that, when governments sponsor or promote activities and events that people value and enjoy, they increase their perceived *legitimacy* in the eyes of citizens.[5] This is the reason many political figures present themselves as friends of sport, even as faithful fans. They may make it a point to attend highly publicized sport events and associate themselves

with high-profile athletes or teams that win major competitions. For example, Canada's prime ministers often are photographed when attending Grey Cup games, and have associated themselves with successful athletes and teams and invited champions to Ottawa for photo opportunities. Of course, Canadian politicians are not the only ones to do this; there are similar examples from other countries. When taken together, these examples provide strong support for the idea that governments and government officials use sports to promote themselves.

---

[5] In historical terms, this is a very old idea. The later Roman emperors instituted a policy of *panem et circensem* (bread and circuses—food and entertainment for the potentially rebellious Roman population) in order to maintain their popularity (see chapter 3). The group opposing Toronto's 1996 and 2008 Olympic bids called itself "Bread not Circuses" in a parody of the Roman policy, and to emphasize the need for social spending rather than mega-event spending.

Promoting Economic Development

Since the early 1980s, government involvement in sports often has been motivated and justified for the purpose of promoting economic development (Schimmel, 2000, 2002). Cities may spend large amounts of money to assemble and submit bids to host the Olympic Games, World Cup tournaments, world or national championships, Grey Cups, All-Star Games, high-profile auto races, golf tournaments, and track and field meets. Although some of these sport events do not show a profit for themselves, they may increase profits for other powerful economic interests in communities.

Governments are also interested in the long-term economic benefits of hosting events. Officials even may use the events as occasions for making contacts with corporations looking for new sites to locate their operations. Or officials may use the events to highlight and promote products made by local businesses. The governments of Japan (1964, 1998), Mexico (1968), and South Korea (1988) invested in hosting the Olympics and in their own national Olympic teams for clear economic development purposes. For Calgary, Vancouver/Whistler, and other hosts of Winter Games, sport events are occasions for promoting tourism and recreational opportunities. In many cases, the hosting of a sport event now combines the interests of civic boosters and government officials in a general effort to enhance the local economy (Huey, 1996). In fact, the policy that governs federal government support for major sport events (*Sport Canada Policy for Hosting International Sport Events*) stipulates that, in order to receive federal funding, an event must be able to generate sport development and economic, social, and cultural benefits: "Economic benefits include job creation, particularly in the small and medium-sized business sector, regional development, increased tourism, increased exports, enhanced infrastructure and increased tax benefit."

Conclusion and Qualification: Critical Issues and Government Involvement in Sports

It is important to raise questions about government involvement in sports and the "public good." Of course, it would be ideal if governments were to promote equally the interests of all citizens, but differences between individuals and groups make this impossible. This means that government involvement in sports usually reflects the interests of some people more than others. Those who benefit most tend to be people capable of influencing policymakers. This does not mean that government policies always reflect the interests of wealthy and powerful people, but it does mean that they are influenced by power struggles among groups within a society.

History shows that, when government intervention occurs, priority is often given to elite sport programmes, rather than to general sport participation. Of course, there are exceptions to this, but seldom are elite programmes ignored or given a low priority. Those who represent elite sports often are organized, generally have strong backing from other organized groups, and can base their requests for support on visible accomplishments achieved in the name of the entire country or community. Those who would benefit from mass participation programmes are less likely to be politically organized or backed by other organized groups, and they are less able to give precise statements of their goals and the political significance of their programmes. This does not mean that mass participation is ignored by government decision makers, but it does mean that it usually has lower priority for funding and support.

Opposition to the priorities that guide government involvement often is defused by the myth that there is no connection between sports and politics. Those who believe this myth seldom have their interests reflected when government involvement occurs. Those who realize that sports have political implications and that governments are not politically neutral arbitrators of differences within societies are likely to benefit the most when government intervention occurs. Sports are connected with power relations in society as a whole; therefore, sports and politics cannot be separated.

SPORTS AND GLOBAL POLITICAL PROCESSES

International Sports: Ideals versus Realities

Achieving peace and friendship between nations has been a longstanding ideal underlying international sports. It was emphasized by Baron Pierre de Coubertin, the founder of the modern Olympic Games in 1896, and by many others since then. The hope has been that international sports would do the following things:

- Open communication lines between people and leaders from many countries
- Highlight shared interests among people from different cultures and nations
- Demonstrate that friendly international relationships are possible
- Foster the cultural understanding needed to eliminate the use of national stereotypes
- Create a model for cultural, economic, and political relationships across national boundaries
- Establish working relationships that develop leaders in emerging nations and that can be used in efforts to close the gap between wealthy nations and poorer nations

During the past century, these ideals have been achieved to some degree on some occasions. International sports have had little impact in the realm of **serious diplomacy,** although they have promoted varying degrees of **public diplomacy.** In other words, when it comes to *serious issues of vital national interest*, sports have had little political impact; government officials do not use sports in their negotiations about crucial national and international policies. However, when it comes to *public expressions of togetherness*, such as cultural exchanges and general communication among officials from various nations, sports have been useful on many occasions. International sports have provided opportunities for officials from various countries to meet and talk, even though sports do not influence what is discussed or the outcomes of the discussions. Furthermore, international sports have brought together athletes, who learn from and about one another; however, athletes have little influence on political decisions, and relationships between athletes have no political significance. These points were illustrated clearly in 1999, when the Cuban National Baseball Team played the Baltimore Orioles in Cuba and then again in Baltimore. Public discourse was affected, but it had no discernible impact on political relations between the two countries, even though politics was involved in arranging these games.

Apart from times when sports are associated with public diplomacy, history shows that most nations have used sports and sport events, especially the Olympic Games, to pursue their own interests, rather than the collective goals of international communication, understanding, friendship, and peace. Nationalist themes have been clearly evident in many events, and most nations have used sport events regularly to promote their own military, economic, political, and cultural goals. This was particularly apparent during the Cold War era following World War II and extending into the early 1990s. In fact, the Olympics often were presented as extensions of so-called superpower politics.

The connection between international sports and politics was so widely recognized in the early 1980s that Peter Ueberroth, president of the Los Angeles Olympic Organizing Committee, said that "we now have to face the reality that the Olympics constitute not only an athletic event but a political event" (U.S. News & World Report, 1983). Ueberroth was not being prophetic when he made this statement; he was simply summarizing his observations of Olympic history. From his perspective in 1983, it was clear that nations seldom put international friendship and world peace ahead of their own interests in connection with the Olympics. The demonstration of national superiority through sports was the major focus for the so-called world powers.

Wealthy and powerful nations have not been the only ones to use international sports to promote political interests. For example, many nations lacking international political and economic power have used sports in their overall quest for international recognition and legitimacy. For them, the Olympics and other international sports have been stages for showing that their athletes and teams can stand up to and sometimes defeat athletes and teams from wealthy and powerful nations. For example, the ability of athletes and teams from the West Indies and India to do well in important cricket competitions against teams from England has been seen by West Indian and Indian people as a symbol of their emerging independence and autonomy in relation to one of the countries that colonized their homelands in the past.

Nation-states also have realized that hosting the Olympics is a special opportunity to generate international recognition, display national power and resources to a global audience, and invite investments into their economies. This is one of the reasons that bid committees from prospective host cities and nations sometimes have used gifts, bribes, and financial incentives to have IOC members vote for them in the bid selection process (see pages 433–434).

The political goals of the nations hosting major international events have been highlighted when other nations have boycotted those events.

> I know why we're here. We're here to spread basketball internationally and make more money for somebody....We're going to win the gold medal, but there won't be any life changing decisions made because of it.... [P]oor people will still be poor and racism and sexism will still exist....
>
> —Charles Barkley, USA Olympic basketball team (1992)

For example, the 1980 Moscow Games were boycotted by Canada, the United States, and some of their political allies to protest the presence of Soviet troops in Afghanistan. The USSR and its allies then boycotted the 1984 Los Angeles Games to protest the commercialization of the games and to avoid potentially threatening behaviour by what they expected to be jingoistic U.S. spectators. However, each of these Olympic Games was held despite the boycotts, and each host nation unashamedly displayed its power and resources to other participant nations. Furthermore, the boycotts had no major effect on national policies in any of the countries involved. However, there is one example where boycotts appear to have been particularly effective: when they were used to bring about the end of apartheid in South Africa in the early 1990s (see the Reflect on Sports box, "Sport Boycotts and the End of Apartheid," on p. 418).

Global media coverage has intensified and added new dimensions to the connection between sports and politics. For example, television companies, especially the U.S. networks, traditionally attracted viewers to their Olympic coverage by stressing political controversies along with national interests and symbols. The theme of their coverage between 1960 and 1988 was less focused on international friendship than on "us versus them" and "this nation versus that nation." The networks justified this coverage by claiming that U.S. viewers prefer nationalistic themes that extolled U.S. values and that claimed U.S. global political superiority. Canada has not been immune to this type of coverage, which was especially evident during the various Canada Cup hockey tournaments, and which is increasingly evident during Olympic coverage.

REFLECT ON SPORTS

Sport Boycotts and the End of Apartheid

Some twenty-nine African, Asian, and Caribbean nations boycotted the Montreal Olympics in 1976. They were responding to calls by the South African Non-Racial Olympic Committee (SANROC) and the Organization of African Unity to boycott any event that included South Africa or any nation that maintained sporting ties with apartheid South Africa. The New Zealand rugby team had recently toured South Africa, and even though rugby is not an Olympic sport, the sporting link between New Zealand and South Africa was enough to trigger the boycott.

Opposition to the apartheid regime in South Africa—in which a minority white population routinely violated the political, social, cultural, and human rights of the majority black and "coloured" population (e.g., no participation in elections or on national sport teams)—was led by the African National Congress (ANC). In addition to attempting to organize economic and other boycotts of South Africa, the popularity of sports with white South Africans was also targeted.

Initially, few first-world nations and national and international sport organizations joined the sporting boycott. The IOC, after declaring that sports and politics should not be mixed, reluctantly endorsed the exclusion of South Africa from the Olympics in 1970. The New Zealand government did not attempt to prevent the national rugby team from competing in South Africa, and the IOC and the Montreal organizing committee did not attempt to prevent New Zealand from competing in the Olympics.

The Montreal boycott seems to have galvanized Prime Minister Pierre Trudeau and the sporting world into more genuine support. At the next meeting of Commonwealth prime ministers at Gleneagles in Scotland, Trudeau managed to include the sporting boycott of South Africa on the agenda. The Commonwealth prime ministers signed the Gleneagles Agreement (1977), endorsing and promising to enforce the boycott. Other governments and sport organizations followed, and, by 1985, South Africa was almost completely isolated from the world sport community.

The end of apartheid was signalled by the release of Nelson Mandela and other members of the ANC (1991) and the first open elections in South Africa (1994), which are now defining moments of the late twentieth century. The first multi-racial team representing South Africa appeared at the Barcelona Olympics (1992). A number of commentators have expressed the view that sporting boycotts were even more successful than trade embargos (which were routinely violated) and consumer boycotts in helping to bring about an end to apartheid. In recognition of his anti-apartheid work, Sam Ramsamy, the president of SANROC, was awarded an honorary doctorate degree by the University of Toronto shortly before the Barcelona Olympics.

Nelson Mandela, who had been an accomplished amateur boxer, said that "sport can create hope where once there was only despair." Although they are unpopular with athletes and sport organizations, we think that boycotts of sports, in a well-planned and well-organized campaign,[1] and in a just cause, also brought about hope. And it could do so in the future. *What do you think?*

---

[1] Two scholars in the social sciences of sports, Bruce Kidd in Canada and Richard Lapchick in the U.S., were actively involved in the campaign against apartheid sports.

• •

Although past media coverage of the Olympics and other international sports encouraged ethnocentrism and a militaristic approach to international relations, more recent coverage has reflected the end of the Cold War and the emerging global market-place. Nationalist themes still exist, but they are not as important as the themes of material consumption and global capitalist expansion. The need to do something about this is highlighted in the Reflect on Sports box, "The Olympic Games," pages 420–421.

Nation-States, Sports, and Cultural Ideology

Sports have been and still are used to promote ideas and orientations that fit the interests of the most powerful and wealthiest nations in the world. For example, participation in major international sport events often has meant that less powerful nations must look to the so-called superpowers for guidance and resources. This has encouraged people in relatively poor nations to deemphasize their traditional folk games and to focus their attention on sports that are largely unrelated to their own values and experiences. Furthermore, it has led them to be involved in events over which they have little control. Generally, if they want to play, they must go along with the conditions determined by people in powerful nations. As Vicky Paraschak (1995) has pointed out, federal funding has been available for the Arctic Games, which include mainstream North American sports, but not for the Northern Games, where there is more emphasis on traditional native activities.

When this occurs, people in poorer nations find that they buy, beg, or borrow everything from equipment to technical assistance from people in wealthy nations. This often promotes dependency on economically powerful nations, and sports become vehicles through which powerful nations extend their control over important forms of popular culture around the world. When people in poorer nations are committed to maintaining traditional cultural practices, including their native games, they resist the ideological influence associated with this type of "cultural imperialism," but resistance can be difficult when the rules and organization of popular international sports are so closely tied to the ideologies of powerful nations. For example, when a U.S. sport such as football is introduced to another country, it comes with an emphasis on ideas about individual achievement, competition, winning, hierarchical authority structures, and the use of technology to shape bodies into efficient machines (Maguire, 1990). These ideas may not be completely accepted by those learning to play and understand football, but they do tend to encourage orientations that work to the advantage of the United States, as well as to the long-term disadvantage of the less powerful nations.

In more developed nations, the influence of Americanization is less clear. For example, Finland has a popular version of baseball known as *pesapallo*. In some ways, the game is quite different from the U.S. version—different equipment and rules—while in other ways, it is quite similar in terms of the uniforms, colour, and "glitz" associated with the higher levels of the game. Finns are quite adamant that the game is different from the U.S. version and that it is representative of Finnish culture; the fact that the game has not become more like baseball attests to that. In Australia, soccer is considered to be a sport of recent immigrants, a second-class sport in comparison to cricket, rugby, and Australian Rules football. Because of that status, the sport has struggled to maintain interest in the rich sporting culture of Australia, and one way that it has been successful is to take on the trappings of North American "showbiz" sports (Rowe, et al., 1994). Thus, in an interesting local paradox, the global process of Americanization has been used to maintain interest in a sport not associated with North American culture.

Ideally, sports can be vehicles for cultural exchanges through which people from various nations *share* information and develop *mutual* cultural understanding. But true fifty-fifty sharing and mutual understanding are rare when two nations have unequal power and resources. This means that sports often become cultural exports from wealthy nations incorporated into the everyday lives of people in other nations. Of course, these imported sports may be revised and reshaped to fit their traditional values and lifestyles. However, even when that occurs, it is likely that the people in the traditional cultures will become increasingly open to the possibility

REFLECT ON SPORTS

The Olympic Games
Are They Special?

Are the Olympics just another international sport event, or are they special in what they do and what they mean? The ideals of Olympism emphasize opportunities for people to learn about and connect with others from different societies and cultural backgrounds. These ideals are important, because our future on this planet depends on human beings working together as global citizens. The goal of this togetherness is not to inspire everyone to think alike or believe that all human beings are basically the same. Instead, it is to establish global processes through which we learn to understand and appreciate our differences and work together to sustain healthy and safe lifestyles for people around the world. If the Olympic Games can be organized and played to promote these goals, they are, indeed, special.

Unfortunately, the Olympic Games clearly fall short of meeting these ideals. Nationalism and commercialism exert so much influence on how the Olympic Games are planned, promoted, presented, and played that the goal of global understanding and togetherness receives only token attention. The current method of selling media broadcasting rights tends to subvert Olympic ideals (Real, 1996). Television companies buy the rights to take the video images they want from the Olympics and combine them with their own commentaries for audiences in their countries. Thus, instead of bringing the world together around a single experience, the coverage presents heavily nationalized and commercialized versions of the Olympic Games. It is, of course, possible for these viewers to impose their own meanings on this coverage, but the coverage itself serves as the starting point for how they think about and make sense of the Olympics.

The IOC issues regular press releases full of rhetoric about friendship and peace, but it has made no concerted effort to take that rhetoric seriously. It has not constructed programmes and processes making it clear to athletes and spectators that the Games are about cultural understanding and working

together in socially responsible ways. Bruce Kidd (1996a), a former Olympian, argues that the time is right to make the Olympic Games special by using them to highlight cultural and social issues and to promote social responsibility around the globe.

Kidd suggests that athletes be selected to participate in the Olympics on the basis of their actions as global citizens, as well as their athletic accomplishments. There also should be a curriculum enabling athletes to learn about fellow competitors and their cultures. The Games should involve formal, televised opportunities for intercultural exchanges, and athletes should be ready to discuss their ideas about world peace and social responsibility during media interviews. The IOC should sponsor projects so that citizen-athletes have opportunities to build on their Olympic experiences through service to others around the world. A proportion of TV rights fees could be used to make this happen. IOC members then could talk about real examples of social responsibility connected with sports. TV viewers may find stories about how the Olympics make the world a better place as entertaining and inspiring as tabloid-like coverage of heartbreaking stories about beating the odds to win medals.

Additionally, the IOC should control both nationalism and commercialism more carefully as it organizes the games and sells broadcasting rights. We offer the following suggestions:

- *Do away with national uniforms for athletes.* Let athletes choose from uniforms designed by artists from various countries to express various cultural themes from around the world. This would minimize nationalism and inspire forms of expression that promote cultural understanding.

- *Revise the opening ceremonies, so that athletes enter the arena with others in their events.* The emphasis would be on unity and fellowship, not on the political and economic systems in which the athletes were born through no choice of their own. Artists from around the world would be commissioned to design flags for various sports. National flags would be displayed collectively in the middle of the field to emphasize unity amid difference.

- *Eliminate national anthems and flags during the award ceremonies.* Present medals in the stadium at the end of each day of competition in such a way that the emphasis during awards ceremonies is on the athletes as representatives of all humanity, rather than of nations.
- *Eliminate medal counts for nations.* National medal counts are contrary to the spirit of the Olympic Movement. They foster chauvinism, intensify existing political conflicts, and distract attention from the achievements of athletes.
- *Eliminate or revise team sports.* Team sports, as they are now structured, automatically focus attention on national affiliations. They encourage players and spectators to perceive games in terms of national honour and pride. If team sports are not eliminated, then develop a method of choosing teams so that athletes from different countries play on the same teams and athletes from any one nation play on different teams (cf., intercrosse; Harvey and Houle, 1994). Then "dream teams" would emphasize international unity, rather than a nationalist and commercial approach to sports.
- *Add to each Games "demonstration sports" native to the cultural regions where the Games are held.* Because television influences how sports are imagined, created, and played around the world, mandate television coverage of these native games, so

viewers have expanded notions of physical activities, which may inspire creative changes in their sport participation.
- *Use multiple sites for each Olympic Games.* This would enable nations without massive economic resources to be hosts. Poorer nations that host only a portion of the events would benefit economically, and multiple sites would enable media spectators to see a wider range of cultural settings while still seeing all the events in the games.
- *Emphasize global responsibility in media coverage and commercials.* Television contracts could mandate an emphasis on global responsibility. Expressions of this theme could be developed by athlete committees working with committees from the Olympic Academy, which includes scholars committed to the spirit of Olympism. This would link corporate sponsors to the special meaning of the Olympics and provide support for athletes as global citizens.

Because the Olympic Games capture the attention of one-third of the world's population, they should be used as something other than global marketing opportunities for transnational corporations and political stages for wealthy nations, which can afford to produce medal-winning athletes. The present is a good time for the Olympics to put into practice the ideals of the Olympic Charter. As this is done, the Olympics should formulate a new motto, one that goes beyond "Citius, Altius, Fortius" ("faster, higher, stronger"), one that takes the Olympics beyond nationalism and commercialism. What about "Excellence for Humanity"? *What do you think?*

• •

of importing and consuming other goods, services, and ideas from the wealthy nations. Unless political power and economic resources are developed in connection with this process, poorer nations are likely to become increasingly dependent on wealthy nations. Of course, this is a complex process, involving many issues in addition to those related to sports.

New Political Realities in an Era of Transnational Corporations

Today, international sports are less likely to be scenes for nationalistic displays than scenes for commercial displays by large and powerful transnational corporations. This was clearly evident at the Olympics in Atlanta (1996),

Nagano (1998), Sydney (2000), and Salt Lake City (2002), and it will be evident in future locations. Global politics have changed dramatically over the past decade. Nation-states have been joined by powerful transnational organizations in global power relations. As noted in chapter 11, about half of the largest economies in the world are corporations, *not* nation-states. As nation-states have lifted trade restrictions, decreased tariffs, and loosened their internal regulations to promote their own capitalist expansion, transnational corporations have become increasingly powerful players in global politics. Many of them are now more powerful in economic terms than the nations in which they have production facilities; this, of course, gives them political power as well.

Therefore, instead of focusing just on international relations when we study sports and political processes, we must broaden our focus to consider *transnational relations*. This enables us to acknowledge that nation-states are now joined by major corporations and other powerful transnational organizations as global political players.

Nationalism still exists in connection with international sports, especially those played in regions where political and economic issues call attention to national differences and interests. However, in the case of many sport events, the differences between national interests and identities and corporate interests and identities are becoming increasingly blurred. This was highlighted by Phil Knight, the CEO of the U.S.–based Nike Corporation, as he explained the basis for his team loyalty during the 1994 World Cup of soccer:

> We see a natural evolution...dividing the world into their athletes and ours. And we glory ours. When the U.S. played Brazil in the World Cup, I rooted for Brazil because it was a Nike team. America was Adidas. (Lipsyte, 1996b)

Knight's point was that he identified teams and athletes in terms of logos, not nationalities. He knew that Nike's markets were not limited to the United States. They were and continue to be worldwide, and this was why Nike gave Brazil's national sport teams US$200 million for the right to use the Brazilian soccer team to market Nike products around the world through the year 2005. Knight sees logo loyalty as more important than national loyalty when it comes to international sports; he sees consumerism replacing patriotism when it comes to identifying athletes and teams; he sees international sport events as sites for Nike and other corporate sponsors to deliver advertising messages promoting their companies' interests, along with the general interests of global capitalist expansion. Furthermore, he and fellow executives from other powerful corporations see this as good for the people of the world. Their conclusion would be similar to conclusions made by those using functionalist theory: sport contributes to economic expansion, and this is good for everyone in the world.

However, to the extent that corporate sponsors influence sport events and media coverage, international sports televised around the world are used as vehicles for presenting to massive audiences a range of messages promoting the interests of corporate capitalism (Donnelly, 1996a). These messages are directed to spectator-consumers, not spectator-citizens. Instead of keying in on patriotism or nationalism, the messages that come with international sports now key in on status consciousness and individual consumption. Sports that do not enable corporations to deliver their messages to consumers with purchasing power are not sponsored. If spectators and media audiences are not potential consumers, corporations see little reason to sponsor events, so, unless the media are publicly owned, they are not likely to cover events viewed by those who have little purchasing power.

Of course, the power of corporations is not unlimited or uncontested, as conflict theorists would have us conclude. Critical and figurational research has identified cases where local populations use their own cultural perspectives to interpret and apply the images and discourses

"I prefer to think of it as my personal 'opening ceremonies.'"

The scandals related to the Olympic site bidding process raised serious questions about the too often assumed "purity" of the Olympic Games.

that come with global sports and global advertising (Donnelly, 1996a; Maguire, 1999; Maguire and Pearton, 1999). However, those who use critical theories also note that global media sports and the commercial messages that accompany them often cleverly fuse the global and the local through thoughtfully and carefully edited images of local traditions, sport action, and consumer products (Andrews and Silk, 1999; Carrington and Sugden, 1999; Jackson and Hokowhitu, 2002; Jackson and Scherer, 2002; Silk, 1999). They argue that these fused images tend to "detraditionalize" local cultures by presenting local symbols and lifestyles in connection with consumer products.

Nike has been especially clever in this regard. As cultural theorist David Andrews points out, Nike commercials that aired in connection with global sport events during the late 1990s masterfully presented images from numerous localities around the world. These local images were "reassembled" and situated in connection with Nike products, such as soccer apparel worn by players from many nations as they kicked a soccer ball in numerous locations around the globe. Andrews argues that Nike captures local traditions and wraps its branded shirts around them until there is little else to be seen or discussed.

The conclusions made by critical theories have not been explored sufficiently in research, but it is clear that, as corporations join or replace nation-states as sponsors of athletes and teams around the world, sports do become framed in new political terms. According to John Horan, the publisher of *Sporting Goods Intelligence*, "It's not the Free World versus Communism anymore. Now you take sides with sneaker companies. Now everybody looks at the Olympics as Nike versus Reebok" (in Reid, 1996, p. 4BB). Horan's conclusion is probably distorted by his hope that global sports are perceived in this way; however, despite some distortion and exaggeration, Horan (and many others like him) expresses the intent of transnational corporations as they spend billions to sponsor sports around the world.

The late Roone Arledge, then president of ABC News and formerly director of ABC Sports in the U.S., noted that this intent is becoming a reality in connection with sport events. He observed that the Olympic Games today are "basically a commercial enterprise that tries every four years to make as much money as it possibly can," and they do not have "much to do with the heroic words that we use to describe them" (in Reid, 1996: 4BB). Reaffirming Arledge's conclusion, Dick Ebersol, president of NBC Sports, explained that NBC paid over $3.5 billion for the U.S. rights to televise all Olympic Games from 2000 to 2008, because the Olympics "has this amazing ability to put the whole family in front of the television together, which is what advertisers are grabbing at" (in Steinbreder, 1996, p. 38).

These statements, made only thirteen years after Peter Ueberroth, president of the Los Angeles Olympic Organizing Committee, described the Olympics as an athletic-*political* event, illustrate the power of corporate capitalism. In just over a decade, the characterization of the largest sport event in the world changed from athletic-*political* to athletic-*economic*.[6] Representatives from many major corporations around the world have come to see the potential of sports to establish new commercial markets and to promote the ideology of consumerism, which drives those markets. Although the sponsorship money coming from these corporations is welcomed by those who benefit from it, the primary goal of those who own and control the corporations is to make profits. Coca-Cola may sponsor the Olympics because it wants to bring people together, but it is primarily interested in selling as many Cokes as possible to the six billion people around the world. This is also the reason that the MARS candy company pays millions to be the official snack food of the Olympics, and that McDonald's uses the Olympics and nearly fat-free athletes' bodies to market hamburgers and fries around the world.

According to Sut Jhally, transnational corporations pay billions of dollars to sponsor global sports in an effort to become "global cultural commissars." Jhally says that, if you listen closely and critically to the advertisements of these sponsors, you'll discover that, in addition to their products, they are selling a way of life based on consumption. They use sports to present images and messages emphasizing individual success through competition, production, and consumption. They know that elite competitive sports are ideal vehicles for presenting these images and messages, because such sports have become primary sources of entertainment around the world. When people are being entertained while watching these sports in person or on television, they are emotionally primed to hear what the sponsors have to say.

Of course, many people ignore the images and messages emphasized by sponsors, or they redefine them to fit local and personal circumstances. But this does not prevent large corporations from spending billions to deliver them. Advertisers understand that sooner or later the images and messages associated with sources of pleasure and entertainment in people's lives will in some form enter the imaginations and conversations of a proportion of those who see and hear them. The images and messages do not dictate what people think, but they certainly influence what people think about, and, in this way, they become a part of the overall discourse that occurs in cultures around the globe.

We should not interpret this description of the new politics of sports to mean that sports around

---

[6] Interestingly, it was probably Ueberroth who triggered this change with his staging of what came to be known as the "hamburger Olympics," and his establishment of the exclusive (US$30 million contribution) sponsor programme which, of course, included McDonald's (Gruneau, 1984).

the world somehow have fallen victim to a global conspiracy hatched by transnational corporations. It means only that transnational organizations have joined nation-states in the global political context in which sports are defined, organized, planned, promoted, played, and presented to the world (Jackson and Scherer, 2002; Silk, 1999).

Other Global Political Issues

As sports have become increasingly commercialized, and as national boundaries have become less relevant in sports, an increasing number of athletes have become global migrant workers. They go where their sports are played, where they can be supported or earn money while they play, or where they can have the cultural experiences they seek. This global migration of athletes has raised new political issues in connection with sports. Another global political issue is related to the production of sporting goods. As the demand for sports equipment and clothing has increased in wealthy nations, transnational corporations have cut costs for those products by having them manufactured in labour-intensive poor countries, where production costs are extremely low. The result has been a clear split between the world's haves and have-nots when it comes to sports: those born into privilege in wealthy nations consume the products made by those born into disadvantaged circumstances in poor nations. This is not a new issue, but it ties sports to global politics in yet another way. These issues receive further attention in the next two sections.

Athletes as Global Migrant Workers Human history is full of examples of labour migration, both forced and voluntary. Industrial societies, in particular, have depended on mobile labour forces responsive to the needs of production. Now that economies have become more global, the pervasiveness and diversity of labour migration patterns have increased (Maguire, 1999; Stead and Maguire, 2000). This is true in sports as well as other occupational categories. Athletes frequently move from their hometowns when they are recruited to play elite sports, and then they may move many times after that, as they are traded from team to team or seek continuing opportunities to play their sports.

As geographer John Bale and sociologist Joe Maguire have noted in a book on athletic talent migration (1994), athletes move from state to state and region to region within nations, as well as from nation to nation within and between continents. They have noted also that each of these moves raises issues related to the following: (1) the personal adjustment of migrating athletes, (2) the rights of athletes as workers in various nations, (3) the impact of talent migration on the nations from and to which athletes migrate, and (4) the impact of athlete migration on patterns of personal, cultural, and national identity formation.

Some migration patterns are seasonal, involving temporary moves as athletes travel from one climate area to another to play their sports. Patterns may follow annual tour schedules, as athletes travel from tournament to tournament around a region or the world, or they may involve long-term or permanent moves from one region or nation to another.

The range of personal experiences among migrating athletes is great. They vary from major forms of culture shock and chronic loneliness to minor homesickness and minor adjustment problems. Some athletes are exploited by teams or clubs, while others make great amounts of money, which enables them to return home when they are not playing games or practising. Some encounter prejudice against foreigners or various forms of racial and ethnic bigotry, while others are socially accepted and make good friends. Some cling to their national identities and socialize with fellow athletes from their homelands, while others develop more global identities unrelated to one national or cultural background. Some teams and clubs expect foreign athletes to adjust on their own, while others provide support for those who need to learn a new language or become familiar with new cultural settings (Klein, 1999).

Athletic talent migration also has an impact on the nations involved. For example, many Latin American nations have their best baseball players recruited by major league teams in the United States. This not only depletes the talent the Latin American nations need to maintain professional baseball in their local economies but also forces them to depend on North American–based satellite television companies to watch the players from their nations. During the television coverage, they often are exposed to images and messages consistent with the advertising interests of corporations headquartered in the United States. There is also a reverse pattern of migration, with North American players who have retired from, or who have not been recruited to, North American teams, playing on European teams in sports such as U.S. football, basketball, volleyball, and hockey (e.g., Maguire, 1996). Dual citizenship and varying definitions of citizenship also create interesting scenarios in terms of sport migration and national team representation, as citizens of one country are able to compete on the Olympic and national teams of another country.

Similar patterns exist in connection with European soccer teams that recruit players from around the world. In fact, soccer has higher rates of talent migration than other sports, although hockey, baseball, track and field, and basketball have high rates as well. The impact of this migration on national talent pools and on the ability of local clubs and teams to maintain economically viable sport programmes is complex. Talent migration usually benefits the nation to which athletes move more than it benefits the nation from which athletes move, but this is not always the case.

The impact of global migration by athletes on how people think about and identify themselves in connection with nation-states is something we know little about. Many people tend to appreciate athletic talent regardless of the athlete's nationality. At the same time, many people tend to have special affections for athletes and teams representing their nations of citizenship or their nations of origin. Leagues such as the NHL are open to athletes of all nations. In fact, even though most of the teams are located in U.S. cities, less than 20 percent of the players are U.S.–born; about 53 percent are from Canada, and nearly 30 percent are from European nations. Other leagues impose quotas limiting the number of foreign-born or foreign-nationality players they may sign to contracts (Greenberg and Gray, 1996). For example, in the early 1990s, Japan banned U.S. women basketball players from its professional league. At the same time, professional leagues in Italy, Spain, and France allowed their teams to have up to two foreign players, many of whom were from the United States. In 1996, England lifted all quotas for both men's and women's pro basketball teams. The current CFL contract permits 17 imports (usually U.S. players) on a roster of 38 or 39, major junior hockey teams permit two imports (i.e., not Canadian or U.S. players) per team, and CIS limits university basketball teams to a maximum of three imports. Currently, some people in the United States are calling for limits on the number of foreign student-athletes who can play on intercollegiate teams—which would affect Canadian students—while many athletic departments are recruiting more student-athletes from outside the United States. Non-Canadian athletes are beginning to play in increasing numbers on Canadian interuniversity teams, but this has not yet been identified as a problem.

As commercial sport organizations expand their franchise locations across national borders, and as they recruit athletes regardless of nationality, talent migration will increase in the future. The social implications of this trend are important to study and understand.

Global Politics and the Production of Sport Equipment and Apparel Free trade agreements (for example, GATT and NAFTA), signed by many nations by the mid-1990s, have created a new global economic environment. In this environment, it is cost-effective for large corporations selling vast amounts of goods to people in wealthy nations to locate production facilities in labour-intensive poor nations. These corporations are taxed at much lower rates when they move products from nation to nation. They can make products in nations where labour is cheap and environmental, worker, health and safety, and other regulations are scarce, and then sell them in wealthy nations where people can afford to buy them.

These political-economic changes mean that, during the mid-1990s, many athletic shoes costing well over $100 a pair in Canada were cut and sewn by workers making less than 25 cents per hour in China and Indonesia, less than 75 cents per hour in Thailand, and less than $2.25 per hour in South Korea (Enloe, 1997). Similar patterns exist in connection with the production of clothes bearing NHL and NBA logos sold in North America (Sage, 1996). Soccer balls sanctioned by FIFA, the international soccer federation, often are hand-sewn by child labourers making far less than poverty-level wages in poor nations, where people are desperate for any kind of work. And, while Nike athletes were making millions of dollars on their shoe endorsements, Nike shoes were being made mostly by young women in Southeast Asia working ten to thirteen hours a day, six days a week under oppressive conditions for 13–20 cents (US) per hour—far below a living wage in China, Vietnam, and Indonesia.

This exploitation attracted worldwide attention among religious, human rights, feminist, and labour organizations, as well as other activist groups. Sport sociologist George Sage (1999; see also Knight and Greenberg, 2002) has described the Nike transnational advocacy network that emerged during the mid-1990s. This network of dozens of organizations from many countries gradually mobilized consciousness and various forms of political action, which, along with other non-governmental organizations

(NGOs) such as Press for Change, Vietnam Labour Watch, Global Exchange, and the Clean Clothes Campaign, influenced various government policies on labour and human rights issues, and Nike's relationship with production contractors in Southeast Asia. The network was so effective that the Nike logo became associated with sweatshops and unfair labour practices in the minds of many consumers. Nike's earnings declined, and its executives began to take responsibility for making some changes in its production facilities; they even downsized the swoosh logo and converted the print logo to *nike* with a small *n* because they wanted to understate their presence and avoid negative attention among potential consumers.[7] The U.S. government formed a new agency, the Fair Labor Association, and Nike has been actively involved. Ideas about "corporate responsibility" began to circulate widely in the latter part of the 1990s; the terminology has now been changed to "global citizenship," and Nike has increased significantly the number of staff it employs to deal with issues of global citizenship.

Sage's case study of the Nike transnational advocacy network is heartening, because it documents the power of people to make change. The Internet and other global communications technologies make it possible for people around the world to mobilize in response to human rights violations and other important social issues. Of course, many factors influence the formation of a transnational advocacy network, but, when issues resonate across many groups of people, a network of organizations and individuals can organize, take action, and have an impact on global political processes. If this were not possible, what would stop transnational corporations, which are accountable to nothing but a generally underregulated global marketplace, from pursuing their interests in whatever ways they wish?

---

[7] In a move that some considered to be controversial, CAAWS accepted Nike sponsorship to promote awareness of girls and sports and to distribute Nike-funded grants.

Making Sense of New Political Realities

It is not easy to explain all the changes outlined in the previous sections. Are sports simply a part of general globalization processes through which various sport forms come together in many combinations? Are we witnessing the modernization of sports? Are sports being Americanized? Europeanized? Asianized? Are we seeing sports simply being diffused throughout the world, with people in some countries emulating the sports played in other countries, or are sports being used in connection with new forms of cultural imperialism and colonization? Are sports tools for making poorer nations dependent on wealthier ones, or are they tools for establishing cultural independence and autonomy in emerging nations? Is it accurate to say that sports are becoming commercialized, or should we say that corporations are appropriating sports for the purpose of global capitalist expansion? Are traditional and folk sports around the world being destroyed by heavily publicized sports based in wealthy nations, or do people take sport forms from other cultures and creatively adapt them to their own circumstances? Are sports becoming more democratic, or have new forms of sponsorship actually restricted people's choices about when and how they will play sports?

Those who study sports as social phenomena now are devoting more of their attention to these and related questions. The best work on these issues involves data on global *and* local levels (Donnelly, 1996a; Guttmann, 1994; Harvey et al., 1996; Maguire, 1999). This work calls attention to the fact that powerful people do not simply impose certain sport forms on less powerful people around the world. Even when sports from powerful nations are played in other parts of the world, the meanings associated with them often are grounded in the local cultures in which they are played. It is important to understand global trends, but it is also important to understand the local expressions of and responses to those trends. Power is a process, not a thing; it is always exercised through social relations, so the study of power must focus on how people agree and disagree with one another as they attempt to live their lives on terms enabling them to achieve a sense of personal significance. This is true in connection with sports, as it is in other dimensions of social life.

POLITICS IN SPORTS

The term *politics* usually is associated with the formal government entities in the public sphere. However, politics includes all processes of governing people and administering rules and policies, at all levels of organization, public and private. Therefore, politics is an integral part of sports, and many local, national, and international sport organizations are referred to as "governing bodies."

If there is one thing that characterizes sport organizations, it is fragmentation. There are so many different organizations, clubs, leagues, multi-sport and service organizations, and ethical and judicial bodies dealing with issues of doping and dispute resolution that they have an extremely difficult time ever speaking with one voice in order to lobby effectively for the sport community. Table 13.2 attempts to capture the diversity and complexity of the sport community in Canada.

Sport organizations do many things, but most are concerned with providing and regulating sport participation opportunities, establishing and enforcing policies, controlling and standardizing competitions, and acknowledging the accomplishments of athletes. This sounds like a straightforward set of tasks. However, they seldom are accomplished without opposition, debate, and compromise. Members of sport organizations may agree on many things, but they also have different interests and orientations. In fact, conflicts often arise as people deal with the following questions surrounding sports and sport participation:

1. What qualifies as a sport?
2. What are the rules of a sport?
3. Who makes and enforces the rules in sports?
4. Who organizes and controls games, meets, matches, and tournaments?
5. Where do sport events take place?
6. Who is eligible to participate in a sport?
7. How are rewards distributed to athletes and other organization members?

Because some people mistakenly assume that sports are pure activities and should be separate from the everyday world, they are sometimes shocked and disappointed when they hear that sports involve politics. However, just as sports are connected with the larger politics of the state, sport events and organizations have politics of their own. These politics affect everyone involved, from athletes, coaches, and administrators in sport organizations to promoters, sponsors, and spectators. The following examples reflect the questions listed in the previous paragraph.

What Qualifies as a Sport?

As noted in chapter 1, there is no universal agreement on the definition of *sports*. What is considered a sport in a society or in a particular event, such as the Olympics, is determined through political processes (Donnelly, 1996b).

The criteria used to identify sports reflect the ideas and interests of some people more than others. In the Summer Olympics, for example, a competitive activity or game for men is not considered for recognition as a sport unless it is played in at least seventy countries; an activity or a game for women must be played in at least forty countries. It also must have an officially designated international governing body, a requisite number of national governing bodies, and a history of international championships before the IOC will consider recognizing it as an Olympic sport.

In these days of multibillion-dollar media contracts, an activity or a game is more likely to

be recognized as a sport if it is attractive to television and if it attracts the interest of younger viewers, who in turn attract new advertisers and corporate sponsors to the Olympics. It also helps if women play the activity, because more women than men watch the Olympics and because the IOC is concerned that its failure to reach gender equity might create bad publicity for the Olympics as a whole.

Of course, this way of defining *sports* favours the nations that historically have had the resources to export their games around the world. Former colonial powers are especially favoured, because they used their national games to introduce their cultural values and traditions to colonized peoples around the world. Wealthy and powerful nations today not only have their national sports broadcast on satellite channels around the world but also have the resources to subsidize the development of these sports, so that they are played in many countries. Therefore, when it comes time for IOC recognition, the sports from wealthy nations are at the top of the list. When these sports are recognized, the cultural values and traditions of wealthy and powerful nations are reaffirmed. In this way, the games of wealthy and powerful nations become the sports of the world.

This is also the reason native games in traditional cultures are not a part of the Olympic Games. Games played in limited regions of the globe usually do not qualify for recognition as sports. However, if they met the criteria outlined above (younger viewers, television friendly, female participation), or if they have substantial political support at the IOC, the criteria are easily waived. This was the case with curling and tae kwan do, which have been included at several Olympics since 1988. Thus, if people from nations with traditional cultures want to participate in the Olympics, they must learn to play activities and games popular in wealthy nations. Since people in traditional cultures lack access to the equipment and facilities needed to train in their homelands, they

Table 13.2 The Canadian Sport Community

INTERNATIONAL

Major Games Federations	International Sport Federations (IFs)	Governments and NGOs
• International Olympic Committee (IOC) • Commonwealth Games Federation (CGF) • International Paralympic Committee (IPC) • FISU (World Student Games) • PASO (Pan-Am Games)	• FIFA (soccer) • IAAF (track and field) •FIS (skiing)	• General Assembly of International Sport Federations (GAISF) •World Anti-Doping Agency (WADA)

REGIONAL

• North American Indigenous Games Association		• Council of Europe

NATIONAL

National Sport Organizations (NSOs)		
• Canadian Olympic Committee (COC) • Canadian Interuniversity Sport (CIS) • Commonwealth Games Canada • Canada Games Council • Canadian Colleges Athletics Association • Special Olympics Canada • Canadian Paralympic Committee • Arctic Winter Games	• Badminton Canada • Skate/Patinage Canada • Rowing Canada Aviron • Patinage de Vitesse Canada • Swimming/Natation Canada	• Heritage Canada/ Sport Canada • Coaching Association of Canada • Canadian Centre for Ethics in Sport • Canadian Academy of Sport Medicine • National Sport Centres • AthletesCAN • CAAWS • Aboriginal Sport Circle • Sport Dispute Resolution Centre

PROVINCIAL

Provincial Sport Organizations (PSOs)		
• Provincial Games Organizations • Provincial Special Olympics • Provincial Disability Sports	• Hockey Québec • Newfoundland Rugby Union • Dancesport BC	• Provincial and Territorial Ministries Responsible for Sport • Provincial Sport Administration Centres

MUNICIPAL/LOCAL

• Schools, colleges, universities	• Sport clubs • Youth sport organizations	• Municipal Parks and Recreation Departments

---

Lists are not comprehensive; • designates examples of organizations/institutions at each level must depend on support from people and organizations in wealthy nations to become international athletes in recognized sports (cf., the Jamaican bobsled team at the Calgary Olympics). In this way, sports become vehicles through which people and organizations in wealthy nations can gain a foothold in traditional cultures and influence social change processes to their own advantage.

This type of political process also occurs in other contexts. For example, for well over one hundred years, the men who have controlled athletic departments in North American high schools and universities have used a power and performance model to designate certain activities as interscholastic or interuniversity sports. Then they have organized these sports to emphasize competition and dominance, so that the sports fit their notions of character and excellence. Over the years, this way of defining and organizing sports seldom has been questioned, but, because gender equity has become an issue, some people now argue that full equity never will be achieved unless such questions are raised. If power and performance sports attract far fewer girls and women than boys and men, it may be time to ask questions about what gets to count as an interschool or interuniversity sport, and why. When we ask these questions, we immediately notice the existence of politics in sports.

The development of the criteria underlying the meaning and organization of sports also occurs on a global scale. Peter Donnelly (1996b) illustrates this in his analysis of the way the ideologies of Olympism and professionalism are being combined to form a global sport monoculture, which he calls "prolympism." Prolympism is quickly becoming the model for determining what activities count and are funded as sports in nations around the world, even in nations where traditional games are clearly inconsistent with professionalism in any form, so the politics of defining *sports* are both local and global in impact.

Wealthy and powerful nations have always had a major share of power in international sports. The games and sports of these nations form the foundation of the Olympic Games. In this historic photo of the 1936 Olympic Games in Berlin, the U.S. team salutes as they represent U.S. interests in pre–World War II Europe. (USOC Archives)

What Are the Rules of a Sport?

Sports are social constructions. This means that people create them as they interact with one another and identify physical challenges within the constraints of environment and culture. The rules that govern sports are also social constructions and, as such, are determined through political processes. Why should the penalty spot in field hockey be located 6.4 metres from the goal line? Why should soccer goals be 7.23 metres wide? Why should the top of volleyball nets be 2.24 metres off the ground in international women's volleyball? Why are pole-vaulters not able to use any type of pole they want? Why are tournament golfers prevented from using any type of golf club or golf ball they want? Why is 6 centimetres the maximum height for the sides of bikini bottoms worn by women in beach volleyball? This list of questions could go on and on. The point is that the rules of sports can be based on many concerns, and this makes them political. Because sports have more rules than most human activities, they are more political than most things we participate in during our lives.

Who Makes and Enforces the Rules in Sports?

The rules of a sport are determined by a governing body of people that is recognized as the official source of information and regulation for those who play the sport. The process of becoming recognized as the *sole* governing body of a sport clearly involves politics (Sugden and Tomlinson, 1998, 1999). Governing bodies have power, status, and control over resources, so it is common for more than one group to claim that it is the rightful rule-making body. The simultaneous existence of various governing bodies can create confusion for athletes and spectators in a sport. Professional boxing, for example, has had at least four governing bodies at the same time (the WBO, the WBU, the WBF, and the IBC), each with its own weight categories and championships and each claiming to be the official rule-making body for boxing. Such new sports as skateboarding and in-line skating have had at least two organizations vying to be official governing bodies. As these organizations seek to establish power over the sports and the athletes who participate in them, they battle each other to recruit dues-paying members and to sponsor competitive events. In the process, their policies confuse athletes and limit participation opportunities. When this occurs, people clearly see the politics in sports.

When rules exist, there is also a need for rule enforcement. This adds another political dimension to sports. Anyone who has ever refereed or officiated a game or match will tell you that rule violations are seldom clear-cut, that identifying violations is difficult, and that few people see violations the same way. Rule violations occur on a regular basis in many sports, but the best referees have learned when to call fouls or penalties in connection with these violations. In fact, referees and officials discuss when they should or should not call fouls during games and matches. Making sports appear to be fair to both athletes and spectators is a political challenge.

Enforcement in the case of off-the-field rule violations is also a political challenge. The process of investigating rule violations, determining innocence or guilt, and punishing rule violators involves determinations of what is good and bad for sports, sport organizations, and various people connected with sports. These determinations may be grounded in ideas about fairness, moral principles, economic interests, personal reputations, organizational prestige, or other factors. How these factors are defined and which ones prevail in the rule enforcement process is a matter for discussion, debate, and compromise.

We also see the politics of rule enforcement in the policies of sport organizations. For example, CIS, the primary governing body for interuniversity sports in Canada, is made up of representatives of member universities located across Canada. Because university sports mean different things from one region of the country to another, these representatives often have contradictory ideas about what is legitimate conduct and what is not. Developing a set of rules and enforcement procedures under these conditions involves intensely political processes. Rule enforcement inevitably creates dissent among the members whose ideas about legitimate conduct are not consistent with what CIS has determined to be "right and official." When this occurs, political processes become heated, as is now the case with the issue of scholarships.

Who Organizes and Controls Games, Meets, Matches, and Tournaments?

Representatives of official governing bodies usually are responsible for the organization and control of sport events. Standards emerge when the governing body is stable, but standards never are established once and for all time. For example, even though officials from governing bodies have devised formal standards for judging performances in sports such as figure skating, diving, and gymnastics, research shows that judges' votes are influenced by political loyalties (Seltzer and Glass, 1991), as became evident in a very public way in "Skategate," the Salé and Pelletier judging scandal at the Salt Lake City (2002) Olympics. Of course, this is disheartening to athletes, but it should be no more disheartening than the knowledge that "cuteness," "hairstyles," "body build," and "eye colour" can influence judges when it comes to women athletes in certain events. This is the reason some athletes spend thousands of dollars on everything from braces for their teeth to plastic surgery for their jaws and noses. Politics comes in many forms.

Now that sports have become commercialized, the organization and control of events may be shared by official governing bodies and a combination of corporate sponsors and media production people. The location and timing of events, event schedules, the choice of people to be given press passes to cover events, the choice of which

television company will have the rights to broadcast the events, the choice of which corporate logos will be associated with the events, and other issues are resolved through political processes. The participants in those processes and their interests change from one event to the next; this means that the politics in sports never end.

Where Do Sport Events Take Place?

The politics of place are an integral part of sports. Site selection decisions are contentious as sports, teams, and events use and are used by towns, cities, and nations for economic purposes.

Certainly, the selection of Olympic sites is a political process, as seen during and after the site selection vote-buying scandal involving the IOC and the Salt Lake Olympic Organizing Committee during the 1990s. It became evident in the 1980s that both political *and* economic benefits could result from hosting the Olympics, and this fuelled an escalating process of wining, dining, bribing, and pressuring one hundred–plus IOC members, whose votes determine which cities would host the games. As investigative journalist Andrew Jennings wrote and talked about the scope of this process and the amounts of money involved, most people thought he was given to exaggeration (Jennings, 1996a; Simson and Jennings, 1992). However, subsequent information has shown that his accusations of corruption and criminal activity were accurate. His most recent disclosures indicate that corrupt political processes still plague the IOC (Jennings and Sambrook, 2000).

The politics of site selection also operate in other ways. For example, Atlanta's bid for the 1996 Games was influenced by everything from the television rights fees anticipated from U.S.–based television companies to the location of the international headquarters of Coca-Cola, the largest corporate Olympic sponsor in the world, in Atlanta. The red-and-white Coke logo was so evident around Atlanta and in Olympic venues that many observers described the games as the "Coca-Colympics."

The involvement of media companies and corporate sponsors in the site selection process is now a key dimension of the politics of place in sports. The fact that NBC paid $3.5 billion for the rights to televise the Olympics from the 2000 Sydney Games through the 2008 Beijing Games guarantees that executives representing NBC's interests will be major players in those politics. This dismays many people around the world who think that U.S. interests have bought political favour from the IOC with sponsorship and television money at the same time that U.S.–based organizing committees have been bribing IOC members.

Site bids for events such as the Grey Cup; All-Star games; CIS championships in (men's) basketball and football; world championships in cycling, swimming, and track and field; as well as other international events, may not cost as much as bids to host the Olympics, but they are just as political.

Sports and the politics of place in many parts of the world also reflect environmental issues (Chernushenko, 1994). For example, the use of open space or agricultural land for golf courses now is being contested in Europe, Japan, and even North America. The Global AntiGolf Movement has developed in connection with widespread objections to the use of chemical fertilizers, pesticides, and massive water resources to keep grass soft and green for golfers representing the economic elite in societies. This organization has 250 member lobbying groups in fifteen countries, and it has coordinated protests and other antigolf campaigns around the world. Ski resort expansion in North America, Europe, and Japan also has been resisted for environmental reasons. The organizers of the 2000 Sydney Games faced severe criticism when they failed in important ways to live up to the environmental principles

"Well, at least nobody can accuse the Olympics of producing **NATIONALISM** anymore."

Nationalism continues to exist in connection with the Olympic Games, but powerful transnational corporations have been successful in combining national identities and the Olympics with an ideology that promotes consumption, competition, and individualism. Corporate logos now are as visible as national flags at most international sport events.

developed by the original bid committee (Lenskyj, 1998, 2002). Such examples highlight the fact that the politics of place in sports often involve local opposition to the hosting of events and the building of facilities.

Who Is Eligible to Participate in a Sport?

Who plays and who does not play is often a hotly contested issue in sports. People in various governing bodies make determinations about participation eligibility. They may use factors such as gender, age, weight, height, ability (and disability), place of residence, citizenship, educational affiliation, grades in university, social status, income, religion, or even race and ethnicity to determine participation eligibility. Although eligibility policies often are presented as if they are based on unchanging truths about human beings and sports, they are grounded in standards debated and agreed upon by groups of officials. These agreements are forged through political processes.

People often have contested the arbitrariness of eligibility rules. For example, in CIS, disputes about eligibility rules have resulted in Policy No. 40 (Eligibility) being one of the longest and most complex to administer. Lawsuits sometimes follow unsuccessful appeals, because people feel they have been excluded unfairly from participation. High school students have made similar challenges when their families have moved from one school district to another and they have found they are ineligible to play inter-school sports. Even in youth sports, there are frequent debates about the age and weight rules used to determine eligibility. Athletes with a disability regularly have challenged rules prohibiting their participation in certain sports. Within events such as the Paralympics, the international event held immediately following the Olympic Games, there are frequent debates about disability classifications and eligibility.

There are literally hundreds of other noteworthy cases of eligibility politics in amateur and professional sports. Sikh boxers in British Columbia and Ontario have challenged boxing regulations that stipulate that boxers who wear a beard are ineligible to box. As globalization increases, there are debates about citizenship and eligibility. The organizers of a popular 10K race in Boulder, Colorado, faced severe resistance when they wanted to change the eligibility rules so that no more than three Kenyan runners could compete. Their justification was that U.S. runners could not beat the Kenyans, and the U.S. corporate sponsors wanted U.S. runners among the top finishers. Amateur sports have been the scene of longstanding debates over the meaning of *amateur* and qualifications for amateur status. Because these meanings are socially determined, they change over time. This always will be the case, and this is one of the many reasons politics always will be a part of sports.

How Are Rewards Distributed to Athletes and Other Organization Members?

The distribution of rewards is an issue at all levels of sport participation. Coaches, league administrators, and parents often must decide who will receive special commendations, certificates of accomplishment, or trophies. "Who gets what?" is a political question, and the answers are not always clear-cut. People discuss, debate, and sometimes argue heatedly over the issue of rewards. As the level of competition increases, so do the stakes associated with participation. At the highest levels of competition, the politics of rewards can involve massive amounts of money and status.

With the increased commercialization of sports, there have been longstanding, heated debates about how revenues should be distributed among sport organizations, organization officials, owners and promoters, athletes, and others connected with sports. As noted in chapter 11, the political processes associated with the distribution of revenues in commercial sports are complex and never-ending. Of course, these processes take various forms and come to different resolutions in different countries and in different sports.

Other debates revolve around questions such as these: Why should professional sport team owners make more money than the best players on their teams? What percentage should agents receive when they negotiate player contracts? Why should Olympic athletes not be paid for their participation when they collectively generate over a billion dollars during a Summer Olympics? Why should the IOC receive 33 percent of the revenues for the Olympic Games, when it does little other than award the games to a particular city and the members get wined and dined in lavish style in the process? Why should professional athletes who receive medals not be allowed during the medal ceremonies to wear warm-up suits made by the companies who pay them endorsement fees? Who owns the surfaces of athletes' bodies, and who may use them for commercial purposes? If athletes' bodies are used in expensive video games that sell millions of copies, how should the revenues from those games be allocated? Who owns the images of athletes (photograph and video) that are taken during major events such as the Olympics, and who decides how they will be used? These and hundreds of similar questions show that the "politics of rewards" is an integral part of sports.

Sometimes rewards involve status or prestige, rather than money. For example, in 1992 there was considerable debate in Japan over whether Akebono (formerly named Chad Rowan), an American sumo wrestler from Hawaii, should be voted into the rank of *yokozuna*, or grand champion, by the Yokozuna Promotion Council. Many Japanese people warned the council that, if such a prized honour were not reserved for native Japanese, Japan might lose control of a celebrated part of its own culture. When the Council voted to name Akebono as the sixty-fourth *yokozuna* in over three hundred years of sumo wrestling, many people voiced objections.

Similar political debates over status occur in connection with the selection of professional athletes for Halls of Fame and All-Star games. And, when combined with athlete migration, it may produce "odd" status awards such as the award for the Outstanding Canadian player in the CFL (an award separate from one for the league's Outstanding Player). Even youth teams have a "politics of status" connected with "the most improved player of the year," "the most valuable player," "the most dedicated player," and so on. When people agree on the players who should receive such awards and special status, they tend to forget that the selection process is political. It is only when they do not agree with the selection that they talk about politics in sports.

SUMMARY

HOW DO GOVERNMENTS AND GLOBALIZATION INFLUENCE SPORTS?

Sports and politics are inseparable. Sports do not exist in a cultural vacuum. They are integral parts of society and culture. Therefore, they influence and are influenced by political forces. Government involvement in sports is related to the need for sponsorship, organization, and facilities. The fact that sports are important parts of people's lives and that sports can be the scene for problems often leads to government regulations and controls. The form of government involvement in sports varies by society; however, when it occurs its purposes are to (1) safeguard the public order, (2) maintain fitness and physical abilities among citizens, (3) promote the prestige and power of a group, community, or nation, (4) promote a sense of identity, belonging, and unity among citizens, (5) reproduce values consistent with the dominant ideology, (6) increase support for political leaders and government structures, and (7) promote economic development.

The rules, policies, and funding priorities set by government officials and agencies reflect the political struggles among groups within any society. This does not mean that the same people always benefit when government involvement occurs, but it does mean that involvement seldom results in equal benefits for everyone. For example, when funds are given to elite sport programmes and the development and training of elite athletes, fewer funds are available for general-participation programmes. Of course, funding priorities could favour mass participation instead of elite sports, but the point is that the priorities themselves are subject to debate and negotiation. This political process is an inevitable part of sports.

History shows that groups with the greatest resources, organization, and outside support and with goals that fit most closely with the political positions of public officials are most likely to be favoured when government involvement in sports occurs. The groups least likely to be favoured are those that fail to understand the connection between sports and politics or that lack the resources to influence political processes effectively. As long as people believe the myth that sports and politics are unrelated, they remain at a disadvantage when rules and policies are made and funds are allocated.

The connection between sports and global political processes is complex. Ideally, sports bring nations together in contexts supportive of peace and friendship. Although this has occurred, the reality is that most nations have used sports to foster their own interests. In fact, displays of nationalism have been and continue to be common at international events. The Olympic Games are a good case in point. The major emphasis among many of those who promote and watch the Olympics is on national medal counts and expressions of national superiority.

Powerful transnational corporations have joined nation-states as major participants in global politics. As a result, sports have been used increasingly for economic as well as political

purposes. Nationalism and the promotion of national interests remain a part of global sports, but consumerism and the promotion of capitalist expansion have become more important since the end of the Cold War. Within the context of transnational relations, athletes and teams now are associated with corporate logos as well as with nation-states. Global sport events are now political *and* economic. They serve as settings for presenting numerous images and messages associated with the interests of nation-states and corporate sponsors. The dominant images and messages are consistent with the interests of the major corporate sponsors, and they tend to promote an ideology infused with capitalist themes of individualism, competition, productivity, and consumption.

Global political processes also are associated with other aspects of sports, such as the migration patterns of elite athletes and the production of sporting goods. Political issues are raised when athletes cross national borders to play their sports, as well as when transnational corporations produce sports equipment and clothing in labour-intensive poor nations and then sell those items in wealthy nations. We best can understand these and other issues associated with global political processes when we study sports on both global and local levels. This enables us to determine when sports involve reciprocal cultural exchanges leading to mutual understanding among people from different parts of the world and when they involve processes through which powerful nations and corporations exercise subtle influence over social life and political events in less powerful nations around the world. Research on this topic suggests that the role of sports in global political processes is very complex.

Politics is also part of the very structure and organization of sports. Political processes exist because people in sport organizations must answer questions about what qualifies as a sport, what the rules of a sport should be and how they should be enforced, who should organize and control sport events, where sport events should occur, who is eligible to participate, and how rewards will be distributed. This is the reason many sport organizations are described as governing bodies: they are the context for the political decision making that affects everyone connected with sports.

Overall, research on the connections between sports and social relations in local, national, and international contexts clearly shows that sports are inseparable from politics and political processes.

SUGGESTED READINGS

Bairner, A. 2001. *Sport, nationalism, and globalization: European and North American perspectives*. Albany: State University of New York Press (analysis of sports and national identity in the context of globalization; analyzes how people in Ireland, Scotland, Sweden, the United States, and Canada have dealt with global forces in connection with sports).

Houlihan, B. 1997. *Sport, policy, and politics: A comparative analysis*. London: Routledge (written from a public policy perspective; focuses on the motives and processes behind sport policies in Australia, Canada, Ireland, the United Kingdom, and the United States).

Jennings, A., and C. Sambrook. 2000. *The great Olympic swindle: When the world wanted its games back*. London: Simon and Schuster (the investigative journalist who published *The Lords of the Rings* in 1992 and *The New Lords of the Rings* in 1996 teams up with a financial writer to outline the operations of the IOC and describe the corruption and criminal actions of those who control Olympic sports; controversial and painstakingly researched).

Kruger, A., and J. Riordan, eds. 1996. *The story of worker sport*. Champaign, IL: Human Kinetics (a unique collection of papers highlighting the ways in which sports have been used for explicitly political purposes by workers in Europe, the former USSR, and Canada; the papers show how sports can be used to inspire a collective consciousness among people at various levels of social organization).

Lenskyj, H.J. 2000. *Inside the Olympic industry: Power, politics, and activism*. Albany: State University of New York Press. (critical analysis of the Olympics as a social phenomenon; emphasis on the internal politics of the games and the impact of the games on the cities and countries that host them).

Maguire, J. 1999. *Global sport: Identities, societies, civilizations*. Cambridge, England: Polity Press (detailed analyses of the complex global processes associated with sports; pulls together over a decade of the author's research on theoretical issues, athletes as global workers, the global sports industry, the global media-sport complex, and globalization and national identity issues).

Miller, T., ed. 2001. *Globalization and sport: Playing the world*. London: Sage (articles focus on how sports are implicated in general processes of cultural production and how sports play a central role in processes of globalization).

WEBSITE RESOURCES

Note: Websites often change. The following URLs were current when this book was printed. Please check our website (www.mcgrawhill.ca/college/coakley) for updates and additions.

www.mhhe.com/coakley8e (click on chapter 13 for information on sports and international relations, gift giving and the Olympic scandal, and politics and the Paralympic movement)

www.ucalgary.ca/library/ssportsite/ (start at this site to find information on "National Sport Structures and Organizations"; links to nearly every established organization in the world that has a website, including National Olympic Committees, government sport organizations around the world, and International Sport Federations)

www.olympic.org (International Olympic Committee; links to National Olympic committees around the world and information about the IOC and its programmes)

europa.eu.int/comm/sport/index_en.html (the site of *Sport and European Union* covers issues related to the development of sports through the European Union; contains information about the politics of coordinating national sport governing bodies with this international governing body)

www.pch.gc.ca/sportcanada (site for Sport Canada contains policy documents and links to all NSOs in Canada)

www.coa.ca (Canadian Olympic Committee site gives a clear indication of the commercialization of the Olympics with its prominent corporate sponsors; also has clear evidence of the COC's new focused high-performance policies, e.g., funding for potential medal winners)

www.sportmatters.ca (site for a sport lobbying group that grew out of the regional meetings during development of the new National Sport Policy; contains news, discussion, and critical commentary on sport policy developments)

www.sport.bc.ca; www.sportnovascotia.com (two examples of provincial sport sites, which give a sense of the amount of sport activity, the number of sport organizations, and the significance of the provincial level in Canadian sport development; check the site for your own province/territory)

http://utenti.lycos.it/dossierisarenas/golf.htm (site for the Global Anti-Golf Movement contains the new manifesto and clippings about struggles over the development of golf courses around the world)

www.iwg-gti.org (International Working Group on Women and Sport; contains information on programs, policy issues, and problems faced by girls and women in nearly 100 countries; information reveals different patterns of government involvement, as well as the cultural issues that influence programmes, policies, and problems; key links to other international sport organizations)

www.ajennings.8m.com (Andrew Jennings, an investigative journalist, has studied the IOC and various national Olympic committees for over a dozen years; this site highlights his work and the work of others who have written articles on the politics and corruption in elite international sports)

www.aafla.com (The Amateur Athletic Foundation in the United States has an outstanding collection of historical and political information about sports, especially international sports; go to "Sports Library")

http://globalmarch.org/index.html (site for The Global March Against Child Labour, an international movement based in India and focused on eliminating exploitive work that condemns millions of children to lives of servitude and suffering; link to its 2002 World Cup project and photos of children in India and Pakistan sewing soccer balls, some with "Child Free Labour" labels on them)

www.nikewages.org (site of *Educating for Justice* formed by former college students who began a grass-roots campaign to end social injustice; its *Nike Corporate Accountability Campaign* is explained at this site)

High school curling photo (*St. Thomas Times Journal*)

Sports in High School and University

Do interscholastic sport programmes contribute to education?

The primary reason…for the existence of school sport is the educational value it imparts to the students.

> —**Colin Hood, executive director, Ontario Federation of School Athletic Associations (1999)**

[G]rowing demands for sophisticated administration and technical programs tend to be beyond the capacity of dedicated volunteers and…the universities and indeed all the educational system are the natural delivery systems for sport in Canada.

> —**Iona Campagnolo, Minister of State for Fitness and Amateur Sport (1977)**

 Online Learning Centre Resources

Visit *Sports in Society's* Online Learning Centre at **www.mcgrawhill.ca/college/coakley** for additional information and study material for this chapter.

The emergence of modern organized sports is closely tied to education in the U.K., the Commonwealth, and North America. However, few schools outside these countries and parts of Japan sponsor and fund interschool sport programmes. Organized sports for adolescents and young adults in most developed countries are tied to community-based athletic clubs funded by members or a combination of public and private sources.

Interscholastic sports have become an accepted and important part of Canadian high schools, colleges, and universities. The term *interscholastic* is used here to refer in a broad sense to organized competitive sports carried out between educational institutions. In general, Canada has three levels of competition:

- Interschool sports (usually between high schools, although competitions are often organized between junior high/middle schools and elementary schools) governed by the Canadian School Sport Federation and ten provincial schools athletic associations;
- Intercollegiate sports (between community colleges and, in Quebec, CEGEPs) governed by the Canadian Colleges Athletic Association and five regional conferences (Atlantic, Quebec, Ontario, Alberta [includes Saskatchewan], and B.C.);
- Interuniversity sports governed by Canadian Interuniversity Sport and four regional conferences (Atlantic, Quebec, Ontario, and Canada West).[1]

There are no essential differences between private and public institutions with regard to interscholastic sports, except that many of the more established private schools have a clear expectation that their students and staff will be involved in extracurricular activities.

Interscholastic sports are distinguished from *intramural* sports, played within an educational institution and organized in various ways. University intramural programmes may have teams organized to represent residences, academic departments, or even ethnocultural communities, as well as teams organized on a more *ad hoc* basis. School intramurals, if they exist at all, are often organized on an ad hoc basis by the student athletic association, although some schools (often private schools) echo the British "house" system in which the whole school is divided into four (usually) named houses that compete against one another in a variety of ways, including sports. There are many variations on these forms of intramural organization. We know of one Ontario elementary school that had a dynamic lunchtime activity programme (organized by an itinerant physical education teacher) in which all the teams were named after vegetables—school announcements would sound like this: "In the gym at lunchtime today, the 'Potatoes' will be playing the 'Cauliflowers,' and the 'Zucchinis' will be playing the 'Carrots' at broomball." The Canadian Intramural Recreation Association (CIRA), which, in 2003, became part of the Canadian Association for Health, Physical Education, Recreation and Dance (CAHPERD), provides leadership in school intramural sports, while many Canadian universities are affiliated with the U.S.-based National Intramural-Recreational Sports Association (NIRSA).

This chapter explores issues related to interscholastic sports, and is organized around five major questions:

1. How do interscholastic sport programmes in Canada compare with those in the United States?
2. What are the arguments for and against interscholastic sports?
3. How are interscholastic sport programmes related to the educational experiences of student-athletes and other students in high schools and universities?

---

[1] This chapter focuses on universities and schools; colleges are excluded because we are not aware of any research on college sports and physical activity in Canada.

4. What effects do interscholastic programmes have for high schools and universities as educational organizations?
5. What are the major problems associated with high school and university sport programmes, and how might they be solved?

COMPARISON BETWEEN CANADIAN AND U.S. INTERSCHOLASTIC SPORTS[2]

Perhaps more than any other aspect of Canadian sports, interscholastic sports, and particularly interuniversity sports, stand in relation to and in comparison with the U.S. system of inter-scholastic sports. While there are striking similarities between the two systems, the differences have become the object of focus. The differences are primarily a question of scale. For example, in many parts of the U.S., high school sports—especially sports such as football and (boys') basketball—are seen as a significant part of the development system for U.S. interuniversity sports. High schools may have an intense focus on basketball, for example, or, in states such as Texas, Michigan, and Ohio, on football. Some of the U.S. programmes may have full-time coaches—we are not aware of any full-time teacher-coaches in Canada. Large paying crowds may attend the games, and a great many school resources are focused on specific (usually male) teams (cf., Foley, 1990; Grey, 1992). This so-called "hothousing" system certainly produces athletic excellence, but critics suggest that this focused excellence is achieved at the cost of failing to provide interschool sport experiences for many other students in a variety of sports (Grey, 1992). While some athletes, and their coaches, at Canadian high schools may have a similar focus in terms of attempting to achieve a

U.S. university scholarship or, increasingly, a Canadian university scholarship, in general, Canadian schools seem to offer a greater diversity of sports and a less intense level of competition. Students may be encouraged to play several sports, and teacher-coaches may encourage individuals who are unsure of their athletic abilities to participate on teams.

Interuniversity sports represent even more of a contrast in terms of scale. While many U.S. universities have interuniversity sport programmes on a scale quite similar to that in Canada, the NCAA (National Collegiate Athletic Association) Division I programmes tend to command attention in Canada, especially in sports such as football, basketball, and, to a lesser extent, hockey. With the widespread availability of U.S. networks on Canadian television, Canadians are exposed to network broadcasts of Division I football and basketball games, including the New Year's Day bowl games in football and the Final Four championships in basketball. Many Canadians also bet on the outcomes of those games. However, the similarity between the two systems is most evident at the National Association of Intercollegiate Athletics (NAIA) level, which is comprised of some 350 small universities in the U.S. Cross-border competitions occur with CIS universities, mostly in Alberta and British Columbia but also other Canadian universities such as Windsor and Laval. These competitions are often in sports (e.g., tennis, softball) that do not have CIS national championships. Cross-border tournaments and exhibition games also extend beyond the NAIA level, but there are no formal arrangements between CIS and the NCAA.

The vast majority of research on interscholastic sport issues has been carried out in the United States—an indication of the concerns associated with the far greater investment in and intensity of some U.S. programmes. The majority of research concerns the benefits of interscholastic sports, and they have produced equivocal results. Some studies show clear benefits, while others

---

[2] For more details on the U.S. system of interscholastic sports, particularly interuniversity, and a review of the research and problems, see the Online Learning Centre.

find no such benefits and point to actual negative aspects of the programmes. The majority of studies also have the same concerns as this chapter—to determine whether there are educational benefits resulting from interscholastic sports. Studies of equity in interscholastic sports are also indirectly concerned with educational benefits. In Canada, a few studies in the 1970s and 1980s addressed similar issues to the U.S. studies, but because there were no significant issues evident in Canadian interscholastic sports, the line of research was dropped. More recently, some research has been concerned with determining how to maintain interschool sports in the face of significant budget cuts to education and poor relations between teachers and provincial governments. No research has yet been carried out on the growing rift in Canadian interuniversity sports over the issue of scholarships.

The comparison between the two systems is evident throughout this chapter. However, because of the pervasiveness and presumed knowledge of the NCAA Division I system in Canada; because comparisons with, and the attractions of, that system in terms of producing athletic excellence and revenue have resulted in a current polarization of Canadian interuniversity sports (see the section, "Interuniversity Sports: Problems and Recommendations," near the end of this chapter); and because most readers of this book are students at Canadian universities, we conclude this section with an examination of the development and organization of organized sports in Canadian universities.

From 1906 to 1965, the original Canadian Interuniversity Athletic Union (CIAU), which changed its name to Canadian Interuniversity Sport (CIS) in 2001, was known as CIAU Central; it involved only male sports in universities from Ontario and Quebec. During that period, other regional university athletic associations were formed in western Canada and in the Maritimes, and CIAU Central provided common rules and regulations. Women's regional university athletic associations were also developed.

The rapid growth of universities, and university athletics, in Canada after World War II saw CIAU Central grow to nineteen universities, "each of which had diverse enrolment, philosophy [sic], and practices both academically and athletically"; this collapsed in 1955 because "there was no forum…to adjudicate conflicts within the organization" (www.cisport.ca). The various regional university athletic associations were brought together under a pan-Canadian CIAU formed in 1961. The women's university athletic associations came together to form the Canadian Women's Intercollegiate Athletic Union in 1969. The two organizations amalgamated under the CIAU in 1978.

The primary purpose of the CIAU, and the former CIAU Central, was to ensure standardized rules of play, determine eligibility to play, and organize championship tournaments. However, when the first pan-Canadian CIAU was organized in 1961, it was in part a response to:

- A recognized need for the formulation of consistent and acceptable sport rules and regulations for all teams represented at national championships;
- Mutually beneficial agreements with other national sport organizations (NSOs);
- Coordination of national and international competition; and
- A need to assist in developing leadership and citizenship of athletic staff (www.cisport.ca).

The re-formation of the CIAU coincided with the passage of Bill C-131, the 1961 Fitness and Amateur Sport Act, which was to have a major impact on Canadian sports, and which also came to have implications for university athletics. In return for some federal funding to the CIAU, and its relocation to the National Sport Centre in Ottawa (Gloucester) in the 1970s, university athletics became implicated in the development of Canada's high-performance sport system. As a part of the professionalization of that system, the Minister of State for Fitness and Amateur Sport, Iona Campagnolo (1977) declared that "growing demands for sophisticated administration and technical programs tend to be beyond the capacity of dedicated volunteers and...the universities and indeed all the educational system are the natural delivery systems for sport in Canada." Federal financial commitments to the CIAU increased in the 1970s to support travel equalization (for example, there are a great many more travel costs associated with competing in western Canada in comparison to Ontario university athletics), national championship travel, and involvement in the World University Games. As federal budgets for sports began to decline, especially in the 1990s, the CIAU shifted to a more corporate basis, seeking sponsorships and negotiating television contracts for university sports (see the direct link between the CIS-SIC website and TSN-RDS). The change in name from CIAU to CIS was intended to be more appealing for marketing purposes. Most recently, the CIS has been involved in establishing gender equity and negotiating the terms and conditions of awarding athletic scholarships across Canada. CIS also mandates performance-enhancing-drug education for all interuniversity athletes in Canada and carries out random drug testing.

While the structure of the CIS is quite similar to other national sport organizations and multi-sport organizations (MSOs) in terms of a voluntary board of directors and a paid staff housed at a central office in Ottawa, the directors of this MSO are somewhat different in that they are all salaried directors (e.g., managers, coordinators) of athletics at their respective Canadian universities. Thus, they function somewhat like a professional association, and all Canadian directors of athletics are involved in the annual general meetings of CIS. In addition to the CIS main office in Ottawa, the CIS International Programs Office is housed at the University of Alberta, and the Vanier Cup (national university football championships) Office is in Toronto. Because the CIS represents university athletics, there are no individual members—the CIS represents forty-nine Canadian universities organized into the four conferences.

According to the CIS website, over 12,000 athletes participate in the eleven sports that have national championships—women only in rugby and field hockey, men only in football, and eight sports for both men and women (www.cisport.ca).

The peak interest in interuniversity sport in Canada seems to have been in the 1950s and 1960s. Associated with the rapid growth of universities at that time, and a significant increase in student numbers, crowds filled the stadia and arenas for games. Competition was especially intense between the four oldest universities in CIAU Central—McGill, Queen's, Toronto, and Western Ontario. Large numbers of students would travel by train to away football games, and an informant recently told us that, for males at the University of Toronto, the single best way to get a date was to obtain a hard-to-find pair of tickets for a Varsity Blues hockey game. By the late 1960s, the counterculture with its critique of authoritarianism, and the anti-(Vietnam) war movement was widespread on university campuses in Canada. Interuniversity sports represented a "school spirit" that was no longer fashionable, and they were seen as a part of the "establishment." Although participation did not decline, the crowds did and it was no longer possible to fill the 20,000 seats at the University of Toronto's Varsity Stadium or the 16,000 seats at McGill University's Molson Stadium on Saturday afternoons in the fall. Interestingly, although the same movements and changes were evident on U.S. university campuses, they had little impact on interuniversity sports.

Some sports on some campuses (e.g., Bishop's University football) were able to retain their spectators, but the long decline continued until the 1990s. Recently, there has been a growing interest. Participation has continued to grow, with new sports being added to the schedules, and gender-equity requirements creating new opportunities and new teams for female student-athletes. Television contracts to broadcast interuniversity games, and well-publicized national championships in football and men's basketball, have revived interest in interuniversity sports, and there have even been some surprises, such as the rapid recent growth of participation and interest in football at francophone universities in Quebec. However, this growing interest has raised some difficult issues about scholarships that are polarizing Canadian universities (see the section, "Interuniversity Sports: Problems and Recommendations," near the end of this chapter).

ARGUMENTS FOR AND AGAINST INTERSCHOLASTIC SPORTS

Most people in Canada take interscholastic sports for granted. The programmes are an expected part of life at school and university. However, budget cutbacks and a few problems in certain high school and university programmes (for example, students extending their high school careers in order to play sports, some incidents of crowd violence at Toronto high school basketball games, and some hazing incidents in university sports) have raised questions about how sports are related to educational goals and the development of young people. Responses to these questions are varied. Programme supporters claim that interscholastic sports support the educational mission of schools and universities, while critics claim that they interfere with that mission. The main points made on both sides of this debate are summarized in table 14.1.

When people enter this debate, they often exaggerate the benefits or the problems associated with interscholastic sport programmes. Supporters emphasize glowing success stories, critics emphasize cases of excess and abuse, and some have suggested that other agencies (e.g., community minor sports programmes) should be given the responsibility of organizing competitive sports for young people. The most accurate descriptions probably lie somewhere in between. Nonetheless, both the supporters and the critics call attention to many of the important issues in the relationship between sports and education. This chapter focuses on some of those issues.

INTERSCHOOL SPORTS AND THE EXPERIENCES OF HIGH SCHOOL STUDENTS

Do interschool sport programmes affect the educational and developmental experiences of high school students? This question is difficult to answer. Education and development occur in connection with many activities and relationships. Even though sport programmes are very important in some schools and for some students, they constitute only one of many potentially influential experiences. Quantitative research on this issue, usually based on functionalist theory, has focused primarily on the characteristics of student-athletes and how they compare with the characteristics of other students. Qualitative research, often guided by interactionist and critical theories, has focused on how interschool sports are connected with the overall school-based culture that exists among high school students.

High School Student-Athletes

Studies carried out in the U.S. have shown consistently that, when compared with students who do not play interschool sports, high school athletes, *as a group*, generally have better grades, more positive attitudes toward school, more interest in continuing their education after graduation, and a slightly better educational achievement rate (see Miracle and Rees, 1994; Rees and Miracle, 2000). These differences usually have been modest, and it has been difficult for researchers to separate the effects of sport participation from the effects of social class, family background, support from friends, and other factors related to educational attitudes, performance, and grades. Membership on a school team is a valued source of status in most U.S.

Table 14.1   Popular arguments for and against interscholastic sports

Arguments For	Arguments Against
1. They involve students in school activities and increase interest in academic activities. 2. They build the self-esteem, responsibility, achievement orientation, and teamwork skills required for occupational success. 3. They provide fitness training and stimulate interest in physical activities among all students in the school/university. 4. They generate the spirit and unity necessary to support the school/university. 5. They promote parental, alumni, and community support for all school/university programmes. 6. They give students opportunities to develop and display skills in activities valued in the society at large and to receive rewards for their athletic skills. 7. They are an important part of non-classroom education, creating opportunities for less formal relationships with teacher-coaches outside the classroom and providing other educational, learning, and leadership opportunities.	1. They distract students' attention from academic activities. 2. They perpetuate dependence, conformity, and a power and performance orientation that is no longer appropriate in postindustrial society. 3. They turn most students into spectators and cause too many serious injuries to student-athletes. 4. They create a superficial, transitory spirit, which has nothing to do with educational goals. 5. They deprive educational programmes of resources, facilities, staff, and community support. 6. They create strong pressure on student-athletes and can support a hierarchical status system in which student-athletes may be given excessive privilege. 7. At a time of declining public sector budgets that have seriously affected public education, it is difficult to justify public expenditure on interscholastic sports when more "core" educational programmes are suffering.

schools, and it seems to go hand in hand with positive educational experiences for some students, reduced dropout rates, and increased identification with the school (Marsh, 1993; McNeal, 1995). However, research has not told us what it is about sport participation that causes those positive experiences.

One of the few Canadian studies to attempt to explain one of these U.S. findings—the effects of high school sport participation on academic achievement—is now over thirty years old (Jerome and Phillips, 1971). The authors tested three explanations:

- The "spill-over" thesis, which suggests that "there is a transfer of positive work habits, attitudes, and values from sport to school work" (p. 18); this is certainly the most widely known explanation, but, like the view discussed in chapter 4 that sports are character-building, no evidence exists that sport participation in and of itself causes such positive changes (Miracle and Rees, 1994)

- The "selection" thesis, that is, "the better, more pro-school students try out for and are selected to membership on school teams" (p. 18)

- The "differential school experiences" of athletes and non-athletes thesis, that is, "athletes are more visible, acquire increased status, and receive more encouragement from school personnel than do non-athletes" (p. 18)

Jerome and Phillips reviewed several Canadian studies from the 1960s, as well as Jerome's own study that was being carried out during that time in Sudbury, Ontario. They found that the results seemed to contradict the relatively consistent U.S. findings. There was no real evidence of a relationship between academic achievement and athletic participation. They argued that if the "spill-over" and/or "selection" explanations were valid, then evidence of the relationship between participation on high school teams and academic achievement would be found in both Canada and the United States. In other words, the positive transfer of work habits, attitudes, and values should occur in whichever country a student-athlete participated, and better students would try out for, and be selected to, school teams regardless of the country. Therefore, they argued, the differences in findings between the two countries must be accounted for by the higher status of, and greater resources used for, school sports in the United States; that is, student-athletes in U.S. high schools had a "differential (and more positive) school experience" from non-athletes.

While the "differential school experience" thesis makes intuitive sense when high school sports in the two countries are compared, Jerome and Phillips' assumptions about the "selection" thesis are not necessarily valid. It is entirely possible that Canadian teacher-coaches could have selected athletes on the basis of athletic ability rather than on other characteristics such as conformity or pro-school attitude. And the studies reviewed by Jerome and Phillips were not focused enough to suggest that there are significant differences between Canadian and U.S. student-athletes in terms of academic achievement and other positive characteristics. Perhaps the best explanation combines the "selection" thesis with the possibility that students involved in high school sports and other extracurricular activities have a different and more positive school experience than those not involved—not the least because of their usually positive interactions with teachers in non-classroom settings.

In fact, selection can lead to differential school experiences, and the most logical explanation for differences between athletes and other students seems to be that interschool

sports, like other extracurricular activities, attract students who already have the characteristics associated with academic and social success in high school. Most studies have not been able to test this explanation, because the researchers do not actually follow students during their high school careers to keep track of how and why changes occur in their lives. Usually, the studies simply report information collected from students at one point in time and then compare students who play on sport teams with students who do not. This makes it impossible for researchers to say whether playing school sports really changes people or whether students who try out for teams, are selected by coaches, and choose to remain on teams are simply different from other students *before* they become student-athletes. The mere fact that young people grow and develop during the same years that they play on school teams does not mean that sport participation *causes* the growth and development. After all, fourteen- to eighteen-year-olds grow and develop in many ways whether they play school sports or do other things. Most studies do not distinguish among all the activities and experiences that might explain growth and development among students.

Fortunately, some U.S. quantitative studies have followed students over time and have measured changes in their lives. These studies suggest that young people who play on varsity sport teams are more likely to come from *economically privileged* backgrounds and have *above-average* cognitive abilities, self-esteem, and academic performance records, including grades and test scores (Fejgin, 1994; Melnick et al., 1988; Rees et al., 1990; Spreitzer, 1995). In other words, students who try out for teams, make teams, and stay on teams often are different in certain ways from other students *before* they become high school athletes.

This type of *selection-in process* is common in most extracurricular activities, not just sports. Students who choose to participate in official, school-sponsored activities tend to be slightly different from other students. These differences are greatest in activities in which student self-selection is combined with formal tryouts, in which teachers or teacher-coaches select students for participation. In the case of school sports, this self-selection and selection by coach process is especially powerful, because it is an extension of a long-term selection-in process, which begins in youth sports and continues through middle school.

Research in the U.S. also suggests that students who play interschool sports for three years during high school are different from those who are cut from or quit teams. Those who are cut or quit are more likely to come from *less advantaged* economic backgrounds and have *lower* cognitive abilities, *lower* self-esteem, and *lower* grades than those who remain on teams (Spreitzer, 1995). Furthermore, student-athletes who have failing grades are usually declared ineligible and then become nonathletes. This guarantees that nonathletes have lower grades when researchers do studies in high schools and compare the grades of athletes and nonathletes! Overall, these findings suggest that, in addition to a *selection-in process*, there also is a complex *filtering-out process* that occurs in interschool sports. These processes combine to influence who does and who does not play.

Further complicating our efforts to learn about the effects of playing high school sports is the fact that many students on teams also participate in other extracurricular activities. Determining whether changes in their lives are due to playing sports or to participating in other activities, such as working on the yearbook, being in a student club or student government, involvement in student theatre or music, or doing community service, is nearly impossible.

Tracking the influence of sport participation in a person's adult life and occupational career is even more challenging. The meanings people give to participation change over time and vary with social and cultural forces related to gender, race and ethnicity, and social class. For

example, information about how many CEOs of Fortune 500 companies played one or more high school sports tells us nothing about the effects of sport participation. The occupational success of these people, most of whom are white men, is related strongly to their family backgrounds, social networks, and the gender and ethnic relations, which have been characteristic in wealthy societies during the past fifty years. Of course, this does not mean that they have not worked hard or that sport participation is irrelevant to who they are and what they do, but the importance of playing sports cannot be understood apart from these other factors.

Several Canadian studies shed light on both of these issues—the effects of involvement in sports and other extracurricular activities, and tracking changes into adult life—by avoiding the traditional problem of collecting data at only one point in time. Norman Okihiro (1984), now a sociologist at Mount Saint Vincent University in Nova Scotia, surveyed over 1,500 Ontario grade 12 students in 1973, and contacted them again in 1979. The study considered a number of factors, including sports and other aspects of extracurricular involvement, grades, career aspirations, actual careers, etc. Okihiro found that both "athletic and social involvement in extracurricular activities play an important role in the process of educational and early job attainment. High school involvement, particularly athletic involvement, raises college expectations…" (p. 346).

However, it is interesting to note that there were no significant differences between those who were involved in sports and other extracurricular activities, and those who were not, in terms of the prestige of their jobs or their income six years later; but, those who were involved in high school were much more likely to be in jobs that involved spending time with people, and to have a self-concept as active persons (those who were active in high school were also likely to be active six years later). Okihiro pointed out that "the major influence of athletic and social involvement on educational and occupational outcomes has something to do with a facility and preference for dealing with people" (p. 346), and although this had not translated into greater job prestige and income after six years, he recognized that such qualities would be a long-term career benefit in the new economy. While Okihiro's findings are similar to those in the U.S., they are more reliable in that they show a clear effect of participation over time.

In a later development of Okihiro's work, a series of studies by Jim Curtis (University of Waterloo), Bill McTeer (Wilfrid Laurier University), and Phil White (McMaster University) employs Bourdieu's framework regarding "capital." Bourdieu argues that an important part of socialization is the acquisition of various forms of "capital" that are of value in later life. Curtis, et al. (1999), found that Canadians involved in school sports were more likely to participate in sports in later life; and Curtis, et al. (2003), found that Canadians who participated in school sports "have higher annual incomes as adults than those who did not participate" (p. 60). They interpret these results in terms of the acquisition, not only of economic capital, but also of physical, social and cultural capital.[3] These studies reaffirm Okihiro's (1984) conclusion:

> To the extent that high school athletic and social [extracurricular] participation carry over into adult activities, add enjoyment to our lives, and constitute potential occupational career assets, the prognosis on their value is favourable. This study suggests that the saying, "It's not the winning that counts, but playing the game," may have more sociological significance than one might expect (p. 347).

The operation of social and cultural forces has also been illustrated in U.S. data on the sexual

---

[3] An earlier study by White and McTeer (1990) found some evidence of a relationship between school sport participation and the development of "cultural capital." Other research has shown clear relationships between cultural capital and social class, and this needs further research in sports.

behaviour of high school students. Interviews with 611 fifteen- to-eighteen-year-old students in New York State indicated that the young women who played varsity sports had *lower* rates of sexual activity (fewer sex partners, lower frequency of intercourse, and later initiation of sexual activity) than their female counterparts who did not play sports (Miller et al., 1998, 1999). However, the young men who played sports had *higher* rates of sexual activity than their male counterparts who did not play sports. The authors suggest that playing on school teams enhances the social status of both young women and men. This gives them more control over the dynamics of their relationships and enables them to regulate sexual activity on their own terms. To the extent that there are control issues that favour males in adolescent sexual relationships, young women may use increased control to resist sexual relationships that may be exploitive, while young men may use their control to gain sexual favours from young women. Therefore, sport participation may affect behaviours and relationships, but we must understand cultural issues and the dynamics of social relations in order to explain how this occurs. Sport participation cannot be understood apart from social meaning, and social meaning is created in a real world, where perceptions of gender, skin colour, sexuality, social class, and other factors have real consequences in people's lives (Godley, 1999a; Hanson and Kraus, 1999).

What We Have Learned from Research What does research tell us about interscholastic sports and the experiences of young people?

1. We should be careful when generalizing about the educational value of interschool sports. Playing school sports does not produce systematic negative effects, but neither does it automatically change high school students in positive ways, making them significantly different from other high school students. Usually, those who try out for teams, are selected by coaches, and stay on

teams for more than one year are somewhat different from other students before they put on their uniforms. Therefore, one-time statistical comparisons between so-called athletes and nonathletes tell us little about the actual experiences of playing sports and how they affect the lives of people.

2. If we want to learn about the effect of interschool sports in the lives of high school students, we must do long-term studies of the overall lives of students, not just their sport lives. Growth and development occur in connection with many experiences—some inside the school and some outside. Unless we know about young people's lives in general, we cannot claim that sport participation is more influential than working at a part-time job, joining the debate team, writing for the school newspaper, or caring for younger brothers and sisters when it comes to overall growth and development.

3. We should examine how the educational lives of student-athletes might be different from the lives of other students. Do those who play sports receive more academic support and encouragement from family, friends, and teachers? Do teachers evaluate them differently? Do they make different academic decisions than other students? How does the issue of eligibility affect those decisions? Do those who play sports sometimes receive privileges that change how they view their schools and their education? Does everyone who plays sports receive similar favourable treatment? If a student participates in a sport outside of school, such as motocross racing, or even community youth sports, does that have the same consequences as playing on a high-profile basketball team?

4. We should study the effect of school sports on the larger student culture that exists in high schools. It may be that the social importance of sports rests in how they are connected with the dynamics of social relations in an entire school. It would seem

to be a higher priority to study this possibility than to focus only on the students who try out for and make teams.

Student Culture in High Schools

Sociologists in the U.S. have long recognized that interschool sports are among the most important social activities sponsored by high schools (Rees and Miracle, 2001). Being a student-athlete may bring a student prestige among peers, formal rewards in the school, and recognition from teachers, administrators, and even people in the community. Athletes, especially males in high-profile sports, may be accorded recognition that enhances their popularity in student culture.

From a sociological perspective, it is important to ask what sports contribute to student culture in a high school. Because these sports and sport events are socially significant activities in the lives of many students, they have the potential to influence students' values and behaviours. For example, do they influence how students evaluate one another or how they think about social life and social relations?

Sports and Popularity For many years, student culture in the U.S. was studied simply in terms of the factors that high school students use to determine popularity. Research usually found that male students wished they could be remembered as "athletic stars" in high schools, while female students wished to be remembered as "brilliant students" *or* "the most popular." These studies were all prompted by James Coleman's classic study of *The Adolescent Society* (1961), in which male high school students in the U.S. were found to value athletics over academics. So popular was this type of research during the 1960s that it even produced a Canadian example. David Friesen (1967) surveyed high school students in cities across Canada, hypothesizing that he would find similar results to the U.S. studies. He was therefore surprised to

Sport participation often gives young women opportunities to establish personal and social identities based on skills respected by peers and the community at large. However, playing sports, for girls such as these New Brunswick field hockey players, may not bring as much popularity to girls in high schools as it does to boys. (CP/*Moncton Times & Transcript*/Viktor Pivovarov)

find that Canadian students did not fit what he assumed was a North American stereotype. High school boys ranked academics over athletics and popularity, while high school girls ranked academics over popularity and athletics.

More recent research indicates that many young men in high school prefer to be known as "scholar-athletes," while young women prefer to be known as "scholars" *and* "members of the leading social group" (Chandler and Goldberg, 1990). Therefore, the link between being popular and being an athlete has traditionally been stronger for male students than for female students. When it comes to popularity for high school women, being in the in-group is crucial, and being an athlete does not by itself put a female student in the in-group.

What do these research findings mean? Are young men in the U.S. more concerned with being athletes than with being scholars? Are young women unconcerned about sports? The answer to both these questions is no. In fact, most high school students *are* concerned with academic achievement. They are aware of the importance of going to college or university, and their parents usually remind them regularly of how important school should be in their lives. However, in addition to academic achievement, high school students in both Canada and the U.S. are concerned with four things: (1) social acceptance, (2) personal autonomy, (3) sexual identity, and (4) growth into adults. They want to be popular enough to fit in with peers and have friends they can depend on; they want opportunities to control their lives; they strive to feel secure about their own sexual identity; and they want to show others that they are mature enough to be taken seriously.

This means that the *social* lives of adolescents revolve around a wide range of important factors. Because males and females in North America are still treated and evaluated in different ways, adolescents use different strategies for seeking acceptance, autonomy, sexual development, and recognition as young adults. As things are now, sport participation is an important basis for popularity for some young men, as long as they do not completely neglect their academic lives. In fact, young men who do not act tough may be marginalized in student culture, so they may put a premium on playing sports, especially contact sports (Eder, 1995).

Sport participation is also important for young women, but being an athlete usually must be combined with other things for a young woman to be popular within the student cultures of most high schools. Young women do not have to be traditionally feminine to be popular, but they usually must show they are something other than tough, competitive athletes; physical attractiveness remains a key factor for a young woman's popularity in student culture, whether she plays sports or not (Eder, 1995). Thus, it seems that the visibility and status gained by high school athletes have different implications for young men than for young women in high school student culture.

Additional Effects of High School Sports

In one sense, everything that we do and experience (both positive and negative) is "educational"—we learn from it, and it adds to who we are as human beings. Thus, interschool sports are always "educational" in a general sense. However, since school sports are frequently justified in terms of their contribution to the educational mission of schools in a more specific sense, we have to conclude that, in and of themselves, sports are not educational. However, if sports are organized and played in certain ways, they do support educational goals, and represent an important component of experiential education, or, in other words, education outside the classroom. For example, when sports are organized so that young people are taken seriously as human beings and valued by those who are important in their lives, sport participation can contribute to their educational development (Mahiri, 1998). However, if school sports are organized in ways that lead young people to think that adults are controlling them for their own purposes, they are developmental dead ends, and students, whether they play sports or not, will become cynical about school and society. In the best case scenarios here, student-athletes will develop strategies of resistance to controlling adults.

Being Noticed and Rewarded Adolescents need to be integral participants in their schools. They need a range of opportunities to develop and display competence in settings where they are noticed and rewarded. They also need chances to prove they are on their way to becoming valued adults in their communities. If interschool sports and other school activities are organized to do these things, they will contribute to education and development, because students will be noticed in positive ways and will be more likely to identify with the school and its educational mission.

Attracting Adult Advocates Interschool sports also are valuable if they provide young people with opportunities to meet adults who can serve as advocates in their lives. This is especially important in schools located in low-income and impoverished areas, such as some inner-city areas or some native reserves, where young people are in serious need of adult advocates who have the resources to facilitate overall development. Sports can give these young people chances to be noticed for something good, rather than for how "bad" they are in the school hallways or on the streets. When adult advocates are scarce in the local neighbourhood, sports can provide young people with the "hook-ups" they need to gain access to opportunities that other young people take for granted.

Providing Occasions for Learning Sports also can be valuable educationally if teacher-coaches take them seriously as learning experiences (Mahiri, 1998). For example, in the U.S., Jomills Braddock and his colleagues (1991) have studied the importance of sports to young black males and have argued that sports in middle schools could be used to spark a commitment to education among many young people ready to give up on classroom learning by the time they are seventh- or eighth-graders. Carl James (1995, 2003), of York University, has shown that for some African-Canadian high school students, high school sport participation provides exactly the experiences that are usually claimed for all students—opportunities to extend one's circle of friends and interact with teachers in non-classroom settings, and increased desire and confidence to achieve academically.

Sports may be used as part of a larger process of giving students responsibility, including them in activities that will help them develop skills, rewarding them for their competence, and connecting them with adults who can exert positive influence in their lives.

The notion of deliberately designing sports to give students responsibility has been emphasized in applied research on moral and social development (Martinek and Hellison, 1997; Shields and Bredemeier, 1995). This research also suggests that, unless adult leaders take care, sport participation may take forms that actually subvert moral development and responsibility among young people. For example, some high school student-athletes may feel that playing sports is more important than anything they do and that they actually deserve special treatment, even if they are not responsible about their schoolwork and even if they fail to follow rules that other students are expected to follow. When this occurs, sports do not provide occasions for learning anything of value.

School Sports and Ideology Research suggests that the most important social consequences of interschool sports may be their effects on ideas about social life and social relations, rather than their effects on grades, on attitudes toward school, or on student popularity. Sports usually have a vocabulary that emphasizes individualism and competition, and they may encourage certain views about gender, race, and social class relations. As we noted in chapter 4, many people believe that "the road to the board room leads through the locker room," and some of the arguments for gender equity in sports are based on the idea that participation will give girls the same ideas, attitudes, and "advantages" that were for so long exclusively for boys.

INTERUNIVERSITY SPORTS AND THE EXPERIENCES OF STUDENTS

Does interuniversity sport participation affect the educational and developmental experiences of university athletes? It seems that this question is only asked in Canada when budget cuts are being considered for athletic programmes. For the most part, interuniversity sports are a normal, but not highly significant part of student life. There are no parallels with the highly-publicized U.S. universities where, in "big time" sport programmes that are like professional sport cartels in every way except the age and income of the players, there is a widespread failure to take the education of student-athletes seriously. However, there are parallels with other levels of university sport in the U.S., such as the NAIA level of competition. CIS eligibility regulations determine that "[a]ll athletes must be demonstrating progress towards furthering their education and maintaining academic success." Student-athletes take at least nine credit hours during the term in which they are competing, and they must achieve passing grades in at least three full/six half (eighteen credit hours) courses in a year. For the most part, student-athletes in Canada are precisely that—students first and athletes second (or equal first). Thus, there is very little research in Canada on the educational and developmental experiences of university athletes. Surprisingly, since there is frequently concern about the conflict between athletics and academics, research on this issue is also relatively scarce in the United States.

The Diversity of Student-Athlete Experiences

In the U.S., many entertainment-oriented interuniversity sport teams are characterized by chronic problems, shamefully low graduation rates, and hypocrisy when it comes to education.[4] However, there are many other teams in

---

[4] A number of Canadian students attending U.S. universities on athletics scholarships have experienced these conditions. Little research has been conducted on the experiences of Canadian student-athletes in the U.S., and an important study may compare the experiences of those who return to Canada after one or two years with those who stay to complete their scholarship eligibility.

The Vanier Cup is one of the biggest events on the interuniversity sport calendar in Canada. In order to develop the media and sponsorship opportunities, CIS maintains an office in Toronto exclusively for the Vanier Cup. Here, the Saint Mary's Huskies celebrate their victory at the SkyDome. (CP/Frank Gunn)

a variety of sports in the U.S., and most university sports in Canada, that are organized in ways that allow student-athletes to combine sport participation with academic and social development. This combination is most likely when student-athletes begin with positive attitudes about the value of a university education, and then receive support for academic involvement and the formation of academic identities (Meyer, 1988, 1990).

Student-athletes in sports that support academic involvement may train very hard and define athletic success as important, but most of them also give priority to academic work and other opportunities apart from training and competition. This awareness usually is grounded in a combination of factors, including (1) past experiences that consistently reaffirmed the importance of education in their lives, (2) social support systems that foster the formation of academic identities, (3) perceived access to career opportunities

following graduation, and (4) social contacts and experiences that expand confidence and skills apart from sports.

Most coaches in these programmes schedule practices and games, where possible, that do not interfere with coursework. Students may miss games and meets because they must study for or take tests, write papers, or give presentations. Team members may discuss academic issues with one another and support each other when it comes to academic performance. In other words, these *are* sport programmes and teams that support the educational mission of higher education.

Grades and Graduation Rates: How Do Student-Athletes Compare with Other Students?

Concerns about the lack of emphasis on education in some U.S. "big time" university athletics programmes has led to the production of a great deal of data about the graduation rates of U.S. student-athletes. These are published annually by the NCAA, as well as by watchdog agencies such as the Centre for the Study of Sport in Society at Northeastern University in Boston. Because there is less emphasis on sports and a greater focus on education at most Canadian universities, there has not been the same concern in Canada about student-athlete graduation rates. McTeer and Curtis (1990), using data from the 1970s and 1980s, showed that there was no reason for concern, as student-athletes and non-athletes had similar grades and graduation rates. However, two more recent studies (Danylchuk, 1995; and an update by McTeer and Curtis, 1999) found lower grades and lower graduation rates for student-athletes, suggesting that there may now be some reasons to monitor this issue carefully.

DO SCHOOLS AND UNIVERSITIES BENEFIT FROM INTERSCHOLASTIC SPORT PROGRAMMES?

The influence of high school and university sport programmes can extend beyond the athletes who play on teams. In this section, we examine the effect of these programmes on schools and universities as organizations. In particular, we examine school spirit and school budgets.

School Spirit

One of the benefits often claimed for school and university sports is that they generate "school spirit." What this means, and how it contributes to the institutions and the education of students is never fully explained. It is associated with a sense of community, belonging, and pride in one's place of education. Of course, this does *not* happen with all sport teams, nor does it happen in all schools or universities. Teams in low-profile sports usually play games without student spectators; teams with long histories of losing records seldom create a spirited response among more than a few students; many students could not care less about the teams that represent their institution; and some students are clearly hostile to sports, and the attention received by some teams and athletes.

While proponents of interscholastic sports say that displays of school spirit strengthen student identification with their places of learning and create the feelings of togetherness needed to achieve educational goals, critics say the spirit created by sports is temporary, superficial, and unrelated to the achievement of educational goals. A football coach at a high school in Florida notes, "[Students] all yell and scream at the pep rally and only a few hundred kids will show up at the game. On Monday morning 70% of them won't know whether we won or lost" (Wahl, 1998: 100).

Being a part of any group or organization is more enjoyable when there are feelings of togetherness that accompany the achievement of goals. However, there is nothing magical about sports. Schools in other countries have used other methods to bring students together and provide enjoyable, educational experiences revolving around recreation and community service.

Critics of interscholastic sports, especially high school sports, are particularly concerned when these sports become elitist activities that involve most students in the passive role of spectator, which produces little in the way of educational experiences. They note that the resources devoted to sports might be used to fund other integrative activities that would involve more than cheering for teams, while providing experiences that actually make young people feel they are valued as contributing members of their communities. King and Peart (1990) note that one of the more significant characteristics of good schools is that they provide a range of extracurricular experiences for students. In response to the belief that sports "keep kids off the streets," critics say that, instead of interschool sports, there should be programmes through which young people can make the streets better places to be.

Budget cuts to interuniversity sports have made it difficult for new sports to become established on the interuniversity schedule. "Club status" is one way that students are able to introduce new sports and establish participation and competition opportunities. While they involve personal costs for students, as in this interuniversity mountain biking event, they also provide leadership opportunities for student-athletes that may not be so available in more established sports. (Kara Dillon and Nick Burdan. Reproduced with permission from the Faculty of Physical Education and Health, University of Toronto, www.utoronto.ca/physical)

The spirit associated with high-profile interuniversity sports is exciting for some students, but only a small proportion of the student body attends most games. Either the students are not interested in attending the games or, in some cases, the athletic department limits student tickets because they can sell seats at a higher price to nonstudents. There is no doubt that the games of high profile sport teams in the U.S., and, to a lesser extent, in Canada, often are major social occasions on university campuses and around televisions in sports bars and in the homes of alumni and other fans. They sometimes inspire displays of spirit on the campus, but there are questions about whether this spirit serves educational functions or simply provides entertaining social occasions for students bored with or stressed out by academic work. If the latter,

then universities may be missing opportunities to critically assess their academic programmes rather than having sports somehow promote the programmes by obscuring problems.

In summary, interscholastic sports may create school spirit. However, for that spirit to have educational significance, it must be part of an overall programme in which students are treated as valued participants and given a sense of ownership in the institution and its programmes. Unless students are actively involved in what happens every day at school, their cheering at weekly games is simply a superficial display of youthful energy having nothing much to do with education.

School Budgets

High Schools What are the financial consequences of interschool sport programmes? Most high school programmes are funded in partnership with the local school board, which provides from 5 percent to 80 percent of the school sport budget depending on the province/board:

> In Ontario it is not unusual to see boards only providing 20-35% of the total funds required. Students often pay a participation fee and there is considerable fund raising by teachers and students. Corporate sponsorship is now an important part of school sport (Hood, 1998).

Participation fees make sport participation less accessible to students from low-income families and, at a time when many students are already not participating because of a need, or desire, to work in their after-school hours, add to the elitist profile that high school sports already have. Sponsorships connect the future of sport programmes with the advertising budgets and revenue streams of private companies. This creates serious problems when advertising budgets are cut or when profits decline. Businesses may then withdraw their support, and programmes are left with even less funds. Other problems occur when the interests of sponsors do not match the educational goals of schools and school sports. For example, promoting the consumption of candy, soft drinks, and fast foods through ads and logos on gym walls, or through vending machine sales, often directly contradicts the health and nutrition principles taught in school classes. This clearly subverts education and makes students cynical about learning and education. It has also led some people to question the educational wisdom of funding sports by selling the student body to businesses. This has intensified debates about how interschool sports should be funded and whether they are worth the expense.

Universities The relationship between sports and budgets is much more complex at the university level. Interuniversity sports in Canada are funded from a whole range of sources, with student fees being the primary source. Smaller amounts may come from gate receipts; from a share of the television income negotiated by the various conferences; and from concessions, logo licence fees, sponsors, alumni, and various other forms of fund raising. For example, one University of Toronto funding campaign is for an endowment (Project Blue) for each of its interuniversity teams in order to reduce their dependency on student fees. No university teams in Canada make a profit, and, despite claims to the contrary, there is little evidence that athletics in "big time" university programmes in the U.S. make a profit.

The critiques of business and corporate sponsorships of high school sport programmes also apply to similar sponsorships of university sport programmes. Universities may have guidelines restricting alcohol or tobacco sponsorships, and some Canadian universities have joined coalitions to ensure fair labour practices in the manufacture of their licensed logo products. However, sponsorships may still produce dependency relationships and subvert the educational mission of the university.

Capital projects and infrastructure are a major concern at a time of restricted budgets in higher education. How are universities to maintain aging facilities, and construct new facilities,

when the budgets are rarely adequate for existing programmes? Sometimes, universities may benefit from provincial donations; or they may be as lucky as McGill University, where the refurbishing of Molson Stadium was paid for by the CFL's Montreal Alouettes in their move from Olympic Stadium. In many cases, universities benefit from their city hosting major games or championships. Examples include the Olympic Oval at the University of Calgary, stadium renovations at McMaster University funded by hosting women's soccer events for the Universiade in Buffalo in 1993 (new facilities at McMaster also figure largely in the plans for Hamilton's bid for the 2010 Commonwealth Games), the 2001 World Championships in Athletics and upgrading University of Alberta facilities, and the new TD Waterhouse stadium at the University of Western Ontario built for the Canada Summer Games in 2001.

HIGH SCHOOL SPORTS: PROBLEMS AND RECOMMENDATIONS

High school sport programmes generally enjoy community support, and many people have vested interests in keeping them the way they are. Many high school sport programmes are doing a good job of providing students with opportunities to develop and display physical skills in ways that have educational relevance. A few seem to have lost direct connections with education and may have subverted the educational process for some students. Problems vary from one high school programme to the next, but the most serious problems include the following: (1) restricted budgets, (2) an overemphasis on "sports development" and big-time programme models, and (3) limited participation access for students.

Restricted Budgets

The significant reductions in public expenditure that occurred across Canada in the 1990s had impacts that are still being felt in areas such as health and education. The effects on school sports were insidious and widespread. Education budget cuts in many provinces resulted in a reduction in the number of teachers, with most reductions coming in those areas of the curriculum designated as ancillary, such as physical and health education and music. This has been most evident at the elementary school level where, in many parts of the country, there are now no physical education specialist positions. The consequences, which vary from province to province, and even from school board to school board, are as follows:

- Physical education programmes have been reduced, and a significant part of the required physical education curriculum is not being taught. An international survey (Hardman and Marshall, 2000) found that 43 percent of required physical education classes in Canada were not taught, compared to 26 percent in the U.S., 13 percent in western Europe, and 7 percent in northern Europe.
- Some sports have been cut from interschool programmes.
- There has been a reduction in athletic facility maintenance.
- Cuts have affected community sports and recreation as school boards have radically increased their facility rental fees.
- Participation fees have been introduced or increased; a great deal of time and effort has been devoted to fund raising; and corporate sponsors now enjoy a far greater presence in school sports.
- Teacher-coaches, who are always reluctant to cut sports, have experienced burnout in their attempts to raise funds and maintain programmes.
- In some provinces (e.g., Ontario), the budget cuts came at a time of major curriculum and workload changes, which led to tense labour relations and job action, with

school sports being implicated in teacher work-to-rule campaigns.
- Some provincial governments have proposed turning school sports over to the community, and merging them with community sport programmes. This has been resisted by provincial schools athletic associations in various ways (e.g., requiring the presence of a teacher at all practices and games if the coach is not a teacher).

Recommendations for Change The Centre for Sport Policy Studies at the University of Toronto held a conference to develop recommendations for resolving the crisis in high school sports (Donnelly, et al., 2001). The delegates, representing all parties interested in school sports, made two key points:

- Better funding of school sports must go hand in hand with enhanced physical education and widely accessible intramural and student activity programmes (see the section, "Limited Participation Access," later in this chapter).
- Increased funding only to school sports would be a problem, and would be seen as elitist, if other forms of extracurricular activity (e.g., music programmes, student theatre, etc.) did not also receive increases.

Thus, increased budgets must be part of a broad-based increase in access to extracurricular activities. This will only occur when there is a commitment to public education, combined with the recognition that good schools have a wide range of extracurricular activities that are an important part of student life (King and Peart, 1990). This is certainly the case in many private schools.

Overemphasis on "Sport Development" Models

Since Canada failed to win any gold medals at the 1976 Montreal Olympics, and the federal government embarked on a strategy to develop high-performance sports, there have been frequent attempts to incorporate sports in high schools and universities in that strategy. As Iona Campagnolo, the first Minister of State for Fitness and Amateur Sport, noted, "the universities and indeed all the educational system, are the natural delivery systems for sport in Canada" (1977). Over twenty years later, Dennis Mills pointed out that schools are the root of sport development in Canada (1998). Because education in Canada is a provincial rather than federal jurisdiction, this has been a difficult strategy to implement, and has been far more successful at the university than at the high school level (see below).

There are two ways to interpret federal government statements on this issue. In the first, schools may be seen as the ideal places to develop a physically literate population by having a wide range of physical education, intramural, exercise, and interschool programmes. A healthy, active population forms an ideal basis for identifying and selecting talented individuals for high-performance programmes, and such a population is more likely to identify with, and be sympathetic to, investing in high-performance sports. In the second interpretation, school sports become part of the elite sport development programme, focusing their resources on individuals who are already talented athletes. These interpretations may be replicated in the increasing interest in developing sports high schools (e.g., in Alberta). In one model, the sports schools are seen in a similar way to arts high schools, where individuals have an opportunity to pursue a variety of interests, and where sports are integrated into the curriculum in a variety of ways (e.g., sport science as part of the science requirements). In the other model, the schools recruit elite athletes and become centres for the development of athletic excellence in a limited number of sports. Unfortunately, it is the latter interpretation that seems to be more likely.

Some high school personnel seem to think that the best way to organize high school sports is to model them after intense sport development programmes. When this happens, people involved with school sports become overconcerned with winning records and presenting tightly organized, high-profile programmes to the community. These programmes often highlight sports such as boys' basketball, but other teams can be highlighted depending on local traditions. In the process of trying to build high-profile sport programmes, teacher-coaches and administrators may overlook the educational needs of all the students.

People who focus on sport development often give lip service to the idea that sports must be kept in proper perspective, but many forget their own words when it comes to the programmes at their schools. In fact, they may even encourage students to specialize in a single sport for twelve months a year, instead of encouraging them to develop a wide range of skills in various sports.

These problems sometimes occur in Canada when community coaches rather than teachers are involved in school sports, and sometimes with young teacher-coaches anxious to establish a reputation as a "winning coach." Older, more experienced teacher-coaches often grow to recognize the cycle of competition in which some years your teams will win, and some years they will lose; and they begin to see themselves as teachers first. Most of the issues that have to be dealt with by provincial schools athletic associations—coaches playing ineligible players, transfers between schools that seem to be motivated by athletics rather than academics, and parents petitioning school boards and suing the athletic associations for preventing their child from an opportunity to be awarded an athletic scholarship to the United States—result from an overemphasis on sport development. In fact, it has been the proximity and lure of U.S. NCAA Division I athletics programmes, and their function as professional farm systems for sports such as football and basketball, and, to a lesser extent, baseball, hockey, golf, and track and field, that has been connected to some of the problems in high school sports. This becomes even more significant for students (and their parents) who have made a major investment in sport participation, sometimes at the expense of academics, and/or who are from less affluent families. They are aware that it is possible to enter some U.S. universities with lower grades than would be required in Canada, and they often believe the wildly exaggerated stories about the number of students who receive full scholarships.

Recommendations for Change Interschool sport programmes ought to be critically assessed on a regular basis. Younger teacher-coaches should be provided with opportunities to learn more about the ways sports can be made into educationally relevant activities. Teacher-coaches also should be given access to coaching education programmes and other professional development opportunities that emphasize student development rather than sport development.

In some cases, teacher-coaches and provincial schools athletic associations might look to students themselves for signs about the directions they might take. Are students paying to participate in private or non-profit fitness programmes when there are often adequate fitness facilities in the schools? Are lots of students in-line skating, or playing hacky sack, pick-up basketball, and Frisbee outside during breaks from classes, but not participating in school-sponsored activities? Colin Hood, executive director of the Ontario Federation of School Athletic Associations (OFSAA) has noted that ultimate Frisbee is the fastest growing sport in high schools, but it is an informal, intramural, and interschool activity usually run by students. Why not give higher priority to sports involving active participation rather than just being a spectator? For example, there could be more combined male/female teams in sports such as long-distance running, doubles tennis and badminton, bowling, golf, cycling and tandem cycling, soccer, hacky sack, wall climbing, archery and shooting, volleyball, swimming, racquetball, and billiards. If a person's

high school years are a time for social development, playing these sports is more valuable than watching spectator sports based on entertainment models. Scoring and handicap systems could be designed to accommodate skill differences and to promote human development and social development, rather than sport development.

Limited Participation Access

Across Canada, approximately 30 percent of the student body participates in interschool sports: "Most schools have the traditional sports programs such as basketball, soccer, hockey, volleyball, track, etc. but there are schools with programs such as fencing, snowboarding, rowing and boxing" (Hood, 1998). Pan-Canadian participation statistics are very difficult to compile; provincial schools athletic associations count participation in different ways (e.g., some count all students participating, while others provide a total of the number participating in each sport—those playing more than one sport are counted more than once). The Canadian School Sport Federation does not keep overall statistics; Ontario has statistics readily available (www.ofsaa.on.ca), tracking participation for the last twenty-five years (Figure 14.1). The graph in Figure 14.1 shows a steady increase in boys' participation, in line with population increases, and a more rapid increase in girls' participation, with new teams in sports such as soccer, rugby, hockey, and even wrestling. Figure 14.1 also shows the dramatic effects of budget cutbacks and tense labour relations on school sport participation since 1996–97, with sharp declines in 1998 and 2000.

The major advantage of interschool sports is that they provide students with opportunities to develop and test their skills, especially physical skills, outside the classroom. However, when high school programmes emphasize power and performance sports, they discourage participation by some males and many females who prefer sports emphasizing pleasure and participation. In fact, this may be the major factor that prevents schools from meeting their gender-equity goals, despite persistent attempts to make sure opportunities are available for females: females may not be as eager to play sports that are built around the idea of "proving who the better man is." At any rate, most high schools have not achieved gender equity when it comes to sport participation.

Budget cuts also have interfered with changing or expanding programmes in creative ways. One of the biggest threats to more open participation in school sports is the use of participation fees. These fees limit access to participation, as does much of the time and energy devoted to fundraising—resources that could be better spent on participation.

Recommendations for Change Not everyone is physically able or motivated to participate in interschool sports based on a power and performance model. Those who do not measure up to their bigger, faster, taller, and stronger classmates need participation alternatives. There is no reason only one team should represent a school in competition. Why not have two or more teams? Why not have a football league with players under 140 pounds, or a basketball league with all players under 5'8" tall, or track meets with height and weight breakdowns for certain events? In places where this has been tried, it has been successful.

There should be efforts to develop new interschool sports in which size and strength are not

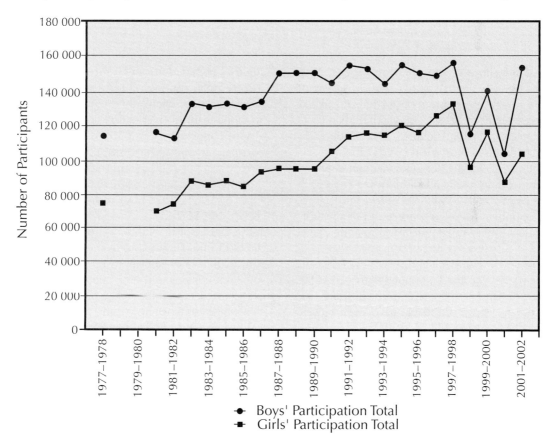

FIGURE 14.1   Ontario School Sport (OFSAA) Participation 1977–2002, www.ofsaa.on.ca/participation_stats/pa

The growth of women's rugby in high schools and universities led to the CIS introducing national championships for women, but not for men's rugby. This helps to establish gender equity in the CIS, given the cost and number of athletes involved in men's football.
(Kara Dillon and Nick Burdan. Reproduced with permission from the Faculty of Physical Education and Health, University of Toronto, www.utoronto.ca/physical)

crucial for success. Too often, the focus is on football and basketball rather than a variety of sports suited for a variety of participants. Why not have teams in Frisbee, racquetball, flag football, softball, in-line skating, or any sport for which there is enough local interest for students to try out? With a little guidance and support, students themselves could administer and coach these teams and coordinate meets and games with opponents at other schools. If responsibility builds autonomy and decision-making skills, why not let students direct their own teams, so that more of them would have opportunities to participate? This has been done with success in some countries, and it costs almost nothing.

Students with a disability have been largely ignored by some school sport programmes. More schools should develop sport participation opportunities for these students. This could occur in a combination of specially designed programmes or by including student-athletes with disabilities on existing school teams, as has sometimes been the case in track and field. This would not work in all sports, but there are certain sports in which competitors with a disability could be included in games, meets, and matches. If there are not enough student-athletes with disabilities in one school, then combine schools or have one team from an entire conference.

Girls' sports still do not have the support that boys' sports enjoy. Of course, this problem has a history that goes far beyond the high school. But the result is that girls still participate at somewhat lower rates than boys, although the gap has closed considerably in recent years. In some areas, there is still an emphasis on boys' teams as the most important teams in the school. Gender equity in school sports could be achieved in some schools through such gender-mixed sports as those recommended in the previous section.

More schools are now using participation fees to save interschool sports. This strategy may work, but it may also limit participation among students from low-income families, even when fee waivers are available. If fees are necessary to save programmes, there should be attempts to enable students to work for the money to pay fees, and there should be ways to encourage community organizations to establish scholarship funds to pay fees for students in need of assistance.

INTERUNIVERSITY SPORTS: PROBLEMS AND RECOMMENDATIONS

Issues in Canadian interuniversity sports are not new. They were summarized by Macintosh (1986), and three of the issues—athletic scholarships, relationships with high-performance sports, and gender equity—were discussed by Hall, et al. (1991). These three, together with budget issues, are still a concern.

Athletic Scholarships

Athletic scholarships in the U.S., as noted previously, offer both advantages and disadvantages to Canadian students. They provide financial assistance, more flexible admission standards, and a potential track to professional/high-performance sports. However, student-athletes may find that they have semi-professional status as "employees" of athletics departments, that the demands of sports may conflict with the demands of education, and that the (usually) partial scholarships do not nearly cover the costs of their (out-of-state/foreign student) tuition and expenses.

Many Canadian university coaches believe that athletic scholarships in Canadian universities will keep student-athletes in Canada who would normally have gone to the U.S., and that a scholarship system will lead to improved standards in Canadian interuniversity sports and add significantly to the Canadian system of sport development. However, others believe that these scholarships will lead to the end of the traditional Canadian emphasis on academics over athletics, that their cost could lead to a limitation of the number of sports available to student-athletes, and that they could create the types of problems and corruption experienced by many U.S. universities.

Since CIS accepted unlimited athletic scholarships at Canadian universities in 2000, they have been extremely divisive. As universities in Ontario and several in other provinces argued for academic standards and limitations on awards, many universities in western Canada threatened to secede from CIS competitions. A compromise was agreed to, but Ontario universities immediately established more restrictive rules—a limit of C$2,500 per year for a student-athlete, a minimum academic average of 70 percent required to receive an award, and no entry (first-year) awards. Universities outside Ontario may make awards that amount to full tuition and mandatory fees, and they can overcome the entry-level limitation by making an award at the end of a student-athlete's first year (an award that may therefore become part of a recruitment offer). Ontario universities have since discussed whether they might secede from CIS national competition, at least in football, arguing that their philosophy of more restrictive awards places them at a competitive disadvantage.

Recommendations for Change Both sides have legitimate arguments, and the problem is clearly difficult to resolve. Academic standards are important if Canada is to avoid the U.S. problems, and some universities have argued that, in order to be eligible for an athletic scholarship, student-athletes should have the grades that would at least make them eligible for consideration for an academic scholarship. As Jack Drover, the athletic director at Mount Allison University, has noted, "We have students on the dean's list here who aren't getting anything, while athletes can get full tuition for just passing their courses" (cited by Sokoloff, 2002). Murray Sperber, a Canadian professor at the University of Indiana forced into hiding following death threats after he criticized the behaviour of basketball coach, Bobby Knight, warned against the slippery slope of athletic scholarships: "Athletes in the U.S. are the only group brought to campuses for entertainment, not academic purposes. It's like paying for rock stars" (cited by Sokoloff, 2002).

Athletic scholarships should be considered in the same category as other non-academic scholarships in, for example, music, art, and drama. They should be adjudicated on the basis of excellence in a non-academic area, but student-athletes should also have grades that make them eligible for academic scholarships. This would also help to counter the "dumb jock" stereotype. Athletic scholarships should also be funded in a way that does not lead to athletic departments cutting sports in order to fund scholarships in just a few sports.

Relationships with High-Performance Sports

Sport Canada has shown ongoing interest in incorporating university sports into Canada's high-performance development system, and has been an advocate of athletic scholarships. Universities are involved in the high-performance development and training system in several ways. For example:

- National Sport Centres (NSCs) are located at universities (e.g., Calgary, Manitoba), or maintain close links with local universities (e.g., Vancouver).
- Sport Canada provides bursaries, through the Athlete Assistance Programme, for national team athletes to attend Canadian universities.

Sport Canada and some NSOs are interested in greater involvement, and there have been proposals for "super leagues" in some sports to provide competition and development opportunities for the best "student" athletes. The NSCs have the advantage, from Sport Canada's perspective, of bringing the best athletes together with a leading coach whose salary is sometimes shared by a university and an NSO, in a location where good facilities and services (e.g., sport science, sports medicine) already exist.

The funding from hosting or linking with NSCs is attractive to cash-strapped university athletic departments, and the presence of high-profile athletes brings publicity to the departments and the universities. National team athletes who are students may be on modified course loads, or may receive special consideration from professors for absences due to international competitions. Such athletes are also eligible for CIS competitions if they meet eligibility requirements.

However, blending the high-performance and university sport systems may mean losing some of the educational principles of university sports (a parallel may be drawn here with attempts to combine community sports with high school sports). It can also lead to a focus on high-performance athletes, and directing resources to a more limited number of sports. This has the effect of depriving many non-elite student-athletes of the interuniversity sport experience.

Recommondations for Change   There is a clear need to negotiate the relationship between university sports and high-performance sports. The negotiations must recognize the mutual advantage that is possible from supporting the needs of high-performance sports, while maintaining and even improving the established "student first, athlete second" interuniversity sport system. This is a balancing act—too much emphasis on high-performance sports can damage the principles of university sports. However, the high-performance system can become a part of the educational environment of university sports.

Gender Equity[5]

Because of the focus on gender equity in the CIAU/CIS in the last ten years, there are now more national championships for females and males as women's sports have been added to the national championship roster in order to create equity. However, in most universities across the CIS, there are fewer female athletes than male athletes, often fewer female sports available than male sports, and lower budgets for female sports

---

[5] It should be noted that concerns about language equity have been an ongoing issue in CIS; however, significant steps have been taken to increase French language capacity and communications in recent years (Donnelly, et al., 2001).

As noted in chapters 8 and 10, the number of women in interuniversity coaching and administration remains disproportionately low. This is one of the gender inequities that has not been addressed very assertively in most universities, although it is a high priority in those, such as the University of Toronto, with a Gender Equity Plan. (Lewko Hryhorijiw. Reproduced with permission from the Faculty of Physical Education and Health, University of Toronto, www.utoronto.ca/physical)

than male sports. Some 54 percent of CIS athletes are male, and 46 percent are female.

Often, the cause of lower budgets and fewer female athletes is football—the sport is expensive and has large rosters of athletes—it is almost impossible to match it in female sports. Some universities (e.g., Dalhousie) have achieved gender equity without football.

When the University of Toronto was grappling with this problem in the 1990s (*Gender Equity Report*), the university found that the only way to achieve equity in budgets was to take football out of the equation. Serious consideration was given to dropping the sport, a problem given the long history of tradition of the Varsity Blues football team, which, in the past, was a Grey Cup–winning team. Their resolution was to establish an alternative source of funding for football, provided by the most outspoken group in favour of keeping the team—the alumni of the team.

The *CIAU Comparative Study* (www.cisport.ca), which compared changes in gender equity between 1992–93 and 1998–99, found that although there had been an increase in the number of female athletic directors and female head coaches, women were still significantly underrepresented in those positions. There is also disparity in athletic scholarships. Out of the 2,439 students who received athletic scholarships in 2001–02, 64 percent were male, and 36 percent were female. Male student athletes received 67 percent of the total amount of money for athletic scholarships, while females received 33 percent.

Recommendations for Change Many of the athletics departments at Canadian universities need to recognize that more than half of the student body is female, and that student fees are their primary source of funding. Departments that do not provide equity for male and female students need to conduct serious gender-equity exercises to ensure fairness in funding of interuniversity sports, and other recreation and intramural programmes on campus, before a student organization brings a human-rights/gender-equity suit against them. Departments that wish to maintain traditional and expensive male sports, and which are unable to provide comparable funding for female sports, need to consider alternative sources of funding for the male sports. Equity exercises also need to consider the availability of coaching and administrative positions, and the distribution of athletic scholarships.

Restricted Budgets

Budgetary constraints are at the root of several of the issues described above, but they also have another consequence—that of providing fewer participation opportunities (interuniversity, intramural, and recreational) for the students who are paying the fees. In terms of interuniversity sports, athletic departments have gone through a number of budget exercises in recent years that have resulted in sports being cut. The decisions usually involve one of the following:

- "Going with your strengths," that is, putting all of the funding towards the few sports in which the university has been most competitive, and/or in which the university employs a full-time coach
- Ranking exercises in which sports are assigned to different categories of funding; for example, the recent exercise at the University of Western Ontario assigned sports to four categories:
  - 1: Sports receive full funding and full services
  - 2: Sports receive basic funding and services
  - 3: "Varsity clubs" are self-funded and receive limited services

- 4: "Sport clubs" involve sports that do not compete in the OUA or the CIS, and receive no athletic department funding or services

While there were attempts to establish gender equity in the Western exercise, it produced some extraordinary inequities. For example, all of the most expensive men's sports—football, hockey, and basketball—were ranked in Category 1. However, women's wrestling was ranked in Category 1, while men's wrestling was ranked Category 2; men's hockey was ranked 1, while women's hockey was ranked 2; women's swimming was ranked 2, while men's swimming was ranked 3—and these latter two teams have to travel together (Kernaghan, 2002; Pyette, 2002).

Recommendations for Change Students, who are paying the fees, must be at the table when budgets are being discussed. The first priority should be to provide interuniversity (and other participation) experiences to as many students as possible. If these experiences—interuniversity, intramural, and recreational—are considered to be valuable, which they are at every university, then they should be available to as many students as possible. Some of the recommendations for extending interschool sport experiences (multiple teams, new sports, etc.) should be considered at universities.

Careful negotiations and planning are necessary in order to determine which expenses are necessary and which are not. For example, at a time when sports are being cut, is it necessary for some teams to travel to play in expensive exhibition tournaments? Who should pay the cost when 120 football players show up to training camp? These are difficult questions, but it is necessary to ask them, and to negotiate their answers in a manner that provides equitable and accessible opportunities to participate in these educational environments.

SUMMARY

ARE INTERSCHOLASTIC SPORTS EDUCATIONAL?

It is difficult to generalize about high school and university sport programmes. They differ from one another in numerous ways. However, interscholastic sports have no place in high schools or universities unless they are legitimate parts of educational programmes and unless they receive their direction from educational purpose. At a minimum, if the programmes do not benefit student-athletes educationally, they cannot be justified as school- or university-sponsored activities.

At this time, there is no consistent evidence that high school sports produce negative consequences for those who participate in them. Of course, some schools, coaches, parents, and student-athletes lose sight of educational goals in their pursuit of competitive success. Sports can be seductive, and people connected with high school teams sometimes require guidance to keep their programmes in balance with the academic curriculum. It is up to school superintendents and principals to oversee what happens in their boards and schools. Parents also should be sensitive to the potential of sports to subvert educational goals. When sport participation interferes with educational achievement, steps must be taken to restore sports to their proper place.

A main theme in this book is that sports are social constructions. That is, sports can be organized and played in many ways, and people can creatively influence the meanings associated with sports to meet specific goals. However, most people associated with interscholastic sports simply have assumed that sports and sport participation *automatically* produce positive results, so they have not taken the time to critically examine sports in student culture as a whole.

The possibility that sport participation might interfere with the educational progress of student-athletes is greatest in U.S. big-time interuniversity programmes. The attractiveness of being an athlete in a big-time programme is often enough to distract students from academic work. In fact, it can make coursework nearly irrelevant in the lives of impressionable young people, especially young men who see their destinies being shaped by sport achievement, not academic achievement.

Interscholastic sport programmes can create school spirit. But it is not known if that spirit contributes to the achievement of educational goals. While it is certain that other activities could be used to bring students together, sports do provide students with high-profile social activities that make schools and universities more interesting places to be. Although they may occupy the everyday attention of a large number of students, it is unknown whether they systematically distract attention from academic matters, or the conditions under which they are most likely to do so.

It is doubtful that high school sport programmes seriously cut into budgets for academic programmes. The money they require is well spent if it provides students with opportunities to explore their physical selves and meet challenges outside the classroom. On the interuniversity level, the funding situation is complex and confusing, and needs to be carefully negotiated in order to maintain the educational goals of university sports.

High school and university sports in Canada are in a time of transition. Careful consideration needs to be given to the educational goals of interscholastic sports, and how they might be maintained. The involvement of students in these negotiations is important.

Interscholastic sport programmes never will be perfect. There always will be a need for critical evaluation and change, just as there is in any part of the curriculum. This means that the educational relevance of these programmes depends on constant evaluation and assessment. A critical approach is the only approach that will enable sports to be meaningful activities in the everyday lives of students and in the social organization of the schools and universities themselves.

SUGGESTED READINGS

There are no books available on interscholastic sports in Canada. Many of the articles cited in this chapter provide valuable insights into sports in high schools and universities. The following address some of the issues we have considered:

Foley, D. E. 1990. *Learning capitalist culture*. Philadelphia: University of Pennsylvania Press (the author pays special attention to high school sports in this excellent ethnography of a small Texas town; focuses on youth, community rituals, and the reproduction of class, ethnic, and gender inequalities).

Gerdy, J. R. 2000. *Sports in school: The future of an institution*. London/New York: Teachers College Press, Columbia University (thirteen articles dealing with four main topics: the educational benefits of sports, the preparation of coaches and athletes, race and gender in sports, and athletics and education).

Miracle, A. W., and C. R. Rees. 1994. *Lessons of the locker room: The myth of school sports*. Amherst, NY: Prometheus Books (a detailed examination of commonly held beliefs about sport in U.S. high schools; uses research to assess those beliefs and shows most of them to be faulty).

Rees, C. R., and A. W. Miracle. 2001. Education and sport. In *Handbook of sports studies* (pp. 277–90), edited by J. Coakley and E. Dunning. London: Sage (a concise overview; provides a brief history, identifies important issues, and reviews relevant research).

Sack, A. L., and E. J. Staurowsky. 1998. *College athletes for hire: The evolution and legacy of the NCAA's amateur myth*. Westport, CT: Praeger (a sociologist and a sport scientist, both former college athletes, use historical and current data to show how the NCAA has systematically developed big-time university sports into

professional and commercial activities while marketing them as amateur sports and denying the fact that student-athletes are workers in a professional sport system; suggestions for reform are offered).

Schulman, J. L., and W. G. Bowen. 2001. *The game of life: College sports and educational values*. Princeton, NJ: Princeton University Press (highly influential book based on data gathered from selected colleges and universities; a thoughtful and provocative analysis that raises serious questions about the educational value of interuniversity sports as they are now organized in many schools).

Sperber, M. 2000. *Beer and circus: How big-time college sports is crippling undergraduate education*. New York: Henry Holt (critique of the state of higher education in the United States; emphasis on how interuniversity sports have been associated with a decline in critical thinking on campuses).

WEBSITE RESOURCES

Note: Websites often change. The following URLs were current when this book was printed. Please check our website www.mcgrawhill.ca/college/coakley for updates and additions.

Interschool sport sites exist at all of the levels outlined in chapter 13.

www.schoolsport.org (site for the International School Sport Federation (ISF), which organizes international competitions)

www.schoolsport.ca (site for the Canadian School Sport Federation only provides links to the provincial associations/federations)

www.asaa.ca; www.fqse.qc.ca (examples of sites of provincial school sport associations [for Alberta and Quebec]; they give an indication of the range of school sports, policies, and statistics)

www.cahperd.ca (site for the Canadian Association for Health, Physical Education, Recreation and Dance includes a great deal of interesting information on school physical education and QDPE programmes; the site now includes the Canadian Intramural Recreation Association)

www.cisport.ca (site for Canadian Interuniversity
Sport [CIS/SIC] contains policies and regulations,
as well as links to the four athletic conferences)

www.ccaa.ca (site for the Canadian Colleges Athletic
Association [CCAA/ACSC] contains policies and
regulations, as well as links to the regional
conferences)

www.knightfdn.org (site of the Knight Foundation;
link to the Knight Foundation Commission on
Intercollegiate Athletics in the U.S., where there
are summaries of the 1991, 1992, and 1993
reports and a copy of the 2001 report *A Call
to Action: Reconnecting College Sports and
Higher Education*)

www.sportinsociety.org (Center for the Study of
Sport in Society collects annual data on the ethnic
and gender composition of U.S. athletic
department employees at major colleges and
universities; click on the "Racial and Gender
Report Card" to find data on the affirmative
action records of Division I institutions in the
United States)

chapter

15

Sports in the Future

What can we expect?

The primary goal of futurists is not to predict the future but to uncover images of possible, probable, and preferable futures that enable people to make informed decisions about their lives.

—W. Bell, futurist (1997)

The effort to create alternatives to the commercial sport culture will continue to be an uphill fight. But such alternatives do exist. They have a long, rich, and proud history.

—Bruce Kidd, educator (1996)

All national and international sports federations will be disbanded and competitive "amateur" tournaments and spectacles beyond the civic level will be prohibited. The Olympic Games, in particular, will be discontinued on the grounds that they have become a hazard to public mental health and to the health of individual competitors.

—Brian Fawcett, author (1990)

Sport is the most dynamic activity in the world today, with the potential to contribute powerfully to a better world . . . . The power and influence of sport is only just being understood.

—Robert Davies, chief executive, International Business Leaders Forum (2002)

 Online Learning Centre Resources

Visit *Sports in Society's* Online Learning Centre at **www.mcgrawhill.ca/college/coakley** for additional information and study material for this chapter.

Discussions of the future are often full of exaggerations, especially at the beginning of a new century. Predicting dramatic changes is always more exciting than predicting that tomorrow will look much like today. Therefore, people often describe the future in science-fiction terms and emphasize extreme hopes and fears. These predictions spark our interest and sometimes leave us temporarily awestruck. However, in most cases, they are neither accurate nor realistic accounts of what is likely to happen.

For better or worse, the future seldom unfolds as rapidly or dramatically as some forecasters would have us believe. Instead, changes usually are tied to a combination of existing social conditions and the efforts of people to shape those conditions to fit their visions of what life should be like. Of course, some people have more power and resources to promote their visions, and those people seldom want revolutionary changes, because their privileged positions depend on stability and controlled change. This tends to slow the rate of deep structural change in societies, although it may speed up changes in technology and the availability and range of consumer products.

As you read this chapter, it is important to remember two things: (1) sports are contested activities, and (2) the future is not determined by fate, computer forecasts, supernatural forces, or sociologists. This means that the future of sports will not unfold according to what is written in this chapter. Much more important are the visions we all have for the future and the choices we make in connection with sports in our lives. Sports will take many forms in the future, and each form will be produced through the collective actions of human beings. Therefore, the primary goal of this chapter is to describe and evaluate the various models of sports that we might use as we envision the future and make choices in our lives.

MAJOR SPORT FORMS IN THE FUTURE

The major theme running through this book is that sports are social constructions: they are cultural practices invented and played by people as they interact with one another and shape social life to fit their ideas of what it should be. Therefore, the dominant sports in any culture are strongly related to the interests and ideas of those who have power in that culture, and they usually celebrate the values and experiences of powerful people. However, not everyone in society accepts the dominant sports. In fact, it is possible for people to modify dominant sports or develop alternative sport forms that challenge the current systems of power relations and promote interests and ideas related to their own lives.

History shows that the dominant sports in most societies have been grounded in the values and experiences of men concerned with military conquest, political control, and economic expansion. As noted in previous chapters and explained in chapter 4, these sports are based on a **power and performance model.**

Although many people have used the power and performance model as the standard for determining the meaning, organization, and purpose of sports, not everyone has accepted it. In fact, some people have maintained or developed other sports, grounded in values and experiences related to their connections with one another and their desire to express those connections through playful and enjoyable physical activities. As noted in chapter 4, these sports are based on a **pleasure and participation model.**

These two models do not encompass all the ways that sports might be defined and played. However, they represent two popular conceptions of sports in people's lives, so they are a practical starting point for thinking about what sports might be like in the future. Even with analyses such as these, we will always be surprised. For example, who would have predicted that football, formerly a power and performance sport associated with anglophones in Quebec, would become so popular with francophones as both participants and spectators? Only a little less surprising on the pleasure and participation side is the recent decision by Vancouver City Council to change its by-laws and open the city's streets to skateboarders.

Power and Performance Sports

Power and performance sports will continue to be the most visible and publicized sport forms in the near future. These sports, based on the "sport ethic" and key aspects of cultural ideology in many postindustrial societies, emphasize the use of strength, power, and speed to push human limits and aggressively dominate opponents (and nature) in the quest for victories and championships.

Although power and performance sports take many forms, they are based on the idea that excellence is proved through competitive success and achieved through intense dedication and hard work, combined with making sacrifices and taking risks. They also encourage people to stress setting records, pushing human limits, using the body as a machine, and viewing technology as a performance aid. According to many athletes in power and performance sports, the body is to be trained, controlled, and constantly monitored, so that it will respond to the challenges and demands of sports efficiently and forcefully; sports are defined as battles in which the opposition is to be intimidated, punished, and defeated.

Power and performance sports also tend to be exclusive. Participants are selected for their physical skills and abilities to achieve competitive success. Those who lack skills and abilities are cut or put in "developmental" programmes. Organizations and teams in power and performance sports feature hierarchical authority structures, in which athletes are subordinate to coaches and coaches are subordinate to owners and administrators. In coach-athlete relationships, it is generally accepted that coaches can humiliate, shame, and derogate athletes as they try to push them to excel. Athletes are expected to respond to humiliation and shame with toughness and a willingness to give all of themselves in the quest for excellence.

The sponsors of power and performance sports know that it is good for them to be associated with people and activities that stress effi-

Some pleasure and participation sports become incorporated into power and performance sports. However, in the case of snowboarding, this is not occurring without a struggle. The sport still has many pleasure and participation elements, including a service component. Instructors Liz Christy and James Roelofsen teach snowboarding to low-income youth. (CP/Bonny Makarewicz)

ciency, organization, competition, hard work, and the endurance of pain for the sake of progress (Hoberman, 1994). Being associated with athletes and teams popularly identified as "winners" is also important. Sponsors use these associations to promote products while establishing favourable public relations profiles. Sponsors assume that their association with winning athletes and teams makes them special in the eyes of consumers and in the lives of people throughout a culture. Of course, as long as the rewards of sponsorship go to those who are successful in power and performance sports, these sports will continue to thrive, and the athletes who play them will continue to be cultural celebrities who are paid to endorse the values of the sponsors. Power and performance sports will remain dominant in most cultures for some years to come; those with power and influence want it to be so.

Pleasure and Participation Sports

Even as power and performance sports have become increasingly visible forms of popular culture, many people have continued to realize two important things: (1) there are many ways to do sports, and (2) power and performance sports may not be consistent with their personal values and experiences. In the past, this dual realization gave rise to sport forms that differ from the sports usually covered in the major media. This will continue to occur in the future.

A trend that will grow more in the future is the creation of alternative sports emphasizing a combination of *pleasure and participation*. These sports involve physical activities in which participants are committed to a combination of challenge, freedom, authenticity, and personal connections—connections between people, mind and body, and physical activity and the environment.

Although pleasure and participation sports take many forms, they generally emphasize an ethic of personal expression, enjoyment, growth, good health, and mutual concern and support for teammates and opponents. They focus on personal empowerment rather than the domination of others, as well as on the notion that the body is to be experienced and enjoyed rather than trained and used as a tool. People who play pleasure and participation sports tend to see their bodies as gardens, which must be cultivated and cared for to promote growth, rather than as machines to be used as tools and then repaired when they break down.

Pleasure and participation sports are characterized by inclusiveness. Playing, not winning, is the most important thing. Differences in physical skills among participants are accommodated informally, or formally through the use of handicap systems, so that players can enjoy competition *with* each other even when they have unequal skills. Sport organizations and sport teams based on this model have democratic decision-making structures characterized by cooperation, the sharing of power, and give-and-take relationships between coaches and athletes. Humiliation, shame, and derogation are inconsistent with the spirit underlying these sports.

The sponsorship of pleasure and participation sports generally is grounded in the ideas that it is socially useful to promote widespread participation in a wide range of physical activities and sports and that overall participation, health, and enjoyment are more important than setting records and recording wins. Unfortunately, many people and corporations with power and money are more interested in sponsoring sports that emphasize power and performance than pleasure and participation. However, not everyone thinks that way, so there will be support for the latter type of sports in the future. Support will grow only as increasing numbers of people choose to include pleasure and participation sports in their lives, and even then it will grow slowly.

FUTURE TRENDS IN SPORTS

The Ongoing Dominance of Power and Performance Sports

Power and performance sports will continue to be the most visible and publicized sport forms in the foreseeable future. Vested interests in these sports are very strong, and those who benefit from them have considerable power and influence. For example, the popularity of power and performance sports is tied to dominant forms of gender relations. When attention is focused on the pushing of physical limits, men will be the centre of that attention, especially when the limits are related to strength, power, and speed. Women athletes will attract increasing attention, but efforts to push human limits will usually celebrate the differences between men and women, and the superiority of men over women (Daniels, 2002). This in itself will preserve the dominance of sports based on the power and performance model for many years to come, as author Mariah Burton Nelson has suggested in a clever book title, *The Stronger Women Get, the More Men Love Football* (1994).

Power and performance sports will remain dominant for another reason: they attract corporate sponsors. American football, the classic

"I love the X Games . . . because they are all about . . . freedom and individual expression."
....

Some athletes in so-called alternative sports are uneasy about what happens when their sports become commercialized.

embodiment of these sports, continues to attract billions of dollars in television rights fees and other revenues, and games are televised in an increasing number of countries around the world, even though few young people play heavy contact football. In the United States, the NFL proudly markets its games under the slogan "Feel the Power." Athletes in the NFL and in other power and performance sports are portrayed in the media as heroic figures and exemplars of corporate images emphasizing productivity, efficiency, and dedication to performance despite pain and injury. Spectators are encouraged to identify with these athletes and their teams and to express their identification through the consumption of licensed merchandise and other products. As long as people identify with teams and athletes in power and performance sports, and as long as their identification can be used to promote consumption in market economies, these sports will continue to receive

the sponsorships and media coverage they need to maintain their dominant position.

Because power and performance sports often involve pushing human limits and some normative limits, they are especially alluring to many people. Attempts to break barriers or do what no one else has done before can be seductive. Sports emphasizing these things are relatively easy to market and sell if they are combined with "storylines" that resonate with the experience of consumers. There are many cases in mainstream sports where people have used technology to push limits for the purpose of competitive success:

- Parents have given synthetic human growth hormone to their children in the hope of "creating" world-class athletes.
- Athletes are in a constant quest to find substances and technological aids to help them become bigger, stronger, and faster.
- People of all ages seek sports equipment made with new, lightweight, strong materials, such as kevlar, titanium, and carbon fibre, so that they can develop new challenges and experiences.
- Some people dream of the day when the Human Genome Project provides information that permits the creation of genetically engineered "designer athletes" (Hoberman, 1992).
- Those people also dream of the day when the brain and central nervous system can be regulated to shape development and facilitate training.

The limits approached so far may be minor, compared with the limits that might be pushed by genetic engineering and its application to power and performance sports.

These changes raise many bioethical issues, but the people who use power and performance sports to form standards for judging what sports should be in the future may find it easy to ignore those issues. For example, many people today grew up with rapidly changing media images that blur the boundaries between human and nonhuman, and they expect that science will provide artificial organs as well as synthetic bones, tendons, and ligaments to those who need them in the future. Therefore, it will not be shocking when superstrong synthetic ligaments, bones, and joints are used to repair bodies injured in power and performance sports. It may not even be shocking when mechanical body parts are used to replace injured limbs and improve performance in sports. In fact, those who watch athletes in power and performance sports will increasingly accept the injuries and the abuse of athletes' bodies as the medical and physical costs of pushing limits, and they will expect science to repair the damage (Hoberman, 1994).

However, this acceptance will not come without resistance. Questions *will* be raised about using technology and pushing limits in sports. Dominant sports in the future will not simply be the result of what is technologically possible. Using technology could eliminate the human element in contests and games, so that athletes reach their potential only when they become machinelike. This approach to sports ultimately subverts creativity, freedom, spontaneity, and expression among athletes, and it turns sports into programmed spectacles involving dramatically presented physical actions—like professional wrestling. Athletes and spectators will have problems with this. Some athletes will resist becoming pawns in such activities, and some spectators will not watch them regularly, because it will be difficult to identify with robot-like athletes playing games lacking human spontaneity and expression. Unless athletes *feel pressure, emotionally respond* to victory and defeat, *make mistakes, work hard* for success, and *have their good and bad days*, spectators may have trouble identifying with them. If this happens, the dominant sports will lose much of their commercial value. The success of power and performance sports depends on fan identification with athletes, and, if technology makes athletes too unlike the spectators who pay to watch them, fan identification could fade. After all, why watch

cyborg athletes when you can buy a video game that enables you to control the images of the same athletes in your own media room at home? The video game costs less than buying a ticket to a game, and it gives you more control than watching a game on television with announcers telling you what you are supposed to see and think.

There are also questions of fairness associated with the use of technology in power and performance sports. When the cost of technology is so high that only wealthy individuals, corporations, or nations can use it to their benefit, many people will question the meaning of athletic success. Will new definitions of *success* emerge? Who will benefit from these definitions? These and many other questions will beg for answers as new forms of pushing limits enter the realm of power and performance sports.

The Growth of Pleasure and Participation Sports

The future will bring diverse sport forms, and many of these forms will embody at least some characteristics of the pleasure and participation model. The reasons for this include growing concerns about health and fitness, participation preferences among older people, new values and experiences brought to sports by women, and groups seeking alternative sports. Each of these reasons is discussed below.

Growing Concerns about Health and Fitness As health-care policies and programmes around the world increasingly emphasize the prevention of illness and injury, and participation in lifelong physical activity, people are becoming more sensitive to health and fitness issues. In North America, for example, health-care programmes in the future will give higher priority to staying well as a strategy for cutting costs (cf., Health Canada's new *Physical Activity Guide*). In connection with this, people may be encouraged to avoid participation in certain power and performance sports and to increase their involvement in pleasure and participation sports for which health benefits are much higher (Waddington, 2000). Health and fitness concerns also will be promoted through changes in physical education curricula. Physical educators will continue to move away from teaching students to play power and performance sports and toward teaching them a range of alternative sports involving lifetime skills, noncompetitive challenges, inclusive participation philosophies, respect and support for other participants, responsible attitudes toward the environment, and concerns for health—all characteristics of pleasure and participation sports. If people realize that healthy exercise can promote personal health, family fun, and a sense of community, there will be powerful incentives for involvement in a wide array of pleasure and participation sports in the future.

Participation Preferences among Older People

As the median age of the population in many societies increases, as people live longer, and as older people represent an increasingly larger segment of the world's population, there will be a growing interest in sports that do not involve intimidation, the use of physical force, the domination of opponents, and the risk of serious injuries. As people age, they are less likely to risk their physical well-being to establish a reputation in sports. Older people are more likely to see sports as social activities and are more interested in making sports inclusive rather than exclusive. Older people also realize that they have but one body, and it can be enjoyed only if it is cultivated as though it were a garden, rather than driven as if it were a machine.

Older people generally are not attracted to power and performance sports. Instead, they prefer noncompetitive physical activities and altered versions of competitive activities. Thus, the future will see more "senior" sport leagues, in which rules are changed to emphasize the pleasure of movement, connections between people, and the challenge of controlled competition. But there

Young people seeking alternatives to organized competitive sports will increase the diversity of pleasure and participation sports in the future. Mountain boarding is a good example. (Jason Lee, Mountain Board Sports)

also will be an increased emphasis on walking, hiking, weightlifting, and other activities, which will be taken seriously but done in settings in which the focus is on health, fitness, and social connections, rather than on setting records or using the body to dominate opponents.

The rising popularity of golf is indicative of general trends we are now seeing in the twenty-first century. Golf involves healthy exercise, it is nonviolent, it does not involve "punishing" the opposition, and it has a handicap system, so that people with different skills can play as equals in competitive events. An important feature is that men and women, and parents and children, can play golf together. Although golf has traditions of exclusiveness and is too expensive for many people to play, older people will develop similar but less expensive pleasure and participation sports as they seek healthy physical activities with aerobic and anaerobic benefits. Bowling has served this purpose for many years, and it remains popular in North America.

Pleasure and participation sports also could be sites for challenging dominant ideas about aging. In the past, aging has been seen as a process involving increasing dependency and incapacity, but the achievements of older athletes support the notion that growing old does not automatically mean becoming weak and incapacitated. "Seniors" and "masters" sport programmes will become increasingly popular; they provide many images of older people who are fit, healthy, and accomplished athletes.[1]

New Values and Experiences Brought to Sports by Women As women continue to gain more power and resources, many of them will emphasize sports that reject the ideology of power and performance sports. Others will continue to seek equity in power and performance sports and, in the process, will challenge the very gender logic on which those sports are organized.

Today, there is a growing number of cases where women have transformed the rules and the spirit of a sport to moderate the emphasis on power and performance and increase the emphasis on pleasure and participation (Fasting, 1996; Griffin, 1998; Hargreaves, 1994; Nelson, 1998; Porterfield, 1999; Theberge, 2000b; Zipter, 1988). Even when women play sports such as rugby, soccer, and hockey, there are indications that they often emphasize inclusiveness and

support for teammates and opponents in explicit ways that are seldom present in the men's versions of these sports. The "in-your-face" power and performance orientation is replaced by an orientation that is expressive of the joy of participation.

Women sometimes encounter difficulties when trying to enlist sponsors for sports such as ringette that differ from men's power and performance sports. Without an emphasis on physical domination, the women's sports often are seen as second rate or not serious enough to attract the attention sponsors seek. However, if women choose such sports in greater numbers, sponsors will respond. As they do, various versions of pleasure and participation sports will receive increased support.

Groups Seeking Alternative Sports Sport participants who reject power and performance sports also will fuel the formation of alternative sports. For example, high school students will continue to form their own sport groups and play games on their own, rather than put up with the constraints of playing on interschool teams, on which coaches sometimes try to control their lives and on which the emphasis on competition and win-loss records is given priority over enjoyment and the experience of participation. Colin Hood, executive director of the Ontario Federation of School Athletic Associations (OFSAA), recently pointed out to us (personal communication, 2002) that the fastest growing sport in Ontario high schools is not administered by the OFSAA and has no teacher-coaches: ultimate Frisbee. Whether more students will look outside the school for alternatives to dominant sports largely depends on how schools organize their sport programmes in the future.

Unique sport subcultures have developed around many alternative sports. For example, studies of skateboarders and snowboarders in Colorado found that many young people in these sports resisted attempts to turn their sport into a commercialized, competitive form (Beal, 1995; Crissey, 1999). Even when the Colorado Skateboard Association sponsored contests,

---

[1] It should be pointed out, however, that master's competitions in a number of sports retain many *power and performance* characteristics. Nonetheless, Seniors Games in many Canadian provinces include many sports and activities based in pleasure and participation principles (e.g., disk golf, bowling, card games, and darts).

many skaters deliberately tried to subvert the formality and the power and performance dimensions of the event. Unregistered skaters crashed the event; registered skaters pinned competition numbers on their shirts, so that they were upside down or difficult to read; they focused on expressing themselves rather than outdoing opponents; and they did not follow the prearranged patterns for warming up and competing. When they were disqualified, their mass protest stopped the event.

There are segments of many sport subcultures that resist attempts to dilute the pleasure and participation emphasis in their activities. They do not want competition and the domination of opponents to replace the expression and support of fellow participants. For example, when a twelve-year-old snowboarder was asked in 1996 what he thought about the possibility of adding his sport to the Olympics, he said, "Don't kill the ride, dude. Let us be free." Even at age twelve, he knew that the ideology of power and performance would subvert the elements of pleasure and participation in his sport. When it was added, Norwegian Terje Haakonsen, reputedly the best boarder in the world, refused to compete in Nagano in 1998. He said, "Snowboarding is about fresh tracks and carving powder and being yourself and not being judged by others; it's not about nationalism and politics and money" (Perman, 1998: 61).

People with a disability or who are physically challenged have sought to develop alternative sports, as well as to adapt dominant sports to fit their needs and physical characteristics. Although some programmes for athletes with a disability clearly have emphasized power and performance sports, others have emphasized a range of sport forms in which pleasure and participation are central. Concern and support for teammates and opponents, as well as inclusiveness related to physical abilities, characterize these sports. When children with a disability are mainstreamed into organized sports, able-bodied children have opportunities to integrate

In the future, people with a disability will not only participate in sports in greater numbers but also influence how sports are played and what new sports are developed. Creatively designed equipment now permits new forms of sports involvement for both the able-bodied and the disabled, as shown in this photo of trail riders. (Rob Schoenbaum)

the characteristics of pleasure and participation sports into their experiences as they interact and play with peers with disabilities. As Jay Coakley's granddaughter with cerebral palsy grows up, he suspects she will favour pleasure and participation sports. However, if she chooses to play in mainstream sports, he suspects she will encourage her peers to qualify their emphasis on power and performance and to remember that connections between people require that we learn how to accommodate difference and uniqueness.

The Gay Games and gay athletic clubs and teams also are an example of an alternative sport form emphasizing participation, support, inclusiveness, and the enjoyment of physical movement (Pronger, 1999). The sixth quadrennial Gay Games, held in Sydney, Australia, in 2002, involved more than 13,000 competitors from eighty-two nations. Although the Gay Games resemble dominant sports in some ways, they explicitly challenge the gender logic that underlies those sports, and they are free of the homophobia that permeates them. Organizers of the 2006 Gay Games in Montreal, a city more accessible than Sydney to major population centres, expect up to 25,000 participants, which would make the 2006 Gay Games the largest international sport event in history.

Gay and lesbian athletes will continue to form sport groups and teams to provide enjoyable experiences in their social lives. One lesbian explains:

> I use sports…to meet people.…Team sports are the main social outlets in my life. I depend on them for emotional support, physical activity, a sense of belonging, a comfortable atmosphere, and an outlet for my competitive nature. (Zipter, 1988: 82)

A gay man in Pronger's study of sports and homosexuality expressed similar feelings:

> The nice thing about playing gay sports is…to interact with gay people…[where you] don't have to be on guard. You can joke around, you can play. That's a good feeling. It's also the sense of community that comes from it.…It's not that I didn't fit in [when I played volleyball at work, but it] is probably more relaxed in gay sports. (Pronger, 1990: 238)

In summary, we will continue to see alternatives to power and performance sports in the future. Most will embody at least some aspects of pleasure and participation sports (e.g., the North American Indigenous Games held in Winnipeg in 2002). One of the challenges we will face in the future is how to maintain alternative sports as sport participation rates increase.

SPECIFIC FORECASTS

Professional Sports

University of Toronto demographer, David Foot (1998), argued that "professional sports in

North America at the millennium are a mature industry. The days of rapid growth and sold-out seasons are over" (p. 151). While Foot may overemphasize the effects of changing age cohorts in the Canadian population at the expense of other factors that influence social change (e.g., economics, international relations, technology, etc.), his arguments should not be ignored and a number of his predictions are now becoming evident.

Foot argued that younger people make up the larger part of the audience (live and on television) for professional sports—"50% of the 18–24 age group attend sports events while only 30% of the 45–64 age group attend" (p. 149). As the largest cohort in the population—the baby boomers—ages, they will be less interested in attending or watching professional sports, and professional sport franchises will become a less lucrative investment. When demographics are combined with other arguments about the problems with professional sports, such as:

- Player strikes and owner lock-outs;
- The immature and sometimes illegal behaviour of millionaire players;
- Weak teams in expanded leagues, and an overall dilution of the quality of play; and
- Competition from the 800-channel universe and other forms of entertainment,

it becomes more clear why leagues such as MLB and the NHL have considered reducing the number of teams, and why some teams that are for sale (e.g., Anaheim Mighty Ducks) are unable to find buyers.[2] Professional team sports have several potential responses to these concerns, and three seem to be under way at this time—increasing globalization, new "total

---

[2] The NFL remains a significant exception to these arguments; some suggest that the limited number of games played in the league (i.e., eight home games during the regular season) make every game important and therefore more attractive to the audience. Unlike the other three leagues, there are few "meaningless" games.

entertainment" stadiums and arenas, and increasing celebrity for "superstar" athletes.

In the future, professional sports will become increasingly global in a number of ways. Leagues will have more teams and more athletes from different countries, and more games will be televised around the world. Sport organizations from wealthier nations will push for international expansion. The political implications of this expansion will be significant, because a North American model of professional and commercial sports will be taken all over the world and presented as the "right" (i.e., most profitable) way to organize, play, and sponsor sports; there will be a "McDonaldization" of sports, with an emphasis on standardization and service provision (Ritzer, 2000). Soccer and basketball will be the most widely played team sports; baseball and hockey will grow in popularity, and football will attract spectator attention but little on-the-field participation in countries outside North America. The number of pro teams and leagues will increase, including those for women, and many will fail, especially those sports that are not already established in a society.

New stadiums for professional teams will be built as "sport malls," where the focus will be on shopping, eating, and drinking, as well as watching games. Pro teams will organize events as total entertainment experiences for spectators. *Entertainment* will be defined in terms of shopping, eating, drinking, and any other form of consumption from which revenue streams can be generated. The goal of team owners will be to induce spectators to spend as many of their entertainment dollars as possible inside the stadium. Public money will continue to be used to subsidize many wealthy owners and their players in the U.S., but support will be less overt in Canada.

Top pro athletes will be global celebrities, and their lives will more closely resemble film and rock music stars. The dynamics of celebrity will enable athletes to capitalize on new publicity and

revenue streams, such as what might be made from fans visiting athletes' Internet sites. The athletes will take their public images more seriously and manage them more assertively.

Professional athletes will gain more autonomy and power in the future, but they will not use their power to make any major changes in the structure of commercial sports or in society as a whole; their primary goal will be to increase control over their careers and enhance their assets.

High School and University Sports

Perhaps even more than professional sports, the future of high school and university sports in Canada is not clear. Sports in these educational sectors are in a time of transition, brought on by a number of factors outlined in chapter 14. However, given the socially constructed nature of sports, times of transition are also times of opportunity. Many readers of this book—i.e., physical education or kinesiology students, university and/or former high school athletes, future teacher-coaches, etc.—are in a position to help determine the future of sports in high schools and universities.

Perhaps the major influence on both sectors is the nearby U.S. model, especially the high-profile aspects that are characterized in media available in Canada. This has led some schools in, for example, the Golden Horseshoe area of Ontario and urban centres in Alberta, to focus on elite development and preparation of athletes who aspire to U.S. university athletic scholarships. In universities, the acceptance of entry-level athletic scholarships in many parts of Canada also suggests a shift towards a U.S.-style model.

Public sector cutbacks throughout the 1990s have also had an impact on both sectors. Because of cutbacks, university students have seen tuition fees increase rapidly in the last ten years; they are reluctant to pay more to support university athletics, and governments are not inclined to reinstate budgets. In high schools, the situation has been even worse, with cutbacks affecting not only school budgets (and consequently, athletics) but also relations between teachers and provincial governments in provinces such as Alberta, Quebec, Ontario, Nova Scotia, and British Columbia. Rather than affect classroom education, teachers have often opted to work-to-rule as a part of their job action—and work-to-rule campaigns have seriously affected extracurricular programmes. Cutbacks have also forced universities and high schools to introduce user fees, and to raise funds in various ways that may compromise the independence and educational character of the programmes.

How might students intervene during this time of transition? First, it is worth re-establishing the principles behind sports programmes in educational institutions. As we state in chapter 14, sports have no place in high schools or universities unless they are legitimate parts of educational programmes and unless they receive their direction from educational purpose. If the programmes do not benefit student-athletes educationally, they cannot be justified as school or university sponsored activities. Second, it is educationally sound to involve students in the organization and decision making of their sports programmes. At the university level, where students are paying fees to support sports programmes, they are entitled to be involved in the decision-making process. Finally, we have argued throughout this book for democratic principles and equity in sports. If sports are good (educational, healthy, fun, etc.), then they should be available to all who are interested in participating, and they should be sensitive to changing student populations and changing interests (e.g., sports applying for club status at many universities indicate shifting gender relations and changing immigration patterns).

Youth Sports

Problems with player, coach, and parent misbehaviour, as well as referee abuse, will continue in youth sports such as soccer and hockey. The revamped National Coaching Certification Programme, and campaigns such as the CHA's "It's Only a Game" series of commercials (www.canadianhockey.ca) will attempt to resolve some of the problems. These changes will help to satisfy parents' demands for more professional approaches to youth sports and to minimize legal liability. Youth programmes will emphasize sport development rather than recreation, and parents will become increasingly concerned about how their children's participation may pay off in the future—in scholarships and in social acceptance. In response to the structured character of youth programmes, many young people will seek out alternative sports, such as skateboarding, as well as various informal games in which they can make up their own rules and develop skills without being under the control of adults. Nine-year-olds, after playing organized sports twelve months a year since they were four years old, will seek to retire from adult-controlled sports, and their parents will force them to continue or sign them up for other organized activities.

Spectators and Spectator Sports

Despite Foot's (1998) claims about an aging population watching less sports, people will continue to watch sports, but not in the same way as in the past. There will be shifts and increasing variation in the sports that people watch. For example, more people may watch soccer, while fewer may watch basketball, and different people will watch a greater range of different sports than ever before, including everything from bass fishing for retired people to various alternative sports for young people. However, people will continue to watch. The media, including the Internet, will encourage this trend with increased sport content. At the same time, more pay-per-view sports, from Little League games to pro games around the world, will be available on cable and satellite television and the Internet.

Spectators and athletes will "connect" via websites for athletes. Fans will be able to ask athletes questions, and athletes will be able to create and present personas that can be converted into valuable commodities and sold back to fans in various forms. Athletes (and their agents) will manage these connections with fans to maximize their commodity value. Athletes' presentations of themselves on the World Wide Web will be consistent with the self-presentations "staged" by film and television celebrities.

Some spectators will form ad hoc organizations to represent their interests when it comes to setting prices for tickets and concessions, controlling the location of team franchises, and guaranteeing fan safety at events. Ad hoc spectator organizations will not be influential, because they will not attract many fans, who already accept commercialized sports, expensive ticket prices, and high salaries for athletes because corporations have built commercial outposts in their heads—and it is difficult to motivate people to resist a foe that has outposts in their heads.

Spectator betting on sports will become more common, and across North America states and provinces will continue to legalize sport gambling. Lotteries and other forms of gambling (e.g., bingo), which, in the past, were used to fund sport activities in various provinces, are now coming under increasing pressure. There is still local fund raising using bingos and breakout tickets, but the claims on the funds from lotteries run by provincial governments are now much more widespread. So, while countries such as the U.K. use their national lottery to fund sports and culture (British Olympic successes in the Sydney Olympics in 2000 compared to the Atlanta Games in 1996 are attributed to the injection of lottery funds into the high-performance system), Alberta is now considering the use of provincial lottery funds to support professional sports—the Calgary Flames and the Edmonton Oilers of the NHL.

An issue will be betting on the Internet, and people will debate whether betting laws should apply to wagering on the Internet, to fantasy leagues with entry fees and cash prizes for winners, and to betting clubs in which wagers involve only individual bettors without a third-party bookie taking a "cut." The increases in sport gambling will be associated with an increase in problem gambling. Problem gambling is an issue for some people at every age, but young people are most involved in gambling, with young males most involved in sport gambling, and it seems likely that they will experience increased levels of problem gambling.

Participant Sports

David Foot (1998), who predicted the decline of spectator sports, also offered predictions about adult participation in sports from a demographic perspective—i.e., what effect an aging ("greying") population will have on the types of sports and recreations in which people participate. Using tennis as an example, he traces the lifecycle of a participant sport. Baby boomers who, in 2003, range in age from thirty-seven to fifty-six, represent almost a third of the Canadian population. A boom in tennis, which started in the early 1970s, peaked in the mid-1980s when there were waiting lists for memberships in tennis clubs in Canada. By the mid-1990s, there were no more waiting lists, and clubs were advertising for members. Of course, there are still many tennis players of all ages, but, Foot argues, the age group most likely to participate grew older. He also suggests that the boomers' children, the "echo generation," will reach peak tennis-playing age during the next ten years, so we should see a mini-boom in the sport.

The boomer generation is probably fitter, and more aware of the benefits of physical activity than any previous middle-aged cohort, but the evidence seems to indicate their declining interest in competitive sports. Curling, swimming, and walking all seem to be activities on the increase. Others have pointed to the growing environmental awareness ("greening") of the Canadian population, and the implications of the greening and greying of a major cohort of the population seems to suggest a major increase in activities such as hiking, snowshoeing, cross-country skiing, gardening, and birding (birdwatching). These activities also produce a major demand for appropriate clothes and equipment, putting businesses such as Mountain Equipment Co-op into a major period of expansion (helped also by the growth in adventure and outdoor sport participation among younger cohorts in the population). Foot reports that 65 million birdwatchers in the United States spend US$5 billion each year on "bird-related products" (cameras, binoculars, bird feed, etc.). With a population in Canada some 10 percent the size of the U.S., but a somewhat more outdoor-oriented and "green" population, it is possible to estimate more than 6.5 million birdwatchers in Canada, spending a great deal of money on their recreation.

Technology and Media

Television and the Internet will provide the visual images and narratives that will influence how sports are imagined, created, and played in many societies around the world. People may not mimic what they see in those images or hear in those narratives, but they will use them as a standard against which they will assess their activities and experiences. Those who control the world's media will have a great influence on discourse about sports and what they should be in the future.

Major private business conglomerates will continue to attempt to connect sport teams, sport events, the media, the entertainment industry, and the Internet. The impact of these connections on sports is difficult to predict; for example, the rush of media and technology corporation convergences from the late 1990s is already coming apart. However, sports increasingly will become online content. As this occurs, sports media will become more interactive. Sports will be presented in new ways, and sport spectators will experience and connect with teams, coaches, and players on the field, in the locker room, and even at home. Internet rights will be tied contractually to broadcast rights in general; such negotiations are now occurring with regard to Olympic sports (previously restricted from Internet coverage). This means that, while spectators will gain more choices about how they will experience sports, the control of sports will become consolidated increasingly in the hands of powerful executives and stockholders, whose interests in sports are peripheral to their interests in expanding their presence and control in the realm of the economy and popular culture. Of course, when spectators participate in interactive ways, they will require detailed knowledge about players, teams, tactics, and strategies—all of which will be available for fees or in a commercial format. The goal of sports media will not change: it will continue to be to sell audiences to sponsors and products or information to audiences.

The Internet will continue to recruit new fans in various fantasy leagues, which allow fans to choose players, construct teams, and qualify for prizes if their teams do well. Improved video games will enable people of all ages to create and coach their own simulated video teams made up of the players they select. Video games will also provide sophisticated new virtual sport experiences. For example, for a few dollars, a person will be able to ski at Mont Tremblant or Lake Louise, select from actual ski runs, face virtual challenges, and fall and break bones—virtual bones, that is.

New medical and genetic technologies will raise numerous ethical problems, as the technologies are used not only to enhance performance and rehabilitation but also to allow athletes to "jump-the-queue" in their access to diagnosis and treatment. Genetic and bio-engineering technologies raise the spectre of cyborg athletes, and offer difficult questions about how to determine which athletes have had their performances enhanced.

Organization and Rationalization

At elite levels of competitive sports, athletes and teams will continue to enlist specialists to help them improve their performances. Therapists and sport psychologists, fitness advisers and drug/substance advisers, aerobics instructors, nutritionists, cooks, biomechanists, and exercise physiologists will make up an expanding corps of "sports advisers" expected to help athletes hit their performance peaks when they compete in important events. Will expectant parents hire these experts because they want their future children to have the benefit of prenatal training and an optimal sports environment in the womb? This is not likely, but it is not out of the question.

An expanding emphasis on the "constructive" use of leisure time will lead to an increasing number of highly organized leisure and sport programmes (Stebbins, 1992). People will link sport participation with rationally chosen "participation goals" and with the consumption of clothing and equipment that will facilitate the achievement of these goals. "Sport experts" will be hired in greater numbers to assist children and adults to play correctly. Wealthier people will join exclusive athletic clubs in increasing numbers, and their social lives and friendships will be more heavily connected with their patterns of participation in sport activities. Their children will learn how to swim, skate, kick soccer balls, hit backhands, ski, sail, and do a variety of other things under trained sport tutors, who will teach them that fun depends on playing sports the right way, by the right rules, with the right equipment, wearing the right clothes and shoes.

Like sport fans and athletes of today, people will continue to be interested in scores, statistics, and records. They will continue to value rationality, hard work, the pursuit of excellence, and the achievement of goals through well-planned efforts and specialized skills. Corporate sponsors will promote these themes in connection with sport media coverage. Sport participation will continue to be linked to character building, although its connection with nationalism will decline in importance.

In general, if physical activity is not organized and controlled by experts, if it does not have winners and losers, if fun is more important than measurable achievement, it will not be considered a sport by many people.

Commercialism and Consumerism

Entertainment and consumption will be the major organizing principles for sports in the future. Financial profits and economic expansion will be the goals of most sports. The ideology and organization of sports will continue to reflect the distribution of resources in society. People with economic and political power will have the most influence on who watches and participates in sports and under what circumstances they will do so. As they have in the past, these people will influence strongly how sports are presented to and defined by the masses of people in societies around the world.

But they will compete increasingly with the "black" and "grey" economies of sports, dealing with everything from stolen satellite signals to sport events and scalped and counterfeit tickets to non-official travel/ticket packages and knock-off replica uniforms (Sugden, 2002).

There are evident problems with media convergence as the high-tech economic boom of the late-1990s continues to decline. Disney has had both of its successful sport teams for sale (MLB's Anaheim Angels was sold in 2003 to Arturo Moreno, who became the first minority person to hold majority ownership in a Major League team; the NHL's Anaheim Mighty Ducks remain on the block), but other media and communications companies, such as News Corp and Rogers, still find it profitable to own teams and link them to their media, entertainment, and Internet divisions. The model of Disney owning ESPN and ESPN owning the X Games will remain popular as corporations use sports to make money and

The marketing of products associated with sports includes an extensive trade in sport memorabilia and collectibles. These Team Canada 1972 bobble-head dolls also market nostalgia. (CP/Kevin Frayer)

sell interconnected products from cartoon videos and toys to shoes and drugs to people around the world. The images of athletes and teams will be used to sell action figures to four-year-olds and drugs to sixty-year-olds, both of whom will want to act as athletes act on television.

Sports equipment manufacturers will continue to sell the idea that involvement in sports requires highly specialized and expensive equipment and clothing. Wealthy people will continue to use sports as contexts for announcing their status and identities through appearance and visual display as much as through their physical abilities; they will buy luxury boxes at games and ski at Sunshine or Whistler with personal instructors and thousands of dollars worth of high-tech gear.

Finally, we will see sport science discourse increasingly used in the marketing programmes of large corporations. This tactic already helps sell everything from athletic shoes to candy products. Pharmaceutical companies will be new players in this realm, and they will use sport science discourse to sell drugs and nutritional supplements to anyone and everyone, regardless of their health.

Gender Equity and Ethnic Diversity

Gender equity will remain an important issue in postindustrial nations, and it will become an increasingly important issue in other nations around the world. Excluding or limiting the participation of half the population in traditional and developing nations will no longer be accepted. The women's movement has become global, and women from around the world are working with each other to raise consciousness and to make changes in their lives. Many of those changes are related to everyday issues of sustenance, but, when standards of living begin to rise, gender equity in sports will emerge as an important social issue, especially in countries that have strong sport programmes for men.

Sociologist Harry Edwards predicted that "the challenge in sports in the 21st century is going to be diversity" (2000: 24). His prediction is grounded in the fact that ethnic diversity is increasing in many nations around the globe. Geographical mobility, labour migration, and political turmoil will push and pull people from diverse backgrounds into new social and political contexts. This will create challenges as governments, communities, and individuals try to come to terms with cultural differences in their lives. Of course, ethnic diversity will increase in sports at all levels, and it will create challenges for players, coaches, spectators, and sport organizations. The number of teams where players speak two or more languages will grow in many sports, coaches will require translators, agents will need courses in cultural issues, diversity training will become common for players, teams will hire language teachers and anthropologists to assist new players making adaptations as they enter and live in new cultures, and family members will need support as they do the same.

Increasing diversity goes hand in hand with globalization. Professional leagues in every nation will recruit more widely on a global basis. Citizenship will become less important than height, weight, and speed. Corporations will scout the world for young athletes who can endorse their products in emerging markets. Issues will be raised about regulating global recruiting. "Age of consent" for signing contracts varies from culture to culture, and different cultures have different norms about what is legal. The political importance of international governing bodies will become more important as these issues are faced in more sports. Conflicts will occur as leagues and teams in wealthy nations recruit star athletes from other nations. Bidding wars for athletes will become international in scope, and they will raise new political issues, which will involve nation-states, transnational corporations, and international governing bodies for sports. Overall, we will face diversity issues that we have not even dreamed of yet as we start a new century. The question will be whether these issues will create a reactionary, jingoistic, and isolationist backlash or new forms of openness and acceptance of cultural differences. To the extent that the former response prevails, conflict will increase; if the latter response prevails, positive new experiences will emerge in sports and in social life generally.

THE CHALLENGE OF MAKING THE FUTURE

The predictions in this chapter are meant to be a challenge for us: *we can make the future*. We are not locked into the predictions offered in this chapter or anywhere else. The meaning, organization, and purpose of sports can be transformed; it is possible to create goals and organizations so that sports are more democratic and more compatible with a wider range of values and experiences.

The growing importance of sports in society makes it more necessary for us to take a closer and more critical look at how sports are defined, organized, and played. As we do this, some of us will

> My Puritan soul burned with indignation at injustice in the sphere of sport. . . . Cricket had plunged me into politics long before I was aware of it. When I did turn to politics I did not have much to learn.
> —C. L. R. James, writer/activist from Trinidad (1963)

call for changes in dominant forms of sports or even reject those forms and call for new and alternative sports. However, we should not expect widespread, revolutionary changes to occur overnight. Social transformation is always a challenging and tedious process. It requires long-term efforts and carefully planned strategies, but it does not occur without a clear vision of possible futures and strategic efforts to turn visions into realities.

Theories Used to Form Visions and Develop Strategies

Playing an active role in transforming the world in which we live is part of being a citizen in a democracy. As noted in chapter 2, theories are useful in constructing our visions and taking actions to promote them. The following are some examples of how theories can be used in making the future.

Functionalist Theory Despite its limitations, this theory is widely used to construct visions of sport in the future. Those with power and influence like functionalism, because it takes the social system for granted and focuses on how sport contributes to maintaining the system. Functionalism usually inspires efforts to improve and expand existing sports and to use *conservative* and *reformist* strategies for making changes.

A *conservative strategy* is based on the assumption that changes in sport, like changes in the rest of society, involve raising more money, developing more effective marketing strategies, and generally strengthening traditional values, definitions, experiences, and organizational structures. A functionalist using a conservative strategy focuses on growth through strengthening what already exists, rather than transforming existing social relations or social structures. A *reformist strategy* focuses on eliminating problems and making sports more socially useful by making it

Social transformation does not occur without a struggle. Producing transformation is always a challenging and tedious process. It requires dedication and long-term commitment, just as some sports require dedication and commitment. Never ever, ever, ever cease to be a critical citizen. (Jay Coakley)

a bigger part of people's lives. A functionalist reformist strategy emphasizes social control more than cultural transformation. The focus is on such things as encouraging girls and women to play sports, eliminating cheating and drug use in sports, making athletes into role models, expanding opportunities to play sports, and tying sports to economic and community development processes. The Canadian Association for the Advancement of Women in Sport and Physical Activity (CAAWS) is an example of an organization that often uses reformist strategies based on a functionalist approach, although it often uses additional strategies grounded in critical and feminist theories as well.

Conflict Theory Conflict theorists envision a society in which sports are expressive and humane activities through which people are free to explore a full range of democratically organized physical challenges. This vision cannot become reality in a society in which the profit motive, economic exploitation, and oppressive forms of class relations destroy the possibility of freedom in and through sports. Therefore, conflict theory emphasizes a *radical strategy* of change in which the goal is the complete transformation of society itself. Unless there are revolutionary changes in the structure of social relations in society as a whole, playing sports will never involve true freedom, liberation, and pleasure. The strategy for bringing about change is to create class awareness in sports and society, thereby enabling people to transform the economic system and the political system that supports it. This involves creating organizations and political action groups through which players and fans could take the control of sports away from those with power and wealth.

Few people have used conflict theory in this way. It was popular during the 1960s and 1970s, and it was centrally involved in the anti-apartheid movement, but the monumental challenges that it presented to its proponents generally discouraged them and kept them from becoming effective agents of broad social change. However, conflict theorists did inspire important efforts to challenge racism, sexism, heterosexism, nationalism, and militarism in connection with sports, and they have inspired athletes to push for representation in sport organizations. This has kept the spirit and visions of conflict theory alive with some people around the world.

Interactionist Theory Interactionists envision sports created from "the bottom up" by the participants themselves. These sports would take many forms, each representing the unique perspectives and definitions of the world formed by participants as they interact with each other. *Conservative, reformist,* or *radical* strategies would be used, but they would all emphasize the importance of participants themselves creating the meaning, organization, and purpose of sports in their lives. Interactionists using *reformist* or *radical* approaches would work to make sports and sport organizations more democratic and inclusive and to inspire the creation of alternatives to existing organized sports.

Critical Theories Critical theorists envision a future in which people resist exclusive, exploitive, and oppressive ideologies and social relations in sports and create new sport forms that represent the interests and experiences of people from many backgrounds. They would use *reformist* and *radical strategies* focused on changing how people think about sports; changing how sports are defined, organized, and played; and using sports to change the structure and dynamics of social relations related to gender, race, class, sexuality, and (dis)ability. A primary radical strategy would be to disrupt structures, relationships, and discourses that help to reproduce forms of power relations that systematically marginalize or erase the identities and voices of particular groups of people in society. The ultimate goal would be to establish process-

es through which underrepresented voices might be heard and through which opportunities are distributed in a fair and representative manner in sports and society.

The Nike transnational advocacy network (Sage, 1999) was a classic example of such a strategy: the groups in the network focused on a specific problem faced by an identifiable group of workers in a sport industry and took political action to produce important changes. Another example of a radical strategy is the scholars in the U.S. who have joined with Native Americans to protest the use of Native American images for mascots and team names.

Feminist Theories Feminist theorists envision sports in which the values and experiences of women are used as central organizing principles and envision a society in which these sports would be funded and supported. They advocate reformist strategies designed to promote equity and radical strategies designed to resist and transform the dominant gender logic, which privileges men and all sports based on men's values and experiences. Feminists also advocate pushing the boundaries of gender, so there would be many accepted ways to "do" gender. Another profeminist strategy is to critique and transform traditional definitions of *masculinity* and create spaces in sports for men who view masculinity in terms of nurturance and support for others, rather than in terms of toughness and dominance over others.

The International Working Group on Women and Sport is grounded in feminist consciousness, and its members around the world use many strategies, including radical strategies aimed at changing ideologies and institutions that systematically exclude women from sports and disadvantage women when they do play sports. Strategies vary from nation to nation, because the problems faced by women are different in different cultures. Conservative strategies are used to increase participation opportunities for girls and women, reformist strategies are used to advance women into positions of power in society and in sport organizations, and radical strategies are used to transform the gender logic on which male privilege is based and female disadvantage is guaranteed.

Figurational Theory Figurational theorists envision sports free of oppressive power, exploitation, and violence. Their primary strategy is to engage in rigorous programmes of research that eventually inspire socially responsible and effective efforts to bring about change and social transformation. They realize that being an effective agent of social change is very difficult in a world where the interconnections between sports and other spheres of life are becoming increasingly complex. However, their hope is that, if research accurately identifies interconnections between collections of people and the processes of power used in social relations, it will be possible to design strategies for challenging and transforming social figurations that are exploitive and oppressive.

Change Means Different Things to Different People

When most people discuss changes in sports, they think in terms of *conservative strategies* grounded in a form of functionalist theory. They see change in terms of expansion and growth, not cultural and social transformation. They focus on *management* issues and strategies for keeping sports organized and profitable. They do not advocate deep changes in how sports are organized and played, or in the structures and ideologies that underlie those sports. Conservative strategies usually emphasize an underlying concern with using sports as tools for social control and teaching people how to conform to traditional values and expectations.

Reformist strategies also emphasize expanding participation opportunities, but they stress that those opportunities must be fair and free of social practices that systematically privilege some groups over others. *Radical strategies* also are concerned with inequities and democratic participation, but they emphasize deep structural and ideological changes; they advocate a combination of the redistribution of power in society, the transformation of social relations, and new ideologies that give voice to the experiences of previously disenfranchised groups of people.

Radical strategies make many people nervous, because they advocate the interests of socially marginalized groups and challenge the structures and ideologies that have privileged select groups of people. This threatens those who live their lives comfortably within the context of those structures and ideologies. Privileged people do not like radicals.

Each of these strategies for change is found in sports today. *Conservative strategies* remain dominant. Those with power tend to be conservative, and they use their resources to convince others to agree with them. They see power and performance sports as excellent vehicles for promoting values consistent with their interests; for them, sports are a means for making money, increasing influence, and promoting consumption and economic expansion. *Reformist strategies* are relatively common, especially among women and others who have lived on the margins of mainstream sports. *Radical approaches* are rare in sports, because most radicals are concerned with issues of poverty, homelessness, health care, quality education for children, accessible public transportation, full employment, and guaranteed minimum standards of living. It is difficult to work on these issues in connection with sports. However, some radicals concerned with ideological issues have used sports as sites for challenging dominant definitions of *masculinity* and *femininity*, raising questions about social class and race, and encouraging people to think critically about the antidemocratic features of hierarchical relationships.

Four Vantage Points for Making Changes

Making the world a better place is a never-ending task. Participating in this process as a change agent is always challenging, regularly frustrating, and sometimes rewarding. For those interested in making changes related to sports and social life, there are four vantage points from which changes might be initiated (Hall et al., 1991):

1. *Work within the system of sports.* You can become involved in sports and sport organizations and then use your position or power to influence and initiate changes. Having an "insider" vantage point can be very effective; sometimes, you can use it even to promote changes in society as a whole. However, becoming an insider often involves adopting the existing values of the organization where you work. This means that, even though you have many ideas about needed changes, your commitment to making those changes may decrease as you move up the organization into positions of increasing power. Once you are in a position to make changes, you may have vested interests in keeping things as they are. This is not inevitable, but it happens often. Although an insider vantage point can be a good place from which to make changes, it is important to be realistic about what insiders can do. This is important to remember when we think of athletes as possible change agents (see the Reflect on Sports box, "Athletes as Change Agents," below.

2. *Join "opposition" groups.* You can become a change agent by forming or joining political groups that challenge problematic sport policies and put pressure on sport organizations that have antidemocratic policies and programmes. For example, such groups might lobby for the building of a community sport centre in a low-income neighbourhood or lobby against using public funds to build a stadium that would serve primarily the interests of already privileged people in your community. Such groups might apply pressure, so that hosting a major sport event such as the Olympics would involve long-term legacies for the community, e.g.,

building low-cost housing for low-income community residents, and ensuring that the facilities built and equipment acquired for the Games are also a legacy, available for all of the community to use once the Games are over. The possibilities are endless.

3. *Create alternative sports.* You can reject or ignore dominant power and performance sports, and the organizations that sponsor them, and develop new sports grounded in the values and experiences of a wide array of different groups of people. This is often difficult to do, because resources are seldom available when you choose this vantage point for making change. However, this vantage point can be effective even when it does not lead to concrete institutionalized changes, because it provides clear-cut examples of new ways to look at and play sports, as well as new ways to look at and interact with other people. These examples then may inspire others to envision how they can create alternative sports in their own lives and communities.

4. *Focus on culture and social relations.* You could ignore sports and work to produce changes in social relations that indirectly raise questions about the organization and structure of sports in society. For example, as people question dominant ideas about masculinity and femininity and the cultural practices associated with these ideas, they may push for changes in the sports that reproduce ideas and practices that are destructive in the lives of many people. This strategy has been used by some groups working to lower sexual assault rates in the United States: they have pressured the NFL, the NCAA, and other sport organizations to support policies that increase awareness of the problem and encourage behavioural changes in connection with gender relations.

Regardless of the vantage point used to make change, any significant social transformation requires a combination of the following three things:

REFLECT ON SPORTS

Athletes as Change Agents
Does It Ever Happen?

Athletes are among the most visible and popular people in many cultures today. Some have the highest name and face recognition of any human beings in history. Such recognition puts them in good positions to act as change agents in society—or does it?

To explore this issue, we must understand that the visibility and popularity of athletes are tied to the public display of physical skills and media images out of which their public personas are formed. Athletes control their sport skills, but their images are controlled by others, including team publicity departments, the media, agents, and advertisers who create and use the athletes' images to promote and sell products. This limits the extent to which athletes can be effective agents of change; if their words and actions do not fit the interests of those who control their images, they risk losing the coverage and support on which their popularity depends. Team owners and corporate sponsors shy away from players who speak out on social issues.

When athletes become involved in community affairs, they usually take a conservative approach. They make speeches and do charity work that reaffirm dominant societal values and strengthen the status quo. They may form foundations to help poor children learn to read, but they will not form organizations to reform or radically alter how resources are allocated to schools. They may make public service announcements supportive of charitable organizations, but they will not identify poverty as a social issue and then call for policy changes related to employment, public transportation, and child care. Even when athletes enter politics, they most often represent conservative political positions aligned with preserving the status quo in society.

Athletes identified as role models are usually those who strengthen the status quo. As spokespersons, they generally represent those who have an interest in keeping things as they are or in selling products to make profits. They do promotions in which they urge children to stay in school, and they do radio and television commercials to sell cars for local dealers. However, they do not advocate *reforms*

Athletes often encounter difficulties when they speak out or demonstrate for certain social issues. Tommy Smith and John Carlos discovered this when they used the victory stand during the 1968 Olympics in Mexico City to protest race relations in the United States and around the world. They were stripped of their medals, expelled from the Olympic village, sent back to the United States amid widespread criticism and condemnation, and subjected to social rejection among many people in the United States. If you look carefully at the photograph, you will see that Peter Norman, the Australian sprinter who won the silver medal, is wearing an Olympic Project for Human Rights button (also worn by Smith and Carlos), showing his support for his two African-American competitors. Norman was not sanctioned.
(AP/Wide World Photos)

Continued

REFLECT ON SPORTS   Athletes as Change Agents continued

or *radical changes* in community processes and structures that intensify poverty, despair, and other social problems. Starting a foundation to help children from low-income neighbourhoods is great, but it does not necessarily call attention to the need for changes in the social system that is failing the children from those neighbourhoods.

When athletes do become real agents of change, they usually do so in connection with established organizations. For example, organizations such as Right to Play (formerly Olympic Aid), which is based in Canada; the Canadian Sport Leadership Corps (run by Commonwealth Games Canada); and Sport Sans Frontières in France all run programmes to bring sports to young people in impoverished communities in developing nations. Former athletes, young coaches, and physical education students all receive the opportunity to spend time in villages, refugee camps, and barrios associated with major cities; they provide equipment, organize and help to run programmes, and teach skills to community members so that they can continue to run sport and physical activity programmes. Some of

these organizations are also showing some sensitivity to local needs and interests rather than attempting to impose Western sports and Western ways of playing sports on local communities.

However, athletes seldom speak out on social issues or initiate political actions on their own. On minor issues such as what shoes or soft drinks to buy, people listen to athletes; however, when athletes talk about racism, sexism, economic exploitation, or violence, many people do not take them seriously, or they reject them outright (except, of course, in the case of Sheldon Kennedy speaking out in order to help prevent the sexual abuse of other young athletes). Look at what happened to Cassius Clay (Muhammad Ali) in the 1970s, when he spoke out on racism and the war in Vietnam. Look at what happened to Tommy Smith and John Carlos when they protested race relations on the victory stand during the 1968 Olympics. Is this why so many athletes now decide to be corporate shills and why they are moral jellyfish when it comes to speaking out on broader issues of social injustice and change? *What do you think?*

• •

1. Visions of what sports and social life could and should be like
2. Willingness to work hard to put visions into actions
3. Political abilities to rally the resources needed to produce results

The future of sports will be created out of this combination of visions, hard work, and politically effective actions.

SUMMARY

WHAT CAN WE EXPECT IN THE FUTURE?

Sports are social constructions; they change as ideas and relationships change in sports and in

society. Although the meaning, organization, and purpose of sports will become increasingly diverse in the future, power and performance sports will remain dominant. They will receive continued funding and sponsorship from those with resources and power in society. Pleasure and participation sports will grow in connection with demographic trends and ideological changes, but they will not receive the funding and support enjoyed by sports organized around the power and performance model.

Sports at all levels will be sites for struggles over who should play and how sports should be organized. The major trends at all levels of sports will be increases in the use of technology, increased coverage through an expanding range of media, a continuing emphasis on organization and rationalization, and a growth of commercialization and the emphasis on consumption that goes with it.

Changing sports remains a difficult challenge. Changes reflect the visions that people have about what they want sports to be in the future. Theories about sports inform and extend our visions of what is possible. Most people, especially those who are advantaged by the status quo, do not want to change sports as much as they want to expand them in their current forms. This conservative strategy fits with the assumptions and goals of functionalist theory. Strategies emphasizing reform and radical changes are more apt to be inspired by conflict theory, interactionist theory, and critical and feminist theories. Figurational theory emphasizes research that builds the knowledge needed to make effective and progressive interventions in the future.

Changes in sports can be made from any one of four vantage points: within sport itself, in connection with opposition groups, through efforts to create new and alternative sport forms, and indirectly by making changes in the society in which sports exist. Regardless of the vantage point, change and transformation depend on clear visions of what sports could be, a willingness to work hard to turn those visions into reality, and the political abilities to produce lasting results. Unless we work to create the sports we want in the future, sports will represent the interests of those who would like us all to play on their terms and for their purposes.

SUGGESTED READINGS

Sociological analyses of the future of sports do not exist. Those who study sports in society usually believe that the best way to understand the future is to critically assess sports today and then promote changes that will make sports more democratic and more open to those who can benefit from participation. Ideas about the future can be gained by creating your own versions of sports to fit the needs and experiences of people who are not often included in dominant forms of sports. Therefore, instead of looking for readings about the future, watch and talk to children as they play sports and develop new sport forms with their friends. They will give you ideas about what is possible in the future. Your visions will inspire a range of strategies for making change.

WEBSITE RESOURCES

Note: Websites often change. The following URLs were current when this book was printed. Please check our website www.mcgrawhill.ca/college/coakley for updates and additions.

www.mhhe.com/coakley8e (predictions on what happens to the control and organization of sports when more people play them; information on the impact of technology on sports and athletes)

www.righttoplay.com; www.commonwealthgames.ca; www.sportsansfrontieres.org (sites for sport aid organizations providing help in developing nations; Right to Play and the Canadian Sport Leadership Corps [run by Commonwealth Games Canada] are both based in Canada and recruit young athletes, coaches, and physical education students who want to help "make a difference")

www.sportinsociety.org (official site of the Center for the Study of Sport in Society; click on all the centre's programmes—Athletes in Service to America, Mentors in Violence Prevention Program, Project TEAMWORK, Urban Youth Sports, SportsCAP, and Additional Outreach Programs—to see examples of how sports can be changed and changes can occur through sports and the work of athletes using their skills to have a positive impact on the social world)

www.abcsports.go.com (this site plus www.espn.com have links to Enhanced TV, an interactive television experience that enables TV viewers to access game-related data and to play along with televised sport events; the future of spectator experiences is being developed in connection with these and related sites)

www.paralympic.org (official website of the
   International Paralympic Committee, an
   international nonprofit organization formed and
   run by 160 National Paralympic Committees and 5
   disability-specific international sports federations)
www.gaygames.com (site of the Federation of Gay
   Games; links to the history of the games, what
   occurred in Sydney at the 2002 Gay Games, and
   what happens in Montreal at the 2006 Gay Games)
www.adventuretime.com (online magazine for
   many outdoor adventure sports; shows
   alternatives to traditional organized sports; there
   are literally thousands of sites like this for
   alternative sports)
www.bmxweb.com/list.cfm (links to more than 500
   sites used by BMX bikers; illustrates that athletes
   in the future will be able to form networks with
   fellow athletes around the world)
www.hotrails.com (the key site for aggressive in-line
   skaters; provides a "feel" for the sport, who
   participates, and the norms underlying
   participation; note gender, racial/ethnic, and social
   class patterns among participants, because they
   provide information about the social dynamics of
   certain alternative sports as they develop)
www.gravitygames.com (is this the site of the future,
   with its heavily commercialized profile and ties to
   the major media and corporations?)

Credits

PHOTOGRAPHS

Chapter 1

p. 1, CP/Steve White; p. 7, Jay Coakley (both photographs); p. 12, CP/Brendon Dlouhy/*Edmonton Sun*; p. 15, Peter Donnelly; p. 18, Margaret MacNeill; p. 23, Peter Donnelly

Chapter 2

p. 30, CP/Ryan Remiorz; p. 33, CP/Adrian Wyld; p. 41, Jay Coakley; p. 46, CP/Crombie McNeil

Chapter 3

p. 69, Bob Jackson, *Colorado Springs Gazette*; p. 71, H. Armstrong Roberts; p. 75, City of Toronto Archives, Fonds 1244, item 477; p. 78, USOC Archives

Chapter 4

p. 83, Anne-Marie Weber/Taxi/Getty Images; p. 87, Photomondo/Taxi/Getty Images; p. 92, Robert E. Daemmrick/Stone/Getty Images; p. 93, CP/Preston Brownschlaigle/*Edmonton Sun*; p. 96, CP/Adrian Wyld; p. 97, CP/Jeff Stokoe/*Red Deer Advocate*; p. 103, Jay Coakley; p. 108, CP/AP/Ng Han Guan

Chapter 5

p. 113, Ron Chapple/Taxi/Getty Images; p. 131, Margaret MacNeill

Chapter 6

p. 147, CP/Jonathan Hayward; p. 150, *Colorado Springs Gazette*; p. 159, CP/Jacques Boissinot; p. 171, CP/Jacques Boissinot; p. 178, Jay Coakley

Chapter 7

p. 186, Jay Coakley; p. 193, CP/Jeff McIntosh; p. 198, CP/Itsou Inouye/AP; p. 204, CP/Ted Jacob; p. 210, CP/Ryan Remiorz; p. 213, CP/Ryan Remiorz

Chapter 8

p. 217, Margaret MacNeill; p. 219, CP/Rob Kruyt; p. 232, CP/Lehtikuva, Jussi Nukari/AP; p. 237, CP/Aaron Harris; p. 242, CP/Jacques Boissinot; p. 249, CP/Frank Gunn

Chapter 9

p. 255, Arthur Tilley/Taxi/Getty Images; p. 260, Lennox McClendon, AP/World Wide Photos; p. 261, CP/Paul Chiasson; p. 274, CP/Frank Gunn; p. 281, CP/Brian Thompson/*Brantford Expositor*; p. 283, CP/Hans Deryk; p. 284, John Terence Turner/Taxi/Getty Images

Chapter 10

p. 294, Laura Robinson; p. 297, Jay Coakley (1st photo), CP/Jonathan Hayward (2nd photo); p. 306, Jay Coakley; p. 309, CP/Andrew Vaughan; p. 316, CP/Bill Sikes/AP; p. 321, Tini Campbell

Chapter 11

p. 325, Alison Derry; p. 334, CP/Ryan Remiorz; p. 347, CP/Frank Gunn; p. 348, CP/Scott MacDonald

Chapter 12

p. 365, Margaret MacNeill; p. 374, CP/Chuck Stoody; p. 380, Margaret MacNeill; p. 390, CP/*Maclean's*/Phill Snel

Chapter 13

p. 403, Peter Donnelly; p. 408, Dick Hemingway Editorial Photographs; p. 414, CP/Fred Chartrand; p. 431, USOC Archives

Chapter 14

p. 440, *St. Thomas Times-Journal*; p. 451, CP/*Moncton Times & Transcript*/Viktor Pivovarov; p. 454, CP/Frank Gunn; p. 456, Kara Dillon and Nick Burdan. Reproduced with permission from the Faculty of Physical Education and Health, University of Toronto, www.utoronto.ca/physical; p. 462, Kara Dillon and Nick Burdan. Reproduced with permission from the Faculty of Physical Education and Health, University of Toronto, www.utoronto.ca/physical; p. 465, Lewko Hryhorijiw. Reproduced with permission from the Faculty of Physical Education and Health, University of Toronto, www.utoronto.ca/physical

Chapter 15

p. 470, unknown; p. 472, CP/Bonny Makarewicz; p. 476, Jason Lee, Mountain Board Sports; p. 478, Rob Schoenbaum; p. 485, CP/Kevin Frayer; p. 487, Jay Coakley; p. 491, AP/World Wide Photos

TEXT CREDITS

Chapter 6

p. 160 From Press Release, "Governor General to launch Canadian Figure Skating Championships and present Elvis Stojko with Meritorious Service Cross," issued by the Government House Press Office, January, 1999 (www.gg.ca).

Chapter 8

p. 251 From ICO Celebrate Humanity advertisement. Used with permission.

Chapter 9

p. 268 From Statistics Canada "Canadian Self-Identifying as Visible Minorities." Accessed via the Statistics Canada web site, www12.statcan.ca/English/census01/products/analytic/companion/etoimm/Canada.cfm.

p. 268 From Statistics Canada "Most Frequently Reported Ethnic Origins" 2001 Census. Adapted from the Statistics Canada web site, www12.statcan.ca/English/census01/products/analytic/companion/etoimm/Canada.cfm.

p. 267–269 From Statistics Canada "Canada's Ethnocultural Portrait." Adapted from the Statistics Canada web site, www12.statcan.ca/English/census01/products/analytic/companion/etoimm/Canada.cfm.

p. 267–269 From Statistics Canada "Increasing complexity of ethnic reporting." Adapted from Statistics Canada's "Canada's Ethnocultural Portrait." Accessed via www12.statcan.ca/English/census01/products/analytic/companion/etoimm/Canada.cfm.

Chapter 10

p. 300 From *The Globe and Mail* "The Top 25–Canada's Sports Leaders 2002," December 6, 2002, by James Christie and William Houston. Reprinted with permission.

p. 305 From Statistics Canada "Recreation participation for children from families above and below the poverty line." Adapted from the Statistics Canada National Longitudinal Survey of Children and Youth (NYSCY) for 1994 and 1996.

p. 311 From *Team Marketing Report*, 2003. Accessed via www.teammarketing.com.

p. 313–314, 321 Based on Parcels, J. (2000), "Straight facts about making it in pro hockey", www.nepeanhockey.on.ca/Docs/MakingIt.htm.

Chapter 13

p. 406–407 From "The development of federal policy for Canadian sport, 1961-2003" (adapted from Green, 2003).

Department of Canadian Heritage. Reproduced with the permission of the Minister of Public Works and Government Services Canada, 2003.

Chapter 14

p. 461 From Ontario School Sport (OFSAA) Participation 1977–2002.

Accessed via www.ofsaa.on.ca/participation_stats/participation%20stats01.htm.

References

Abdel-Shehid, G. 2000. Writing hockey through race: Rethinking black hockey in Canada. In *Rude: Contemporary Black Canadian cultural criticism* (pp. 69–86), edited by R. Walcott. Toronto: Insomniac Press.

Abdel-Shehid, G. 2002. Raptor morality: Blacks, basketball and national identity. In *Changing identities: Reading and writing ourselves* (pp. 131–38), edited by S. Fogel and L. Thoman. Toronto: Canadian Scholars Press.

Abney, R. 1999. African American women in sport. *Journal of Physical Education*, Recreation and Dance 70 (4): 35–38.

Acosta, R. V., and L. J. Carpenter. 1996. *Women in intercollegiate sport: A longitudinal study—Nineteen year update*, 1977–1996. Brooklyn, NY: Photocopied report.

Acosta, R. V., and L. J. Carpenter. 2000. *Women in intercollegiate sport: A longitudinal study—Twenty-three year update, 1977–2000*. Brooklyn, NY: Photocopied report.

Acosta, V. 1999. Hispanic women in sport. *Journal of Physical Education, Recreation and Dance* 70 (4): 44–46.

Adang, O. 1993. Crowd, riots, and the police: An observational study of collective violence. *Aggressive Behavior* 19: 37–38.

Adler, P. A., and P. Adler. 1991. *Backboards and blackboards: College athletes and role engulfment*. New York: Columbia University Press.

Adler, P. A., and P. Adler. 1998. Peer power: Preadolescent culture and identity. New Brunswick, NJ: Rutgers University Press.

Adler, P. A., and P. Adler. 1999. College athletes in high-profile media sports: The consequences of glory. In *Inside sports* (pp. 162–70), edited by J. Coakley and P. Donnelly. London: Routledge.

Alfred University. 1999. *Initiation rites and athletics: A national survey of NCAA sports teams*. See www.alfred.edu/news/html/hazing_study.html

Allison, L. 1993. *The changing politics of sport*. Manchester, England: Manchester University Press.

Allison, L. 2000. Sport and nationalism. In *Handbook of sports studies* (pp. 344–55), edited by J. Coakley and E. Dunning. London: Sage.

Anderson, E. 1999. *Comparing the black and gay male athlete: Patterns of oppression*. Paper presented at the annual conference of the North American Society for the Sociology of Sport, Cleveland, OH (November).

Anderson, E. 2000. *Trailblazing: America's first openly gay track coach*. Hollywood, CA: Alyson.

Anderson, S., and J. Cavanagh. 1996. The top 200. Washington, DC: Institute for Policy Studies.

Andrews, D. 1996. The fact(s) of Michael Jordan's blackness: Excavating a floating racial signifier. *Sociology of Sport Journal* 13 (2): 125–58.

Andrews, D. (ed.) 1996a. Deconstructing Michael Jordon: Reconstructing Postindustrial America. Special issue of the *Sociology of Sport Journal* 13 (4).

Andrews, D., and R. Pitter. 1997. Serving America's underserved youth: reflections on sport and recreation in an emerging social problems industry. Quest 49 (1):85–99.

Andrews, D., and M. Silk. 1999. *Football consumption communities, trans-national advertising, and spatial transformation*. Paper presented at the annual conference of the North American Society for the *Sociology of Sport*, Cleveland, OH (November).

Andrews, D. 2000. Posting up: French post-structuralism and the critical analysis of contemporary sporting culture. In *Handbook of sports studies* (pp. 106–38), edited by J. Coakley and E. Dunning. London: Sage.

Andrews, D.L., and S.J. Jackson. 2001. Sport stars: The cultural politics of sporting celebrity. London/New York: Routledge.

Andrews, V. 1998. African American player codes on celebration, taunting, and sportsmanlike conduct. In *African Americans in sport* (pp. 145–81), edited by G. Sailes. New Brunswick, NJ: Transaction.

Anonymous. 1999. Confessions of a cheater. ESPN—*The Magazine*, 1 November, 80–82.

Arbena, J. L. 1988. *Sport and society in Latin America: Diffusion, dependency, and the rise of mass culture.* Westport, CT: Greenwood Press.

Armstrong, G. 1994. False Leeds: The construction of hooligan confrontations. In *Game without frontiers: Football, identity, and modernity* (pp. 299–325), edited by R. Giulianotti and J. Williams. Aldershot, England: Arena (Ashgate).

Armstrong, J. 2000. Coors Field is not the patient's place. *The Denver Post*, 24 April, 3D.

Armstrong, J. 2003. He's no poser, dude. *Globe and Mail*, 17 May, p. F4.

Armstrong, P. 1984. *Labour Pains: Women's Work in Crisis.* Toronto: Women's Press.

Arnold, E. 2002. *Whose puck is it anyway?: A season with a minor novice team.* Toronto: McClelland & Stewart.

Ashe, A. 1993. *A hard road to glory.* 3 Vols. New York: Amistad.

Athletics Administration, April 1993, p. 22.

Atkinson, M. 2000. Brother can you spare a seat?: Developing recipes of knowledge in the ticket scalping subculture. *Sociology of Sport Journal* 17 (2), 151–70.

Atkinson, M., and K. Young. 2002. Terror games: Media treatment of security issues at the 2002 Winter Olympic Games. *Olympika* 11, 53–78.

Atkinson, M. In press. It's still part of the game: Dangerous masculinity, crime, and victimization in professional ice hockey. In *Sexual sports rhetoric and violence: Teaming up gender with the language of sport*, edited by L. Fuller. New York: The Haworth Press.

Atlanta Journal/Constitution. 1996. America's Olympic teams are increasingly marked by less diversity, more elitism. 1 October, H7. Special report.

Bagnato, A. 1995. The buck stops nowhere. *Chicago Tribune*, 6 August, 1, 5.

Bairner, A. 1996. Sportive nationalism and nationalist politics: A comparative analysis of Scotland, the Republic of Ireland, and Sweden. *Journal of Sport & Social Issues* 20 (3): 314–34.

Bairner, A. 2001. *Sport, nationalism, and globalization: European and North American perspectives.* Albany: State University of New York Press.

Baker, W. J. 1988. *Sports in the Western world.* Urbana: University of Illinois Press.

Bale, J., and J. Maguire (eds.) 1994. *The global sports arena: Athletic talent migration in an interdependent world.* London: Frank Cass.

Ball, D. 1973. Ascription and position: A comparative analysis of 'stacking' in professional football. *Canadian Review of Sociology and Anthropology* 10, 97–113.

Ballard, S. 1996. Broken back doesn't stall Indy winner. *USA Today*, 28 May, A1.

Bamberger, M., and D. Yaeger. 1997. Over the edge. *Sports Illustrated* 86 (15), 14 April: 60–70.

Banet-Weiser, S. 1999. Hoop dreams: Professional basketball and the politics of race and gender. *Journal of Sport & Social Issues* 23 (4): 403–20.

Banks, D. 1993. Tribal names and sports mascots. *Journal of Sport & Social Issues* 17 (1): 5–8.

Barnes, B. A., S. G. Zeiff, and D. I. Anderson. 1999. Racial difference and social meanings: Research on "Black" and "White" infants' motor development, 1931–1992. *Quest* 51 (4): 328–45.

Bartimole, R. 1999. *The city and the stadia (panel).* Presentation at the annual conference of the North American Society for the Sociology of Sport, Cleveland, OH (November).

Baxter, V., A. V. Margavio, and C. Lambert. 1996. Competition, legitimation, and the regulation of intercollegiate athletics. *Sociology of Sport Journal* 13 (1): 51–64.

Beal, B. 1995. Disqualifying the official: An exploration of social resistance through the subculture of skateboarding. *Sociology of Sport Journal* 12 (3): 252–67.

Beal, B. 1999. Skateboarding: An alternative to mainstream sports. In *Inside sports* (pp. 139–45), edited by J. Coakley and P. Donnelly. London: Routledge.

Beal, C. R. 1994. *Boys and girls: The development of gender roles.* New York: McGraw-Hill.

Beamish, R., and J. Bowery. 1988. *Q. What do you do for a living? A. I'm an athlete.* Kingston, Ontario:

Sport Research Group.

Beamish, R. 1990. The persistance of inequality: an analysis of participation patterns among Canada's high performance athletes. *International Review for the Sociology of Sport* 25 (2): 143–55.

Beaton, R. 1993. Mexicans best-suited to pitch, scouts say. *USA Today Baseball Weekly*, 24 February–2 March, 11.

Beauchesne, L. 1990. *The Dubin Inquiry's political purpose*. Paper presented at the conference, "After the Dubin Inquiry: Implications for Canada's High Performance Sport System." Queen's University, Kingston, ON, September.

Becker, D. 1999. Leaping past the pain. *USA Today*, 1 April, 1E, 4E.

Becker, D. 1996. Nothstein: "I enjoy the pain." *USA Today*, 24 July, 14E.

Begg, D. J., J. D. Langley, T. Moffitt, and S. W. Marshall. 1996. Sport and delinquency: An examination of the deterrence hypothesis in a longitudinal study. *British Journal of Sport Medicine* 30 (4): 335–41.

Begley, S. 1995. Three is not enough. *Newsweek*, 13 February, 67–69.

Bellamy, R. V., Jr. 1998. The evolving television sports marketplace. In *MediaSport* (pp. 173–87), edited by L. A. Wenner. London/New York: Routledge.

Bellefleur, M. 1986. *L'Église et le Loisir au Québec avant la Revolution Tranquille*. Sillery: Presses de l'Université du Québec.

Bellefleur, M. 1997. *L'Évolution du Loisir au Québec*. Sillery: Presses de l'Université du Québec.

Beller, J. M., and S. K. Stoll. 1995. Moral reasoning of high school athletes and general students: An empirical study versus personal testimony. *Journal of Pediatric Exercise Science* 7: 352–63.

Benedict, J. 1997. *Public heroes, private felons: Athletes and crimes against women*. Boston: Northeastern University Press.

Benedict, J. 1998. *Athletes and acquaintance rape*. Thousand Oaks, CA: Sage.

Benedict, J., and A. Klein. 1997. Arrest and conviction rates for athletes accused of sexual assault. *Sociology of Sport Journal* 14 (1): 86–94.

Benedict, J., and D. Yaeger. 1998. *Pros and cons: The criminals who play in the NFL*. New York: Warner Books.

Bentz, R. 1996. Robinson for three. *Sports Spectrum*, June, 14–15.

Berck, P. 2003. Personal communication. 20 March.

Berger, J. 1999. Alone at the top. *ESPN—The Magazine*, 29 November, 128–31.

Berlage, G. 1982. Are children's competitive team sports socializing agents for corporate America? In *Studies in the sociology of sport* (pp. 309–24), edited by A. Dunleavy, A. Miracle, and R. Rees. Fort Worth: Texas Christian University Press.

Billings, A., and S. Eastman. 2002a. Selective representations of gender, ethnicity, and nationality in American television coverage of the 2000 Summer Olympics. *International Review for the Sociology of Sport* 37 (4), 351–70.

Billings, A., and S. Eastman. 2002b. *Gender and national bias in the announcing of the 2002 Winter Olympics*. Paper presented at the annual meeting of the North American Society for the Sociology of Sport, Indianapolis, IN, 9 November.

Birrell, S. 2000. Feminist theories for sport. In *Handbook of sports studies* (pp. 61–76), edited by J. Coakley and E. Dunning. London: Sage.

Birrell, S., and D. M. Richter. 1994. Is a diamond forever? Feminist transformations of sport. In *Women, sport, and culture* (pp. 221–44), edited by S. Birrell and C. L. Cole. Champaign, IL: Human Kinetics.

Bissinger, H. G. 1990. *Friday night lights*. Reading, MA: Addison-Wesley.

Blain, N., R. Boyle, and H. O'Donnell. 1993. *Sport and national identity in the European media*. Leicester, England: Leicester University Press.

Blake, A. 1996. *The body language: The meaning of modern sport*. London: Lawrence and Wisehart.

Blinde, E. M., and D. E. Taub. 1992. Women athletes as falsely accused deviants: Managing the lesbian stigma. *The Sociological Quarterly* 33 (1): 521–33.

Blinde, E. M., D. E. Taub, and L. Han. 1993. Sport participation and women's personal empowerment: Experiences of the college athlete. *Journal of Sport & Social Issues* 17 (1): 47–60.

Blinde, E. M., D. E. Taub, and L. Han. 1994. Sport as a site for women's group and societal empowerment: Perspectives from the college athlete. *Sociology of Sport Journal* 11 (1): 51–59.

Bloom, G. A., and M. D. Smith. 1996. Hockey violence: A test of the cultural spillover theory.

Sociology of Sport Journal 13 (1): 65–77.

Bloom, M. 1998. Slower times at American high schools. *New York Times*, 29 January, C27.

Blumstein, A., and J. Benedict. 1999. Criminal violence of NFL players compared to the general population. *Chance* 12 (3): 12–15.

Bodley, H., and E. Brady. 1999. Baseball's new caste system. *USA Today*, 2 April, 1C, 2C, 13C.

Boileau, R., F. Landry, and Y. Trempe. 1976. Les Canadiens-français et les Grands Jeux Internationaux. In *Canadian Sport: Sociological Perspectives* (pp. 141–69), edited by R. Gruneau and J. Albinson. Don Mills, ON: Addison Wesley.

Bolin, A. 1992a. Beauty or beast: The subversive soma. Unpublished manuscript.

Bolin, A. 1992b. Flex appeal, food, and fat: Competitive bodybuilding, gender, and diet. *Play and Culture* 5(4), 378–400.

Bolin, A. 1992c. Vandalized vanity: Feminine physiques betrayed and portrayed. In *Tattoo, torture, mutilation, and adornment: The denaturalization of the body in culture and text* (pp. 79–99), edited by F. Mascia-Lees and P. Sharpe. Albany: State University of New York Press.

Bolin, A. 1998. Muscularity and femininity: Women bodybuilders and women's bodies in culturo-historical context. In *Fitness as cultural phenomenon* (pp. 187–212), edited by K. Volkwein. Munster, Germany: Waxman.

Booth, D. 1999. Gifts of corruption? Ambiguities of obligation in the Olympic Movement. *OLYMPIKA: The International Journal of Olympic Studies* 8: 43–68.

Bouchier, N. 2003. *For the love of the game: Amateur sport in small-town Ontario*, 1838–1895. Montreal and Kingston: McGill-Queen's University Press.

Bourdieu, P. 1986. *Distinction: A social critique of the judgment of taste*. London: Routledge.

Boyd, R. 1996. Genetic basis for race a skin deep fallacy: Biological, DNA advances tell us we're all the same. *Toronto Star*, 13 October, A14.

Boyd, T. 1997. *Am I black enough for you? Popular culture from the 'hood and beyond*. Bloomington: Indiana University Press.

Boyle, R. H. 1970. Oral Roberts: Small but OH MY! *Sports Illustrated* 33 (22), 30 November: 64.

Braddock, J., et al. 1991. Bouncing back: Sports and academic resilience among African-American males. *Education and Urban Society* 24 (1): 113–31.

Brady, E. 1996. Some legislators say Baltimore's money misspent. *USA Today*, 6 September, 19C.

Brady, E. 1999a. Colleges help to make the grade. *USA Today*, 19 October, 3C.

Brady, E. 1999b. Term of non-endearment? *USA Today*, 12 May, 1C, 2C.

Brady, E., and D. Howlett. 1996. Ballpark construction booming. *USA Today*, 6 September, 13C, 21C.

Bray, C. 1984. Gender and the political economy of Canadian sport. In *Sport and the Sociological Imagination* (pp. 104–24), edited by N. Theberge and P. Donnelly. Fort Worth: Texas Christian University Press.

Bray, C. 1988. Sport and the Canadian state: Gender and class issues. *Resources for Feminist Research* 17 (3), 75–77.

Bredemeier, B., E. B. Carlton, L. A. Hills, and C. A. Oglesby. 1999. Changers and the changed: Moral aspects of coming out in physical education. *Quest* 51 (4): 418–31.

Brennan, C. 1996. *Inside edge: A revealing journey into the secret world of figure skating*. New York. Scribner.

Bretón, M. 2000. Field of broken dreams: Latinos and baseball. *ColorLines* 3 (1): 13–17.

Bretón, M., and J. L. Villegas. 1999. Away games: *The life and times of a Latin baseball player*. Albuquerque: University of New Mexico Press.

Bricknell, L. 1999. The trouble with feelings: Gender, sexualities, and power in a gender regime of competitive sailing. *Journal of Sport & Social Issues* 23 (4): 421–38.

Brooks, D., and R. Althouse. 2000a. African American head coaches and administrators: Progress but ....? In *Racism in college athletics: The African-American athlete's experience* (pp. 85–118), edited by D. Brooks and R. C. Althouse. Morgantown, WV: Fitness Information Technology.

Brooks, D., and R. Althouse. 2000b. Fifty years after Jackie Robinson: Equal access but unequal outcome. In *Racism in college athletics: The African American athlete's experience* (pp. 307–20), edited by D. Brooks and R. Althouse. Morgantown, WV: Fitness Information Technology.

Brooks, D., R. Althouse, and D. Tucker. 1998. African American male head coaches: In the "red zone," but can they score? In *African Americans in sport* (pp. 217–40), edited by G. Sailes. New Brunswick, NJ: Transaction.

Brownell, S. 1995. *Training the body for China: Sports in the moral order of the People's Republic.* Chicago: University of Chicago Press.

Bruce, T. 1998. Audience frustration and pleasure: Women viewers confront televised women's basketball. *Journal of Sport & Social Issues* 22 (4): 373–97.

Bryshun, J., and K. Young. 1999. Sport-related hazing: An inquiry into male and female involvement. In *Sport and gender in Canada* (pp. 269–92), edited by P. White and K. Young. Don Mills, Ontario: Oxford University Press.

Burstyn, V. 1999. *The rites of men: Manhood, politics, and the culture of sport.* Toronto: University of Toronto Press.

Burstyn, V. 2000. The sporting life. In *Taking Sport Seriously: Social Issues in Canadian Sport* (pp. 22–28), edited by P. Donnelly. Toronto: Thompson Educational Publishing.

Bylsma, D., and J. Bylsma. 1998. *So your son wants to play in the NHL?* Toronto: McClelland & Stewart.

Bylsma, D., and J. Bylsma. 2000. *So you want to play in the NHL: A guide for young players.* Chicago: McGraw-Hill/Contemporary Books.

CAAWS-ACAFS news release. 1997. Coverage of women's sports plummets despite strike, lockout. In *Taking Sport Seriously: Social Issues in Canadian Sport* (pp. 289–90), edited by P. Donnelly. Toronto: Thompson Educational Publishing.

CAAWS. 2002. Presentation to the Sub-Committee on the Study of Sport in Canada: Bill C-54, *The Sport and Physical Activity Act.* 22 May.

Cagan, J., and N. deMause. 1998. *Field of schemes: How the great stadium swindle turns public money into private profit.* Monroe, ME: Common Courage Press.

Calhoun, C. 1998. Editor's comments. *Sociological Theory* 16 (1): 1–3.

Campagnolo, I. 1977. *Toward a national policy on amateur sport: A working paper.* Ottawa: Ministry of State, Fitness and Amateur Sport.

Campbell, M. 2003. Long Shots series. *Toronto Star,* 1 June.

Campbell, M. 2003. Join the dots on politics, fitness, sports and schools. *Globe and Mail,* 13 May, p. A9.

Campbell, N. 1995. Tense clash of cultures surrounds Mann Cup. *Globe and Mail,* 14 September, p. C8.

Canadian Journal for Women in Coaching. 2000.

www.coach.ca/WOMEN.

Canadian Press. 1994. Équipe canadienne de hockey aux Jeux: un seul francophone à Lillehammer. *Le Devoir,* 24 January.

Cantelon, M. 2001. *The Canadian Football League: Radically Canadian?* Unpublished master's thesis, University of Ottawa.

Capouya, J. 1986. Jerry Falwell's team. *Sport* 77 (9): September, 72–83.

Carlston, D. 1986. An environmental explanation for race differences in basketball performance. In *Fractured focus* (pp. 87–110), edited by R. Lapchick. Lexington, MA: Lexington Books.

Carnegie, H. 1997. *A fly in a pail of milk: The Herb Carnegie story.* Oakville, ON: Mosaic Press.

Carr, C. N., S. R. Kennedy, and K. M. Dimick. 1996. Alcohol use among high school athletes. *The Prevention Researcher* 3 (2): 1–3.

Carrington, B., and J. Sugden. 1999. *Trans-national capitalism and the incorporation of world football.* Paper presented at the annual conference of the North American Society for the Sociology of Sport, Cleveland, OH (November).

Caudwell, J. 1999. Women's football in the United Kingdom: Theorizing gender and unpacking the butch lesbian image. *Journal of Sport & Social Issues* 23 (4): 390–402.

Cavalli-Sforza, L. L., and F. Cavalli-Sforza. 1995. *The great human diasporas: The history of diversity and evolution.* Reading MA: Perseus Books.

Cavallo, D. 1981. *Muscles and morals.* Philadelphia: University of Pennsylvania Press.

Chafetz, J., and J. Kotarba. 1999. Little League mothers and the reproduction of gender. In *Inside sports* (pp. 46–54), edited by J. Coakley and P. Donnelly. London: Routledge.

Chalip, L., and B. C. Green. 1998. Establishing and maintaining a modified youth sport program: Lessons from Hotelling's location game. *Sociology of Sport Journal* 15 (4): 326–42.

Chamberlain, M. 1983. *Soccer, multiculturalism and the Canadian state.* Unpublished Master's thesis, University of Alberta.

Chandler, T. J. L., and A. D. Goldberg. 1990. The academic all-American as vaunted adolescent role-identity. *Sociology of Sport Journal* 7 (3): 287–93.

Chernushenko, D. 1994. *Greening our games: Running sports events and facilities that won't cost the earth.* Ottawa: Centurion Publishing.

Chisholm, A. 1999. Defending the nation: National bodies, U.S. borders, and the 1996 U.S. Olympic women's gymnastics team. *Journal of Sport & Social Issues* 23 (2): 126–39.

Christie, J. 1998. Limpert won't create Commonwealth flap. *Globe and Mail*, 14 August, p. S1.

Christie, J. 2000. COA running bilingual operation. *Globe and Mail*, 25 May, p. S6.

Christie, J. 2003. COC head takes aim at Ontario's failures. *Globe and Mail*, 9 May, pp. S1–S2.

Churchill, W. 1994. *Indians are us? Culture and genocide in Native North America.* Monroe, ME: Common Courage Press.

Ciborowski, T. 1997. "Superstition" in the collegiate baseball player. *The Sport Psychologist* 11 (3): 305–17.

Clancy, F. 1999. Warriors. *USA Weekend*, 12–14 February, 4–6.

Clark, C. 2000. National sport programs weak in French, report says. *Globe and Mail*, 15 June, p. S2.

Clarke, A. 2003. Picturing diversity through wrong eyes. *TVO*, 8, 10 February.

Clarke, J., et al. 1978. Football and working class fans: Tradition and change. In *Football hooliganism: The wider context* (pp. 37–60), edited by R. Ingham. London: Inter-Action Inprint.

Cluer, S., P. Donnelly, M. MacNeill, and G. Knight. 2001. *Lessons learned: A case study of CBC coverage of men's and women's diving at the Sydney Olympics.* Paper presented at the North American Society for the Sociology of Sport Annual Conference, San Antonio, TX, 31 October–3 November.

Coakley, J. 1983a. Play, games, and sports: developmental implications for young people. In *Play, games and sports in cultural contexts* (pp. 431–50), edited by J. C. Harris and R. J. Park. Champaign IL: Human Kinetics.

Coakley, J. 1983b. Leaving competitive sport: Retirement or rebirth? *Quest* 35: 1–11.

Coakley, J. 1985. When should children begin competing? In *Sport for children and youths* (pp. 59–63), edited by D. Gould and M. R. Weiss. Champaign, IL: Human Kinetics.

Coakley, J. 1992. Burnout among adolescent athletes: A personal failure or social problem? *Sociology of Sport Journal* 9 (3): 271–85.

Coakley, J. 1993a. Socialization and sport. In *Handbook of research on sport psychology* (pp. 571–86), edited by R. N. Singer, M.

Murphey, and L. K. Tennant. New York: Macmillan.

Coakley, J. 1993b. Sport and socialization. *Exercise and Sport Science Reviews* 21: 169–200.

Coakley, J. 1997. Ethics, deviance, and sports: A critical look at crucial issues. In *Ethics, sport, and leisure: Crises and critiques* (pp. 3–24), edited by A. Tomlinson and S. Fleming. Aachen, Germany: Meyer and Meyer Verlag.

Coakley, J. 2002. Using sports to control deviance and violence among youths: Let's be critical and cautious. In *Paradoxes of Youth and Sports* (pp. 13–30), edited by M. Gatz, M. Messner, and S.J. Ball-Rokeach. Albany, NY: State University of New York Press.

Coakley, J., and A. White. 1999. Making decisions: How young people become involved and stay involved in sports. In *Inside sports* (pp. 77–85), edited by J. Coakley and P. Donnelly. London: Routledge.

Coakley, J., and E. Dunning, eds. 2000. *Handbook of sports studies.* London: Sage.

Coakley, J., and P. Donnelly, eds. 1999. *Inside sports.* London: Routledge.

Cochrane, J., A. Hoffman, and P. Kincade. 1977. *Women in Canadian life: Sports.* Toronto: Fitzhenry & Whiteside.

Cole, C. L. 2000a. Body studies in the sociology of sport. In *Handbook of sports studies* (pp. 439–60), edited by J. Coakley and E. Dunning. London: Sage.

Cole, C. L. 2000b. The year that girls ruled. *Journal of Sport & Social Issues* 24 (1): 3–7.

Comité sur la place du Québec dans le système sportif Canadien. 2001. *Le Québec dans le système sportif Canadien.* Report presented to the Ministre délégué au Tourisme, au Loisir et au Sport.

Concerned American Indian Parents. 1988. *Nicknames, logos and mascots depicting Native American People.* Photocopy report distributed by the National Conference of Christians and Jews and Martin-Williams Advertising, Inc., Minneapolis.

Conniff, R. 1996. New day for women's sports. *The Progressive* 60 (9): 11.

Conroy, P. 1986. *The prince of tides.* Boston MA: Houghton Mifflin.

Coombe, R. J. 1999. Sports trademarks and somatic politics: Locating the law in a critical cultural studies. In *SportCult* (pp. 262–88), edited by

R. Martin and T. Miller. Minneapolis: University of Minnesota Press.

Corbett, D., and W. Johnson. 2000. The African American female in collegiate sport: Sexism and racism. In *Racism in college athletics: The African American athlete's experience* (pp. 199–226), edited by D. Brooks and R. Althouse. Morgantown, WV: Fitness Information Technology.

Corsello, A. 1999. Hallowed be thy game. *Gentlemen's Quarterly* (September): 432–40.

Coulombe, S., and M. Lavoie. 1985. Les francophones dans la Ligue nationale de hockey: Une analyse économique de la discrimination. *L'Actualité économique* 61 (1), 73–92.

Cousins, S. O., and P. Vertinsky. 1999. Aging, gender, and physical activity. In *Sport and gender in Canada* (pp. 129–52), edited by P. White and K. Young. Don Mills, Ontario: Oxford University Press.

Cox, B., and S. Thompson. 2000. Multiple bodies: Sportswomen, soccer and sexuality. *International Review for the Sociology of Sport* 35 (1): 5–20.

Creager, E. 1999. Sports dropouts. *Colorado Springs Gazette*, 7 October, LIFE1–LIFE2.

Creedon, P. J. 1998. Women, sport, and media institutions: Issues in sports journalism and marketing. In *MediaSport* (pp. 88–99), edited by L. A. Wenner. London/New York: Routledge.

Crissey, J. 1999. Corporate cooptation of sport: The case of snowboarding. Unpublished Thesis, Colorado State University, Ft. Collins.

Critcher, C. 1979. Football since the war. In *Working class culture* (pp. 161–84), edited by J. Clarke. London: Hutchinson.

Crompton, J. L. 1993. Sponsorship of sport by tobacco and alcohol companies: A review of the issues. *Journal of Sport & Social Issues* 17 (3): 148–67.

Crosset, T. 1995. *Outsiders in the clubhouse: The world of women's professional golf.* Albany: State University of New York Press.

Crosset, T. 1999. Male athletes' violence against women: A critical assessment of the athletic affiliation, violence against women debate. *Quest* 51 (3): 244–57.

Crosset, T., and B. Beal. 1997. The use of "subculture" and "subworld" in ethnographic works on sport: A discussion of definitional distinctions. *Sociology of Sport Journal* 14 (1): 73–85.

Curry, T. 1991. Fraternal bonding in the locker room: A profeminist analysis of talk about competition and women. *Sociology of Sport Journal* 8 (2): 119–35.

Curry, T. 1993. A little pain never hurt anyone: Athletic career socialization and the normalization of sports injury. *Symbolic Interaction* 16 (3): 273–90.

Curry, T. 1996. *Beyond the locker room: Sexual assault and the college athlete.* Presidential Address, North American Society for the Sociology of Sport Conference (Birmingham AL).

Curry, T. 1998. Beyond the locker room: Campus bars and college athletes. *Sociology of Sport Journal* 15 (3): 205–15.

Curry, T., and R. H. Strauss. 1994. A little pain never hurt anybody: A photo-essay on the normalization of sport injuries. *Sociology of Sport Journal* 11 (2): 195–208.

Curtis, J. and Ennis, R. 1988. Negative consequences of leaving competitive sport?: Comparative findings for former elite hockey players. *Sociology of Sport Journal* 5: 87–106.

Curtis, J., and P. White. 1992. Toward a better understanding of the sport practices of francophone and anglophones Canadians. *Sociology of Sport Journal* 9 (4), 403–22.

Curtis, J., and W. McTeer. 1990. Sport involvement and academic attainment in university: Two studies in the Canadian case. In *Psychology and Sociology of Sport II: Selected Research*, 2 (pp.177–92), edited by L. VanderVelden and J. Humphrey. New York: AMS Press.

Curtis, J., W. McTeer, and P. White. 1999. Exploring effects of school sport experiences on sport participation in later life. *Sociology of Sport Journal* 16, 348–65.

Curtis, J., W. McTeer, and P. White. 1999. Exploring effects of school sport experiences on sport participation in later life. *Sociology of Sport Journal* 16 (4): 348–56.

Curtis, J., W. McTeer, and P. White. 2003. Do high school athletes earn more pay?: Youth sport participation and earnings as an adult. *Sociology of Sport Journal* 20 (1), 60–76.

Dacyshyn, A. 1999. When the balance is gone: The sport and retirement experiences of elite female gymnasts. In *Inside sports* (pp. 214–22), edited by J. Coakley and P. Donnelly. London: Routledge.

Dallaire, C. 2000. At the Alberta Francophone Games. In *Taking Sport Seriously: Social Issues in Canadian Sport*, 2nd Edition (pp. 126–27), edited by P. Donnelly. Toronto: Thompson Educational Publishing.

Dallaire, C., and C. Denis. 2000. "If you don't speak French, you're out": Don Cherry, the Alberta Francophone Games, and the discursive construction of Canada's Francophones. *Canadian Journal of Sociology* 25.

Daniels, D. 1999. *Body display: Women athletes' bodies as ornamental surfaces.* Paper presented at the annual conference of the North American Society for the Sociology of Sport, Cleveland, OH (November).

Daniels, D. 2000. Gazing at the new black woman athlete. *ColorLines* 3 (1): 25–26.

Daniels, D. 2002. Woman/athlete: Can you tell me when you see one? *Canadian Women's Studies/les cahiers de la femme* 21 (3), 64–72.

Danylchuk, K. 1995. Academic performance of intercollegiate athletes at a Canadian university. Comparisons by gender, type of sport and affiliated faculty. *Avante* 1 (2): 78–93.

Davis, C. 1999. Eating disorders, physical activity, and sport: Biological, psychological, and sociological factors. In *Sport and gender in Canada* (pp. 85–106), edited by P. White and K. Young. Don Mills, Ontario: Oxford University Press.

Davis, L. 1994. A postmodern paradox? Cheerleaders at women's sporting events. In *Women, sport, and culture* (pp. 149–58), edited by S. Birrell and C. L. Cole. Champaign, IL: Human Kinetics.

Davis, L. 1997. *The swimsuit issue and sport: Hegemonic masculinity in Sports Illustrated.* Albany: State University of New York Press.

Davis, L., and O. Harris. 1998. Race and ethnicity in U.S. sports media. In *MediaSport* (pp. 154–69), edited by L. A. Wenner. London/New York: Routledge.

Decker, D., and K. Lasley. 1995. Participation in youth sports, gender, and the moral point of view. *The Physical Educator* 53: 14–21.

Deford, F. 1976. Religion in sport. *Sports Illustrated*, 44 (16): 19 April, 88–100.

Department of Athletics and Recreation. 1994. Report of the Task Force on Gender Equity. University of Toronto.

Department of Canadian Heritage. Reproduced with the permission of the Minister of Public Works and Government Services Canada, 2003.

Devereaux, E. 1976. "Two Ball Games" (30 min.). Consortium of University Films Centre, Cornell University, Ithaca, NY.

Devereaux, E. 1976. Backyard versus Little League baseball: The impoverishment of children's games. In *Social Problems in Athletics* (pp. 37–56) edited by D. Landers. Urbana: University of Illinois Press.

DiPasquale, M. G. 1992. Editorial: Why athletes use drugs. *Drugs in Sports* 1 (1): 2–3.

Dobie, M. 1987. Facing a brave new world. *Newsday*, 8 November, pp. 28, 32.

Dodd, M. 2000. Morals clause seals Hancock's renewal of sponsorship. *USA Today*, 16 February, 9C.

Domi, T. 1992. Tough tradition of hockey fights should be preserved. *USA Today*, October 27, C3.

Donnelly, P. 1981. Four fallacies, III: Climbing is character building. *Mountain* 82:20–23.

Donnelly, P. 1988a. Sport as a site for "popular" resistance. In *Popular cultures and political practices* (pp. 69–82), edited by R. Gruneau. Toronto: Garamond Press.

Donnelly, P. 1988b. Subcultures in sport: Resilience and transformation. In *Sport and social development: Traditions, transitions, and transformation* (pp. 119–46), edited by A. Ingham and J. Loy. Champaign, IL: Human Kinetics.

Donnelly, P. 1993. Democratization revisited: Seven theses on the democratization of sport and active leisure. *Loisir et société/Society and Leisure* 16 (2): 413–434.

Donnelly, P. 1993. Problems associated with youth involvement in high-performance sports. In *Intensive participation in children's sports* (pp. 95–126), edited by B. R. Cahill and A. J. Pearl. Champaign, IL: Human Kinetics.

Donnelly, P. 1996a. The local and the global: Globalization in the sociology of sport. *Journal of Sport & Social Issues* 20 (3): 239–57.

Donnelly, P. 1996b. Prolympism: Sport monoculture as crisis and opportunity. *Quest* 48 (1): 25–42.

Donnelly, P. 1997. Child labour, sport labour: Applying child labour laws to sport. *International Review for the Sociology of Sport* 32 (4), 389–406.

Donnelly, P. 1999. Who's fair game? In *Gender and Sport in Canada*, edited by P. White and K. Young. Toronto: Oxford University Press.

Donnelly, P. 1999. Who's fair game? Sport, sexual harassment, and abuse. In *Sport and gender in*

Canada (pp. 107–28), edited by P. White and K. Young. Don Mills, Ontario: Oxford University Press.

Donnelly, P. 2000. Youth sport in Canada: Problems and resolutions. In *Sociology of Sport: Theory and Practice* (pp. 167–86), edited by R. Jones and K. Armour. Harlow, England: Pearson Education.

Donnelly, P. 2002. George Herbert Mead and the development of an interpretive sociology of sport. In *Theory, sport and society* (pp. 83–102), edited by J. Maguire and K. Young. London: Elsevier.

Donnelly, P., and J. Coakley. 2002. *The role of recreation in promoting social inclusion.* Toronto: Laidlaw Foundation Working Papers on Social Inclusion (www.laidlawfdn.org).

Donnelly, P., and J. Harvey. 1996. *Overcoming systemic barriers to access in active living.* Ottawa: Fitness Branch, Health Canada, and Active Living Canada.

Donnelly, P., and J. Harvey. 1999. Class and gender: Intersections in sport and physical activity. In *Sport and gender in Canada* (pp. 40–64), edited by P. White and K. Young. Don Mills, Ontario: Oxford University Press.

Donnelly, P., and K. Young. 1999. Rock climbers and rugby players: Identity construction and confirmation. In *Inside sports* (pp. 67–76), edited by J. Coakley and P. Donnelly. London: Routledge.

Donnelly, P., and R. Sparks. 1997. Child sexual abuse in sport. In *Taking sport seriously: Social issues in Canadian sport* (pp. 200–05), edited by P. Donnelly. Toronto, Ontario: Thompson Publishing, Inc.

Donnelly, P., B. Kidd, J. Harvey, S. Laberge, and G. Rail. 2001. Plus ça change…: Patterns of association in Canadian Hockey. Report for the project, *Patterns of Association in Canadian Civil Society: Linguistic Relations in Non-Governmental Organizations.*

Donnelly, P., C. McCloy, L. Petherick, and P. Safai. 2000. *The crisis in school sport: Issues and resolutions.* University of Toronto: Centre for Sport Policy Studies Reports.

Drahota, J. T., and D. S. Eitzen. 1998. The role exit of professional athletes. *Sociology of Sport Journal* 15 (3): 263–78.

Drakich, K. 2002. Personal communication.

Dubin, C. 1990. *Commission of inquiry into the use of drugs and banned practices intended to increase athletic performance.* Ottawa: Ministry of Supply and Services.

Dufur, M. 1998. Race logic and "being like Mike": Representations of athletes in advertising, 1985–1994. In *African Americans in sport* (pp. 67–84), edited by G. Sailes. New Brunswick, NJ: Transaction.

Duncan, M. C., and M. A. Messner. 1998. The media image of sport and gender. In *MediaSport* (pp. 170–85), edited by L. A. Wenner. London/New York: Routledge.

Dunk, T. 1991. *It's a working man's town: Male working class culture.* Montreal and Kingston: McGill-Queen's University Press.

Dunn, K. 1994. Just as fierce. *Mother Jones*, November/December: 35–39.

Dunn, R., and C. Stevenson. 1998. The paradox of the Church Hockey League. *International Review for the Sociology of Sport* 33 (2): 131–41.

Dunning, E. 1999. *Sport matters: Sociological studies of sport, violence, and civilization.* London: Routledge.

Dunning, E., and K. Sheard. 1979. *Barbarians, gentlemen, and players: A sociological study of the development of rugby football.* New York: New York University Press.

Du Pree, D. 1992. Petty issues won't change the world. *USA Today*, 5 August, 7E.

Duquin, M. 1993. One future for sport: Moving toward an ethic of care. In *Women and sport: Issues and controversies* (pp. 289–96), edited by G. Cohen. Newbury Park, CA: Sage.

Dyck, N. 2001. *Immigration, integration and sport in Canada.* Paper presented at the Policy Research Seminar on Identity, Halifax, NS.

Early, G. 1998. Performance and reality: Race, sports, and the modern world. *The Nation* 267 (5): 11–20.

Eastman, S. T., and A. C. Billings. 1999. Gender parity in the Olympics: Hyping women athletes, favoring men athletes. *Journal of Sport & Social Issues* 23 (2): 140–70.

Eddington, B. 2000. Lacrosse: Little brother of war. *The Beaver*, October–November, 8–14.

Eder, D. (with C. C. Evans and S. Parker). 1995. *School talk: Gender and adolescent culture.* New Brunswick, NJ: Rutgers University Press.

Edwards, H. 1973. *Sociology of sport.* Homewood, IL: Dorsey Press.

Edwards, H. 2000. The decline of the black athlete (as interviewed by D. Leonard). *ColorLines* 3 (1): 29–24.

Eisen, G., and D. K. Wiggins, eds. 1994. *Ethnicity and sport in North American history and culture*. Westport, CT: Greenwood Press.

Eitzen, D. S. 1988. The myth and reality of elite amateur sport. *The World and I* 3 (10): 549–59.

Eitzen, D. S. 1999. *Fair and foul: Beyond the myths and paradoxes of sport*. Lanham, MA: Rowman and Littlefield.

Eitzen, D. S. 2000. Public teams, private profits: How pro sports owners run up the score on fans and taxpayers. *Dollars and Sense*, March/April; see www.DollarsandSense.org/2000/0300eitzen.html

Elias, N. 1978. *The civilizing process: The history of manners, Vol. 1*. Oxford, England: Basil Blackwell.

Elias, N. 1982. *The civilizing process: State formation and civilization, Vol. 2*. Oxford, England: Basil Blackwell.

Elias, N. 1999. Fathers focus increased care on boys. *USA Today*, 14 June, 6D.

Elias, N., and E. Dunning. 1986. *Quest for excitement*. New York: Basil Blackwell.

Eliasoph, N. 1999. "Everyday racism" in a culture of political avoidance: Civil society, speech, and taboo. *Social Problems* 46 (4): 479–502.

Elkind, D. 1981. *The Hurried Child: Growing Up Too Fast Too Soon*. Don Mills, Ontario: Addison Wesley.

Engh, F. 1999. *Why Johnny hates sports*. Garden City Park, NY: Avery.

Enloe, C. 1995. The globetrotting sneaker. *Ms.* 5 (5), March/April: 10–15.

Entine, J. 2000. *Taboo: Why black athletes dominate sports, and why we are afraid to talk about it*. New York: Public Affairs.

Eskes, T. B., M. C. Duncan, and E. M. Miller. 1998. The discourse of empowerment: Foucault, Marcuse, and women's fitness texts. *Journal of Sport & Social Issues* 22 (3): 317–44.

ESPN. 1999. High school athletes: Do jocks rule the school? www.espn.com/gen/features/jocks, 20 June–24 June (edited by T. Farrey for ESPN's television show, *Outside the Lines*).

Essed, P. 2002. Everyday Racism. In *A Comparison of Race Studies* (pp. 202–16), edited by D.T. Goldberg and J. Solomos. Oxford: Blackwell Publishers.

Etue, E., and M. Williams. 1996. *On the Edge: Women Making Hockey History*. Toronto: Second Story Press.

Evans, R.G., M. Barer, and T. Marmor. 1994. *Why Are Some People Healthy and Others Not?* New York: Aldine de Gruyter.

Ewald, K., and R. M. Jiobu. 1985. Explaining positive deviance: Becker's model and the case of runners and bodybuilders. *Sociology of Sport Journal* 2 (2): 144–56.

Faber, M. 1998a. Beware! *Sports Illustrated* 89 (15): 12 October, 98–106.

Faber, M. 1998b. Stitches in time: Culture of pain. *Sports Illustrated* 89 (15): 12 October, 88–96.

Falk, B. 1995. Bringing home the violence. *Newsday*, 8 January, 12–13.

Farrey, T. 1998. New stadiums, new fans. espn.sportszone.com/gen/features/stadiamnia/_monday.html (Part 1 of a five-part series).

Fasting, K. 1996. *40,000 female runners: The Grete Waitz Run—Sport, culture, and counterculture*. Paper presented at International Pre-Olympic Scientific Congress, Dallas (July).

Fausto-Sterling, A. 2000. *Sexing the body: Gender politics and the construction of sexuality*. New York: Basic Books.

Feeney, R. 1995. *A Catholic perspective: Physical exercise and sports*. N.p.: Aquinas Press.

Fejgin, N. 1994. Participation in high school competitive sports: A subversion of school mission or contribution to academic goals? *Sociology of Sport Journal* 11 (3): 211–30.

Ferguson, A. 1999. Inside the crazy culture of kids sports. *Time* 154 (2): 12 July, 52–61.

Feschuk, S. 1998. COA chastised for language faux pas. *Globe and Mail*, 18 March, p. A4.

Field, R. In press. *The ties that bind: Ted Rogers, Larry Tanenbaum, and the Toronto sport elite*. University of Toronto: Centre for Sport Policy Studies Working Papers.

Fine, G. A. 1987. *With the boys: Little League baseball and preadolescent culture*. Chicago: University of Chicago Press.

Fish, M. 1993. Steroids riskier than ever. *The Atlanta Journal-Constitution*, 26 September, A1, A12–A13. Part I of four parts.

Fish, M. 1998. Pay dirt! Bought & paid for: How booster clubs help turn out the state's best football teams. *Atlanta Journal-Constitution* (archives: www.ajc.com).

Fish, M., and D. A. Milliron. 1999. The gender gap

(8 day series). *Atlanta Journal-Constitution*, 13 December–21 December, www.ajc.com.

Florey, B. 1998. Snow job. *Independent* (Colorado Springs), 28 January–4 February, 9–14.

Foley, D. 1990a. The great American football ritual: Reproducing race, class, and gender inequality. *Sociology of Sport Journal* 7 (2): 111–35.

Foley, D. 1990b. *Learning capitalist culture*. Philadelphia: University of Pennsylvania Press.

Foley, D. 1999a. High school football: Deep in the heart of south Tejas. In *Inside sports* (pp. 133–38), edited by J. Coakley and P. Donnelly. London: Routledge.

Foley, D. 1999b. Jay White Hawk: Mesquaki athlete, AIM hellraiser, and anthropological informant. In *Inside sports* (pp. 156–61), edited by J. Coakley and P. Donnelly. London: Routledge.

Foot, D., and D. Stoffman. 1998. *Boom, Bust & Echo 2000: Profiting from the Demographic Shift in the New Millennium*. Toronto: Macfarlane Walter & Ross.

Franseen, L., and S. McCann. 1996. Causes of eating disorders in elite female athletes. *Olympic Coach* 6 (3): 15–17.

Fraser, D. 1999. Rogers calls for massacre reparations. *Rocky Mountain News*, 30 November, 7A, 10A.

Freeman, M. 1998. Surviving in a violent world. *New York Times*, 6 September, section 8:1.

Freeman, M. 2000. Daunting issue of off-field violence. *San Francisco Examiner*, 9 January, D-9.

Friedman, S. (2002). *Body Thieves*. Vancouver: Salal Books.

Friesen, D. 1967. Academic—athletic—popularity syndrome in the Canadian high school society. *Adolescence* 3 (1), 39–52.

Frisby, W., S. Crawford, and T. Dorer. 1997. Reflections on participatory action research: The case of low income women accessing local physical activity services. *Journal of Sport Management* 11, 8–28.

Fudzie, V., and A. Hayes. 1995. *The sport of learning: A comprehensive survival guide for African-American student-athletes*. North Hollywood, CA: Doubleplay Publishing Group.

Fusco, C. 1995. Lesbians and locker rooms. In *Taking sport seriously: Social issues in Canadian sport* (pp. 91–94), edited by P. Donnelly. Toronto: Thompson Educational.

Galasso, P. 1988. *Philosophy of sport and physical activity*. Toronto: Canadian Scholars' Press.

Garber, G. 1999. What's in a name? www.espn.go.com/otl/americans/mascots.html (*Outside the Lines*, 18 November).

Garrity, J. 1989. A clash of cultures on the Hopi reservation. *Sports Illustrated* 71, (21): 20 November, 10–17.

Gems, G. R. 1993. Working class women and sport. *Women in Sport & Physical Activity Journal* 2 (1): 17–30.

George, J. 1994. The virtual disappearance of the white male sprinter in the United States: A speculative essay. *Sociology of Sport Journal* 11 (1): 70–78.

Giacobbi, P. R., and J. T. DeSensi. 1999. Media portrayals of Tiger Woods: A qualitative deconstructive examination. *Quest* 51 (4): 408–17.

Giddens, A. 1989. *Sociology*. Cambridge: Polity Press.

Giulianotti, R. 1994. "Keep it in the family": An outline of Hibs' football hooligans' social ontology. In *Game without frontiers: Football, identity, and modernity* (pp. 327–58), edited by R. Giulianotti and J. Williams. Aldershot, England: Arena (Ashgate).

Giulianotti, R., N. Bonny, and M. Hepworth, eds. 1994. *Football, violence, and social identity*. London: Routledge.

Globe and Mail. 1999. Playing by linguistic rules (editorial). 10 November, p. A20.

Godley, A. 1999a. *The creation of the student/athlete dichotomy in urban high school culture*. Paper presented at the annual conference of the North American Society for the Sociology of Sport, Cleveland, OH (November).

Godley, A. 1999b. *Transforming softball: Using a competitive model of sport to foster non-competitive adolescent peer culture*. Paper presented at the annual conference of the North American Society for the Sociology of Sport, Cleveland, OH (November).

Goodman, C. 1979. *Choosing sides: Playground and street life on the lower east side*. New York: Schocken Books.

Gordon, M. 1964. *Assimilation in American life*. New York: Oxford University Press.

Gould, D. 1996. Personal motivation gone awry: *Burnout in competitive athletics*. Quest 48 (3): 275–89.

Gould, D., S. Tuffey, E. Udry, and J. Loehr. 1997. Burnout in competitive junior tennis players: III. Individual differences in the burnout experience. *The Sport Psychologist* 11 (3): 257–76.

Gouldsblom, J. 1977. *Sociology in the balance.* Oxford, England: Blackwell.

Green, M. 2003. An analysis of elite sport policy change in three sports in Canada and the United Kingdom. Unpublished doctoral thesis, Loughborough University, UK.

Green, T. S. 2000. The future of African American female athletes. In *Racism in college athletics: The African American athlete's experience* (pp. 227–43), edited by D. Brooks and R. Althouse. Morgantown, WV: Fitness Information Technology.

Greenberg, J., G. Knight, P. Donnelly, and M. MacNeill. In press. Negotiating news: Structural constraints and strategic inaction in television coverage of the Olympics. In *Selected Proceedings of the Qualitative Research Conferences*, edited by C. Miall, D. Pawluch, and W. Shaffir.

Greenberg, M. J., and J. T. Gray. 1996. Citizenship based quota systems in athletics. *Marquette Sports Law Journal* 6 (2): 337–56.

Greendorfer, S. L. 1993. Gender role stereotypes and early childhood socialization. In *Women in sport* (pp. 3–14), edited by G. L. Cohen. Newbury Park, CA: Sage.

Grenier, G., and M. Lavoie. 1992. Discrimination and salary determination in the National Hockey League: 1977 and 1989 compared. In *Advances in the Economics of Sport*, volume 1 (pp. 153–77), edited by G. Scully. Greenwich: JAI Press.

Grey, M. 1992. Sports and immigrant, minority and Anglo relations in Garden City (Kansas) High School. *Sociology of Sport Journal* 9 (3), 255–70.

Grey, M. 1999. Playing sports and social acceptance: The experiences of immigrant and refugee students in Garden City, Kansas. In *Inside Sports* (pp. 28–36), edited by J. Coakley and P. Donnelly. London: Routledge.

Griffin, P. 1998. *Strong women, deep closets: Lesbians and homophobia in sport.* Champaign, IL: Human Kinetics.

Gruneau, R. 1984. Commercialism and the modern Olympics. In *Five ring circus: Money, power and politics at the Olympic Games* (pp. 1–15), edited by A. Tomlinson and G. Whannel. London: Pluto Press.

Gruneau, R. 1988. Modernization or hegemony: Two views of sports and social development. In *Not just a game* (pp. 9–32), edited by J. Harvey and H. Cantelon. Ottawa, Ontario: University of Ottawa Press.

Gruneau, R. 1989. Making spectacle: A case study in television sports production. In *Media, Sports & Society* (pp. 134–54), edited by Lawrence Wenner. London: Sage.

Gruneau, R. 1999. *Class, sports, and social development.* Champaign, IL: Human Kinetics.

Gruneau, R., and D. Whitson. 1993. *Hockey Night in Canada: Sport, identities, and cultural politics.* Toronto: Garamond Press.

Gruneau, R., and J. Albinson. 1976. *Canadian Sport: Sociological Perspectives.* Toronto: Addison-Wesley.

Gulick, L. 1906. Athletics do not test womanliness. *American Physical Education Review* 11 (3): September, 158–59.

Guttmann, A. 1978. *From ritual to record: The nature of modern sports.* New York: Columbia University Press.

Guttmann, A. 1986. *Sport spectators.* New York: Columbia University Press.

Guttmann, A. 1988. *A whole new ball game: An interpretation of American sports.* Chapel Hill: University of North Carolina Press.

Guttmann, A. 1994. *Games and empires: Modern sports and cultural imperialism.* New York: Columbia University Press.

Guttmann, A. 1998. The appeal of violent sports. In *Why we watch: The attractions of violent entertainment* (pp. 7–26), edited by J. Goldstein. New York: Oxford University Press.

Guttmann, A. 2000. The development of modern sports. In *Handbook of sports studies* (pp. 248–59), edited by J. Coakley and E. Dunning. London: Sage.

Hall, A. 1999. Creators of the lost and perfect game?: Gender, history, and Canadian sport. In *Sport and gender in Canada* (pp. 5–23), edited by P. White and K. Young. Toronto: Oxford University Press.

Hall, A. 2002. *The girl and the game: A history of women's sport in Canada.* Peterborough, ON: Broadview Press.

Hall, A., T. Slack, G. Smith, and D. Whitson. 1991. *Sport in Canadian society*. Toronto: McClelland & Stewart.

Hall, S. 1985. Signification, representation, ideology: *Althusser and the post-structuralist debates. Critical Studies in Mass Communication* 2 (2): 91–114.

Hanford, G. 1974. *An inquiry into the need for and the feasibility of a national study of intercollegiate athletics*. Washington, DC: American Council on Education.

Hanford, G. 1979. Controversies in college sports. *Annals of the American Academy of Political Science* 445: 66–79.

Hanson, S. L., and R. S. Kraus. 1999. Women in male domains: Sport and science. *Sociology of Sport Journal* 16 (2): 92–110.

Hardman, K., and J. Marshall. 2000. The state and status of physical education in schools in international context. *European Physical Education Review* 6 (3), 203–29.

Hargreaves, J. 1994. *Sporting females: Critical issues in the history and sociology of women's sport*. London: Routledge.

Hargreaves, J., and I. MacDonald. 2000. Gramscian/cultural studies. In *Handbook of sports studies* (pp. 48-–60), edited by J. Coakley and E. Dunning. London: Sage.

Harrison, C. K. 1995. Perceptions of African American male student-athletes in higher education. Unpublished dissertation, School of Education, University of Southern California.

Harrison, C. K. 1998. Themes that thread through society: Racism and athletic manifestation in the African-American community. *Race, Ethnicity, and Education* 1 (1): 63–74.

Harrison, L. 1995. African Americans: Race as a self-schema affecting physical activity choices. *Quest* 47 (1): 7–18.

Harrison, L., A. M. Lee, and D. Belcher. 1999. Race and gender differences in sport participation as a function of self schema. *Journal of Sport & Social Issues* 23 (3): 287–307.

Hart, L. E., and A. L. Pipe. 1997. Enhancing athletic performance: when ethics and evidence clash [editorial]. *Clinical Journal of Sport Medicine* (B9T), Jan; 7 (1): 1–2.

Hart, M. M. 1981. On being female in sport. In *Sport in the sociocultural process* (pp. 450–60), edited by M. M. Hart and S. Birrell. Dubuque, IA: William C. Brown.

Harvey, J. 1988. Sport and the Quebec clergy, 1930–1960. In *Not Just a Game: Essays in Canadian Sport Sociology* (pp. 69–84), edited by J. Harvey and H. Cantelon. Ottawa: University of Ottawa Press.

Harvey, J. 1999. Sport and Quebec nationalism: Ethnic or civic identity? In *Sport in Divided Societies* (pp. 31–50), edited by J. Sugden and A. Bairner. Aachen: Meyer & Meyer Sport.

Harvey, J., and A. Law. In press. Resisting the global media oligopoly?: The Canada Inc. response. In *Sport and Corporate Nationalism*, edited by M. Silk and D. Andrews. New York: Berg Publishers.

Harvey, J. and F. Houle. 1994. Sports, world economy, global culture and new social movements. *Sociology of Sport Journal* 11 (4), pp. 337–55.

Harvey, J., A. Law, and M. Cantelon. Forthcoming. North American professional team sport franchises ownership patterns and global entertainment conglomerates. *Sociology of Sport Journal*.

Harvey, J., and R. Proulx. 1988. Sport and the state in Canada. In *Not just a game* (pp. 93–120), edited by J. Harvey and H. Cantelon. Ottawa, Ontario: University of Ottawa Press.

Harvey, J., G. Rail, and L. Thibault. 1996. Globalization and sport: Sketching a theoretical model for empirical analysis. *Journal of Sport & Social Issues* 20 (3): 258–77.

Hasbrook, C. 1999. Young children's social constructions of physicality and gender. In *Inside sports* (pp. 7–16), edited by J. Coakley and P. Donnelly. London: Routledge.

Hasbrook, C. A., and O. Harris. 1999. Wrestling with gender: Physicality and masculinities among inner-city first and second graders. *Men and Masculinities* 1 (3): 302–18.

Haut Commissariat à la Jeunesse, aux Loisirs et aux Sports. 1978. Situation des Québécois dans le secteur du sport sur l'échiquier canadien: Rapport final. Québec: Gouvernement du Québec.

Hawes, K. 1999a. Dangerous games: Athletics initiation—Team bonding, rite of passage, or hazing? *The NCAA News*, 13 September, 1, 14–16

Hawes, K. 1999b. Weighing in. *The NCAA News*, 36 (24), 22 November, 1, 24–25.

Hawkins, B. 1998. The dominant images of black men in America: The representation of O.

J. Simpson. In *African Americans in sport* (pp. 39–52), edited by G. Sailes. New Brunswick, NJ: Transaction.

Hayes, D. W. 1993. Sports images and realities. *Black Issues in Higher Education* 10 (20): 15–19.

Haynes, R. 1993. Every man(?) a football artist: Football writing and masculinity. In *The passion and the fashion: Football fandom in the New Europe.* (pp. 55–76), edited by S. Redhead. Aldershot, England: Avebury.

Heine, M. 1991. The symbolic capital of honor: Gambling games and the social construction of gender in Tlingit Indian culture. *Play & Culture* 4, 346–58.

Heine, M. 1995. Gwich'in Tsii'in: A history of Gwich'in Athapaskan Games. Unpublished doctoral thesis, University of Alberta.

Henry, F., and C. Tator. 2002. *Discourses of Domination: Racial Bias in the Canadian English-Language Press.* University of Toronto Press.

Heywood, L. 1998. *Bodymakers: A cultural anatomy of women's bodybuilding.* New Brunswisk, NJ: Rutgers University Press.

Hilliard, D. C., and J. M. Hilliard. 1990. *Positive deviance and participant sport.* Paper presented at the annual conference of the North American Society for the Sociology of Sport, Las Vegas (April).

Hoberman, J. 1992. Mortal engines: *The science of performance and the dehumanization of sport.* New York: The Free Press.

Hoberman, J. 1994. The sportive-dynamic body as a symbol of productivity. In *Heterotopia: Postmodern utopia and the body politic* (pp. 199–228), edited by T. Siebers. Ann Arbor: University of Michigan Press.

Hoberman, J. 1995. Listening to steroids. *The Wilson Quarterly* 19 (1): 35–44.

Hoberman, J. 1997. *Darwin's athletes: How sport has damaged black America and preserved the myth of race.* Boston: Houghton Mifflin.

Hoffer, R. 1996. Real deal. *Sports Illustrated* 85 (21): 18 November, 28–37.

Hood, C. 1998. *The status of high school sport in Canada.* Report presented to the International School Sport Federation.

Hooks, Bell. 1992. Theory as liberatory practice. *Yale Journal of Law and Feminism* 4 (1): 1–12.

Horne, J., A. Tomlinson, and G. Whannel. 1999.

Understanding sport: An introduction to the sociological and cultural analysis of sport. London: E and FN SPON.

Horovitz, B. 2000. Coaches calling business plays. *USA Today,* 14 March, B1–B2.

Houlihan, B. 1994. *Sport and international politics.* Hemel Hempstead, England: Harvester-Wheatsheaf.

Houlihan, B. 1999. *Dying to win: Doping in sport and the development of anti doping policy.* Strasbourg: Council of Europe Publishing.

Houlihan, B. 2000. Politics and sport. In *Handbook of sports studies* (pp. 213–27), edited by J. Coakley and E. Dunning. London: Sage.

House, T. (with T. Kurkjian). 1999. Law and order: The edge. *ESPN—The Magazine,* 1 November, 84.

Houston, W. 2003. Saturday night hockey famine could continue. *Globe and Mail,* 6 May, p. S1.

Hovden, J. 2000. Gender and leadership selection processes in Norwegian sporting organizations. *International Review for the Sociology of Sport* 35 (1): 75–82.

Howell, C. 2001. *Blood, sweat and cheers: Sport and the Making of Modern Canada.* Toronto: University of Toronto Press.

Howell, D., and P. Lindsay. 1981. Social gospel and the young boy problem, 1895–1925. In *Sports in Canada: Historical Readings* (pp. 220–33), edited by M. Mott. Toronto: Copp Clark Pitman.

Huey, J. 1996. The Atlanta game. *Fortune* 134 (2): 22 July, 43–56.

Hughes, C., and S. Griffiths. 1992. *No level playing field: Recreation and poverty in Scarborough—A community report.* Toronto: Laidlaw Foundation.

Hughes, R., and J. Coakley. 1991. Positive deviance among athletes: The implications of overconformity to the sport ethic. *Sociology of Sport Journal* 8 (4): 307–25.

Hughson, J. 2000. The boys are back in town: Soccer support and the social reproduction of masculinity. *Journal of Sport & Social Issues* 24 (1): 8–23.

Humber, W. 1983. *Cheering for the Home Team: The Story of Baseball in Canada.* Erin, Ontario: Boston Mills Press.

Humphrey, J. 1986. No holding Brazil: Football, nationalism, and politics. In *Off the ball* (pp. 127–39), edited by A. Tomlinson and G. Whannel. London: Pluto Press.

Hunt, J. C. 1995. Divers' accounts of normal risk. *Symbolic Interaction* 18 (4): 439–62.

Ingham, A. G., B. J. Blissmer, and K. W. Davidson. 1999. The expendable prolympic self: Going beyond the boundaries of the sociology and psychology of sport. *Sociology of Sport Journal* 16 (3): 236–68.

Ingham, A., and A. Dewar. 1999. Through the eyes of youth: "Deep play" in Peewee ice hockey. In *Inside sports* (pp. 7–16), edited by J. Coakley and P. Donnelly. London: Routledge.

Ingham, A., and P. Donnelly. 1990. Whose knowledge counts? The production of knowledge and issues of application in the sociology of sport. *Sociology of Sport Journal* 7 (1): 58–65.

Ingham, A., and P. Donnelly. 1997. A sociology of North American sociology of sport: Disunity in unity, 1965–1996. *Sociology of Sport Journal* 14 (4): 362–418.

Institute for Social Research. 1996. Injuries incurred by Ontario residents during participation in sport and other physical recreation activities. Toronto: York University.

Jackson, D. 1999. BC wins the Gap Bowl. *Boston Globe*, 29 December, A27.

Jackson, D. 2000. Kansas State closes the gap. *Boston Globe*, 3 January, A23.

Jackson, S. A., and M. Csikszentmihalyi. 1999. *Flow in sports*. Champaign, IL: Human Kinetics.

Jackson, S.J. 1998, Life in the (mediated) Faust lane: Ben Johnson, national affect and the 1988 crisis of Canadian identity. *International Review for the Sociology of Sport* 33 (3), 227–38.

Jackson, S.J., and B. Hokowhitu. 2002. Sport, tribes and technology: The New Zealand All Blacks Haka and the politics of identity. *Journal of Sport and Social Issues* 26 (1): 125–39.

Jackson, S.J., and J. Scherer. 2002. *Screening the Nation's Past: Adidas, Advertising and Corporate Nationalism in New Zealand*. Paper presented at the North American Society for the Sociology of Sport Conference, Indianapolis.

James, C. 1995. Negotiating school through sports: African Canadian youth strive for academic success. *Avante* 1(1), 20–36.

James, C. 1999. *Seeing ourselves: Exploring race, ethnicity and culture, 2nd edition*. Toronto: Thompson Educational.

James, C. 2003. Schooling, basketball, and the U.S. scholarship aspirations of Canadian student athletes. *Race, Ethnicity and Education* 6 (2), 123–44.

James, C. L. R. 1984. *Beyond a boundary*. New York: Pantheon Books.

Jamieson, K. 1998. *Navigating the system: The case of Latina student-athletes in women's collegiate sports*. Paper presented at the annual conference of the American Alliance for Health, Physical Education, Recreation and Dance, Reno, NV (April).

Jamieson, K. 1999. *Advance at your own risk: Latinas making paths toward collegiate basketball*. Paper presented at the annual conference of the North American Society for the Sociology of Sport, Cleveland, OH (November).

Jenkins, H. 1997. "Never trust a snake": WWF wrestling as masculine melodrama. In *Out of bounds: Sports, media, and the politics of identity* (pp. 48–78), edited by A. Baker and T. Boyd. Bloomington: Indiana University Press.

Jennings, A. 1996a. *The new lords of the rings*. London: Pocket Books.

Jennings, A. 1996b. Power, corruption, and lies. *Esquire*, May, 99–104.

Jennings, A., and C. Sambrook. 2000. *The great Olympic swindle: When the world wanted its games back*. New York: Simon and Schuster.

Jerome, W., and J. Phillips. 1971. The relationship between academic achievement and interscholastic participation: A comparison of Canadian and American high schools. *Journal of the Canadian Association for Health, Physical Education and Recreation* 37, 18–21.

Jhally, S. 1984. The spectacle of accumulation: Material and cultural factors in the emergence of the sports/media complex. *The Insurgent Sociologist* 12 (3), 41–57.

Johns, D. 1992. *Starving for gold: A case study in overconformity in high performance sport*. Paper presented at the annual conference of the North American Society for the Sociology of Sport, Toledo, OH (November).

Johns, D. 1996. Positive deviance and the sport ethic: Examining weight loss strategies in rhythmic gymnastics. *The Hong Kong Journal of Sports Medicine and Sport Science* (May): 49–56.

Johns, D. 1997. Fasting and feasting: Paradoxes in the sport ethic. *Sociology of Sport Journal* 15 (1): 41–63.

Johnson, C. 2000. America's pastime crisscrosses the globe. *USA Today*, 17 March, 16C.

Johnson, J. 1999. *Sport hazing experiences in the context of anti-hazing policies: The case of two Southern Ontario universities*. Unpublished master's thesis. Toronto: University of Toronto.

Jones, R., A. J. Murrell, and J. Jackson. 1999. Pretty versus powerful in the sports pages: Print media coverage of U.S. women's Olympic gold medal winning teams. *Journal of Sport & Social Issues* 23 (2): 183–92.

Joravsky, B. 1995. *Hoop dreams: A true story of hardship and triumph*. New York: HarperCollins.

Joyce, G. 1997. White rules. In *Taking Sport Seriously: Social Issues in Canadian Sport* (pp. 325–35), edited by P. Donnelly. Toronto: Thompson Educational.

Kane, M.J. 1995. Resistance/transformation of the oppositional binary: Exposing sport as a continuum. *Journal of Sport and Social Issues* 19 (2), 191–218.

Kane, M. J., and H. J. Lenskyj. 1998. Media treatment of female athletes: Issues of gender and sexualities. In *MediaSport* (pp. 186–201), edited by L. A. Wenner. London/New York: Routledge.

Kaplan, D. 2002. The end of baseball again. Newsweek 140 (9), 26 August, 46–47.Kearney, J. 1999. Creatine supplementation: Specifics for the trained athlete. *Olympic Coach* 9 (2): 3–5.

Keith, S. 1999. Native American women in sport. *Journal of Physical Education, Recreation & Dance* 70 (4): 47–49.

Kelley, B. C., S. J. Hoffman, and D. L. Gill. 1990. The relationship between competitive orientation and religious orientation. *Journal of Sport Behavior* 13(3): 145–56.

Kellner, D. 1995. *Media culture*. London: Routledge.

Kelly, M.C. 2001. *Hanging it out on Camera 3: Canadian sports in the media era*. Toronto: Prentice Hall Canada.

Kennedy, E. 2000. Bad boys and gentlemen: Gendered narrative in televised sport. *International Review for the Sociology of Sport* 35 (1): 59–73.

Keri, M. G. 2000. Take me out of their ball game. *Utne* Reader, No. 97, January/February, 55.

Kernaghan, J. 2002. Search for equity leads to unequal teams. *London Free Press*, 17 May.

Kesterton, M. 2002. Social Studies. *Globe and Mail*, 14 June, p. A24.

Kidd, B. 1980. *Tom Longboat*. Toronto: Fitzhenry & Whiteside.

Kidd, B. 1984. The myth of the ancient games. In *Five-ring circus* (pp. 71–83), edited by A. Tomlinson and G. Whannel. London: Pluto Press.

Kidd, B. 1987. Sports and masculinity. In *Beyond patriarchy: Essays by men on pleasure, power, and change* (pp. 250–65), edited by M. Kaufman. New York: Oxford University Press.

Kidd, B. 1988. The philosophy of excellence: Olympic performance, class power, and the Canadian state. In *Philosophy of sport and physical activity: Issues and Controversies* (pp. 11–31), edited by P. Galasso. Toronto: Canadian Scholars Press.

Kidd, B. 1992. The culture wars of the Montreal Olympics. *International Review for the Sociology of Sport* 27 (2), 151–63.

Kidd, B. 1995. Inequality in sport, the corporation, and the state: An agenda for social scientists. *Journal of Sport & Social Issues* 19 (3): 232–48.

Kidd, B. 1996a. Taking the rhetoric seriously: Proposals for Olympic education. *Quest* 48 (1): 82–92.

Kidd, B. 1996b. Worker sport in the New World: The Canadian story. In *The story of worker sport* (pp. 143–56), edited by A. Kruger and J. Riordan. Champaign, IL: Human Kinetics.

Kidd, B. 1997. *The struggle for Canadian sport*. Toronto: University of Toronto Press (2nd printing).

King, A.J.C., and M.J. Peart. 1990. *The good school: Strategies for making secondary schools effective*. Toronto: Ontario Secondary School Teachers' Federation.

King, P. 1996. Bitter pill. *Sports Illustrated* 84 (21): 27 May, 25–30.

Kinkema, K. M., and J. C. Harris. 1998. MediaSport studies: Key research and emerging issues. In *MediaSport* (pp. 27–54), edited by L. A. Wenner. London/New York: Routledge.

Kirby, S., L. Greaves, and O. Hankivsky. 2000. *The dome of silence: Sexual harassment and abuse in sport*. Halifax, NS: Fernwood Publishing.

Kjeldsen, E. 1984. Integration of minorities into Olympic sport in Canada and the USA. *Journal of Sport and Social Issues* 8(2), 29–44.

Klein, A. 1991. *Sugarball: The American game, the*

Dominican dream. New Haven, CT: Yale University Press.

Klein, A. 1993. *Little big men: Bodybuilding subculture and gender construction*. Albany: State University of New York Press.

Klein, A. 1999. Coming of age in North America: Socialization of Dominican baseball players. In *Inside sports* (pp. 96–103), edited by J. Coakley and P. Donnelly. London: Routledge.

Klein, A. M. 1997. *Baseball on the border: A tale of two Laredos*. Princeton, NJ: Princeton University Press.

Knight Foundation. 1991. *Report of the Knight Foundation Commission on Intercollegiate Athletics*. (Note: available through NCAA.)

Knight, G., and J. Greenberg. 2002. Promotionalism and subpolitics: Nike and its labor critics. *Management Communication Quarterly* 15 (4): 541–70.

Knisley, M. 1996. Rupeat. *The Sporting News*, 1 January, S1–S28. Special section: The 100 most powerful people in sports.

Kohn, A. 1992. *No contest: The case against competition*. Boston: Mariner Books.

Kooistra, P., J. S. Mahoney, and L. Bridges. 1993. The unequal opportunity for equal ability hypothesis: Racism in the National Football League. *Sociology of Sport Journal* 10 (3): 241–55.

Koppett, L. 1994. *Sports illusion, sports reality*. Urbana: University of Illinois Press.

Kornheiser, T. 1999. Six billion? Where's mine? *ESPN—The Magazine*, 13 December, 46.

Koukouris, K. 1994. Constructed case studies: Athletes' perspectives of disengaging from organized competitive sport. *Sociology of Sport Journal* 11 (2): 114–39.

Kozol, J. 1991. *Savage inequalities*. New York: Crown.

Krane, V. 1996. Lesbians in sport: Toward acknowledgement, understanding, and theory. *Journal of Sport & Exercise Psychology* 18 (3): 237–46.

Kuhlemeyer, G. 1999. Taxpayer cost of Mile High name. *The Denver Post*, 7 November, Section B.

Laberge, S. 1986. *Rapport de l'Enquéte sur le 'Fait Français.'* Présenté à La Direction du Sport d'Élite, Ministere du Loisir, de la Chasse at de la Peche.

Laberge, S. 1988. Quelques constats et problématiques sur le 'fait français' dans la sport amateur. Unpublished paper.

Laberge, S. 1995. Sports et activités physique: modes d'alliénation et pratiques émancipatoires. *Sociologie et Sociétés* 27 (1), 53–74.

Laberge, S., and D. Sankoff. 1988. Physical activities, body habitus, and lifestyles. In *Not just a game* (pp. 267–86), edited by J. Harvey and H. Cantelon. Ottawa: University of Ottawa Press.

Laberge, S., and M. Albert. 1999. Conceptions of masculinity and of gender transgressions in sport among adolescent boys: Hegemony, contestation, and social class dynamic. *Men and Masculinities* 1 (3): 243–67.

Laberge, S., and Y. Girardin. 1992. Questioning the inference of ethnic differences in achievement values from types of sport participation: A commentary on White and Curtis. *Sociology of Sport Journal* 9(2), 295–306.

LaFlamme, A. 1977. The role of sport in the development of ethnicity: A case study. *Sport Sociology Bulletin* 6(1), 47–51.

Lamb, L. 2000. Can women save sports? An interview with Mary Jo Kane. *Utne Reader*, No. 97, January/February, 56–57.

Landry, F., C. St-Denis, and C. Turgeon. 1966. Les Canadiens-français et les Grands Jeux Internationaux. *Mouvement* 1 (2), 115–32.

Landry, F., R. Boileau, and Y. Trempe. 1972. Les Canadiens-français et les Grands Jeux Internationaux. *Mouvement* 7 (1–2), 81–92.

Lang, G.E. 1980. Riotous outbursts at sports events. In *Handbook of Social Science of Sport*, edited by G. Luschen and G. Sage. Champaign, IL: Stipes Publishing.

Lapchick, R. 1984. *Broken promises: Racism in American sports*. New York: St. Martin's/Marek.

Lapchick, R. 1995. Front court. Preface. In *The sport of learning: A comprehensive survival guide for African-American student-athletes* (pp. 5–7), V. Fudzie and A. Hayes, eds. North Hollywood, CA: Doubleplay.

Lapchick, R.E., and K. Matthews. 2002. *Racial and gender report card* (for 2001). Boston: Center for the Study of Sport in Society (Northeastern University).

Laqueur, T. 1990. *Making sex*. Cambridge, MA: Harvard University Press.

Latimer, C. 2000. Where have all the shooters gone? *Denver Rocky Mountain News*, 16 April, 28–29C.

Lavoie M., and W. M. Leonard II. 1994. In search of

an alternative explanation of stacking in baseball: The uncertainty hypothesis. *Sociology of Sport Journal* 11 (2): 140–54.

Lavoie, M. 1998. *Désavantage numérique: Les Francophones dans la LNH*. Hull: Vent D'Ouest.

Lavoie, M. 2000. Economics and sport. In *Handbook of sports studies* (pp. 157–70), edited by J. Coakley and E. Dunning. London: Sage.

Layden, T. 1995a. Better education. *Sports Illustrated* 82 (14), 3 April: 68–90.

Layden, T. 1995b. Book smart. *Sports Illustrated* 82 (15), 10 April: 68–79.

Layden, T. 1995c. You bet your life. *Sports Illustrated* 82 (16), 17 April: 46–55.

Lee, V. 1996. Wimps or warriors? *Sports Spectrum* (December): 22–25.

Lefkowitz, B. 1997. *Our guys: The Glen Ridge rape and the secret life of the perfect suburb*. Berkeley: University of California Press.

Leizman, J. 1999. *Let's kill 'em: Understanding and controlling violence in sports*. Lanham, MD: University Press of America.

Leland, J. 2000. Why America's hooked on wrestling. *Newsweek* 135 (6): 7 February, 46–55.

Lenskyj, H. 1986. *Out of bounds: Women, sport, and sexuality*. Toronto: Women's Press.

Lenskyj, H. 1991. Combating homophobia in sport and physical education. *Sociology of Sport Journal* 8 (1): 61–69.

Lenskyj, H. 1998. Sport and corporate environmentalism. *International Review for the Sociology of Sport* 33 (4): 341–54.

Lenskyj, H. 1999. Women, sport, and sexualities: Breaking the silences. In *Sport and gender in Canada* (pp. 170–81), edited by P. White and K. Young. Don Mills, Ontario: Oxford University Press.

Lenskyj, H. 2000. *Inside the Olympic industry : Power, politics & activism*. Albany, NY: State University of New York Press.

Lenskyj, H. 2002. *The Best Olympics Ever? Social Impacts of Sydney 2000*. Albany, NY: State University of New York Press.

Leonard, W. M., II. 1995. Economic discrimination in major league baseball: Marginal revenue products of majority and minority groups members. *Journal of Sport & Social Issues* 19 (2): 180–90.

Leonard, W. M. II. 1996. The odds of transiting from one level of sports participation to another.

Sociology of Sport Journal 13 (3): 288–99.

Lieblich, J., and R. N. Ostling. 2000. Little prayer of resolving church and state debate. *Denver Rocky Mountain News*, 16 January, 2A, 63–64A.

Life. 1984. The victors and the vanquished. *Life*, Summer (Special Issue): 31.

Ligutom-Kimura, D. A. 1995. The invisible women. *Journal of Physical Education, Recreation and Dance* 66 (7): 34–41.

Lipsyte, R. 1996a. Little girls in a staged spectacle for big bucks? *New York Times*, 4 August, 28.

Lipsyte, R. 1996b. One fell swoosh: Can a logo conquer all? *New York Times*, 7 February: 9 (Section B).

Lipsyte, R. 1998. A step in the healing process. *New York Times*, 5 March, C22.

Lipsyte, R. 1999. The jock culture: Time to debate questions. *New York Times*, 9 May (online).

Longman, J. 1996. Slow down, speed up. *New York Times*, 1 May, B11.

Lopiano, D. 1991. Presentation at the Coaching America's Coaches Conference, United States Olympic Training Center, Colorado Springs, CO (June).

Lowe, P. 1998. Rodeo women over a barrel, champion racer says. *The Denver Post*, 24 January: F-01.

Lowes, M. D. 1999. *Inside the sports pages: Work routines, professional ideologies, and the manufacture of sport news*. Toronto: University of Toronto Press.

Loy, J., and D. Booth. 2001. Emile Durkheim, structural functionalism and the sociology of sport. In *Theory, sport and society* (pp. 41–62), edited by J. Maguire and K. Young. Oxford: Elsevier Science.

Loy, J., D. L. Andrews, and R. Rinehart. 1993. The body in culture and sport. *Sport Science Review* 2 (1): 69–91.

Loy, J.W. 1995. The dark side of agon: Fratriarchies, performative masculinities, sport involvement and the phenomenon of gang rape. In *International Sociology of Sport: Contemporary Issues* (pp. 263-282), edited by K.H. Bette and A. Rutten. Stuttgart: Verlag SN.

Lupton, D. 2000. The social construction of medicine and the body. In *The handbook in social studies in health and medicine* (pp. 60–63), G. Albrecht, R. Fitzpatrick, and S. Scrimshaw, eds. London: Sage.

Lüschen, G. 1967. The interdependence of sport and culture. *International Review of Sport Sociology* 2: 127–41.

Luxton, M. 1980. *More than a labour of love: Three generations of women's work in the home*. Toronto: The Women's Press.

Lyman, S. L. et al. 1998. Youth pitching injuries. *Sports Medicine Update* 13 (2): 4–9.

MacAloon, J. 1990. Steroids and the state: Dubin, melodrama, and the accomplishment of innocence. *Public Culture* 2, 41–64.

Macintosh, D. 1986. Intercollegiate athletics in Canadian universities: An historical perspective. In *The role of interuniversity athletics: A Canadian perspective* (pp. 3–7). London, ON: Sports Dynamics.

Macintosh, D., and D. Whitson. 1990. *The game planners: Transforming Canada's sport system*. Kingston and Montreal: McGill-Queen's University Press.

Macintosh, D., and M. Hawes. 1994. *Sport and Canadian diplomacy*. Kingston and Montreal: McGill-Queen's University Press.

Macintosh, D., T. Bedecki, and C. Franks. 1987. *Sport and politics in Canada: Federal government involvement since 1961*. Kingston and Montreal: McGill-Queen's University Press.

MacMillan, H.L., et al. 1997. Prevalence of child physical and sexual abuse in the community: Results from the Ontario Health Supplement. *The Journal of the American Medical Association* 278:131–135.

MacNeill, M. 1996. Networks: Producing Olympic ice hockey for a national television audience. *Sociology of Sport Journal* 13 (2): 103–24.

MacNeill, M. 1998. Sex, lies and videotape: The political and cultural economics of celebrity fitness videos. In *Sport and postmodern times*, edited by G. Rail. Albany, NY: State University of New York Press.

MacNeill, M. 1998. Sports journalism, ethics, and Olympic athletes' rights. In *MediaSport* (pp. 100–15), edited by L. Wenner. London: Routledge.

MacNeill, M. 1999. Social marketing, gender, and the science of fitness: A case study of ParticipACTION campaigns. In *Sport and gender in Canada* (pp. 215–31), edited by P. White and K. Young. Toronto: Oxford University Press.

MacNeill, M. In press. Remote control: Canadian youth, access to physical activity, and contradictory relationships with the media. In *Sport for all in Canada: Building on the european experience*, edited by P. Donnelly and B. Kidd. Toronto: Canadian Scholars' Press.

Madan, M. 2000. "It's not just cricket!" World series cricket: Race, nation, and diasporic Indian identity. *Journal of Sport & Social Issues* 24 (1): 24–35.

Maguire, J. 1988. Race and position assignment in English soccer: A preliminary analysis of ethnicity and sport in Britain. *Sociology of Sport Journal* 5 (3): 257–69.

Maguire, J. 1990. More than a sporting touchdown: The making of American football in England, 1982–1990. *Sociology of Sport Journal* 7 (3): 213–37.

Maguire, J. 1994. Globalisation, sport and national identities: "The Empires Strike Back?" *Society and Leisure* 16: 293–323.

Maguire, J. 1995. Blade runners: Canadian migrants and global ice hockey trails. *Journal of Sport and Social Issues* 20 (3), 335–60.

Maguire, J. 1998. Globalization and sportization: A figurational process/sociological perspective. *Avante* 4 (1): 67–89.

Maguire, J. 1999. *Global sport: Identities, societies, civilizations*. Cambridge, England: Polity Press.

Maguire, J., and B. Pearton. 1999. *The media-sport advertising complex and the 1998 FIFA World Cup*. Paper presented at the International Conference on Football and Fans, Queensland, Australia (July).

Maguire, J., and D. Stead. 1996. Far pavilions? Cricket migrants, foreign sojourn, and contested identities. *International Review for the Sociology of Sport* 31 (1): 1–24.

Maguire, J., and K. Young (eds.) 2002. *Theory, sport & society*. Oxford: JAI.

Mahany, B. 1999. Parents drive free time from lives of kids. *Chicago Tribune*, 27 May, LIFE1.

Mahiri, J. 1998. *Shooting for excellence: African American youth culture in New Century Schools*. London/New York: Teachers College Press, Columbia University.

Majors, R. 1986. Cool pose: The proud signature of black survival. *Changing Men: Issues in Gender, Sex, and Politics* 17: 184–85.

Majors, R. 1998. Cool pose: Black masculinity and sports. In *African Americans in sport* (pp. 15–22), edited by G. Sailes. New Brunswick, NJ: Transaction.

Maki, A. 1999. Train Olympians bilingually or lose funds, centres told. *Globe and Mail*, 9 November, pp. A1, A5.

Malcomson, R. W. 1984. Sports in society: A historical perspective. *British Journal of Sports History* 1 (1): 60–72.

Mannon, J. M. 1997. *Measuring up: The performance ethic in American culture*. Boulder, CO: Westview Press.

Markula, P. 1995. Firm but shapely, fit but sexy, strong but thin: The postmodern aerobicizing female bodies. *Sociology of Sport Journal* 12 (4): 424–53.

Marple, D. 1975. Analyse de la discrimination que subissent les Canadiens-français au hockey professionnel. *Mouvement* 10 (1), 7–13.

Marsh, H. W. 1993. The effect of participation in sport during the last two years of high school. *Sociology of Sport Journal* 10 (1): 18–43.

Marsh, P. 1982. Social order on the British soccer terraces. *International Social Science Journal* 34 (2): 247–56.

Marsh, P., and A. Campbell, eds. 1982. *Aggression and violence*. Oxford, England: Basil Blackwell.

Martin, R., and T. Miller, eds. 1999. *SportCult*. Minneapolis: University of Minnesota Press.

Martinek, T. J., and D. R. Hellison. 1997. Fostering resiliency in underserved youth through physical activity. *Quest* 49 (1): 34–49.

Marty, M. E., and R. S. Appleby, eds. 1995. *Fundamen-talisms comprehended* (Vol. 5 of The Fundamentalism Project). Chicago: The University of Chicago Press.

Mason, D. 2002. "Get the Puck Outta Here!" Media Transnationalism and Canadian Identity. *Journal of Sport and Social Issues* 26 (2), 140–67.

May, R. 1972. *Power and innocence: A search for the sources of violence*. New York: W. W. Norton.

Mayeda, D. T. 1999. From model minority to economic threat: Media portrayals of major league baseball pitchers Hideo Nomo and Hideki Irabu. *Journal of Sport & Social Issues* 23 (2): 203–17.

McAll, C. 1992. English/French Canadian differences in sport participation: Comment on White and Curtis. *Sociology of Sport Journal* 9(2), 307–13.

McCall, N. 1997. *What's going on: Personal essays*. New York: Random House.

McChesney, R. W. 1999. The new global media: It's a small world of big conglomerates. *The Nation* 269 (18), 29 November: 11–15.

McClung, L. R., and E. M. Blinde. 1998. *Negotiation of the gendered ideology of sport: Experiences of women intercollegiate athletes*. Paper presented at the annual conference of the North American Society for the Sociology of Sport, Las Vegas (November).

McCormack, J. B., and L. Chalip. 1988. Sport as socialization: A critique of methodological premises. *The Social Science Journal* 25 (1): 83–92.

McDaniel, S. R., and C. B. Sullivan. 1998. Extending the sports experience: Mediations in cyberspace. In *MediaSport* (pp. 266–81), edited by L. A. Wenner. London/New York: Routledge.

McDonald, I. 1999. "Physiological patriots"?: The politics of physical culture and Hindu nationalism in India. *International Review for the Sociology of Sport* 34 (4): 343–58.

McDonald, M. G. 2000. The marketing of the Women's National Basketball Association and the making of postfeminism. *International Review for the Sociology of Sport* 35 (1): 35–47.

McDonald, M., and S. Birrell. 1999. Reading sport critically: A methodology for interrogating power. *Sociology of Sport Journal* 16 (4): 283–300.

McGraw, D. 1997. The national bet. *U.S. News and World Report* (7 April): 50–55.

McGregor, M. 1997. Canadian sports editor's speech. In *Taking Sport Seriously: Social Issues in Canadian Sport* (pp. 291–304), edited by P. Donnelly. Toronto: Thompson Educational Publishing.

McGregor, R. 2003. Temples of gloom: Big arenas haven't been the panacea hockey clubs had hoped for. *Globe and Mail*, 9 January, p. A2.

McKay, J. 1975. Sport and ethnicity: Acculturation, structural assimilation, and voluntary association involvement among Italian immigrants in metropolitan Toronto. Unpublished Master's thesis, University of Waterloo.

McKay, J. 1997. *Managing gender: Affirmative action and organizational power in Australian, Canadian, and New Zealand sport*. Albany: State University of New York Press.

McKay, J. 1999. Gender and organizational power in Canadian sport. In *Sport and gender in Canada* (pp. 197–215), edited by P. White and K. Young. Don Mills, Ontario: Oxford University Press.

McKenzie, B. 1999. Retiring from the sideline: Building new identities on new terms. In *Inside sports* (pp. 232–36), edited by J. Coakley and P. Donnelly. London: Routledge.

McMurtry, R. 1974. *Investigation and inquiry into violence in amateur hockey*. Report to the Honourable René Brunelle, Ontario Minister of Community and Social Services. Toronto: Ontario Government Bookstore.

McNeal, R. B., Jr. 1995. Extracurricular activities and high school dropouts. *Sociology of Education* 64: 62–81.

McShane, L. 1999. Winner take all (Associated Press). *Colorado Springs Gazette*, 4 July, LIFE4.

McTeer, W., and Curtis, J. 1999. Intercollegiate sport involvement and academic attainment: A follow-up study. *Avante* 5 (1), 39–55.

Mead, C. 1985. Black hero in a white land. *Sports Illustrated* 63 (13): 16 September, 80–101.

Meisel, J., and V. Lemieux. 1972. Amateur hockey associations. In *Ethnic Relations in Canadian Voluntary Associations* (pp. 55–70), Documents of the Royal Commission on Bilingualism and Biculturalism—13. Ottawa: Supply and Services.

Melnick, M. J., B. Vanfossen, and D. Sabo. 1988. Developmental effects of athletic participation among high school girls. *Sociology of Sport Journal* 5 (1): 22–36.

Mennesson, C. 2000. "Hard" women and "soft" women. *International Review for the Sociology of Sport* 35 (1): 21–33.

Merron, J. 1999. Running on empty. *Sportsjones*, 3 June (www.sportsjones.com/running.htm).

Messner, M. 1990. When bodies are weapons: Masculinity and violence in sport. *International Review for the Sociology of Sport* 25 (3): 203–19.

Messner, M. A. 1992. *Power at play*. Boston: Beacon Press.

Messner, M. A. 1996. Studying up on sex. *Sociology of Sport Journal* 13 (3): 221–37.

Messner, M. A., D. Hunt, and M. Dunbar. 1999. *Boys to men: Sports media messages about masculinity*. Oakland, CA: Children Now.

Messner, M.A. 2002. *Taking the field: Women, men, and sports*. Minneapolis: University of Minnesota Press.

Metcalfe, A. 1978. *Working class physical recreation in Montreal, 1860–1895*. Working papers in the sociological study of sports and leisure 1 (2): 1, 12–14002E

Metcalfe, A. 1987. *Canada learns to play: The emergence of organized sport, 1807–1914*. Toronto: McClelland and Stewart.

Metro Interschool Athletic Association. 1997. Metro schools' female athletes angered by lack of media attention. In *Taking sport seriously: Social issues in Canadian sport* (pp. 309–10), edited by P. Donnelly. Toronto: Thompson Educational Publishing.

Meyer, B. B. 1988. *The college experience: Female athletes and nonathletes*. Paper presented at the North American Society for the Sociology of Sport Conference, Cincinnati, OH (November).

Meyer, B. B. 1990. From idealism to actualization: The academic performance of female collegiate athletes. *Sociology of Sport Journal* 7 (1): 44–57.

Michaelis, V. 1996. Dream team: Capitalism on the hoof. *The Denver Post*, 19 July, 8D.

Micheli, L. J. 1990. *Sportsense for the young athlete*. New York: Houghton Mifflin.

Midol, N. 1999. *Sport and modernity: The sociology of structuralism, of post-structuralism, of deconstruction, and of simulation*. Paper presented at the annual conference of the North American Society for the Sociology of Sport, Cleveland (November).

Midol, N., and G. Broyer. 1995. Toward an anthropological analysis of new sport cultures: The case of whiz sports in France. *Sociology of Sport Journal* 12 (2): 204–12.

Miedzian, M. 1991. *Boys will be boys: Breaking the link between masculinity and violence*. New York: Anchor Books.

Miller, K. E., D. F. Sabo, M. P. Farrell, G. M. Barnes, and M. J. Melnick. 1998. Athletic participation and sexual behavior in adolescents: The different world of boys and girls. *Journal of Health and Social Behavior* 39: 108–23.

Miller, K. E., D. F. Sabo, M. P. Farrell, G. M. Barnes, and M. J. Melnick. 1999. Sports, sexual behavior, contraceptive use, and pregnancy among female and male high school students: Testing cultural resource theory. *Sociology of Sport Journal* 16 (4): 366–87.

Miller, L., and O. Penz. 1991. Talking bodies: Female bodybuilders colonize a male preserve. *Quest* 43, 149–63.

Miller, T., ed. 2001. *Globalization and sport: Playing the world*. London: Sage.

Mills, C.W. 1959. *The Sociological Imagination*. Oxford: Oxford University Press.

Mills, D. 1998. *Sport in Canada: Everybody's Business—Leadership, Partnership and Accountability*. Report of the Standing Committee on Canadian Heritage, Sub-Committee on the Study of Sport in Canada.

Miracle, A. W., and C. R. Rees. 1994. *Lessons of the locker room: The myth of school sports*. Amherst, NY: Prometheus Books.

Montville, L. 1999. Shall we dance? *Sports Illustrated* 91 (22): 6 December, 98–109.

Morris, G. S. D., and J. Stiehl. 1989. *Changing kids' games*. Champaign, IL: Human Kinetics.

Morrow, D. 1986. A case study in amateur conflict: The athletic war in Canada, 1906-1908. *British Journal of Sports History* 3: 173–90.

Morton, D. 1983. *A short history of Canada*. Edmonton: Hurtig Publishers.

Mott, M., ed. 1989. *Sports in Canada: Historical readings*. Toronto: Copp Clark Pittman.

Mrozek, D. 1987. Games and sport in the Arctic. *Journal of the West* 26(1), 34–46.

Mrozek, D. J. 1983. *Sport and American mentality, 1880–1920*. Knoxville: University of Tennessee Press.

Murphy, G. M., A. J. Petipas, and B. W. Brewer. 1996. Identity foreclosure, athletic identity, and career maturity in intercollegiate athletics. *The Sport Psychologist* 10 (3): 239–46.

Murphy, P., Williams, J., and E. Dunning. 1990. *Football on trial: Spectator violence and development in the world of football*. London: Routledge.

Murphy, P., Sheard, K., and I. Waddington. 2000. Figurational/process sociology. In *Handbook of sports studies* (pp. 92–105), edited by J. Coakley and E. Dunning. London: Sage.

Murphy, S. 1999. *The cheers and the tears: A healthy alternative to the dark side of youth sports today*. San Francisco: Jossey-Bass.

Myers, J. 2000. *Afraid of the dark: What whites and blacks need to know about each other*. Chicago: Lawrence Hill Books.

Nabokov, P. 1981. *Indian running: Native American history and tradition*. Santa Fe, NM: Ancient City Press.

Nack, W. and L. Munson. 1995. Sports' dirty secret. *Sports Illustrated* 83 (5): 31 July, 62–75.

Nack, W., and D. Yaeger. 1999. Every parent's nightmare. *Sports Illustrated*, 91(10): 13 September, 40–53.

Nakamura, Y. 2002. Beyond the hijab: Female Muslims and physical activity. *Women in Sport and Physical Activity Journal* 11 (2), 21–48.

Nakamura, Y. 2003. The samurai sword cuts both ways: Japanese and American media representations of Ichiro. Unpublished paper, University of Toronto.

Nash, B., and A. Zullo. 1986. *The baseball hall of shame* (2). New York NY: Simon and Schuster.

Nash, H. L. 1987. Do compulsive runners and anorectic patients share common bonds? *The Physician and Sportsmedicine* 15 (12): 162–67.

Naughton, J. 1996. Alcohol abuse by athletes poses big problems for colleges. *The Chronicle of Higher Education* 43 (4): A47–A48.

Nauright, J. 1996a. "A besieged tribe"?: Nostalgia, white cultural identity, and the role of rugby in a changing South Africa. *International Review for the Sociology of Sport* 31 (1): 69–108.

Nauright, J. 1996b. *"It's the world in union": Rugby tours, the Rugby World Cup, nostalgia, and memory in maintaining the "Old (boys)" world order*. Paper presented at the annual conference of the North American Society for the Sociology of Sport, Birmingham, AL (November).

Nauright, J. 1997. Masculinity, muscular Islam, and popular culture: "Colored" rugby's cultural symbolism in working class Cape Town c. 1930–70. *The International Journal of the History of Sport* 14 (1): 184–90.

Nauright, J., and White, P. 1996. Nostalgia, community, and nation: Professional hockey and football in Canada. *Avante* 2 (3), 24–41.

NCAA. 1999a. *NCAA Division I graduation-rate report*. Indianapolis, IN: NCAA Publications.

NCAA. 1999b. *NCAA Divisions II and III graduation-rate report*. Indianapolis, IN: NCAA Publications.

NCAA. 1999c. Sportsmanship survey. *The NCAA News* 36 (9): 26 April, 2.

NCAA News. 1998. Survey shows increase in deficits. *The NCAA News* 35(34), 12 October: 1, 25.

Neal, W. 1981. *The handbook on athletic perfection*. Milford, MI: Mott Media.

Nelson, J. (ed.). 1990. News: Stereotypes by six. *Journal of Physical Education, Recreation and Dance*

61 (8): 9.

Nelson, M. B. 1991. *Are we winning yet?* New York: Random House.

Nelson, M. B. 1994. *The stronger women get, the more men love football: Sexism and the American culture of sports.* New York: Harcourt Brace & Company.

Nelson, M. B. 1998. *Embracing victory: Life lessons in competition and compassion.* New York: William Morrow & Company.

Nixon, H. L. II. 1993a. Accepting the risks and pain of injury in sport: Mediated cultural influences on playing hurt. *Sociology of Sport Journal* 10 (2): 183–96.

Nixon, H. L. II. 1993b. A social network analysis of influences on athletes to play with pain and injuries. *Journal of Sport & Social Issues* 16 (2): 127–35.

Nixon, H. L. II. 1994a. Coaches' views of risk, pain, and injury in sport, with special reference to gender differences. *Sociology of Sport Journal* 11 (1): 79–87.

Nixon, H. L. II. 1994b. Social pressure, social support, and help seeking for pain and injuries in college sports networks. *Journal of Sport & Social Issues* 18 (4): 340–55.

Nixon, H. L. II. 1996a. Explaining pain and injury attitudes and experiences in sport in terms of gender, race, and sports status factors. *Journal of Sport & Social Issues* 20 (1): 33–44.

Nixon, H. L. II. 1996b. The relationship of friendship networks, sports experiences, and gender to expressed pain thresholds. *Sociology of Sport Journal* 13 (1): 78–86.

Nixon, H. L. II. 2000. Sport and disability. In *Handbook of sports studies* (pp. 422–38), edited by J. Coakley and E. Dunning. London: Sage.

Noll, R., and A. Zimbalist (eds.) 1997. *Sports, jobs, and taxes.* Washington, DC: The Brookings Institution.

Norcliffe, G. 2001. The ride to modernity: The bicycle in Canada, 1869–1900. Toronto: University of Toronto Press.

Nosanchuk, T. A. 1981. The way of the warrior: The effects of traditional martial arts training on aggressiveness. *Human Relations* 34 (6): 435–44.

Novak, M. 1976. *The joy of sports.* New York: Basic Books.

O'Brien, R. 1992. Lord gym. *Sports Illustrated* 77(4): 27 July, 46–52.

O'Ree, W. 2002. *The autobiography of Willie O'Ree: Hockey's black pioneer.* Toronto: Key Porter Books.

Office of the Commissioner of Official Languages (OCOL). 2000. *Official Languages in the Canadian Sports System,* vols. 1 and 2. Ottawa: Minister of Public Works and Government Services.

Offord, D., E. Lipman and E. Duku, *Sports, the Arts and Community Programs: Rates and Correlates of Participation.* Applied Research Branch, Strategic Policy, Human Resources Development Canada. October 1998 (W-98-18E).

Oglesby, C., and D. Schrader. 2000. Where is the white in the Rainbow Coalition? In *Racism in college athletics: The African-American athlete's experience* (pp. 279–93) edited by D. Brooks and R. Althouse. Morgantown, WV: Fitness Information Technology, Inc.

Okihiro, N. 1984. Extracurricular participation, educational destinies and early job outcomes. In *Sport and the Sociological Imagination* (pp. 338–49), edited by N. Theberge and P. Donnelly. Fort Worth: Texas Christian University Press.

Orlick, T. 1978. *The cooperative sports & games book: Challenge without competition.* New York: Pantheon Books.

Orlick, T., and C. Botterill. 1975. *Every kid can win.* Chicago: Nelson-Hall Co.

Ormsby, M. 1997. Survey ignores realities of sports– and news. In *Taking sport seriously: Social issues in Canadian sport* (pp. 305–6), edited by P. Donnelly. Toronto: Thompson Educational Publishing.

Osterland, A. 1995. Field of nightmares. *Financial World* 164 (4): 14 February, 105–7.

Overdorf, V. G., and K. S. Gill. 1994. Body image, weight and eating concerns, and use of weight control methods among high school female athletes. *Women in Sport and Physical Activity Journal* 3 (2): 69–79.

Overman, S. J. 1997. *The influence of the Protestant Ethic on sport and recreation.* Brookfield, VT: Ashgate.

Oxendine, J. B. 1988. *American Indian sports heritage.* Champaign, IL: Human Kinetics.

Ozanian, M. K. 1995. Following the money. *Financial World* 164 (4): 14 February, 27–31.

Palmer, B. 1979. *A culture in conflict: Skilled workers and industrial capitalism in Hamilton, Ontario, 1860–1914.* Montreal and Kingston: McGill-Queen's University Press.

Palmer, J. 2000. Bad call. In *Taking sport seriously:*

Social issues in Canadian sport, 2nd Edition (pp. 155–57), edited by P. Donnelly. Toronto: Thompson Educational Publishing.

Palmer, J. 2002. Bread and circuses: The local benefits of sports and cultural businesses. *C.D. Howe Institute Commentary* 161, March.

Paraschak, V. 1982. The heterotransplantation of organized sport: A Northwest Territories Case Study. In *Proceedings of the 5th Canadian Symposium on the History of Sport and Physical Education*, edited by B. Kidd. Toronto: School of Physical Education, University of Toronto.

Paraschak, V. 1989. Native sports history: Pitfalls and promises. *Canadian Journal of History of Sport* 20(1), 57–68.

Paraschak, V. 1995. The native sport and recreation program, 1972–1981: Patterns of resistance, patterns of reproduction. *Canadian Journal of History of Sport* (December): 1–18.

Paraschak, V. 1996. An examination of sport for Aboriginal females on the Six Nations Reserve, Ontario, from 1968 to 1980. In *Women of the First Nations. Power, Wisdom, and Strength* (pp. 83–96) edited by C. Miller and P. Chuchryk. Winnipeg: University of Manitoba Press.

Paraschak, V. 1997. Variations in race relations: Sporting events for native peoples in Canada. *Sociology of Sport Journal* 14 (1): 1–21.

Paraschak, V. 1999. Doing race, doing gender: First Nations, "sport," and gender relations. In *Sport and gender in Canada* (pp. 153–69), edited by P. White and K. Young. Don Mills, Ontario: Oxford University Press.

Parcels, J. 2000. *Straight facts about making it in pro hockey*. www.nepeanhockey.on.ca/Docs/MakingIt.htm.

Park, R. 1950. *Race and Culture*. Glencoe: The Free Press.

Parkhouse, B. L., and J. M.Williams. 1986. Differential effects of sex and status on elevation of coaching ability. *Research Quarterly for Exercise and Sport* 57 (1): 53–59.

Pastore, D. L., S. Inglis, and K. E. Danylchuk. 1996. Retention factors in coaching and athletic management: Differences by gender, position, and geographic location. *Journal of Sport & Social Issues* 20 (4): 427–41.

Patterson, O. 2002. Beyond compassion: selfish reasons for being unselfish. *Daedalus* (Winter): 26–38.

Perman, S. 1998. The master blasts the board. *Time*, 19 January, 61.

Perrucci, R., and E. Wysong. 1999. *The new class society*. Lanham, MD: Rowman and Littlefield.

Phillips, B. 1997. *Sports supplement review* (3d issue). Golden, CO: Mile High.

Picard, A. 2003. High-fees slam-dunk children's basketball. *Globe and Mail*, 13 May, p. A9.

Pilz, G. A. 1996. Social factors influencing sport and violence: On the "problem" of football hooliganism in Germany. International Review for *Sociology of Sport* 31 (1): 49–68.

Pipe, A. L. 1993. J. B. Wolffe Memorial Lecture. Sport, science, and society: Ethics in sports medicine. *Med Science Sports Exercise* (MG8), Aug; 25 (8): 888–900.

Pipe, A. 1998. Reviving ethics in sports: Time for physicians to act. *The Physician and Sportsmedicine* 26 (6): June, 39–40.

Pitter, R. 1996. The state and sport development in Alberta: A struggle for public status. *Sociology of Sport Journal* 13 (1), 31–50.

Pitter, R., and D. Andrews. 1997. Serving America's underserved youth: Reflections on sport and recreation in an emerging social problems industry. *Quest* 49 (1), 85–99.

Pluto, T. 1995. *Falling from grace: Can pro basketball be saved?* New York: Simon and Schuster.

Polsky, S. 1998. Winning medicine: professional sports team doctors' conflicts of interest. *Journal of Contemporary Health Law Policy* (IDD), Spring; 14 (2): 503–29.

Ponic, P. 2000. A herstory, a legacy: The Canadian Amateur Sports Branch's Women's Program. *Avante* 6 (2), 51–63.

Ponomaryov, N. I. 1981. *Sport and society*. Translated by J. Riordan. Moscow: Progress (and Chicago: Imported).

Pooley, J. 1981. Ethnic soccer clubs in Milwaukee: A study in assimilation. In *Sport in the Sociocultural Process* (pp. 430–447), edited by M. Hart and S. Birrell. Dubuque, Iowa: Wm. C. Brown.

Porterfield, K. 1999. Late to the line: Starting sport competition as an adult. In *Inside sports* (pp. 37–45), edited by J. Coakley and P. Donnelly. London: Routledge.

President's Council on Physical Fitness and Sports. 1997. *Physical activity and sport in the lives of girls.* Minneapolis: Center for Research on Girls and Women in Sport, University of Minnesota.

Price, S. L. 1997. What ever happened to the white athlete? *Sports Illustrated* 87 (23): 8 December, 31–55.

Pronger, B. 1990a *The arena of masculinity: Sports, homosexuality, and the meaning of sex.* New York: St. Martin's Press.

Pronger, B. 1990b. Gay jocks: A phenomenology of gay men in athletics. In *Sport, men and the gender order* (pp. 141–52), edited by M. Messner and D. Sabo. Champaign, IL: Human Kinetics.

Pronger, B. 1995. Rendering the body: The implicit lessons of gross anatomy. *Quest* 47 (4): 427–46.

Pronger, B. 1999. Fear and trembling: Homophobia in men's sport. In *Sport and gender in Canada* (pp. 182–97), edited by P. White and K. Young. Don Mills, Ontario: Oxford University Press.

Pronger, B. 2002. *Body fascism: Salvation in the technology of physical fitness.* Toronto: University of Toronto Press.

Putler, D. S., and R. A. Wolfe. 1999. Perceptions of intercollegiate athletic programs: Priorities and tradeoffs. *Sociology of Sport Journal* 16 (4): 301–25.

Pyette, R. 2002. Mustangs assigned their corrals. *London Free Press*, 17 May.

Rabey, S. 1992. Competing for souls in Barcelona. *Colorado Springs Gazette*, 8 August, B1.

Raboin, S. 1998. A family torn apart. *USA Today*, 9 December, 1C–2C.

Raboin, S. 1999. Bela is back on U.S. team. *USA Today*, 16 November, 1A–2A.

Rail, G. 1998. *Sport and postmodern times.* Albany: State University of New York Press.

Rail, G., V. Gaston, and J. Harvey. 1995. *Quebec 2002 and the confrontation of nationalisms.* Paper presented at the annual meeting of the North American Society for the Sociology of Sport, Sacramento, CA.

Rains, P. 1984. The production of fairness: Officiating in the National Hockey League. *Sociology of Sport Journal* 1 (2): 150–62.

Real, M. R. 1996. The postmodern Olympics: Technology and the commodification of the Olympic movement. *Quest* 48 (1): 9–24.

Real, M. R. 1998. MediaSport: Technology and the commodification of postmodern sport. In *MediaSport* (pp. 14–26), edited by L. A. Wenner. London/New York: Routledge.

Rees, C. R., and A. W. Miracle. 2000. Sport and education. In *Handbook of sports studies* (pp. 277–90), edited by J. Coakley and E. Dunning. London: Sage.

Rees, C. R., F. M. Howell, and A. W. Miracle. 1990. Do high school sports build character? *Journal of Social Science* 27 (3): 303–15.

Regroupement des organismes nationaux de loisir du Québec, Secteur Sport. 1983. Rapport de la Conférence de Presse Dénonçant l'Unilinguisme Anglais dans les Organismes Canadiens de Sport.

Reid, E. 1997. My body, my weapon, my shame. *Gentlemen's Quarterly*, September, 361–67.

Reid, S. M. 1996. The selling of the Games. *The Denver Post* (21 July): 4BB.

Reiss, S. 1998. *Sports and the American Jew.* Syracuse, NY: Syracuse University Press.

Riggs, M. T. 1991. *Color adjustment* (video tape). San Francisco: California Newsreel.

Rimer, E. 1996. Discrimination in major league baseball: Hiring standards for major league managers, 1975–1994. *Journal of Sport & Social Issues* 20 (2): 118–33.

Rinehart, R., and C. Grenfell. 1999. *Icy relations: Parental involvement in youth figure skating.* Paper presented at the annual conference of the North American Society for the Sociology of Sport, Cleveland, OH (November).

Rinehart, R., and S. Sydnor (eds.) 2003. *To the extreme: Alternative sports, inside and out.* Albany: State University of New York Press.

Rinehart, R. E. 1998. *Players all: Performances in contemporary sport.* Bloomington: Indiana University Press.

Rintala, J., and J. Bischoff. 1997. Persistent resistance: Leadership positions for women in Olympic sport governing bodies. *OLYMPIKA: The International Journal of Olympic Studies* 6: 1–24.

Riordan, J. 1993. Soviet-style sport in Eastern Europe: The end of an era. In *The changing politics of sport* (pp. 37–57), edited by L. Allison. Manchester, England: Manchester University Press.

Ritchie, I., and R. Beamish. 2002. *The forgotten history of drug prohibition in high performance sport.*

Paper presented at the annual meetings of the North American Society for the Sociology of Sport, Indianapolis, IN, 7 November.

Ritchie, I., and R. Beamish. 2003. Personal communication.

Ritzer, G. 2000. *The McDonaldization thesis* (New Century Edition). Thousand Oaks CA: Pine Forge Press.

Robbins, R. 1996. Josh Davis: Overcoming the trials. *Sports Spectrum*, June, 20–21.

Robidoux, M. 2001. *Men at play: A working understanding of professional hockey*. Montreal and Kingston: McGill-Queen's University Press

Robinson, L. 1995. Indigenous Games offer new goal to girl athletes. *NOW*, March 9–15, p. 31.

Robinson, L. 1997. Canoe race gracefully protests Hydro devastation. In *Taking sport seriously: Social issues in Canadian sport* (pp. 342–44), edited by P. Donnelly. Toronto: Thompson Educational Publishing.

Robinson, L. 1998. *Crossing the line: Violence and sexual assault in Canada's national sport*. Toronto: McClelland and Stewart.

Robinson, L. 2000a. Games boys play. In *Taking sport seriously: Social issues in Canadian sport*, 2nd Edition (pp. 79–83), edited by P. Donnelly. Toronto: Thompson Educational Publishing.

Robinson, L. 2000b. Prairie priorities on thin ice. In *Taking sport seriously: Social issues in Canadian sport*, 2nd Edition (pp. 114–15), edited by P. Donnelly. Toronto: Thompson Educational Publishing.

Robinson, L. 2002a. *Black tights: Women, sport and sexuality*. Toronto: HarperCollins.

Robinson, L. 2002b. *The nightmare of residential school: A story of ten indigenous runners in Canada*. Paper presented at the Playing the F+Game Conference, Copenhagen, Denmark, 9–14 November.

Romanow, R. 2002. *Building on Values: The Future of Health Care in Canada* (Ch. V). Ottawa: Government of Canada Publications.

Rose, A., and J. Friedman. 1997. Television sports as Mas(s)culine cult of distraction. In *Out of bounds: Sports, media, and the politics of identity* (pp. 1–15), edited by A. Baker and T. Boyd. Bloomington: Indiana University Press.

Rosentraub, M. 1997. *Major league losers: The real cost of sports and who's paying for them*. New York: Basic Books.

Routon, R. 1991. The standard of a new age.

Colorado Springs Gazette Telegraph, 2 June, C1.

Roversi, A. 1994. The birth of the "ultras": The rise of football hooliganism in Italy. In *Game without frontiers: Football, identity, and modernity* (pp. 359–81), edited by R. Giulianotti and J. Williams. Aldershot, England: Arena (Ashgate).

Rowe, D. 1999. *Sport, culture, and the media: The unholy trinity*. Buckingham, England: Open University Press.

Rowe, D., G. Lawrence, T. Miller, and J. McKay. 1994. Global sport?: Core concern and peripheral vision. *Media, Culture & Society* 16, 661–75.

Rowe, D., J. McKay, and T. Miller. 1998. Come together: Sport, nationalism, and the media image. In *MediaSport* (pp. 119–33), edited by L. A. Wenner. London/New York: Routledge.

Rubenstein, L. 2003. Most Canadians at U.S. colleges see dreams turn to nightmares. *Globe and Mail*, 18 January, p. S5.

Ruck, R. 1987. *Sandlot seasons: Sport in black Pittsburgh*. Urbana: University of Illinois Press.

Russo, R. D. 1999. Root, root, root for the home team. *The Denver Post*, 14 June, 1D, 7D.

Ryan, J. 1995. *Little girls in pretty boxes: The making and breaking of elite gymnasts and figure skaters*. New York: Doubleday.

Sabo, D., and S. C. Curry. 1998. Prometheus unbound: Constructions of masculinity in sports media. In *MediaSport* (pp. 202–17), edited by L. A. Wenner. London/New York: Routledge.

Sabo, D., and S. C. Jansen. 1998. Prometheus unbound: Constructions of masculinity in sports media. In *MediaSport* (pp. 202–20), edited by L. A. Wenner. London: Routledge.

Sabo, D., K. Miller, M. Farrell, G. Barnes, and M. Melnick. 1998. *The Women's Sports Foundation report: Sport and teen pregnancy*. East Meadows, NY: Women's Sports Foundation.

Sabo, D., S. C. Curry, D. Tate, M. C. Duncan, and S. Leggett. 1996. Televising international sport: Race, ethnicity, and nationalistic bias. *Journal of Sport & Social Issues* 20 (1): 7–21.

Sack, A. L., and E. J. Staurowsky. 1998. College athletes for hire: The evolution and legacy of the NCAA's amateur myth. Westport, CT: Praeger.

Safai, P. 2001. Healing the body in the 'culture of risk,' pain and injury: Negotiations between clinicians and injured athletes in Canadian competitive intercollegiate sport. Unpublished

Master's thesis. Toronto: University of Toronto.

Safai, P. 2002. Boys behaving badly: Popular literature on the misbehaviour of male team sport athletes in North America. *International Review for the Sociology of Sport* 37 (1): 97–102.

Sage, G. H. 1996. Public policy in the public interest: Pro franchises and sports facilities that are really "yours." In *Sport in contemporary society* (pp. 264–74), edited by D. S. Eitzen. New York: St. Martin's Press.

Sage, G. H. 1998a. Does sport affect character development in athletics? *Journal of Physical Education, Recreation and Dance* 69 (1): 15–18.

Sage, G. H. 1998b. *Power and ideology in American sport: A critical perspective.* Champaign, IL: Human Kinetics.

Sage, G. H. 1999. Justice do it! The Nike transnational advocacy network: Organization, collective actions, and outcomes. *Sociology of Sport Journal* 16 (3): 206–35.

Sailes, G. 1998. The African American athlete: Social myths and stereotypes. In *African Americans in sport* (pp. 183–98), edited by G. Sailes. New Brunswick, NJ: Transaction.

Sandomir, R. 1996. Word for word: The Jackson-Rodman papers. *New York Times*, 9 June, Section 4, p. 7.

Sapolsky, R. 2000. It's not all in the genes. *Newsweek*, 10 April, 68.

Savage, H., ed. 1929. *American college athletics.* Bulletin No. 23. New York: Carnegie Foundation.

Savage, J. 1997. A sure thing? Sports and gambling. Minneapolis: Lerner.

Scanlan, L. 2002. *Grace under fire: The state of our sweet and savage game.* Toronto: Penguin Canada

Scheinin, R. 1994. *Field of screams: The dark underside of America's national pastime.* New York: W. W. Norton.

Scherer, J. 2001. Globalization and the construction of local particularities: A case study of the Winnipeg Jets. *Sociology of Sport Journal* 18 (2), 205–30.

Schimmel, K. 2000. Take me out to the ball game: The transformation of production-consumption relations in professional team sport. In *Cultural Production and Consumption: Readings in Popular Culture* (pp. 36–52), edited by C. Harrington and D. Bielby. Oxford: Blackwell.

Schimmel, K. 2002. The political economy of place: Urban and sports studies perspectives. In *Theory, Sport and Society* (pp. 335–53), edited by J. Maguire and K. Young. Oxford: Elsevier Science.

Schimmel, K., A. G. Ingham, and J. W. Howell. 1993. Professional team sport and the American city: Urban politics and franchise relocations. In *Sport in social development* (pp. 211–44), edited by A. G. Ingham and J. W. Loy. Champaign, IL: Human Kinetics.

Schroeder, J. J. 1995. Developing self-esteem and leadership skills in Native American women: The role sports and games play. *Journal of Physical Education, Recreation and Dance* 66 (7): 48–51.

Schultz, B. 1999. The disappearance of child-directed activities. *Journal of Physical Education, Recreation and Dance* 70 (5): 9–10.

Schulze, L. 1990. On the muscle. In *Fabrications: Costumes and the Female Body* (pp. 59–78), edited by J. Gaines and C. Herzog. New York: Routledge.

Scraton, P. 1999. *Hillsborough: The truth.* Edinburgh: Mainstream Publishing.

Scully, G. W. 1995. *The market structure of sport.* Chicago: University of Chicago Press.

Segrave, J. 1994. The perfect 10: "Sportspeak" in the language of sexual relations. *Sociology of Sport Journal* 11 (2): 95–113.

Sellers, R., and S. Keiper. 1998. *Opportunity given or lost? Academic support services for NCAA Division I student-athletes.* Paper presented at the annual conference of the North American Society for the Sociology of Sport, Las Vegas (November).

Seltzer, R., and W. Glass. 1991. International politics and judging in Olympic skating events: 1968–1988. *Journal of Sport Behavior* 14 (3): 189–200.

Sewart, J. 1987. The commodification of sport. *International Review for the Sociology of Sport* 22 (3): 171–92.

Sheehan, R. G. 1996. *Keeping score: The economics of big-time sports.* Lakeville, IN: Diamond Communications.

Shields, D. 2000. Vince Carter as African-American. In *Taking Sport Seriously: Social Issues in Canadian Sport*, 2nd Edition (p. 118–19), edited by P. Donnelly. Toronto: Thompson Educational.

Shields, D. L. L., and B. J. L. Bredemeier. 1995. Character development and physical activity.

Champaign, IL: Human Kinetics.

Shields, D. L. L., B. J. L. Bredemeier, D. E. Gardner, and A. Bostrom. 1995. Leadership, cohesion, and team norms regarding cheating and aggression. *Sociology of Sport Journal* 12 (3): 324–36.

Shilling, C. 1994. *The body and social theory.* Thousand Oaks, CA: Sage.

Shogan, D., and M. Ford. 2000. A new sport ethics. *International Review for the Sociology of Sport* 35 (1): 49–58.

Shropshire, K. 1996. *In black and white: Race and sports in America.* New York: New York University Press.

Shropshire, K. 1999. *Who should pay for new sports facilities?* Wharton Real Estate Review 3 (2): 1–6.

Sigelman, L. 1998. Hail to the Redskins? Public reactions to a racially insensitive team name. *Sociology of Sport Journal* 14 (4): 315–25.

Silk, M. 1999. Local/global flows and altered production practices. *International Review for the Sociology of Sport* 34 (2): 113–23.

Silk, M., and J. Amis. 2000. Institutional pressures and the production of televised sport. *Journal of Sport Management* 14 (4): 267–92.

Silver, J. 1996. *Thin ice: Money, politics, and the demise of an NHL franchise.* Halifax: Fernwood.

Simpson, K. 1996. Sporting dreams die on the "rez." In *Sport in contemporary society* (pp. 287–94), edited by D. S. Eitzen. New York: St. Martin's Press.

Simri, U. 1983. *A concise world history of women's sports.* Netanya, Israel: Wingate Institute for Physical Education and Sport.

Simson, V., and A. Jennings. 1992. *The lords of the rings: Power, money, and drugs in the modern Olympics.* London: Simon & Schuster.

Smith Maguire, J. 2002. Bodies fit for consumption: The cultural production of the fitness field. Unpublished doctoral thesis, City University of New York Graduate School, New York.

Smith, A. 1999. Back-page bylines: Newspapers, women, and sport. In *SportCult* (pp. 253–61), edited by R. Martin and T. Miller. Minneapolis: University of Minnesota Press.

Smith, B. 2000. Keep courts out of sport, lawyer says. *Globe and Mail*, 21 August, p. S5.

Smith, D. 1997. Score: How the millionaire owners of the Winnipeg Jets got the public to pay for their hockey team. In *Taking sport seriously: Social issues in Canadian sport* (pp. 240–43), edited by

P. Donnelly. Toronto: Thompson Educational.

Smith, E. 2000. Stacking in the team sport of intercollegiate baseball. In *Racism in college athletics: The African American athlete's experience* (pp. 65–84), edited by D. Brooks and R. Althouse. Morgantown, WV: Fitness Information Technology.

Smith, E., and C. K. Harrison. 1998. Stacking in major league baseball. In *African Americans in sport* (pp. 199–216), edited by G. Sailes. New Brunswick, NJ: Transaction.

Smith, G., and C. Grindstaff. 1972. Race and sport in Canada. In *Training: Scientific Basis and Application*, edited by A. Taylor and M. Howell. Springfield, IL: Charles C. Thomas.

Smith, M. 1983. *Violence and sport.* Toronto: Butterworths.

Smith, R. E. 1986. Toward a cognitive-affective model of athletic burnout. *Journal of Sport Psychology* 8 (1): 36–50.

Smith, Y. 2000. Sociohistorical influences on African American elite sportswomen. In *Racism in college athletics: The African American athlete's experience* (pp. 173–98), edited by D. Brooks and R. Althouse. Morgantown, WV: Fitness Information Technology.

Snyder, E. E. 1994. Interpretations and explanations of deviance among college athletes: A case study. *Sociology of Sport Journal* 11 (3): 231–48.

Snyder, E. E., and E. Spreitzer. 1992. Social psychological concomitants of adolescents' role identities as scholar and athletes. *Youth and Society* 23 (4): 507–22.

Sokoloff, H. 2002. Universities spend $6.2m to aid athletes. *National Post*, 31 January.

Solomon, A. 2000. Our bodies, ourselves: The mainstream embraces the athlete Amazon. *The Village Voice*, 19–25 April (www.villagevoice.com/issues/0016/solomon2.shtml).

Solomon, N. 2000. What happened to the "Information Superhighway"? *Z Magazine* 13 (2): February, 10–13.

Sparks, R. 1992. "Delivering the male": Sports, Canadian television, and the making of TSN. *Canadian Journal of Communications* 17 (3): 319–42.

Spence, C. 1999. *The skin I'm in: Racism, sports and education.* Halifax: Fernwood Publishing.

Sperber, M. 1990. *College Sports, Inc.: The athletic department vs the university.* New York: Henry Holt.

Sports Québec. 1998. Brief presented to the Sub-Committee on the Study of Sport in Canada of the House of Commons Standing Committee on Canadian Heritage.

Spreitzer, E. A. 1995. Does participation in interscholastic athletics affect adult development: A longitudinal analysis of an 18–24 Age Cohort. *Youth and Society* 25 (3): 368–87.

Starr, M. 1999. Voices of the century: Blood, sweat, and cheers. *Newsweek*, 25 October, 44–73.

Starr M., and A. Samuels. 2000. A season of shame. *Newsweek* 135 (22): 29 May, 56–60.

Staurowsky, E. J. 1998. An act of honor or exploitation? The Cleveland Indians' use of the Louis Francis Sockalexis story. *Sociology of Sport Journal* 15 (4): 299–316.

Staurowsky, E. J. 1999. American Indian imagery and the miseducation of America. *Quest* 51 (4): 382–92.

Stead, D., and J. Maguire. 2000. "Rite of passage" or passage to riches?: The motivation and objectives of Nordic/Scandanavian players in English Soccer League. *Journal of Sport & Social Issues* 24 (1): 36–60.

Stebbins, R. 1987. *Canadian football: The view from the helmet*. London, ON: Centre for Social and Humanistic Studies, University of Western Ontario.

Stebbins, R. 1992. *Amateurs, Professionals, and Serious Leisure*. Montreal and Kingston: McGill-Queen's University Press.

Stebbins, R. 1998. *After work: the search for an optimal leisure lifestyle*. Calgary: Detselig Enterprises.

Steinbreder, J. 1996. Big spender. *Sky* (Delta Airlines magazine), July, 37–42.

Stevens, N. 1999. Stojko earns medal of different sort. Ottawa: Canadian Press, 26 January.

Stevenson, C. 1999. Becoming an elite international athlete: Making decisions about identity. In *Inside sports* (pp. 86–95), edited by J. Coakley and P. Donnelly. London: Routledge.

Stokes, M. 1996. "Strong as a Turk": Power, performance, and representation in Turkish wrestling. In *Sport, identity, and ethnicity* (pp. 21–42), edited by J. MacClancy. Oxford, England: Berg.

Stoll, S. K. 1995. A comparison of moral reasoning scores of general students and student athletes in Division I and Division III NCAA member collegiate institutions. *Research Quarterly for Exercise and Sport* 66, March (Supplement), A-81.

Stoll, S. K., and J. M. Beller. 1998. Can character be measured? *Journal of Physical Education, Recreation and Dance* 69 (1): 18–24.

Stratta, T. 1995. Cultural inclusiveness in sport—Recommendations from African-American women college athletes. *Journal of Physical Education, Recreation and Dance* 66 (7): 52-–56.

Stratta, T. P. 1997. Contextual analysis of African-American women college athletes at a predominantly white university. *Research Quarterly for Exercise and Sport* 68 (1): March (Supplement), A115–A116.

Strug, K. 1999. Life in Romania, Texas. *Newsweek*, 134 (17): 25 October, 73.

Sugden, J. 1996. *Boxing and society: An international analysis*. Manchester, NH: University of Manchester Press.

Sugden, J. 2002. *Scum Airways: Inside Football's Underground Economy*. London: Mainstream Publishing.

Sugden, J., and A. Tomlinson. 1998. *FIFA and the contest for world football: Who rules the peoples' game?* Cambridge, England: Polity Press.

Sugden, J., and A. Tomlinson. 1999. *Great balls of fire: How big money is highjacking world football*. Edinburgh, Scotland: Mainstream.

Sugden, J., and A. Tomlinson. 2000. Theorizing sport, social class, and status. In *Handbook of sports studies* (pp. 309–21), edited by J. Coakley and E. Dunning. London: Sage.

Suggs, W. 2000. Uneven progress for women's sports. *The Chronicle of Higher Education* 46 (31): A52 (http://chronicle.com/free/v46/i31/31a05201. htm).

Sundgot-Borgen, J. 1993a. Knowledge and practice of top level coaches about weight control and eating disorders. *Medicine and Science in Sports and Exercise* 5, Supplement 25, 180.

Sundgot-Borgen, J. 1993b. Prevalence of eating disorders in elite female athletes. *International Journal of Sport Nutrition* 3 (1): 29–40.

Sundgot-Borgen, J. 1994a. Eating disorders in female athletes. *Sports Medicine* 17 (3): 176–88.

Sundgot-Borgen, J. 1994b. Risk and trigger factors for the development of eating disorders in female elite athletes. *Medicine and Science in Sports and Exercise* 26 (4): April, 414–19.

Swain, D. 1999. Moving on: Leaving pro sports. In *Inside sports* (pp. 223–31), edited by J. Coakley and P. Donnelly. London: Routledge.

Taylor, I. 1982a. Class, violence, and sport: The case

of soccer hooliganism in Britain. In *Sport, culture, and the modern state* (pp. 39–97), edited by H. Cantelon and R. Gruneau. Toronto: University of Toronto Press.

Taylor, I. 1982b. On the sports violence question: Soccer hooliganism revised. In *Sport, culture, and ideology* (pp. 152–97), edited by J. Hargreaves. Boston: Routledge and Kegan Paul.

Taylor, I. 1987. Putting the boot into a working-class sport: British soccer after Bradford and Brussels. *Sociology of Sport Journal* 4 (2): 171–91.

Temple, K. 1992. Brought to you by....*Notre Dame Magazine* 21 (2): Summer, 29.

Theberge, N. 1987. Sport and women's empowerment. *Women's Studies International Forum* 10 (4), 387–93.

Theberge, N. 1988. Making a career in a man's world: The experiences and orientations of women in coaching. *ARENA Review* 12 (2), 116–27.

Theberge, N. 1993. The construction of gender in sport: Women, coaching and the naturalization of difference. *Social Problems*, 40, 301–13.

Theberge, N. 1995. Gender, sport, and the construction of community: A case study from women's ice hockey. *Sociology of Sport Journal* 12 (4): 389–402.

Theberge, N. 1999. Being physical: Sources of pleasure and satisfaction in women's ice hockey. In *Inside sports* (pp. 146–55), edited by J. Coakley and P. Donnelly. London: Routledge.

Theberge, N. 2000a. In *Handbook of sports studies*. (pp. 322–33), edited by J. Coakley and E. Dunning. London: Sage.

Theberge, N. 2000b. *Higher goals: Women's ice hockey and the politics of gender*. Albany NY: State University of New York Press.

Theberge, N. 2002. Challenging the gendered space of sport: Women's ice hockey and the struggle for legitimacy. In *Gender and sport: A reader* (pp. 292–302), edited by S. Scraton and A. Flintoff. London: Routledge.

Thomas, R. 1996. Black faces still rare in the press box. In *Sport in society: Equal opportunity or business as usual?* (pp. 212–33), edited by R. Lapchick. Thousand Oaks, CA: Sage.

Thompson, R., and R. T. Sherman. 1999. Athletes, athletic performance, and eating disorders: Healthier alternatives. *Journal of Social Issues* 55 (2): 317–37.

Thompson, S. 1999a. The game begins at home: Women's labor in the service of sport. In *Inside sports* (pp. 111–20), edited by J. Coakley and P. Donnelly. London: Routledge.

Thompson, S. 1999b. *Mother's taxi: Sport and women's labor*. Albany: State University of New York Press.

Thompson, W. 1999. Wives Incorporated: Marital relationships in professional ice hockey. In *Inside sports* (pp. 180–89), edited by J. Coakley and P. Donnelly. London: Routledge.

Tirone, S. 1999–2000. Racism, indifference, and the leisure experiences of South Asian Canadian teens. *Leisure* 24 (1–2), 89–114.

Tirone, S., and A. Pedlar. 2000. Understanding the leisure experiences of a minority ethnic group: South Asian teens and young adults in Canada. *Loisir et Sociètè/Society & Leisure* 23 (1), 145–69.

Todd, T. 1987. Anabolic steroids: The gremlins of sport. *Journal of Sport History* 14 (1): 87–107.

Tofler, I. R., et al. 1996. Physical and emotional problems of elite female gymnasts. *New England Journal of Medicine* 335 (4): 281–83.

Tomlinson, A. 1998. Power: Domination, negotiation, and resistance in sports cultures. *Journal of Sport & Social Issues* 22 (3): 235–40.

Toohey, K., and A.J. Veal. 2000. *The Olympic Games: A social science perspective*. Wallingford, U.K.: CABI Publishing.

Torbert, M. 2000. *Follow me: A handbook of movement activities for children*. St. Paul, MN: Redleaf Press.

Trujillo, N. 1995. Machines, missiles, and men: Images of the male body on ABC's Monday Night Football. *Sociology of Sport Journal* 12 (4): 403–23.

Trulson, M. E. 1986. Martial arts training: A novel "cure" for juvenile delinquency. *Human Relations* 39 (12): 1131–40.

Tuggle, C. A., and A. Owen. 1999. A descriptive analysis of NBC's coverage of the centennial Olympics: The "Games of the Woman"? *Journal of Sport & Social Issues* 23 (2): 171–82.

Turner, B. S. 1997. *The body and society*. London: Sage.

U.S. News and World Report. 1983. A sport fan's guide to the 1984 Olympics. May 9, 124.

University of Toronto. 1994. Report of the Task Force on Gender Equity. Department of Athletics and Recreation.

Unwin, P. 2001. Who do you think I am?: A story of Tom Longboat. *The Beaver*, April–May, 20–26.

Urquhart, J., and J. Crossman. 1999. The Globe and Mail coverage of the Winter Olympic Games: A cold place for women athletes. *Journal of Sport & Social Issues* 23 (2): 193–202.

Urquhart, J., and J. Crossman. 1999. The Globe and Mail coverage of the Winter Olympic Games: A cold place for women athletes. *Journal of Sport & Social Issues* 23 (2), 193–202.

USOC. 1992. *USOC drug education and doping control program: Guide to banned medications.* Colorado Springs: United States Olympic Committee.

Veblen, T. 1899. *The theory of the leisure class.* New York: Macmillan. (See also 1953 paperback edition, New York: A Mentor Book.)

Veri, M. J. 1999. Homophobic discourse surrounding the female athlete. *Quest* 51 (4): 355–68.

Verma, G., and D. S. Darby. 1994. *Winners and losers: Ethnic minorities in sport and recreation.* London: The Falmer Press.

Vertinsky, P. 1990. *The eternally wounded woman: Women, exercise and doctors in the late nineteenth century.* Manchester: Manchester University Press.

Vertinsky, P. A. 1987. Exercise, physical capability, and the eternally wounded woman in late nineteenth century North America. *Journal of Sport History* 14 (1): 7–27.

Vertinsky, P. A. 1992. Reclaiming space, revisioning the body: The quest for gender-sensitive physical education. *Quest* 44 (3): 373–96.

Vertinsky, P. A. 1994. Women, sport, and exercise in the 19th century. In *Women and sport: Interdisciplinary perspectives* (pp. 63–82), edited by D. M. Costa and S. R. Guthrie. Champaign, IL: Human Kinetics.

Vine, C., and P. Challen. 2002. *Gardens of shame: The tragedy of Martin Kruze and the sexual abuse at Maple Leaf Gardens.* Vancouver: Douglas and McIntyre.

Wacquant, L. J. D. 1992. The social logic of boxing in Black Chicago: Toward a sociology of pugilism. *Sociology of Sport Journal* 9 (3): 221–54.

Wacquant, L. J. D. 1995a. The pugilistic point of view: How boxers think and feel about their trade. *Theory and Society* 24: 489—535.

Wacquant, L. J. D. 1995b. Pugs at work: Bodily capital and bodily labour among professional boxers. *Body & Society* 1 (1): 65–93.

Wacquant, L. J. D. 1995c. Why men desire muscles. *Body & Society* 1 (1): 163–79.

WADA. 2003. World Anti-Doping Code, v. 3, 20 February. www.wada-ama.org.

Waddington, I. 2000. Sport and health: A sociological perspective. In *Handbook of sports studies* (pp. 408–21), edited by J. Coakley and E. Dunning. London: Sage.

Wagner, G. G. 1987. Sport as a means for reducing the cost of illness—Some theoretical, statistical, and empirical remarks. *International Review for the Sociology of Sport* 22 (3): 217–27.

Wahl, G. 1998. Unintentional grounding. *Sports Illustrated* 89 (20): 11 November, 92–108.

Walton, T. 2001. The Sprewell/Carlesimo episode: Unacceptable violence or unacceptable victim. *Sociology of Sport Journal* 18 (3): 345–57.

Wasielewski, P. L. 1991. Not quite normal, but not really deviant: Some notes on the comparison of elite athletes and women political activists. *Deviant Behavior: An Interdisciplinary Journal* 12: 81–95.

Weber, M. 1958. *The Protestant Ethic and the spirit of capitalism.* Translated by T. Parsons. New York: Scribner's.

Weber, M. 1968 (1922). *Economy and society: An outline of interpretive sociology.* Translated by G. Roth and G. Wittich. New York: Bedminster Press.

Wechsler, H., et al. 1997. Binge drinking, tobacco, and illicit drug use and involvement in college athletics. *Journal of American College Health* 45, 1 March, 195–200.

Wee, E. L. 1995. Youth sports hit families in the wallet. *Washington Post*, 15 October, A1.

Weiler, K. H., and C. T. Higgs. 1999. Television coverage of professional golf: A focus on gender. *Women in Sport and Physical Activity Journal* 8 (1): 83–100.

Weiner, J. 1999. What do we want from our sports heroes? *Business Week*, 25 February, 77.

Weiner, J. 2000. Sports centered: Why our obsession has ruined the game. *Utne Reader* 97, January/February, 48–50.

Weinstein, M. D., M. D. Smith, and D. L. Wiesenthal. 1995. Masculinity and hockey violence. *Sex Roles* 33 (11/12): 831–47.

Weir, T. 1999. The next century: Sports. *USA Today*, 31 December, 7C.

Weir, T. 2000. Americans fall farther behind. USA Today, 3 May, 3C.

Weiss, O. 1996. Media sports as a social substitution pseudosocial relations with sports figures.

International Review for the Sociology of Sport 31 (1): 109–18.

Welch, W. M. 1996. Federal taxpayers shut out of stadium payoff. *USA Today*, May 31, A1.

Wenner, L. A., and W. Gantz. 1998. Watching sports on television: Audience experience, gender, fanship, and marriage. In *MediaSport* (pp. 233–51), edited by L. A. Wenner. London: Routledge.

Wenner, L. A., ed. 1998. *MediaSport*. London: Routledge.

Wertheim, J., and D. Yaeger. 1999. The passing game. *Sports Illustrated*, 14 June, 90–102.

Whannel, G. 2002. Media sport stars: Masculinities and moralities. London/New York: Routledge.

Whannel. G. 2000. Sport and the media. In *Handbook of sport studies* (pp. 291–309), edited by J. Coakley and E. Dunning. London: Sage.

Wheeler, G. D., et al. 1996. Retirement from disability sport: A pilot study. *Adapted Physical Activity Quarterly* 13 (4): 382–99.

Wheeler, G. D., et al. 1999. Personal investment in disability sport careers: An international study. *Adapted Physical Activity Quarterly* 16 (3): 219–37.

White, A., et al. 1992. *Women and sport: A consultation document*. London: The Sports Council.

White, P., and J. Curtis. 1990a. Participation in competitive sport among anglophones and francophones in Canada: Testing competing hypotheses. *International Review for the Sociology of Sport* 25, 125–39.

White, P., and J. Curtis. 1990b. English / French Canadian differences in types of sport participation: Testing the school socialization hypotheses. *Sociology of Sport Journal* 7, 347–68.

White, P., and K. Young. 1997. Masculinity, sport, and the injury process: A review of Canadian and international evidence. *Avante* 3 (2): 1–30.

White, P., and K. Young. 1999. Is sport injury gendered? In *Sport and gender in Canada* (pp. 69–84), edited by P. White and K. Young. Don Mills, Ontario: Oxford University Press.

White, P., and W. McTeer. 1990. Sport as a component of cultural capital: Survey findings on the impact of participation in different types of sport on educational attainment in Ontario high schools. *Physical Education Review* 3, 66–71.

Whitson, D. 1998. Circuits of promotion: Media, marketing, and the globalization of sport. In *MediaSport* (pp. 57–72), edited by L. A. Wenner.

London/New York: Routledge.

Whitson, D., and D. Macintosh. 1996. The global circus: International sport, tourism, and the marketing of cities. *Journal of Sport & Social Issues* 20 (3): 278–95.

Wieberg, S. 1994. Conley nears end of six-year career. *USA Today*, 17 November, 8C.

Wieberg, S. 2000a. A judgement in Vermont. USA Today, 3 February, 16C.

Wieberg, S. 2000b. A night of humiliation. *USA Today*, 4 February, 1C–2C.

Wiggins, D. 1994. The notion of double-consciousness and the involvement of Black athletes in American sport. In *Ethnicity and sport in North American history and culture* (pp. 133–56), edited by G. Eisen and D. K. Wiggins. Westport, CT: Greenwood Press.

Wiggins, D. 2000. Critical events affecting racism in athletics. In *Racism in college athletics: The African American athlete's experience* (pp. 15–36), edited by D. Brooks and R. Althouse. Morgantown, WV: Fitness Information Technology.

Wiggins, D. K., ed. 1995. *Sport in America: From wicked amusement to national obsession*. Champaign, IL: Human Kinetics.

Wilkerson, M. 1996. Explaining the presence of men coaches in women's sports: The uncertainty hypothesis. *Journal of Sport & Social Issues* 20 (4): 411–26.

Williams, R. (with D. LeBatard). 1999. Everything hurts. *ESPN—The Magazine*, 12 December, 78–82.

Wilmore, J. 1996. Eating disorders in the young athlete. In *The child and adolescent athlete* (pp. 287–303), edited by O. bar-Or. Vol. 6 of the Encyclopaedia of Sports Medicine—a publication of the IOC Medical Commission. London: Blackwell Science.

Wilson, B. 1997. "Good Blacks" and "Bad Blacks": Media Constructions of African-American Athletes in Canadian Basketball. *International Review for the Sociology of Sport* 32 (2), 177–89.

Wilson, B. 1999. "Cool pose" incorporated: The marketing of black masculinity in Canadian NBA coverage. In *Sport and gender in Canada* (pp. 232–53), edited by P. White and K. Young. Don Mills, Ontario: Oxford University Press.

Wilson, B., and R. Sparks. 1996. "It's Gotta Be the

Shoes": Youth, Race, and Sneaker Commercials. *Sociology of Sport Journal* 13 (4), 398–427.

Wilson, B., and R. Sparks. 2001. Michael Jordan, Sneaker Commercials, and Canadian Youth Cultures. In *Michael Jordan Inc.: Corporate sport, media culture, and late modern America* (pp. 217–55), edited by D. Andrews. Albany, NY: State University of New York Press.

Wilson, J. 1994. *Playing by the rules: Sport, society, and the state*. Detroit, MI: Wayne State University Press.

Winlock, C. 2000. Running the invisible race. *ColorLines* 3 (1): 27.

Winn, M. 1984. *Children without childhood*. New York: Viking Penguin.

Wolf, N. 1991. *The beauty myth*. New York: Anchor Books.

Wolfe, T. 1979. *The right stuff*. New York: Farrar, Strauss, Giroux.

Wolff, A., and D. Yaeger. 1995. Credit risk. *Sports Illustrated* 83 (6): 7 August, 46–-55.

Womack, M. 1992. Why athletes need ritual: A study of magic among professional athletes. In *Sport and religion* (pp. 191–202), edited by S. Hoffman. Champaign, IL: Human Kinetics.

Wong, J. 1999. Asian women in sport. *Journal of Physical Education, Recreation and Dance* 70 (4): 42–43.

Woog, D. 1998. *Jocks: True stories of America's gay male athletes*. Los Angeles: Alyson Books.

WOSPORT WEEKLY, 1999. Quotes of the week. 28 June (online newsletter covering women in sports).

Yeung, W. J. 1999. Multiple domains of paternal involvement with children. Unpublished paper, Institute for Social Research, University of Michigan, Ann Arbor.

Yeung, W. J., J. F. Sandburg, P. E. Davis-Kern, and S. L. Hofferth. 1999. Children's time with fathers in intact families. Unpublished paper, Institute for Social Research, University of Michigan, Ann Arbor.

Young, K. 1993. Violence, risk, and liability in male sports culture. *Sociology of Sport Journal* 10 (4): 373–96.

Young, K. 2000. Sport and violence. In *Handbook of sports studies* (pp. 382–409), edited by J. Coakley and E. Dunning. London: Sage.

Young, K. 2000. *Toward a more inclusive sociology of sports-related violence*. Paper presented at the North American Society for the Sociology of Sport, San Antonio, TX.

Young, K. 2002a. From "sports violence" to "sports crime": Aspects of violence, law, and gender in the sports process. In *Paradoxes of youth and sport* (pp. 207–24), edited by M. Gatz, M. A. Messner, and S. J. Ball-Rokeach. Albany, NY: State University of New York Press.

Young, K. 2002b. Standard deviations: An update on North American crowd disorder. *Sociology of sport journal* 19 (3): 237–75.

Young, K., and P. White. 1995. Sport, physical danger, and injury: The experiences of elite women athletes. *Journal of Sport & Social Issues* 19 (1): 45–61.

Young, K., and P. White. 1999. Career-ending injuries: Just part of the game? In *Inside sports* (pp. 203–13), edited by J. Coakley and P. Donnelly. London: Routledge.

Young, K., ed. 2003. *Sporting bodies, damaged selves: Sociological studies of sport-related injury*. Oxford: Elsevier Press.

Young, K., P. White, and W. McTeer. 1994. Body talk: Male athletes reflect on sport, injury, and pain. *Sociology of Sport Journal* 11 (2): 175–95.

Zeman, B. 1988. *To run with Longboat: Twelve stories of Indian athletes in Canada*. Edmonton: GMS Ventures.

Zhang, J. J., et al. 1996a. Impact of TV broadcasting on the attendance of NBA games. *Research Quarterly for Exercise and Sport* 67, March Supplement, A12.

Zhang, J. J., et al. 1996b. Negative influence of entertainment options on the attendance of professional sport games: The case of a minor league hockey team. *Research Quarterly for Exercise and Sport* 67, March Supplement, A113.

Zhang, J. J., et al. 1997. Impact of broadcasting on minor league hockey attendance. *Research Quarterly for Exercise and Sport* 68, March Supplement, A117.

Zimbalist, A. 1999. *Unpaid professionals: Commercialism and conflict in big-time college sports*. Princeton, NJ: Princeton University Press.

Zipter, Y. 1988. *Diamonds are a dyke's best friend*. Ithaca, NY: Firebrand Books.

Name Index

Abdel-Shehid, Gamal, 263, 285, 286
Adam, Dyanne, 278
Adang, O., 210f
Adler, Patricia A., 116, 138, 145
Adler, Peter, 116, 138, 145
Aga Khan IV, 255
Albert, Mathieu, 240, 308
Albinson, J., 107, 273, 304
Alcott, Amy, 102
Ali, Muhammad (Cassius Clay), 492
Allayne, Kristi, 284
Allison, L., 405, 411
Alou, Felipe, 289
Amis, J., 386
Anderson, Eric, 247
Anderson, S., 332
Andrews, D., 108, 109, 115, 408, 423
Andrews, D.L., 401
Arbena, J.L., 412
Arledge, Roone, 424
Armstrong, G., 210f
Armstrong, J., 241
Armstrong, P., 307
Arnold, E., 143, 145
Astophan, Jamie, 147
Atkinson, M., 187, 191, 350, 408
Austin, Tracy, 126

Bairner, A., 411, 438
Baker, Russell, 39
Baker, W.J., 59, 60, 62, 80
Bale, J., 292, 425
Ball, David, 136
Ball, Donald, 282, 283

Bamberger, M., 148
Barkley, Charles, 417
Barnes, Stuart, 403
Barrett, Danny, 289
Bartimole, R., 349
Beal, B., 12, 101, 115, 135, 477
Beal, C.R., 132
Beamish, R., 127, 181, 294, 304, 351, 353, 355f, 360, 361
Beauchesne, L., 175
Becker, D., 196
Beckham, David, 326
Bedard, Myriam, 274, 275, 276
Beddoes, Dick, 1, 123
Bedecki, T., 411
Beers, George, 277
Begley, S., 258f
Bell, W., 470
Bellamy, R.V., Jr., 333, 375, 376
Bellefleur, M., 76, 115, 271
Beller, J.M., 94, 95, 167
Benedict, J., 165, 201
Benedict, J.R., 215
Berck, P., 266
Berger, J., 236
Berlage, G., 107
Best, J.C., 174, 175, 430
Bettman, Gary, 299, 300
Billings, A., 390
Birrell, S., 42, 47, 52, 108, 235, 236, 252
Bischoff, J., 315
Blackhurst, M., 175, 430
Blain, N., 393
Blainey, Justine, 229, 231, 234

Blake, A., 21
Blinde, E.M., 225, 236
Bloom, G.A., 201
Bloom, M., 263
Blumer, Herbert, 40
Blumstein, A., 201
Boileau, R., 272, 273
Bolin, A., 243, 244
Bompa, 122
Bone, Jamie, 282, 283
Booth, D., 52, 264
Botterill, C., 121, 122, 124
Boucher, Gaetan, 270
Bouchier, N., 63, 68, 80
Bourdieu, P., 305, 449
Bowen, W.G., 468
Bowery, J., 127, 294, 353, 360, 361
Bowlen, Pat, 351
Boyd, R., 259
Brace, Rick, 300
Braddock, Jomills, 452
Brady, E., 349, 351
Brashear, Donald, 190, 191
Bray, C., 307
Bredemeier, B.J.L., 95, 167, 196, 197, 225, 453
Brennan, Christine, 104
Breton, M., 292
Brill, Debbie, 325
Brisco, Ryrie, 414
Brown, George, 269
Brownell, S., 21, 27
Broyer, G., 115
Bruce, T., 392
Brunt, 128
Brunton, H., 313, 314, 321

Bryden, Rod, 301
Bryshun, J., 162, 164, 165
Buono, Wally, 300
Burke, Brian, 158
Burstyn, V., 1, 18, 20, 28, 47, 73, 74, 77, 105, 109, 175, 215, 237, 241, 246, 250, 252, 327
Bylsma, D., 145
Bylsma, J., 122, 145

Cagan, J., 346, 364
Cahill, B.R., 145
Calhoun, C., 32
Calvin, John, 63
Campagnolo, Iona, 315f, 406, 440, 443, 459
Campbell, A., 209
Campbell, Clarence, 1 86, 212
Campbell, Colin, 300
Campbell, Hugh, 300
Campbell, M., 310
Campbell, N., 279
Cantelon, M., 125, 282, 326
Capriati, Jennifer, 126
Caray, Chip, 400
Carlesimo, P.J., 170, 172
Carlos, John, 491–492
Carnegie, Herb, 288f, 292
Carrington, B., 423
Carter, Anson, 289
Carter, Vince, 3, 108, 300, 335, 392, 394
Caudwell, J., 250
Cavalli-Sforza, F., 259
Cavalli-Sforza, L.L., 259
Cavanagh, J., 332
Chafetz, Janet, 131

Chalip, L., 94, 142
Challen, P., 215
Chamberlain, M., 281
Chandler, T.J.L., 451
Chastain, Brandi, 224
Chebet, Joseph, 335
Chernushenko, D., 434
Cherry, Don, 194, 283, 367, 390
Chrétien, Jean, 414
Christie, J., 275, 300
Clark, C., 278
Clarke, Austin, 285
Clarke, Bobby, 165
Clemons, Mike, 289
Cluer, S., 221, 390
Coakley, Jay, 7, 13, 28, 41, 52, 84, 89, 90, 91, 103, 111, 120, 130, 132, 133, 137, 145, 155, 172, 178, 191, 236, 288, 297, 299, 306, 323, 408, 478, 487
Cochrane, J., 74, 81
Cocker, Joe, 161
Coderre, Denis, 275, 300
Cole, C.L., 21, 236
Coleman, James, 450
Comaneci, Nadia, 125
Conniff, R., 221
Conroy, Pat, 190
Costas, Bob, 339
Coulombe, S., 274
Cowart, V.E., 185
Cox, B., 242
Creedon, Pam, 391
Crissey, J., 387, 477
Crooks, Charmaine, 320
Crosset, T.W., 101, 103, 169, 201, 215, 236
Crossman, J., 388
Csikszentmihalyi, M., 109
Cummings, Gail, 231
Curry, T., 100, 157f, 165, 201
Curtis, J., 85, 91, 274, 317, 323, 449, 455

Dacyshyn, A., 93, 319
Dales-Schuman, Stacey, 244
Daley, Trevor, 289
Dallaire, C., 266
Daniels, D., 473
Danylchuk, K., 455
Davies, Robert, 470
Davis, C., 157
De Coubertin, Pierre, 403, 416
Deford, Frank, 30
DeKnop, P., 145
deMause, N., 346, 364
Devereaux, E., 120
Dewar, A., 132, 195
Di Pasquale, M.G., 181
Diefenbaker, John, 411
Dobie, M., 308
Dolan, Larry, 349
Domi, Tie, 206
Donnelly, Jay, 178
Donnelly, Liam, 202
Donnelly, Peter, 14, 15, 23, 25, 41, 46, 52, 88, 94, 101, 109, 111, 116, 117, 121, 125–130, 145, 157, 169, 172, 202, 247, 265, 266, 271f, 278, 281, 288, 304, 306, 310, 323, 330, 331, 386, 422, 423, 428, 429, 431, 458, 464f
Dragila, Stacy, 217
Drahota, J.T., 93
Drakich, K., 224
Drapeau, Jean, 403
Drover, Jack, 463
Dryden, Ken, 83
Dubin, Charles, 181
Duku, E., 305
Dumont, Fernand, 32
Duncan, M.C., 387, 389, 391
Dunk, T., 111
Dunn, K., 198
Dunn, R., 98
Dunning, E., 28, 50, 52, 53, 59, 60, 64, 68, 69, 70, 80, 81, 167, 188, 189, 208, 210, 215, 329
Duquin, M., 250
Duthie, Jim, 122
Dyck, N., 266

Early, Gerald, 54, 411
Eastman, S., 390
Eberts, Mary, 360
Eddington, B., 76, 277
Eder, D., 451, 452
Edwards, Frank, 255
Edwards, H., 255, 256, 287, 294, 397, 485
Eichler, Margrit, 32
Eitzen, D.S., 93, 184, 344, 349
Elias, N., 50, 53, 58, 80, 329
Elkind, D., 121
Elway, John, 335
Engstron, L.-M., 145
Enloe, C., 427
Ennis, R., 91
Eskes, T.B., 236
Essed, P., 257
Etue, E., 217, 245
Euchner, Charles, 351
Euripides, 58
Evans, R.G., 306
Ewald, Keith, 157

Fasting, K., 220, 477
Fausto-Sterling, A., 21, 239, 252
Fawcett, Brian, 470
Fejgin, N., 447
Ferguson, A., 117
Ferguson, John, 165
Feschuk, S., 275
Field, R., 384
Findlay, Hilary, 191
Fine, G.A., 145
Florey, B., 387
Foley, D., 442
Foley, D.E., 468
Foot, David, 479, 481, 482
Ford, M., 181
Franks, C., 411

Franseen, L., 157f
Freud, Sigmund, 43
Friedman, J., 392
Friedman, S., 224
Friesen, David, 450
Frisby, W., 307
Fusco, C., 100

Galasso, Pat, 127
Gantz, W., 395, 397
Gaston, Cito, 289
Gems, G.R., 307
George, J., 263
Gerdy, J.R., 468
Giddens, A., 306
Giese, Rachel, 217
Gilbert, Doug, 125
Gill, K.S., 157f
Gillett, George Jr., 300
Girardin, Y., 274, 275
Giulianotti, R., 210
Glass, W., 433
Glassford, Gerry, 277
Godfrey, Paul, 300
Godley, A., 262, 449
Goffman, Erving, 32
Goldberg, A.D., 451
Goodenow, Bob, 299, 300
Gordon, M., 264
Gould, D., 13, 91
Gowan, Geoff, 407f
Gramsci, Antonio, 43, 105, 106
Gray, J.T., 426
Greaves, L., 215
Green, B.C., 142
Green, Mick, 405, 406
Green, Roy, 17
Greenberg, J., 427
Greenberg, J.G., 375
Greenberg, M.J., 426
Greendorfer, S.L., 132
Grenier, G., 272
Gretzky, Wayne, 123, 193, 300, 335
Grey, M., 265, 442
Griffin, P., 225, 244, 246, 247, 252, 477
Griffiths, S., 305

Grindstaff, C., 282
Gruneau, R., 28, 32, 42, 52, 56, 64, 66, 68, 71, 81, 107, 273, 296, 304, 323, 338, 386, 424
Grunwald, Glen, 300
Guttmann, A., 56, 59, 62, 64, 69, 70, 81, 188, 208, 428

Haakonsen, Terje, 478
Hall, A., 68, 74, 81, 115, 116, 117, 231, 243, 253, 266, 271, 273, 280, 282, 463, 490
Hall, M.A., 52
Hall, S., 17
Hankivsky, O., 215
Hanson, S.L., 449
Hardman, K., 458
Hargreaves, J., 44, 52, 132, 224, 477
Harris, J.C., 369, 393, 394
Harris, Mike, 301
Harris, O., 132, 241
Harrison, L., 241
Hart, M.M., 74
Harvey, J., 32, 75, 76, 115, 271, 304, 306, 404f, 409, 421, 428
Hasbrook, C., 132, 241
Hawes, K., 157f, 162
Hayden, Frank, 78
Haynes, R., 210f
Heine, M., 277, 280
Hellison, D.R., 453
Henderson, Paul, 165
Henry, F., 285–286
Heywood, L., 224, 243, 244
Higgs, C.T., 390, 391
Hillaird, D.C., 157
Hillaird, J,M,, 157
Hitler, Adolf, 78
Hoberman, J., 21, 173, 184, 329, 472, 474, 475
Hoffman, A., 81, 98, 315

Hokowhitu, B., 423
Hood, Colin, 440, 456, 460, 477
Hood, Graham, 320
Hooks, B., 31
Horan, John, 423
Horne, J.A., 28
Houle, F., 421
Houlihan, B., 184, 405, 411, 412, 438
Houston, William, 300
Hovden, J., 233
Howell, C., 71
Howell, D., 114
Howlett, D., 351
Huey, J., 415
Hughes, C., 305
Hughes, R., 155
Hughson, J., 213
Humber, W., 54, 270
Humphrey, J., 411

Igali, Daniel, 286
Iginla, Jarome, 259, 289, 300
Ingham, A., 14, 25, 90, 132, 157, 195
Innis, Harold, 32
Isray, Robert, 349

Jackson, R., 407f
Jackson, Russ, 282
Jackson, S.A., 109
Jackson, S.J., 286, 401, 423, 425
Jackson, Stu, 289
Jacobs, Richard, 349
Jaeger, Andrea, 126
James, C., 257, 262, 286, 452
James, C.L.R., 44, 54, 486
James, Graham, 104, 123
Jansen, S.C., 391, 392, 393
Jennings, A., 170, 177, 184, 303, 433, 438
Jericho, Chris, 9
Jerome, Wendy, 446, 447
Jhally, Sut, 373, 424

Jiobu, Robert, 157
Johns, D., 157, 224
Johnson, Ben, 175, 180, 181, 276, 286, 406
Johnson, C., 331
Johnson, Dave, 271
Johnson, J., 162, 164, 165
Johnson, Lyndon, 228
Johnson, Magic, 244, 245
Joravsky, B., 324
Jordan, Michael, 108, 332, 335
Joyce, G., 262

Kane, Lori, 300
Kane, M.J., 230, 240, 391
Kaplan, D., 345, 358
Kariya, Paul, 197
Keane, Paul, 165
Kearney, J., 177f
Kelly, M.C., 401
Kennedy, Sheldon, 202, 492
Keri, M.G., 120
Kernaghan, J., 466
Kesterton, M., 119
Kharmalov, Valeri, 165
Kidd, Bruce, 30, 32, 58, 71, 72, 73, 76, 77, 81, 127, 139, 173, 229, 237, 241, 270, 272, 277, 292, 298, 304, 360, 365, 418, 420, 470
Kincade, P., 81
King, A.J.C., 455, 458
Kinkema, K.M., 369, 393, 394
Kirby, S., 202, 215
Kirke, Gordon, 300
Kirke, Graham, 202
Kjeldsen, E., 273
Klein, A., 102, 284, 425
Klein, A.M., 330
Knight, Bobby, 463
Knight, G., 386, 427
Knight, Phil, 422
Knisley, M., 383
Kohn, A., 124

Koppett, L., 138, 374, 386, 397, 398, 399
Kotarba, Joe, 131
Kournikova, Anna, 245
Krane, V., 244
Kraus, S.J., 449
Kruger, A., 81, 438
Kwan, Michelle, 340

L'Heureux, Bill, 120
Laberge, S., 240, 270, 274, 275, 305, 308
LaFlamme, A., 265
LaForge, Patrick, 300
Landry, F., 272
Lang, G.E., 208
Lapchick, R., 288, 289, 315, 393, 418
Laqueur, T., 21
Lasch, Christopher, 325
Latimer, C., 339
Lavoie, M., 272, 273, 274, 292, 346, 362, 364
Lay, Marion, 407f
LeBlanc, Romeo, 160
Leduc, Mark, 247
Lee, Nancy, 300, 390
Lefkowitz, B., 165, 201
LeMay Doan, Catriona, 271
Lemieux, Mario, 186, 197, 299, 300
Lemieux, V., 271
Lenskyj, H., 74, 76, 132, 225, 245, 303, 391, 435, 438
Leonsis, Ted, 325
Levesque, Rene, 270
Lewis, Carl, 175
Lewis, Lennox, 300
Ligutom-Kimura, D.A., 223
Limpert, Marianne, 275
Lindros, Eric, 344f, 357f
Lindsay, P., 114
Lipinski, Tara, 242
Lipman, E., 305
Lipsyte, R., 165, 422
Longboat, Tom, 277

Longman, J., 159
Lopiano, D., 234
Louati, Samir, 414
Lowe, P., 236
Lowe, Sidney, 289
Lowes, M., 111, 386
Lowes, M.D., 401
Loy, J., 21, 52, 201, 249, 264
Lupton, D., 21
Luther, Martin, 63
Luxton, M., 307
Lyman, S.L., 117
Lyons, Lew, 147
Lysko, Mike, 300

MacAloon, J., 175, 405
MacDonald, I., 44, 52
Macfarlane, John, 30
MacGregor, Roy, 113, 135
Macintosh, D., 411, 463
MacKay, Jim, 266
MacLean, Ron, 300
MacNeill, Margaret, 223, 224, 236, 286, 386, 393, 398, 409f
Macrozanaris, Nicholas, 261
Maguire, J., 50, 52, 53, 56, 167, 284, 330, 331, 411, 412, 419, 423, 425, 426, 428, 438
Mahiri, J., 52, 452
Majors, Richard, 263
Makosky, L., 175, 430
Malcolmson, Robert, 63
Malone, Karl, 339
Mandela, Nelson, 418
Manley, John, 301
Mannon, J.M., 135
Marchment, Bryan, 195
Marcotte, Gaston, 205
Markula, P., 12, 223
Marple, D., 272
Marsden, Rachel, 202
Marsh, H.W., 446
Marsh, Lou, 277
Marsh, P., 209

Marshall, J., 458
Martel, Yvan, 255
Martin, R., 9
Martinek, T.J., 453
Marx, Karl, 37, 43
Mason, D., 383
Matheson, Dan, 365
Matsui, Hideki, 375
Matthews, K., 288, 289, 315
May, Rollo, 212
Mayeda, D.T., 393
McAll, C., 274
McCann, S., 157f
McChesney, R.W., 368, 383
McClung, L.R., 236
McCormack, J.B., 94
McDaniel, S.R., 371
McDonald, Les, 113
McDonald, M., 42
McDonald, M.A., 215
McGregor, M., 315, 388
McGregor, R., 301
McGuire, Bart, 127
McGwire, Mark, 175
McKay, J., 223, 231, 232, 233, 234, 253, 281, 315, 316, 324
McKegney, Tony, 288
McKenzie, B., 92, 157, 319
McLuhan, Marshall, 6, 32
McMahon, Vince, 338
McNeal, R.B., Jr., 446
McNeil, Crombie, 46
McPherson, C.B., 32
McSorley, Marty, 190, 191
McTeer, W., 85, 159, 323, 449, 455
Mead, George Herbert, 40
Meehan, Don, 300
Meisel, J., 271
Melnick, M., 447
Mennesson, C., 242
Mercer, Rick, 264
Merron, J., 263

Messner, M.A., 194, 196, 199, 247, 253, 308, 309, 318, 319, 387, 389, 391, 392, 394, 402
Metcalfe, A., 66, 67, 68, 71, 72, 81
Meyer, B.B., 454
Michaelis, V., 341
Micheli, L.J., 117
Midol, N., 115
Miller, K.E., 449
Miller, L., 244
Miller, T., 9, 438
Mills, D., 13, 271, 459
Ming, Yao, 331
Miracle, A.W., 95, 168, 184, 445, 446, 450, 468
Modell, Art, 349, 363
Moreno, Arturo, 484
Moriarty, Dick, 122
Morris, Alwyn, 281
Morris, G,S,D., 129, 142
Morrison, David, 229
Morrow, D., 72
Morton, D., 270f
Mosca, Angelo, 147
Mott, M., 81
Mrozek, D., 280
Munro, John, 228, 272, 304, 407f
Munson, L., 201
Murdoch, Rupert, 383
Murphy, G.M., 93
Murphy, P., 49, 53, 210f, 211
Murphy, S., 141, 142

Nabokov, Peter, 66
Nack, W., 201, 247
Naismith, James, 3
Nakamura, Y., 284, 375, 393
Nash, B., 208
Nash, H.L., 157
Nash, S., 300
Naughton, J., 169
Nauright, J., 411

Navritalova, Martina, 186, 247
Nelson, J., 132
Nelson, M.B., 107, 165, 198, 225, 235, 236, 245, 250, 473, 477
Nichol, Lori, 300
Niland, John, 200
Nixon, H.L. II, 133, 197, 198
Noah, Yannick, 259
Nolan, Ted, 279, 290, 316
Noll, R., 346
Norcliffe, G., 81
Norman, Peter, 491
Nothstein, Marty, 196
Nyad, Diana, 370

O'Neal, Shaquille, 335, 358, 394
O'Ree, Willie, 270, 288, 289, 292
Obodiac, Stan, 241
Offord, D., 305
Oglesby, C., 290
Okihiro, Norman, 317, 448–449
Orlick, T., 121, 122, 124, 129
Ormsby, M., 388
Osterland, A., 350
Overdorf, V.G., 157f
Owen, A., 389
Owens, Jesse, 70, 78, 413
Oxendine, Joseph, 65, 66

Palmer, B., 66
Palmer, J., 346
Paopao, Joe, 289
Paraschak, V., 109, 277, 279, 280, 292, 419
Parcels, J., 313, 321, 356
Parizeau, Jacques, 270
Park, R., 263
Pastore, D.L., 232, 233
Patterson, Orlando, 107
Pearl, A.J., 145
Peart, M.J., 455, 458
Pearton, B., 423
Peddie, Richard, 300

Pedlar, A., 285
Pelletier, David, 170, 300, 433
Pelley, Keith, 300
Penz, Otto, 244
Perman, S., 478
Perrucci, R., 295
Petitclerc, Chantal, 30
Phillips, B., 177
Phillips, J., 446, 447
Picard, A., 310
Pilz, G.A., 167, 196, 210f
Pippen, Scottie, 341
Pitter, R., 115, 404f, 408
Pluto, T., 339
Pollack, Susan, 315
Ponic, P., 220
Ponomaryov, N.I., 413
Poole, Jack, 300
Pooley, Jim, 266
Porter, John, 32
Porterfield, K., 89, 477
Prince, Skip, 300
Pronger, B., 52, 100, 107, 237, 245, 246, 247, 391, 478, 479
Proulx, R., 404f, 409
Pugliese, Dan, 407f
Pyette, R., 466

Quarrington, Paul, 255
Quinn, Pat, 300

Radcliffe, Paula, 173
Rail, G., 9, 270
Ramsamy, Sam, 418
Read, Ken, 365
Real, M.R., 367, 393, 420
Rees, C.R., 95, 168, 184, 445, 446, 447, 450, 468
Reeves, Keanu, 411
Reid, E., 201
Reid, S.M., 333, 423, 424
Ricciardi, J.P., 300
Richard, Maurice, 212, 325
Richter, D.M., 108, 236
Riesman, David, 106
Rigauer, B., 52
Riggs, M.T., 393

Riley, Pat, 197
Rinehart, R., 1, 9, 12, 115, 145, 372
Rintala, J., 315
Riordan, J., 65, 81, 413, 438
Ritchie, Grace, 74
Ritchie, Ian, 181
Ritzer, G., 480
Robidoux, M., 101, 102, 112, 324, 356, 358
Robinson, Jackie, 270, 288
Robinson, Laura, 104, 165, 184, 201, 215, 231, 247, 253, 279, 412
Rogers, Rand, 139
Rogers, Ted, 300
Romanow, Roy, 409
Roosevelt, J. West, 74
Rose, A., 392
Rosentraub, M., 346
Roversi, A., 210f
Rowan, Chad, 436
Rowe, D., 369, 385, 393, 402, 419
Roy, Patrick, 300
Rubenstein, 314, 321
Rudge, Chris, 309
Russo, R.D., 400
Ryan, J., 104, 126, 145, 224, 241

Sabo, D., 391, 392, 393
Sack, A. L., 468
Safai, P., 158, 165
Sage, G.H., 95, 296, 352, 364, 427, 488
Salazar, Alberto, 159–160
Sale, Jamie, 170, 300, 433
Sambrook, C., 170, 177, 184, 433, 438
Sang, J., 292
Sankoff, D., 305
Sauvageau, Danielle, 290
Scanlan, L., 123, 215
Scheinin, R., 167, 208
Scherer, J., 411, 423, 425

Scherer, Karl Adolph, 194
Schimmel, K., 344, 415
Schrader, D., 290
Schulman, J.L., 468
Schultz, B., 138
Scott, Becky, 173, 300
Scraton, P., 14
Segrave, J., 251
Seles, Monica, 207
Seltzer, R., 433
Sewart, J., 363
Sheard, K., 53, 69
Sherman, R.T., 157f
Shields, D., 108, 392
Shields, D.L.L., 95, 167, 196, 197, 453
Shilling, C., 21
Shogan, D., 181
Shropshire, K., 290, 317, 349
Silk, M., 386, 423, 425
Silver, J., 351, 411
Simcoe, John Graves, 269
Simri, U., 58
Simson, V., 433
Sinclair, Christine, 300
Skirstad, B., 145
Slaney, Mary Decker, 159–160
Smith, D., 32, 351, 411
Smith, E., 94
Smith, G., 282, 365
Smith, M., 118, 124, 189, 210
Smith, M.D., 201
Smith, R.E., 13
Smith, T., 491–492
Smythe, Conn, 288f
Snyder, Eldon, 172
Sokoloff, H., 463
Solomon, N., 372
Solomon, Patrick, 263
Sorenstam, Annika, 224
Sparks, R., 117, 247, 263, 285, 379
Spence, C., 262
Sperber, M., 463, 468
Spreitzer, E.A., 447, 448

Sprewell, Latrell, 170, 172
St-Hilaire, Caroline, 275
Staurowsky, E.J., 468
Stead, D., 412, 425
Steadward, Bob, 78
Stebbins, R., 112, 484
Stein, G., 364
Steinbreder, J., 424
Stevens, N., 160
Stevenson, C., 87, 88, 89, 98
Stiehl, J., 129, 142
Stojko, Elvis, 160
Stoll, S.K., 94, 95, 167
Strauss, R.H., 157f
Stronach, Frank, 300
Struna, N., 81
Sugden, J., 215, 296, 324, 331, 423, 432, 484
Sullivan, C.B., 371
Sundgot-Borgen, J., 157f
Sutton-Brown, Tammy, 244
Suzuki, Ichiro, 331, 375
Swain, Derek, 91
Sydnor, S., 12, 145

Tannenbaum, Larry, 300
Tanner, Elaine, 83
Tator, C., 285–286
Taub, D.E., 225
Taylor, I., 122, 209, 210f
Teitel, Jay, 138
Temple, Kerry, 369
Tenebaum, 128
Tewksbury, Mark, 247
Theberge, N., 17, 32, 99, 102, 103, 112, 192, 198, 232, 235, 236, 240–242, 245, 247, 253, 477
Theodore, Jose, 300
Thomas, Isiah, 289
Thomas, R., 392, 393
Thompson, Dan, 300
Thompson, S., 131, 145, 242, 253, 307, 324
Thompson, W., 157
Tirone, Susan, 285

Todd, T., 173
Tofler, I.R., 224
Tomlinson, A., 28, 42, 296, 324, 331, 432
Toohey, K., 375
Torbert, M., 129, 142
Trempe, Yves, 272
Trudeau, Pierre, 148, 265, 270, 405, 418
Trujillo, N., 251
Trulson, M.E., 170, 204
Tuggle, C.A., 389
Turner, B.S., 21
Tymowski, Gabriela, 126

Ueberroth, Peter, 416, 424
University, Alfred, 162
Unwin, P., 276, 277
Urquhart, J., 388

Van Hellemond, Andy, 300
Vanbiesbrouck, John, 288
Veal, A.J., 375
Veblen, T., 67
Veri, M.J., 225
Vertinsky, P., 74, 75
Villegas, J.L., 292
Vine, C., 215

Wacquant, L.J.D., 204, 309
Waddington, I., 53, 177, 198, 199, 409, 476
Wagner, G.G., 409
Wahl, G., 455
Walker, Larry, 300
Wallin, Jesse, 159
Walton, T., 172
Wasielewski, P.L., 157
Watters, Brad, 300
Weber, M., 404
Weiler, K.H., 390, 391
Weiner, Jay, 332
Weinstein, M.D., 195, 196
Weir, Mike, 300
Weir, T., 263
Weiss, M., 145

Weiss, O., 396
Wenner, L., 402
Wenner, L.A., 385, 395, 397
Weschler, H., 169
Wetzel, D., 364
Whannel, G., 28, 402
Wheeler, G.D., 92
White, A., 89, 132
White, P., 85, 157f, 159, 192, 195, 196, 198, 199, 236, 237, 247, 253, 274, 323, 411, 449
Whitson, D., 28, 71, 81, 338, 375, 411
Wickenheiser, Hayley, 231–232, 244, 300
Wieberg, S., 158, 162
Wilberforce, William, 269
Wilkens, Lenny, 289
Wilkerson, M., 232
Williams, M., 217, 245
Williams, R., 107
Williams, Serena, 359
Williams, Venus, 359
Willis, Michael, 269
Wilmore, J., 157f, 224
Wilson, B., 108, 262, 263, 285, 286, 392
Wilson, J., 28, 364, 405
Wolf, N., 224
Wolfe, Tom, 162
Woods, Tiger, 259, 260, 375
Woog, D., 100, 248, 253
Wyld, Adrian, 33
Wysong, E., 295

Yaeger, D., 148, 247, 364
Yalden, Max, 275
Yesalis, C.E., 185
Young, K., 52, 88, 157f, 159, 162, 164, 165, 185, 187, 189, 190, 192, 195, 196, 198, 199, 208, 209, 210, 212, 215, 216, 236, 237, 247, 253, 408

Zeman, B., 279, 292
Zhang, J.J., 396
Ziegler, John, 325
Zimbalist, A., 301, 346
Zipter, Y., 477, 479
Zullo, A., 208

Subject Index

ABC, 381
Abuse in youth sports, 128
Academics. *See also* College sports; High school sports
athlete detachment from, 453–454
cheating rates, 167
graduation patterns, 454–455
Acceptance, 88
Accommodation, 264–268
Accommodation of interest test, 227
Action, in youth-controlled sports, 129–130
Administrators
"deviant" behaviour examples, 170
racial/ethnic patterns, 289
women, 208, 223, 230–234, 314–315
Advertising. *See also* Commercialization of sports; Media influence
branding of sports with, 333–336, 422, 423–424
glorification of overconformity, 160
spending levels, 20, 105–106, 333, 335, 380
Aesthetic versus heroic orientations, 339–341

African-Americans. *See* Racial/ethnic issues
Agents, "deviant" behaviour example, 170, 173
Aggression. *See also* Masculinity; Violence in sports
compared to violence, 188
media theme, 393–395
Aggro rituals, 209
Aging beliefs, 76
Air Canada Centre, 301, 333, 348, 350
Air Jordan, 332
Akebono, 436
Alcohol, 169, 384–385
Alienation theory, 90
Alternative sports, 121
characteristics, 96–97
trends, 477–479
X Games, 135–136, 336, 380
Amateur, 68
word origins, 296
Amateur sports
governing bodies, 352–353
incomes of athletes, 361–362
rights of athletes, 360–361, 408
American Airlines Center, 352
American Indian Sports Heritage (Nabokov), 66
Americanization with sports, 72–73
Anarchy, 156

Anderson, Eric, 248
Assimilation, 264–268
Association of Tennis Professionals, 357
Associations for sports study, 24–25
Athletes in Action, 99
Attendance at sports events
costs of, 310–312
media influence, 396
Authority, defined, 404
Auto racing, sponsor branding, 334

Baltimore Colts, 349
Baltimore, stadium subsidies, 349
Baseball
broadcasting rights, 345, 484
cultural ideologies of, 19
globalization of sports, 330–331
professional career opportunities, 313–314
racial/ethnic issues, 288–290
racism, 289–290
rules and commercialization, 336–337
salaries, 356t, 358
sponsorship development, 68
television revenues, 375
ticket prices, 310–312
Basketball
invention of, 3

Olympic team benefits, 330–331
professional career opportunities, 313–314
salaries, 314, 356t, 358, 359
ticket prices, 310–312
violence sanctioned, 196–197
BBC, 368
Beach volleyball, 56
"Beehive soccer," 129
Bell Centre, 333
Big-time programmes, college
academics/sports balance, 453–454
graduation patterns and, 454–455
limitations as model for high schools, 457–462
Bilingualism, 278–279
Binge drinking, 167
Biotechnology, 483
BMXing, 139, 336
Body (physical), cultural images, 21–22
Bodybuilders, 102, 243–244
Boston Marathon, 335
Bowlen, Pat, 351
Boxing
governing bodies, 432
social world study, 204–206
socioeconomics, 308–309
sponsorship control, 357

Boy Scouts, 114
Branding of sports, 333–336, 422, 423–424
Brazil, 410, 422
Brighton Declaration, 220
Broadcasting rights/ revenues, 20, 343–344, 380–384, 484
Brooklyn Dodgers, 288
Budgets, interscholastic sports, 456–457
Bureaucratization, as competitive sports characteristic, 70
Burke, Brian, 158
Burnout, 13, 91

CAAWS, 230, 235, 388–390, 398, 487
Calgary Olypmic Park, 303
Calgary Saddledome, 302
Canada, fitness programs, 409–410
Canadian Association for Health, Physical Education, Recreation and Dance, 441
Canadian Association for the Advancement of Women in Sports. See CAAWS
Canadian Human Rights Act, 220
Canadian Interuniversity Athletic Union. See CIS
Canadian Interuniversity Sport. See CIS
CanWest Global, 377, 384
Career changes study, 92–93
Career opportunities, comparisons coaching/

administration, 314–315
post-athletic, 317–320
professional athletics, 312–317
Carlesimo, P. J., 172
Catholic Church, medieval sports, 61, 62
Catholic Youth Organization, 114
CBC television, 20, 221, 367, 368, 370, 375, 379–381, 390, 399
Celebrity feminism, 236
CFL, 368
designated import rule, 282
migrant athletes, 426
Change agent research, 122
Change agents, 489–492
Character logic, 19, 72–73, 93–95
Charles I (king), 63
Charter of Rights and Freedoms, 220, 227–228, 229, 408
Chastain, Brandi, 224, 225
Cheating rates, 167
Chebet, Joseph, 335
Cheerleaders, 224
Children. See Youth sports
China, 427
CIAU. See CIS
CIS, 6, 23, 432, 442–445, 453
athletic scholarships, 463
gender equity, 464
Citizenship, 426
Civic pride, government promotion, 410–411
Class logic, 19, 298
Class relations, 295
commercialization of sports, 327–328
Cleveland Browns, 349
Cleveland Indians, 349

Cleveland, stadium subsidies, 348–349
Clubs, sports, 68, 310
CNBC, 381
Coaches
"deviant" behavior examples, 170
overconformity promotion, 162, 163–166
racial/ethnic patterns, 289
women, 223, 230–234, 314–315
Coaching Association of Canada, 398
Coaching certification, 121–122
Coaching education, 121
Coca-Cola, 105–106, 332, 333, 433
College sports
academic conflicts, 453–454
budgets, 457
graduation patterns and, 454–455
predictions about, 480–481
proposed changes, 463–466
reading recommend- ations, 468
school spirit and, 455–457
summary, 467–468
Web resources, 468–469
Colorado Springs, youth sports complex, 350–351
Commercialization of sports. See also Owners, 327–328
amateur sports, 352–353
branding process, 333–336
class relations, 327–328

globalization, 330–333, 422–425
impact on athletic performances, 339–341
legal rights of athletes, 353–357
media importance, 299–303, 373–377, 400–401
organization changes, 341
ownership of professional sport teams, 340–341
predictions about, 479–480, 484–485
reading recommendations, 364
requirements for, 327–328
salaries of athletes, 358–360
socioeconomic classes, 327–328
structural changes, 336–338
summary, 327, 362–363
team advertiser benefits, 328–329, 332–335
violence and, 192–194
Web resources, 364
Commitment development, 87
Commonwealth Stadium, 302
Competitive activities, 5
Confirmation, 88
Conflict theory
described, 37–40
"deviance", 154–155
future of sports, 487–488
socialization, 85–86, 90
Conformity and hazing, 164

Conservative strategy of change, 488, 489
Construction, 88
Consumerism as media theme, 393–395
See also Commercialization of sports; Globalization, sports
Contested activities, sports as, 9–10
Contract negotiations (athlete), 344, 353–357
Convention on the Elimination of all Forms of Discrimination against Women, 220
"Cool pose," 263
Cooperative games, 121, 124, 125
Corel Centre, 301, 333, 350
Corporations. See Commercialization of sports; Globalization, sports
Cosmetic fitness, 223, 224, 475–476
Creatine, 177n
Crime rates, 169
Critical theory approach described, 42–49
"deviance", 155–157
feminist theories of sports, 51
future of sports, 488
socialization, 86
Critical transformation model, 27
Crowd violence. *See* Spectators
CRTC, 367
CTV, 381, 399
Cuba and baseball, 416
Cubs game, spectator violence, 208
Cultural creation, 259

Cultural encouragement, 227
Cultural ideology, 44, 237
overview, 17–20
Cultural issues and media influences, 393
Cultural mosaic, 265–267
Cultural practices, sports as, 3–11
Culture of caution, 136
Culture, defined, 3
Curling, 429–431
rules and commercialization, 338

Dallas Cowboys, 344
De Coubertin, Pierre, 416
Delinquency rates, 168–169
Delinquency relationships, 171–172
Denver, stadium subsidies, 350–351
Designer athletes, 474
"Deviance"
delinquency study, 171–172
overconformity as, 156–157
reading recommendations, 184–185
research, 166–169
research difficulties, 148–153
sport ethic and, 157–160
substance use, 173–183
summary, 183–184
theoretical perspectives, 153–157
Web resources, 185
DHEA, 177
Differential school experience, 446–447

Diplomacy, sports, 416–418
Disabilities and sports, 462, 478
Disappointment Games, 388–389
Distinction norm, 158
Dolan, Larry, 349
Dominant ideology, overview, 17–20
Dominant sport forms, study, 69–70
Doping, defined, 174, 176
Dramatic spectacle in sports, 6, 9–11
Dream pursuit norm, 158–159
Dropping out of sports, decision making, 90–93
Drug testing, 179–180
Dual citizenship, 426
Dubin Commission, 175

e-mail, 367n
EBU, 381–382
Economic development, 346–351
government-sponsored sports, 415
stadium subsidies, 301–303, 346–351
Economic power, conflict theory approach, 37–40, 85–86, 154–155
See also Globalization, sports; Socioeconomic classes, sport participation
Education. *See* Academics; Interscholastic sports
Elderly, sport participation, 76, 475–477

Electronic media, described, 366
Eligibility rules, political influences, 435
Elite athlete studies, 87–90
Elitism in youth sports, 125, 126–129
Elway, John, 335
Emotional contagion, 212
Empowerment discourses, 236
Enforcers (hockey), 196–197
England
soccer studies, 209–210
sports history, 63
Enlightenment Era, sports history, 64
Entrepreneurialism, 72
Entry fees, league, 344
Equality, as competitive sports characteristic, 69, 70
Equity definitions (gender), 227–230
ESPN, 381, 484
Ethnic group, 257
Ethnic issues. *See* Racial/ethnic issues
Ethnic logic, 19
Ethnicity, defined, 256–258
European Broadcast Union (EBU), 381–382
Everitt, Diana, 227–230
Exhibition Stadium, 348
Exxon Mobil, 332

Fabiola, 236
Fair play leagues, 123, 205
Family life
role of youth sports, 114–118, 130–131
sports importance, 20
Fan Cost Index, 311

Fascism, 156
Fédération Internationale
de Ski (FIS), 5
Felony rates, 169
Femininity, alternate
definition, 249–250
Feminist theories of
sports, 47–48,
488–489
critical theory
approach, 51
Figurational theory,
49–51, 489
Filtering-out-process,
high school sports,
445–449
Fitness
cosmetic, 223, 224
government
promotion, 409–410
health incentives, 221,
475–476
Fitness and Amateur
Sports Act, 405
Flow experiences,
109–110
Football
designated import in
Canadian game, 282
globalization tactics,
330–331
league entry fees, 344
owner revenues, 352,
375–376
professional
opportunities,
313–314
reserve system,
355–357
rules and
commercialization,
336–337
salaries, 356t, 359
socialization studies,
106–107
ticket prices, 310–312
Ford Motor Company,
332
Ford Stadium, 333

Fox Television, 383–384
Franchises. See Owners,
team
Free agency, 355–357
Functionalist theory
approach
described, 32–37, 40
"deviance", 153–154,
155
future of sports,
486–487
socialization, 84–85,
86, 90

Gambling, 396, 482
GATT, 426–427
Gay athletes, 100,
245–248, 478–479
See also Homophobia
Gay Games, 478–479
Gender
defined, 238–239
high school sports, 450
Gender logic. See also
Masculinity; Women
in sports
described, 237–240
feminist theoretical
critiques, 47–48,
488–489
sexual assaults and,
201–203
sport tradition of,
17–18, 73–75
Gender marketing, 391
General Motors, 332
General Motors Place.
See GM Place
Genetic engineering, 483
Global Television, 375
Globalization, sports, 404
See also Politics
athlete migration,
425–426
economic orientation,
330–333, 417–418,
421–425
political impact,
416–418

production of
equipment/clothes,
426–427
reading
recommendations,
438
summary, 436–438
Web resources,
438–439
Globe and Mail, 299–300
GM Place, 301, 333
Golf
appeal to advertisers,
328, 380
commercialization,
328
professional career
opportunities,
313–314
rules and
commercialization,
338
salaries, 359
television revenues,
375
women's tour study,
102–104
Goons (hockey), 196–197
Government
defined, 404
equity legislation,
219–220, 227–230,
464–466
sport involvement
purposes, 78f,
404–415
Grades and athletes,
445–449, 454–455
Graduation rates,
454–455
Grants/scholarships, 320,
321–322, 463–464
Gravity Games, 139
Greece, sports history,
57–59
Gretzky, Wayne, 335
Group identity
government
promotion, 410–413

overconformity and,
162–165
sexual assault, 201–203

Haakonsen, Terje, 478
Hazing, 164
Hegemony, 72, 106
Hera, 58
Heraean Games, 58
Heroic versus aesthetic
orientations,
339–341
High school sports
athlete/non-athlete
comparisons,
441–453
budgets, 456
predictions about,
480–481
reading
recommendations,
468
recommendations,
457–462
school spirit and,
455–457
socialization studies,
450–452
socioeconomic
influences, 309–310
summary, 467–468
Web resources,
468–469
High-risk sports and
overconformity, 162
History of sports
Greece, 57–59
Industrial Revolution
Era, 64–68
modern developments,
68–78
pre-industrial Europe,
60–64
prehistoric origins, 56
reading
recommendations,
80–81
Rome, 59–60
summary, 55–56,
79–80

violence, 188–189
Web resources, 82
Hit men (hockey),
196–197
Hitler, Adolf, 413
Hockey
appeal to advertisers,
328
commercialization,
328
entry fees, 344
fair play leagues, 205
globalization tactics,
330–331
migrant athletes, 426
monopoly, 344
nationalism, 411
owner revenues, 351
player strike, 355
professional career
opportunities,
313–314
race logic, 262
racism, *288–290*
"role engulfment"
study, 101–102
salaries, 356t, 358, 359
social world study, 104
socialization study,
99–100, 192
television revenues,
375
ticket prices, 310–312
travel sports, 134
violence, 196–197
youth programmes,
122
youth sports, 134
youth team costs, 117
Hockey Night in Canada,
337, 381
Homogeneous
masculinity, 101
Homophobia, 225, 227,
242, 245–248, 391
Homosexuality, 391
House leagues, 122
Hubris, 198
Hubris, defined, 163

Human Genome Project,
259, 474
Hypo-descent rule, 259

Identification, 88
Identity, 40
Identity formation. *See
also* Masculinity;
Socialization and
sport participation,
research
athlete retirement,
319–320
interactionist theory
of, 40–42
Ideology. *See* Cultural
ideology, overview
In-line skating, 432
Indian Running
(Nabokov), 66
Indianapolis, stadium
subsidies, 349
Individualism as media
theme, 393–395
Indonesia, 427
Industrial Revolution, 64
Industrial Revolution
Era, sports history,
64–68
Informal youth sports,
133–134, 137–138
Injuries and pain, 18–19,
158–160, 198–199
Institutionalization, 5
Institutionalization
process, 8–9
Interaction, 88
Interactionist theory
described, 40–42
"deviance", 155–157
future of sports, 488
socialization, 86
Internalization models of
socialization, 84–86
International Olympic
Committee (IOC),
5, 126, 298, 390, 408
See also Olympic
Games

corruption in, 170,
433–435
doping definition, 174
globalization
approach, 330–331
Internet rights, 375
sex tests, 239n
sports definition,
429–431
women members, 226,
232
International Sociology of
Sport Association
(ISSA), 24
International Working
Group on Women
and Sport, 220, 488
Internet, 367
See also Web resources,
sport topics
characteristics,
371–373
marketing uses by
athletes, 335
predictions about,
482–483
television rights and,
375
Interscholastic sports.
See also College
sports; High school
sports
Canadian and United
States comparison,
442–445
pro/con arguments,
445, 446t
prominence, 23
reading
recommendations,
468
school spirit and,
455–457
summary, 467–468
Web resources,
468–469
Intimidation, defined,
188
Intramural sports, 441

Introduction, 87
Involvement, 87
Irsay, Robert, 349
Ivor Wynne Stadium,
302

Jacobs, Richard, 349
James I (king), 63
Japan, baseball values, 19
Job creation with stadium
subsidies, 301–303,
346
Johnson, Ben, 180–181
Johnson, Magic, 244
Jordan, Michael,
108–109, 332, 335
Journalists, sport,
397–400
Journals of sport study,
19, 24–26
"Jumping genes,"
260–262

Kane, Mary Jo, 230
King's Book of Sports, 63
Knight, Phil, 422
Knowledge-building
model, 27
Kwan, Michelle, 340

Labor issues
contract negotiations,
353–357
migration of athletes,
425–426
production of sporting
goods, 426–427
youth sports, 127–128
Ladies Professional Golf
Association, 357
Language of sports, 110,
194–195, 250–251,
395
Legal status of athletes,
353–357, 360–361
Lesbian label, 225, 227,
236, 242, 245–248,
391
Life chance, 295
Lipinski, Tara, 242

Little Big Men (Klein), 102
Los Angeles Dodgers, 383
LPGA, 357

Magazines
importance of sports, 378–379
sport coverage styles, 386
Major League Baseball (MLB). *See also* Baseball, 479, 484
broadcasting rights, 345
globalization strategies, 330–331
professional career opportunities, 313–314
racial/ethnic issues, 288–290
racism, 289–290
salaries, 356t
ticket prices, 310–312
Malone, Karl, 339
Manchester United Football Club, 335, 383
Marchment, Bryan, 195
Martial arts, 171–172, 204
Maryland, stadium subsidies, 349
Masculinity. *See also* Gender logic; Socialization and sport participation
"cool pose" purpose, 263
homogeneous, 101
language and sports and, 110, 250–251
media emphasis, 387–392
redefining, 238, 248–249
sexual assaults, 201–203

sports as celebration of, 18, 240–241, 387
violence, 194–195, 198–199, 206
youth sport socialization, 73, 132–133, 308–309
MCI Center, 333
McKenzie, Bette, 157
McMahon, Vince, 338f
Media, sport world portrayed in, 104
Media influence. *See also* Advertising
content, 367
image/message themes, 385–392
Internet role, 371–373
journalist types and, 397–400
overview, 366–370, 400–401
reading recommendations, 401–402
television commercialization and, 20–21, 299–303, 373–377, 417–418
spectator interest, 328–330
sport globalization, 417
sport-related activities and, 395–397
video games, 373
Web resources, 402
women's sports, 221–222, 226–227, 387–391
Medieval Europe, sports history, 60–62
Métis, 259
Migration, athlete, 425–426
Minority group, defined, 256–258
Mitsubishi, 332

MLB. *See* Major League Baseball (MLB)
Modell, Art, 349
Monopolies, owner, 342–346, 355f
Monopsony, 355f
Montreal Expos, 345
Montreal Olympic Stadium, 301, 302
Moral entrepreneurs, 71
Moral lessons, 98
Motivation, 13
MSNBC, 381
Multiculturalism, 265–267
Murdoch, Rupert, 383–384

NAFTA, 426–427
Naismith, James, 3
Naming rights, pricing, 351
National Association of Intercollegiate Athletics (NAIA), 442–445
National Basketball Association (NBA). *See also* Basketball
Olympic team benefits, 330–331
professional career opportunities, 313–314
salaries, 356t
ticket prices, 310–312
violence sanctioned, 196–197
National Collegiate Athletic Association (NCAA), 442–445
National Football League (NFL). *See also* Football, 368
broadcast revenue, 381–383
franchise prices, 345
free agency, 35–357
globalization tactics, 330–331

monopoly benefits, 344
owner revenues, 351, 375–376
salaries, 356t
ticket prices, 310–312
National Hockey League (NHL), 114, 337, 344, 479, 482, 484
See also Hockey
broadcast revenues, 381–383
globalization tactics, 330–331
owner revenues, 351
pain and injury, 199
player strike, 356
racism, 288–290
salaries, 356t
ticket prices, 310–312
violence, 199
National Intramural-Recreational Sports Association, 441
National Sports Centres, 464
National sport organizations (NSOs), 352–353
Nationalism, 282–284
government promotion, 78f, 410–414, 416–418
media theme, 393–395
Native peoples
racial/ethnic issues, 276–281
sport participation, 63–66, 76
Navratilova, Martina, 247
Nazi Germany, 78f, 413–414
NBA. *See* National Basketball Association (NBA)
NBC television, 338f, 368, 370, 380, 381, 423–424, 434

Nelson, Mariah Burton, 235

New York Yankees, 345

Newspapers, sports, importance, 378–379

NFL. See National Football League (NFL)

NHL. See National Hockey League (NHL)

NightHoops, 408

Nike
branding of journalists, 335
globalization strategies, 422, 423–424
glorification of overconformity, 160
Jordan sponsorship, 332
labour issues, 426–427, 488

Nike Transnational Advocacy Network, 488

Niland, John, 200

Noah, Yannick, 259

North American Free Trade Agreement (NAFTA), 332

North American Indigenous Games, 479

North American Society for the Sociology of Sport, 25

NSOs (national sport organizations), 352–353

OFSAA, 460, 477

Olympic Advertising Index, 340

Olympic Games, 368
advertising costs, 20
broadcasting revenues, 20, 380–382

commercialization effects, 417–418, 423–424
corruption, 170, 433–435
event addition factors, 56, 336–338
gender opportunities compared, 226–227, 228f
globalization strategies, 330–333
government purposes, 78f, 413–414, 416–418
Greek origins, 57–59
impact on Atlanta, 302–303
media coverage style, 221, 368–370, 417–418
modern ideals, 416
proposed changes, 420–421
site selection factors, 433–435
socioeconomic participation patterns, 296, 303
sponsorship benefits, 105–106, 332, 333, 417–418

Olympic Games, advertising, expenditures, 20

Olympic Stadium, 350

Ontario Federation of School Athletic Associations . See OFSAA

Open Ice Summit, 123

Organizations for sport study, 24–25

Organized sports for youth. See also "Deviance"
controlling, 163–166
described, 156–157
motivations for, 160–165

non-athlete examples, 170, 172
sport ethic and, 157–160, 190–192
underconformity relationships, 163

Ottawa Senators, 344

Outdoor Life Network, 368

Owens, Jesse, 78f, 413

Owners, team
athlete contracts, 344, 353–357
"deviant" behaviour examples, 170
monopoly trends, 342–346
overview, 341–344
revenue sources, 351–352, 374–375
stadium subsidies, 301–303, 346–351

Pain norm, 18–19, 158–160, 198–199

Parents. See Family life

ParticipACTION, 409

Participation in sports, 89
See also Racial/ethnic issues; Socialization and sport participation; Women in sports; Youth sports
disabled, 462, 478
elderly, 76, 475–477
media influences, 395–396

Pengrowth Centre, 302, 333

Performance, 13

Performance ethic in youth sports, 123, 125, 126–129

PGA, 357

Physical activities, 5

Pippen, Scottie, 341

Platform for Action (United Nations), 221

Play, 6

Play versus sports, 9

Player-controlled youth sports, 137–138

Pleasure and participation model, 99
See also Alternative sports
predictions about, 475–479
summarized, 96–97, 471–473

Politics. See also Globalization, sports
defined, 404
government purposes in sport involvement, 78f, 404–415
influence on sports, 22–23, 428–436
reading recommendations, 438
summary, 436–438
Web resources, 438–439

Popularity, high school, 448–449

Postructuralism, described, 105n

Power. See also Commercialization of sports; Socio-economic classes, sport participation
conflict theories of, 37–40, 85–86, 154–155
critical theories of, 42–49
defined, 404
sponsorship of pleasure and, 105–106

Power and performance model
predictions about, 473–475

summarized, 96–97,
471–472
Power and performance
sports, 98
Print media
defined, 366
sport coverage style,
386, 399–400
sports importance,
378–379
Privatization
impact on
girls/women's sports,
222–223
youth sports, 116–118
Production ethnography,
386
Professional Golf
Association, 357
Professional Rodeo
Cowboys
Association, 357
Progress test, 227
Prolympism, 431
Promotional culture,
339–341
Proportionality test, 227
"Prowess ethic," 103–104
Psychology/sociology of
sport, compared,
12–13
Public subsidies
government sport
promotion, 404–415
stadiums, 301–303,
346–351
Publications for sport
study, 26
Puritans, influence on
sports, 63–64

Quantification, as
competitive sport
characteristic, 70
Quebec, sports in, 115
Quiet Revolution, 115
Quotas (foreign players),
427

Race, 257

Race logic, described, 19,
75–76, 260–263
Racial/ethnic issues
aboriginal, 276–281
accommodation,
264–268
African-Canadians,
285–286
Asian relations,
284–285
assimilation, 264–268,
280–281
bilingualism, 279–279
Canada compared to
United States,
269–270
Canada, in, 263–269
Canadian/American
relations, 281–284
challenges, 286–291
cultural, 271–276
cultural mosaic,
265–267
definitions/
classifications,
256–260
diversity, dealing with,
288–289
dynamics in Canadian
sports, 270–286
eliminating, 287–288
ethnic origin, 267–269
future, 209–291
historical ideologies,
67, 68, 260–263
language, 272–276,
278–279
media influences,
392–393
modern ideologies,
108–109, 263–269,
463–464
multiculturalism,
265–267
nationalism, 282–284
natives, 276–281
participation rate
comparisons,
272–275

power and control,
289–290
predictions about,
485–486
racism, 277–279
reading
recommendations,
292
social stratification,
295
summary, 291–292
violence in sports,
194–195, 212–213
Web resources, 293
Racism(s), 257, 277–279
Radical strategies of
change, 489
Radio, sports importance,
377–378
Rational recreation, 68
Rationalization, as
competitive sport
characteristic, 69–70
Readiness for
competition
(children), 129–130
Reading recommend-
ations, sport topics
commercialization,
364
globalization, 438
history, 80–81
interscholastic, 468
media influence,
401–402
race/ethnic issues, 292
socialization, 111–112
socioeconomic classes,
323–324
sociology, 27–28
substance use, 184–185
theories, 52–53
violence, 215–216
women, 252–253
youth, 145
Records, as competitive
sport characteristic,
70
Reformation Era, sports
history, 63–64

Reformist strategy of
change, 488, 489
Regulation of sports,
352–353, 404–409,
432–433
See also Rules
Religion
historical influences on
sports, 56, 57,
63–64, 65–67
modern influences on
sports, 23–24,
72–73, 75–76
sport stories, 98–99
Renaissance Era, sports
history, 62–63
Renaissance women, 62
Reporters, sports,
397–400
Reserve system, 354–357
Retirement, success
factors, 92–93,
319–320
Reward distribution,
political aspects,
435–436
Riley, Pat, 196–197
Robinson, Jackie, 288
Role conflict, 99
"Role engulfment" study,
101–102
Role theory, 90
Romanow Report, 409
Rome, sports history,
59–60
Rowan, Chad, 436
Rules. See also Regulation
of sports
adult-controlled youth
sports, 137–138
commercialization
influences, 336–338,
375
player-controlled
youth sports,
137–138
political aspects,
432–433

Sacrifice norm, 158

Salaries, athlete, 20, 314,
    356t, 358–360
Salazar, Alberto, 159–160
Scholar-athlete, 62
Scholarships/grants, 320,
    321–322, 463–464
School spirit, 455–457
Scientific expert model,
    27
Secularism, as
    competitive sport
    characteristic, 69, 70
Selection-in-process,
    high school sports,
    445–449, 447–448
Seles, Monica, 207
Self-esteem, 2
Self-image, 2
Sex, 238
Sex tests, 239n
Sexism. *See* Gender logic;
    Masculinity; Women
    in sports
Sexual assaults, 201–203
    violence in sports, 214
Significant others, as
    socializing agents, 85
Site selection, political
    aspects, 433–435
Skateboarding, 132, 432,
    477–478
SkyDome, 301, 348, 350
Skyreach Centre, 333
Slaney, Mary Decker, 159
Snowboarding, 477, 478
Soccer
    beehive version, 129
    branding of teams,
    334–335
    crowd violence,
    209–210
    globalization, 381
    rules and
    commercialization,
    336–338
    value in U.S., 73
    viewership, 375
Social classes, 295

See also Socioeconomic
    classes, sport
    participation
Social construction,
    sports as, 3
Social constructions, 37
Social Darwinisn, 261
Social mobility, defined,
    312n
Social phenomena, of
    sports, 2
Social stratification, 295
Social systems and
    theories of sports
    conflict, 37–40
    critical, 42–49
    figurational, 49–51
    functionalist, 32–37
    interactionist, 40–42
Social worlds, research,
    101–104
Socialization and sports.
    See also "Deviance"
    character building,
    93–95
    decision-making
    processes, 86–93
    experiential-oriented,
    95
    ideology-oriented,
    104–106
    limitations of, 109–110
    participation, research
    reading
    recommendations,
    111–112
    social world approach,
    101–104
    summary, 110–111
    theoretical approaches,
    84–86, 90–93
Society, defined, 3
Socioeconomic classes,
    sport participation
    career opportunities
    compared, 314–317,
    321–322
    commercialization of
    sports, 327–328

definitions of terms,
    294–296
historical highlights,
    57, 58–59, 60,
    61–68, 71–72
impact of sport
    subsidies, 301–303
modern patterns,
    303–312
reading suggestions,
    323–324
summary, 322–323
wealth/power
    influences, 296–303
Web resources, 324
Sociology, defined, 2
Sociology of sport
    discipline status, 24–25
    goals of, 11
    psychology of sport
    compared, 12–13
    reading suggestions,
    27–28
    summary, 27
    uses of, 13–16
    Web resources, 28–29
Sociology, described, 2–3
South Korea, 427
Soviet Union, 413, 417
Specialization, as
    competitive sport
    characteristic, 69, 70
Spectators
    creation of, 328–330
    "deviant" behaviour
    examples, 170, 172
    predictions about,
    481–482
    violence and, 206–214
Spill-over thesis, 446
Sport ethic
    norms of, 157–160
    violence and, 190–192
Sportainment, defined,
    369–370
Sporting News, The, 299
Sports
    alternative definition,
    8–11

defined, 5
defining, 8–12,
    429–431
societal definition,
    8–11
study purposes, 2–4,
    13–16, 16–24
Sports Canada, 408, 464
Sports Illustrated, 378
Sportsnet, 368
Sprewell, Latrell, 172
Stadiums
    branding of, 333
    public subsidies,
    301–303, 346–351
    revenue sources,
    351–352
Status, 2
Story perspective of
    socialization,
    105–106
Stress, 13
Strikes, player, 355–357
Structural uncertainty,
    103
Student-athletes. See
    College sports; High
    school sports;
    Interscholastic
    sports
Substance use,
    performance-
    enhancing
    controlling, 178–179,
    180–183
    definition/ban
    difficulties, 174–177
    motivations for, 173,
    178–179
    reading
    recommendations,
    184–185
    summary, 183–184
    testing for, 179–180
    Web resources, 185
Success ideology
    class logic and, 98–99,
    298
    media emphasis, 387

role in spectator interest, 329
Summaries, sport topics
  commercial, 327, 362–363
  globalization, 436–438
  history, 79–80
  interscholastic, 467–468
  media influence, 400–401
  race issues, 291–292
  socialization, 110–111
  socioeconomic classes, 322–323
  sociology, 27
  substance use, 183–184
  theories, 51–52
  violence, 214–215
  women, 251–252
  youth, 143–145
Summer sport programmes, 134
Super Bowl, 382
Super Bowl, advertising expenditures, 335, 380
System needs, 33

Tae Kwon Do, 431
  study, 171–172, 204
Team owners. *See* Owners, team
Teamwork as media theme, 393–395
Technological body, 107
Telelatino, 368
Television. *See also* Media influence
  advertising costs, 20, 335, 380
  announcer characteristics, 399–400
  broadcasting rights/revenues, 20, 343–344, 351, 374–375, 380–384, 484–485

impact on sport-related activities, 395–397
  representation versus reality, 369–370
  spectator interest creation, 329–330
  sports importance, 379–384
  viewer violence, 207
Tennis
  appeal to advertisers, 380
  rules and commercialization, 338
  salaries, 359
Thailand, 427
Theories of sports
  compared, 34–35
  conflict, 37–40
  critical, 42–49
  figurational, 49–51
  functionalist, 32–37, 40
  interactionist, 40–42
  purpose, 31–32
  reading recommendations, 52–53
  summary, 51–52
  Web resources, 53
Ticket prices, 310–312
Title IX, 220, 227–230
Tobacco advertising, 367–368
Toronto Blue Jays, 348
Toronto Raptors, 348
Toronto SkyDome, 301, 348, 350
Toronto, stadium subsidies, 348
Total entertainment experiences, 338
Tournaments, Medieval European, 60–62
Travel leagues, 122
TSN, 368
TV5, 368

TVA, 377
U.S. President's Commission on Olympic Sports, 360–361
Ueberroth, Peter, 416
Underconformity, "deviant", 156–157, 163–165
United Center, 333
United States, high school football culture, 450–452
URLs. *See* Web resources, sport topics

Video games, 373
Violence in sports
  celebratory, 208
  commercialization, 192–194
  contextual factors, 212
  control of crowd, 213
  controlling, 199–200
  crowding dynamics, 211
  defining, 187–188
  effect on society, 214
  general factors, 210–213
  historical overview, 58–59, 60, 188–189
  location, 211
  masculinity issues, 194–195
  National Hockey League, 199
  noncontact sports, 194–195
  off-field, 200–206
  reading recommendations, 215–216
  research, 209
  role of sport ethic, 190–192
  sexual assaults, 214
  situational factors, 211

spectators, 206–214
  strategic uses, 196–198
  summary, 214–215
  theory, 209
  types, 189–190
  Web resources, 216
Visible minority, 257
Volleyball, 469

WADA, 180
Wages, manufacturing, 427
Web resources, sport topics
  commercialization, 364
  future of sports, 493–494
  globalization, 438–439
  history, 82
  interscholastic sports, 468–469
  media influence, 402
  race issues, 293
  socialization, 112
  socioeconomic classes, 324
  sociology of sport, 28–29
  substance use, 185
  theories of sports, 53
  violence, 216
  women in sports, 253–254
  youth sports, 146
Women in sports. *See also* Gender logic
  advertiser discovery of, 380
  athlete support, 230
  body building, 102, 243–244
  budgets, 222–223
  coaching/administration, 223, 230–234, 314–315
  cultural obstacles, 71, 73–75, 132–133, 222–225, 237

equity legal
definitions, 227–230
feminist theories,
47–48, 488–489
golf tour study,
102–104
historical highlights,
57–59, 60, 62–63, 68
lesbian label, 225, 227,
242, 245–248
media coverage,
221–222, 226–227,
387–391
participation, 477
participation
opportunities,
14–16, 225–230,
462, 464–466
professional
opportunities,
313–316
proposed equity
strategies, 234–235,
248–249
racial/ethnic
influences, 284–285
reading
recommendations,
252–253
sex tests, 239n
socialization/ideology
studies, 99–100, 108
socioeconomic
influences, 307–308
softball team study,
108
summary, 251–252
support, 230
supporting trends, 115,
218–222
trivialization, 224–225
violence, 192, 198
Web resources,
253–254
Women's Sports
Network, 222
Women's Tennis
Association, 126
Woods, Tiger, 259–260

World Anti-Doping
Code, 176
World Conference on
Women (United
Nations), 221
World Trade
Organization
(WTO), 332
World Wrestling
Federation, 338f
Wrestling, 338f
WTSN, 222, 368, 390

XFL (football), 338f
X Games, 136, 139, 336,
380

YMCA/YWCA, 24, 68,
114
Youth sports. *See also*
High school sports
abuse, 123
alternative sports,
135–136, 139
assumptions, 118–125
changing, 133–139
child readiness for,
129–130
class relations
compared to, 298
coaching certification,
141–142
costs, 117
development of,
114–118
fair play, 123
family dynamics and,
130–131
future, 141
gender socialization,
132–133, 308–309
good games, 141
growth of, 143–145
hockey, 134
informal sports,
139–143
performance ethic,
123, 135
personal involvement,
140–141

player versus adult-
controlled, 137–138
reading
recommendations,
145
socioeconomic
influences, 307–308
spectator interest
development and,
329
sponsors of, 309–310
summary, 143–145
summer sport
programmes, 134
trends, 116–118, 481
Web resources, 146

Zeus, 58